THE GERMAN
WAY OF WAR

THE GERMAN
WAY OF WAR

From the Thirty Years' War
to the Third Reich

Robert M. Citino

UNIVERSITY PRESS OF KANSAS

Published by the University Press of Kansas (Lawrence, Kansas 66049), which was
organized by the Kansas Board of Regents and is operated and funded by Emporia
State University, Fort Hays State University, Kansas State University, Pittsburg State
University, the University of Kansas, and Wichita State University

ISBN 0-7006-1410-9

Printed in the United States of America

To my daughter Emily

Contents

Illustrations and Maps

Illustrations

Maps

Preface

The Problem: The German Way of War

Consider, if you will, this practically forgotten scene from the pages of German military history:

They came up out of the dark forests, mounted and mobile, driving deep into the flank and rear of their enemy. The shock and surprise of their sudden assault carried all before them. So rapid was the advance that it overtook every attempt by the defenders to form a cohesive position. The attackers were not simply faster than their opponents. Moving in a compact, mobile column, they were also more agile, more flexible, and far more responsive to the commands of their officers. This great mobile column chopped the bewildered enemy force in front of it into uncoordinated segments, each with little more on its mind than flight. It was a near-perfect marriage between the best available technology, a flexible system of command and control, and officers who understood the possibilities of both. It was war in a new, faster tempo.

And now, a quiz: from whence comes this scene? Is it a description of the Tannenberg campaign of 1914? Perhaps a moment from the dramatic victory of German armor during Case Yellow, the invasion of France, in 1940? Does it perhaps describe one of those stunning armored drives into the Soviet Union with which the German Wehrmacht opened Operation Barbarossa, leading to yet another stunning encirclement?

Any of the three would certainly be a good guess, but each would be wrong. In fact, the preceding passage describes a military action of Friedrich Wilhelm I, the "Great Elector" of Brandenburg. It marked the climax of his highly successful winter campaign of 1678–1679 in East Prussia and Samogitia. The routed enemy was Swedish, and the mounted force launching the devastating mobile assault and pursuit was actually riding sleighs. Centuries before anyone had ever heard of a panzer maneuver, there was the "great sleigh drive."

Is there a German way of war? The answer may seem obvious.

There are few notions in modern history more secure than that of German military excellence. Many absolute monarchs were soldier-kings, but Frederick the Great was *the* Soldier-King,[1] an apparently seamless combination of enlightened despot and gifted field commander. During the nineteenth century, the Prussian army carried out a military revolution that culminated in the toppling of Austria from its dominant perch in Germany, the toppling of France from its dominant perch in Europe, and the creation of a new German Empire, a "second Reich" that was a very different creature indeed from the old Holy Roman Empire. During World War I, the German army came within an ace of victory in the opening weeks, held off a vast coalition of Great Britain, France, Russia, and the United States for four long years of positional warfare, and then came within an ace of victory again in the spring of 1918. In the interwar era, the Germans carried out a *second* military revolution, devising a potent and deadly method of integrating the new mechanized mobility of tank and aircraft into field operations. The world would call it blitzkrieg, although the Germans themselves did not invent or use that term in any official way. In the opening years of World War II, German mechanized armies again went from victory to victory, a run that climaxed in the campaign against the Soviet Union. In the opening six months of Operation Barbarossa, the Germans inflicted the staggering total of four million casualties on the Soviet army, a majority of which were prisoners taken in one huge "battle of encirclement" (*Kesselschlacht*) after another.

Upon closer inspection, however, these facts don't answer the question. Although it is true that the Germans seem to have been good at war, they haven't had a monopoly on military excellence. There have been many "great captains" over the years, and the membership list is instructive. For the modern period up to 1850, for example, we have a Swede (King Gustavus Adolphus), an Englishman (John Churchill, the Duke of Marlborough), a Franco-Italian (Eugene of Savoy), a Prussian (Frederick the Great), and a Frenchman, or to be more precise, a Corsican (Napoleon I). Most historians still regard the "Emperor of the French," in fact, as having been the greatest of them all.

Moreover, the Germans themselves repeatedly and vehemently denied having any special or unique system for conducting their wars. War, they claimed, was an art. Mastering it required long years of study and monastic devotion, like any art, and no one could ever reduce it to a system or a prescriptive set of principles. A good commander found a way to win; he did not follow a list of rules. This is a conceptual link between Frederick the Great through the great philosopher of war, Carl Maria von Clausewitz, and later key figures like the elder Helmuth von Moltke, Count Alfred von Schlieffen, and Hans von Seeckt. Each of them rejected any schema of war that was valid at all times. Lists of rules like the U.S. Army's famous principles of war were, Clausewitz once said, "absolutely useless."[2]

A third problem in devising any easy formula on this topic is the simple adjective "German." When we discuss the Germans in this volume, we are usually referring to the kingdom of Prussia and its successor regimes: the united Bismarckian Reich, the Weimar Republic, and the Nazi dictatorship. A great deal of historical work of late has analyzed the other Germanies: the Holy Roman Empire and its successor state, the Habsburg Empire, as well as the various smaller member-states of the Empire and the German Confederation: Hanover, Saxony, Baden, Württemberg, Bavaria, and so forth.[3] A true "German way of war" would include them all, and many of the greatest battles in "German" military history, Frederick the Great's victory at Leuthen, or Moltke's triumph at Königgrätz, take on quite a different face when you realize that they actually came at the expense of a fellow "German" state, Austria. The 1866 war, for example, shows up repeatedly in the contemporary literature as a "war of brothers" (*Brüderkrieg*). In postmodernist terms, historians have tended to "privilege" Prussian history at the expense of that of the other German states.

To such a crime this work will plead guilty in advance. It will argue that there is indeed a German way of war and that it had its origins within the Kingdom of Prussia. The rulers of this small, relatively impoverished state on the periphery of European civilization, the "sandbox of the empire," recognized early that Prussia's wars had to be "*kurtz und vives*" (short and lively). Prussia, and later Germany, was *die Macht in der Mitte*, the power in the center of Europe. Crammed into an unfortunately tight spot in the heart of the continent, ringed by enemies and potential enemies, more often than not the chessboard on which others played out their strategies,[4] it had neither the resources nor the manpower to win long, drawn-out wars of attrition. Even by drafting every available man and squeezing out every last taler in taxes, Prussia could not fight and win a long war. Prussia's military problem from the start, then, was to find a way to fight short, sharp wars that ended rapidly in a decisive battlefield victory, a front-loaded conflict that left the enemy too weak or frightened to consider a second round.[5]

The solution, found in embryo form in the wars of the Great Elector, developed further by Frederick the Great, then brought to maturity in the career of the elder Helmuth von Moltke, was to emphasize an intermediate level of warfare known as the *operational*. It exists in a conceptual space between *tactics* (the movement of small units like battalions, companies, and squads on the battlefield) and *strategy* (the realm of the politico-military leadership of the respective warring nations). The operational level involves the movement and command of large units: armies, corps, and divisions. Prussian, and later German commanders, sought to maneuver their operational units—sometimes their entire force—in a rapid and daring fashion. The Germans called it *Bewegungskrieg* ("bev-AY-goongs-kreeg")—the war of movement on the operational level. The term did not refer to tactical mobility or ground speed in miles per hour. Instead, it meant the maneuver of large units to strike the enemy a sharp, even annihilating blow as rapidly as possible. It could be a surprise assault on an unprotected flank or, better yet, both flanks—or even better than that, his rear. Such a vigorous operational posture implied certain other characteristics, as we shall see: an army with an extremely high level of battlefield aggression, an officer corps that tended to launch attacks no matter what the odds, and a flexible system of command that left a great deal of initiative, sometimes too much, in the hands of lower-ranking commanders.

Thus, the Germans evolved a certain pattern of war making from their culture and traditions, and especially their geographic position. Other nations, with radically different situations, evolved different patterns. Need to land a huge amphibious force on foreign shores? Call the Americans. Interested in deep strikes and consecutive operations on a vast scale of men and matériel? Study the Red Army in its prime. War as a means of colonial aggrandizement? Look to the British. Levels of firepower large enough to turn the enemy homeland into a parking lot? It's back to the Americans.

In all the contemporary discussion about military doctrine, one fact tends to be ignored. Doctrine is not something you put on like a coat. National armies make war in various ways. They train intensively to learn some things well, usually at the expense of deemphasizing other things. For all the skill that the Germans have shown in operational-level maneuver and the battle of annihilation, they have shown serious and persistent weaknesses in other areas. The problem of logistics has rarely been on the front burner. A quick and decisive battlefield victory obviates the need for a deep logistics net and, in fact, in seeking the former the Germans have traditionally campaigned on a logistical shoestring. Intelligence and counterintelligence have been among the worst in European military history. One could argue, for example, that in the 1930s German intelligence lagged far behind even second-rank powers like Poland (the country that cracked the German Enigma machine).

Moreover, the German pattern of *Bewegungskrieg* had its origins in the need to fight campaigns in the relatively restricted theater of central and western Europe, with its fine road network and its temperate climate. After 1941, when Germany's national leadership pointed the army toward higher goals, the conquest of the Soviet Union and the maintenance of a defensive position from Archangel on the Arctic Ocean to Astrakhan on the Caspian Sea, for example, or the prosecution of logistics-heavy campaigns in the vast and faraway deserts of North Africa, we see the German war machine breaking down completely.

The Work

The German Way of War offers a detailed look at operations of the Prussian, and later the German, army from the first major campaign of the Great Elector, Frederick William, to the crushing defeat in front of Moscow in 1941. It is an attempt at something that, to my knowledge, has not yet been done, a study of the historical phenomenon of Prussian-German war making over an extremely long period of time, what French historian Fernand Braudel called the *longue durée*.[6] The benefit of such an approach is that many developments that seem revolutionary and utterly new—the notion of blitzkrieg, for example—in fact turn out to be rooted firmly in the past. It also attempts, wherever possible, to go beyond what actually happened and give a nod to what the Germans—especially professional military opinion—thought they were doing. In other words, it attempts to say something of the operational *mentalité* of the German officer corps. The work traces the role played by the Prussian army in elevating a small and impoverished state to the ranks of the European great powers by the mid-eighteenth century. It analyzes the operations of Frederick the Great, starting with the early battles of Mollwitz and Hohenfriedeberg in the Silesian Wars, then proceeding to three of his greatest battles in the Seven Years' War: a masterful humbling of a Franco-Imperial army twice the size of his own at Rossbach in November 1757; the improbable triumph at Leuthen in December 1757 over the Austrians; and the bloody slugfest at Zorndorf, a hard-fought win over the Russians under a broiling August sun in 1758. It looks at the reasons for the collapse of the Prussian army against Napoleon in 1806, its rapid rebirth, and its participation in the final campaigns to rid Europe of Napoleon's tyranny. It looks carefully at the nineteenth century, the age of Carl von Clausewitz and General Helmuth von Moltke. The former created what he called a "metaphysic of war," an explanation of war as an ideal that is still compelling. The latter, working in an era of dramatic technological change that saw the introduction of the rifle, the telegraph, and the railroad, succeeded beyond any contemporary figure in integrating the new machines into plans for war and actual military operations alike. The climax of his career came with decisive victories over Austria in the Seven Weeks' War of 1866, and over France in the Franco-Prussian War of 1870–1871. Although both these wars were dramatic and rapid victories, it is plain that they were far from flawless.

These victories made the German army the leading military institution in Europe, and the rest of the world attempted to emulate its training techniques, its command doctrine, and even its uniforms. This work looks closely at the years from 1871–1914, the "classical period" of Prussian-German military history—an era dominated by Field Marshal Count Alfred von Schlieffen. During this period, the Germans seemed to have cornered the market on meticulous peacetime planning, a more rapid and efficient mobilization system than their neighbors, and a high-tempo war of maneuver that could destroy an enemy force in the opening weeks of the fighting. The existence of such an apparently invincible military machine went a long way toward keeping Europe in a nearly permanent state of diplomatic crisis during those years.

Then, in 1914, it all came crashing down. World War I was the largest and bloodiest conflict that the world had ever seen, and its course seemed to show the absolute futility of offensive operations in the grand style of German *Bewegungskrieg*. After a mobile opening phase, the western front exhibited stasis for the next three years of the conflict, and in the end, after an impressive but unsuccessful flurry of mobile operations in 1918, Germany lost a war of attrition. We examine German operations in the war in some detail, especially the very real chance for victory in the dramatic opening campaign.

The interwar period saw German military planners undertaking an arduous reappraisal of virtually every area of their repertoire, seeking to find out, first, what had gone wrong, and second, how those things might be put right in some future war. The result was a doctrinal renaissance of sorts, as German officers rediscovered the things that had made their army formidable before it was ground down by three years of trench warfare and overwhelming numerical superiority. They rediscovered the art of *Bewegungskrieg*, for all its attendant risks still Germany's best chance to win a future war. They then set about designing a military force that would be able to prosecute it. The result was the Wehrmacht, the panzer division, and the Luftwaffe. This work analyzes German operational performance in this greatest of all wars, seeking to define exactly what it was that made the German army so formidable, particularly in the early years of the war, the years of the *Kesselschlacht* and of "Hurryin' Heinz" Guderian. It focuses also on those German failings that led to the debacle in front of Moscow in 1941.

Although there is a mountain of books on various aspects of the German army, it has its share of flaws. It is an amazing fact for such a critical topic, but there is still hardly any agreement on just what it was that the Germans brought to modern warfare, or on the exact characteristics of the new era they supposedly inaugurated in 1939–1940. We see the same problem throughout the period under discussion. Frederick the Great is an iconic figure in much eighteenth-century historiography, one of the great battlefield commanders of his era, but there is to this day no real agreement about how his battles were fought, or just what he contributed to Prussia's art of war. Analysts use the term *oblique attack*, for example, to mean any number of different things, as we shall see. Originating in the nineteenth century, *Auftragstaktik* has come to be used as a buzzword by modern American officers, again without a great deal of care taken in defining it. As for the twentieth century, the term *blitzkrieg* remains the classic example of conceptual fuzziness. It can mean so many things that, in the end, it has come to mean nothing.

As in my previous works *Quest for Decisive Victory: From Stalemate to Blitzkrieg in Europe, 1899–1940* and *Blitzkrieg to Desert Storm: The Evolution of Operational Warfare*, the emphasis in this work is on action rather than theory, on actual operations rather than doctrine. Operational history, once synonymous with military history, has become something of a historiographical stepchild of late. The "new military history" of the 1960s and 1970s—with its emphasis on social and political methodologies—seemed willing to discuss everything about armies but the actual wars they fought. It has been an unfortunate state of affairs that has taken a field in which there is still intense public interest and left it to buffs, amateurs, and dubious interpretations.[7] A scholarly look into Prussian-German military operations provides new insights into a phenomenon that is often studied in the abstract, as a matter of philosophy or doctrine. It helps to answer some simple, but fundamental, questions. What, historically, did the Germans do well? What did they do poorly? Is there a "typical" German operation? And yes, there is more on the great "sleigh drive" (the *Schlittenfahrt*, the Germans called it), of the Great Elector against the Swedes. It was a milestone in the development of *Bewegungskrieg*—the German way of war.

Acknowledgments

No one can write without inspiration, and this is a good opportunity to thank the many scholars and colleagues whose work has stimulated my thoughts on this topic. Dennis E. Showalter deserves special mention. Reading any of Dennis's numerous books and mountain of articles is both a challenge to the intellect and a delight to the senses. Geoff Wawro is a close second; his recent books on *The Austro-Prussian War* and *The Franco-Prussian War* are models of scholarship, concision, and great writing. Likewise, the works of James Corum have always inspired me with their intellectual rigor, honesty, and plainspokenness. Every time I read a new piece by Richard L. DiNardo, I see the bar being raised in the field of German military history, and the same thing goes for the work of Geoff Megargee. German-language historians, too, are making a major impact, from established scholars like Stig Förster to fresh faces like Dierk Walter. The field is currently in a vibrant state, and these scholars are the reason why.

Other thanks go to the staff of the Harlan Hatcher Graduate Library at the University of Michigan. The Hatcher is one of academe's special places, not only for its immense holdings in all subject areas, but also for the wonderful people who work there. It would be hard to imagine a more professional, dedicated, and helpful group. I also would like to acknowledge a Danish cyber-friend of mine, Christian Ankerstjerne, for allowing me to use some of the many rare German army photographs in his possession. The help and support he lent to me on this project prove once again that you really can meet the nicest people on the Internet. Those interested in sampling Christian's wares might point their browsers to www.panzerworld.net.

Twenty years ago, I was a doctoral student at Indiana University. I was fortunate to be working with two renowned scholars who also happened to be among the most caring and concerned people I have ever met: Barbara and Charles Jelavich. They gave me the advice I needed and more attention than I deserved, and for that I will always be grateful.

Finally and most important, every book that I write is also a testimony to the love and support I receive on a daily basis from my family: my wife, Roberta, and my daughters, Allison, Laura, and Emily. All of them put up with a lot, including piles of old issues of the *Militär-Wochenblatt* in every corner of our house and mini-lectures on obscure topics breaking out at any moment. It can't be easy, and I thank for them for their patience.

1

The Great Elector and the Origins of Prussian War Making

A Question of Origins

It is tempting to begin a military history of Germany with some ancient encounter between the Germanic tribesmen and their Roman neighbors. Perhaps we might trace the origins of German military might to Hermann's destruction of three Roman legions under Varus in the Teutoburger Forest (9 A.D.).[1] Perhaps we might look to the later barbarian invasions of the Roman Empire. The triumph of Visigothic cavalry over the forces of the Eastern emperor at Adrianople in 378 figures prominently in ancient history texts,[2] as do the devastating sacks of Rome by the Goths under Alaric and the Vandals under Gaiseric. Later, Charles the Great (*Karl der Grosse*) would establish a reputation as a great warrior and a wise ruler, conquering neighboring kingdoms, reestablishing an empire in the West in 800 and relighting the lamp of civilization in western Europe. In the next century, it was Otto the Great rescuing Europe from the depredations of the barbarian Magyars at the battle of the Lechfeld. In fact, it is possible to come away from a typical university course in Western Civilization—and many students do—thinking of the Germans as a fierce warrior race from first to last.

The problem is that none of these wars, campaigns, and battles say much one way or the other about the Germans of yore and even less about the Germans of the modern era. To begin, it is difficult to reconstruct any one of them to any acceptable degree of historical detail, so analyzing their significance or drawing their "lessons" is simply an interesting academic exercise, utterly divorced from reality. We don't even know exactly where most of these great encounters took place. It is valuable to recall, however, that Hermann wasn't invading anyone, but defending his homeland from the rapacious Romans. He also would probably not have answered to the name *German;* more accurately, he was a chieftain of the Germanic tribe known as the Cherusci. He had served in the Roman army from 1–6 A.D., had studied Roman military techniques, and was himself a Roman citizen. At any rate, a punitive expedition under Germanicus Caesar, the adopted nephew of Emperor Tiberius, soon taught Hermann the error of his ways. As to the barbarian invasions of Rome, historians have been hammering away for decades at the very concept.[3] It seems the Germanic tribes found themselves driven into the Empire by Hunnish raiders to the east (probably the "Hsiung-nu" who figure prominently in Chinese chronicles of the day and who had just been taught the error of their ways by the Han dynasty). The Visigoths actually asked to be allowed to cross the Danube River into Roman territory, hoping to find protection against these fierce newcomers. Once there, the mysteries of the money economy and debt slavery soon drove them into revolt, it is true. Finally, history has transformed Karl der Grosse, once a Germanic Frank, into a Frenchman, far better known to the world as Charlemagne. Incidentally, he fought his bloodiest campaigns, replete with atrocity and massacre on both sides, against a fellow Germanic tribe, the Saxons.[4]

Frederick William and the Rise of Brandenburg-Prussia

For German army officers of the nineteenth and twentieth centuries, however, there was no mystery about the origins of their military prowess. They looked back to the seventeenth century, in particular to the reign of Frederick William I (1640–1688) of the Hohenzollern dynasty.[5] There was at the time no "Germany" in the sense of a unified nation-state, and there wouldn't be until Bismarck's founding of the Reich in 1871. In fact, there wasn't even a Kingdom of Prussia yet. Frederick William was the ruler of a principality in northeastern Europe known as Brandenburg. Because of its location on what most Europeans considered the frontier of civilization, it was also called the Mark, from the German for "marchlands."[6] Frederick William was the Margrave (*Markgraf,* or "Count of the Mark") of Brandenburg and also held the status of Elector (*Kurfürst*), since the ruler of Brandenburg was one of the seven imperial princes (divided between secular and religious authorities) who had the right to cast a vote to elect the Holy Roman Emperor.[7]

No one should confuse Brandenburg in this era with a great power. The territories under Frederick William's control sprawled haphazardly across northern Europe from the Rhine to the Niemen River, and there was little uniting them except the person of the Elector. Besides Brandenburg in the north German plain, there were the small but lucrative territories of Cleves and Mark on the lower Rhine to the west, as well as the Duchy of Prussia to the east. Formerly the possession of the religious order known as the Teutonic Knights, this separated province was destined to play a key role in the fortunes of Frederick William's house and to figure prominently in German nationalist and military myth.[8]

The Knights had invaded the region in 1231, part of the expansion of German culture to the east known as the *Drang nach Osten*. They conquered the original tribal inhabitants—the Prussians, a Baltic people neither Germanic nor Slav—and ruled the territory as feudal overlords. Their castles remained long after they were gone, at Marienwerder, Thorn, Kulm, and especially Marienburg, seat of the Order's authority. The Prussians never stopped resisting the Knights, however, and made good use of the dense forests of this still wild province. Whatever crusading or religious impulse might have been present among the Knights at the start soon disappeared in favor of brutal repression of the native population.

Although the Knights were able to bring that threat under control by the end of the thirteenth century, they soon found another, more dangerous challenger: the great Polish-Lithuanian state, then at the height of its power. The Knights found their territory gradually whittled down, and as Polish authority expanded toward the Baltic Sea, they began to fear for their landward communications back to Germany proper. In 1410, Grand Master Ulrich von Jungingen assembled an army, largely heavy cavalry, and marched out to contest Polish-Lithuanian supremacy. The subsequent battle of Tannenberg (July 15) is impossible to reconstruct with any degree of accuracy. One source, Detmar's *Lübeck Chronicle*, assigns the Polish-Lithuanian force the fantastic size of 5.1 million men; another chronicler gives a figure of no less than 630,000 dead. A better total may be a knightly force of ten to eleven thousand men facing fifteen thousand Poles. What is certain is that Ulrich and his men went to their doom against a larger and more nimble enemy force. The *Drang nach Osten* had come to an emphatic end, although internal weaknesses within Poland precluded an actual conquest of the province.[9] Later generations of German historians, particularly in the nineteenth century, would construct Tannenberg as a heroic but doomed attempt to save German territory from the depredations of the Slav, and of course, the place name would once again figure prominently in the opening days of World War I.[10]

It was not the Poles but the Protestant Reformation that finally laid the Knights low. In 1523, the order elected a new Grand Master, Count Albrecht of Hohenzollern-Ansbach. Like many ambitious rulers of the day, he decided to break with the Church, adopt Lutheranism, and transform Prussia into a secular duchy. He became the first Duke of Prussia in 1525. Although still a vassal of the Polish crown, he had nonetheless laid the dynastic groundwork for the union of Prussia with Brandenburg under the main Hohenzollern line, an event that took place in 1591.

Even as Brandenburg slowly developed into Brandenburg-Prussia, however, there was little to distinguish it from the three hundred other petty principalities of the Holy Roman Empire. After the nineteenth-century unification of Germany under Otto von Bismarck, a school of historians arose who saw the rise of Prussia to a dominating position within Germany as inevitable. Exemplified in the writings of Heinrich von Treitschke and Johann Gustav Droysen, this so-called "Borussian" school (from the Latin name for Prussia) has remained influential to the present day.[11] We must resist it, however, since it has little to do with the political realities facing Frederick William when he ascended to power in 1640.

Frederick William was an energetic prince, in many ways typical of the age of absolutism, and much of the later political and social structure of the Prussian kingdom had its origins in his reign. Well-connected to the main currents of political Protestantism, his mother was the sister of the "Winter King," Frederick V of the Palatinate, whose accession to the Bohemian throne touched off the Thirty Years' War. His aunt was married to the great Swedish warrior-king Gustavus Adolphus. After the king's death in battle at Lützen, eleven-year-old Frederick William actually accompanied the casket as it was loaded onto the ship at Wohlgast for transport back to Sweden. The dynasty had converted to Calvinism during the reign of John Sigismund (1608–1619), and Frederick William spent much of his youth in the Calvinist Netherlands, going to study in Leyden in 1634. Here he became acquainted with modern systems of government, administration, and taxation, and more important, modern military science, then in its full flowering in the Dutch Republic. In the camp of Frederick Henry of Orange, the young Elector-to-be learned the value and necessity of drill, the use of firearms, and techniques of command. There could not have been a better introduction to what we call the "Military Revolution" of the seventeenth century: warfare based on firearms and trained, thoroughly drilled professional armies.[12]

Brandenburg-Prussia's role in the Thirty Years' War was no more or less honorable than that of dozens of the other petty German states. It started out neutral, family and confessional ties to the Winter King notwithstanding, backed Sweden when Gustavus Adolphus sailed to Germany to rescue the Protestant cause in its darkest hour, and then, when the Swedes had carried all before them and began to present a clear and present danger to Brandenburg itself, switched sides yet again. At issue was the disposition of the Duchy of Pomerania, stretching along the southern coast of the Baltic Sea. With the death of reigning duke Bogislav XIV in 1637, Brandenburg moved to enforce a claim that it had by marriage.[13] That claim rang hollow given the presence of Swedish troops actually on the ground in Pomerania. Such shifts in policy were typical of an era in which the cause of religion had given way to *raison d'état* as the principal motivation for going to war.

Internally, he was a typical royal figure of his time. That is, he imposed new taxes, brought the estates of his disparate territories to heel, and tried to pass laws encouraging commerce and nascent home industries alike. One of his crowning achievements was the construction of a canal linking the Oder and Spree Rivers.[14] He treated with his nobles not in the style of Louis XIV, who built a pleasure palace for them at Versailles, but by enrolling them in royal service. In return he granted them an ever tighter hold on their peasants and serfs. With allowances made for regional variation, this was the basic recipe for absolutism.

Such internal activities aimed at one goal. The lesson that Frederick William learned from the Thirty Years' War was the importance of a standing army. Essential to making one's weight felt in international affairs, it was equally handy in intimidating the estates of the realm and recalcitrant nobles. The standing army thus played a central role in state building in the seventeenth century. The new technology of fire weapons, artillery in particular, gave the monarch what is often called a "monopoly on violence" within the state. Apart from the power-political aspects, a standing army could potentially help to integrate the separate portions of his state, with soldiers from Ducal Prussia being employed in the defense of Cleves, and vice versa.

By the nineteenth century, it was common among historians to argue that Brandenburg-Prussia's development was an example of the *Primat der Aussenpolitik* (the primacy of foreign policy).[15] Because of

Prussia's geographical vulnerability, so the argument ran, Frederick William had no real choice. He had to bend all his power (and spend virtually all his tax revenues) on a strong army. Within the twentieth century, leftist historians like Eckart Kehr stood that proposition on its head, arguing that the Prussian-German elite used army building (later, fleet building) and military adventurism abroad to cement their position at home and to maintain a regressive and authoritarian social structure. Kehr, in other words, argued that domestic considerations took precedence (*Primat der Innenpolitik*) and thus should be the primary ground of study for the historian.[16]

As is typical in such polemical debates, the only sensible position is to say that both were true. A well-drilled standing army ready to march at any moment gave the state prestige abroad, and perhaps a diplomatic triumph or two. That was a coin that could be traded on the domestic market as well, keeping the ruler popular and giving people a reason to continue to pay taxes. Internal stability, prosperity, and "calm and order" (*Ruhe und Ordnung*), in turn, made it easier to recruit, equip, and pay for troops, cannon, and the ever-greater expense of fortifying the cities. At the same time, however, it cannot be denied that in the seventeenth century there was a certain autonomy to foreign and military affairs. Frederick William considered these areas to be the personal prerogative of the monarch—a situation that obtained not only in Prussia. One-sided attempts to find the source of Prussian "militarism" in Frederick William's reign fail to note that the same things were happening all over Europe.

Frederick William's standing army, established in 1643–1644, started as a modest venture. It was only about 5,500 men at first, although it included an elite unit of 500 musketeers that served as the Elector's bodyguard.[17] It grew steadily during his reign, however, and as his rising prestige in international affairs turned into concrete gains, he could afford to make it larger still. Thus, when the Treaty of Westphalia awarded him Eastern Pomerania (*Hinterpommern*), he had a new territory contributing revenue to his coffers, as well as its stalwart sons to the ranks of his military. In addition, once his army proved itself in battle, neighboring powers were willing to hire it, as it were, in the ongoing series of late seventeenth-century conflicts. This was the age in which Louis XIV was striving for mastery of the continent, and a European-wide coalition (the Holy Roman Empire, the Netherlands, and eventually England) was trying to stop him. The result was a series of conflicts: the Devolution War (1667–1668), the Franco-Dutch War (1672–1678), and the Nine Years' War (1688–1697).[18] Throughout the period, Frederick William lent himself out to the highest bidder, which usually was the coalition, but sometimes was Louis XIV. During the Nine Years' War, for example, Brandenburg received about a third of its total military expenses from foreign subsidies—6,545,000 talers to be exact.[19]

More important, however, were the domestic arrangements he made to fund the army. In 1653, he came to an agreement with the Brandenburg Diet, the famous "Brandenburg Recess."[20] The estates agreed to provide him with the princely sum of 530,000 talers, to be paid in annual installments over six years. They didn't mind; most of the revenue was going to come from the commoners and peasants. In return, he granted them wholesale privileges: tax exemption, absolute ownership of their lands (as opposed to the old system that recognized land ownership only in the feudal context of the fief), autonomy in the handling of their serfs, and the right to be recognized as the legal authority in their local districts. Not only did the agreement allow him to expand the army to some eight thousand men, it was also the start of Prussia's distinctive social contract, a contract between monarch and nobility (*Junker*) only, at the expense of everyone else. Such arrangements kept the money flowing into the treasury. By his death in 1688, the force amounted to some twenty-nine thousand men, a considerable figure given the small population of the state and the relatively underdeveloped nature of its economy.

The First Northern War and the Battle of Warsaw

From the start, Frederick William was able to put his new army to good use in foreign affairs. The First Northern War (1655–1660) is a good example of this new Brandenburger military diplomacy in action.[21] In 1655, King Charles X (Gustav) of Sweden approached the Elector about a joint invasion of Poland. Frederick William hesitated before deciding on neutrality in the upcoming conflict. The invasion went ahead anyway, and Swedish forces quickly overran most of Poland, forcing Polish king John Casimir to flee the country for Upper Silesia. Frederick William was now in a corner, with strong Swedish forces just a few days march away from Brandenburg and no regional counterweight to Sweden. Bowing to the inevitable, he concluded an alliance with the Swedish king in the Treaty of Königsberg (January 1656). Ducal Prussia now became a Swedish fief, rather than a Polish one, and Frederick William morphed from a Polish into a Swedish vassal. Swedish conquest soon touched off a popular uprising in Poland, however. Leading the national rally was the Catholic Church, which had no desire to submit to Poland's new Lutheran overlords. John Casimir was able to return to the country, assemble an army, and chase the Swedes back from whence they had come. Charles X wished to return the next campaigning season, but found that his Brandenburg ally had now upped the ante, demanding a share of Polish territory if the country were conquered. The two powers concluded a new alliance, signing the Treaty of Marienburg in June. It promised significant territories in the event of victory: the districts of Posen, Kalisch, Lencycz, and Sieradz.[22]

Together, the allies reinvaded Poland and marched on Warsaw. Here they fought a murderous three-day engagement against Polish forces defending the capital. The Elector proved himself to be a field commander of some skill, with energy, boldness, and a good eye for the terrain. His troops impressed observers with their march discipline, their bearing in this, their first combat, and their relatively more humane treatment of the civilian population, the last being a clear contrast to the rapacious Swedes. Charles X's success in Poland aroused the attention of the rest of Europe, however, and soon the Dutch, the Russians, and the Emperor were sending assistance to John Casimir. Once again, there was trouble in Poland as well, with the Swedish-Brandenburger supply lines coming under attack by light cavalry and Tatars. With Sweden increasingly isolated, Frederick William was able once again to renegotiate the terms of the alliance, demanding Swedish recognition of his sovereign rights over Prussia. Now it was Charles, bereft of friends, who had no choice but to sign the Treaty of Labiau in November 1656.[23]

Sweden's situation went from bad to worse when Denmark entered the war. Charles had to redeploy his forces in the north to face this grave threat to Swedish interests. At this point, Frederick William quietly renounced his twice-renegotiated alliance with Sweden and opened talks with John Casimir. In the Treaty of Wehlau (September 1657) he won Polish recognition of his complete sovereignty over Prussia. With remarkably little fighting, three days in front of Warsaw, in fact, Frederick William had won a province. The Peace of Oliva, concluded in 1660, thus ended any foreign claim to the Elector's major territories. It was a shrewd, even brilliant, diplomatic performance.

The new Prussian army had arrived, as well. The battle of Warsaw (July 29–31, 1656) was the first combat for the Elector and his standing army, and it deserves closer attention than it usually receives in modern histories of the German army (that is to say, none at all).[24] Beyond the incredible irony of the first major Prussian military operation being a lightning strike against Warsaw, the battle displays many attributes that would later come to be seen as characteristic of the German army.

The allied armies approached Warsaw from the north, marching along the right bank of the Vistula River, with Charles X's cavalry on the right, Swedish-Brandenburg infantry in the center, and Frederick William's cavalry on the left. Together they commanded some 18,000, of whom just under half—8,500—were Brandenburgers. The Polish force was much larger, perhaps 35,000–40,000 men; estimates that place it at 70,000, 100,000, or even 200,000, although increasing the drama of the upcoming contest, are fantasy.[25] The Poles did, however, have an uncounted number of Crimean Tatar cavalry auxiliaries active in the countryside, harrying the supply lines and march columns of the invaders. The center of the Polish position, held by most of their forces, was the fortified suburb of Praga, directly across the Vistula from Warsaw. The first day, July 18, saw the cavalry on both sides making contact and feeling each other out, but no decisive action on either side. The Poles were confident in their entrenched position; the allies were waiting to bring up their main body before attempting any serious stroke against a numerically superior enemy.

As the two allied commanders arrived on the field that evening, they spotted trouble. The space between the river and the Białołenka forest to the northeast was too narrow for the entire force to deploy—and room for the firing lines had become the sine qua non of battle in this era. In addition, the Poles had thrown up heavy earthworks and entrenchments in this bottleneck, standing square athwart the Swedish-Brandenburger line of advance. Although Polish forces were nowhere near their adversaries in terms of armaments, training, or discipline, this was a position that even relatively inferior troops could hold for a long, long time.

It is unclear who first decided on the operational response to this problem. A postbattle publicity war between Frederick William and Charles X saw the two rulers casting aspersions galore on each other and on their respective armies.[26] Nevertheless, they decided to begin the next day with a left flank march around the offending bottleneck, to strike a blow against the weakly defended Polish right flank. It was a risky decision. The hostile forces were practically in contact with each other, the flanking march was taking place no more than two miles from the enemy camp, and much of it had to pass through the dense Białołenka forest. It also involved a complete allied redeploy-

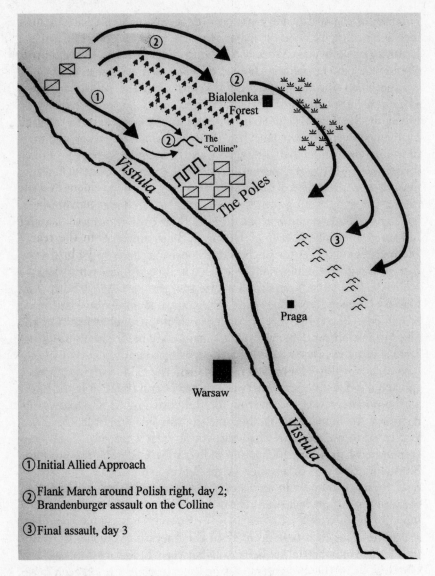

The Debut: The Battle of Warsaw, July 29–31, 1656

ment, with the Swedes, currently on the right, countermarching to the left of the line. In the words of a nineteenth-century German staff officer who analyzed the campaign, "it was a bold gamble, one that could only be accomplished by troops who were securely in the hands of their commanders."[27]

Morning dawned on July 30, and the allies prepared their columns for the flank march. Frederick William, carrying out a personal reconnaissance, now took note of a hill, marked on maps as the Colline, which was hard up against the forest and commanded a good view of the route the allies had marked out. Before the flank march could begin, he had a force of infantry and dragoons from the advance guard storm the Colline.[28] His troops immediately established heavy guns on the height, and successfully defended it from vigorous counterattacks launched by the Poles out of a nearby fortified work. With the Brandenburgers fixing Polish attention to the struggle for the Colline, the Swedes began their flank march. It went without incident at first, but soon a large force of Tatar cavalry (estimates range from two thousand to six thousand horse) came riding down from the north, lapping around the Swedish flanks and even taking Charles X in the rear.[29] From his position on the Colline, Frederick William had a bird's eye view of the action, and in fact sent a small force of his own cavalry to ride to his ally's aid, assistance that helped drive off the threat to the Swedish columns. Soon, however, trouble aplenty embroiled the Brandenburgers on the hill. The Colline was now the right wing of Frederick William's position, and a large force of Polish cavalry attempted to outflank it to the right, while a large Tatar force on the left drove around into his rear. The stalwart infantry on the hilltop drove back the assaulting force, mainly by fire, and as always the Tatars were more interested in attempting to plunder the baggage, unsuccessfully, than in achieving an operational goal against his army. Frederick William could look on with some satisfaction as Charles X completed his flank march, wheeled to his right and now faced southwest, directly toward the Vistula.

It was roughly 4 o'clock in the afternoon. The allies had just won the battle of Warsaw, although it was probably not yet obvious to a single man on the field. The allied maneuver had levered the Poles out of their tough fortified line between the Białołenka and the great river and forced them into a hasty redeployment. The upcoming battle would be in relatively open country, with room enough for the combined allied force to deploy. It was a spot ideally suited to display the benefits of superior training, discipline, and weaponry. Above all, the Poles would no longer have the benefits of fighting from the prepared position, the traditional equalizer between forces of notably different quality.

This is not to say that the Poles made it easy or passively accepted the inferiority of their new situation. In fact, they spent the rest of that day redeploying troops from the Vistula-Białołenka bottleneck to face the new threat and rushing them into the assault. The result was a series of dangerous, though uncoordinated, blows against the entire face of the allied position that caused no lack of anxious moments in both the Swedish and the Brandenburger camps. The high point of the Polish attacks was the bold charge by Aleksandr Połubinski's hussars, some eight hundred strong, against the left flank of the combined army, that is, against the Swedish cavalry (ably supported by a few regiments of Brandenburger infantry). Slashing through a first and then a second line of Swedish horse, they were unable to break through a third. This was not some anachronistic "cavalry against tank" charge, of the type that western historians insist on writing when the subject is the Polish military. This was, after all, an age in which infantry still fought with either the pike or the matchlock musket, with its slow rate of fire and short range. A Polish hussar therefore had a good chance of riding down his adversaries, and if he did that, acquainting them with the sharp end of his lance.[30] There are reports of Charles X engaging in hand-to-hand combat in halting Połubinski's charge. Although such information is, as always, difficult to substantiate, the reports are a clear sign of how desperately the Swedes viewed the situation.

There was action all over the field, however. The Tatar threat to the baggage trains, in particular, added to the anxiety and soaked up much of the Swedish reserves. A Brandenburg regiment, the Foot Guards (*Leibgarde zu Fuss*) played a crucial role in helping the Swedes restore their position in this area. As daylight waned, the Polish attacks began to peter out. Nightfall saw the allies holding the position they had seized that morning, and both monarchs met to plan for a general assault on the Poles the next day.

The assault would have to reckon with a long sandy knoll, covered on its southern end by a small copse of trees. The Poles had hastily fortified the position in the night, and garrisoned it strongly with infantry and artillery.[31] It is a measure of the ferocity of the second day's fighting, and its impact on the Swedes, that the war council decided to have Frederick William's forces lead the assault, which would clearly be the decisive stroke, one way or the other. Leading the assault group, including most of the Brandenburger infantry and guns, was Master of Ordnance (*Feldzeugmeister*) Otto Christof von Sparr. He began with an hour-long preparatory bombardment, followed by a charge by his pikemen that succeeded in driving out the Polish defenders. Simultaneously, the Elector himself led a group of cavalry to Sparr's right, toward a chain of sandy hills that extended out of the copse. Driving off a force of Polish hussars here, he drove into the rear of the Polish position. Hit in their front and with their rear threatened, the Poles now simply came apart. Their losses had been heavy, they had fought valiantly against a better armed and trained adversary for three days, even after their main position had been turned, and they had now had enough. Leaving behind most of their artillery, some fled across the main bridges to the far bank of the Vistula. Others simply vanished to the north and south, still on the near side of the Vistula. Such a hurried, all-points-of-the-compass retreat is the traditional prerogative of the light cavalry army. The next day, Elector and king entered Warsaw, not the last time in history that a German military commander would tour the conquered city. Losses had been considerable on both sides, some seven hundred for the allies, several thousand for the Poles.

The battle of Warsaw was the first time that the young Brandenburger army had faced the test, and it had passed with distinction. Frederick William's nineteenth-century biographer, Martin Philippson, gave a verdict that is typical: "Prussia's fame at war begins with Warsaw; this battle was the first leaf in the rich laurel wreath of the Brandenburg-Prussian army," he wrote.[32] The new army had fought on an equal footing alongside the Swedes, an army that still had a reputation as the finest in Europe, and in fact it had probably outperformed them. Frederick William's men had stormed the Colline to get the great flank march under way, succored the Swedes on several occasions during the fight, and carried out the final and decisive storm against the main Polish defensive position.

All arms could look back at the battle with some satisfaction. The infantry, whose missions included both positional defense and a desperate charge into the teeth of an entrenched position, had proven equally adept at both. The pikemen, in particular, came away from Warsaw with a reputation for excellence. Dragoons had cooperated well with the foot soldiers, and the cavalry (*Reiterei*) displayed aggression and flexibility, redeploying, charging, and reforming without loss of cohesion. In an age of cumbersome infantry, the cavalry was clearly Frederick William's arm of decision and, in fact, he led it in person for most of the last two days of fighting.

As to the Elector himself, he had shown not only personal bravery, as commanders were expected to do in that age, but a cleverness and agility of mind that were remarkable for one fighting his first major battle. His eye for the terrain and for the operational opportunity, as well as his ability to size them up in a single glance (what Napoleon called the *coup d'oeil*), were particularly worthy of mention. The key to the battle was the operational maneuver onto the Polish flank, which may well have been his own idea. The battle of Warsaw was a worthy beginning for the career of both the commander and the army.

Frederick William spent much of his reign joining alliances and then changing sides as the situation dictated. After Warsaw, he switched sides on Charles X, and spent the last few years of the First Northern War in a successful campaign to drive out Swedish forces from Western Pomerania (*Vorpommern*). The campaign, which saw the Elector commanding his largest force yet, thirty thousand men of the anti-Swedish alliance, included a land drive into Schleswig-Holstein, an amphibious assault on the island of Ahlsen (September 2, 1658), and the conquest of most of Pomerania, save the key port of Stettin.[33] However, once Sweden had been chastened and the balance of power restored in the region, Frederick William found himself abandoned by his great power allies, and in the Peace of Oliva (1660) had to restore Western Pomerania to the Swedes. It was a deeply disappointing turn of events after sipping the heady wine of victory. It was also a signal lesson about the limits of Brandenburg's power, as well as the problems of fighting in a coalition with larger powers whose interests would always trump his own. This may well be the source of Frederick William's famous quote: "Alliances are good, to be sure, but it is better to rely on one's own forces."[34]

The Day of Victory: Fehrbellin

Warsaw was a good start, but most later Prussian officers would point to June 28, 1675, and the battle of Fehrbellin as the true birthday of the Prussian army.[35] Here, Frederick William faced not indifferently armed Poles or their Tatar auxiliaries, but the mighty Swedes themselves, and beat them soundly. The shock reverberated throughout Europe, and Frederick William got a new nickname: the Great Elector. In many ways, Fehrbellin was not a typical battle for Brandenburg's new army. Fought almost exclusively by cavalry, it involved only a fraction of Frederick William's forces. Yet the circumstances in which it was fought form a dramatic backdrop that is still gripping today, and its later status as the Prussian army's "creation myth" makes it a crucial part of our narrative.

The wars of Louis XIV saw the Elector up to his typical behavior and also reinforced his dim view of what he could expect to gain through coalition warfare. In the Dutch War, Frederick William first joined the anti-French coalition. He offered twenty thousand men to the Netherlands in return for a subsidy that paid half his costs. When things went badly on the Rhine, however, he cut his losses and signed a separate peace with the French king, the Peace of Vossem (1673). The only alternative was the loss of his western provinces (Cleves and Mark) to the French. When promised French subsidies failed to materialize rapidly enough, however, he turned around again and signed on to the coalition. Such a policy smacked of inconstancy to later generations of patriotic German historians, particularly the times when they had to explain the Elector aiding the French against the Holy Roman Empire, and an apologetic tone crept into the scholarly writings.[36] It is pointless, however, to describe it as cynicism, as some modern historians persist in doing. This simply was the way foreign affairs were done in the age of cabinet diplomacy. As the English chancellor put it at the time to the Brandenburger ambassador in London, Otto von Schwerin, "The Lord Elector thinks only of pursuing his own affairs," and that seems a fair description.[37] At any rate, Brandenburger troops dutifully marched off to the Upper Rhine in 1674 to defend Europe from the depredations of the French.

Campaigning in Alsace, saddled with allies who each sought different things from the war, and facing the wily French commander Henri Turenne, Frederick William found the campaign an exercise in frustration. On one occasion, near Marlenheim, an allied war council representing the various contingents—imperial troops, Brandenburgers, troops from Brunswick, Münster, Electoral Saxony, and the Electoral Palatinate—rejected his suggestion for an attack on Turenne. Frederick William's fiery cavalry commander, Field Marshal Georg von Derfflinger, had reconnoitered the enemy position personally and had found an unoccupied height on Turenne's flank. If the allies could muscle some guns up the hill, he was sure that the entire French position would be vulnerable. The council rejected the plan, supposedly because of the "exhaustion of the troops," although it is hard to say why they should have been exhausted; they'd hardly been doing anything. Frederick William put most of the blame for the weak showing in Alsace on the shoulders of the allied commander, the Imperial general Alexander Graf von Bournonville, described as a "complete incompetent" by a later Prussian source. Derfflinger actually stormed out of the discussion at this point, in response to the "insult" to his monarch.[38] That evening, Turenne evacuated his vulnerable position and the chance for a decisive victory had vanished. Later, at the battle of Turkheim, another war council similarly decided to retreat after an indecisive battle that the allies could well have renewed on the following day. The Allied retreat back over the Rhine marked the final surrender of Alsace to the French. In late 1674 the army of Brandenburg, along with a deeply disillusioned Elector, went into winter quarters in the Franconian city of Schweinfurt.

At this point, real disaster struck. While the allies had dithered in Alsace, Louis had been active on the diplomatic front. He concluded an alliance with king Charles XI of Sweden that granted the northern kingdom large subsidies in return for an invasion of Brandenburg. Although it might appear that the Swedes would have been only too happy to do so, given the checkered nature of their past relationship to Frederick William, that is not the case. There was divided counsel within Sweden over the venture, but France was Sweden's only ally, and there seemed little choice but to accept Louis' offer.[39] So in December 1674, Swedish forces invaded Brandenburg with two corps, about twenty thousand men in all. They plundered, as was their wont, and then went almost immediately into winter quarters. With most of the army abroad, the defense of Brandenburg was in the hands of Johann Georg, the Prince of Anhalt, in his capacity as viceroy (*Statthalter*). His troops were too few to resist the Swedes, however. Protests to the Swedish commander General Karl Gustaf Wrangel received the rejoinder that the Swedes would leave "as soon as the Elector had made his peace with France."[40]

For the Elector, the Swedish invasion was a nightmare. While he had been wasting his time far from home as a useless cog in an expeditionary force, the enemy had succeeded in striking at his heartland. Negotiations with his allies in Alsace came to naught. No one was predisposed to rush forces to faraway Brandenburg while the French lay poised on the Rhine. Frederick William would have to go it alone. Once weather permitted, he struck camp in Schweinfurt and set out across Germany. In a sense, emergency had liberated him: "As he recognized that he would now establish his immediate future by his own good sword, there was no more hesitating. His actions were as bold and rapid as lightning. He could now bring his own energy to bear, free from diplomatic considerations."[41]

The operational problem was simple to state, but more difficult to carry out: bring an army clear across Germany as rapidly as possible to catch the Swedes by surprise. Armies of the day did not travel light. Not only did they drag along a trail of wagons carrying supplies, munitions, and luxuries for the officers, but a horde of camp followers as well, suttlers and pages, even the wives and children of soldiers. There were, perhaps, two or three of them to each soldier. Things were different, however, as the Brandenburgers departed Schweinfurt on May 26, 1675. With the sixty-nine-year-old Derfflinger in over-all operational command, the army marched rapidly in small, widely separated contingents.[42] There were three wings, the left under Prince Friedrich II of Hesse-Homburg, the right under General Joachim Ernst von Görtzke, and the center under Derfflinger, accompanied by the Elector himself. To liberate the army from the tyranny of its supply columns, the soldiers had orders to buy their provisions from the local townspeople, but to leave crops and horses unmolested. Derf-flinger disbursed funds for the purpose. The major obstacle was the Thuringian Forest, with its dense woods, mountains, and roads that wound seemingly to nowhere. The left and right wings, mainly cav-alry, could skirt it, but the center contained the infantry and artillery, and it had to pass straight through. In fact, the center wing itself had to be divided into three columns to make the passage of the forest possible at all. With the army operating in at least five major seg-ments and spread out over some 120 kilometers of terrain, command and control became crucial. Cavalry detachments and mounted liaison officers maintained daily, sometimes hourly, contact between the vari-ous columns, and Derfflinger and the Elector even employed runners and trumpeters as a primitive means of traffic control.

There certainly were problems along the way. The Thirty Years' War a generation before had hit the area hard, and it still hadn't re-covered. There was often precious little to buy from the locals, and sometimes no locals from whom to buy. Moreover, a sizable gap soon opened up between the cavalry wings and the rest of the force, and Derfflinger had to crack the whip more than a few times to keep things moving forward. Nevertheless, on June 11, the army arrived in Mag-deburg, the cavalry coming up first, the infantry straggling in over the next few days. Derfflinger had covered 250 kilometers in just over two weeks—one of the great marches of the era.

Meanwhile, within Brandenburg, the harshness of foreign occupa-tion had begun to tell on the peasantry, and soon a rural uprising had begun. The peasants formed irregular militia units, eventually reach-ing company strength, and picked off the occasional Swedish soldier or patrol. On their banners they carried the slogan:

Wir sein Bauern von geringem Gut
Und dienen unserm gnädigsten Kurfürsten mit unserm Blut[43]

("We are poor farmers with little land
and serve our most gracious Elector with our blood")

The Swedes, following the path of most occupation armies, responded
with violence and even atrocity, a situation that apparently became
worse once their commander, Wrangel, became ill and ceased to exercise a firm hand over his subordinates.

With Swedish attention fixed on the difficulties of occupation duty,
Frederick William saw an opportunity. His sources inside Brandenburg assured him that the Swedes were still unaware that he had even
left the Rhine, and immediately after arriving in Magdeburg he had
the gates closed so that no news of his coming would leak out. Swedish
forces had become dispersed over the months, typical of an occupation
army being called hither and yon against domestic targets. Two main
bodies lay on the Havel River, one at Alt-Brandenburg, west of Berlin,
and the other at Havelberg to the north. Frederick William therefore
cast his gaze at the little walled town of Rathenow. It was a well-chosen
target, lying on the Havel a day's march between the two Swedish
forces. Its occupation would split the Swedish army in two and give
Frederick William flexibility in choosing his next target.

The evening of June 12 saw his army cross the Elbe and advance by
a circuitous route on Rathenow. The attack took Rathenow by stealth,
rather than force. Surreptitiously contacting his chief official in the
town, *Landrat* Briest, the Elector inquired as to the best way to open
the gates. Some sources describe a banquet that Briest threw for the
officers of the Swedish garrison, the Wangelin Dragoon Regiment.
As the Swedish officers gave themselves over to drink, the Elector's
troops took up position around the town.[44] He even commandeered
ships to carry troops across the Havel, to make the ring around Rathenow airtight. In the assault itself, the redoubtable Derfflinger again
took the lead. Claiming to be a Swedish officer who had escaped from a
Brandenburger patrol, he got the Swedish watch on the Havel to lower
the gate. He then personally led a charge of dragoons into the town
and opened the gates to the rest of the Brandenburger force. It was
June 15, just twenty days since he had left Schweinfurt.

Frederick William's bold stroke had utterly transformed the situation in Brandenburg. His original plan had called for a pause to wait
for the infantry to arrive. It was clear, however, that there was not a
moment to lose. Now that the secret was out and the Swedes knew
that they had trouble on their hands, they had moved immediately to
concentrate their forces. The main Swedish body at Alt-Brandenburg,

deployed farthest to the south, was in the most danger. Soon it was in motion to the north, seeking to escape the trap. The Elector ordered his cavalry at Rathenow to set out for Lauen, astride the road from Alt-Brandenburg. The Swedish force, commanded by Field Marshal Wrangel's half-brother, General Volmar Wrangel, got through Nauen just hours before the Elector cut off the route. There was real desperation in the Swedes now. A raiding party under Colonel Joachim Hennigs, one hundred cavalry and thirty dragoons, scoured the country around the Swedes, destroying bridges and blocking roads.[45] Their activity, as well as the uncertain state of the countryside, severely limited Wrangel's options. His choices ran out altogether when his force attempted a crossing of the Rhin River at the small town of Fehrbellin early on the morning of June 18. Not only did they find the bridge there destroyed, the last link in the chain that Hennigs and his men had been forging, they also saw riders approaching from the southeast. Brandenburg had arrived. Frederick William had closed the trap.

It was the advance guard of the Elector's horse, 1,500 men in nine squadrons under the Prince of Hesse-Homburg. With nowhere to run and no choice but to fight, Wrangel reluctantly put his men into battle array to the south of Fehrbellin. He had eight brigades of infantry and twenty-four squadrons of horse, some 10,600 men in all. With some of his infantry detailed to guard the guns that were en route to Fehrbellin, there were probably some 7,000 men in the line itself.[46]

His best chance for victory, or at least for respite while his engineers worked feverishly to rebuild the bridge over the Rhin, was a bold spoiling attack on the much smaller force facing him. The Prince of Homburg, by contrast, had orders to reconnoiter the Swedish position and push back enemy pickets, but not to launch a general assault. The aggressiveness that was already becoming the Brandenburger trademark soon won out, however, and it was the Prince who struck first. The situation seemed too favorable to let pass. The Swedes had a downed bridge behind them, and impassable marshes on both left and right (the Rhin and Havelland bogs, respectively). Their headlong flight had been suddenly and unexpectedly interrupted and they were fighting a battle for which they seemed to have little stomach. Against orders, the Prince ordered his squadrons forward into the attack. He could make little impression on the much larger force in front of him, but his attacks did have the effect of pinning it in place.

When riders brought the news to the Elector in his camp at Nauen, he immediately set his entire mounted army on the road to Fehrbellin, arriving there about noon. His eye for terrain almost immediately

Dorf
Hakenberg —

Rechts das
Rhinluch —

Schweden —

Rechts
Homburgs —
Reiterei

Derfflingers —
Dragoner
auf dem
Hügel

Branden-
burgische —
Reiter

Fehrbellin 1675

A period rendering of the battle of Fehrbellin, with the Rhin River bordering the battlefield to the east. Near the bottom of the scene, the Prussians have just seized the crucial hills on the Swedish right and are in the process of launching their enveloping assault.

settled on a line of small sand hills on the right flank of the Swedish position.[47] How he must have smiled, remembering a nearly identical situation on Turenne's flank at Marlenheim.[48] There he had failed to convince his allies to go along with his ideas for an attack; this time he had only to give the order. Quickly, the Elector had them occupied, with artillery emplaced on the heights. From here, his guns could take the entire Swedish position in enfilade.

Wrangel's failure to garrison the hills is another sign of how reluctantly he had taken up this fight and of the confusion within the Swedish camp. In fact, his entire handling of the battle is only explicable in moral terms. He felt that he was about to be beaten, and his only thought was to get the bridge back up and to escape. Later German commentators would question the "schematic" nature of his battle line, infantry in the center, cavalry on both wings, and his seemingly willful ignorance of the terrain.[49] A better question might be, Why didn't he attack when he had the chance?

The guns on the hills opened fire soon after noon, and began to deal out punishment to the right wing of the Swedish forces below them. Once Frederick William had his entire force in line, some 5,600 riders, he began to press hard on the open Swedish right flank, seeking to envelop it. For their part, the Swedes were trying to storm the hills to silence the guns. This was the only spot on the field where movement was possible; the Swedish left was well anchored, pressing hard up against the Rhin swamp. Throughout the fighting, the Elector was on the point of the assault, a highly visible figure. In fact, his gray drew so much fire that, according to legend, his Master of the Horse, Emanuel Froben, offered to trade horses on the excuse that Frederick William's horse was balking. They made the exchange, and Froben was killed in the fighting.[50] There was tough fighting here, and on at least one occasion the Elector had to intervene to keep a fleeing unit in the line.

The Elector's cavalry finally put to flight the Swedish horse on the right flank. Now it could turn in on the uncovered and vulnerable infantry. One unit, the Delwig Foot Regiment, which had been trying with leveled pikes to get at the Brandenburg guns, bore the brunt of the attack. The Elector's cavalry cut it to pieces. Still, the Swedish right put up just enough resistance to allow most of the left and center to retreat toward Fehrbellin in relatively good order. As night fell, the Swedes managed to repair the bridge over the Rhin and salvage most of the army, although Wrangel had to abandon eight guns and many vehicles on the southern bank. With a Swedish rear guard still holding the town, and with much of the Brandenburg army not yet present, there was no pursuit. Frederick William was content to camp on the ground where he had just won his greatest victory. The next day, however, he sent his riders over the Rhin, along with some fresh cavalry just up from Berlin, to harry the Swedish retreat.

In terms of size and scope, Fehrbellin might appear to be a minor affair. Brandenburger losses amounted to some five hundred men, Swedish losses not much higher, at least on the day of battle itself. The defeated Swedes, however, now had to retreat through a countryside of sullen, often hostile peasants who took their share of parting shots at their hated occupiers. By the time the Swedes passed through Ruppin and Wittstock to the safety of Mecklenburg, their force probably amounted to no more than four thousand men.

The importance of the battle goes well beyond mere numbers, however. To attempt to argue away the significance of Fehrbellin, or to label it essentially a victory for the Elector's postbattle propaganda machine, as does one modern scholar, is to miss the point entirely.[51]

When Frederick William woke up on June 18, Brandenburg was a minor player on the European scene. Neighboring powers saw his army as an interesting addition to a friendly coalition, but no more than that. Now it had single-handedly faced the forces of a country that was considered to be a Great Power, perhaps the preeminent military force in Europe, and had smashed them with ease. From our perspective in the twenty-first century, a victory over Sweden might not be all that impressive; it is crucial to remember, however, that the world of the seventeenth century saw things differently. There was celebration in the Netherlands at the news of the victory over Louis XIV's ally; in Alsace, popular songs suddenly appeared praising him.[52] Frederick William had arrived. When he went to bed that evening, he was the Great Elector.

Operationally, the battle must be seen as the culmination of a remarkable campaign. The sudden quitting of Franconia, the rapid and dispersed march across Europe, the successful attempt to keep the march a secret for as long as possible, the recognition of Rathenow as the key to the Swedish position—all these are the product of a first-class operational mind. His goals remained flexible. It is likely that he had no thought beyond freeing Brandenburg from foreign occupation. Once the Prince of Homburg had the Swedes in his sights south of the ruined bridge of Fehrbellin, Frederick William did not hesitate. It is clear that he aimed at nothing less than the complete destruction of the force facing him. In battle, he showed the same eye for terrain as he had in front of Warsaw and at Marlenheim. Recognizing the key to the Swedish position in an instant, he blended movement, fire, and shock into a potent combination. From "the Rhine to the Rhin,"[53] there was hardly a false step in the Great Elector's art of war.

Schlittenfahrt: The Great Sleigh Drive

Further proof of Fehrbellin's importance was the fact that Frederick William went from victory to victory against the Swedes over the next few years. He had clearly gained a moral advantage over his bitterest adversary. His infantry was in the theater by July, and he could now assume a more aggressive operational posture. In September he gained an ally, King Christian V of Denmark, always eager to strike a blow at the Swedes and even more eager to do so while they were weak. Likewise, contingents from the Empire, from Brunswick and Münster, now arrived to fight at his side, a reminder of the broader conflict, the Dutch War, still raging in the background.

With the Danish and Dutch fleets putting pressure on the Swedes, the campaign against Western Pomerania (*Vorpommern*) began in earnest. He outnumbered the Swedes and could therefore threaten more places than they could legitimately defend. He drove into Mecklenburg, took Warnemünde, and threw the Swedes back into Wismar, cutting off their communications between Pomerania and Bremen-Werden. Still, the enemy held several fortresses: Demmin, Anklam, Greifswald, Stralsund, the island of Rügen, and the real prize of the campaign, the port of Stettin. Levering them out of all these places would be difficult. It would be a long, drawn-out campaign, typical of any campaign of the era that aimed at large-scale territorial aggrandizement. Nevertheless, the Great Elector's progress was steady: Demmin in 1676, Stettin in December 1677, Rügen and Stralsund in September and October 1678, respectively. It appeared that all of Pomerania, a long-term objective of his foreign policy, now lay in his grasp.[54]

There was one more great campaign in this war, however, and although it has nearly vanished down the modern memory hole, it was of tremendous significance for later Prussian-German military operations. It was the winter campaign of 1678–1679.[55] Despite the loss of Pomerania, Sweden still remained a danger, and French subsidies continued to flow into its coffers. In late 1678 a Swedish force of twelve thousand men under the command of Field Marshal Heinrich Horn left its base in Riga, marched south through Kurland, and crossed the Memel River into Prussia. It's fair to say that the invasion caught the Great Elector, then involved in the siege of Stralsund, utterly flatfooted. Prussia was virtually empty of troops, with viceroy Duke Ernst of Croy having at his disposal just 2,500 regulars and an equal number of local militia.[56]

Slowly the Swedes advanced to the south, through Tilsit, toward Insterburg and then Wehlau. The defenders retired ahead of them, the regulars hurriedly and the militia panicking, especially at the first sign of cannon fire. In the course of their retreat, they emptied the land of cattle and supplies, as well as wagons and boats for river crossings. Reinforcements arrived from Brandenburg, some two thousand men under General von Görtzke, but the rout simply swept them up. Soon, Croy's regiments had withdrawn to the region south of Königsberg.

The Great Elector met the invasion calmly. Long years of warfare against the Swedes had apparently left him unconvinced of the gravity of the threat. A small regular force and a call-up of the province's militia should suffice, he felt. He left Stralsund and arrived in Berlin on December 12, where he intended to remain. His mind changed suddenly, however, when news arrived on December 14 that the Swedes had breached the Memel line and crossed the small stream to the south, the Rus. It now appeared that the Duchy was in danger, and the specter loomed of having conquered Pomerania only to lose Prussia. He issued orders for a major operation in Prussia, involving considerable forces:

Six regiments of cavalry	3,700 men
Two regiments of dragoons	1,400 men
Five battalions of infantry	3,500 men
Total:	8,600 men[57]

In addition, the operation would call upon thirty-two cannon and two howitzers. Along with their crews, the Great Elector was able to lead some nine thousand men to the relief of Prussia.

These were high times for Frederick William. Never before or again would he have so many men under arms. Four years of battle against the Swedes, much of it bankrolled by foreign subsidy, had swollen the size of his army to 45,000 men: 31,000 infantry, 9,700 cavalry, and 3,400 dragoons, with artillery and staff making up the difference.[58] He had come a long way from those first 5,000 men.

As always, speed was Frederick William's stock in trade. He left Neustettin on January 1, 1679, and arrived in Buchholz that evening (55 kilometers), Tuchel the next day (35 kilometers), and Marienwerder the day after that (80 kilometers). At Marienwerder his men were able to cross the frozen Vistula on the fly, without any of the normal delays attendant upon a bridge crossing. After this hot start over some pretty miserable roads, he allowed his army two days of rest. Here he heard that the Swedes had reached Schippenbeil in their southward march. Only now, apparently, did he set an operational goal: the town of Preussisch Holland, south of Königsberg. Here he would rendezvous with Görtzke's corps and then launch the combined force into an immediate attack on the Swedes.

The Swedes had experienced this sort of thing before, and the news that the Great Elector was driving toward Prussia led them into retreat. It appears, in fact, that the original intent of the invasion had been to relieve pressure on Stralsund, and it had already fallen. On January 22, Görtzke took up the pursuit with his cavalry and one thousand mounted infantry. The news only spurred Frederick William into

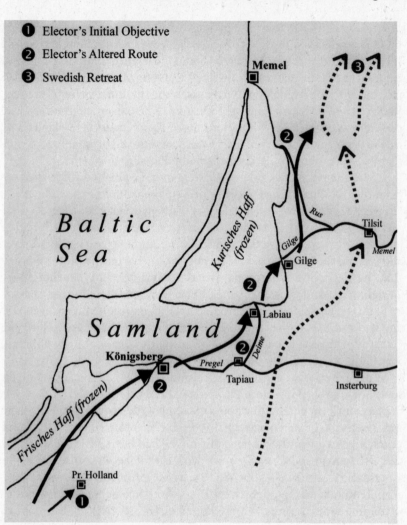

The Great Sleigh Drive, Winter 1678–1679

greater speed, and a changed objective. Now, instead of Preussisch Holland, for a prudent prebattle concentration, it was pursuit through Königsberg and Tilsit. "I intend to cut them off,"[59] he wrote at the time to the Emperor. But how to get there as rapidly as possible?

As on similar occasions in the past, the Elector's solution merged "cleverness with boldness."[60] First he ordered Görtzke to continue the pursuit with his force, now 2,800 cavalry and dragoons. He then sent orders to the fortress city of Königsberg to have 1,200 large sleighs, 600–700 horses, and provisions for eight days ready upon his arrival. In Marienwerder, he had already procured sleighs to mount as many of his men as possible, and he now set out on one of the most improbable pursuit rides of his career. On January 23, the main column reached Preussische-Mark, fifty kilometers from Marienwerder, the next day they made thirty-two kilometers more to Preussisch-Holland. The ride on January 25 was truly prodigious, amounting to some sixty kilometers and ending in the Carben-Heiligenbeil region.

It was the next day's ride that later generations of German staff officers would immortalize: January 26 saw the column driving over the frozen Frisches Haff and Pregel Rivers to Königsberg, turning what was a winding coastal road into a perfectly straight line and advancing another fifty-five kilometers. The new equipment waiting in the city allowed him to forge ahead in his pursuit. News reached him that day that the Swedes were in retreat toward Insterburg, and that their force of eight thousand contained at least two thousand sick. Late in the day on January 27 the main column departed Königsberg and by the next day had reached Labiau, another bound of fifty kilometers. Here the Great Elector finally had his rendezvous with Görtzke. The combined force now amounted to some fifteen thousand men.

With Horn now in full retreat toward Tilsit, Frederick William sent Görtzke ahead in close pursuit and ordered him to fix the Swedes in place until the main force could come up to destroy them. The drive was starting to take its toll on the Great Elector; he was fifty-eight years old and given the amount of time he had been in the field during the last four years, it was not surprising that he was suffering from a number of ailments—gout and breathing problems. His increasing corpulence made it impossible for him to mount a horse without assistance. The temperatures, which dipped below –25 degrees Fahrenheit, could not have helped.

Beyond simple exhaustion, however, was an operational problem: the sleigh columns were finding it increasingly difficult to keep order. They tended to string out during the course of the day, as they moved in single file through the forest roads, then bunch up when they reached a bottleneck of any sort, a particularly narrow stretch of road or a bridge. The problems seemed to be getting worse as men and animals tired. Still, onward they drove, with another ice crossing on January 29, as Frederick William crossed the Kurisches Haff toward Gilge, making another twenty-three kilometers.

The Great Elector as he appeared in 1683, at the age of 63. Failing health and increased corpulence had made it nearly impossible for him to get into the saddle.

On that same day, Görtzke ran into the Swedes near Tilsit. His advance guard under Colonel Joachim Hennigs von Treffenfeld (the hero of the Fehrbellin bridge, whom Frederick had ennobled for his heroism) had made contact near the village of Splitter, three kilometers west of the city. In a sudden attack they had inflicted several hundred casualties on the Swedes, took eighty prisoners, and plundered a great deal of the enemy baggage train. Unfortunately, Görtzke's failure to reinforce Hennigs in a timely manner meant that the principal result of the encounter at Splitter was to let the Swedes know that trouble was closing in and that they had best redouble the speed of their retreat. Frederick William promoted Hennigs, a son of peasant stock, to Major General on the spot; his words for Görtzke have, unfortunately, not entered the historical record.

Splitter was the campaign's turning point. In fact, both sides were reaching the limit of their endurance. By the end of January, the Swedish army had been without quarters for five days and had not been fed for two. On January 30, Frederick William had to halt his columns altogether outside Tilsit to allow his dispersed, straggling columns to close up. As a result, a planned attack on the main Swedish body on January 31 struck air. The Swedes had already recrossed the Memel, heading north. Görtzke's belated attempts to maintain contact with the enemy went for naught. With the Elector racing for Heidekrug, directly on the coastal road, the entire Swedish main body was in danger of being cut off. Horn parried by taking an interior route to the north, well away from the coast, and a much more difficult place from which to provision his troops. In the absence of reliable reconnaissance, Frederick William failed to recognize the change of direction, and the Swedes escaped the trap.

Some of them had, at any rate. The Swedish force that made it back to Riga on February 14 was a remnant of the original invasion force. Nearly three-quarters of Horn's men, some nine thousand out of twelve thousand, were casualties. Many of them had been victims of disease or frostbite, the price of campaigning in the winter. He had also lost twenty-eight of his original thirty-six cannon, always a sign in this era that things had gone amiss. If it had not been quite as bad as Napoleon's retreat from Moscow, the comparison made by Thomas Carlyle in his *History of Frederick the Great*, it had certainly been bad enough.[61]

Despite the lack of any significant battle, the Winter Campaign of 1678–1679 wrote another important chapter in the military career of the Great Elector. The parallels to the 1675 campaign are striking.

Once again he faced invasion of the homeland while he was tied up in operations abroad. Once again he was able to whip together a significant force, march it across hundreds of miles to the threatened territory, and then triumph. Once again these were the Swedes that he had shattered. Horn's orders to retreat do nothing, from the perspective of history, to lessen the size of the victory. He saw his command essentially destroyed in the retreat, and that was mainly because it had to take place so rapidly. Tarrying a single day, with Frederick William's sleigh columns coming up out of the forest at him, would surely have meant disaster. Even so, if Colonel Treffenfeld had been General Treffenfeld *before* the rear guard action at Splitter, Horn's entire force probably would have perished there.

The Great Elector and German Military Operations

Historians have spilled their share of ink over the Great Elector's domestic policies. They have noted his transformation of Brandenburg-Prussia into a machine seemingly designed for one purpose: to finance a standing army. They have analyzed the Brandenburg Recess and the allegedly fateful consequences for later social development in Prussia and Germany. They have looked carefully at institutions like the General War Commissariat (*Generalkriegskommissariat*), which systematized administration and funding of the army, and which often made it seem as if the state served the army, rather than the other way around. They have made a case for the birth of militarism during his reign. About his military operations, indeed, his "operational art," they have had much less—hardly anything, in fact—to say.[62]

A good point of departure is to note that his military successes brought him little of what he desired. His minor participation in the Thirty Years' War had netted him Eastern Pomerania, and all his wars after that added not an acre to his territory. Even the dramatic victories over Sweden from 1675 to 1679 brought him nothing. He returned from the great winter campaign to find that his allies had decided on a separate peace with France and that he was going to have to give all his Pomeranian conquests of that war back to Sweden. When he hesitated, Louis XIV underlined the demand by looting and burning an undefended Cleves. The Elector responded, as he often did, by switching sides in the European power struggle and becoming a French ally. If he could not gain Pomerania against France, his reasoning went, perhaps he would gain it with France. In this too he would be disappointed.

Yet the lesson drawn by later generations of German officers, and much of the population at large, was not the emptiness of even a glittering operational victory. Rather, it was the speed, boldness, and aggressive nature of the Great Elector's way of war. The same adjectives appear again and again in later Prussian and German writings: bold, clever, energetic, rapid, daring. The decision to launch a risky flank march against the Polish positions in front of Warsaw; the dramatic march across Germany to clear the "foreign guests," as Frederick William was wont to call the Swedes, from the Mark; the quick eye for terrain, displayed at Fehrbellin, along with the snap decision to attack a numerically superior enemy; the improvised pursuit of the same Swedes by foot, hoof, and sleigh in the winter campaign: later German officers were convinced that this was the only kind of war their country could fight. In central Europe, surrounded by dangerous foes and inconstant allies, a passive policy of defense would only stave off inevitable defeat. Paradoxically, the very danger of their position meant that Prussian and German armies had to prepare, train, and equip themselves for aggressive and high-tempo offensive warfare, the bold operational thrust, the war of movement.

Any balanced analysis of the Great Elector's campaigns must also allot a complete role to several talented subordinates. They include Sparr for the artillery and Derfflinger for the cavalry and dragoons. The former played a key role in the battle of Warsaw, the latter was the heart and soul of the new Prussian army, a commander who did not mellow with age, but in fact grew more aggressive with each passing year. Derfflinger was an interesting personality: an Austrian, a journeyman tailor, a young man so poor he "couldn't afford to pay the boatman for passage over the Elbe." He entered military service, he would later explain, because soldiers got across for free. He had fought for Sweden in the Thirty Years' War and had gained a special reputation for harshness toward civilians and for the scale of his exactions on the local towns, not unusual in that conflict. He was also a rogue and a hard drinker. He came into the service of Brandenburg at the age of forty by purchasing a piece of property that his wife's indebted relatives could no longer afford to keep. The settled conditions in his new land were hard to bear after all those years of camp life, however. He and a few friends once went on a drunk in the town of Kölln and things got completely out of hand. Derfflinger wound up threatening to shoot the *Bürgermeister* and his family, as well as several officials who tried to intervene.[63]

Field Marshal Georg von Derfflinger was the first in a long line: a tough, ambitious, and slightly unsavory foreigner in the service of the Prussian crown. Bust by Andreas Schlüter.

His relationship with Frederick William was a stormy parade of contretemps, moments of wounded vanity, and tendered resignations. Upon agreeing to serve Brandenburg in the Polish campaign, he gave the Elector a series of conditions, including the incredible "No one advances ahead of me." On another occasion, after Frederick William chose the Prince of Anhalt for a field command on the Rhine, Derfflinger resigned. When things went bad in the campaign, the Elector begged him to return. Derfflinger's conditions: "Salary of three hundred taler. A fixed 'amusement' from every haul of booty. Half the number of all imprisoned officers. The losses of my regiment made good by the Elector. I pick my adjutants myself. I may choose and dismiss all my own officers on my discretion, at least in Your Highness's absence. What else? No disgrace upon me if I lose a battle."[64]

Derfflinger was the first example of what would become a Prussian tradition, an ambitious, slightly unsavory foreigner rising to the top of the Hohenzollern bureaucracy. Such men often wound up in key positions in both the civil and military hierarchy. Their numbers would increase greatly when Louis XIV's revocation of the Edict of Nantes drove so many French Protestants into exile. Frederick William welcomed them with open arms, as the presence of later surnames like Du Moulin and François would attest. The population of Brandenburg was so small that Frederick William welcomed every able body he could get. If they had talent, as did Derfflinger, so much the better.

Frederick William believed in giving these men general missions, but not in overseeing the details. Officers of all ranks who showed initiative in combat might find a promotion waiting them at the end of the day, as was the case with Treffenfeld. Here it is possible to see the kernel of what became known as *Auftragstaktik*, or flexible command. We should keep in mind the true nature of its social background, however. The compact between the monarch and the estates of the realm—the nobles, in other words—was the basis of the Prussian state. Toward those of the lower orders under his control, whether on the land or in the army, a Prussian Junker had not just privilege, but absolute sovereignty. The granting of operational prerogatives to the nobles in combat was not just a good idea; it was of a piece with the social contract of the Prussian state. For the monarch to insist on close supervision of a subordinate commander's plan of action would have been a grievous infraction. In other words, *Auftragstaktik* grew directly out of Prussian culture.

Finally, the fame of the *Schlittenfahrt*, the "sleigh drive," has barely survived to the present day. One recent standard scholarly work on the Northern Wars mentions it not at all. However, among later German officers, the drive was a model of maneuver-oriented war, of improvisation, of bold and aggressive command. Consider this evaluation, written by a German staff officer in 1927:

> The winter campaign 1678–79 was a complete success, but not because of successful battles (in fact most of the tactical encounters were either indecisive or even entirely unfavorable). Rather, it was the moral effect of the relentless pursuit, pressure on the retreat routes, and especially the tremendous speed of the Brandenburger advance that convinced the exhausted Swedes that only the fastest possible retreat could save them from destruction.
>
> In the fifteen days between January 18th and February 2nd, the Elector's troops covered 540 kilometers, that is 36 kilometers daily, and this despite bad roads, snow, and ice. The rough winter was in many respects a comrade to a commander like the Great Elector. River crossings could proceed without any time lost due to bridges. In fact, the water courses and bays actually served as excellent routes, open plains over which the sleds of the infantry and artillery sleighs—procured with such great energy—could both advance rapidly and preserve their strength. The use of sleighs was an improvisation, and thus doubly noteworthy. The drive brought *Bewegungskrieg* directly to the enemy.[65]

The staff officer also noted that although the speed of the drive was a benefit, the tendency of the columns to stretch out along the roads was a disadvantage when it came to concentrating the power necessary for actual combat. He no doubt began to ponder that problem deeply, and to turn it over in his mind for the next ten years. He was just a young major at the time, but he had an interesting future ahead of him. His name was Heinz Guderian.

The Origins of Frederician Warfare

The Age of Limits?

There is a well-established consensus that the eighteenth century was an age of limited war, "limited in aims and means alike and gentlemanly in conduct."[1] It was an age of maneuver, so the argument goes, in which battles were fought sparingly, if at all, and only when both sides desired them. As a host of writings from the period attest, there were numerous theorists who claimed that battle had become superfluous: maneuver was precise and geometric, and only a fool would choose the uncertainties of battle over it. A widely quoted aphorism of the day, one that often shows up in the writings of the generals themselves, was to ask "whether the advantages you would derive by winning exceed in degree the damage you would sustain if you lost." Usually, they wrote, the answer was no. The service regulations for the Saxon army in 1753 went so far as to say that "the greatest generals refrain from giving battle, except for urgent reasons."[2]

There certainly were reasons to have a prejudice against battle. Soldiers were simply too expensive to train and replace to waste them frivolously. Each casualty, on the average, meant a waste of three years of training and expense—much less for the infantry soldier and much more for the cavalry trooper. The taxation and revenue systems were far too underdeveloped to make good the losses. As a result, the wise eighteenth-century general attempted wherever possible to maneuver against the magazines, depots, and supply lines of his adversary, to get him to retire from the theater. In addition, the relatively small size of the armies involved imposed its own set of limitations on what was possible. As Hans Delbrück, the civilian bane of the German General Staff in the nineteenth century, wrote: "The military means at hand did not suffice to destroy the enemy state completely. To annihilate his forces or to occupy his capital and the better part of his provinces was impossible, even after a great victory." The utter overthrow of an enemy in a single day's battle, in other words, was a fantasy. In all ways, an age of limited resources could only sustain limited warfare. Forcing an enemy into compliance meant not so much overthrowing him, as exhausting him.[3] Although it might be achieved through battle, Delbrück argued, it was also possible through "clever marches." A general could seek a position where it was equally possible to threaten the magazines and supplies of the enemy while simultaneously protecting one's own from the enemy.

Although the idea continues to percolate through a great deal of our contemporary military history, there is just one problem with it. If indeed the entire European military system of the time supposedly aimed away from battle and toward elegant, geometric maneuver, it certainly seemed to produce more than its fair share of battles: repeated and bloody battles, a simple list of which for the eighteenth century alone could fill a book. If indeed the contestants recognized that they were living and fighting in an age of limits, then they certainly gave a good imitation of seeking the utter destruction and overthrow of their enemies. It is difficult to read the account of any eighteenth-century battle, which typically found two lines of hostile infantry blasting away at each other at extremely close range, with casualties often in the 30–40 percent range, and come away with a sense that one had just experienced a kind of limited warfare. It is also useful to remember that following such bloodletting, with its huge losses of supposedly "irreplaceable" manpower, the antagonists then often did it again a few miles up or down the road. In a great conflict in the middle of the eighteenth century, they actually repeated this pattern for seven full years. Apparently, infantry wasn't all that irreplaceable.

The misapprehension, of course, comes from comparing eighteenth-century warfare with what came later: the French Revolution and the *levée en masse*; Napoleon and the *manoeuvre sur les derrières*; Moltke and the *Kesselschlacht*; the Schlieffen Plan, not to mention the horrors of the twentieth century.[4] Historians have dubbed the nineteenth and twentieth centuries the "age of total war," and by any reasonable standard the wars of Frederick the Great don't qualify. It is certainly permissible for historians to compare the eighteenth century with later periods. It is ahistorical in the extreme to *define* eighteenth-century warfare only in terms of later developments of which the participants could not possibly be aware. If one could interview the soldiers who just fought the battle of Zorndorf, a brutal and bloody Prussian assault against a stolid Russian adversary during the third campaigning season of the Seven Years' War, one suspects that they would be surprised to find that they had just been fighting a "limited war."

Two views of Frederick the Great of Prussia, fresh-faced at the start of his reign (left) and older, grayer, and perhaps wiser toward the end (right). The strain of long years in the field had obviously taken its toll.

In fact, no single individual better defies the alleged spirit of his age than Frederick II (the Great), king of Prussia from 1740 to 1786.[5] In many areas of his life, he may well have been a careful and calculating enlightened despot. His literary and musical pursuits, his friendship with Voltaire, his belief that religion was a childish fairy tale that no thinking adult could possibly take seriously: in all these things, he was clearly a figure of the Enlightenment. In war, however, he usually saw one path to victory, and that was fixing the enemy army in place, maneuvering near or even around it to give himself a favorable position for the attack, and then smashing it with an overwhelming blow from an unexpected direction. He was the most aggressive field commander of the century, perhaps of all time, and one who constantly pushed the limits of the possible. According to one modern scholar, "The King was also more consistently willing than any of his contemporaries to seek decisions through offensive operations."[6] When later generations of Prussian-German staff officers looked back to the age of Frederick, they saw a commander who repeatedly, even joyfully, risked everything on a single day's battle—his army, his kingdom, often his very life.

Learning Curve: The Battle of Mollwitz

Since the death of the Great Elector, two monarchs had ruled in Berlin. The first was Elector Frederick III, no warrior, but a refined man and a lover of fine things. He was a sponsor of the arts, patron to the historian Samuel von Pufendorf, founder of the University of Halle and its Prussian Academy of the Arts.[7] The culmination of his reign was being crowned King Frederick I. Although the title originally covered the king only when he was in Ducal Prussia, that is, outside imperial territory, Frederick essentially ignored this restriction. Soon "King in Prussia" became "King of Prussia." Brandenburg-Prussia had now become the Kingdom of Prussia, recognized as a major player on the European scene.

The second was King Frederick William I.[8] As his father loved art and sculpture and architecture, he loved soldiers and uniforms and guns. In most ways he seems perfectly sane to us. He greatly increased the size of his army, and even the fact that he dispatched recruiting parties across Europe to kidnap young men for the service doesn't disqualify him as a rational actor in an age when "impressment" was a basic recruiting tool. Other areas of his personality, his preference for tall men in the ranks—the taller the better—for example, or his highly abusive treatment of his son and crown prince Frederick, might land us in murkier psychological waters.

The army, in short, was Frederick William's obsession, and he trained and drilled it obsessively, putting it through paces quite unlike the training regimen of any other European state. As a result, it could load and shoot faster, change formation more smoothly, and pass through some of the most complex tactical evolutions imaginable without losing its cohesion. Prussian infantry could "form up more rapidly than any other troops on earth," Frederick once wrote.[9] Such rote training worked best in the single most mechanical area of eighteenth-century soldiering, where thinking could actually get you into trouble: handling the flintlock musket. That single advantage, the ability to loose off four to five shots per minute when their adversaries were achieving two to three, would be a major factor in the history of eighteenth-century Europe.[10] Although the "soldier-king" Frederick William I never fought a battle, he did bequeath a highly trained, highly disciplined force to his son.

Certainly Frederick did not spring into action as a fully grown master of the art of war. His opening campaign in Silesia was hesitant, even amateurish.[11] The march into the province in December 1740 saw an army that had for years done nothing but eat and drill suddenly plunge into the uncertainty of actual operations. Men and officers rediscovered the facts of life: it rains; horses get sick; maps don't always tell you where you're going if you hold them upside down at night by the light of a flickering candle. They also discovered that a twenty-nine-year-old who has never commanded anything larger than a regiment—and that in peacetime—needs a shakedown cruise or two to find his bearings.

The first battle, at Mollwitz, showed that Frederick needed to develop the skills to go along with his aggressive battlefield nature.[12] Having been outmaneuvered by the Austrian Field Marshal Wilhelm Neipperg—a common theme of both Silesian Wars, no matter who was commanding his enemies—Frederick found himself in early April chasing the Austrian army, which had bypassed him while he was still in winter quarters. It was a miserable affair, with swirling snows and near-zero visibility. The Austrian target was Neisse, one of the few cities in Silesia that had held out against Frederick's initial offensive. Frederick kept pace with the Austrians, the two armies moving parallel and roughly northward, Frederick to the east, Neipperg to the west.[13] The Austrians reached Neisse, relieved the town, crossed the nearby river (of the same name), and were now interspersed between the Prussian army and home. Frederick had to attack. He was in a spot often identified as the worst possible by armchair generals: on the strategic defensive (defending the newly won province of Silesia, to be precise) but the tactical offensive, with no choice but to risk the high casualties attendant on attacking.

On April 10, 1741, Frederick caught up with the Austrians. Using information gleaned from captured Austrian prisoners and the local farmers, he was able to get a fix on Neipperg's camp, in front of the town of Mollwitz, southeast of Ohlau. Neither side had a decisive numerical advantage. The Prussian army included thirty-one battalions of infantry, thirty cavalry squadrons, and three squadrons of hussars, for a total of 21,600 men, plus thirty-seven regimental and sixteen heavy guns. The Austrians had sixteen infantry battalions, fourteen grenadier companies, two regiments of hussars, plus a large mass of cavalry: six cuirassier (heavy cavalry) and five dragoon regiments. The Austrians nearly matched the Prussians in total manpower (19,000 to 21,600 men), vastly outnumbered them in cavalry (8,000 to 4,000), and were equally inferior in infantry (10,000 to 16,800) and artillery (nineteen field guns to the fifty-three Prussian, the latter a mixed force of field guns and heavies).[14] All battles are asymmetrical, and this one was no exception: Austrian cavalry would try its luck against the Prussian infantry and artillery.

Of course, like the rest of the Austrian army, the men of those cavalry regiments weren't going to do any good while they were sleeping. Frederick was literally able to march his entire force to within two thousand paces of Neipperg's camp without the Austrians stirring. While the modern mind screams, "storm the Austrian camp," such a thought simply did not occur to the eighteenth-century commander. Armies of the day did not execute all those firing drills and practice all those intricate tactical evolutions for nothing.

Instead, Frederick now gave the army orders to deploy. Five columns marched up and swung to the right, forming a battle line. On the surface, it was a by-the-numbers procedure that resulted in two parallel lines, or echelons (*Treffen*): a first line under the command of General Kurt Christoph von Schwerin, and a second, supporting echelon under Hereditary Prince (*Erbprinz*) Leopold of Anhalt. Cavalry stood on both the right and left flanks: the right wing under the command of Count Adolf Friedrich von der Schulenberg and the left under the command of Colonel von Posadowsky. The artillery deployed to the front of the first echelon, to cover the entire friendly front with its fire, but also to move forward with the infantry as it advanced.

This was the first time that Frederick had ever performed this act for real, however, and it showed. In fact, the entire exercise proved to be vastly more difficult to perform on the battlefield than it had been on the exercise square, especially with two feet of snow on the ground, sun glare making the estimation of distances a matter of guesswork, and the jitter of men and troops who knew that they are about to go into battle. A major problem soon arose. There turned out to be a considerable narrowing of the open plain from the spot where Frederick began his approach march (*Anmarsch*) to the spot where the deployment from column into line (*Aufmarsch*) would take place. Such calculations, made on the spot and at a glance, were part of the repertoire of experienced officers, but not a new battlefield commander. Apparently, some of the older hands among his officers tried to tell the king about the problem. Not only did he refuse to listen, he would later blame at least one of them for the problem itself.[15] At any rate, there certainly was not room to deploy all the forces originally intended for the front line. Amounting to seven battalions of infantry and the entire cavalry of the left wing, these were a not inconsiderable portion of the king's fighting strength.

The Prussian king and his commanders had to come up with expedients, and their solutions show a great deal about the complexity of battle in the age of linear tactics. Since there was no room for the orphan units in the first echelon, they came under the operational control of Prince Leopold, commander of the second echelon. For the most part he employed them for protection of his open right flank. This was the fate of the Kleist Grenadier Battalion and the two battalions of the Prince Dietrich Regiment, for example. In fact, he actually deployed the Kleist Grenadiers and the 1st Battalion of the Prince Dietrich Regiment in the open space in front of his echelon, facing outward, that is, to the right, at a right angle to the rest of his line. It was a decision that would have interesting consequences, as we shall see. As for the rest, the 2nd Battalion of Prince Dietrich deployed on the right of the second echelon. The Prince Leopold Regiment and the 2nd Battalion of the Schwerin Regiment, too, were in the no man's land between the echelons, this time on the left. The Puttkamer Grenadier Battalion deployed in column behind the first echelon, ready to move up if the opportunity presented itself. Finally, the entire left wing cavalry had to wait in column behind the left wing of the second echelon. It must have been difficult for men and officers of these three regiments (five squadrons of the Prince Frederick Regiment, five squadrons of the Platen Dragoons, and six squadrons of the Bayreuth Dragoons) to imagine how they would ever be able to get into this fight, and in fact they barely did.

It took ninety minutes, but the Prussians had finally gotten their troops into line. Their left (southwest) rested on a good position, the village of Neudorf, hard up against the Kleiner Bach, a small stream whose steep and swampy banks made it essentially unflankable. The line then stretched toward the northeast in two echelons, 240 paces apart, passing through a flat plain and ending in a group of trees 400 meters to the west of the village of Hermsdorf. All told, the front line extended some 2,750 meters—about 800 meters too short for all the intended troops to deploy.[16]

The Prussians had their troubles, but the Austrian situation bordered on the catastrophic. The first Neipperg learned of the Prussian army's approach "was when he looked out of his quarters and saw it in battle array."[17] Moreover, he wasn't even facing Frederick, who was coming up from the southeast. In expectation of the next day's march on Ohlau, he was facing northwest—in exactly the opposite direction. The cavalry of his right wing lay at Mollwitz, his infantry at Laugwitz, in the center, and his cavalry of the left wing in Bärzdorf. A small force of hussars rounded out the deployment on the extreme right at Grüningen. All in all it was a rough arc facing in the wrong direction.

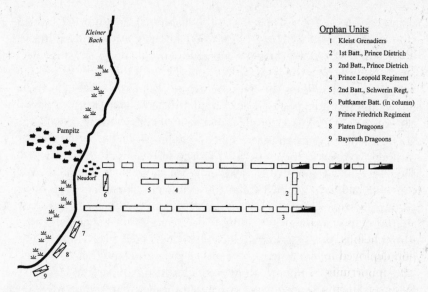

On-the-Job Training: Frederick's Deployment at Mollwitz, April 10, 1741

Camps are not tactical formations, at least they are not meant to be, but being caught in the rear forced the Austrians to go through a complex series of evolutions—one is tempted to call them gyrations—before they could meet the enemy. Their right wing cavalry, for example, commanded by Field Marshal Römer, now had to become the left of their battle line, and vice versa. Moreover, the Austrian commanders would have to perform these complex evolutions under fire from the superior Prussian artillery—also a very different experience from that on the parade ground. Only the delay in the Prussian deployment allowed Neipperg to shake his men out of camp reasonably well.

By 1:00 P.M. both armies were in motion. The Prussians advanced first, both echelons moving in step with "trumpets blaring, drums beating, and banners waving," in the words of more than one source.[18] The artillery moved forward several hundred meters, unlimbered, and lobbed a few shells off in the direction of some enemy hussars, driving them off. So far, it was a display of skills learned on the parade ground. No army in Europe could pull this off better than the Prussians, since no one drilled, exercised, or maneuvered in peacetime with their degree of intensity. The Austrians, still rushing their troops into line, were in danger of suffering a killing blow before they were even in the fight. There was as yet no real Austrian strength—not a single formed unit—visible on the battlefield.

It is unclear who in the Prussian ranks first spotted the approach of trouble. But suddenly all eyes went to the Windmill Hill east of the village of Mollwitz. A mass of enemy cavalry was approaching, six regiments—four cuirassier and two dragoon—under the command of Field Marshal Römer. Originally forming the Austrian right wing, they were now the left of the gradually forming battle line. This was the wing closer to Mollwitz, and thus the most vulnerable portion of the Austrian position. His orders were to undertake no decisive action until the entire army had been deployed. His troopers began to grumble, however, standing under Prussian artillery fire. "There were loud voices saying that it was better to get at the enemy than to be sacrificed uselessly."[19] Finally, Römer could wait no longer and launched his regiments into a grand charge against the Prussian right wing.

Römer's charge, involving some 4,500 horses, hit the Prussian cavalry opposite like a storm. There is controversy over Schulenberg's deployment and leadership of the Prussian right. His monarch accused him of failing to garrison Hermsdorf and of belatedly trying to extend toward the village. According to Frederick, Schulenberg's squadrons were actually making a quarter-turn to the right to reach the village, and in the process offering Römer their left flank. The Prussian official history offers a more logical account. As Römer's cavalry swung out to the left to take Schulenberg in the right flank, the latter tried a last second wheel to the right to meet it.[20] It was too late, and the charge caught the Prussians at the worst possible time: in the vulnerable moment when they were changing their facing.

As to the charge itself, again, there are differing accounts. Frederick states that Römer did not even bother to deploy into line, but made the charge while still partially in column formation. The Prussian official history, supported by Austrian sources, argues that as Römer's two lines of cavalry approached at speed, the lagging of the slower horses and the springing ahead of the faster ones might have made the impression of a column. Neipperg himself described it as a fairly wild ride, a charge made "à la hussarde."[21]

About one aspect there is no controversy: Schulenberg received it flat-footed. In fact, that sums up the entire tale of the Prussian cavalry at Mollwitz. It did not function as an arm of decision in the attack, and it failed even to defend itself. Schulenberg's lack of aggressive intent is clear from the fact that he had deployed two grenadier battalions in the midst of his cavalry array. It was a clear sign of a defensive mentality, since they certainly wouldn't be able to keep up with a cavalry charge. Neither was Frederick innocent of inculcating a defensive mentality in his cavalry. He had apparently read of the mixed formation in a book about Gustavus Adolphus's art of war, and decided to try out these tactics, by now more than a century old and at least fifty years out of date.[22]

Giving his horses their head, Römer crashed into the unsteady Prussian right wing "with wild cries and pistol shots."[23] His thirty Austrian squadrons hit just ten Prussian, and scattered them. The first targets were the four squadrons of the Schulenberg Horse Grenadiers; they melted away. Some Prussian cavalrymen fled among the infantry of the first line, others rode off into the gap between the first and second lines, and others betook themselves to the safety of villages off to the flanks or in the rear. In fact, according to Frederick, "they would have ridden down their own infantry, if the latter had not fired at them, in the process slowing down the charge."[24] In fact, Römer's charging regiments took a great deal of fire: from the grenadiers interspersed among the cavalry, from the two "orphan" battalions facing outward, and from the battalion guns standing off to the flank—their canister tearing into the thick ranks of Austrian horse.

The king was on the right wing. He now looked on, shocked, as his first-ever battle plan went utterly to pieces, and he did what many young commanders would have done in his position. He recklessly exposed himself to the enemy in order to rally his troops. With more bravery than wisdom, he gathered a couple of squadrons of the 11th Cuirassiers, along with Schulenberg, and rode off to halt the rout of his right wing.[25] It was a *beau geste*, magnificent, perhaps, but not war. As he admitted later, in a candid assessment of the uselessness of his own action, "broken and hastily reassembled troops have no powers of resistance,"[26] and the attempt was a miserable failure. For a time, Frederick was carried along in the rout of his own cavalry between his own echelons, an extremely dangerous spot.

It was at this point that Frederick's senior commander, Count Schwerin, asked him to leave the field for his own safety. Schwerin didn't say so, of course, but perhaps he also felt that it would be easier to get down to the business of rescuing the army without the young man present. Frederick at first refused, but eventually allowed himself to be convinced. He could not have been pleased, however, and relations between him and Schwerin would never be warm again. Frederick,

Count Kurt Christoph von Schwerin. He commanded the Prussian first echelon at Mollwitz and ordered Frederick to leave the field after the rout of the Prussian cavalry. Relations with his monarch would be cool after the victory. Schwerin would be killed at the battle of Prague in 1757.

incidentally, spent the rest of the day wandering around the countryside, and he came close to being captured by a party of Austrian hussars at Oppeln. A swift horse, the famous "Mollwitz gray," was the king's salvation. He did find time that day, however, to send a note to the Prince of Anhalt saying that the battle was lost.[27]

Back on the field, Austrian cavalry, having dispersed their opposite number on the Prussian side, now turned in on the infantry and artillery. Schulenberg was wounded, and then, while trying once again to rally some remnant of his force, killed. Although the Austrians had dispatched the Prussian horse, however, and even succeeded in putting out of action several of the Prussian guns that had been in front of the right wing, they finally met their match in the infantry. Without orders, Prussian battalions faced right and began to fire into the ranks of the Austrian horse. Austrian losses to Prussian fire were extremely heavy, and with both Prussian lines firing, often toward each other, so were Prussian losses. Soon, the momentum of the great Austrian charge was spent. Frederick would later credit the infantry battalions displaced from the first line in the original deployment.[28] Trapped, homeless, between the two Prussian echelons, they served as a kind of impromptu flank guard for the entire Prussian right.

It was a bitter struggle, however, and fierce fighting would continue here for nearly five hours. Austrian infantry came up and joined the fray unit by unit; Prussian infantry poured their fire into the onrushing horse, and then used their bayonets to throw enemy riders from the saddle. Somewhere in the melee, the man who started it all, Römer, was shot dead, so that both wing commanders met their deaths in this encounter. As the fight dragged on, Prussian infantry went through their supply of powder and ball, and began to scrounge from those fallen on the battlefield.[29] The older officers were aghast, waiting for the moment when they would simply have to surrender. It never came. Frederick would later write that "younger officers might learn from this not to despair too quickly."[30] Bit by bit, the Prussians restored the situation, halting the Austrians, and slowly driving them back in this sector.

Frederick's departure was, coincidentally or not, the turning point of the battle of Mollwitz. Schwerin began with some remedial work in the area of morale. In another of those moments, virtually unknown outside Germany but part of the mythology of the German army, one of the senior commanders asked for the direction of the retreat: "Over the body of the enemy!" Schwerin responded.[31] He then sent Prince Leopold an order to get the second echelon to stop firing, a necessity if some semblance of order was to return to the ranks. Then he addressed a few words to the 1st Battalion of the Guard Regiment, holding firm in the center of the first echelon. It all seems quite simple when one draws up a list. Nonetheless, it was an impressive achievement.

Despite having been wounded himself, Schwerin was confident. The battle on the Prussian right wing had taken up most of the enemy's attention, energy, and troops. However, by late afternoon, the Prussian infantry was fully master in that sector, dealing out death to the Austrians—infantry and cavalry alike—through a constant rolling thunder of fire by platoons. A telling sign was the increasing hesitation of Austrian troops in the second echelon to march up to fill gaps in the first. That, after all, was precisely what the second echelon was for. But it began to look like suicide to a great number of Austrian soldiers.

Action now shifted to the other flank. The Austrian cavalry on the right, here, led by Field Marshal Graf von Berlichingen, also launched a series of powerful assaults against the Prussian left.[32] At one point his troopers broke through the Markgraf Friedrich Regiment, but flanking fire from Prussian infantry forced them to draw back. At another, a group of Austrian dragoons broke through, only to feel the wrath of infantry fire from the Prince Leopold Regiment, one of the orphan units on the left wing, between the echelons. Austrian hussars even managed to get through the Prussian line, plunder the Prussian baggage at Pampitz, and set fire to the town. The situation deteriorated further when the Prussian hussars, sent to protect the baggage, apparently joined in the looting. Nevertheless, the Austrians could win no decision on this flank, and soon Neipperg decided to commit much of Berlichingen's cavalry to the battles still raging on the Prussian right.[33]

With the Austrian cavalry of both wings spent and much of their infantry committed on their left, the time had come to deliver the telling blow. Sometime around 5:00 P.M., Schwerin ordered a general advance by the infantry on his left wing, deployed along the Kleiner Bach. It may have been an enveloping attack.[34] So many gaps had occurred in the Austrian line by now that it may have been the sharp frontal rap they needed to come apart. For all the chaos on the field, the advance by the bluecoats was a moment for eighteenth-century lovers of *l'esprit géometrique*, including at least one Austrian officer: "I can indeed say that I have never seen a prettier sight in my life. They marched with great steadiness, as straight as a line, as if they were on a parade-ground. The musket glistening in the sun had the most beautiful effect, and their fire was like nothing so much as a steady thunder. Our army felt its courage sink completely."[35]

The Prussian infantry, marching silently, pausing to fire, reloading while on the march, and then firing again, was too much for the Austrians, and the defenders lost all formation. They clumped together in huge masses, and the gaps between them became large enough for entire cavalry units to pass through—if the Prussians had possessed an aggressive cavalry. Still, the Austrians were now offering even more lucrative targets to Prussian fire, especially artillery fire. "It was a pity," one Austrian observer noted, "to see these poor recruits hiding one behind the other."[36] Their casualties rose ever higher, and finally, many of them broke and ran. Neipperg ordered a general retreat at 6:00 P.M., in order to save his army from complete dissolution. It was a disordered retreat, to be sure, but not a wild flight, and with much of the Prussian cavalry used up in the first moments of the battle, there was no pursuit.

Mollwitz Evaluated

The battle of Mollwitz was over. It had been a bloody day, typical of the eighteenth century, with casualties nearly even on both sides: 4,551 (or 24 percent) for the Austrians, 4,659 (or 21 percent) for the Prussians. The cavalry had taken a particularly severe mauling. More than four hundred officers on both sides had also lost their lives, a reminder of the price exacted by the old regime's ideas of *noblesse oblige*.[37]

Mollwitz had been a Prussian victory, but it certainly was not a decisive one. In fact, it vividly displays how battles of the era tended toward indecision. Circumstances here certainly seemed to lend themselves to a decisive victory. One side actually surprised the other in his camp. The other recovered, launched a great cavalry charge, and blew away most of his enemy's right wing. Then the first side recovered and launched a decisive punch on the enemy's flank that apparently destroyed the foe's morale and drove him into a hurried retreat. Circumstances endemic to the era, however, conspired to rob either side of complete victory. Linear tactics were necessary to maximize the firepower of high-technology weapons like flintlock muskets, but getting into line took time, lots of time. The command structure was primitive.[38] Control of troops, especially cavalry troops that had just attacked or been attacked, was nearly impossible.

Beyond those problems, Mollwitz offers a mixed picture of the Prussian army at war. The cavalry's performance had been abysmal, "damned worthless" in Frederick's words. Its major accomplishment at Mollwitz was to serve as a target for its more aggressive Austrian counterpart. On the right wing, Schulenberg's cavalry had received a major Austrian charge while at the halt. The impact simply scattered them to the four winds, and at least some of them careened into their own infantry, causing major disruption and even some casualties. The deployment of grenadiers among the cavalry only anchored the horsemen in place. Although the grenadiers did help to wear down the rush of Römer's cavalry and eventually rejoin the main body of infantry on the right flank, they would have been better off starting there.

The Prussian infantry, by contrast, had saved the day. "Our infantry is like Caesar's," wrote the king.[39] For the most part, they had fought in a new three-rank formation, rather than the prewar four, to maximize their firepower. The troops had been practicing it for months under their drill instructors at home, and it paid off in combat, as realistic training always does. One nineteenth-century German staff officer wrote that it was a victory essentially won "on the exercise squares at home,"[40] and that is a fair assessment. The Austrian commander, Field Marshal Neipperg, would later say that the Prussians had outshot his men, five rounds to two.[41] The infantry may have been cumbersome and slow in getting into line. It had also been an awesome sight in the advance, filling the air with its own fire and augmenting it with the light field guns accompanying it every step of the way, and it had eventually succeeded in putting the Austrians to flight.

The commander had been terrible, perhaps understandable in one so young and inexperienced. To his credit, however, he knew it and he admitted it. "The king and Field Marshal Neipperg outdid one another in errors," he would later write. He emphasized especially the need to strike quickly when one has won the advantage of surprise. "As the king arrived at Mollwitz, where the Austrians were encamped, he could have attacked from the march and routed them."[42] It's a doubtful case. With the Austrians encamped in three separate villages, the Prussians themselves would have had to disperse to attack them, with unforeseen consequences. That he must be ready to take advantage of opportunities as they presented themselves, however, was a lesson he never forgot.

To his further credit, Frederick learned from his brush with catastrophe. "Mollwitz was my school," he wrote.[43] Even before the end of the First Silesian War, he began a series of wholesale reforms to incorporate the lessons of Mollwitz. They began within days of the battle, in fact, while his army was still encamped on the field. Training exercises, maneuvers, and a king who enjoyed beginning his inspections at 4:00 A.M.—this was the state of the victorious Prussian army in the six weeks following Mollwitz. Royal directives also began to flow in a steady stream of letters to Prince Leopold von Anhalt-Dessau, his trusted "old Dessauer," who was even then training the reserve forces in their camp at Cöttin, back home in Brandenburg.[44]

This was a fertile time for Frederick, who seemed to churn out a new regulation on a weekly basis. They emerged even as the war still raged, and the Prussian army won another close-fought victory at Chotusitz (May 17, 1742).[45] There was the *Battle Instruction for Cavalry* (*Instruction für die Kavallerie im Fall einer Bataille*) of March 17 and the *Disposition for the Infantry Regiment* (*Disposition für die sämmtlichen Regimenter Infanterie*) of March 25, which would eventually expand into the *Regulation for the Cavalry and Dragoons* (*Reglement für die Kavallerie und Dragoner*) and *Instruction for the Infantry* (*Instruction für die Infanterie*), both in June. In 1743, he would issue a comprehensive new set of *Infantry Drill Regulations*, and in 1744 his handbook for the higher officers *Orders for the Generals* (*Ordres für sämmtliche Generale*).[46] Rather than formulate a theory of war, these were highly specific documents that spoke to situations that the army had either already faced in Silesia or would be likely to face in a future war. This was something new, the first time that an army had drawn up a formal body of shared principles and procedures. It was the tentative birth of what we today call doctrine.[47]

If we can sum up this new doctrine in a word, it was "aggression." The entire army was now geared to an aggressive, offensive battlefield approach. It was particularly evident with the cavalry, with Frederick issuing a famous standing order promising to cashier any cavalry officer who failed to get his charge in first and meet the enemy at a gallop. His father had favored tall men on tall horses, "giants on elephants" (*Kolosse auf Elefanten*), Frederick called them, mockingly. He downsized the arm, with smaller men riding smaller mounts. Lighter and more nimble than the cumbersome troopers he had inherited, increased speed allowed them to pack a punch. Increasingly, the cavalry would become the arm that "rode the king's ideas into reality."[48] Likewise, to help the infantry get forward, the artillery received new regimental guns, light three-pounders, that were nimble enough to move up over the most varied terrain. At first they met a mixed reception, with old hands complaining about their lack of hitting power and range. They certainly couldn't fight artillery duels with the heavier Austrian guns. With an average of two guns assigned to every regiment, however, Frederick achieved his goal of increased firepower at the point of contact.

Another important reform was the increasing importance accorded to the hussar cavalry. From their origins as one of his father's "luxury troops," Frederick made them an integral part of the army, adding the distinct blush of light cavalry to his palette. Under their commander Hans Joachim von Ziethen, a "short man with a weak voice,"[49] a taste for drink, a mean temper, and a penchant for duels, they carved out a reputation for themselves as Prussia's equivalent of the Austrian *Grenzer*. Although they lacked the latter's firepower and flexibility, the hussars were useful for scouting, skirmishing, and threatening the enemy's baggage train. They also lent an aura of dash, "a light, mobile flair"[50] to an army that essentially had to plod along at the pace of the foot soldier.

Although all these reforms resulted in a fiercer, more aggressive force, his first encounters with the Austrians taught Frederick something even more important. He received a new insight into operations. More and more, he came to agree with the Great Elector that Prussia had to keep its wars "short and lively" ("*kurtz und vives*"). To do that, he had to place a higher emphasis on battle than on maneuver. Already the Austrian light infantry, Croats and *Grenzer* from the military frontier in the southeast of the Habsburg Empire, had proven to be a tough problem to Frederick in a pure war of maneuver.[51] Prussian supply columns, magazines, and foraging parties alike had all made the acquaintance of the Croats, usually to the delight of the latter.

During the opening campaign of the Second Silesian War in 1744, for example, Frederick's thrust into Bohemia and occupation of Prague would end not in near-disaster—but in the real thing. As the ruins of his starving force straggled back into Silesia without having fought a single battle, Frederick found himself forced into a reappraisal. He was still a young, inexperienced general, and he had found that his Austrian elders were far more practiced at this highly stylized art of maneuver. He had also found that they were not particularly adept at actual fighting. Indeed, Frederick got into his worst trouble in all of these wars when he tried to outmaneuver his opponent in some clever fashion. When he actually fought, things went much better. From now on, he decided, he would fight, seeking to lure enemy armies into battle and, if possible, destroy them. Let the Austrians try to weave their web of maneuver, levering him off his supply lines and placing him in a false position. That might take months of work, an ornate and delicate *objet d'art* that he could shatter in a single bloody afternoon.

A second issue arose from the preference for battle. The linear tactics of the day were not configured for decisive victory, but for mutual mauling. Two firing lines at close range were mutual killing machines, to be sure, but they lacked the flexibility and maneuverability to achieve anything more decisive. The best they could hope for was to drive the enemy from the field. Frederick's solution was the "oblique attack" (*schräge Schlachtordnung*): massing combat power on one wing and using it strike a blow against the weaker wing or even flank of the enemy, while holding back ("refusing") one's own weaker wing.[52] "By attacking in the flank, an army of 30,000 might defeat an army of 100,000," he wrote.[53]

It is common knowledge that the concept and the term come from antiquity, in particular the triumph of the great Theban commander Epaminondas over the Spartans at the battle of Leuctra in 371 B.C., as well as that of Alexander the Great over the Persians at Gaugamela.[54] It might be more charitable, however, to say that because of the paucity of source materials on these and other ancient battles, Frederick's oblique order actually derived from a contemporary construction of what these ancient encounters might have been like. The Enlightenment was awash in love for the ancients, and all sorts of movements for political or social reform attempted to gain legitimacy by claims that they were actually restorations of traditions from the Classical period. So it was in eighteenth-century military affairs: "Indeed, intelligent officers knew far more about Classical military history than they did about the events of their own time. An acquaintance with Caesar's *Commentaries* was part of the mental equipment of every well-read gentleman, and the writers defer constantly to the authority of figures like Polybius, Homer, Herodotus, Xenophon, and 'our historian' Thucydides."[55]

This "power of ancient precedent," in the words of one modern authority, was based on the notion that the principles of war were unchanging from age to age. This is a highly debatable proposition, unless one is prepared to accept the equally problematic notion that what worked for troops armed with hacking and slashing weapons also worked for firearms.

This is not to say we should discard the term "oblique" in reference to Frederick's battles. He himself used the term, and it does have a certain utility in helping us understand his methods once the armies had clinched. It is to argue, however, that the "oblique attack" was not some sort of secret weapon that Frederick trotted out whenever he needed it. If it were, and if it were so effective, why did his enemies not copy it? They certainly saw enough of it over the years. Military historians, therefore, should not fetishize the term in the way that they have. In point of fact, many of the battles described (and diagrammed) in history books and atlases as "oblique" were actually something far more dramatic: prebattle, or operational, maneuvers designed to bring a large chunk of Frederick's army down upon the flank or rear of his unwitting adversary.

The Dawn of Victory: Hohenfriedeberg

Frederick spent the years between the First and Second Silesian Wars acting like his father. The army drilled relentlessly. He put new formations and tactical combinations to the test in highly realistic field maneuvers, the first ever in what was to become a tradition in the Prussian-German military: the fall maneuver (*Herbstübung*). The first one took place on September 2, 1743, at Schöneberg: hussars attacking a village occupied by grenadiers, and then falling upon a force of cuirassiers who were moving up. On September 30, a mixed infantry-cavalry exercise explored ways to seize a fortified position. The point was not to work out a schema or "school solution," but merely to expose officers and men to many of the problems involved in these operations. It was a busy time. In 1743 alone, Frederick personally inspected no fewer that 85 battalions and 153 squadrons.[56] He would see the results of these labors in the Second Silesian War and, at Hohenfriedeberg, would experience his first decisive victory.[57]

Perhaps we should add the word "eventually." It had to be a bitter pill for all concerned on the Prussian side that, after all the work in the interwar era, the Second Silesian War opened with an absolute disaster. In 1744, the army invaded Bohemia through Saxony (whose small but sturdy force would play a crucial role in this war), seizing the great city of Prague. They then advanced into the southern reaches of Bohemia, marching down the east bank of the Moldau River, seizing Budweis and Tabor. Such a direct thrust of the dagger toward the Habsburg heartland was sure to lure the Austrian army into battle, Frederick reasoned. The wily Austrian commander Field Marshal O. F. von Traun, however, was neither the first nor the last general to outmaneuver Frederick in these wars. With the Prussians far from home, at the end of long supply tether, Traun entered Bohemia from the west.

Along with twenty thousand Saxon auxiliaries, he simply ensconced himself in a heavily fortified position athwart Frederick's line of communications. This "Camp of Marschowitz" was too large either to ignore or to attack with any hope of success. With his supply magazines, depots, and even field bakeries being swallowed up by light Austrian forces in the rear, Frederick had to retreat from Bohemia. With Saxony now hostile territory, the route out was much harder than the route in: through the mountains. Freezing cold, typhus, dysentery, general exhaustion, the impossibility of foraging when the countryside was firmly in the hands of Austrian light infantry—all these conspired against Frederick, and he now had the experience of watching much of his force melt away. The Austrians would later state that they had accepted no less than seventeen thousand deserters from the Prussian army, not all that much less than the size of Frederick's whole army at Mollwitz.[58] There are many sources who speak of a chastened Frederick in the next year's campaign: more willing to listen, slower with the sarcastic tongue or the biting rejoinder. If so, he had every reason to be.

Even his natural aggression seemed to have deserted him. There would be no invasions of enemy territory in 1745, he told his French allies. Instead, he would wait for an opportunity, luring his opponent out of the heights into the Silesian plain and striking a sharp blow on advantageous terms as they debouched from the mountains. "If the Austrians come at me, I shall let them cross the hills in peace, after which I shall march directly against them." Traun might never have fallen for it, but his success had led Maria Theresa to promote him to command Austrian forces in western Germany. With Prince Charles of Lorraine (her brother-in-law, the brother of Francis Stephen) now in overall command, Frederick saw a good chance for some "stupid mistakes" on the part of his adversary.[59]

There would actually be quite a few of them. Frederick benefited in this campaign from fighting against a coalition. The assembly of the allied army took time, as the Austrians came from their winter quarters at Königgrätz and the Saxons from Jung-Benzlau and Köninghof. The rendezvous of Prince Charles's fifty thousand Austrians with their nineteen thousand Saxon counterparts at Trautenau did not occur until quite late in May. Frederick would later claim that the ponderous movements of the enemy host were predictable to the day and hour.[60]

This was one of the most carefully laid plans in Frederick's long career. He even made good use of a double agent, later identifying him as a certain "man from Schönberg" in one source, and as an "Italian from Schmiedeberg" in another.[61] Whoever he might have been, Frederick filled him with misinformation that he knew would eventually reach the Austrian camp. The Prussians had no intention of contesting an Austrian invasion of Silesia, Frederick told him. Instead, they were going to pull back to Breslau before the Austrians crossed the mountains. To put the final touch on the ruse, the king even began improvements to the roads back to Breslau. The spy dutifully brought these plans to the Austrian camp.

On the allies came, moving deliberately into the mountain range known as the Riesengebirge. Prussian scouts reported details back on a daily basis about the exact position of the host. There is little doubt that the allies were suffering from a bout of overconfidence. They had whipped Frederick in Bohemia in 1744, his military coalition was on the verge of falling apart, and now he seemed to be on the run. As they neared the important Prussian-held crossroads town of Landeshut, Frederick gave his General Winterfeldt orders to retreat upon their approach. After a brief but well-handled defense of the town, he did so, falling back on the advance guard under Lieutenant General Peter Du Moulin, then stationed at Schweidnitz.[62] "At the same time you should as cleverly as possible let the rumor leak out that the Prussians intend to leave the foot of the mountains and seek shelter under the cannon of Breslau," Frederick added. Our man from Schönberg took it all in, as the king knew he would, and brought the news to the Austrians, confirming to them that the Prussians had no stomach for a fight. As Frederick wrote, looking back on the campaign many years later, "In war, cunning is often more useful than strength."[63]

In fact, the Prussians had no intention of retreating anywhere. Frederick had made his camp at Frankenstein, in the plain on the other side of the Riesengebirge. As Charles and his Saxon allies were attempting to cross the mountains into Silesia, moving northeast through Landeshut and Hohenfriedeberg, Frederick was on the other side of the mountains, shadowing them, steadily sliding to the northwest. On May 27–28, he broke camp at Frankenstein, reached Reichenbach on May 29, and by June 1 stood at Schweidnitz. Meanwhile, Du Moulin's advance guards, reinforced now by Winterfeldt's corps, were on the march, arriving at the heights around Striegau, overlooking the river of the same name (*Striegauer Wasser*). In addition, a detachment under Lieutenant General Christoph Ernst von Nassau was in the *Nonnen-busch*, a small forest to the southeast of Striegau, and the main Prussian body was encamped between alt-Jauernick and Schweidnitz.[64]

Even centuries later, the asymmetry of the situation is stunning. These were two armies of nearly identical size. Once Frederick had concentrated the Prussian army for action, it added up almost exactly to the allied force it faced: fifty-nine thousand men. The two forces possessed virtually identical weapons, ammunition, and systems of command. Nevertheless, the situation could not have been better for the Prussians. "There was," Frederick would write, "a ten mile wide stretch between Striegau and Schweidnitz occupied by an almost un-broken line of Prussian troops." Well might he say that "the king's situation was highly favorable."[65] Two lines of approach were heading toward the intersect point. No matter where the allies crossed the mountains, they were in for some serious trouble. The only problem was that Frederick was aware of it, and the allies were not.

At times it must have seemed to him as if the allies were refusing to play their part. They arrived in Landeshut on May 27 and stayed there for five full days. It seems to have been mainly the work of the Saxon commander, the Duke of Weissenfels, who argued for allowing the men to recuperate and the heavy artillery to come up.[66] On June 2, Charles and Weissenfels held a council of war on the Gallow's Hill (*Galgenberg*) outside Hohenfriedeberg. Both agreed that the time had come. Evidently their intelligence had been correct. The Prussians were still at Schweidnitz, quite out of the way. The crossing would take place tomorrow.

At 7:00 A.M. on the morning of June 3, then, the allied commanders met once again on the *Galgenberg* to work out their final plans. By noon, the allied army was descending into the plain, passing between Hohenfriedeberg and Kauder. There is nothing quite like an army coming down from the mountains, with the beautiful country that it is about to conquer laid out before it. Since this impressive force was only hours from being destroyed, the scene is rife with poignancy and, indeed, virtually every source on the battle has described it in detail: the sheer pageantry, the banners fluttering in the breeze, the drum and trumpets, the perfectly ordered ranks of men and horse, eight columns strong, infantry in the center, cavalry on the wings.[67]

It was late in the afternoon, perhaps 4:00 P.M., when the march was finished. The Prussians were nowhere to be seen, and the satisfied allied commanders decided to give their men a well-earned rest. The Saxons lay on the left, around the village of Pilgrimshain, the Austrians on the right, from Halbersdorf to Günthersdorf, with the two separated by a nearly one-kilometer gap. All in all, the position was nearly seven kilometers long, but there were only enough troops for a four-kilometer position. No serious thought was given to seizing useful terrain for the defense, no fieldworks went up, and there were no preparations for battle, since there was no enemy. The Saxons even left their artillery behind.[68] One later German source would remark on the "careless and noisy way the Allied army had entered the Silesian plain."[69]

The long period of waiting had allowed Frederick and his commanders a great deal of time to formulate a response, to prepare his troops, and generally to put things in readiness. Frederick was probably feeling even better on May 29, when General Winterfeldt handed over a copy of the entire Austrian order of battle, courtesy of an Austrian deserter. That same day, the general sent Frederick a long letter outlining his thoughts on the probable moves of the enemy and the appropriate potential countermoves. All in all, the camp was brimming with confidence. Since the dark days of 1744, Frederick had managed to restore a great deal of the morale lost as a result of the Bohemian debacle. According to one observer, "from the highest to the lowest, you couldn't ask for more good will in such a difficult matter. . . . Like everyone else in this camp, I am of the opinion that if God doesn't decide differently and nothing unusual happens, I expect it to go well, and perhaps very well with His Majesty, should it come to a decisive affair."[70] Early on the morning of July 3, the Prussians could see smoke rising from the allied encampment, a sure sign that the cooks were at work and the army about to get on the move.

That night, Frederick suddenly and rapidly set his regiments into motion. In another legacy of the obsessive drill forced on the army by Frederick William I, no force in the world could break camp, shake out into march column, and get on the road faster than the Prussians. The plan was a simple concept: a nighttime march to the right, across the face of the allied position, through the villages of Gräben and Striegau, and across the Striegauer River, onto the left (Saxon) flank. Once the army had achieved that position, it would launch a sudden and powerful early morning assault that should simply sweep the allies away. Even the tactical directives leaned in this direction. Once in battle, the infantry was to move smartly and rapidly to the assault, not bothering to shoot until it was two hundred paces from the foe. At thirty paces, it should make the final charge with the bayonet. What he did not want was a long, drawn-out firefight. The allies were going to be shocked by his sudden appearance, and he did not want to allow them time to recover their equilibrium. If all went well, they would not even have time to form a cohesive line.

In fact, about 90 percent of Frederick's plan worked as he envisioned it. The marching columns moved out smoothly at 8:00 P.M., General Du Moulin's advance guard in the lead, the main body following up an hour later, artillery on the roads, cavalry and infantry on either side. Things moved swiftly at first, helped by the fact that the Prussians had made improvements to the roads they were using in the approach, yet another benefit of the long preparation time they had enjoyed. To fool inquisitive enemy eyes, the tents were left standing and the watch fires burning, the men ordered to keep complete silence and forbidden to smoke. A force descending from the mountains into the plain has only one rival for drama: the flank march by night, and once again the sources let us share in that drama: "Across the Striegauer numerous enemy watch fires were burning. It was a crisp, starry night, during which 60,000 Prussians impatiently awaited the battle which would decide the survival or fall of the House of Brandenburg." Says another, "The night was still and starry. Fog billowed up out of the damp marshes. Numerous watchfires burned at the foot of the mountains and in the broad plain of Rohnstock."[71]

And then things began to go wrong, shattering the idyll. Du Moulin's first operational objective after crossing the Striegauer River was a pair of hills northwest of the town of Striegau, the Fuchsberg and the Spitzberg. They were supposed to be unoccupied, but Du Moulin found that he had a fight on his hands. In fact, these were Saxon units of the advance guard under General von Schlichting, uhlans and a number of grenadier companies, along with two guns. Du Moulin's orders expressly forbade him to launch a night attack. Not only would it be risky, as are all night engagements, but it would remove the element of surprise for the main attack. It was 9:00 P.M., and he now halted the advance.[72] He was puzzled; the Saxons weren't supposed to be this far to the east; the Saxons, for their part, felt that the Du Moulin force had to be a weak detachment that they could push back when the sun came up. By midnight the main body had come up to the Striegauer River crossings. Here it rested for two hours, Frederick among them wrapped in his cloak, no doubt working to come up with "plan B."

The new plan merged the aggressive nature of the original flanking attempt with the new realities of a large enemy force sitting off to the left. At 4:00 A.M., Du Moulin's cavalry, simply ignoring the small forces on the heights, launched an assault on the main Saxon position in front of the village of Pilgramshain. This forced the Saxon units on the heights to make their way as rapidly as possible back to their main body, to avoid being cut off. The Prussians held all the cards in this opening assault. They were in hand and in good tactical formation, and they were facing an army that was completely unready for action, in fact, that was quite literally sleeping. The rest of the course of the battle makes sense only when one keeps that fact in mind.

The Duke of Weissenfels did manage to get his cavalry deployed in front of Pilgramshain, a mixed force of Austrian and Saxon horse. They soon ran into heavy fire from Du Moulin's artillery and from six 24-pounders that the king had quickly placed on the Fuchsberg. Now Du Moulin's cavalry came forward, along with the right wing cavalry of Field Marshal Buddenbrock, into the attack. This was no longer the timid Prussian cavalry of Mollwitz, but an aggressive force with blood in its eye. Although the Saxons fought gamely here, they were driven back by 6:00 A.M. It was early, and both sides were disoriented, the one by being up all night, the other by being rudely shaken out of bed to go fight. The later German official history describes the situation as a "general brawl."[73] As the mass of riders untied itself, the allies were in flight to the south and west.

Now came the turn of the Saxon infantry. Although things were far too chaotic to claim this as a part of the plan, the Prussians were rolling down on the allies from the north, peeling off one wing at a time. Under Prince Dietrich von Anhalt, the Prussian infantry of the first echelon now launched a hastily formed attack on the Saxon infantry in the "Gule," a narrow lowland or gully between Pilgramshain and Günthersdorf.[74] Here, Frederick's admonitions to act aggressively in the attack also bore fruit:

> The Prussian attack went irresistibly forward, even in the face of devastating canister fire. Its own heavy batteries on the Fuchsberg passed over it, taking the Gule under fire with good result. At 200 paces, the Saxons began well-aimed musket fire, to which the Prussian battalions on the wings began a platoon fire while continuing to move forward. In the center the Anhalt Regiment, led personally by Hereditary Prince Leopold, drove against the Nordbusch, without taking a shot and with muskets shouldered.[75]

With an easterly wind blowing the dust and smoke toward the Saxon position, men and officers alike were blinded. The already unstable line now began to waver, and then gave way altogether. By 7:00 A.M., it was all over. The Prussian attack had dismantled the Saxon army, and the entire left wing of the allied army, along with it.

It may seem incredible, but the Austrians on the right wing were only now getting themselves into position.[76] Actually, it is another sign of the complete surprise that Frederick managed to achieve in his attack, and the advantage that it gave him throughout the battle. The battle against the Saxons had at least forced the Prussians into a completely new deployment. Rather than continue the operational maneuver onto the Saxon flank, much of the Prussian army, heading north in march column, now simply changed facing to the west and advanced toward the allied position. Prince Charles of Lorraine, hearing cannon fire in the morning, first thought it must be the Saxons evicting Du Moulin's weak Prussian force from the town of Striegau. Not until about 6:30 A.M., in other words about the time the Saxon army was in its death throes, did he order his forces to deploy.

This sector of the battlefield contained three evenly spaced towns that form a line facing northeast: Günthersdorf, Thomaswaldau, and Halbendorf. The first Austrians in line were the cavalry, between Thomaswaldau and Halbendorf. The Prussians took a scare here early. As their cavalry was crossing the Striegauer to get into action, the main bridge at the village of Gräben broke. Ten squadrons of Prussian cuirassiers now rode boldly against an Austrian force twice that number, unaware that they were all alone. Soon, however, Ziethen found a usable ford over the Striegauer, bringing with him another ten squadrons and allowing the Prussians to get the rest of their forces across the river and into action. Charge led to countercharge, with neither side able to get the upper hand. The decisive act was the seizure of the village of Thomaswaldau by Prussian infantry. The sudden appearance of their fire on the flank of the Austrians broke their already shaky morale, and they fled the field en masse.

Three down, one to go. All that was left now was the Austrian infantry, the last major portion of the allied force to reach the field, deployed between Thomaswaldau and Günthersdorf. It must have known by now that it was about to plunge into disaster. Its Saxon allies were gone, infantry and cavalry alike. Its own cavalry could be seen, when the smoke and dust temporarily cleared, fleeing the battlefield. The Prussian infantry, the steadiest soldiers in Europe—and the best shots—were moving toward them with a glint in the eye. All the ingredients for a quick rout were there.

It was not to be. For whatever reasons—pride, loyalty, fear of their officers, love for their empress—they fought. Volley followed volley, with the Austrians keeping steady and matching the Prussians. Huge gaps were torn in both sides' lines, filled rapidly by troops from the second echelon. Stymied in the center, the Prussian infantry moved to seize the villages on the flanks. We have already seen that their entry into Thomaswaldau materially affected the cavalry battle to the south. Likewise, Günthersdorf was soon in Prussian hands as well. Although Frederick was heard to exclaim that "the battle is won," there was still no surrender from the Austrians.

The battle wasn't yet won, but it was about to be. The Austrians were reaching their breaking point. Not only were casualties rising as the Prussian fire began to tell, but it was clear that the overall situation was hopeless. On the Prussian side, the ferocity of the Austrian fire and the emphasis on the flanking villages had opened gaps between the various units of the first line. Behind one such gap, facing the Austrian center almost directly, lay the oversize Bayreuth Dragoon Regiment.

To this day, controversy persists over who ordered it, but the signal to charge rang out, and the regiment suddenly leaped into action. The 1,500 horsemen—ten squadrons—passed through the gap in their own infantry, deployed into line, and moved forward. Starting with a walk, then a trot, and finally moving into a full gallop, the regiment careened into the increasingly unsteady soldiers of the Austrian first line, scattered them, and then did the same to the second line. Where the Austrian center used to be, there was now literally a hole. With flight looking hopeless, hundreds of Austrian soldiers began to surrender. The charge had scattered the better part of twenty Austrian infantry battalions. All told, the regiment took 2,500 prisoners and captured sixty-six flags. Its own losses were a negligible ninety-four.[77] It was the most celebrated moment in the battle of Hohenfriedeberg, one of those feats that entered the lore of the Prussian army. It was also, perhaps, the battlefield event that solidified Frederick's military reputation all over Europe.

Hohenfriedeberg Evaluated

The battle was over. The Prussians had demolished four separate enemy wings in what can only be described as workmanlike fashion. Unusually for battles of the era, their own losses were a fraction of their enemies: 4,700 to 13,360. The former total was largely the result of the heroic last stand of the Austrian infantry; the latter included 5,655 prisoners, a very difficult thing to achieve in the age of slow-moving linear battle formations. In that sense, the battle of Hohenfriedeberg was the forerunner of later German victories in 1866, 1870, and 1940: decisive and about as complete as one could hope, with friendly losses that hardly registered compared to typical battles of the era.

It is possible, of course, to find fault with Frederick's generalship. The original plan had gone awry, for reasons never satisfactorily explained. A general who had paid double agents, led opponents into his trap with plausible misinformation, and seemed to think of every detail from leaving the watch fires burning to forbidding his soldiers to smoke on the great flank march also failed to carry out an elementary reconnaissance of the march route beforehand. An argument that it might have given away the entire plan is not convincing. As we have seen, the allies would not have been overly worried by Prussian patrols.

It is always possible, however, to fault the generalship in any battle. This approach is so common that it has come to appear as the essence of military history. This general turned left, we write, when he ought to have turned right; this general was too timid, this one too impetuous. This is the approach that Dennis Showalter calls "military Calvinism," a belief that victory and defeat is a judgment on the military righteousness of the commander. Those who fail to act on "war's revealed truths" are cast into the lake of fire; those who walk "the "straight and narrow path are admitted to the scholar's Valhalla."[78] Unfortunately, despite the attempt of analysts—academics and operators alike—to construct them over the centuries, there is no such thing as a "Ten Commandments of Warfare," a detailed instruction manual to bring victory and ward off defeat. On the operational level, war will always be a colossal gamble. Generals commanding large bodies of troops are always leading into the unknown. They make plans and, as Clausewitz wrote, have to watch helplessly as those plans are ground down in an unstoppable process of friction. Little things start to go wrong, and eventually add up to big things. Good generals do not draw up brilliant plans. They draw up flexible ones, then they have the ability to make up a second plan on the spot, and a third and a fourth, if necessary. Not everyone can do it. It is an art, not a science. We may debate these ideas today, but generations of German officers in the nineteenth and twentieth centuries recognized them as incontestable truths.

Frederick's triumph at Hohenfriedeberg is a classic example of this argument. The easiest exercise in the world, for a military historian, would be to draw up a list of generals who would have fallen to pieces if a carefully laid plan for a flank march had bumped into enemy forces deployed where they ought not to be. By midnight of June 4, 1745, a handful of Saxon battalions had just ruined an ornate plan, a carefully prepared timetable of troop movements involving every unit in the force to some degree, and using every spare inch of the available road network. The halt of the Prussian advance guard under Du Moulin had the potential to act like a car hitting its brakes on a rush-hour highway. Instead, new plans emerged. Du Moulin threw himself into a direct assault on the Saxons to his west; virtually the entire force switched its facing from north to west, and marched into battle; a battle plan that depended on an attack from the flank now turned into one that relied on the moral shock to the allied soldiers of seeing the Prussian army before their morning coffee. In the end, that was enough.

It wasn't just Frederick who displayed this flexibility and ability to improvise. Since the days of the Great Elector, the Prussian army had relied on a talented officer corps who had near-absolute freedom to handle their units—and themselves—as they saw fit. Hohenfriedeberg is impossible to imagine without Du Moulin's decision *not* to fight for the

heights west of Striegau during the night, and his morning decision to ignore threats to his flanks and attack the Saxon position at Pilgramshain.
It is unthinkable without the irrepressible hussar Ziethen taking it upon
himself to find a ford over the Striegauer River and leading his squadrons
over the river to assist the Prussian cuirassiers in their lonely struggle
against superior numbers. It is unthinkable without the brigade commanders of the Prussian infantry, stymied by Austrian fire to their front,
shifting the weight of their attack onto the villages on the flanks. Above
all, it is unthinkable without the charge of the Bayreuth Dragoons, a unit
that was lucky enough to be in the right place at the right time, but that
also had the ability to recognize and seize a decisive opportunity. There
is no "principle of war" that covers all of these various decisions and actions. *Auftragstaktik*, the current buzzword, may help to describe it, but
it may not be a teachable, or even a transferable, concept.

Hohenfriedeberg was an extremely important battle in the evolution of Prussian-German operational methods. The progression from
Mollwitz to Hohenfriedeberg is instructive. At the former, Frederick
managed to march to an advantageous and unsuspected site outside the
enemy's camp, but then deployed so deliberately that he lost any advantage he might have gained from the march. At Hohenfriedeberg, he
made a much more daring attempt to get around the enemy's flank and
attack him. Although he failed ultimately in that quest, he came close
enough to give a thorough rattle to the enemies, who never did manage
to recover their equilibrium. In the attack, his entire force—infantry, artillery, and cavalry alike—was much more aggressive than it had
been four years earlier, and that aggression proved enough to cover a
multitude of sins. Historians over the years, both scholarly and popular, have described the battle as an example of the "oblique attack," but
that only shows how meaningless the term truly has become—another
buzzword of military history.[79] It elevates the tactical over the operational. It also makes a daring, dangerous stratagem seem to be much
more formalized and organized than in fact it was.

We shall see his art of war develop to its fullest potential in the
Seven Years' War. Some of his greatest triumphs in that bloody conflict—Rossbach and Leuthen, for example—were examples of the
operational maneuver onto the enemy's flank and rear, followed by a
pounce, or at least as much of a pounce as an eighteenth-century army
deploying from column into line could manage. Long after the linear
battle tactics of the day had disappeared, German staff officers would
look back at this aspect of Frederick's art of war, and recognize in it
Bewegungskrieg: the war of movement on the operational level.

Frederick in the Seven Years' War

The *Federkrieg*

Like any valuable estate, the legacy of Frederick the Great was the subject of a protracted, often angry quarrel among his inheritors. The nineteenth century would see a great debate over Frederick's generalship. On one side lay the big guns, the General Staff, especially its Military History Section (*Abteilung für Kriegsgeschichte*), with all the considerable resources of the German army at its disposal. On the other side, disputing virtually everything they said, stood a civilian military historian by the name of Hans Delbrück.[1]

At issue in this "war of the pen" (*Federkrieg*) was the precise way in which to characterize Frederick's military art. From the official side, best characterized in General Theodor von Bernhardi's biography *Frederick the Great as Commander* (*Friedrich der Grosse als Feldherr*, 1881), came the image of Frederick as military radical, as the pursuer of a "strategy of complete destruction" of the enemy (*Niederwerfungsstrategie*).[2] In an age in which his contemporaries were willing to settle for limited territorial gains and victory by maneuver, Frederick aimed for nothing less than the battle of annihilation (*Vernichtungsschlacht*). He therefore started the transformation of warfare that would continue under Napoleon and reach its apogee under the great Helmuth von Moltke.

From Delbrück came Frederick the limited, a rational commander who understood that his resources did not suffice for a strategy of destruction. Rather, he pursued a strategy of exhaustion (*Ermattungsstrategie*) against his foes. Throughout Frederick's career, Delbrück argued, he aimed at quite limited goals. He fought battles only as a last resort, and in that sense he was completely rooted in the view of war that was traditional in his own day.

Along with the two types of strategy, Delbrück posited two operational poles: battle (which, he argued, was more appropriate to a strategy of destruction) and maneuver (more appropriate to the strategy of exhaustion), and argued that Frederick had, more often than not, pursued the latter. He was, in sum, a traditional general of his era:

> As penetrating, and indeed as earth-shaking, as were the changes in tactics from the Renaissance to Frederick the Great, the principles of strategy remained the same. The closely formed deep squares of infantry became threadlike lines; the spearmen and halberdiers became musketeers; the knights who fought individually became closely formed squadrons; the few, cumbersome cannon became countless batteries. But the art of the commander presents the same countenance through all the centuries. Again and again we find the same situations and decisions initiated in the same manner and similarly motivated. Seldom did the two sides move directly against one another in order to bring on the decision.[3]

 Indeed, he argued, "the decisions made by Gustavus Adolphus to fight at Breitenfeld and Lützen were made in a manner completely similar to the decisions of Frederick before the battles of Leuthen and Torgau." Frederick fought battles not to annihilate, but solely for the purpose of freeing himself to turn on his next foe, in the hopes that eventually his enemies would tire of the struggle and seek a negotiated peace.

Who was right? Much depends on one's point of view and the prejudices that go with it. Military men may recognize in Delbrück a typical civilian gadfly whose mission in life is to make their jobs more difficult. There is some truth to the image. For all its scholarly brilliance, there is in Delbrück's writing a tendency toward the ex cathedra pronouncement on matters that can never be more than educated guesses. His four-volume masterwork *History of the Art of War* is filled with them, in fact, on topics ranging from the individual load carried by the Roman legionary[4] to the size of the Burgundian army under Charles the Bold at the battle of Grandson in 1476, both of which, he argued in typical demythologizing fashion, were far smaller than previously thought.[5]

His major work on Frederick, *The Strategy of Pericles Interpreted through the Strategy of Frederick the Great*, is idiosyncratic, to put it mildly. It includes one chapter in the form of a "methodological parody," analyzing the strategy of Frederick's opening campaigns of the Seven Years' War as it would be seen by an advocate of the strategy of annihilation.[6] Judged by the standards of the annihilationist, Frederick was a "strategic bungler."[7] He accuses the king of the high crime of "feinting" and of repeatedly letting his opponents off the hook when he might have destroyed them. "Is world history decided though feints?" Delbrück's parody asks.[8] It is a funny piece, but not everyone got it. Beyond the rights and wrongs of his analysis, Delbrück was attacking the icon not only of the Prussian military caste, but of the new German Reich, and the reaction could not have surprised him in the least. It might be added here that Delbrück came under just as much fire from fellow academics, classicists in particular, who called him a heretic for daring to question the veracity of *their* icon, Herodotus. At issue was the father of history's legendary claim that Xerxes led an army of 4,200,000 men into Greece in 480 B.C., and here we may say that Delbrück's attack was on much firmer ground.[9]

Likewise, civilian analysts may recognize in Bernhardi and his brethren the stereotypically blinkered "military mind," refusing to see the truth when it comes from outside the uniformed community. There is more than a grain of truth here, as well. In the course of the *Federkrieg*, writers far less learned than Delbrück mocked him as a "lectern strategist" and treated his works with contempt simply because they were the work of a scholar and not an operator, a civilian who had not been initiated into the sacred mysteries of the officer corps.[10] This fact alone has probably had a great deal to do with the positive treatment that Delbrück has received in the writings of the scholarly community.[11]

Today, it should be easy to see that both sides had their points. The General Staff was not fantasizing in its portrait of Frederick as the most aggressive commander of the century. Attempts to paint him as a timid, eighteenth-century maneuverist, a Prussian version of Marshal Traun, for example, would hardly have been recognizable to his own contemporaries. There may indeed have been a preference toward attritional, maneuver warfare among many eighteenth-century generals, but Frederick wasn't one of them. Even Delbrück eventually had to admit that his description of Frederick was much more applicable to the post-1760 period, that is, to the last three years of the Seven Years' War, by which time the king had already fought enough battles to satisfy even the purist.

Delbrück could also argue, however, that attempts to forge a direct link between Frederick and Napoleon were absurd in a historical sense. Napoleon sought European rule and even universal empire—he was truly a man without limits. Frederick fought a series of wars for Silesia. A ruler as gifted as Frederick surely recognized that there were limits beyond which Prussia could not go. Moreover, he soon learned (whatever he may have thought in 1740) that his enemies were capable of weathering even severe blows like Hohenfriedeberg and remaining in the field. The military establishment, likewise, eventually came to admit that Frederick understood, and had to work within, the limits of his time.[12]

For our purposes, then, the debate was between two schools that no longer exist. It is a "period piece," in the words of Christopher Duffy.[13] It generated an enormous monographic literature, with Delbrück's doctoral students matching General Staff works one for one. Much of the discourse revolves around arcane points. A central point of the debate, for example, revolved around Frederick's praise for his cautious, maneuver-minded brother Prince Henry as "the general who never made a mistake." Delbrück took it at face value.[14] Bernhardi pointed out that Frederick said it as part of a toast at a banquet he threw for his generals to celebrate the Peace of Hubertusberg.[15] It was hardly, Bernhardi argued, a doctrinal statement.

Such trivia no longer has much of a place in modern discussion of the king's military career. The greatest weakness of both sides in the debate lay in positing a false dichotomy of two strategic options, and trying to plug Frederick into one of them: either as a general who sought to destroy the enemy or one who sought to attrite him, or as one who tried to crush the enemy in battle or outmaneuver him. This is a gross simplification of warfare on any level. Maneuver and battle stand in close relationship with one another, similar to the basic concepts of movement and fire.[16] There is an entire continuum to war, in other words. It can include attrition, annihilation, maneuver, battle, and so much more besides.

There cannot, at this late date, be a major interpretational breakthrough on Frederick the Great—there are simply no new sources to inform us. What we can do is to open the window a little more broadly by insisting on the importance of the *operational level* in any discussion of Frederick's art of war. It finds its space between the discourse on tactics, where there is general agreement on Frederick's use of the oblique attack, and strategy, where there is equal agreement on his use of interior lines. This chapter emphasizes his achievement on the operational level. This is one key to understanding Frederick, especially his influence on later German patterns of war making. We analyze three of his most famous campaigns, Rossbach, Leuthen, and Zorndorf, from this perspective. When we view his campaigns from the operational level, we can see a clear link between Frederick, Napoleon, and the great Moltke—no matter how much larger the resources and the armies of the latter two may have been.

Operations in 1757: From Prague to Kolin

There has long been general agreement among historians, even between Delbrück and his General Staff antagonists, that Frederick made skillful use of "interior lines" during the Seven Years' War.[17] The conflict found him facing a great power coalition of France, Austria, and Russia, along with Swedish and imperial troops. His enemies, therefore, sat on the arc of a rough circle around him, while he occupied the midpoint. The impossibility of coordinating their efforts to any degree made it possible for Frederick to deal a hammer blow to whichever army first came within his reach, then to turn and do the same to the next available enemy. As is always the case, it sounds easier than it was in reality. It certainly kept him busy, marching and countermarching across central Europe and, as exhausting as they were, the marches were not ends in themselves. At the end of each one he had to bring his opponent to battle quickly, attack him, and beat him. Then he had to march off and do the entire process all over again. It would be amazing to add up the number of miles covered by Frederick's main body in the course of these campaigns. It was a true backpack tour of Central Europe.

Frederick opened the war in 1756 with a preemptive strike against his enemies.[18] He coupled a lightning drive into Saxony (the unfortunate kingdom whose resources would fund a great deal of this expensive war) with a drive into western Bohemia. Neither action went well. There was tougher than expected Saxon resistance at the fortified camp of Pirna, plus a bloody check delivered by the reformed and revitalized Austrian army at Lobositz (October 1). At the latter battle, Frederick impetuously launched an attack against what he perceived to be an Austrian rear guard. It turned out to be a main force and, although the battle was a tactical victory for the Prussians, it was a very bloody one. Once again, incidentally, Frederick had ridden away in the midst of battle. With the surrender of Pirna, major actions for the year were done and both sides went into winter quarters.

He was back in 1757, this time with a much larger and more ambitious plan—an all-out invasion of Bohemia by four widely separated columns: one from Chemnitz in western Saxony under Prince Moritz von Anhalt-Dessau; the main army under the king coming down from Dresden; one from Lusatia under August Wilhelm, the Duke of Bevern; and a fourth from Silesia under Count Schwerin—some 115,000 men in all. With the columns spread out over 210 kilometers of terrain, the plan bore more than a passing resemblance to Field Marshal

Austrian Field Marshal Leopold Josef Maria von Daun. The victor of Kolin, a master of the eighteenth-century art of maneuver, and a worthy adversary for Frederick the Great.

Helmuth von Moltke's campaign against the Austrians in 1866.[19] The four columns resolved into two at Leitmeritz in the west and Jungbunzlau in the east. Coordination problems on the march were few, and the result was the concentration of the entire Prussian army in front of Prague. Here Frederick fought the Austrians in a messy battle east of the city on May 6, driving them back into Prague and initiating a siege.

With their main force bottled up in Prague, the Austrians dispatched a large relief force under Marshal Leopold Josef Maria von Daun. Characteristically, Frederick did not wait for it to arrive, but marched out to attack it at Kolin (June 18). He badly underestimated its numbers and misjudged its position, however, and received the first defeat of his career. Although his army managed to retreat in relatively good order, his casualties were heavy, and the Austrians captured many cannon and standards, the currency of victory in those days. Frederick had no choice but to retreat from Bohemia. This attempt to win a decisive victory over the Austrians and perhaps drive them from the war miscarried badly. Whatever aura of infallibility the king still carried was now gone, apparently forever, and that went equally for his own men and his adversaries.

Both of these battles—Prague and Kolin—had shared one attribute: in both cases, Frederick had attempted an operational march onto the enemy's flank. At Prague, the strong position of the enemy led Frederick to attempt a leftward march to get around the Austrian right flank. The terrain was much more difficult than he had anticipated, to include a morass of swamps, drained fishponds, and silt. The march took much longer than expected and the Austrians were able to puzzle out the king's intentions. They managed a hasty redeployment of forces from their main body onto the right, so the attack caught not the Austrian flank but a new line of infantry, and there was hard going from the start. Frederick's field commander, Count Schwerin, was killed in the fighting on this wing, and Winterfeldt seriously injured. Eventually superior Prussian fighting qualities told, caving in both the northern (left) wing and the southern (right) Austrian wings. The Austrian armies retired in some disorder into Prague. With twenty-four thousand Austrian and eighteen thousand Prussian casualties, Prague was "one of the most murderous battles of the entire century," according to the king.[20] In the end, however, it was without decision. Frederick lacked the means to prosecute a siege of a large city. He wheeled up his artillery and began a bombardment, but it seemed to have little effect, and he ran out of ammunition before Prague ran out of buildings. Siege warfare—slow, deliberate, and expensive—would never be Prussia's game, and in fact one modern authority labels them "incompetent" at it.[21]

As bad as Prague had been, however, Kolin was far worse. Here Frederick once again ordered a flank march to the left, based on a

Ziethen.   Friedrich II.   Belling.   Keith.   Seydlitz.
Friedrich II., nach der Schlacht ausruhend. (Seite 1038.)
(Brief von R. v. Heyden in Graf Moltke's Arbeitszimmer.)

What now? A weary Frederick, surrounded by his generals, ponders his next move after the defeat at Kolin.

rudimentary personal reconnaissance. Many of his officers apparently tried to argue against the attack, simply on the basis of the relative size of the forces: Frederick had, perhaps, thirty-five thousand men, while Daun was in command of more than fifty thousand. Opposition to the royal will, however, was a tricky proposition in an absolute monarchy. They were not the king's advisers, but his vassals, and honor demanded that they follow where he led. The flank march dutifully got under way, only to be changed in midstream for reasons that will never be adequately explained. Instead of marching to get on the Austrian flank, Frederick ordered his regiments to wheel right, form battle line, and storm the well-prepared Austrian position, stocked with far more artillery and men than he could command. There are those who simply accuse Frederick of misjudging the situation and changing his mind. The king, for his part, blamed overzealous unit commanders, especially General Manstein on the refused right flank, who threw his men into the fray against orders when his command came under fire from Croat light forces holding advanced positions in front of the Austrian line. The result was predictable, although there would be much hard fighting before the Prussians had to withdraw from the battlefield. Once again, Prussian attacks, both infantry and cavalry, were irresistible and cut great gaps in the Austrian ranks opposite. Caught in a frontal attack against a larger enemy, however, Frederick lacked the reserves to exploit these successes. "Four more fresh battalions," he wrote, "and the battle would have been won,"[22] although Delbrück, for one, would later label that assessment a delusion.[23]

It is important to point out the limits of these operational maneuvers. On both occasions, Frederick attempted flank marches to strike the enemy at a vulnerable point. However, he undertook these marches at such close proximity to the enemy that they actually proceeded under fire. Both times, the Austrian commanders were able to rush enough forces to the threatened sector to form a two-echelon defensive position. Although we must not underestimate the shaky nature of the hastily improvised lines, we also cannot say that Frederick succeeded in getting onto the enemy's flank.

A word or two about the Austrians is in order. Virtually every commentator, Hans Delbrück in the late nineteenth century, Christopher Duffy and Dennis Showalter today, paint a portrait of a revived Habsburg army. Under the administration of Count Friedrich Wilhelm von Haugwitz, recruitment, training, and armaments alike had all received a thorough upgrade after Hohenfriedeberg. Perhaps von Haugwitz's most important achievement was getting the estates in the Habsburg crown lands and Bohemia to agree to the raising of recruit quotas for a ten-year period (the so-called "decennial recess"), which made long-range planning a possibility for the first time.[24] The new model army fought well at Lobositz in 1756, even better at Prague, and best of all at Kolin, where it won an undisputed victory. What generally goes unmentioned, however, is the utter lack of operational imagination or initiative that the Austrians showed in any of these campaigns. In each one, their art of war on the operational level consisted of one thing: choosing a decent piece of ground and grimly defending in place. They fought well tactically. Although their musketry never reached Prussian levels in either speed or effect, they shot, launched infantry assaults on key terrain features, and sent cavalry into dramatic charges or countercharges. This cannot disguise the fact, however, that they rarely did more than fight a static war of position. Their monarch, Maria Theresa, stated repeatedly that Austria was fighting to humble Prussia, perhaps transform it once again into a "starveling duchy."[25] But Austrian operations in these wars rarely reached the empress's level of intensity. If the Austrian army wanted to win back Silesia and punish the miscreant who had stolen it, at some point it was going to have to go out and get Frederick. A passive *Stellungskrieg* would not get the job done.

Rossbach[26]

Still licking his wounds from Kolin, and desperately trying to scrounge up replacements for his shattered infantry units, Frederick now had to turn and face a new threat: a combined French-Imperial army advancing from the west. The adversary has not gotten a great deal of respect from historians, it is true. The French commander, Marquis Charles de Soubise, received his appointment though the good graces of the royal mistress, Madame Pompadour, rather than for his ability. The commander of the "Imperial Army of Execution" (*Reichsexecutionsarmee*), Austrian prince Joseph von Sachsen-Hildburghausen, was "a resoundingly titled non-entity," according to one recent history.[27] His army consisted of contingents of varying quality from no less than 231 of the states of the Holy Roman Empire. It is easy to paint the upcoming Prussian victory as an inevitable triumph over some sort of polyglot rabble and, indeed, historians have even found it hard to resist taking a swipe at the impossibly tangled designation of the force: in this campaign, Frederick would be taking on the "Combined Imperial Reichs-Execution and French Army."

This is reading history backward. The inevitability of victory certainly was not so apparent to Frederick at the time. His strategic position was horrible, with enemies closing in from all points. In the south, the Austrians were bestirring themselves after Kolin, but that, as he knew, would be a fairly slow process. The Russians, likewise, were advancing from the east, but given the underdeveloped state of roads in that district, their armies moved ponderously at best. The Franco-Imperial advance into Thuringia, however, used the best road network in Europe and could overrun Frederick's prosperous western territories and threaten his position in Saxony in just a handful of marches. At the moment, this posed the most serious threat to Prussia, and the iron logic of interior lines meant that Frederick had to go out to meet it.

Leaving behind a covering force in Silesia under the Duke of Bevern, Frederick and his army set out from Dresden on August 31. The army wasn't large, just twenty-five thousand men, nor were these the fresh and well-fed troops of the spring. They were the remnant of that army, understrength units made up of exhausted men, led by commanders whose faith in the king had no doubt been shaken. A noticeable exception was General Friedrich Wilhelm von Seydlitz. A cavalry commander and one of the few officers who had impressed Frederick at Kolin, he was now in command of the advance guard, as the little army made its way across Germany.[28] Two Austrian hussar regiments under General Szecheny, detailed to the Reichsarmee for the duration of the campaign, fell back in front of the Prussians, occasionally turning to skirmish with Seydlitz, and another detachment of hussars and Croats harassed them along their left flank. Nevertheless, the king moved quickly. Traveling light and leaving behind all unnecessary baggage, he supplied his troops from the countryside and quartered them in civilian homes along the way—a rarity for the magazine-based warfare of the day.[29] He crossed the Saale River on September 10 and drove into Thuringia, reaching Erfurt on September 13. He had marched his army 170 miles in thirteen days.[30] Two days later Frederick was in Gotha. Seydlitz's advance guard got there so quickly, in fact, that he came within a hair of capturing both allied commanders.

Frederick may have intended a lightning campaign, but it opened with a great deal of sparring. His advance to Gotha found the allies staying just out of reach; his withdrawals found them advancing carefully without giving him the opening he sought. The principal allied problem was not the talent (or lack thereof) of either commander. It was that there were two of them—a textbook case in the problems of divided command. Soubise preferred maneuver to seeking a battle. Hildburghausen, technically his superior, the opposite. He no doubt recognized that centrifugal forces might go to work at any time on his disparate army. Sometimes, however, the two commanders switched sides, with Soubise suddenly for aggression, and Hildburghausen turning on the caution.[31] There was little cooperation between them, and on occasion their forces operated as separate armies. Frederick, too, had to be cautious. His intelligence reports estimated the size of the combined force at 55,000–60,000, almost three times the size of his own.[32] Several times he withdrew to see if he could lure some or all of the Franco-Imperial army out into the open field, but the allies refused to bite. Back and forth the two sides darted, looking for an opening, with the Saale River the approximate operational boundary between them.

There now intervened in the campaign what can only be called an intermission. On October 12, Frederick received news that an Austrian raiding party was marching on Berlin. They broke into the city four days later. Under Count Hadik, a force of 3,400 men had assaulted the gates, fought a series of small but pitched battles with garrison troops in the suburbs, and generally terrorized the citizenry. He had departed the next day, but only after extorting a payment of two hundred thousand talers, plus another fifteen thousand talers in "refreshment money" for his troops. It had been a small raid, but it had certainly caused some anxious moments, and the city governor had hurriedly

Andreas Count Hadik. Commander of the daring and successful Austrian raid on Berlin, October 16, 1757.

bundled off the queen and crown prince to the fortress of Spandau.[33] Hurrying back to rescue his capital from what seemed like an all-out assault, Frederick turned back again to the west once he realized the limited scale of the operation.

As it turned out, the Hadik raid played a role in the war out of all proportion to its size. Frederick's departure for Berlin was just the sort of opening even a command-paralyzed army might exploit, and on October 24, the Reichsarmee drove across the Saale. This was the news for which the king had been waiting. He now rushed back, determined to force the issue. By October 31, the Prussian main body, reinforced by the troops of Prince Moritz and Prince Ferdinand of Brunswick, had once again closed up to the river. Frederick's lightning thrust back into Thuringia finally seemed to concentrate the minds of the allied commanders. Hildburghausen, whose bold thrust across the Saale had gone unsupported by Soubise, again withdrew behind the river upon news of Frederick's approach. On November 2, the two allied armies linked up, with the Reichsarmee coming up from the southeast and joining the French camp at St. Micheln. Together, the two armies contained 10,900 imperial troops and 30,200 French, for a total of 41,100 men. It was far less than the 60,000 Frederick feared, but still a formidable force.

Frederick crossed the Salle at Weissenfels on November 3. Linking up with another detachment under Marshal Keith, coming down from Halle, the Prussian army made camp between the village of Braunsdorf and the Geisel stream, facing to the west, about three miles to the east of the allies. Even after calling in the various detachments, the Prussian force still consisted only of a mere twenty-seven battalions, forty-five squadrons, and twenty-five heavy guns, just twenty-two thousand men.[34]

Although they had linked up, the allied commanders now had a difficult time agreeing on how to proceed against Frederick. The site of the camp and the dispositions within it appeared suicidal to Hildburghausen. It was actually facing north, based on Soubise's belief that the Prussian main body was crossing the Saale at Halle and would come down on him from that direction. Hildburghausen, whose advance guards had been in contact with Frederick at Weissenfels, could not convince Soubise that Frederick was actually lurking to the east. The fact that his Reichsarmee formed the right wing of the camp, and thus would bear the brunt of any Prussian attack from that direction, might have contributed to his anxiety. The hastily erected camp, Hildburghausen said at the time, was the "most confused thing I have ever seen in my life."[35] The command headquarters, for example, were actually located to the north of the troops, that is, in front of the camp. Hildburghausen argued for an immediate change of front to the east. Soubise at first resisted, no doubt simply to preserve form, but then eventually agreed. Even he seems to have accepted the inevitability of a showdown with Frederick by this time, and there are reports of him spending most of November 3 scouting the surrounding area for a good potential battlefield.[36]

The two armies were now just a few miles apart, but unaware of each other's exact location. On November 3, Frederick's reconnaissance patrols were the first to clarify the situation. They reported late in the day that the allies were in camp facing north, and thus offering Frederick their right flank. This was a situation that the king usually had to work hard to attain. Now it had apparently fallen into his lap. Not surprisingly, he decided on an attack the next morning. That evening, however, with the allies receiving disturbing reports about activity on their right flank, the commanders finally ordered a shift in the facing of the camp. The new position faced east, with its anchors roughly on Mückeln in the north and Branderoda in the south, parallel to the Prussian position.

On the morning of November 4, Frederick led his army to attack the allied camp. As he often did, he undertook a personal reconnaissance before launching the attack. Instead of a voluntary offering of the enemy flank, he saw instead a heavily fortified defensive position. A frontal attack could not have had much appeal so soon after Kolin. He could probably have taken the position, he later wrote, but only at the cost of twenty thousand men, men he no longer had.[37] He now had his army take up a new position of its own, its right wing anchored on Bedra in the north and on Rossbach to the south, with the king's headquarters in the latter.

Many eighteenth-century campaigns can be quite challenging to analyze. With relatively small main armies and as many as three or four detachments all in simultaneous movement, the effect can be a confusing swirl. By November 4, however, the situation on this front had sorted itself out nicely. The two armies sat facing each other in parallel lines, about two and a half miles apart. Both were oriented north to south, the combined army to the west, the Prussians to the east. At first glance, it might appear to be a map exercise for beginners. From the operational situation it is almost impossible to conceive of one of these armies winning a decisive victory the very next day.

To this day it is difficult to reconstruct the exact reasons that the allies decided to launch an attack on Frederick. It is possible to make a few observations, however.[38] The supply situation, particularly for the profligate French, made it impossible to stay put. Both allied armies had been parading back and forth across the region for months, and the resources of the local countryside had been exhausted.[39] Soubise and Hildburghausen knew enough about Frederick's abilities to see that retreat, too, was no longer an option. With the Prussians so close, Frederick would surely take the opportunity to attack them while they were in an unfavorable position. At the very least he would set upon their rear guard.

That left one option. On the evening of November 4, the allied commanders decided to advance against Frederick. They didn't necessarily mean to attack him. Perhaps a maneuver around Frederick's flank, one that threatened his communications back to Weissenfels and the Saale, would lever him out of his position and force him to fall back. If he didn't, they would, at the very least, be on his left flank by the evening of November 5. They would establish their camp between Obschütz and Reichartswerden, and launch their attack on the morning of November 6. Hildburghausen objected to the lack of specificity, and early on the morning of November 5 had Soubise put his intentions to attack Frederick in writing—a true indication of the depressing level of cooperation within the allied command. Nevertheless, it was a sound plan, and against most eighteenth-century generals it might have worked.

On November 5, Prussian reconnaissance indicated that the allies had broken camp and were moving to their right. Frederick did not immediately jump into action. The allies could well be heading south in retreat toward Freiburg, he felt, to reprovision themselves. Perhaps they were even retreating across the Unstrut River. There was no need, he argued, to hurry or rush into a precipitate deployment.[40] He had already seen something of the maneuver capability of the enemy army, and the energy of its commanders, in the preceding weeks and had been none too impressed. Their intentions would be clear soon enough, and whatever they decided to do, they had spared him the difficulty of a frontal attack on a prepared position. Just to be prudent, however, he did prepare a force of ten battalions from his right wing and all his hussars and dragoons to attack the allied rear guard if Soubise and Hildburghausen had indeed ordered a general retreat.

For an army carrying out what was by any standard a daring maneuver, the allies certainly did take their time. The French, in particular, had a great deal of difficulty breaking their camp and sorting themselves out into formation. Even with Hildburghausen urging the greatest haste, the maneuver onto the right did not begin until noon. The advance guard consisted of six squadrons of Austrian hussars, followed by the main body in three columns. The left column, the first echelon, consisted of sixteen German squadrons, followed by sixteen French battalions, and finally twelve French squadrons; the middle column contained seventeen German squadrons followed by sixteen French battalions; the right column held the French reserve corps and the infantry of the Reichsarmee, the least reliable units in the force, followed by the German artillery reserve.[41] The French artillery formed a small column all its own between the second and third columns. The force headed almost due south for the first hour, then turned east at Zeuchfeld, a ninety-degree wheel by four closely packed columns that led to a great deal of confusion. Soon, four columns had become five. The march held its order, but by all accounts it was no thing of beauty.

It was 2:00 P.M. The allied columns had halted so that the commanders could reconnoiter the Prussian camp. There had been no contact yet, and what was by now a predictable argument had broken out between the two commanders. Soubise still spoke of establishing a new camp between Obschütz and Reichardtswerden, while Hildburghausen was for an attack as soon as they reached the Prussian flank. The complete absence of any discussion at all among the allies about what the Prussians might be doing is striking, as is the thought of taking a long pause during the execution of a bold flanking maneuver—both of which failings were products of the allied command tussle. On the positive side, the break did allow the German infantry contingents, which were already straggling badly, to close up to the rest of the army.

It is unclear who among Frederick's entourage first detected the allied wheel at Zeuchfeld. The honors certainly do not go to the king himself. Even with the day wearing on, Frederick still refused to believe either that the allies intended to attack him or that they were trying to get onto or past his flank. The fact that a succession of officers tried to apprise the king of the situation over his lunch apparently led to harsh royal words for a few of them. In fact, the first reports he received spoke only of enemy cavalry heading east. These, Frederick argued, might well be reconnaissance patrols. Only a patrol that clearly identified infantry formations on the march convinced Frederick that the allies were coming against him.

As obstinate as he had been in refusing to believe the reports of his own scouts, he was now equally decisive in fashioning a response to the allied advance. It seemed apparent to him almost immediately that he could achieve something all too rare in his own day: catching an entire enemy army on the march, hitting it before it had a chance to deploy, and scattering it. It is impossible to say whether the king had been mulling over this very subject in the days before November 5. He certainly never claimed that it was so. It seems, rather, to have been a sudden inspiration deriving from the moment.

At 2:30, Frederick set his army into motion. The Prussians, in stark contrast to their adversaries, broke camp like lightning and were soon on the march. Some sources say minutes, but it was more likely half an hour.[42] In the van rode Seydlitz with the Prussian cavalry. Although he was the youngest of Frederick's cavalry generals, the king recognized talent when he saw it and had placed him in command of thirty-eight squadrons. Seydlitz took off almost due east, toward Klein Kayna. The path took him behind a long hill called the Janus Berg. The Prussian infantry soon followed.

Incredibly, the allied generals had watched the scene from the town of Luftschiff where they had halted. They could clearly see the Prussian army breaking camp, heading east, and vanishing altogether behind the Janus Berg. A quick council of war convened to discuss this new information. The prognosis: the Prussians were in retreat, probably to Merseburg and then back over the Saale.[43] This was Hildburghausen's moment. For months he had been advocating an aggressive attitude toward Frederick, and events had now borne out the wisdom of what he'd been saying. The army should speed up and attack the Prussians while they were in full retreat. Soubise and the other French generals agreed. Within all the columns, the cavalry now came to the fore, and set out in pursuit of the apparently beaten, or at least demoralized, foe. The axis of approach switched to the northeast as the allies tried to overtake Frederick before he slipped away over the Saale. The rest of the army started out once again.

The allied pause had enabled Seydlitz to complete his encircling maneuver. His ride had taken him first due east toward Klein Kayna, then to the south through Gross Kayna. The entire maneuver had been out of the allied line of sight, hidden first by the Janus Berg (for the eastward leg), its extension, the Pölzen Hügel (for the southern). When he suddenly came over the rise of the Pölzen Hügel at 3:30 P.M., he had achieved the dream of every battlefield captain: utter and complete surprise. No less than seven Prussian cavalry regiments were in the first charge: three in the first echelon (the Czettritz Dragoons, the Meinicke Dragoons, and the Leib Hussars) and four in the second (the *Garde du Korps*, the *Gensd'armes*, the Rochow Cuirassiers, and the Driesen Cuirassiers). An eighth regiment, the Szekely Hussars, formed the extreme left flank of Seydlitz's position. It was a powerful force, fifteen squadrons in the first echelon and eighteen in the second, riding like the wind—one of the greatest moments in the history of the horse arm.

The allied horse had just passed Reichardtswerden to their right when the charge hit. Given the shock of the moment, being struck by an enemy who was supposedly in full retreat, it is incredible that the allied cavalry did not simply flee. The two lead regiments of Austrian cuirassiers actually managed to deploy, the Bretlach Regiment into line, the Trautmannsdorff Regiment into a loose net of individual squadrons.[44] The initial fight was a tough one, eventually degenerating into a melee of individual hand-to-hand combats, and in fact the Austrians did manage to hold up Seydlitz's first echelon. With his second echelon moving to envelop the allied cavalry on both the right and the left, however, the defenders' position was soon hopeless. A charge by the Szekely Hussars against the deep right wing of the enemy was the finishing stroke, throwing the allied cavalry into complete disarray. When the French Mailly Regiment attempted to form line, to give just one example, it was first disrupted by fleeing cavalry of its own side, and then overrun completely by the Prussian *Gensd'armes*. It had apparently allowed them to pass its flank, thinking they were friendly cavalry of the Reichsarmee.[45] Soon the entire allied cavalry was in flight to the rear.

Up until now, the allied infantry had only the dimmest idea of what was going on ahead of them. Then, a series of rapid events put them into the picture. First, they saw riding toward them a mob of cavalry. As they loomed closer, it was clear that it was the remnants of their own force, which had just moments before set out in pursuit of the retreating Prussians. It was also clear that some disaster had befallen them. Without formation and apparently terrified, the fleeing horsemen rode past, and sometimes simply through, the densely packed formations of friendly infantry. And then, in literally the next seconds, a line of Prussian infantry, echeloned to the left, crested the Janus Berg. They advanced east of the town of Lunstädt and wheeled to the right, sealing off the allied infantry's avenue of advance. Dennis Showalter has described it as "crossing the T," and the naval metaphor aptly describes what had happened.[46] The allies were still in march formation, of course, not at all ready for combat. Only the forward regiments managed to form any sort of line at all. Some French regiments threw themselves into column formation and attacked where they could. This was not yet the Napoleonic era, however. Without the cover afforded by thick clouds of skirmishers, French columns were simply huge targets for the Prussian muskets. As the Prussians smartly extended their line on both sides, forming a "V" around the enemy, panic began to spread in the ranks of the allied army. Frederick now wheeled up the artillery that he had originally emplaced on the Janus Berg and redeployed the guns in Reichardtswerden. From here they poured canister at point-blank range into the milling allied columns, who now had no higher direction and no place to go.

It is fitting that the final blow of the battle came from the Prussian cavalry. After the complete success of Seydlitz's first charge, he had done what many cavalry officers of the day consistently failed to do: he had regrouped and reorganized his cavalry. Redeploying them to the southwest, between Tagewerben and Storkau, he now launched a general charge into the right flank of the wavering allied army. It served as the signal for a general advance of the Prussian infantry, as well. Under these hammer blows, the French-Imperial army simply dissolved. Individuals, groups, and then entire units lost all discipline, throwing down their weapons and fleeing to the rear. Only a handful of units managed anything like a retreat in good order, protected by a remnant of the allied cavalry that had managed to fight its way back. A large portion of the allied artillery, virtually all the heavy guns, and an incredible baggage train—this was the French army, after all—fell into Prussian hands.

It was the casualty list at Rossbach, however, that was the best indication of what had just happened. The allies had lost more than 10,000 men, including more than 5,000 prisoners. Prussian killed had amounted to just 169 and 379 wounded.[47] In an era when even successful battles consisted of long lines of infantry firing at each other at point-blank range and hand-to-hand cavalry melee, this was not merely unusual. It was unique, the easiest and most complete victory in Frederick's career. It had taken just ninety minutes. Large portions of his already tiny army hadn't even gotten into the action; Frederick himself would say that virtually all the infantry fighting fell on the backs of just seven battalions, and few of their soldiers fired more than twelve to fifteen rounds. Other units stood and watched with their muskets shouldered.

There is no need to canonize Frederick for his generalship at Rossbach, and in fact historians have tended not to. They repeatedly point out the incompetence of the enemy he faced there. Delbrück's "methodological parody" on Frederick calls the allied army "miserable, and their commanders even worse."[48] The Reichsarmee was not an army, but a collection of contingents. The French army displayed huge weaknesses from the lowliest soldier to the highest commander. Its officers were venal and corrupt, its rank and file half-hearted, its doctrine in a state of utter confusion. As much as modern military historians seem to love the infantry column, it was tried and found wanting on the field at Rossbach. The two armies combined were even worse, unable to make the simplest campaign decision without it degenerating into an argument between the joint commanders. Frederick, it is often argued, had given this combined army a little knock, and it had simply collapsed into a mob.

This argument falls apart, however, when we look at the actual course of the campaign and culminating battle. For all its problems, Frederick had a great deal of difficulty bringing the combined army to battle. When he finally did, he had to call off his first attack due to the allied redeployment. In the eyes of recent research, and this is confirmed repeatedly in period sources, its manpower—both French and German—seems to have been no worse or better than any of Frederick's adversaries.[49] Although the sources indicate that Frederick had a disrespect for the allied army that bordered on contempt, we must keep in mind that this is the same commander who had just launched a frontal assault against a much larger Austrian force at Kolin. He had contempt for just about everyone at this stage of his career.

The key to Rossbach can only come when we analyze it on the operational level. Although virtually every battle in Frederick's career found him trying to get to his adversary's flank, he had previously attempted it through a flank march while already in contact with the enemy. It was a tactical maneuver, in other words. Often, his men performed the march while under enemy fire, which tended to slow it down (Prague) or disrupt it altogether (Kolin). At Rossbach, however, Frederick had a clear field. He was able to carry out his flanking move completely out of sight and range of the enemy force, and then to swoop down on it from out of nowhere. In an era of set piece battles, of linear tactics and parallel battle lines, Frederick actually managed to catch an enemy army strung out in a long march column, and thus nearly helpless in the face of his attack. Rossbach was not simply a triumph of a better-trained and better-led army over a rabble. Nor was it, classically speaking, an example of an oblique attack. Instead, Frederick triumphed through an operational maneuver that allowed him to take his penchant for the flanking maneuver to the next level. The allies had served it up to him, of course, but he had intuitively recognized the opportunity and exploited it in style. In the process, he cemented his military reputation, drove the French into a military funk from which they would not emerge for forty years, and demonstrated conclusively that numbers, in and of themselves, are not decisive in war. It is no exaggeration to say that at Rossbach, Frederick inadvertently and unconsciously discovered the art of operational-level warfare.

Leuthen

Even though Rossbach took place in November, this incredible year of battles was not yet over. According to the king, the victory at Rossbach "strictly speaking, only gave me the freedom to seek out new dangers."[50] On November 13, Frederick set out from Leipzig with a small but satisfied army of eighteen battalions and twenty-nine squadrons, once again rapidly countermarching back across central Europe and, again, quartering his troops among the civilian population.[51] His target this time was Silesia. The Austrians had spent the months since Kolin methodically reconquering the province against an inept defense led by the Duke of Bevern. The key fortress of Schweidnitz had fallen; the Austrians had stormed the Prussian camp outside Breslau; the Prussian army was in retreat back across the Oder River. As he entered Silesia on November 28, he heard more bad news: Breslau itself had fallen, and Bevern himself had fallen into Austrian hands while on a personal reconnaissance. Not only had the Prussian army in Silesia dissolved, Frederick no longer even had a decent base of operations in the province.

Every piece of bad news only served to increase the king's pace. Frederick arrived in Silesia in late November. Skirting Austrian-held Liegnitz, he made straight for Parchwitz. After a brisk fight between his advance guard and a surprised enemy detachment that netted him three hundred prisoners, Frederick entered Parchwitz on November 28. Even by Frederick's standards, it had been another remarkable march: from Leipzig to the Oder, a little more than 140 miles of mostly muddy winter roads, in just thirteen days.

Speed wasn't the only thing on the king's mind, however. As his main body made contact with the remnants of Bevern's Army of Silesia, he could see he had some remedial work to do. The men had just been through a series of defeats under a commander who had completely lost his nerve, and they bore the marks of the experience. Frederick had to lift spirits, and he did so in several ways: having the veterans of Rossbach tell their tales of glory; meeting with the men around their campfires, highly unusual behavior for a Hohenzollern; and even increasing the size of the wine ration. As confidence grew in the camp, it spread to the surrounding countryside. One result was the return of many deserters who had fled the debacle at Breslau. This morale-boosting peaked in perhaps the most famous episode in the king's entire career: the war council that he held on December 3 with his senior commanders and staff. Here he stated the terms of the upcoming battle as victory or death and asked for the resignations of any officer not prepared for either of those options.[52]

On December 4, Frederick and his advance guard of hussars approached Neumarkt. It bore all the signs of a soon-to-be Austrian base: Pandours in occupation and a field bakery up and running. If the Austrians settled into Neumarkt, the heights behind the city would give them a real tactical advantage in any battle. Frederick decided to storm the place. The only problem was that he had no troops for that kind of work. His hussars weren't in the assault business, and he had no infantry at hand—they wouldn't be coming up until evening. "The king," Frederick later wrote, "decided to make a virtue out of a necessity."[53] Ordering several hussar squadrons to dismount, he had them storm the town gates. A still-mounted regiment then sprang through at a full gallop, while another scoured the suburbs near the Breslau Gate. It ended with the town, eight hundred Croat prisoners, and some eighty thousand bread rations in Frederick's hands. Upon entering, it was clear from engineer markers and surveying stakes that the Austrians had indeed intended to use Neumarkt as their headquarters.

In fact, he had arrived not a moment too soon. As the king's main body was hastening up to Neumarkt that evening, Frederick received news that the Austrians were advancing toward him. Moving out of their fortified encampment on the Lohe River near Breslau, they had crossed the Weistritz River at Lissa and established a position near the town of Leuthen. Their right wing lay near the village of Nippern in the north, moving down through the villages of Frobelwitz, Leuthen, and then to their left at Gohlau. Frederick's forces lay roughly between Neumarkt and Stephansdorf. As at Rossbach, the two encamped armies faced each other in roughly parallel lines, arrayed north to south, with the Prussians lying to the west.

By any rational accounting, the battle of Leuthen should have been the end of Frederick's career.[54] He faced, once again, a much larger enemy force. His always sketchy intelligence reports, or perhaps merely his wishful thinking, estimated that the Austrian army was thirty-nine thousand men. In fact it was closer to sixty-five thousand: 85 battalions, 125 squadrons, some 235 pieces of artillery. The king himself had just thirty-five thousand (48 battalions, 133 squadrons, and only 78 guns).[55] Moreover, he was facing an army that had defeated him at their last encounter and whose commanders, Prince Charles and Marshal Daun, were thus distinctly unimpressed by the Frederician mystique. Although it might have seemed like a hundred years to the soldiers in both armies, Kolin was only six months in the past.

Nevertheless, Frederick was determined to attack them. Anything less would leave a substantial portion of Silesia in Austrian hands over the winter, and that might well translate into the loss of the province altogether.[56] He had, in fact, intended to attack them even if they had remained entrenched on the Lohe. Now they had done him the favor of coming out toward him. "The fox has come out of his hole," Frederick laughed to a subordinate on the eve of the battle, "and now I want to punish him for his insolence."[57] Since he had denied them their new base at Neumarkt, they were more or less encamped in the open, and in fact, the Austrians spent the entire night of December 4 under arms. Such was the price of camping in close proximity to Frederick.

Even with these advantages, the problem was still a daunting one. A frontal assault, even against a cold and tired army, would surely end in disaster. Frederick had, once again, to conceive of a way to get onto his opponent's flank. Six months ago he simply would have ordered a march in full view of the enemy, with mixed results, as we have seen. Here, fresh from Rossbach, he was thinking in more radical terms.

The plan he conjured up, seemingly overnight, involved one of the most complex approach marches in the entire history of linear warfare. The Prussian cavalry would deploy in front of the Austrian position, launching an attack on the forward Austrian position at Borne. It would then align itself as if it were to spearhead an attack on the Austrian right between Nippern and Frobelwitz. This would fix enemy attention to this sector. Meanwhile, as his main body approached the Austrians behind the cavalry, it would suddenly perform a mass wheel to the right, turning south. A line of low hills, including the Schleierberg and the Sophienberg, would screen his subsequent movements from the Austrians. It is often said that Frederick only noticed the hills that morning, more evidence of his coup d'oeil. In fact, the entire area had been a Prussian army maneuver ground between the Silesian and Seven Years' Wars, and Frederick knew it intimately. At any rate, as far as the enemy camp was concerned, the Prussians would simply vanish. Once they were safely out of sight, near the village of Lobetinz, the three main columns (advance guard farthest east, first echelon in the middle, second echelon farthest west) would once again wheel, this time to the left, heading east. At the end of this complicated set of formation changes, wheels, and deployments, the entire Prussian army would be sitting on the dangling left flank of the Austrian position, arrayed into line and prepared to land a devastating blow.

The maneuver worked almost exactly as Frederick had drawn it up. The Austrians swallowed the bait whole. Daun and Charles reacted

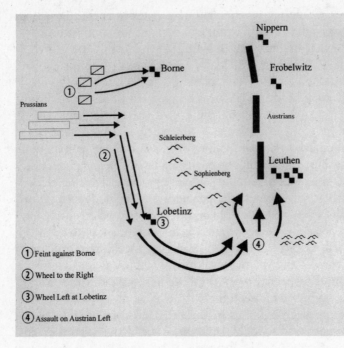

The Maneuver on Leuthen, December 5, 1757

to the Prussian cavalry attack on Borne and subsequent advance by rushing troops toward what looked like the threatened sector in the north. The "fog of war" is always an operational problem for both sides, but here the real thing actually played a role, with morning fog further obscuring Prussian movements and intentions. The Austrian commanders interpreted the Prussian vanishing act as a retreat by an outnumbered Prussian army that had decided not to try conclusions with a much larger force. On the list of famous last words, there can be few more pungent than Charles's comment as the Prussian columns moved away to the south: "The good fellows are leaving; let's let them go."[58] Perhaps the king had found the Austrian position too strong, Charles reasoned. Perhaps Frederick felt that there was not enough daylight left for an attack. Most likely, he was marching south in an attempt to threaten Austrian communications with Bohemia, and thus lever the Austrians out of their position without a fight. According to the Prussian official history, it was "a notion entirely in the spirit of the age."[59] Perhaps deluded by such comfortable thoughts, Charles and

Daun were no doubt as surprised as anyone when a massive Prussian infantry attack suddenly erupted from the south, smashing into their unprepared left wing. It was a little after 1:00 P.M. Before a single shot had been fired, the Prussians had won the battle of Leuthen.

Numerous histories describe the actual fighting. Suffice it to say that even after Frederick's operational surprise, the battle offered its share of nail-biting moments to all concerned. Given the weaponry and tactics in use at the time, such a thing was inevitable. The first wave of the Prussian attack in the south, with General Wedel's brigade leading on the right, hit the imperial German contingents. These were Württembergers, to be precise. No doubt Charles and Daun had placed them here for the very reason that it was expected to be a fairly quiet sector of the battlefield. They were Protestants for the most part, men who had little desire to fight against Prussia and for Catholic Austria, and they lasted only a few moments before they dissolved.

The shocked Austrian command now had to switch the axis of their entire force ninety degrees to the south, a maneuver difficult enough to pull off on the parade ground, but almost impossible under fire. With their own refugees streaming all over the area, and with Prussian infantry advancing determinedly to the north, the results ranged from decidedly mixed to nightmarish. Rather than present a cohesive battle-front against the Prussian attack, Charles and Daun threw in a few hastily redeployed units at a time, and the results were predictable.

Still, as the Prussians drove north, the sheer number of Austrians engaged made for some tough fighting. This was particularly true of the village of Leuthen itself, laid out west to east and thus a natural breakwater in the center of the Austrian position. Austrian cavalry, always showing a good deal of dash, did manage to get into action on the flanks of the battle, and as always, there was some hard fighting here, too. It had its opportunities to attack the Prussian infantry, whose advance to the north had uncovered both of its own flanks. On both flanks, however, the Prussian cavalry managed to drive back their Austrian counterparts, with Ziethen's fifty-three squadrons covering on the right flank, and a force of forty more on the left under Lieutenant General Wilhelm von Driesen. Once again, knowledge of the ground was crucial. To the right of the Prussian line, the broken terrain made it difficult for entire cavalry formations to deploy. Ziethen, however, had ridden over this exact ground in the Silesian Maneuver of 1754 and knew it intimately.[60]

Meanwhile, the Austrian infantry, never agile under the best of circumstances, did what it always tended to do when the situation got difficult. It bunched up, making itself an attractive target for Prussian musket fire, as well as for the Prussian artillery deployed on the high ground south of Leuthen. Eventually, when Austrian losses rose high enough, their infantry broke and ran en masse. Prussian hussars pursued them, with one regiment alone (the Ziethen Hussars) taking more than two thousand prisoners.

Given the relative size and configuration of the forces, Leuthen could not be a painless victory for the Prussians. They took significant casualties, some six thousand in all, or one-sixth of their total force. Battering the Austrians was always a bloody business, as Frederick well knew. Austrian infantry, in particular, fought well whenever it managed to find shelter or a position upon which to anchor itself. Much of the Prussian total, in fact, came from the murderous fighting for Leuthen village itself, by which time the hopelessness of the Austrian operational situation was obvious to all. Nevertheless, the Austrians had suffered far worse: some twenty-two thousand men. Of that number, a staggering ten thousand were prisoners.[61] Four hours of combat against a better-led and better-trained force had destroyed about one-third of the Austrian army.

The significance of Leuthen ranged far beyond the battlefield losses, however. The battle meant the collapse of the entire Austrian position in Silesia. In the next few days, Prussian hussars roamed the countryside, rounding up Austrian prisoners in the villages around Leuthen, capturing some four hundred wagons of baggage. Charles and Daun reacted to the catastrophe by deciding to retreat from Silesia altogether. Harried all the way by Prussian cavalry under Ziethen and Fouqué, with the men demoralized and the commanders in shock, it was an ugly operation. The Austrian army that crossed the Bohemian border on December 31 was just about one-fourth the size of the one that had entered the province back in September. The retreat, in turn, spelled doom for the various Austrian fortress garrisons within the province, which Charles had to abandon if he were to have any chance to save his army. On December 19, to give just one example, another seventeen thousand men of the Breslau garrison surrendered to the Prussians.[62] By the end of the year, the Prussians had taken some forty thousand prisoners and seized four thousand wagons of supplies. On December 21, Frederick entered Breslau, the capital of his now secure Silesian province. Here he made his winter quarters.

The battle of Leuthen appears in virtually every history book, both general works and those that deal more specifically with military history. It is almost always portrayed as the classic example of the "oblique attack."[63] Certainly, Frederick's actual attack against the Austrian left flank was echeloned to the right, that is, with his right wing leading and his left drawn back or "refused." However, all the tactical ability in the world would not have brought Frederick the kind of victory he won on December 5. He had tried that path at Prague and Kolin, and failed. Instead, this triumph was the result of operational maneuver, the flank march while out of sight and out of contact with the enemy. "The battle of Leuthen," Napoleon would later write, "was a classic work of movement, of maneuver, and of resolution." The maneuver let Frederick hide his intentions from his enemy. It gave him a chance to achieve complete surprise. Finally, it allowed him to reemerge back onto the situation map and strike a massive blow at the time and place of his choosing. He succeeded in getting not just a lone regiment, or even a wing, onto the enemy flank—but his entire army. Moreover, this was not the result of happenstance or enemy bungling, as had arguably been the case at Rossbach. In fact, Frederick seems to have contemplated just this sort of flanking maneuver from the moment he arrived in Silesia. In that sense, Leuthen was the first conscious example of what would become known as the German way of war: the operational war of movement.

There were other crucial factors at Leuthen. One, mentioned repeatedly in nineteenth-century German accounts, was the independence of the Prussian commanders in battle. "From the moment that their royal army commander gave the command to attack, his generals acted with an understanding for his intentions, with a skill and an independent energy as in no other previous battle," the Prussian official history would write. "Nowhere was there a mention of personal directives from the king." Indeed, Frederick set the standard for the later ideal of the German army commander, devising a mission for his officers, then allowing them to carry it out as they saw fit:

The bearing of his commanders showed how the Parchwitz speech had inspired them to give their best. No rash foolhardiness, like Manstein at Kolin; instead the tranquil calm of the general who understands how to wait for the correct moment. With remarkable skill, each of the arms fulfilled its own mission and supported the others. On the right wing, infantry and cavalry competed with each other in a hard struggle to drive the enemy from position to position. In the open order struggle for the villages, the infantry was resourceful and agile, and those same battalions, despite their exertions and their losses, were immediately reassembled in preparation for new attacks. Driesen and his riders won the decision on the left flank at the precise moment that the infantry reached the exhaustion point . . . and he succeeded when they were no longer capable of proceeding alone.[64]

The artillery, too, had played a crucial role, with even the heavy twelve-pounders trundling forward over the frozen ground, never leaving the infantry without supporting fire.

It is interesting to note how the German account links the concepts of independent command and combined arms. Indeed, analyses of Leuthen often read like a modern manual on cooperation of the various arms. Such cooperation, in the German scheme, was intimately tied up with the independence of the various field commanders. No supreme commander, no matter how gifted or how advanced the means of communication at his fingertips, can effectively coordinate the fire and shock capabilities of the various arms in battle. That has to be the work of the commanders actually on the scene. The German skill at combined arms coordination stands in intimate relationship to *Auftragstaktik*.

Zorndorf

Although Rossbach and Leuthen had brought Frederick hopes that his enemies might make peace, in fact they seem to have hardened attitudes in Paris and Vienna. Maria Theresa, "the only real man amongst his opponents,"[65] remained intransigent, and her enmity and determination to see the struggle through guaranteed that the war would go on. The rest of the war would find Frederick attempting to repeat the success of Leuthen, and often with the same pattern of a prebattle operational maneuver onto the flank. He would find, however, that even victorious battles rarely worked as smoothly as Leuthen had.

Frederick opened the campaigning season of 1758 with a strike into Moravia. He was unable to draw Marshal Daun into battle, however. Even with a vastly larger army than Frederick's, Daun had no wish to take part in a repeat of Leuthen. The campaign turned into a siege of the principal Austrian fortress of Olmütz, which opened on May 31. Daun lurked in the vicinity, fortifying himself at a camp near Skalitz, and with Prussian supply lines back to Silesia increasingly threatened by the Croats, Frederick was unable to bring the campaign to a successful conclusion. Its climax came on June 30, with a successful ambush of a vital Prussian supply convoy containing some three thousand wagons near Domstadtl. Frederick had to raise the siege.[66] It was, in other words, a "routine eighteenth century operation" in every way.[67]

By now, in the typical dynamic of this war, a more dangerous situation had arisen, this time in the east.[68] The ponderous advance of the Russians had finally brought them within operational range. The Russian commander, General Fermor, had invaded East Prussia, overrun the province, and occupied Königsberg. From here, they had advanced to the Oder, and on August 15 had opened a siege of the fortress town of Küstrin, only fifty miles from Berlin. Frederick now hurried eastward with a small force, just eleven thousand men. He covered nearly 125 miles in just twelve days—once again a rapid pace for those days, especially considering the torrid heat—and linked up with his eastern commander, General Dohna, at Gorgast on August 22. With Dohna's twenty-six thousand, the Prussian force now totaled thirty-seven thousand men. As always, numbers would tilt in favor of his enemies: Fermor's army was at least forty-five thousand men.

Frederick, by now a master of the art, intended to prosecute the war of movement against the Russians. It was clear from their own operations thus far that they would be even more immobile than the Austrians. They would do little more than defend in place, in other words, although he had little knowledge about their fighting qualities. Frederick's task was to find some way to turn their line, place them in a false position, and then hammer them from the flank. For that reason, he considered, then discarded, the thought of simply crossing the Oder at Küstrin, debouching from the fortress, and striking them a frontal blow. Instead, he crossed the river at Güstebiese, about fifteen miles downstream, that is, to the northwest. The crossing took place on August 23. The Russians, surprised by Frederick's sudden arrival, did not contest it. The next day, he set out due east, reaching a position between Darrmietzel and the Neudammer Mill.

With an enemy field army now marching toward him, Fermor adopted the orthodox posture for the era. He lifted the siege of Küstrin and readied the Russian army for battle. Since reports from the countryside said that Frederick was coming down on him from the north and west, Fermor placed himself in a rough line near Zorndorf. He spent most of August 24 working on the position, which faced north toward the Mietzel River, but with a refused left protecting his flank, as well. The terrain of the battlefield was extremely difficult. Although a quick glance would perceive a relatively flat plain, there are actually numerous hillocks and depressions, along with three gullies running northwest to southeast: from the west, the Zaberngrund, Galgen-grund, and Langengrund. All three were deep, some ten to fifteen meters below the plain.[69] Each presented difficulties to the movement of men, horses, and guns, and in fact finding crossing points over them would be crucial for both armies during the fighting. With the entire region also dotted with small ponds and pools of brackish water, this was definitely not linear tactics country. Nevertheless, by evening of August 24, Fermor had his men in line, a solid two-echelon position anchored on the Zaberngrund in the west, and strongly protected by cavalry on both flanks.

Frederick seems once again to have conceived of his maneuver scheme on the fly, that is, as he was crossing the Oder. Once again, this was terrain that Frederick knew intimately, from his younger days as a prisoner in Küstrin. At 3:00 A.M. on August 25, he set the army in motion from its camp at Darrmietzel. Engineers had established two bridges over the Mietzel River for the infantry, while the cavalry crossed farther upstream at Kerstenbrügge, about four miles to the northeast. Only after emerging from the swampy banks of the Mietzel did the king form his order of battle, moving from right to left: the advance guard of eight battalions under Manteuffel, the first infantry echelon, and then the second. Protecting the right flank of the march were the hussars, ready to tangle with the ubiquitous Cossacks in Russian service. The lines formed up, and Frederick now directed them on a leftward march, heading southeast toward the village of Batzlow. There they would wheel right, heading southwest toward Wilkersdorf.[70]

This was the most ambitious maneuver Frederick had yet undertaken. It aimed not at a mere flanking maneuver, but a march clear around the Russian force to come up on their right rear. As at Leuthen, he had the benefit of terrain: the undulations would keep the Prussians hidden until the moment they were ready to spring their trap from the Wilkersdorf area.

So single-minded was he about fighting a decisive battle that even a piece of great fortune did not sway him. As the Prussian columns passed the villages of Gross- and Klein-Kammin, they saw an incredible sight: the entire Russian heavy baggage train drawn up in encampment. Its capture would almost surely have forced Fermor to retreat without a battle.[71] This was classic eighteenth-century warfare as described by generations of historians—with strikes against supply lines rather than battles determining the campaign—but apparently Frederick hadn't read the manuals. Onward he drove his columns toward his real target: the Russian army itself.

As the columns emerged from the forests, Frederick rode on ahead with a hussar escort to the high ground southwest of Wilkersdorf. Here he carried out his by now customary personal reconnaissance. Although it was only 7:00 A.M., the dust and the haze of what was about to become a scorching August day made it difficult to get an accurate fix on the Russian positions. There seemed to be a great deal of activity in the Russian line, as if it were just shaking itself out in good order. He could see a general outline, however, enough to tell him the one thing he needed to know. His great march onto the rear had failed. The Russian position now faced south.

Even though it was still early morning, Fermor had already had a very busy day. As reports came in from his Cossacks and hussars that the Prussians were on the march to the east, it seemed clear that Frederick would attempt to get around his flank. Fermor knew his men as well as anyone, their strengths and their limitations. A hasty redeployment under fire had broken the Austrian army at Leuthen. Its consequences would have been incomparably worse for the Russians, particularly given the relatively low standard of their noncommissioned officers. He began to make arrangements to turn the army toward the threat looming from the east. Once the sun rose, however, Fermor could clearly see the dust cloud kicked up by the Prussian army, a combination of thousands of feet and hooves, blistering weather, and sandy roads. It was clear that the Prussians were riding around him altogether, and intended to come up on his rear. Once he had clarified that situation, it was equally clear how he should proceed: the army simply turned around in place. The former right wing, facing the Mietzel River, was now the left; the former left now the right. His second echelon became his first. The principal trouble was redeploying the artillery, but that was soon made good by the strength of thousands of hands and hundreds of horses.

That had been the activity that Frederick was seeing from Wilkersdorf. The king had to have been dispirited. He had just led his army on an exhausting march, and it had achieved nothing. The Russians had turned to meet him, and although still shaking themselves out into battle array, they seemed well enough prepared. By the time the rest of the army caught up with the king, there was nothing to do but continue on to the west, toward Zorndorf, transform the columns into lines, and launch a frontal assault.

It wasn't until 8:00 A.M. that the Prussian army was in place: the advance guard under Manteuffel on the front left, its own left anchored against the Zaberngrund. Behind him, the left wing under General

Kanitz (nine battalions) and the right wing under Dohna (eleven battalions). Behind them there was a thinly spread second echelon of ten battalions under Lieutenant General Forcade. The twenty-seven cavalry squadrons of General Schorlemer stood on the open right flank, with thirty-six more under the command of General Seydlitz on the far left. Finally, twenty more squadrons formed a *corps de reserve* behind the left wing. The artillery was in typically aggressive posture, in forward positions covering the entire line.[72] Seydlitz actually started the battle across the Zaberngrund from the rest of the army, and would have to find a crossing point over the gully to get into action. As we'll see, he managed to do just that.

As Frederick came closer and surveyed the Russian dispositions more closely from the high ground north of Zorndorf, he could see the impossibility of getting around the Russian flanks. Still, the Russian deployment offered him opportunities. The speed of the Russian turnaround, as well as the conformation of the ground, had led to deep cleavages in what had first appeared to be a solid wall of troops. Sixteen battalions of the right wing lay between the Zaberngrund and the Galgengrund. East of the latter lay twenty-four more battalions of the center, then fourteen more of General Browne's "Observation Corps," troops who had just joined up with the main body, who extended the line to the Langengrund. The Russian left consisted of a large body of cavalry under General Demiku. All in all, the Russian position was a shallow inverted "V" with the wings thrust slightly forward toward the Prussians and the center held back. The space between the echelons was filled with battalion-strength reserves, and the entire array gave the impression of a solid, dense mass. Since flanking this position was impossible, Frederick decided on a frontal assault on the Russian right wing. The shock troops would be Manteuffel's advance guard, with Kanitz echeloned behind him directly to the right.[73] With his right wing (Dohna) refused, Frederick hoped to chew through the Russian right and roll up their line from there.

A frontal assault should be the simplest approach in the military textbook, but this one went wrong from the start. The attacking wings advanced to the north of the burning village of Zorndorf at 8:30, and the Prussian artillery began its preliminary bombardment fifteen minutes later. Two grand batteries, one of twenty guns to the northwest of Zorndorf, and one of twenty a few hundred meters to the east, targeted the Russian guns. The range was too great to do much damage, however, and so the guns were brought forward to the open terrain just south of the Fuchsberg, a small hillock between the two armies.

Their crew laid them out skillfully; Russian reports say that only the muzzles were visible.[74] From this much closer range, they had a much more lucrative target, the dense infantry formations to their front. The Russian guns responded but were at a disadvantage: on lower ground, with the bright August sun in their eyes, and soon smothered by a thick cloud of dust and smoke.

Meanwhile, Manteuffel's advance wing was struggling into formation, since only four of its battalions could pass through the bottleneck between Zorndorf village and the Zaberngrund to the west. The other four had to pass through the roads of the burning village. They overcame that obstacle, however, and reformed their line to the north. Behind them came the troops of the first and second echelons. As they advanced to contact, the guns on both sides opened up with murderous canister fire, followed by musket fire from both sides, and soon the smoke and dust had blinded troops and commanders on both sides.

If they could have parted the smoke for a moment, they would have seen a textbook case of an infantry attack misfiring: Manteuffel was about where he should have been. With his left anchored on the Zaberngrund, staying in alignment was no problem. But instead of Kanitz on the right flank and five hundred paces to the rear, as the king's orders had specified, he had drifted unaccountably to the right.[75] As the air filled with smoke and dust, he had inadvertently come abreast of Manteuffel. He would later explain that he was trying to maintain some degree of contact with the Prussian right under Dohna, who had advanced slightly from his own starting position. There was a small but dense copse of trees directly in Kanitz's path (the Steinbusch). He feared that if he passed to the west of it, there would be a huge gap looming in the Prussian line. His explanation, although condemned by later Prussian staff officers, makes perfect sense. It might be equally true to say that he simply became disoriented on a low-visibility battlefield.

About forty paces away from the Russian line, Manteuffel's advance guard suddenly burst out of the smoke and dirt. Many of the Russians opened fire; those who had already expended their ammunition leaped into an impromptu bayonet attack. Manteuffel was soon in trouble, all the more so as he discovered that the expected support on his flank was not there. The king's original plan for a concentrated blow on the Russian right by twenty-three battalions, an immense force by Prussian standards, had come to naught. Instead, a thin line of Prussian infantry, extending over two thousand meters, was launching an unsupported frontal assault. Poor Kanitz had it worst of all: his wing careened directly into the center of the Russian position. It had been wholly untouched by Prussian fire, and given the angle it formed it was able to take the unfortunate Prussian infantry under a blazing crossfire. The final blow to the opening attack came on the Russian right. Here General Gaugreben's cavalry now managed to squeeze itself through the line with the Zaberngrund on its right, form up for an attack, and launch a grand charge on Manteuffel's already wavering advance guard. On came the Russian horse: four full regiments, including the Kargopol Horse Grenadiers, Novotroizk Cuirassiers, Tobolsk Dragoons, and Serbian Hussars. Manteuffel's infantry had had enough by this point. They fled, throwing off all discipline, followed by Kanitz's wing to the east, which had reached the breaking point at almost the same time. Back the Prussians fled, most to the relative safety of Zorndorf and Wilkersdorf, others to the neighboring woods, pursued by an increasingly disorganized mass of Russian cavalry and infantry. Among the Russian gains were the twenty guns of the left Prussian battery, which had advanced just west of the Fuchsberg and now lay undefended.

Saving the day for the Prussian army was the cavalry. Frederick had watched the rout from his position in the middle battery, and immediately sent orders to Seydlitz to ride to the assistance of the hard-pressed infantry. Until this point, the great cavalryman and his troopers had been spectators in the battle, deployed safely across the Zaberngrund. He couldn't quite make out the situation yet but had sent parties to reconnoiter suitable crossing points through the gully. In the meantime, an impatient Frederick dispatched some cavalry directly from the "reserve corps" into battle. These were the three dragoon regiments of Baron Marschall von Bieberstein: Plettenberg, Alt-Platen, and bit a farther to the east, Schorlemer. The Plettenberg Dragoons contacted the enemy first, with Prince Moritz of Anhalt-Dessau at their head.[76] Riding directly into the path of the onrushing enemy cavalry, they were able to slow it down, or at least to divert it from spearing fleeing Prussian infantrymen.

But now, from the west, emerging suddenly from the depths of Zaberngrund, came Seydlitz. Finally sorting out what had happened to the advance guard, he had crossed the gully in three columns. Lacking time, and probably space, for a full deployment, he put the squadrons of each regiment into line, one behind the other, and launched these improvised "regimental columns" into battle. It should be difficult for six brightly accoutered cavalry regiments to catch an opponent napping, but the fact that it happened is yet another sign of the role that poor visibility played on this day.[77] The *Garde du Corps*, the *Gensd'armes*, and the Czettritz Dragoons struck the right wing of Russian advance; to their left (north) the Seydlitz Cuirassiers took the Russians in the flank; and farther to the left the Ziethen and Malachowsky Hussars struck practically into their rear. Hit from all four points of the compass by a well-handled opponent in full stride, the Russian cavalry melted away, fleeing to the north as far as the village of Quartschen, the backstop of the Russian position, and essentially taking itself out of the battle. The infantry was hard hit as well, but the Prussian cavalry's incomplete deployment left relatively large gaps in the attack. Although Seydlitz did wreck the Russian advance, a surprisingly large number of their infantry managed to filter back to the safety of their own lines, even if their units as such had dissolved.

It was 2:00 P.M., and both sides now paused for breath. A little more than five hours into the battle, the Prussian advance guard and most of the left wing were gone. The same held true for the Russian cavalry and most of the infantry on the right wing. Frederick's plan had gone spectacularly wrong, but his army had battered the Russians, as well. The rest of the day would see Frederick ready his right wing for battle. Dohna's battalions were, in effect, his last fresh force. As they advanced to the attack, however, the Russians managed to launch a surprise cavalry blow of their own on this wing. Again, it is explicable only by reference to the conditions. The Prussian cavalry soon joined the melee. The Russians captured another Prussian battery in front of Dohna's line; the Prussians recaptured it. At one point, Prussian infantry mistook their own cavalry, riding behind the Prussian line to assist the battle on the right flank, for Russian, and the rumor that there were Russian horsemen behind the line caused the rout of at least one battalion.[78]

Gradually, however, the Prussians reestablished order in their ranks and began to drive back the Russian right wing. The Russians were unable to deliver much more than the occasional local counterpunch, but kept defending themselves tenaciously. Their gunners, in particular, repeatedly died at their guns, delivering canister against the attacking Prussians until the last moment. And so it went—both sides taking and delivering horrible amounts of punishment. Both armies pivoted, the Prussians throwing their right forward, the Russians pulling back their left until it rested on the village of Quartschen. It could have only worked because more than half of each force was out of the fight, good for little more than defending in place. A last attack ordered by Frederick at 7:00 P.M. fell apart before it started, and the Prussians had nothing left to throw at their adversary. As night fell, incredibly, the dance had gone so far that each army was essentially sitting in the position that the other had occupied in the morning, the Russians facing northeast from Quartschen to the Fuchsberg, the Prussians southwest.

When both sides totaled their losses the next day, the cost of Zorndorf became obvious. A Russian force of some forty-five thousand men had taken more than twenty-two thousand casualties, nearly 50 percent of the force. Even by the standards of bloody eighteenth-century battle, this was a shocking loss. Fermor, in fact, would be the one to retreat, although the two sides spent several days glowering at one another. The Prussians, who had misfired early, then rallied and hounded their opponent from one end of the battlefield to the other without managing to break him, had suffered thirteen thousand, about one-third of their total force. It is interesting to note that in this "victory," their casualties had approximated those of the Austrians at Leuthen. They had also taken a good haul of the standard trophies of the era: 103 guns and twenty flags. Not so standard was their capture of a wagon with part of the Russian field treasury, a stroke of luck that netted 858,000 rubles.[79] It is a sign of the back-and-forth nature of the fighting that each side held some two thousand prisoners at battle's end.

Zorndorf continues to fascinate on many levels. Strategically, there has been no lack of commentary that it was the battle that announced the arrival of the Russians on the European stage. Previously consigned to the geographical margins, battling the Swedes for control of Courland or Livonia, the Russians had managed to get an army within operating distance of Berlin, and once there, to maul the same army that had so recently beaten the French and the Austrians. Clearly, the Russians were in the European heartland to stay.

Likewise, as a tactical encounter, Zorndorf contained enough twists and turns to keep analysts arguing for centuries. The rightward drift of the Prussian attacking force, the mutual cavalry attacks on inviting flanks, the continuing ability of both sides to land surprise blows—all these certainly give the lie to any arguments that eighteenth-century linear battles were schematic and overly stylized. The adrenaline, the exhilaration, and the sheer panic felt by both sides rival any battle of our era. Clausewitz was right when he observed that "this battle is without doubt the most remarkable of the Seven Years' War, perhaps in all of modern military history, because of its remarkable course."[80]

It is on the operational level, however, that Zorndorf assumes its real importance to the German art of war. Frederick had advanced on the Russians fully intending to "Leuthen" them. The approach march to the battlefield was a classic of German *Bewegungskrieg*. Here was the war of movement on the operational level: one army literally marching a ring around its opponent, passing through the wilderness to emerge, deploy, and land a well-timed blow against a flat-footed opponent. Only in this way, Frederick had by now concluded, could a smaller force hope to fight a decisive battle against its opponent. Interior lines gave him the strategic possibilities; the oblique attack was a tactical marvel for achieving local superiority on a relatively parallel battle-field. The operational maneuver, however, had been the backbreaker for the enemy at Rossbach and at Leuthen, placing an impossible burden on the primitive and already overloaded command structure of the day. Simply getting these armies into line, with their left, middle, and right wings (and their first, second, and reserve echelons) was dif-ficult enough. Turning them on a dime was a nightmare. We can sym-pathize with Fermor. Those two hours after sunrise, as he took note of the ominous dust cloud on his flank, must have seemed like an eternity to him.

In the end, Frederick's turn onto the field at Zorndorf fizzled. Para-doxically, although the sudden realignment to a threatened flank was difficult for armies of the day, a shift to the rear was much easier. Each wing, each unit—each man, one can say without that much exaggera-tion—simply turned around in place. Problems might arise as the left wing became the right and vice versa, but it required only several min-utes for most of the work to be done. Frederick now had to face the possibility of a frontal assault. Instead of revisiting Leuthen, he was back at Kolin. He attempted to isolate a weakened portion of the Rus-sian line and threw two hours of artillery preparation at it, an unheard-of thing for this age.[81] What most accounts of the battle fail to take into account, however, is that even a successful blow at the Russian right would have still left the Prussians with a very thorny problem.

The question posed by Zorndorf is, What happens when the op-erational maneuver doesn't work? We might broaden it to ask, What happens when the rapid maneuver-based victory eludes an army that is trained only to achieve one? It is a question not without significance for later German war making, and the answer given by Frederick's behavior at Zorndorf is not encouraging. He fought, literally, down to the last man and shell, leaving behind a field soaked in blood, and then had the audacity to declare, "For the first time, my troops let me down."[82] It is the single most unattractive moment of his military career.

Not every legacy of Zorndorf was negative, however. It can be argued that a history of the German way of war is also a history of the idea of flexible command: the supreme commander deciding on a mission while his battlefield leaders exercise discretion in the ways and means of achieving it. Although it is a concept that was already well established in Prussian military circles, mentioned repeatedly in analyses of Leuthen, as we've seen, Zorndorf provides a magic moment that, while perhaps apocryphal, nevertheless entered the lore of the Prussian army. It is said that as Frederick ordered his cavalry into action on the left flank on that fateful day, he became perturbed at Seydlitz's refusal to jump into action. At issue was not the cavalry master's shyness in getting into the fight, but his search for the best path across the Zaberngrund. After another order arrived, replete with threats if he did not move, Seydlitz told the messenger, "Tell the king that after the battle my head is at his disposal, but meantime I hope he will permit me to exercise it in his service."[83] Seydlitz made good on his promise to the king, but on his terms and in his own way. It was one of the key noble prerogatives in the peculiar social contract of old Prussia.

Conclusion

In his *History of the Art of War*, Hans Delbrück pondered the role that "chance, that completely blind incalculable factor," played in Frederick's greatest battles. At Lobositz, for example, "the Austrians had actually won the battle, and the Prussians carried the day only because Browne did not realize his advantage, did not pursue, and withdrew in the night." At Prague, Dauns's vanguard (Puebla's corps) was just miles from a linkup with the main body. "That corps was 9,000 men strong, and, considering the wavering aspect of the battle, it could have given the decisive blow against the Prussians." There are more: the chain of hills at Leuthen, fortuitously placed to hide the king's great flank march, or the Russian corps of thirteen thousand men north of the fight at Zorndorf that "could very easily have joined forces with the Russian main army."[84]

Although no doubt written in such a manner as to annoy his opponents in the debate over Frederick's legacy, it contains a point worth pondering: happenstance played a huge role in virtually every one of the king's battles, sometimes bringing him victory, at others unexpectedly rescuing him from catastrophe. He was, perhaps, Frederick the Great, but he was certainly Frederick the lucky. To which one is

A painting of the young Friedrich Wilhelm von Seydlitz, the aggressive Prussian cavalry commander and man of the hour at both Rossbach and Zorndorf.

tempted to add: anyone who is this lucky eventually receives an invitation to leave the casino.

Delbrück moves on from this simple list to try to explain just why Frederick was lucky and to provide an explanation as to why Frederick's enemies so often seemed to favor him with their worst blunders at the worst possible time (which is another kind of luck, of course). He concluded that the very scale of Frederick's audacity made his defeats just as impressive as his victories. The attempt to surround and capture the entire Austrian army at Prague, for example, and the assault on an army that had him outnumbered two to one at Kolin were rash, it is true:

> But victories like defeats of this kind had a spiritual significance that extended beyond the military result and was almost completely independent of that result. That was the tremendous respect which the king gained in the eyes of the opposing commanders. Why did they so seldom take advantage of the favorable opportunities that he offered them frequently enough? They did not dare. They believed him capable of everything.[85]

We might add, paraphrasing, that they also believed him capable of anything. A moral advantage accrued to Frederick, Delbrück argued, from his enemies' "constant fear of being attacked."[86]

Delbrück here put his finger on Frederick's significance for later German commanders. German officers of the nineteenth and twentieth centuries consistently saw their task as winning a decisive victory in the shortest possible time. In so far as they marched in Frederick's footsteps, they were men in a hurry. No matter that Frederick's war lasted for seven long years. Virtually every campaign he fought was a rapid one, planned on the fly and executed against the backdrop of a merciless timetable that permitted him no leeway. However long the war went on, be it seven weeks in 1866, eleven months in 1870–1871, or the titanic world struggles of the twentieth century, the German commander still aimed at "short and lively" campaigns that ended in decisive victory over the enemy's main field force.

The only way to reach that difficult goal was the war of movement on the operational level, or *Bewegungskrieg*. In the same manner that Frederick had made himself the terror of Europe, later German commanders attempted to maneuver their army onto the flank or rear of the adversary and crush him. The pace had to be as rapid as Frederick's pounding marches from Bohemia to Thuringia in the Rossbach campaign, or from Moravia to the eastern reaches of the Oder before Zorndorf. Speed and audacity would bewilder the opponent and force him to fight before he was mentally prepared, or not fully deployed, or facing the wrong way—or perhaps all three. The very fact that the army trained and prepared to wage war in this manner would be a moral advantage even before a shot was fired, officers believed, and the history of Prussia-Germany had borne it out again and again.

In 1905, a German staff officer wrote a short biography of Frederick in the *Educator of the Prussian Army* series (*Erzieher des preussischen Heeres*). He drew an explicit connection between the spirit of the great king and the German army in his own day:

> Frederician too was the spirit of the offensives which we conducted in 1866 and 1870. In the same spirit are our brave troops today bearing up under all the toils and privations, fighting all-day engagements under the burning sun for their emperor and fatherland. In this Frederician spirit, which is now the property of the entire German army, we will also march out to battle and victory, if our Emperor gives the call.[87]

From Hohenfriedeberg to Leuthen to Königgrätz to the burning sands of the Kalahari Desert in southwest Africa, where the German army was engaged in some of the most brutal campaigns in the entire history of the age of imperialism, the spirit of Frederick endured through the ages. It was the spirit of offensive warfare: attacking the enemy "even if he should be on top of the Zobtenberg," as Frederick remarked before Leuthen.[88] He was, in the words of a twentieth-century German officer, "the most offensive-minded general in the world."[89] It was a preference burned into the corporate memory of the Prussian-German officer corps.

Frederick bequeathed a magnificent reputation as commander to later generations of soldiers, as well as an excellent military machine and even a doctrine for employing it decisively. He was the greatest soldier in Prussian history. There was also a danger lurking in the legacy, however. As they approached the twentieth century, Germany's neighbors found themselves living next to a powerful country whose army was trained overwhelmingly for large-scale offensive operations within weeks of the outbreak of war. It was hardly a comfortable situation, or a recipe for long-term stability in international relations. What if, as happened in 1756, such an aggressive posture aroused enough fear in those neighbors to forge another grand coalition against Germany? The answer, provided again and again in German military literature, was that German commanders should follow the example of Frederick, who had "conducted a war of five million against 80 million": they should defy the world and fight on alone.[90] Many of them—far too many, one might say—would get a chance to do just that in the twentieth century.

4

"Disgrace and Redemption"[1]:
The Prussian Army in the Napoleonic Wars

It began on October 14, 1806, at Jena and Auerstädt, where the Prussian army had just come apart under two simultaneous blows of the Napoleonic hammer. The army of Frederick the Great, the institution around which the entire Prussian state revolved, one that had managed even during its defeats to maintain a reputation for invincibility, collapsed in a single short day of battle. As two twin streams of refugees, one from each of the defeats, crashed into one another on the high road to Weimar, something that had rarely been seen even in the darkest days of the Seven Years' War now suddenly made its appearance: panic. It was a *sauve qui peut*. There was general indiscipline and even looting, curses, and threats of violence against officers who tried to reestablish order. There were also hundreds and eventually thousands of Prussian infantry—reputedly the finest soldiers in Europe—who wanted nothing more than to find a Frenchman to whom they could surrender. It is said that as he began the pursuit of the fleeing Prussians at Jena, Napoleon's cavalry commander, Marshal Joachim Murat, laughingly wielded a riding whip rather than his customary saber. It was a gesture of contempt, but who could blame him?

It would end less than nine years later, on June 18, 1815, at a village named Plancenoit. All day long, Napoleon had been locked in a death struggle with the army of the Duke of Wellington. The English, mainly wily veterans of the Peninsular War, along with their Dutch and German allies, had been conducting a tenacious defense of the ridge south of Mont St. Jean against a series of increasingly desperate French assaults. Both supreme commanders were waiting for reinforcements: Napoleon for the wing of Marshal Emmanuel Grouchy, and Wellington for the Prussian army under Marshal Gebhard Leberecht von Blücher, a "rough, remarkably ill-educated man,"[2] but a soldier nonetheless, and a man animated by a seemingly implacable hatred of the French. He had been there, that horrible day at Auerstädt.

As a cloud of dust billowed up on the far eastern flank around 4:00 P.M., Napoleon had reason to be optimistic that it was the result of French boots. He himself had given Blücher's army a good hammering just two days ago at the battle of Ligny, and the Prussians must still be licking their wounds, probably retreating far to the east at this very moment. Perhaps Wellington had been thinking the same thoughts. It may have been a surprise to both men, therefore, when out of the cloud materialized a Prussian army corps under General Friedrich Wilhelm von Bülow, the lead troops of Blücher's army. They immediately launched a spirited assault against Plancenoit, the extreme right wing of the French position.

It ended at Waterloo.

The Impact of the French Revolution and Napoleon

THE REVOLUTION

Historians have traditionally viewed the French Revolution as a complete and dramatic break in the history of the western world. No matter what the field—politics, society, or economics—they have seen the Revolution discarding old, outmoded ways of thought and substituting fresh new ones. Absolute monarchy made way for participatory democracy; aristocratic privilege and a society of orders had to yield to equality before the law; physiocracy, mercantilism, and the economic restrictions of the guilds vanished in favor of capitalism and the free market. The revolutionaries, wrote Jules Michelet, "found despotism in heaven and earth, and they instituted law."[3] It was nothing less than the death of the traditional and the birth of the modern.

So too, the argument runs, the Revolution and the Napoleonic period that followed it witnessed the downfall of an archaic method of making war and the rise of a new one. No longer limited by a tacit gentleman's agreement among monarchs, the new warfare pitted nation against nation, with the ideologies, passions, and hatreds of the masses bringing a new ferocity to the fighting. With the whole people now enlisted in the war effort via the *levée en masse*, France's revolutionary armies grew to monstrous size. The "nation in arms" simply swamped the smaller professional forces of the traditional monarchies. It was the age of total war, a conflict that knew no limits in terms of size, aims, and, unfortunately, casualties.

The revolutionary armies were not just bigger, they were quali-
tatively different. No longer made up of the dregs of society or of
foreigners dragooned by the agents of the king, they now consisted
of free and independent citizens. They fought not merely to escape
the lash, but for elevated concepts of liberty, equality, and brother-
hood. That being the case, their commanders could ask, even demand,
more of them than ever before, without fearing desertion or mutiny.
These new citizen soldiers made possible new tactical concepts like
"skirmishing," essentially harassing fire by individual light infantrymen, that were impossible for the traditional armies of Europe. The
Prussian army, for example, could not employ skirmishers, because the
men were sure to desert. Likewise, long unwieldy lines of musketeers,
the mainstay of the traditional professional army, now gave way to
dense "infantry columns," perhaps forty men wide by twelve deep,
the only kind of tactical formation a hastily assembled citizen army
could master. Instead of relying on superior firepower in the manner
of Frederick the Great, the revolutionary armies, with their hordes of
enthusiastic manpower, threw column after column in bayonet attacks
against the thin lines of their enemies, and eventually broke them.

Just as the traditional narrative about eighteenth-century "limited
war" has been undergoing revision, however, so too has the belief that
the French Revolution marks a complete rupture in the history of
warfare.[4] Scholars have become increasingly skeptical that political
and social events of 1789 were mirrored immediately in military transformation. Armies are inherently conservative bodies, of course, and
rarely take to innovation lightly. It is now generally recognized that
the infantry column, for example, was not the invention of the French
Revolution, but a tactical experiment conceived by military reformers during the monarchy. Some French infantry battalions, as we have
seen, went into column at Rossbach in 1757. Skirmishing, too, was simply the French equivalent of the Austrian light infantry, the "Croats"
who made Frederick's life so miserable. As for the bayonet attack, it
has always existed far more in the fantasies of literature (and, today,
film) than it ever has on the actual battlefield.[5] Revolutionary and Napoleonic armies lived and died by fire. Certainly, the French Revolution marked a critical break in many areas of European life. The realm
of infantry tactics was not among them—here, developments were far
more evolutionary than radical. Even the magic moment enshrined in
generations of western civilization textbooks, the "battle" of Valmy
in 1792, has lost some of its luster. The encounter that guaranteed the
survival of the revolutionary experiment in France had no infantry

component at all. It was instead a rather desultory exchange of artillery fire, and the artillery, interestingly enough, was probably the arm of the French army least affected by the Revolution.[6]

Certainly, tactics were important. What the French revolutionary armies—and later, Napoleon—succeeded in doing was in fashioning a new tactical synthesis out of elements that were already present. It still used the line (*ordre mince*) to maximize firepower. It also used columns (*ordre profond*) for rapid movement across the battlefield and for shock, or at least the threat of shock. It also made extensive use of "open order" skirmishers, with the infantry fighting as small, irregular groups of *tirailleurs* to harass the enemy and screen friendly formations. In fact, it is generally accepted today that French infantry often deployed in a combination of all three (*ordre mixte*) for maximum flexibility. Infantry in line provided the firepower, infantry in column provided the threat of assault, and skirmishers screened the formed units from enemy fire and assault.[7]

As important as these tactical reforms were, however, they would have been much less effective without similar developments on the operational level. Perhaps the most important contribution of the era was the development of command echelons above the level of the regiment, divisions for the revolutionary armies and corps for the Napoleonic. These were large formations consisting of all arms, with permanent commanders, staff, and administration.[8] They were able to march independently and to fight on their own for at least a limited time. The Frederician army consisted of a general and his regiments (and their component battalions and squadrons). He had to concentrate them for battle, conceive of a deployment scheme, and then send them off against the enemy on the spot. Frederick often personally directed his regiments into battle, pointing to a windmill or a hill in the distance as the point around which they should deploy.[9] The development of divisions and corps made it possible for a supreme commander to lead a much larger army more effectively than ever before. It was far more responsive to his commands, since corps and divisional staffs mediated his orders to the rest of the army. Divisions and corps were, in modern parlance, operational-level units. They made it possible for a commander to devise combinations that were beyond the dreams of even a gifted general like Frederick the Great.

It has been interesting to watch the scholarly revision unfold on all these questions. Even more interesting is that most analyses of the era now have generally come around to the same views that German officers held at the turn of the twentieth century. For example, in a 1903

German General Staff study entitled *Success in Battle* (*Der Schlachter-folg*) the change in warfare during the revolutionary and Napoleonic periods is a major theme. It was not the skirmisher or the emphasis on shock that the General Staff found most important: "The revolution-ary wars led to many reforms in the area of organization as well as the employment of forces. They led the French, first of all, to form divi-sions—formations of all arms—and to employ them as strategic units. Divisions raised the mobility of the army and allowed operations with widely separated columns instead of maneuvers by a unified linear battle front."[10] Not surprisingly, given their history and preferences, Prussian-German officers looked to changes in the operational level of warfare. It was here that they awarded Napoleon the praises usually reserved for one of their own. Looking back, we must label their judg-ment as authoritative. If anyone had earned the right to speak about the operational abilities of Napoleon and the *Grand Armée* at their height, it was the Prussians.

THE IMPACT OF NAPOLEON

Although the Revolution had given rise to certain new patterns of war making, Napoleon Bonaparte first realized their true potential. He was both the originator and the master of the corps system.[11] On the march, his army was dispersed into *corps d'armée* of perhaps twenty thousand men apiece. He often arranged them in what he jokingly called a "battalion square" (*bataillon carré*), but they were a lot more powerful than that. Each corps was generally one day's march away from its neighbors. It was, theoretically, able to engage and fight even a much larger foe for one day, at which point it would be reinforced by the others. The system offered many advantages. It broke up a huge force into smaller sections, allowing for the most rapid possible move-ment. It was capable of sudden changes of direction while on the march (a crucial advantage, as we shall see, in the 1806 campaign). Finally, it disguised Napoleon's true objective, giving the appearance of an ill-coordinated scatter while allowing rapid concentration and bringing the largest possible number of men to the battlefield in the shortest possible time. Napoleon had found "a new way of making war." Ac-cording to the well-known words of one French soldier, "He uses our legs instead of our bayonets."[12]

A second, specifically Napoleonic, innovation was its deemphasis on magazines and supply lines. There is a limit to how far and fast men can march, but he was able to increase the mobility of his forces in several ways. First, in a throwback to the seventeenth century, he dispensed with supply lines and had his men live off the land, "foraging" or "requisitioning" their supplies.[13] Although these are fancy terms for stealing and looting from the civilians among whom they campaigned, Napoleon also made use of purchasing officers. Sent out in front of the army, their mission was to arrange for food and fodder. His enemies, tied to bulky supply convoys, might as well have been moving in slow motion.

A third key characteristic was a fairly advanced system of command and control over his forces. The *Grande Armée* possessed an expert staff, led by Marshal Alexandre Berthier, whose task it was to execute Napoleon's commands (and sometimes read between the lines of those commands). With each corps having its own staff, and the same for each division within the corps, the French army possessed a nervous system that was far superior to the traditional command structure of France's enemies. These typically consisted of a king or emperor, his close relatives and princes of the blood, and other royal cronies. As always, the dramatic victories from 1805–1807, victories without parallel in military history, are attributable not just to Napoleon's genius or superior tactics, but to French superiority in crucial "software" areas like command and control.[14]

The Franco-Prussian War, 1806

The tale of how the Prussian army came to face Napoleon in a one-on-one contest is an unedifying one. Historians have tended to assume a tone of wounded moral outrage when discussing it, accusing the once-proud kingdom of Frederick the Great of dishonesty, disloyalty to its allies, and all manner of perfidy. In particular, the indictment revolves around sitting off to the side while Austria and Russia fought Napoleon. One historian uses the terms *pusillanimous, degraded,* and *duplicity* with regards to Prussian policy in the period—all in a single paragraph.[15] Another describes the king, Frederick William III, as the "Hohenzollern Hypocrite."[16]

In fact, it was more a matter of bad timing. The Prussian position before 1806 may be described thus: Frederick William III stayed neutral in the war between Napoleonic France and the Third Coalition, and then tried to time his entry so as to maximize his leverage. He was on the verge of doing so—he had already drawn up an ultimatum to France—when Napoleon destroyed the allied armies at Austerlitz. The ultimatum hurriedly turned into a message of congratulations to Napoleon.[17]

The next year brought more humiliations, with Napoleon imposing the Convention of Vienna on the Prussians, forcing it to renege
on previous treaty commitments to Britain and Russia, requiring it
to join any economic measures he chose to levy against Britain, and
stripping it of territories like Jülich and Neufchâtel. In return, Napoleon awarded Prussia a territory it had long coveted: the electorate of
Hanover. Since the Elector was the king of England, however, this last
clause guaranteed Prussia only the enmity of England (as well as historians' outrage for eternity, apparently). Soon a war party came to the
fore in the Prussian government (led by the queen, "the only real man
in Prussia," according to Napoleon, Frederick's exact assessment of his
adversary, Maria Theresa),[18] and in the fall of 1806, Prussia declared
war on the French Empire.

Now began the parade of disasters. To say that the Prussians were
unready for war is to understate the case considerably. The army was
an ossified relic. Frederick the Great's successors had preserved his
standards of training, tactics, and weaponry as carefully as a fly in
amber. The three-rank linear formation, in two echelons, remained
Prussian doctrine, and so did the oblique order. The musket was the
1754 model, called "the worst in Europe" by one authority.[19] Tied to
its system of slow-moving supply columns and magazines, dragging
along "an infinite quantity of baggage,"[20] it was making good time if it
marched ten to twelve miles per day, at a time when the *Grand Armée*
could do twenty. Where France had mobilized the entire nation for
war, Prussia still exempted five hundred thousand men from service
and made up the lack by continuing to recruit foreigners. By one accounting, some two hundred thousand non-Prussians served in the
ranks, well over half the army.[21]

The most serious problem lay in its commanders, however. This
was a group of men long past their sell-by date, many of whom had
soldiered faithfully during the Seven Years' War—now fifty years in
the past. The field commander was the Duke of Brunswick, who was
seventy-one. The king's chief military adviser, General von Mollen-
dorf, was eighty-two. Of 142 generals in the army, 77 were over the
age of 60, and those numbers were reflective of the officer corps as a
whole.[22] Few of these men were particularly aware of military developments in the last two decades, nor should we expect them to have
been. Although a handful of younger officers had been suggesting reforms, they had not been able to win the ear of either the king or his
gerontocracy. Thus, Prussia went to war without any real staff and
with no permanent commands above the regimental level. There were

some reforms after 1805, but they were halting. The king did order the formation of divisions to "make our army more like the French," for example, but those directives went out only as the army was on the march in the 1806 campaign.

Some things never change, however. The Prussians deployed their forces in a highly aggressive posture, made to order for a campaign of maneuver, at least as it had been conceived in Frederick's day. By this time in the history of the officer corps, they could probably do no differently. They opened the war in their traditional "when in doubt, invade Saxony" mode, impressed several divisions of Saxons into their service (who, as before, would fight indifferently at best), and did their best to poise themselves for offensive operations against the French. A purely defensive posture would have found their main force units behind the Elbe River, but in fact that was far from being the case. The Prussians not only opened the war already over the Elbe, but massed far to the west and south, over the Saale River deep in Thuringia.

There were three groups in the initial deployment. The main army, under the Duke of Brunswick (fifty-eight thousand men) was at Erfurt, with its advance guard under the Duke of Weimar between Emleben and Schwabhausen.[23] A second force, under Prince Hohenlohe straddled the Saale from Blankenhayn in the west to Roda in the east; it consisted of forty-six thousand men, once he had incorporated some twenty thousand Saxons; its advance guard, under Prince Louis Ferdinand, stood at Rudolstadt, with his forward troops hard up against the Thuringer Wald. Finally, a smaller force of twenty-two thousand men under General von Rüchel stood at Erfurt, acting as the reserve behind Brunswick and Hohenlohe. All in all, it was a strong force of some 126,000 men, well arranged to strike south or west against the French lines of communication and supply, or perhaps to deal a powerful blow to the left flank of any French drive toward Berlin.

In fact, Brunswick's original plan of operations contemplated four options, all of them offensive: (1) a move through the eastern Thuringer Wald from Hof toward Bamberg; (2) a move through the western Wald to threaten Frankfurt; (3) passing directly through the Wald and advancing on Würzburg; and (4) dividing the army to threaten two or three of the above points.[24] He settled on the third option, since it offered the best chances for a quick, decisive encounter with the French while guaranteeing the highest possible security for Prussian communications. He would command the main army, while the forces under Rüchel and Hohenlohe would essentially protect his flanks.

The plan almost immediately came under attack by other factions within the Prussian command structure. Hohenlohe and his principal military adviser, Massenbach, submitted their own ideas. As might be expected, they objected to the minor role that they would play in the Brunswick plan. Hohenlohe suggested an advance by the more easterly route from Hof to Bamberg, in which he would play a leading role. Members of the Prussian *Ober Kriegs Kollegium*, a kind of nascent military council, staff, and inspectorate rolled into one, had their own suggestions. It is incredible to contemplate, given the storm about to break over all of them, that the Prussians held a council of war as late as October 5 to dissect and discuss each of these various plans. Present were the king, his three commanders, and several other staff officers and royal favorites, twelve men in all. Such a talk-fest could only have continued in the absence of direction from the top. "The Duke decided, therefore, to remain behind the Saale and await developments," wrote Clausewitz, "if one can speak of a personal decision at all where such a hydra-headed staff, in a state of chaos and perpetual vacillation, was concerned."[25] The king now declared a recess until October 8, the very day that the French invaded Saxony.

Perhaps they should have consulted Napoleon. As the crisis heated up and a Prussian declaration of war seemed imminent, the emperor had gathered powerful forces on the upper Main, between Bamberg and Bayreuth. Large forces were already in Bavaria and southern Germany, stretching from the Inn River and the Böhmerwald to the upper Rhine (essentially the quadrilateral Amberg-Lichtenfels-Schweinfurt-Würzburg-Nuremberg).[26] Six army corps, along with his elite Guard formations, 180,000 men in all, stood ready to invade Saxony and "threaten the heart of the Prussian monarchy,"[27] in Napoleon's own words. He had also had scouts out reconnoitering all the points that might play a role in the upcoming campaign. These included the roads leading from Bamberg to Dresden and Berlin, the numerous river crossings he was likely to encounter (the Saale, Elster, Luppse, Pleisse, Mulde, Spree, and especially the Elbe crossing at Wittenberg), as well as the state of the fortresses on the Elbe (Dresden, Torgau, and Magdeburg).[28]

Napoleon first seems to have felt that the Prussians would hold themselves in a sensible defensive position along the Elbe. As more and more reports came in about activity to the west, however, it became more difficult for him to get a fix on the Duke of Brunswick's intentions. If the Prussians really were to be found west of the Saale, then an opportunity beckoned. Such a forward deployment meant that the enemy was offering him its own left flank. Moreover, the Prussians would be uncovering their communications—and there was no army in Europe more sensitive about protecting its lines of communications.

The plan, then, had to process a good deal of uncertainty. The *Grande Armée* would concentrate enormous strength on its right, "leaving the space between the Rhine and Bamberg completely empty of troops," Napoleon wrote to his IV Corps Commander, Marshal Soult.[29] The various corps would form a gigantic *bataillon carré* of nearly two hundred thousand men, pass through the Franconian Forest (the eastern extension of the Thuringer Wald), and head north for Berlin via Leipzig and Dresden. Predicting the course of events at that point would be difficult, as a great deal depended on where the Prussians actually were. If they were to be found on the Elbe, the *Grande Armée* would meet them there. If, however, they lay to the west, then all six corps would simply execute a gigantic wheel left. The principal difficulty of the plan lay in the passage of the forest. If the Prussians aggressively contested the French forces debouching from the forest, there might be trouble. Given the numerical disparity in the campaign, what he called his "immense superiority,"[30] Napoleon was reasonably sure that he would find a path somewhere. At any rate, he was confident that a gigantic thrust toward Berlin would soon smoke out the Prussians, forcing them not only to reveal their positions, but to give battle in defense of the capital.

On October 8, the *Grande Armée* invaded Saxony from Bavaria—and this in a war, let us remember, that Prussia had declared. Three great multiple-corps columns advanced on a concentrated front to the northeast. The leftmost column, consisting of V Corps (Marshal Jean Lannes) and VII Corps (Marshal Augereau), advanced from Coburg into the Thuringer Wald toward Saalfeld; the central column (I Corps under Bernadotte and III Corps under Davout) from Kronach toward Schleiz; and the right column (the IV Corps of Marshal Soult and the VI Corps under Marshal Ney) from Bayreuth toward Hof. A thick and very aggressive cavalry screen covered all these movements, a Napoleonic trademark and the work of the redoubtable Marshal Joachim Murat, commander of the so-called "Cavalry Reserve."

What happened over the next few days is the stuff of legend. Historians have been able to recount the movements in detail—one of the benefits of such a brief campaign. The French columns passed through the forest, brushed aside a handful of Prussian pickets, and emerged without incident. Over the next few days, French cavalry found a vacuum in front of them except for Prussian hussars. There was a certain amount of tension in the Napoleonic camp by this time. The emperor himself continued to have his eyes fixed straight ahead. A defensive position behind the Elbe seemed so sensible that he was unable to conceive that the Prussians had marched their entire body so far out to the west. As Bernadotte's corps at the head of the central column reached Schleiz, it tussled with a small detachment of Hohenlohe's army under General Tauenzien (eight and a half battalions, nine squadrons, and a battery, some nine thousand men), forced it back to Mittel-Pöllnitz, then immediately lost contact with it. The right column (Soult and Ney's corps) passed through Hof and reached Gross-Zöbern by October 9, observing, but not contacting, small forces retreating in front of it. A slew of bewildering intelligence poured into Napoleon's headquarters, that placed large Prussian forces left, center, and right—there were reports, for example, that spoke of a force of fifty thousand men concentrated for the defense of Dresden. Napoleon seemed to be getting frustrated, and in fact reproved Murat for excessive dispersion of his cavalry forces.[31]

It is an amazing thing to pause and contemplate. An immense French phalanx of concentrated fighting power was passing to the northeast, toward Gera, then Leipzig, with its ultimate destination Berlin. On its left flank, standing as still as a statue, was the Prussian host: three separate "armies"; Hohenlohe on the Prussian left, Brunswick to his right, Rüchel in reserve. Opportunities there were aplenty for a drive into the French left, or a leap onto Napoleon's communications back to France, or for any number of things. Instead, the Prussians sat and watched the parade go by.

It is relatively easy to explain why this was so. The Prussian commanders had only just arrived at their respective positions and were still sorting out their battle array, arranging their camps, and establishing their supply lines. Divided councils within the command had left the overall operation in doubt, and no one had any definite orders as yet. Most important, these were men who were old and out of touch, and were simply unused to the pounding pace of Napoleonic operations. It was, by and large, a young man's game.

It was the left column, V Corps of Lannes and VII of Augereau, that made first contact. By October 9, they were at Grafenthal and Coburg, respectively, after an uneventful passage of the Thuringer Wald. On the morning of October 10, Lannes bumped into Hohenlohe's advance guard under Prince Louis Ferdinand at Saalfeld.[32] The prince had just four Prussian and six Saxon battalions, as well as ten squadrons, and two and a half batteries, just 8,300 men in all. Nevertheless, he attacked Lanne's columns as they debouched from the hills

south of Saalfeld. Lannes, one of the most gifted of Napoleon's marshals, handled his corps skillfully. One division under General Suchet
gradually worked its way around Louis's right flank. In attempting to
restore his position, Louis personally led his cavalry in a charge and
was killed in the fighting. There was nothing particularly surprising
here. These were veteran French troops, men who had done this to
other armies on other battlefields many times. Most of the Prussians,
by contrast, were seeing combat for the first time.

What is less explicable is why Louis had fought this action at all.
Hohenlohe, to whose army he belonged, had already decided to recross
the Saale heading east and to concentrate his force between Roda and
Mittel-Pöllnitz. His orders to Louis on the morning of October 10
failed to make that clear, however, and in consequence Louis was defending a position that no longer existed. The entire episode shows the
dangers of having an excessive number of detachments: Hohenlohe had
deployed his army in no less than four separate groupings (Prussians,
Saxons, the Tauenzien detachment, and Prince Louis Ferdinand's advance guard). Even before there had been a major battle, the French
had already handled one of them (Tauenzien) quite roughly, and destroyed another.

The news of the action at Saalfeld, not to mention the death of a very
popular prince, seems to have spread consternation through all levels
of the Prussian army. To the commanders, it seemed as if a French
breakthrough to Leipzig was imminent—which in fact it was. Brunswick now drew up orders for the retirement of his main army toward
the Elbe, covered by Hohenlohe's corps, once again with Rüchel in
support.[33] In addition, Saalfeld seemed to have brought the indecision
and bumbling of the higher commanders to the attention of the Prussian rank and file for the first time. They began to consider the awful
possibility that their leaders were not at all on top of the situation.

Saalfeld had little immediate impact on Napoleon. The presence
of a sizable advance guard here fit in perfectly with his preconceived
notions about the Prussian deployment. He felt that Lannes had contacted the center or right of the enemy position as the Prussians were
pulling back to the Elbe. Even now, the notion that the Prussian army
had deployed out on a limb and that he was hitting the extreme left wing
of the entire enemy position seemed like lunacy to him. He therefore
ordered the advance to the northeast to continue, expecting Brunswick
to attempt a concentration at Gera. Confident in his mobility and his
corps commanders, he wrote that "I doubt, however, whether he can
unite before I can."[34]

It was not until October 11 that French reconnaissance began to clear up some of the fog. Patrols to the north continued to show an empty hole as far as the river Elster and Leipzig. Meanwhile, on the French left, Lannes continued to report the presence of large numbers of Prussian campfires on the left bank of the Saale, in the vicinity of Jena. Against all expectations, and his own common sense, a flabbergasted Napoleon was finally forced to admit that he'd been wrong: the Prussian army lay not to his north, but to his west. Even now, however, Napoleon wasn't sure how far to the west the Prussians lay. His orders, in fact, indicate that he expected battle no earlier than October 16 at Weimar, west of Jena.[35]

Having found the enemy, Napoleon now drew up orders for October 12. The entire army would wheel to the left toward Jena and assault the Prussian forces there. The leading corps of the original array (Lannes's V and Soult's IV) would still constitute the "front," with Lannes on the left and Soult on the right. They would now be facing west, however, rather than north.[36] Behind them in reserve, coming up later in support, would be the VII Corps of Augereau and the VI of Ney. The central column had pushed on most rapidly of all three in the original direction toward Gera, and it received special orders. The corps of Davout, with Bernadotte in support, would continue to the north, reach Naumburg, wheel to the southwest through Auerstädt and thence to Apolda. He would therefore come down on the rear of the Prussian army, a maneuver that would cut the Prussian army's line of retreat and turn its defeat into its utter destruction. No Napoleonic plan rivals this one as a "battle of annihilation."

On October 12–13, the French bataillon carré swung to the left. With Lannes in the lead, it contacted the Prussians over the Saale at Jena. By the morning of October 14, Napoleon had concentrated the better part of two full corps in a small bridgehead over the Saale, seized on Lannes's initiative the night before. With Napoleon looking on, Lannes led off the attack in the morning against the Prussian right. Two divisions advanced abreast (Gazan on the left and Suchet on the right) and drove a wedge into Prussian positions. Augereau soon joined in to the left of Lannes. Ney arrived on the battlefield and, on his own initiative, wedged himself in between his fellow Marshals without orders.[37] His impetuosity made for some tense moments as his leading units outstripped the two flanking corps, but his neighbors soon fought their way up to his relief.

Things weren't going well for the Prussians, but as the infantry of Major General von Grawert's division arrived, it seemed as if Hohenlohe might yet save something of this day. In one of those moments seemingly invented to demonstrate the changeover from one military era to another, however, they deployed far too slowly for the attack. "Solemnly, as if on the parade ground," they halted and formed line within range of the French skirmishers in front of the village of Vierzehnheiligen.[38] The French had already taken them under fire, and their own fire by volleys was utterly ineffective against small clumps of men under cover in and around the village. There they would stand for nearly two hours, being cut down one by one not just by enemy skirmishers, but by a new way of war.

Finally they broke, but by then it hardly mattered. The Prussians had already abandoned their initial position on the elevated plateau known as the Dornberg, and their line was leaking everywhere. It broke into a flood as yet another French corps arrived, Augereau's. General Rüchel's reserve, summoned in the early morning, arrived just in time to be caught in a general rout. By midafternoon, the Prussians were in full flight from the Jena battlefield, outmaneuvered, outhustled, and outfought. The French *bataillon carré* had worked to perfection: seeking out the enemy, finding him, then closing on him like a fist and crushing him.

The only problem was that the fist had closed on the wrong army.

Unbeknownst to Napoleon, his masterstroke had completely missed the main Prussian force. Brunswick wasn't even at Jena, but in retreat to the north. Napoleon had gathered the concentrated combat power of four full corps in a battle against nothing more spectacular than Hohenlohe's force. He had smashed it, as well he should have given his gross numerical superiority. The battle had also, luckily, engulfed the Prussian reserve under Rüchel, who had picked the worst possible time to do his duty. Nevertheless, the debacle had left Brunswick's main army untouched. Jena, in other words, had been a victory, but not at all the complete triumph that Napoleon had envisioned.

Those laurels went to perhaps the greatest marshal of them all: Davout. Ordered to advance his III Corps through Naumburg toward Apolda and come down on the rear of the Prussian position at Jena, he had unwittingly crashed into Brunswick's main army in retreat toward the Elbe. At Auerstädt, fought concurrently with Jena, Davout's single corps, a mere twenty-seven thousand men, had taken on Brunswick's sixty thousand—and thrashed them soundly.[39] Here the French displayed their entire tactical package, with aggressive skirmishers covering the rapid movement of their infantry columns around a broken battlefield. Meanwhile the Prussians tried desperately to find enough flat ground to deploy into lines in order to employ the oblique attack. It should also be kept in mind that Brunswick was in the midst of a retreat caused at least partly by a morale collapse that had set into his already jittery army at the news of Saalfeld. What Davout encountered, therefore, was not the concentrated might of a full Prussian army, but a unit-by-unit procession toward the battlefield without any central direction. Apart from a handful of veterans of the Valmy and Flanders campaigns of the 1790s, the manpower was seeing combat for the first time. A younger, more active commander might have been able to help them through it, but Brunswick took a musket ball through the eyes early in the battle and fell mortally wounded.

Even the day after the battle of Jena, Napoleon still believed that he had crushed the main Prussian army. There is confusion as to his reaction to the stunning news of the battle of Auerstädt. Depending on the source you read, he either resented Davout's success or treated him magnanimously; even his leading biographer tries to have it both ways. What is not ambiguous is Napoleon's feelings about Marshal Bernadotte's performance. In the midst of two of the greatest battles of the age, he hadn't taken part in either. He had left Davout in the lurch at Auerstädt, contrary to Napoleon's explicit orders to support him, yet he had not bothered to march on Jena, either.[40]

What is equally incontestable is the utter collapse of the Prussian army after these twin defeats. In part, it was the result of two defeated forces desperately trying to shift themselves onto the same road network in retreat. It was partly the result of the original deployment to the west of the Saale. With the French to their front and slipping around their left, the mass of the Prussian army was cut off from home. Of course, it was also partly the result of one of the most successful pursuits of all time, the moment in which Murat came into his own as an operational commander. Rarely pausing for breath, and never letting up the pressure on the demoralized columns trudging along ahead of him, Murat's troopers completed the destruction of the Prussian army. It began in battle, but ended in pursuit. Even well-led cavalry, however, should not expect to receive the surrender of fortress after fortress, as Murat's troopers did. The morale of the army had simply vanished.

There were two notable exceptions. One was the last-ditch defense of the fortress of Kolberg by a young officer, August Wilhelm von Gneisenau, along with the heroic mayor of the town, Nettelbeck.[41] In January 1945, the Nazi regime would release one of the last feature films in the history of the Third Reich on this very subject, as a means of rallying the people to fight another invader, this time the Red Army. The other was the repeated refusal of General Blücher to surrender his division. Not until the French had run him to ground near Lübeck near the Baltic coast did he agree to stack his weapons, a remarkable achievement given the complete military and political dissolution going on around him.[42]

Napoleon's campaign had not been perfect—far from it. From the start, he had misjudged the position of the Prussian main body, thinking it was in front of him, when in fact it was to his left. Then, when he finally discovered it on his left, he thought it must be farther to the west. The great battle planned for October 16 had turned into two separate battles on October 14. Murat's reconnaissance, the perfection of which has been filling historical tomes since Napoleon's own day, failed completely to uncover much of anything. Napoleon fought a battle at Jena against what he thought was the entire Prussian army, which turned out to be an oversized rear guard, leaving Davout to make things right at Auerstädt, and it was entirely appropriate that the marshal would henceforth be known as the "Duke of Auerstädt." Even then, however, Murat's pursuit took off in the wrong direction, to the west toward Erfurt when most of the Prussian army was fleeing north. In the end, these were just the sorts of uncertainties that Napoleon's art of war, above all the flexibility of the corps system, was designed to handle—especially when the opponent sat and waited to be destroyed.

Early Rebirth: The Eylau Campaign

Despite having suffered the worst and most complete defeat of the entire Napoleonic period, Prussia was still in the war against the French. The king had fled to the fortress of Königsberg in the extreme northeast of his kingdom, surrounded by a small but faithful remnant of his once powerful army. Moreover, the Russians had arrived in the theater. They had moved immediately to the aid of their Prussian allies, but the rapidity of the collapse at Jena and Auerstädt had rendered direct assistance moot. Nevertheless, Napoleon had marched off to oppose their entry into Europe, attempting to meet them as far to the east as possible, and by November the French army had reached Warsaw without meeting any significant opposition beyond a few Cossack patrols. Only in December did a sizable Russian force arrive, as an army of fifty-five thousand men under General Bennigsen reached the north (right) bank of the Vistula. The last corps of the Prussian army, some fifteen thousand men under General L'Estocq, stood at the fortress of Thorn.

Fighting broke out by the end of 1806, but the campaign ended with the indecisive battle of Pultusk on December 26.[43] As Napoleon would find out again in the future, an art of war that appeared unbeatable in the cozy confines of western Europe, with a world-class road net and a prosperous agricultural system, looked much more fallible in the primitive hinterland of eastern Europe. The roads, poor in the summer, were terrible in the winter, and the land was sparsely populated and underdeveloped. Neither foraging nor requisitioning could do much about it, and as it always does when supplies run low, morale in the *Grande Armée* plummeted. Marshal Lannes reported from Schneide-mühl that "the country from Stettin to this place is exactly similar to that which we traversed when we marched from Egypt to Syria except that here the sand makes the roads even worse. It is impossible to get one day's bread ration for any army corps here."[44] The disappearance of the occasional French courier at the hands of Prussian partisans in the forests didn't help matters, and in January, they bagged even bigger game in the form of divisional commander Claude Victor (who would soon be exchanged for a prisoner in French hands: General Blücher). It was yet another problem of campaigning in the wilds. Napoleon was, indeed, a long way from Paris.

In January 1807, the Russians came out of their winter quarters in eastern East Prussia, moving westward to the line Deutsch Eylau-Osterode-Allenstein. The move had three aims: to threaten Napoleon, then in quarters in central Poland, on his left wing; to gain a favorable jumping off point for spring operations farther to the west; and to firm up contacts with L'Estocq's Prussian corps at Freystadt. The Russian action had caught Napoleon napping. He was neither the first nor the last great general to underestimate Russian operational vigor. As was typical, however, he reacted swiftly and set the army on the march in early February. Napoleon had the resources of the entire French Empire behind him—essentially all of Europe west of the Vistula—but he couldn't campaign forever this far away from France. To get back home, he needed a complete victory as rapidly as possible.

In early February 1807, Napoleon launched an offensive against the Russians from his Vistula bridgehead.[45] He gathered all available forces on the west-east line from Allenstein to Wartenburg, that is, facing north. The *Grande Armée* now moved forward in three columns. On his left lay the VI Corps of Marshal Ney; Napoleon himself, along with his Guard and the corps of Soult (IV) and Augereau (VII), formed the central column; to his right lay the trusty Davout and his III Corps. Even farther to the right lay the cavalry, guarding the eastern flank of the advance at Bischofsburg. His staff officers carried out the redeployment with their by-now accustomed swiftness and precision. Within a week, Napoleon had turned the tables. Once the threatened, he was now the threat, with a concentrated force ready to advance against the extreme left flank and rear of the Russian position in East Prussia, threatening their communications and almost certainly forcing them into a battle. A frontal attack or a blow to the Russian right would simply force Bennigsen into a retreat, and Napoleon had no desire to chase him back to Russia.

In his later study *Cannae* (1913), the chief of the German General Staff Count Alfred Schlieffen described it as a classic example of Napoleonic warfare: "meeting envelopment with envelopment, a threatened attack with the real thing."[46] The plan was to proceed directly against Bennigsen with the main column and bring him to battle, at which point either Ney or Davout—hopefully both of them—would swing in on the flanks or rear of the Russian army and enable Napoleon to fight a battle of annihilation. Ney's mission included a second component, however: keeping an eye on the Prussian corps of L'Estocq, which now stood at Osterode to the west, and preventing its junction with the main Russian force.[47]

The campaign that followed would be one of Napoleon's most difficult. His advance threw Bennigsen into headlong retreat. Although the Russians were prepared to accept a frontal assault, they kept a careful watch for any threat to their flanks. There was a nearly daily series of tough rearguard clashes, but Napoleon could not bring the enemy to battle. It was a difficult time for all concerned—howling winds, deep snow, and a thinly settled land without much in the way of accommodations for the armies. In what was highly unusual behavior for this era, the Russians carried out no less than four successive night marches to keep ahead of the French columns, which were having their own problems by this time.[48] The main column had the best road, from Allenstein through Jonkendorf and Landsberg. Davout continued his encirclement attempts from Guttstadt to Heilsberg. Ney kept pace in the west, reaching Wormditt, to keep L'Estocq's Prussians separate from the Russians. On February 6, the Russians put up a particularly strong rearguard action at Hof, strong enough to make Napoleon think he had hit the main body. He drew Davout close to gather strength for the upcoming battle, but as the truth of the situation dawned on him, he once again sent the Marshal off on his continuing flank march to the east and north toward Beisleiden.

On February 7, Bennigsen finally offered battle just east of the village of Preussisch-Eylau. His own army was coming apart by this time. A steady regimen of stiff rearguard fights and ice-cold night marches were taking their toll. Western tales of Russian primitivism to the contrary, his men had to eat, rest, and sleep just like Napoleon's did. One source speaks of a "gradual dissolution" of the Russian army as it desperately tried to escape Napoleon's clutches, and that seems a fair statement.[49] In addition, the terrain here was relatively open, and thus far more suited to Russian mass tactics than the hilly country they had been passing through. Above all, however, the position allowed him to keep the principal roads—and communications arteries—in his hands. Just behind his position lay the major roads to Königsberg (north) and Friedland (east).

There are sources aplenty that describe the battle of Eylau, a hellish encounter over a land of frozen lakes and rivers and four-foot snow-drifts that made the simple movement of men and horses nightmarish.[50] After a stiff fight on the evening of February 7 between the Russian rear guard and the French advance guard for the village of Eylau itself, the battle proper began the next day. Napoleon's plans, as always, were ambitious. Soult's corps would launch a pinning attack in the center. It would divert Russian attention and hopefully draw in Russian reserves. Meanwhile, the main event would be unfolding on the French right, where Davout's corps would strike the enemy's left, once again with an eye to levering the Russian army away from its communications.[51] The VII Corps of Augereau, along with Murat's cavalry, would form the *masse de décision*, to be inserted at the crucial moment, and the Imperial Guard would be in reserve.[52] If Ney managed to arrive on the left, the French might achieve a complete encirclement of the entire Russian force.

Little went right with the plan, and the problems started early. Davout's corps was still in the process of coming up—it seemed to Napoleon that nothing went smoothly on this road network—and Soult's pinning attack had to be extended to the Russian right as well as its center. Along with the cavalry corps of Lasalle, Soult dutifully attacked and was soon in full flight back to Eylau in the face of an attack by the Russian division of Tutchkov. Russian cavalry on the left was active, harassing Friant's Division, the lead elements of Davout's corps, as it was coming up. The Russians were here to fight, not to be the passive object of a Napoleonic encirclement battle. They were obviously going to be excessively jealous of their left, to protect their communications. In fact, as Napoleon surveyed the battlefield, both of his own flanks now seemed endangered.

This seems to have been what was on his mind when he ordered Augereau's Corps out of the *masse de décision* to launch a great attack on the Russian left, held by Tolstoy's division. It was one of the greatest fiascoes of the entire Napoleonic period and bears more than a passing resemblance to what happened to Frederick the Great's left wing against these same Russians at Zorndorf. A combination of smoke, snow, and glare—and perhaps an overly complex choice of formation— led Augereau's advance to veer far off course. He struck the Russians not in their left, but directly in their center, up to now completely untouched by the fighting and fronted by nearly the entire Russian artillery park. No doubt as surprised as the French at what had happened, they opened fire with canister at point-blank ranges—well under one hundred yards—at the French columns suddenly emerging out of the driving snow. As the Russian guns opened up, so did the French to their front, unaware that they were also firing on Augereau. Soon the ragged remnant of what had been an army corps just a few moments before fell back in disorder, pursued by the Russian infantry.

It was 10:30 A.M., and Napoleon's army was falling apart left, right, and center. Once again, another unit from the *masse de décision* had to go in. At 11:30 Murat led more than ten thousand horse of the Cavalry Reserve—eighteen complete regiments—on one of history's greatest cavalry charges.[53] Although Napoleon normally employed Murat to deliver the final blow or the pursuit after victory, however, this was simply remedial work. It sliced through the center of the Russian line, reformed, and then sliced its way back out again. The Russian center now had its own remedial work to do, and by early afternoon, the line was essentially reestablished for both sides at where it had stood in the morning.

Not until 1:30 P.M. was Davout prepared to launch his strike on the Russian left. When it went in, however, it made excellent progress; the Russians, too, were committed all along the line. As Davout's regiments ground forward inexorably, Bennigsen's position came to resemble a ninety-degree angle, with the eastern extremity drawn back to Kutschitten. The situation was dire. As a German staff officer described it in his 1913 history, "The Russians had lost. Crowded together in an acute angle of which the point was the front of Eylau and the branches lay along the tracks to Lampasch and to Schmoditten, they were in no condition to resist much longer. Already the interior of the angle was filled with wounded and demoralized men. The line of retreat to Domnau, Allenburg, and the home country was severed."[54] Indeed, a glance at the map tells the tale of a French victory, with the Russian army finally pried away from its communications and soon to be driven off into the wilderness.

That, however, was not the way it went. At 3:30 Bennigsen's redemption arrived in the form of General L'Estocq and his Prussian corps, the last operational unit in the Prussian army. He had been playing a game of cat and mouse with his pursuer Marshal Ney, but the game was on L'Estocq's own turf, over terrain that he knew intimately and that his French antagonist knew only from poorly drawn maps. Both he and Ney, in fact, had received messages from their commanders recalling them to Eylau. Although they were sent at the same time, Bennigsen's message arrived first, and L'Estocq had spent the day eluding Ney's pursuit and driving hard for Eylau. Interestingly enough, Ney was within easy reach of the battlefield all day, and the thunder of the cannon would normally have been enough to summon him. "Marching to the sound of the guns," however, was much more difficult when falling snow and howling wind muffled the roar. In fact, L'Estocq himself would later say that he "saw" the battle raging to his east rather than heard it, as the white snow and gray sky reflected the glare of explosions.[55]

L'Estocq did not bring a very large force, just eight battalions, twenty-eight squadrons, and two batteries of horse artillery. Even with the Russian stragglers he swept up on his approach, he certainly had less than the nine thousand men some sources credit. He probably had some seven thousand, and with allowance for stragglers of his own, perhaps less than that. Some of the corps were still holding the rear guard against Ney. The exact employment of the force was, therefore, a crucial issue. Arriving at Althof, on the extreme northwest of the battle area, L'Estocq conferred with his "assistant" (Gehilfe), General Gerhard von Scharnhorst. The position of "chief of staff" was as yet unknown in the Prussian army, still struggling its way forward in the new age of divisions and corps.[56] They could see the grave position of the Russian army overall, and perhaps the smart thing to do was to get in the battle as soon as possible. Such a consideration argued for driving due south, taking up a position on the Russian right or in the center, and attacking the first French formations they could find. The problem was that this would place the Prussian attack against the part of the French line that had, as yet, been least touched by battle, the left. L'Estocq's strength would probably not suffice to make much of a difference here. Bennigsen's preference, expressed by Russian officers whom he had sent to meet the Prussians at Althof, was to split up the corps to provide relief at various points along the line. Scharnhorst refused immediately, given the already weakened state of the corps.

The more closely he considered the situation, it seemed to Scharnhorst that the real danger for the Russians lay on their left. Not only had Davout driven them away from their communications, seizing their lines of retreat, but their flank was now dangling, unanchored in any natural terrain or village. Nor could he exclude the possibility of further French attacks in this sector. Quickly, he made his decision. Although one biographer has him standing dramatically on a hilltop at Althof surveying the entire battlefield, later scholars would point out that there was no hill at Althof.[57]

Be that as it may, the already exhausted Prussian corps now set out on a swift ride clear across the rear of the Russian army. They came up into attack position at Kutschitten, prepared themselves for the assault, and slammed into Davout's exhausted and freezing troops. The attack drove the French back in complete disorder. With renewed heart, the Russians soon joined in, with the divisions of Kamenskoi and Bagavout driving forward on L'Estocq's right and recovering the village of Anklappen.

It had certainly been a long day for L'Estocq. Since the afternoon of February 2 the corps had already marched eighty to ninety miles.[58] On February 7, his march from Engelswalde to Rossitten was eighteen miles as the crow files, more like twenty-four as the column marches, when one figures in the winding roads and obstacles in rural and heavily forested East Prussia. The heavy frost cut the soil into deep ruts, and it was literally impossible to ride any faster than a man could walk. As a result many of his men had not even reached camp until well after midnight. The morning of February 8 had seen him in motion once again. Some of his men had been in camp only a few hours and immediately had to fall in again with little rest and no food. It was a grueling approach march toward Eylau. The front of the columns had fought their way through Ney's patrols the entire way, and there were nearly constant rearguard actions as well. In fact, the French and Prussians cut through each other's march columns all day. Yet, he had persisted. A later analyst would call it "a model of the way in which a flank march in the face of a near and powerful adversary should be conducted."[59] His day then culminated in a daring maneuver and a surprise assault on a French force that was by now utterly fought out. It was not a bad day's work for a man just this side of seventy.

It is interesting to compare Ney's arrival on the battlefield with L'Estocq's. The French marshal arrived at Althof, having by now lost contact altogether with the Prussians, at 7:30. Acting in an utterly orthodox fashion, he simply fell in on the French left, launched an attack on the Russian right toward Schloditten, then fell back to take up a position in the French line to the left of Soult's corps. L'Estocq's 9,000 men had utterly transformed the battle through clever and daring operational maneuver; Ney's corps, 14,500 men, achieved much less with far more. As night fell, once again, the lines were about where they had stood in the morning.

The battle was over, as both armies collapsed in exhaustion. It would turn out to be one of the bloodiest encounters in the whole Napoleonic era. The *Grande Armée* had lost about a third of its strength, or twenty-five thousand men, the Russians at least fifteen thousand, and the Prussians eight to nine hundred.[60] Needless to say, the wounded died in droves in the succeeding days, as they lay out on a bitterly cold, snow-blown open field.

Who had won? As after the bloodletting at Zorndorf, the question of retreat now arose. Scharnhorst was for continuing the fight on the next day. Bennigsen, who knew how close he had come to being destroyed, decided to retreat north, toward Königsberg. That evening, Scharnhorst wrote to General Kleist, the king's aide-de-camp: "It is a great misfortune that the battle was not renewed on the following morning. The troops were extremely fatigued, it is true, but after all the enemy was in similar plight." Even worse, he felt, was Bennigsen's choice of direction. Königsberg was the nearest available fortress, true, but to fall back on a fortified place in Napoleon's presence was foolish. It could be a repeat of Ulm. In addition, a retreat to Königsberg meant the abandonment of his communications to Russia, a short-term fix with potential long-term consequences.

Thus it was that Scharnhorst and L'Estocq came to the second fateful decision of the day. Continuing their pattern of independent operations, they decided to head east toward Friedland. It was somewhere around midnight, and the Russian retreat north was already well under way, when the Prussian generals reached their decision. It was a dramatic moment, captured well by Scharnhorst's great nineteenth-century biographer Lehmann:

It was difficult to find the way in the darkness. In the deserted villages no one could be discovered who could have undertaken to act as guide on the snow-covered roads. At last two grenadiers were discovered who were natives of that region, and with these two seated on a gun in front the column was set in motion. They marched as far as Domnau, and then on to Friedland the same day, unmolested by the enemy, who probably would have credited anything sooner than the retreat of the victor.

The independent retreat of L'Estocq's corps was crucial for two reasons. First, the difficulties of following this "excentric" or divergent retreat, as well as his own crippling losses, made Napoleon forgo his trademark pursuit. No fact could say more about how he truly viewed the outcome at Eylau, despite the flurry of positive-sounding dispatches he now dictated for the French and European public. Second, and more important, a Prussian corps standing at Friedland would hold open the lines of communication back to Russia. "For the second time," wrote Lehmann with some justice, "the Russian army had been saved."[61]

The arrival of L'Estocq's tiny corps was not only the transforming event of the battle of Eylau. Later German analysts would view it as much more, indeed, as a historical turning point for the Prussian army. One historian, writing in 1906, regretted how completely the name "Jena—1806" had cast into shadow the name "'Preussisch Eylau —1807." At Eylau, he wrote, "the glory of the Prussian army, forfeited wholesale by the neglect and senility of its leaders at Jena, was most honorably retrieved in detail."[62] A General Staff officer and well-known writer on military affairs, Colmar Freiherr von der Goltz, wrote in 1913 that "it was at Eylau in 1807, and not the War of Liberation in 1813, that the old army vindicated itself before the tribunal of history." To Goltz, success came from a combination of Scharnhorst's intellect and old L'Estocq's itch to get into a fight. The general, "the last of Frederick the Great's school to hold a high command," had "vigor, alertness, and daring enough to make the victory on 8th February possible." He not only recognized his assistant's "keener insight," but "assumed full responsibility for its consequences." Scharnhorst, for his part, had provided "the idea of carrying out the glorious flank march in the face of Ney's attempt at interception." Likewise, it was he who "made the dispositions for keeping off the French, who chose the direction of attack on the battlefield, and who fixed the line of retreat afterwards."[63] The German army's interest in Eylau would continue well into the twentieth century. In 1937, a Wehrmacht captain would write of "the success of L'Estocq's exhausted Prussian troops" in the battle, a sign of the preeminence of moral factors in war. "The battle of Preussisch-

Eylau," he continued, "especially the storming of Kutschitten, was the first gleam of light in that dreary age." Indeed, it was nothing less than "the first step towards the rebirth of the Prussian army and people."[64] Indeed, just four months after the collapse, the Prussian army had returned with a vengeance on the man who had destroyed it.

Reform

For many Prussian subjects, the decisive defeat of the army raised a series of fundamental questions: What was Prussia? Was it, truly, as Count Mirabeau had once stated, an army that had a country attached to it?[65] Was it a fatherland to which they owed allegiance? Or simply a hostile agency that coerced, taxed, and recruited them? There was by now an active commercial middle class in all the Prussian cities, often quite prosperous. Should it not be playing a role in the state commensurate with its economic influence? Did the monarchy's reliance on an increasingly narrow stratum of the population—the Junker elite—make sense? In fact, in the face of the French onslaught, was it even possible to maintain the traditional monarchy?

The best illustration of the difference between revolutionary France and absolutist Prussia was their reaction to invasion. In 1792, the French had cried out as one, "La Patrie en danger!", had imposed the *levée en masse*, and had moved ruthlessly to still any voices opposing war against the invaders. Men went into the army by the hundreds of thousands, women and children rolled bandages and cast musket balls, and the elderly took themselves into the town squares "to preach the hatred of kings."[66] In 1806, by contrast, the Berlin commandant actually put up signs informing the population of the city that, "The King has lost a battle. It is your civic duty to stay calm."[67]

In the eyes of many Prussian officials, this was an untenable situation. Enlightened ministers like Friedrich Karl vom und zum Stein and Karl August von Hardenberg enacted a comprehensive series of domestic reforms.[68] They transformed backward, semifeudal Prussia into a modern state: abolishing serfdom; granting self-government to towns, with elected town councils replacing royal appointees; and formally emancipating the Jews, granting them full citizenship for the first time, even if full social acceptance remained wanting. In general, the purpose of the reformers was to forge a new Prussian patriotism. In giving the Prussian people a stake in defending the state, making them citizens and not merely subjects, the reformers hoped to harness the dynamism of the French Revolution. At the same time, they consciously hoped to avoid its wrenching and violent social transformation. It was revolution from above, a phenomenon that would be seen again in Prussian and German history.

Most important to our account was the transformation of the Prussian army. A group of military reformers now came to the fore who, in many cases, had been staunch advocates of change well before 1806. Their requests had fallen on deaf royal ears before, but that was then. Now, with all seemingly lost, the king was deep in the midst of what educators call "a teachable moment." He no longer had any prerogatives, any turf, worth protecting. The reformers included Gneisenau, who had carried himself bravely at Kolberg while all was dissolving around him, and Scharnhorst, who had shone at Eylau in the heat of battle. The latter headed a new Military Reorganization Commission in 1807, with Gneisenau at his side. It included a number of other reform-minded generals, Wilhelm Heinrich von Grolman and Hermann von Boyen, for example, and even some civilian members like Stein and Könen, the Prussian auditor-general. Five of the group would later become chiefs of the Prussian General Staff.[69] As these new men came forth, many others receded: of the 142 generals in the Prussian army in 1806, 17 were cashiered and 83 honorably dismissed—a purge of unprecedented proportions that would dwarf any subsequent event in the army's history with the possible exception of Hitler's mass dismissal of his Wehrmacht generals in early 1942.[70]

The Scharnhorst-Gneisenau reforms certainly do constitute an impressive list. In August 1808, a new law opened the officer corps to all classes of the population, ending the Junker monopoly, although certain educational qualifications remained; in November, promotion was tied to a system of examinations testing both military and general education. In March 1809, the king created a Ministry of War to regularize and systematize military decisions that had formerly been his personal prerogatives. The reformers also did what they could to evade restrictions on Prussia's armaments. Although Napoleon had imposed a limit of forty-two thousand men on the Prussian army, each year a few men (typically three to five from each company) went on extended leave, while new recruits took their place. This was the "Krümper system," a term whose exact etymology continues to be elusive. Likewise, estimates of its effectiveness vary widely, with numbers of these hastily trained soldiers ranging from 30,000 to 150,000.[71] At any rate, it did give Prussia a larger reserve with at least minimal training than would otherwise have existed. Apart from the numbers involved, these new soldiers represented a break with an old Frederician army that relied almost completely on long-term conscripts. It was, in the words of one modern scholar, "the first step along the path to an army of short-term compulsory service."[72]

In fact, it is easy to exaggerate the impact of all these reforms. The Ministry of War, for example, would have a checkered history. Frederick William III set it up but then refused for years to appoint a minister. Arguments about the responsibilities of the office would continue well into the imperial period. The new officer corps, likewise, was far more open in theory than in fact, since old regimental officers still had the right to vote on the selection of candidates. Finally, although Scharnhorst was interested in some form of conscription to replace the venerable canton system, a militia or *Landwehr* to stand alongside the regular army, that suggestion broke on the reefs of royal and conservative opposition. Only in 1813, and only through the demands of a population aroused by the War of Liberation against Napoleon, did the Prussians finally form a *Landwehr*. Although it gave a decent account of itself, its very existence would continue to be controversial to conservative officers.

Perhaps the most important reform of the era, one that was actually adopted and implemented in full, was a new field manual. The Regulations of 1812 was largely the work of General Hans Yorck and was, as might be expected, an amalgam of old and new. Skirmishers, infantry columns, and the *ordre mixte* now made their appearance in Prussian garb. It stressed combined arms, perceived as one of the most important French strengths, and tied cavalry and artillery more closely to the infantry support role. The assault was a complex process of initial skirmishing, followed by the gradual introduction of battalions, either firing in line or charging in column, and required a great deal more initiative and understanding from company and battalion commanders. The entire process was also to be a lot faster: infantry was now to make all field movements at the pace of 108 steps per minute—up from 75 in the Frederician army. It would later become the U.S. Army march pace, and in fact, it still is today.

There were also two crucial reforms on the operational level. First of all, it was impossible to form divisions while French troops were in occupation of Prussia and the country was essentially disarmed. Nevertheless, large "brigades" now made their appearance. These were all-arms formations. In wartime, they would consist of two infantry regiments, a grenadier battalion, ten to fourteen squadrons of cavalry, and two artillery batteries (one light foot and one horse). Two brigades would constitute a corps in wartime.[73]

Second, this period saw the genesis of the Prussian army staff system. Scharnhorst felt that an overhaul in the system of military education was imperative to train well-rounded commanders and staff officers who also were up-to-date in military developments. In 1810, he convinced the king to open several new schools for junior officers (*Fähnrichs-Kriegsschulen*) as well as an Officer's War College (*Offiziers-Kriegsschule*), developments parallel with the opening of the University of Berlin and the overhauling of civilian education.[74] From the beginning, Scharnhorst envisioned the *Kriegsschule* as an elite institution with a rigorous curriculum, and in fact the original plans called for just fifty students. Enthusiasm among younger officers ran so high, however, that he decided to raise the figure to eighty-five. Not a single cavalry officer, the type who had always emphasized personal dash over book learning, passed the first entrance examination. It was proof, Scharnhorst said, of how badly they needed the instruction, and he decided to admit many of them anyway.[75] The faculty included both military and civilian instructors, and the curriculum was quite liberal: physics and French alongside tactics and strategy.[76] It would later become the famous War Academy (*Kriegsakademie*).

Scharnhorst also wrung from the king an 1813 decree assigning a chief of staff to each commander in the field, responsible for giving advice on all operational decisions. The system had its origins in Scharnhorst's own career. Chief of staff to Brunswick during the catastrophic Jena campaign, he had served largely as a factotum. Brunswick was under no requirement even to listen to what he might have to say. At L'Estocq's side at Eylau, his advice had largely been responsible for saving the day. The chief of staff was not a co-commander, a surrogate commander, or even a vice-commander. He was simply a highly trained officer, sharing the same educational background and coursework as his fellow officers at the *Kriegsakademie*, who could give sound advice. In the Prussian system, the army or corps commander still had a great deal of leeway in deciding how to proceed. Although he was ultimately responsible for making the decision, a wise commander also listened carefully to the advice of his chief of staff. The Prussian command structure combined the man of action with the man of intellect in a highly potent mix.

Liberation: The Leipzig Campaign

The 1813 campaign would see Prussia once again a full partner in the war against Napoleon, first as an ally of Russia during the spring, then, after a summer armistice, as a member of a broadly based coalition that included Austria, Russia, and Sweden. Both of these campaigns displayed certain characteristics of Prussian war making that both harked back to the past and would be significant for the future.[77]

First, the Prussian army was the most aggressive of the allied forces in the field. Despite the fact that the Russians were the dominant party in the spring, and the Austrians in the fall, it was the Prussian army that went into the attack at the first great engagement of the spring, at Lützen (May 2), and that held most tenaciously and counterattacked most fiercely at the second great battle, at Bautzen (May 20–May 21). This was due partly to the team in charge of the Prussian-dominated "Army of Silesia": Blücher in command, first with Scharnhorst at his side and, after the latter's death at Lützen, Gneisenau. Gneisenau's cooler head and analytical abilities were useful in channeling the drive and aggression of "Marschall Vorwärts" (General Forward), as Blücher was known. The marshal's inveterate hatred of the French in general and Napoleon in particular kept the emotional fires burning. The result was a reasonably proficient army on the operational level.

Of course, before getting too far ahead of ourselves and crowning the Prussian army with laurel wreath, it is necessary to point out that it was on the losing side at both Lützen and Bautzen. The conclusion of both battles, in fact, found the Prussians and Russians streaming away from the field in some disorder. In neither case was Napoleon able to administer the final blow, or carry out the careening pursuits of the old days. He blamed his own lack of cavalry, the arm that had been hit hardest during the Russian campaign, and most historians concur. Also at work, however, was a new dynamic of battle, in which far more flexible Prussian and Russian forces were not only able to take a great deal of punishment, but to dish it out as well. Every great moment of Napoleon's career inevitably finds him punctuating it with a famous witticism or bon mot, but perhaps the best of all is his offhand comment after Lützen: "These animals," he said, referring to his Prussian adversaries, "have learned something."[78]

The postarmistice fall campaign of that year found a huge but lumbering allied coalition following a somewhat contradictory strategy. On the one hand, it was desperately trying to figure out a way to bring its massive combat power to bear on Napoleon. On the other, it didn't

August Wilhelm von Gneisenau, the "Enlightened soldier": defender of Kolberg, one of the key Prussian military reformers, and Blücher's chief of staff during the Leipzig campaign.

want to fight a battle with him directly. Those divergent impulses found their way into a series of operational schemes, eventually coalescing into the so-called Trachenberg Plan of August 15. There would be three armies in the allied order of battle: the Army of the North, under former French Marshal Bernadotte, now the Crown Prince of Sweden; the Army of Bohemia in the south, the main allied body under the command of Austrian Karl Philip Schwarzenberg; with Blücher's Army of Silesia sandwiched between them. The plan called on each of the three to give way whenever confronted directly by Napoleon. The other two were then to advance and threaten French communications. It is a remarkable testament to the moral advantage that the emperor still held over his adversaries, and it certainly made sense based on what had happened at Lützen and Bautzen.

For all the sense the Trachenberg Plan made on paper, however, actually carrying it out was another story. It implied a constant series of marches and countermarches in response to Napoleon's own movements, and more than a few times to false reports of those movements.[79] The troops of all three allied armies found themselves bewildered on more than a few occasions, as they passed the same town or rock formation for the third time in a week, heading in different directions. General Yorck, a corps commander under Blücher, wrote to the king at the time, "Blücher's leadership is hasty and inconsistent. In its ignorance of the practical elements of waging war he has . . . put the Silesian army in such a state that it cannot expect a favorable result in the face of a powerful enemy offensive." That was all of eight days into the renewal of operations. Clausewitz would later describe the campaign as being "notable not for any length of march, but for a series of movements to and fro."[80] The seemingly aimless movements were also draining of supply—the allies by now had some six hundred thousand men in the field. Above all, it promised no early end. Hitting an isolated French corps was satisfying to officers who had tasted defeat at the hands of the French on too many occasions, but at some point they were going to have to come to grips with the man himself. In the back of most allied commanders' minds lurked the nightmare: sticking out their neck a bit too far, precipitating a battle, and suddenly hearing the cries of "Vive l'Empereur" from the French troops opposite.

That is precisely what happened to the Army of Bohemia at Dresden (August 26–27). It launched an assault on what looked liked the isolated XIV Corps of Marshal Gouvion St. Cyr. Fighting from prepared positions, he managed to hold off the assault until Napoleon and the main body could come up. Day two saw a concentrated French attack out of the city against the allied flanks. Napoleon used Dresden as a kind of gigantic sally port to form troops for the assault and to re-form them after action. A huge rain during the night had converted the Weisseritz River into an unfordable torrent, cutting off the allied left from the formations of the main body, and hammer blows from the Cavalry Reserve under Murat and Marshal Victor's II Corps had smashed it, taking no less than thirteen thousand prisoners. The evening of August 27 once again saw the allies in a hurried and disorganized retreat.[81]

As in the earlier battles of 1813, however, there was no successful pursuit. Historians line up the typical suspects: the muddy ground, the lack of sufficient French cavalry, and as always when Napoleon has made some puzzling decision, the emperor's health. Other factors were at work, however. At the same time as the two sides were joining battle at Dresden, Blücher had caught Macdonald's small "Army of the Bobr" strung out and vulnerable and had routed it in a sharp action at the Katzbach River, taking fifteen thousand prisoners of his own. Soon thereafter came news of another French disaster. On August 29, Vandamme's I Corps, pursuing out of Dresden, crashed into elements of Ostermann's Corps (Russian) in a confused fight at Kulm. The battle culminated with Kleist's Prussian corps, also fleeing from Dresden, inadvertently slamming into Vandamme's rear. The marshal himself, along with thirteen thousand French prisoners, fell into allied hands.[82]

The cause of these twin disasters was not lack of cavalry or a sudden indigestion on Napoleon's part. It was the first example of a problem that would increasingly bedevil military operations in the nineteenth century. The manageable army of fifty thousand to seventy-five thousand men had now turned into the horde, the unmanageable mass army of five hundred thousand. No single commander, no matter how gifted, could possibly process all the possibilities and potential combinations of that many men and that many corps. Assistance in the form of highly trained staff officers might help, as the Prussians were discovering, but given the primitive means of commanding and controlling these forces, the occasional unit was bound to drop off the commander's mental situation map from time to time.

Dresden was the last major action for two complete months, as the allies wrestled with their seemingly insoluble problem. The front had reached what a later German staff officer characterized as "a dead point." Even Napoleon seemed stumped, and as the French came to a standstill, so too did the allies. That was the dynamic of the Trachenberg Plan—it left all the initiative in Napoleon's hands. If he didn't move, then they wouldn't either. The allies confronted Napoleon in a rough arc, with Bernadotte, Blücher, and Schwarzenberg arrayed from north to south, and the mighty Elbe River protecting both sides. Allied "operations" in this period consisted mainly of repeated calls, then urgent requests, and finally demands from Schwarzenberg to Blücher for more troops. Since the Army of Silesia was already the smallest of the three armies, Blücher and Gneisenau stood fast against detaching any units to the south. Past experience being any guide, they would simply enlarge the Army of Bohemia without improving its fighting abilities, and diminishing either of the two smaller armies would place the entire allied posture in jeopardy. For his part, Schwarzenberg rarely seemed to want to go beyond a posture of the "deliberate offensive" (*abgmessenen Offensive*), unlikely to free Europe from the Napoleonic yoke.[83]

The solution to the conundrum emerged within the Prussian command in early October 1813. It is unlikely to have been Blücher's idea, more likely Gneisenau's. The only way to get the front into motion again was to move. Specifically, on October 3, the Army of Silesia slid northwest along the Elbe toward its own right, slipping around Napoleon's left and crossing the Elbe at Wartenburg against light opposition. Yorck's corps was in the van—he had been calling for more aggressive action, as we've seen—and hereafter he would be known as Yorck von Wartenburg.[84] The general and his chief of staff managed to talk Bernadotte into crossing as well. In coming down from the north and west, the two armies would be exposing their communications to Napoleon, but he had already shown that he wasn't the fast-moving dynamo of prior years. When Napoleon did, indeed, turn on Blücher at Düben on October 9, the Army of Silesia retreated not back north over the Elbe, but west toward the Saale (that is, the allies were retreating toward France). It was a "very unconventional move,"[85] to say the least, and once again both Blücher and Gneisenau had to work overtime to prevent a precipitate retreat by Bernadotte and keep the Army of the North in the game. Meanwhile, Napoleon's preoccupation with Blücher had allowed Schwarzenberg's main body to advance from the east and south, pushing the other major wing of the French army, under Murat, toward Leipzig.

The maneuver on Wartenburg and the retreat to the Saale had now surrounded Napoleon's main body. Old verities about the "superiority of the central position" no longer obtained. Analysts are wont to use such phrases until they take on the aura of revealed truth, but in fact it was no longer an operative concept. What had worked for Frederick the Great, with his relatively nimble armies of thirty thousand or less—twenty-two thousand at Rossbach, for example—was simply not possible with armies of two hundred thousand men. They couldn't

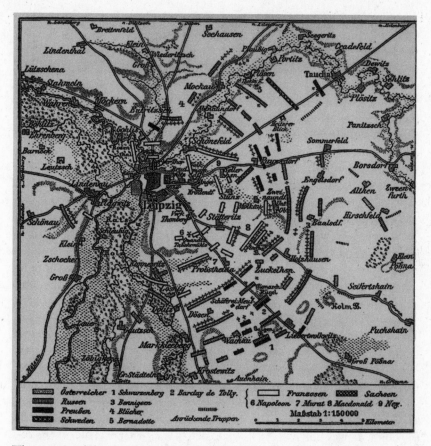

The mammoth battle of Leipzig, the first great concentric assault by "separated portions of the army," from *Meyers Konversationslexikon* (4th edition), published in 1888.

turn easily, and they couldn't pounce rapidly, and reorganizing them after a battle was even harder. They took time to get into motion, and whichever way Napoleon was likely to turn, two other armies would have had a clear shot at him from behind.

The climax of the fall campaign was the great "battle of nations" (*Völkerschlacht*) at Leipzig. Here the combined forces of Austria, Russia, and Prussia formed a great arc around the city in a three-day battle the likes of which the world had never before seen. Even Bernadotte showed up—on the third day. The numbers involved were stupendous. Gneisenau wrote to his wife on the morning of the third day: "We have the French emperor completely surrounded. A half million men stand concentrated in a tight space, ready to destroy each other."[86] The fighting was bloody, especially on the first and third days, with the heaviest fighting in the south, where Schwarzenberg and the Army of Bohemia launched repeated assaults against the French positions between the villages of Wachau and Liebertwolkwitz. The emperor's plans for a great counteroffensive in this sector came to naught, however. The failure was at least partially because of Blücher's pressure from the north, pressing in on the French perimeter near Möckern. Napoleon had to feed first one, and then a second corps earmarked for the blow against Schwarzenberg into the furnace at Möckern. The Prussian Marshal was in his element: in the heat of battle, driving forward, and not to put too fine a point on it, killing Frenchmen.[87] The inability to bring the northern front under control played a material role in Napoleon's decision to retreat on day three, a decision that ended in disaster when a jittery grenadier exploded the demolition charges over the causeway to the west of the city, while it was still crowded with retreating French troops.

Conclusions

The Elbe crossing at Wartenburg, the retreat forward over the Saale, and the drive on Möckern are a convenient way to end this discussion of the Prussian army during the Napoleonic wars. To later generations of German staff officers, the 1813 campaign was an operational breakthrough. It was not merely its size, or the fact that it marked the rebirth of Prussia as a great power. Instead, it marked a conceptual link between the wars of Frederick the Great, the art of war as practiced by Napoleon, and the great nineteenth-century campaigns of Helmuth von Moltke. The concept involved in all three, according to Lieutenant General Waldemar Erfurth in 1939, was "the combined action of separated bodies of the army" (*Zusammenwirken getrennter Heeresteile*). In all these cases, armies had marched separately, completely out of contact with each other, and had linked up only on the battlefield itself. Frederick the Great's invasion of Bohemia in 1757 had been a forerunner, with various detachments linking up in front of Prague. It had occurred mainly because of the geographical conformation of the Bohemian-Silesian border, however. At Leipzig, the pattern had appeared again. It did not appear to have been a conscious operational choice, and in fact it was counterintuitive to everything that contemporary soldiers had learned about war:

If one considers the many unending difficulties that had to be over-come in order to conceive and execute this first great concentric operation with separate bodies of the army, then one can get a mea-sure of how strange and unusual the operation must have appeared to the army commanders of 1813. . . . The battle of the nations, if viewed overall and rightly, was only a result of the conditions. It had not yet sprung out of the soul of a supreme commander.[88]

Later, Moltke's great victories over the Austrians and the French would rely consciously on the same pattern of "concentric operations." Moreover, Erfurth argued that it had become a normative pattern for operations under modern conditions, and was certainly normative for the German army. The triumph at Leipzig had been, in effect, the first *Kesselschlacht:* the battle of encirclement.

But 1813 is important for another reason. There is a tendency in studies of the German military to focus on the elusive concept of its "doctrine," largely as it has been enunciated in the writings of military intellectuals: Scharnhorst, Clausewitz, the great Moltke, Schlieffen, and others. Clausewitz literature continues to pour out in a flood.[89] More recently scholarship has investigated the work of lesser known individuals like Hugo Freiherr von Freytag-Loringhoven[90] and Gen-eral Sigismund von Schlichting.[91] Certainly, there is a great deal of profit in such an approach. The writings of Clausewitz, in particular his masterwork *On War*, continue to stimulate commentary, analysis, and criticism, and are as much of a lodestar to the contemporary U.S. Army as they were for the nineteenth-century German.

We must resist the temptation, however, to view German patterns of war making as an intellectual exercise, carried out in a clinical fash-ion by highly trained staff officers who calculated each occurrence to a mathematical probability. In so far as we view German military his-tory that way, it can be a distorting lens. Certainly, German officers respected their intellectual forebears. In their military writings, how-ever, they devoted just as much attention to the man of pure action. No one could confuse Frederick's cavalry master Seydlitz with a military intellectual; he was a roué and a cad, but he knew how to lead a charge on the battlefield without being ordered. Likewise, Marshal Blücher offers the historian little in the way of thoughtful writings or papers; he was a genuinely strange character, perhaps mentally unstable, but he despised the enemy, he hated having to withdraw in his presence, and he liked nothing better than going after him. Kaiser Wilhelm II, he of the famous indiscretions, once offended a British visitor by stat-

Napoleon's nemesis: Field Marshal Gebhard Leberecht von Blücher. Even in his seventies, energy, aggression, and hatred of the French were the principal command traits of "Marschall Vorwärts."

ing that Blücher "had rescued the English army from destruction at Waterloo,"[92] but he was only stating what generations of later German officers firmly believed. It may even be true. In later periods it would be Frederick Charles, the "Red Prince" of Moltke's wars, who would emulate Blücher. He had no more understanding of Moltke's "concentric operations by separate bodies" than a modern undergraduate would, but he was aggressive, he almost always attacked first, and he triumphed more often than not.[93] In World War II, it would be Rommel, no intellectual, but a man blessed with a "bias for action," who embodied the same spirit.[94] From Frederick the Great down to 1945, the German officer who acted aggressively would be confident that he was acting in the best traditions of the service, and he could also be reasonably certain that the commander of the neighboring formation thought the same way. To sit and wait for the opponent's move was to be Schulenberg, Frederick's cavalry commander at Mollwitz, or Prince Hohenlohe at Jena.

This is not to argue for an anti-intellectual or know-nothing approach to military history. It is simply to argue for a restoration of campaign history—especially on the operational level—to its rightful place in the study of war, alongside the study of doctrine. A German military proverb, later inserted into the Wehrmacht's military manual *Truppenführung*, stated the proposition clearly: "Inaction and neglect incriminate [the officer] more severely than a mistake in the choice of means."[95] When doctrine failed, as it often does on a real-life battlefield, the commander had to be ready to act. The German way of war matched intellect and drive, and one who studies it must give equal time to "the genius of Gneisenau and the aggression of Blücher."[96]

Moltke's Art of War:
Innovation and Tradition

During the nineteenth century, the Prussian-German army entered what we might call its classical phase. It fought a series of enormously successful wars, and in the process it solved one of the most vexing foreign policy issues of the day: the German question. This was the era in which "Prussia conquered Germany," in the words of Golo Mann,[1] toppling the Habsburg Empire from its perch atop the German-speaking world and reshaping the German Confederation into a "little German empire" (*Kleindeutschland*), a new Reich dominated by Prussia.[2] For better or worse, that political structure has been the predominant shape of the German nation-state ever since. It has even survived Prussia itself.

Led by its brilliant chief of the General Staff, Helmuth von Moltke, the Prussian army not only defeated Austria in 1866 and France in 1870–1871, but it did so in record time and, in the first instance at least, with remarkably few casualties. Both the Austrian War (the "Seven Weeks' War") and the Franco-Prussian War appeared at the time as models of successful military operations and still excite the interest of scholars and operators alike in our own day. The current U.S. military, in particular, has studied them deeply and has derived a number of lessons from them. It is a process that began in the late 1970s and is still going on, although there have from time to time been warnings both within and without the military establishment against falling into a certain overenthusiasm for things German.[3]

Beyond its battlefield success, the Prussian army also seemed to have cornered the intellectual market, thinking its way through a remarkable spectrum of military issues—from weaponry and systems of command and control to abstract and metaphysical notions of war as an idea. In this context, it is enough to mention the name of Carl von Clausewitz, author of the weighty tome *On War* (*Vom Kriege*).[4] He acquired a position as the preeminent philosopher of war in the mid-nineteenth century that he has still not relinquished today. From theory to practice, war doctrine to actual fighting, the nineteenth century was the age of Prussia, an era in which the rest of the world wanted to learn "what Prussia had to teach."[5]

The terms crowd in one after another. *Auftragstaktik*. Striking at the enemy's "center of gravity." *Kesselschlacht*. "War is the continuation of policy by other means." *Schwerpunkt*. "No plan survives contact with the enemy's main body." Modern military operations, in both theory and practice, are unthinkable without these Prussian concepts. For present-day analysts, such terms define the German way of war: an intricate combination of carefully wrought doctrine and theory. As we shall see, however, they do not necessarily tell us all that much about what actually happened in the German wars of the nineteenth century.

The Impact of Clausewitz

In attempting to analyze the meaning of Clausewitz's *On War* for the nineteenth-century Prussian army, we must first acknowledge the difficulty in assessing its meaning at all. Most scholars still consider *On War* to have been unfinished at Clausewitz's death. His wife, Marie, had the unenviable task of whipping it into some kind of publishable shape. She tried to assume the blame for its organizational weaknesses, apologizing that her husband's work was "far beyond my intellectual horizon,"[6] but she was being modest about her own intellectual attainments, and it is impossible to think of anyone else in the world who could have done better. *On War* sprawls, shifting somewhat haphazardly from topic to topic. Attempts to establish a "metaphysic of war"—discussing War in the absolute, ideal sense—stand awkwardly next to detailed operational and tactical concepts like "Defensive Mountain Warfare"[7] or "Attack on an Enemy Army in Billets."[8] It is at once a work of German idealist philosophy in the manner of G. W. F. Hegel or J. G. von Herder and a detailed manual for actual operations, and the combination has left readers puzzled (and scholars arguing) over its true intent ever since it first appeared in 1832. At times it is, as critics have said, "heavy going,"[9] and the reader will sympathize with Hubert Camon's criticism that reading this "most German of the Germans" is like being caught up "in a metaphysical fog."[10] At other times, for example in the discussion of the Jena and Auerstädt campaign[11], Clausewitz is much more a thoughtful operational military historian than a mad German professor, although the connection in such sections to his broader idealist attempt can often be difficult to perceive.

It is probably best to read *On War*, as John A. Lynn has recently argued, not as a work that expresses certain eternal truths about war, but within the intellectual context that generated it. It is a Romantic work, and like the broader intellectual and cultural movement of Romanticism, it cannot be understood apart from the intellectual paradigm that it challenged: the rationalism of the Enlightenment.[12] In the eighteenth century, there were many who argued that war was, above all, a science, a rational activity that was susceptible to natural law. This was a point made most forcefully by the Baron Antoine Henri de Jomini, a Swiss officer who had served with both the French and allied armies during the Napoleonic wars.[13] He used that experience to distill Napoleon's art of war into a small number of universal principles. His two-volume *Précis de l'Art de la Guerre* (1838) is still a classic statement of military rationalism, a veritable handbook of guidelines, prescriptions, maxims, and geometrical diagrams. It includes nothing less than "the one great principle" underlying all military operations: "To throw by strategic movements the mass of an army, successively, upon the decisive points of a theater of war, and also upon the communications of the enemy as much as possible without compromising one's own."[14] Jomini believed he had uncovered the key to military success in a concept he called "interior lines." Both Frederick the Great and Napoleon, he argued, tended to establish themselves in some central position between or among their foes, to deal successively with each of them in turn. With their enemies operating on the edge of a circle, widely separated from one another and therefore unable to coordinate their activities to any real degree, Frederick and Napoleon were able to mass their entire strength against them one at a time—and to triumph against the odds.[15]

Standing as the nemesis of Jomini, who based his teachings on a scientific, rational approach, was Clausewitz. Just as nineteenth-century Romantics criticized the Enlightenment for its stress on dry rationalism and for ignoring the unruly passions that drove human activity, Clausewitz painted a radically different portrait of war than Jomini's. Far from being a rational activity, war arose out of "primordial violence, hatred, and enmity." Rather than a schematic exercise in copybook geometry, war was an "instrument of policy"; it was "the continuation of policy by other means," and each war was understandable only in the context of both sides' political aims. Finally, far from being the servant of rules and regulations and Jomini's "one great principle," war was about "the play of chance and probability within which the creative spirit is free to roam." One could understand war, he wrote, only by giving equal weight to each leg of this "paradoxical trinity."[16]

Where Jomini's work offered prescriptions, then, Clausewitz gave analysis. War was not a science to be taught, not a measurable and structured object, but an organism, operating under an internal logic that we can only dimly penetrate. It is the domain of violence, "an act of force to compel our enemy to do our will."[17] It is the domain of danger, physical exertion, and suffering. Here is Clausewitz at his most effective and least opaque:

> Let us accompany a novice to the battlefield. As we approach the rumble of guns grows louder and alternates with the whir of cannonballs, which begin to attract his attention. Shots begin to strike close around us. We hurry up the slope where the commanding general is stationed with his large staff. Here cannonballs and bursting shells are frequent, and life begins to seem more serious than the young man had imagined. Suddenly someone you know is wounded; then a shell falls among the staff. You notice that some of the officers act a little oddly; you yourself are not as steady and collected as you were: even the bravest can become slightly distracted.

We have not yet even arrived at the battle. At the front, the guns of both sides are hammering away and "shot is falling like hail." We report to the brigadier, a man whom we know to be brave, and even he is taking cover "behind a rise, a house, or a clump of trees." Grapeshot rattles on the roof, "cannonballs tear past, whizzing in all directions, and musketballs begin to whistle around us." For our "final shock," of course, we arrive in the firing line, and here "the sight of men being killed and mutilated moves our pounding hearts to awe and pity."[18]

War was not a rational activity. Those men with their "pounding hearts" will not necessarily behave in predictable patterns, or indeed in any patterns at all. Thus, war is the domain of uncertainty. Although "everything in war is very simple, the simplest thing is difficult." Both sides develop plans, and then have to watch helplessly as they are ground down in an inexorable process that he called "friction." It may be the most oft-quoted term in all of On War. His description is therefore worth quoting in full:

> Imagine a traveler who late in the day decides to cover two more stages before nightfall. Only four or five hours more, on a paved

highway with relays of horses: it should be an easy trip. But at the next station he finds no fresh horses, or only poor ones; the country grows hilly, the road bad, night falls, and finally after many difficulties he is only too glad to reach a resting place with any kind of primitive accommodation. It is much the same in war. Countless minor incidents—the kind you can never really foresee—combine to lower the general level of performance, so that one always falls far short of the intended goal.[19]

Likewise, the problem of accurate information was ever present. Information was always going to be sketchy at best: "all action takes place, so to speak, in a kind of twilight, which, like fog or moonlight, often tends to make things seem grotesque and larger than they really are."[20] Like Napoleon at Jena, then, all generals were commanding into the unknown. As a result of these factors, war could never possess mathematical certainty but was instead a matter of assessing probabilities, a gamble: "No other human activity is so continuously or universally bound up with chance."[21] Guesswork, luck, and fortune are the watchwords here, not the geometry of interior lines.

The section of *On War* that links Clausewitz most closely with his time is the discussion of genius. Here is clear evidence of the impact of Napoleon on his contemporaries. This, Clausewitz felt, was where Jomini and all other systematizers had gone furthest astray. "It is only analytically that these attempts at theory can be called advances in the realm of truth; synthetically, in the rules and regulations they offer, they are absolutely useless," he wrote. They ignored moral factors, such as the experience of the troops or their patriotic spirit, and they seemed to conceive of war as a "unilateral action," rather than an "interaction of opposites." Even worse, they ignored the role of the great commander, his boldness, his audacity, his will. Genius, he wrote, "rises above all rules":

> Pity the soldier who is supposed to crawl among these scraps of rules, not good enough for genius, which genius can ignore, or laugh at. No; what genius does is the best rule, and theory can do no better than show how and why this should be the case.[22]

"What genius does is the best rule": Clausewitz's apt phrase is the perfect distillation of the Napoleonic legacy. The Prussian army had learned it at Jena.

Clausewitz was a profound thinker—perhaps too profound for his target audience. The general take on Clausewitz today is that *On War* is one of those "far more often quoted than read" classics, not unlike the Bible—and that is a fair characterization.[23] Certainly that was true of many German military intellectuals in the nineteenth and twentieth centuries, who believed that Clausewitz was the "teacher and guide to present day officers, even if in the majority of cases it is unconscious."[24] Their writings are filled with quotes from Clausewitz, to be sure, quotes that were used so often that they become literary tropes—turns of phrase whose meaning was instantly and unambiguously clear to the reader, even if Clausewitz himself might have meant them in a more subtle or nuanced way. Certain narrow portions of *On War* thus became foundation stones of Prussian-German military discourse over the next century: the claim that war was an art and not a science, and was, therefore, not susceptible to a schema or a system, for example, and its corollary, that the commander was an artist and had to be allowed absolute creative freedom.

Above all, however, when a German officer referenced Clausewitz, chances are he was referring to one specific idea: the philosopher's admonitions—expressed repeatedly in *On War*—that "the direct annihilation of the enemy's forces must always be the dominant consideration" in wartime[25]; that "the destruction of the enemy's forces is admittedly the purpose of all engagements"[26]; and that "the grand objective of all military action is to overthrow the enemy—which means destroying his armed forces."[27] This "annihilation concept" (*Vernichtungsgedanke*) was not simply something that Clausewitz invented, but had its roots deep in the Prussian past.[28] As one officer accurately wrote in 1905, "these teachings led us to Königgrätz and Sedan; they also derived from the experiences of the great warlike era at the start of the 19th century."[29] This was the Clausewitz that most German officers knew, rather than the sage who wrote that "war is the continuation of policy by other means."

Technology: Rifles and Railroads

If Clausewitz really was trying to identify and analyze what was eternal and unchanging about war, he did so at an unusual time, against a backdrop of restless change in every area of western life. The Industrial Revolution had unchained technology and was now busily transforming society, economy, and culture. It was an age of questions. There was the "social question": how best to alleviate the poverty and suffering of the new industrial working class, or "proletariat." There was the "national question": how better to harmonize state boundaries in Europe with the new principle of ethnic nationality. In virtually every European state, there was the "constitutional question": how best to reform political structures to give "the people," variously defined, more of a say in the running of the state. Not surprisingly, the age of questions was also the age of new ideologies, ready-made systems of thought that provided answers to all these problems and more. Revolution was in the air, and not just in industry and the economy.

It should not be surprising, then, that the age also witnessed the transformation of war. It was the age of the mass army, "railroads and rifles,"[30] and the telegraph. The growth of industry allowed military forces to expand to unheard-of size. In 1757, Frederick the Great triumphed over the French at Rossbach with an army that totaled twenty-two thousand men; at Königgrätz in 1866, well over four hundred thousand men would be contesting the issue, and Austrian casualties alone, some forty-four thousand men, would be precisely twice as large as Frederick's victorious host at Rossbach. The railroad allowed these hordes to move, quite literally, twenty-four hours a day, and the problem of the slow-moving supply column that had bedeviled military operations from time out of mind seemed to have been solved.

For each advantage of the new technology, however, there was a problem. It was soon clear that commanding and controlling the mass army was a huge, even insurmountable problem. It is generally agreed that Napoleon I had serious problems in this area in 1812, and that he was at his best with armies that totaled eighty-five thousand men or less.[31] It was foolish to expect an army of several hundred thousand men to maneuver nimbly across the countryside, wheel like a company, and whack the opponent a surprise blow in the flank. In fact, getting them to maneuver at all was a stretch. The telegraph was a modern marvel, true, but the vision it offered of total control of far-flung operations turned out to be a mirage. Tied to a static system of poles and wires, it was far more useful to the defender than to the attacker, and it was nearly useless in any kind of mobile campaign.[32] The mass army, then, was a huge body with a small brain that had a difficult time doing much more than marching straight ahead and crashing into whatever happened to be in front of it.

At that point, a mutual slaughter began. The other great technological advance of the era was the introduction of new firearms—the rifled musket, or simply "rifle." It dramatically improved the range and firepower of infantry, and the 1860s would see another break-through, the breechloader, which greatly increased rate of fire. With long-range rifles now in the hands of the defenders, assault columns could theoretically be shot to pieces long before they struck home. In place of the old-style assault, there now arose the firefight, with extended skirmish lines on both sides replacing the formations of line and column. It was an "open order revolution," the logical culmination of tactical developments since the French Revolution.[33] Open order tactics, however, rarely allowed enough concentration of fighting power for a successful assault. Both sides lined up and fired. There were casualties, enormous casualties, often for little gain. It was the great conundrum of the era.

The Impact of Moltke

It is important to keep these problems in mind when assessing the career of General Helmuth von Moltke, the chief of the Prussian General Staff from 1857 to 1888.[34] More than any contemporary figure, he seemed able to work within the new technology of the era, reconciling it with older German traditions of war handed down from the Great Elector, Frederick the Great, and Scharnhorst. Like them, he was offensive-oriented, aggressive, and always in search of rapid victory. Moltke did not discover anything new, but rather blended the new machines into a way of war that was very, very old. It was not always seamless, but it created a more effective operational package than any other army of the day.

Even as a thoughtful young staff officer, he noted the changes. He could see that war was becoming a far more complex affair and that improvising an operation, as Napoleon had done in the weeks before Jena, was no longer possible. Detailed planning had now become the key. After 1857, he expanded the Prussian General Staff and vastly extended its influence, using it for systematic, peacetime war planning. A Mobilization Section, for example, drew up detailed plans for the initial moves of a future war, compiling railroad schedules in huge volumes. A Geographical-Statistical Section was responsible for estimates of foreign armies, cartography, and weather charts of potential theaters of war. A Military History Section wrote histories of past campaigns, distilling the key lessons for modern officers. In the place of the quick coup d'oeil, Moltke substituted a filing cabinet filled with plans, scenarios, and mobilization schedules, often requiring only the entry of a date.

He also drew up a series of standardized operational regulations. His *Instructions for Large Unit Commanders* (1869) was the first handbook for warfare on the operational level. In it, Moltke standardized several traditional Prussian concepts: "The modern conduct of war is marked by the striving for a great and rapid decision. Many factors press for a rapid termination of the war: the struggle of the armies; the difficulty of provisioning them; the cost of being mobilized; the interruption of commerce, trade, business, and agriculture; the battle-ready organization of the armies, and the ease with which they may be assembled."[35] Indeed, Frederick the Great could have written these words. Prussia's relatively small population, resource base, and tax revenues had always favored wars that were "*kurtz und vives.*"

To teach both tactics and operations, the General Staff ran a busy schedule of maneuvers and war games (*Kriegsspielen*), played on large sand tables and umpired by senior officers. There was also an annual staff ride (*Führerreise*), in which staff officers played a simulated war while touring the actual terrain over which they were fighting. Each game featured an initial scenario (*Lage*), the issuing of realistic orders, situation reports from the umpires, and, by far the most important component, a final discussion (*Schlussbesprechung*) analyzing each side's performance.[36] These may have been games, but they were very serious business. A slip-up in a war game, or a shoddily prepared analysis in a final discussion, could place a serious limit on an officer's advancement.

They were the elite, these General Staff officers, a kind of secular priesthood. For all their influence, however, they were not expected to become public figures. Moltke himself advised them to remain "faceless." Leo Caprivi, the chief of staff of X Corps in the Franco-Prussian War and later Imperial Chancellor, once wrote that "the role of an army corps chief of staff is always full of self-denial. If things go wrong, he is a scapegoat. If they go right, then he works *ad majorem gloriam* (for the greater glory of) his general."[37] In wartime, each army, corps, and divisional commander had a chief of staff at his right hand, a General Staff officer, educated at the *Kriegsakademie*, who could guide the commander's thinking onto the right path. In addition, each chief of staff could be sure that on either flank was another one just like him, a man who had studied the same curriculum and endured the same training, whose behavior he could predict with reasonable certainty.

Along with his theoretical and administrative efforts, Moltke also rearmed and reequipped the Prussian army. Most important was his adoption, in 1858, of the first production model breech-loading rifle. This was the Dreyse Needle Gun, named for the narrow firing pin that struck the back of the cartridge and ignited the charge.[38] The breech-loader greatly increased the soldier's rate of fire. It could also be loaded in a number of positions in which the old muzzleloader was useless, kneeling behind cover, for example. Instead of three shots a minute for a well-trained soldier, the needle gun raised it to ten. Moreover, Moltke helped to give strategic direction to a huge railroad-building program in Prussia, with major lines leading to all the likely deployment points along the country's borders. If the nineteenth century was the age of rifles and railroads, then Moltke personified it.

These reforms alone would have made Moltke an important figure, a latter-day Scharnhorst. Taking him onto a different level altogether, however, was his stature as one of the century's great field generals.[39] He commanded the Prussian army in the three wars of German unification: the Danish War of 1864, the Seven Weeks' War against Austria in 1866, and the Franco-Prussian War of 1870–1871. As we analyze his campaigns, we may detect three constants in his art of war. The first was the importance he attached to the initial deployment (*Aufmarsch*) of the army. Because of the fixed nature of the railroad, a mistake made here could be a disaster. "If the views shaping original deployment are incorrect, the work is completely without value. Even a *single* error in the original assembly of the armies can hardly ever be made good again during the entire course of the campaign. However, all measures for the assembly can be thoroughly thought out long in advance."[40] A well-planned initial deployment, he argued, "must invariably lead to the desired result."

Second, Moltke had a distinct preference for concentric operations by "separated parts of the army" (*getrennter Heeresteile*).[41] The mass army had become too unwieldy to operate as a single body. Drawing it up in one place, he once wrote, was nothing less than a "calamity,"[42] since it was impossible either to move or to feed it. Once assembled, it had only one option: fight a decisive battle as quickly as possible.[43] Moltke's solution envisioned portions of the army operating from different bases, with completely separate lines of communication, sometimes moving directly toward one another. Their purpose was to pin the foe in the front with one army, then hit him simultaneously in the flank and rear with another.

The relatively short-range flank attack (*Umfassung*) had become obsolete in the age of rifles and long-range artillery; Moltke was thinking in terms of a larger scale "turning movement" (*Umgehung*), a maneuver on the operational level.[44] If all went well, the result would be a *Kesselschlacht* (cauldron battle), or more simply a battle of encirclement.[45] Achieving this goal required widely separated armies that had to "march separately but fight jointly,"[46] linking up only on the battlefield. It was a risky scheme, since dispersed armies invited an enemy concentration and attack against one of them, but it was also the only operational approach that offered the possibility of a quick and decisive victory. Once again, this was no theoretical breakthrough, but a broadening of the Prussian approach of Frederick the Great, leavened by study of the great fall campaign of 1813.

Finally, Moltke saw no certainty in war. "Strategy," he once wrote, "is a system of expedients," and on another occasion, "No plan survives contact with the enemy's main body." While it was on the march, an army had to be ready for anything, not hamstrung by rigid orders. "Only the layman perceives the campaign in terms of a fixed original conception, carried out in all details and rigidly followed until the end," he wrote.[47] His solution was something that has become known as *Auftragstaktik* (mission tactics).[48] The commander devised a mission (*Auftrag*), explained it in a short, clear order, and then left the methods and means of achieving it to the officer on the spot.

> One does well to order no more than is absolutely necessary and to avoid planning beyond the situations one can foresee. These change very rapidly in war. Seldom will orders that anticipate far in advance and in detail succeed completely to execution. This shakes the confidence of the subordinate commander and it gives the units a feeling of uncertainty when things develop differently than what the high command's order had presumed.[49]

The basic rule was that "the higher the authority, the shorter and more general" the orders. It was the responsibility of lower echelons to fill in the necessary detail.

In the wars of German unification, Moltke's command touch was light indeed, so light that he came under attack from analysts both inside and outside Prussia. For the most part, his army commanders did what they thought was best and reported it to him afterward. On several occasions in the 1866 campaign, for example, armies of over one hundred thousand men went a day or two without any orders at all, an incredible notion by modern standards. At other times, commanders received his orders and ignored them. And in one celebrated incident, a Prussian general received an order from Moltke and snorted, "This is all very good, but who is General Moltke?"[50] They wouldn't be asking that question for long.

The War of 1866[51]

LANGENSALZA: A PRUSSIAN TRADITION?

The war of 1866, usually described as "Austro-Prussian," was actually a highly complex affair that saw the Prussian army fighting in two widely separated theaters. A small Army of the West under General Vogel von Falckenstein (commander of Prussian VII Corps) had to defeat Austria's allies in western Germany.[52] On paper, they looked like a potentially threatening combination. North of the Main River were the armies of Hanover and Hesse-Cassel (or "Electoral Hesse"). South of it were the VII (Bavarian) and VIII (South German) Corps of the Federal Army, the latter consisting of contingents from Baden, Württemberg, and Hesse-Darmstadt. Moltke's plan was to mop up northern Germany first, then turn on the southern German states. He needed a quick victory to protect the strategic right flank of Prussia's great armies forming farther to the east, as well as to secure the link between Prussia's Brandenburg heartland and the great industrial provinces of the Rhineland.

Falckenstein had precisely three divisions to carry out the task. A sizable chunk of his men were not even line troops, but *Landwehr* reserves, fortress garrisons, and units from the small north German states that had sided with Prussia. Operations began on June 15. Two Prussian divisions invaded Hanover, the "Corps Manteuffel" (really an ad-hoc division) moving south from Holstein and the Goeben Division northeastward from Minden, while a third (the Beyer Division, from the Hohenzollern enclave at Wetzlar) drove into Hesse-Cassel. Both enemy capitals soon fell to the invaders, although in each case the defenders managed a hurried evacuation before the Prussians arrived in strength. The Hanoverian army under blind King George V, with Major General Friedrich von Arentsschildt in operational control, fled south by rail toward Göttingen; the Hessians toward Fulda. Their strategic aim was a linkup with the Bavarians, coming up over the Main from the south. As it turned out, the latter took so long to mobilize and showed so little inclination to cross the natural defense line of the Main that such a link was more of a theoretical consideration than a real danger.

Nevertheless, the small Prussian army had no choice but to struggle south on foot after their rail-bound adversaries, who were systematically demolishing the lines as they went. Falckenstein was neither a good general nor an energetic one, and his lagging kept headquarters in Berlin in a constant state of uproar. The day after taking Hanover, for example, he declared a day of rest for his troops, and both he and his divisional commanders complained repeatedly to Berlin about the heat, lack of supplies, and exhaustion of the men.[53] Falckenstein's major operational stroke was to order all three of his divisions to march on Göttingen as rapidly as possible, a course to which he adhered even after being informed that the Hanoverian army had evacuated the place and was heading farther south.

Luckily, the Hanoverians were having problems of their own. The declaration of war had found the army in the midst of its annual operational maneuvers, which in the Hanoverian case were brigade exercises. Although this meant that most units were ready to go at the outset of the war, it also meant that a large number of new recruits were with the colors, and they now found themselves dragged along on a hard march to the south. The evacuation of the capital, in particular, had been pure pandemonium.[54] To maintain any sort of march discipline, Arentsschildt had to declare periodic days of rest—an unusual posture in the midst of a flight. The hurried departure from Hanover also meant huge supply problems for the force: food, artillery, and small arms ammunition alike.

By June 26, this low-speed chase seemed to have come to an end. Falckenstein had brought the exhausted and starving Hanoverians to bay near the town of Langensalza. He had three divisions coming down from the north, and Moltke had managed to assemble a sizable force of nine thousand men near Gotha under General Eduard von Flies. With Falckenstein's army to the north and the Flies detachment to the south, Arentsschildt, George V, and the entire Hanoverian army were trapped.

During the entire ten days of the campaign, there had been a constant stream of directives from Moltke ordering Falckenstein to get a move on, to pursue the Hanoverians more vigorously, and to attack and destroy them when they were found. When these seemingly had no effect, there was a harshly worded royal order to the same effect, on June 26.[55] Falckenstein's recommendations had warded off those of Moltke by arguing that lack of supply would soon force the Hanoverians to surrender without a fight. He had to respond to the king, however, and he now began preparing for the attack. Just as he was launching the final drive to the south, surprising news came in: Gen-

The contenders at Langensalza. On the left, General Eduard von Flies. His rash assault against an enemy who vastly outnumbered him led to disaster for the Prussians. On the right, the victorious Major-General Friedrich von Arentsschildt, field commander of the Hanoverian army. Within days of the battle, the kingdom in whose name he had triumphed would cease to exist.

eral Flies had taken it upon himself to advance to the north and attack the Hanoverians just northeast of Langensalza.

The decision seems insane. The Hanoverian force outnumbered the Prussians by two to one in both manpower and artillery: 19,000 men to 8,900, 42 guns to 22. The defenders had all the advantages of the terrain. Their line faced southwest, with the Unstrut River to the front. The center of the Hanoverian position was the village of Merxleben, held by the De Vaux Brigade. To its right, toward the village of Thamsbrück, lay the Bülow Brigade, and to its left, at Nagelstädt, the Bothmer Brigade. De Vaux also had pickets in Langensalza itself, along with an advance guard at Hennigsleben, across the Unstrut. Reserves in the form of the Knesebeck Brigade were well in hand, concentrated a few kilometers to the north. Three batteries of artillery bristled on the high ground outside Merxleben, the Kirchberg, with individual batteries placed right and left of the town. Protecting much of the riverbank between Merxleben and Thamsbrück was a meter-high dike. All told, it was about as good a defensive position as you could find in this part of western Germany.

As for Flies, he was commanding what we can only call a scratch force. About two thirds of his force were regular regiments (five Prussian line battalions and a regiment from tiny Gotha, one of the north

German allies); the other third were elements of three *Landwehr* regiments (the 20th, 27th, and 32nd), five battalions in all, as well as three replacement companies. The *Landwehr*, consisting largely of middle-aged men, "lawyers and oculists,"[56] were the sort of troops that don't get the pick of any army's most modern equipment, and indeed they were carrying Minié rifles rather than needle guns.[57] Still, they were on the road early on this dreadfully hot day, kicking up huge clouds of dust as they approached the battlefield.

Given the terrain and the balance of forces, Flies had little option besides a frontal assault, and that's exactly what he did. At 10:00 A.M., the Prussian advance guard under Colonel von Fabeck drove its Hanoverian counterpart from Hennigsleben, back down toward the river. The Prussian main body (Colonel Baron von Hanstein) followed up, establishing batteries on the hill northeast of Langensalza called the Judenhügel, along with its extension to the east, the Erbsberg. Both sides were deluded as to the situation. Flies apparently seemed to think he was dealing with a light Hanoverian rear guard; Arentsschildt a light Prussian probe. In fact, Arentsschildt initially ordered his Hanoverians over the river to make sure that Langensalza was securely in hand. The Knesebeck Brigade came out of the reserve and crossed the river through the narrow defile at Merxsleben. At almost that same moment, however, the Hanoverian Advance Guard came fleeing back toward the town, reporting that the Prussians had arrived in strength. Not sure of the exact situation, and having trouble getting a fix on faraway troop movements in the shimmering heat, at 11:00 A.M., Arentsschildt ordered his troops to form up in and on either side of Merxleben along the river bank and "assume a defensive posture until a further clarification of the situation."[58]

For the next two hours, both sides exchanged artillery fire, and the Hanoverians got the better of it. The main Hanoverian gun position lay on the Kirchberg, the Prussians on the Judenhügel. Neither side had the most modern artillery, with many smoothbores on each side, and the distance between the two hills, some 1,600 meters, meant that not a great deal of damage was done on either side. Just downstream (southeast) of Merxleben, however, the conformation of the Unstrut allowed the Hanoverians to deploy a battery of four 6-pounder guns in a position that was able to take the entire Judenhügel in the flank.

By now, the Prussian main body had reached Langensalza itself. From here, it began its advance. Making use of the numerous gullies in the area, much of the infantry was able to approach the bank of the Unstrut River, and in a few cases crossed it. For the most part, how-

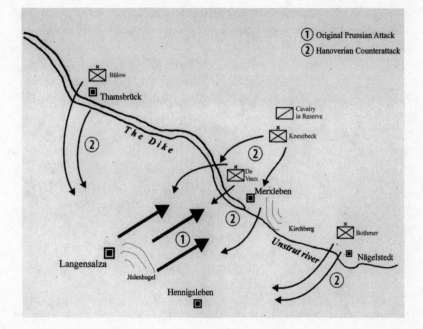

A Prussian Tradition? The Battle of Langensalza, June 27, 1866

ever, they were stuck, facing an unbroken line of Hanoverian infantry deployed along a very steep riverbank. They were close enough, however, to begin peppering Hanoverian artillery on the Kirchberg with needle gun fire, which silenced some of the guns.

The Prussians had now shown their hand, and Arentsschildt could see what a small force he was facing. At 1:00 P.M., he ordered a general advance across the river, striking the Prussians frontally and also in both flanks. Much of the Prussian force gave way at this point, with the *Landwehr* leading a charge to the rear—at least those *Landwehr* who had not already straggled their way out of the battle as soon as the shooting started. The regulars managed to retreat in fairly good order, moving back toward Langensalza. There was little else they could do; there were no Prussian reserves to speak of, and General Flies was at that very moment attempting to recover from a spell of dizziness brought on by the intense heat.

With the Prussians still in the open field, Arentsschildt now hit them with the pursuit: five Hanoverian cavalry regiments (for the record, the *Gardes du Corps*, the Guards Hussars, the Guards Cuirassiers,

GEFECHT BEJ LANGENSALZA
Avanciren gegen die hannöverische Aufstellung bei Merxleben

The Battle of Langensalza. The frontal advance of the Prussian army against the Hanoverian defensive position at Merxleben.

the Cambridge Dragoons, and the Queen's Hussars).[59] It was one of the most interesting tactical moments of the late nineteenth century. The infantry managed to form "square," actually two large, irregular clumps of manpower, but presenting enough of a firing line to give the cavalry a taste of the needle gun. The *Gardes du Corps* rode against the western square, the 2nd Squadron against its "front," the 3rd against its eastern corner, and the 1st echeloned to the right rear. A series of well-timed volleys drove the 3rd Squadron off to the left, the other two to the right. The *Gardes'* casualties amounted to eighteen men and forty-two horses in just a few minutes. The eastern square, after receiving and rejecting a Hanoverian demand to surrender, had to ward off an attack by the Guards Cuirassiers from the north, and then the Cambridge Dragoons from the south. Prussian fire managed to drive the Cuirassiers off to the left, but a portion of the charge ripped through a corner of the square, springing several dozen Prussian soldiers from its protection. Scarcely a minute later, the Cambridge Dragoons struck from the south. Attacking "with great valor,"[60] they broke through the square altogether. Although the Prussians managed to re-form it almost immediately, a considerable number of prisoners fell into Hanoverian hands. The Cuirassiers then struck again, from the north, although this time they had little success. With each blow, infantry fire dealt out considerable punishment, and eventually the cavalry attacks on this brutally hot day petered out. The Prussians continued their retreat, and the Hanoverians ruled the field. Losses on both sides had been significant: the Prussians had suffered 845 casualties and had lost another 878 prisoners; Hanoverian losses numbered 1,429.

Most historians see Langensalza as a pointless battle. Flies was a fool to attack, they say, and George and the Hanoverians had no strategic options even after their victory. On the very day after the battle, in fact, Falckenstein's army arrived in force. The Hanoverians had to continue to retreat in the only available direction, east, but they were literally surrounded by Prussian-controlled railways. Without hope of reinforcement or a linkup with the Bavarians, George V surrendered his army at Nordhausen. It was June 29. Hanover handed back its Prussian prisoners just two days after taking them.

In fact, Flies's decision to attack was absolutely predictable. It was the Prussian way, dating back to the Great Elector, to attack the enemy whenever and wherever he presented himself. Other kingdoms and other armies might coolly add up the odds, deciding on a course of action based on a head- or gun-count of the enemy, the terrain, or the overall strategic situation. The Prussian officer was expected to attack. As Frederick the Great had stated on numerous occasions, the Prussian army always attacked, even when the odds seemed to be against it. The Great Elector at Fehrbellin, Frederick at Kolin, L'Estocq at Eylau: the history of the Prussian army is studded with these events.

Nor was it entirely without positive effect. It was precisely this reputation for aggression, Hans Delbrück once argued, that kept neighboring powers in a constant state of anxiety about going to war with Prussia and made them commit errors in operations and combat once they did. By any conventional reckoning, Flies may indeed have made the most stupendously wrong-headed decision of all time. He may indeed have been one of those "bad generals" who clog the pages of military history, and he had suffered a bloody defeat for his troubles. Nevertheless, any close reading of Prussian military history tells us that his decision to attack was entirely in keeping with the aggressive nature of Prussian military operations as they had evolved over time. Viewing the attack at Langensalza as a mistake ignores the Prussian military culture that nurtured such decisions. No student of nineteenth-century warfare should want to "rehabilitate" the reputation of Eduard Flies, a crusty old hussar who had only contempt for the *Landwehr* citizen-soldiers in his ranks. Criticizing him, however, is almost beside the point. In its senseless bloodletting, Langensalza was a Prussian tradition.

THE CAMPAIGN IN BOHEMIA

The main event in 1866 was the face-off with Austria for supremacy in Germany.[61] This was not the first time that Berlin and Vienna had gone to war with one another and, in a sense, both sides had it down to a drill. First, to protect his own westward flank and seize a favorable base for operations, Moltke started this war much as Frederick had started the Second Silesian War in 1744 and the Seven Years' War in 1756, and the same way that Brunswick had started the war of 1806 with Napoleon: with an invasion and occupation of Saxony. As in 1756, the Saxon army retreated before *force majeure*, moving south and east and linking up with the Austrians. Second, Prussia mobilized and deployed three separate armies along the Austrian border, outside the Bohemian-Moravian arc, creating an initial situation map that appears almost identical to Frederick the Great's invasion of Bohemia in 1757.[62]

Moltke's initial deployment generated a great deal of comment from contemporary analysts—and continues to do so. In a sense, it was an inversion of Napoleonic warfare. Rather than employing "interior lines," Moltke was using his rail net to operate on "exterior lines," keeping the armies well separated, with the only possibility of uniting them being a concentric advance into enemy territory. There was no shortage of dissenting voices in the Prussian command warning of the dangers of Moltke's heresy. To Moltke, however, an initial concentration of all available Prussian forces was simply not in the cards. The layout of the rail net and the conformation of the border virtually demanded the initial separation of the armies. The latter factor had also been at work in 1757.

The initial deployment, then, would find the Elbe Army (General Karl Herwarth von Bittenfeld) overrunning Saxony and forming the right wing of the Prussian advance at Torgau; 1st Army (under Prince Frederick Charles, the king's nephew) was in the center, deployed at Görlitz in Lusatia; and finally 2nd Army (under the crown prince, Frederick William) on the left, at Glatz in Silesia. Rather than the lightning blow that had been such a prominent feature of previous Austro-Prussian campaigns, the political situation meandered on the brink of war for months during the spring of 1866, and both sides had a great deal of time first to deploy, then to redeploy. As the crisis dragged on, with King Wilhelm hemming and hawing about war with

Austria, Moltke tightened up his line a bit: both Elbe and 1st Armies carried out a shift to their left, reducing the gap with 2nd Army from 270 miles to just 210.[63]

Likewise, when Austrian deployment patterns became clearer, the Prussians changed theirs again. The Austrian commander, *Feldzeug-meister* Ludwig Benedek, had deployed his Army of the North in a most orthodox way: assembling it in one great mass around the town of Olmütz in Moravia. The chief Austrian threat now lay to the east, King Wilhelm felt, and at his urging Moltke shifted the crown prince's 2nd Army farther to the east, from Glatz to Neisse, to cover the crucial industrial region of Upper Silesia. In addition, the crown prince found his command beefed up, first with the addition of I Corps, then with the Guards Corps, both of which moved over from 1st Army.

Moltke's plan for the Bohemian campaign was little more than a sketch. As operations commenced, Elbe Army (forty-six thousand men) and 1st Army (ninety-three thousand men, three infantry and one cavalry corps) would sweep into western Bohemia from the west and north, respectively. They would link up on the Iser River, where he believed they would meet stiff Austrian resistance, since the Iser formed one of the few defensible positions in this corner of Bohemia. To the east, the four corps of 2nd Army (Guards, I, V, and VI) would have the unenviable task of crossing the wall of the *Riesengebirge* (literally, the "Giant Mountains"), heading almost due west toward a linkup with the two armies to the west. Geography demanded that one corps at a time would have to cross the mountains at four widely separated passes, and there were certainly some nervous stomachs at 2nd Army headquarters at the prospect. Hitting a march column as it straggles out of the mountains has traditionally been the easiest maneuver in the playbook of a competent military force—it remained to be seen whether the Austrians qualified. Once through the mountains, 2nd Army would have a long march, indeed, heading toward a rendezvous with Elbe and 1st Armies at Gitschin. In fact, the march demands on 2nd Army throughout the campaign would be prodigious. After their shift to the east toward Neisse, they would have a long way to go to the west merely to reach their crossing points.

It is hard to find a starker contrast in modern war than the operational plans of the two sides. Moltke's directives were utterly flexible: advance in a concentric fashion, find the Austrian main body, fix it in place wherever it happened to be, then effect a junction of all three Prussian armies to destroy it. If it lay to the east, Frederick William would pin it, while Elbe and 1st Armies slammed into its left flank; if it lay to the west, the latter two armies would hold it in place for a killing blow from 2nd Army. It was a simple, but effective concept, that would not require much in the way of fine tuning or close control from the center, two things that Moltke felt were impossible in any event.

By contrast, Benedek didn't seem to know what he wanted to do. The original deployment in Olmütz threatened a vital Prussian province, and Moltke had responded to it. The concentration of Austrian forces—at a time when the Prussians were still sorting themselves at their widely dispersed railheads—offered Benedek a chance to launch an invasion of Prussia, but he didn't take it. Secondarily, it offered him the opportunity to hit the first Prussian force that came within his reach a concentrated blow—that would be 2nd Army. He didn't take that, either. Instead, having found to his consternation that the Prussians had deployed major strength on his far western flank, he now launched his entire North Army—whose concentration at Olmütz had been laborious and not without problems of administration and supply —on a long flank march to the west. Out of Moravia and into Bohemia it crawled, a hard march in relentlessly scorching heat through some rough and even desolate country. His supply systems broke down almost immediately. It is no exaggeration to say that Benedek's sudden lurch to the left helped to break the Habsburg Army, never a cohesive institution under the best of circumstances, even before it met the Prussians.[64]

The war in Bohemia opened with a series of sharp engagements along the line of the *Riesengebirge*. As isolated corps of 2nd Army came through the mountains, Benedek dispatched individual corps from his flank march to stop them. There were times when the entire North Army was within marching distance of a single Prussian corps, a lucrative operational target for the Austrians. With a level of determination that has continued to provide fodder for his critics, Benedek forswore the opportunity to win any such victory and doggedly continued the march to his left. Meanwhile, the pace of the march slowed, straggling increased, and the centrifugal forces of the multinational Habsburg Army increased.

This is not to say that Frederick William had an easy time getting over the passes. Benedek might not have been a hard charger, but many of his corps commanders were. In all these crossing battles— Nachod and Trautenau on June 27, Burkersdorf (Soor) and Skalitz on June 28—Austrian infantry formed up into dense columns and charged the first Prussian unit they met.[65] Such "shock tactics" (*Stosstaktik*) had been the Austrian army's response to the defeat of 1859.[66] Blamed on a passive defensive doctrine that allowed fast-moving French columns to dictate the pace of the engagement, shock arguably made sense for a low-cohesion, polyglot, largely peasant army.[67] In a sense, the best remedy for its internal weaknesses was to group every last man together and send them at the enemy.

In fact, shock would have made almost perfect sense against any European army except the one that the Austrians were facing. They charged forward in deep battalion columns with fifty-man frontages, and again and again were torn apart by volleys of Prussian fire. In virtually every one of these early encounters, Austrian losses were four to five times those of the Prussians: at Nachod, 5,719 to 1,122; at Trautenau 4,787 to 1,339; at Burkersdorf, 3,819 to 713; and at Skalitz, 5,577 to 1,367.[68] In all of them, the Austrians left huge numbers of dead and wounded on the field who fell into Prussian hands, and numerous unwounded prisoners who surrendered rather than try their luck against the needle gun. Finally, in one case where the Austrians did succeed in throwing back the Prussians, at Trautenau, the victory was utterly without strategic issue. General Ludwig Gablenz's X Corps managed to force back the Prussian I Corps of General Adolf von Bonin, and suffered heavy losses in doing so. Gablenz then had no choice but to retreat, however, for fear of being cut off from Benedek's main body as it made its way slowly to the left.

Similar disasters occurred to the west, where the Austrians were unable to hold the Iser line. At Münchengrätz on June 28, the I Austrian Corps (General Eduard Clam-Gallas) and its Saxon allies (under the command of Saxon Crown Prince Albert) came under attack by the combined forces of Frederick Charles and General Herwarth. In the first of numerous such instances, Frederick Charles simply ignored Moltke's directive to proceed at all speed to the east to bring relief to the 2nd Army, currently under a great deal of pressure to its front. Moltke could advise and recommend, but he could not command. Rather than hurry east, Frederick Charles changed direction to the south, hoping to pin a *Kesselschlacht* on the Austro-Saxon forces in conjunction with a frontal assault by General Herwarth's Elbe Army coming from the west. The timing of the blow misfired and there was no battle of encirclement. But once again, Austrian casualties had been huge, and they had failed even to defend themselves in place. Nor did Clam-Gallas and Crown Prince Albert have much better luck when attacked at Gitschin on June 29. Here, a well-handled Prussian attack drove the allies from an extremely strong defensive position on the heights north and west of the town.

Indeed, after the first week of fighting, the entire Austrian position in Bohemia was in shreds. Two of the three Prussian armies were now operating side by side, and although the situation map showed several corps arrayed in front of 2nd Army, many of them were in fact the shaken and understrength remnants of corps that had tried to oppose Frederick William's entry into Bohemia. Even when the two sides had blundered into one another, Prussian tactical superiority had been nearly absolute. It wasn't just the needle gun, but the Prussian ability to maneuver in smaller units, especially their nimble company columns—a product of the greater time and money the Prussians spent on peacetime drill and field exercises.[69]

Benedek now made the controversial decision to concentrate his main body near Sadowa, west of the Elbe. It was about time, certainly. There had been at least six major engagements, and the North Army had not seen any action at all, although individual corps had engaged the Prussians. If the timing was right, however, the exact spot was much more problematic. It does not require a degree in higher strategy to realize the difficulties in defending with a major river at one's back. That was precisely the situation here, however. If North Army had to retreat at any point, it would essentially have to do so over a single Elbe river bridge toward the fortress of Königgrätz.

At Sadowa, Benedek had his engineers hastily prepare a position on the Chlum Heights, just behind the tiny Bistritz (Bystrice) River. With its center on Chlum, and both of its wings bent back, the position resembled a horseshoe with its center curved out toward the enemy and its wings drawn back. There have been analysts who have criticized it, since a retreat on either wing could potentially lead to catastrophe, but in the age of rifles and long-range weapons, armies have shown themselves able to hold elevated positions in a variety of unusual shapes.[70] Just three years earlier, in fact, the Union army had managed to do just fine in one of the strangest lines of all time—the famous "fishhook" at Gettysburg.

As in all campaigns of the era, intelligence was not simply imperfect, but more like nonexistent. On July 1, Moltke was still not sure where Benedek's main body actually was. The absence of pursuit after each battle meant a breaking of contact between the hostile armies. On July 2, Frederick Charles solved the mystery, when his cavalry literally bumped into the Sadowa position in the early evening. He now did three things. First, he decided, on his own initiative and following the long-standing Prussian tradition, to launch an attack on the Austrian army at 10:00 A.M. the next morning. It was clear that he was facing a huge force, but that had rarely stopped Prussia's great captains of the past. Second, he notified his neighboring army commanders: telling Herwarth on his right to ready Elbe Army for an advance to the Bistritz, and sending a dispatch to the crown prince at 2nd Army headquarters at Köninghof, asking him to send at least a corps to support the attack. Third, almost an afterthought, he informed Moltke of what he had just done.[71]

Moltke had by this time left Berlin for the front, since he was finding it difficult to impose his will on his subordinates at such a great distance. Along with Bismarck and the king, he was now at Gitschin. Lieutenant General Konstantin von Voigts-Rhetz, 1st Army's chief of staff, brought him the message in the night. Moltke immediately realized the significance of the news—and the opportunity that beckoned. "Gott sei Dank!" he is supposed to have cried as he rose from his bed.[72] He now drafted two short orders: one to the crown prince, telling him to send not just a corps but to move "with all forces against the right flank of the presumed enemy order of battle, attacking him as soon as possible";[73] and one to Frederick Charles, ordering him to attack earlier in the morning, to pin Benedek in place until 2nd Army could arrive to destroy him.

What happened next would become the stuff of Prussian military legend. The attack went in at 8:00 A.M. in a heavy rain, with 1st Army driving directly over the Bistritz in a frontal assault, and the Elbe Army hitting the Austrian left flank, defended largely by the Saxon Army under Crown Prince Albert in the position between the villages of Problus and Nieder-Prim. South of Nieder-Prim, the Saxon line trailed off into air, and an attack might have offered rich prospects, but the very small Elbe Army was not the force to take advantage of it. Herwarth would eventually turn Albert's left flank late in the afternoon, but the Prussians had already won the battle elsewhere. The situation was far different in the center. Here, 1st Amy's advance bogged down almost immediately in the face of Austrian fire. Rifled artillery on the Chlum Heights—firing from elevated terrain and prepared shelters, with aiming points and range fixed well in advance—silenced the Prussian batteries over the Bistritz, and then began methodically chewing up the infantry. For seven hours, 1st Army was pinned in a killing ground between the Bistritz and Chlum, the men lying in the mud and rain, finding it difficult either to advance or to retreat.

The king was now present with 1st Army, and from his perch on the Roskosberg just northwest of Sadowa, the old soldier knew that he was looking at trouble. "Moltke, Moltke, we are losing the battle,"

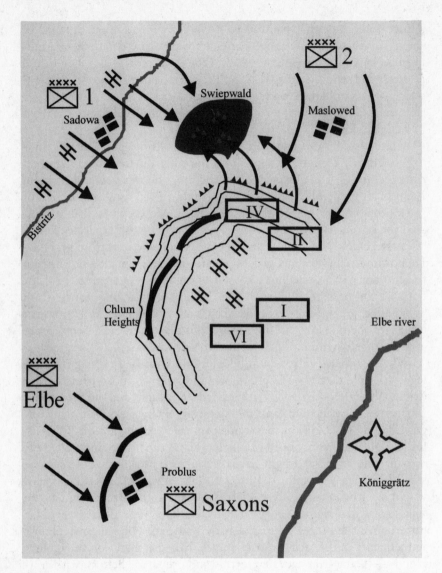

Moltke's Masterpiece: Königgrätz, July 3, 1866

the king told his chief of staff. There are witnesses who heard Moltke calmly disagree. "Your majesty will today win not only the battle but the campaign," he is supposed to have said.[74] Other stories, far more improbable, have him actually delivering a stern pep talk to the king: "This is about Prussia's very existence!" ("Hier geht es um Preus-

PRINCE FREDERICK CHARLES OF PRUSSIA

Prince Frederick Charles of Prussia, the "Red Prince." His bold attack against an Austrian army twice his size began the battle of Königgrätz.

sen!").[75] His exact words notwithstanding, Moltke does seem to have remained calm during what must have been a long morning.

It was command problems that would eventually sink the Austrians. The two formations on the Austrian right wing, the IV Corps under Tassilo Count Festetics de Tolna, and II Corps under Karl Count von Thun-Hohenstedt, spent the first few hours of the battle puzzling over their mission. Benedek had them in place to handle the Prussian 2nd Army, if and when it should arrive. He had not told them that, however. In fact, he had not apprised any of his corps commanders of the overall operational situation, even though he had called them together for a "council of war" the night before.[76] By midmorning, an increasingly restive Festetics looked down to the battlefield and could clearly see Prussian forces moving into the Swiepwald, a sturdy patch of forest a mile long and half-mile deep on 1st Army's left. These were troops of the Prussian 7th Division, under General Eduard von Fransecky. He was attempting to use the Swiepwald as an assembly point where his brigades could shelter and organize themselves to resume their advance toward Chlum. This represented a clear danger to the Austrian position, and Festetics reacted by wheeling his corps from the north to the west and advancing into the Swiepwald. Thun, whose vague orders were firm on only one point—that he was to remain aligned with IV Corps—dragged his corps along. Soon both IV and II Corps were engaged in a confused, close-range fight in the forest with the Prussian infantry, and suffering horrible casualties from the fire of the needle gun.[77]

It might seem that a supreme commander like Benedek would have parked himself in some good vantage point where he could survey most of the action. In fact, that had become nearly impossible because of the size of the forces engaged—over four hundred thousand men between the two armies—and the immense sprawl of the battlefield. He spent most of the day riding at top speed from point to point, outpacing his aides and his staff, and was repeatedly missing when an important decision was required. Still, sometime around noon, Benedek discovered what had happened, and sent orders to his two corps to return to their start line. By this time, however, it was simply impossible. Both corps were far too heavily engaged.

This was the situation when Prussian 2nd Army began arriving on the field after midday. Believing that his two corps had returned to their original position, he met the news with calm, a calm that was shattered the next moment when Festetics's chief of staff arrived to argue *against* pulling out of the Swiepwald. The attack by Prussian 2nd Army, spearheaded by the elite Guard Corps, therefore, caught II and IV Corps still facing to the west. It hit Benedek's position not in the right wing, but in an open, dangling flank. The Guards drove into Maslowed village at 1:00 P.M., then charged up the Chlum Heights by 2:00 P.M., overrunning the guns there, scattering the Austrian reserves, and actually dispersing Benedek's headquarters with wild volleys of needle gun fire. It is always difficult to explain exactly why an army breaks, but the storming of Chlum seemed to have done it for the Austrians. Benedek himself was, as usual, not present, and he greeted

The crown prince of Prussia, Frederick William, an army commander in the wars with Austria and France and later, for an all-too-brief period, Kaiser Frederick III.

the news that Prussian Guardsmen were in his headquarters with a shocked, "Quit talking rubbish—that's impossible!"[78] An hour ago, he might have won a decisive victory over the Prussian 1st Army; certainly there was no shortage of corps commanders demanding that Benedek set them loose in a counterattack against the sorely pressed Prussian troops directly in front of them. That moment had passed, however, and now another Prussian army had suddenly appeared, moving and firing at full throttle. The Austrian formations in and around Chlum came apart, and the men were fleeing south in confusion. There was one abortive counterattack at 3:30 P.M., by Austrian VI and I Corps, but Prussian rifle fire shattered it before it even got moving.

By 5:00 P.M. it was all over. Benedek's army was streaming away to the south in some confusion, desperately trying to get across the Elbe River into Königgrätz. It is often said that a brave rearguard action by the Austrian cavalry helped to save the army. Recent research has exploded it as a myth. The Austrians did engage their heavy cavalry for the purpose of a rear guard, but it was pounded mercilessly by Prussian artillery, now firing south from Chlum, as well as rifle fire. It wasn't the Austrian cavalry that saved the remnants of North Army. It was, as always in the nineteenth century, the inability of the victor to pursue. Even without the pursuit, however, it had certainly been bad enough for North Army. Austrian and Saxon losses topped forty-four thousand men, including some twenty thousand prisoners of war. Prussian casualties totaled nine thousand men, the vast majority from 1st Army's very difficult frontal attack.

1866: OBSERVATIONS

It is not necessary to romanticize any of this, or to use the victory to make specious claims for Moltke's infallibility. Luck had played a leading role in the triumph. During the ride home from Königgrätz, an aide turned to Bismarck and said: "Your excellency, now you are a great man. If the crown prince had arrived too late, you would be the greatest villain."[79] That judgment applies even more directly to Moltke. Indeed, if Frederick William had arrived even a single hour later, Moltke might be sitting where Benedek is today: in front of the bar of history answering some very difficult questions. A huge number of things had gone wrong in the course of the campaign, including the virtual collapse of the entire Prussian supply net. The bread supply for the entire 1st Army, for example, was being baked in Berlin.[80] It had to compete with other pressing needs for space on the Prussian rails, and usually lost. Prussian logistics throughout the campaign were even worse than Benedek's, which is saying something.

Still, Königgrätz was the most decisive battle of the era and deserves close scrutiny. The only problem is that many of the analytical tools used to explain it are less useful than they might at first appear. Many point to the concept of *Auftragstaktik* (or "flexible command") as a key to the victory, but that is hard to accept. The Bohemian campaign was an example of *Auftragstaktik* only if having subordinate commanders

General Albrecht von Manstein. "This is all very good," he declared as a divisional commander at Königgrätz, "but who is General Moltke?"

ignore your directives, march south when you've distinctly ordered them to march east, and treat you with barely disguised contempt are truly a form of "flexible command." Frederick Charles of the 1st Army, for example, had no understanding at all of Moltke's strategy, didn't much like the parts he did understand, and was loath to follow anything but a direct order from his uncle, the king. He dawdled when Moltke ordered him to move, turned away to attack the Austrian forces at Münchengrätz when he was supposed to be heading east to the succor of the 2nd Army, and launched an attack on Benedek that some analysts still see as premature. Divisional commander Albrecht von Manstein's single entry into the list of famous military quotations, "This is all very good, but who is General Moltke?" was as much a snort of contempt as it was a question born of ignorance.[81]

Likewise, the term *Kesselschlacht* ("the battle of encirclement") appears often in analysis of the battle. What happened at Königgrätz was many things, but a *Kesselschlacht* it was not. No one was encircled. A true battle of encirclement might have found 2nd Army remaining on the left bank of the Elbe and coming up from the south to hit Benedek's rear or cut off his line of retreat. Given the foot speed of a great nineteenth-century army, as well as its immense supply requirements, such a thing would have been plainly impossible. Instead, 2nd Army had made a relatively short sweep, with its right wing coming up against 1st Army's left. Under ordinary conditions, Frederick William's advance should have struck Benedek's right wing, not his open flank. The shocking level of command confusion within the Austrian camp, with the guilt shared by Benedek and his corps commanders alike, had made it much worse than it should have been.

Even if we dispense with the buzzwords, however, Moltke's victory at Königgrätz was the most impressive battlefield achievement from the Napoleonic era to World War II. He deserved every one of the accolades that he received. He had devised a simple, sound operational framework, not a plan, but a sketch, based on a clear-headed analysis of the strengths and weaknesses of contemporary armies, as well as his insight into the difficulties of commanding mass armies in the field. As the campaign unfolded, he had altered his vision as circumstance and opportunity dictated. He had given his subordinate army commanders a huge amount of leeway, and although he and they made several miscalculations and mistakes, when the time came, he managed to direct the crucial maneuvers of the campaign, bending it, just barely, to his will. In battle, he had persevered through the difficult morning in front of the Chlum Heights, coolly watching what looked like a disaster in the making, no doubt casting the occasional anxious glance to the northeast to look for signs of the crown prince, yet still displaying admirable calmness under fire. It may not have been a *Kesselschlacht*, but Königgrätz was still very, very impressive.

He had not invented a new way of war. There is a clear conceptual link between Moltke's conduct of the 1866 campaign and earlier Prussian traditions. It is *Bewegungskrieg*, the "short and lively" war of movement on the operational level. The armies had grown exponentially in size, the supply requirements more onerous, the weaponry more terrible, but in the end, Moltke was still prosecuting war the way Frederick the Great had: trying and usually succeeding in getting onto the flank or rear of the enemy force, hitting him with unexpected blows from seemingly impossible directions. Although the lag in mobilization at the start of the campaign had Moltke first thinking about defense, that spell lasted for only a brief moment. The Prussian army always attacked, not in a purely tactical sense (although it was often true there, as well), but on the operational level. It was a recipe so ingrained in Prussian officers that it might no longer have been conscious.

As always in Prussia's wars, the pace had to be quick. In 1866, Prussia fought two wars: one big one, involving most of the army, against Austria and its Saxon ally; and one small one, involving pocket-sized forces on each side, against the smaller German states. The war in central Germany had to go first and end quickly, so that Prussia's main armies could proceed without worries about their flanks or communications. Likewise, the campaign against Austria had to be over before neighboring powers like Russia or France began to get nervous about what a Prussian victory might do to the balance of power. As always in the Prussian tradition, Moltke was a man in a hurry.

A final word about Frederick Charles is in order. For most historians, the "Red Prince" is either Moltke's nemesis or the comic relief of the campaign. No great military intellectual, he seemed particularly at sea for much of it. On the march, he formed his huge army into a relatively compact mass, with cavalry deployed in the rear, ready to deliver the final charge in battle.[82] As a result he marched much more slowly than he might, and with no reconnaissance arm out in front of his main body, he rarely had any idea what he was facing. Moltke's repeated admonitions to him to hurry to ease the pressure on 2nd Army had no effect at all. In the battle itself, historians have often accused him of attacking too early, before 2nd Army was within safe distance, and therefore courting disaster.

But just as Moltke had been crucial to the success of the operation, so too had Frederick Charles. It was a simple thing he did: daring to launch an attack on a huge enemy force, twice his size, in fact. He was able to survive for the better part of a day against heavy odds, and in the process he attracted more and more attention from neighboring Austrian corps, luring them forward into the Swiepwald and paving the way for the crown prince's arrival. Hans Delbrück, certainly no friend of the officer corps, made this very point, arguing that Frederick Charles's gamble on that sticky July morning had been in the best Prussian tradition of boldness, "which, by daring to lose a battle, wins it."[83]

The Franco-Prussian War[84]

Another analytical tool for 1866, Moltke's use of "exterior lines," also requires qualification. Certainly, it is a fair description of the König-grätz campaign, and Moltke himself used the term in his theoretical writings. Before we can speak of exterior lines as part of a "Moltkean system," however, we must take into account the war with France, especially the opening campaign of 1870. Here, we find a very different war. Rather than the dispersed deployments of the Bohemian campaign, we see a close-order assembly of three full armies, a veritable phalanx. In his winter 1868–1869 *Denkschrift* that formed the basis for operations in 1870, Moltke identified the primary task as interposing his main strength between "two French forces at Strasbourg and Metz, separated by the Vosges mountains." In other words, he intended to exploit interior, not exterior lines: "In the Palatinate we will stand on the inner operational line between both enemy groupings."[85] On the tactical level, too, this war was quite a bit different from the last one. Rather than a reliance on the superior fire of the needle gun, the guar-antor of victory in 1866 no matter what the Austrians tried to do, the Prussian infantry would have to struggle forward against the finest breech-loading rifle of the day, the French Chassepot, not to mention the primitive machine gun known as the *mitrailleuse*. For Moltke, war in the real world always took precedence over war in theory.

Both sides began their mobilization in mid-July, and by the end of the month, a combination of careful planning by Moltke's staff and the highly developed Prussian rail net had resulted in the assembly of more than four hundred thousand men. Deployed in the Bavarian Palatinate along the border of French Lorraine, this mass was organized into three armies: the small 1st Army, under General Karl von Stein-metz, was on the right at Trier; 2nd Army, under Frederick Charles, stood between Mainz and Kaisersläutern; and 3rd Army, under Crown Prince Frederick Wilhelm, was between Landau and Karlsruhe. The last was a sign of the new times. With Prussia now the dominant power in Germany, and German nationalism aroused by the war with France, two of the four corps in Frederick William's command were Bavarian (I and II Bavarian Corps, thoroughly reorganized along Prussian lines between 1866 and 1870), and there were also individual divisions from Baden and Württemberg in his force. It was not, strictly speaking, a Franco-Prussian war, but a Franco-German one.

Moltke had no firm plan for the operation against France. He never had one for any of his campaigns. In directives to the General Staff on

May 5, 1870, he played it close to the vest, speaking only of "several marches into the French interior in the general direction of Paris in order to bring about a battle with the enemy army."[86] His posthumously published history of the war went much further, claiming that "from the start the plan of campaign had the capture of the enemy capital in view. Along the way we intended to drive enemy forces away from the fertile southern regions towards the leaner hinterland in the north,"[87] although this may well be dressing up the matter in hindsight.

It is safe to say that he envisioned the centrally located 2nd Army advancing against the French main body—the "Army of the Rhine," it was called, optimistically—and pinning it in place, most likely with the assistance of 1st Army. As at Königgrätz, Frederick William would then have an opportunity to come up on the extreme right flank of the French force and destroy it. It was possible that Steinmetz might also play a flanking role against the French left, leading to a double envelopment. Or perhaps the situation would be reversed, with the crown prince pinning and 2nd Army landing the telling blow. Then again, one or both of the main armies could drive toward Paris and get astride the French lines of communication, literally forcing the French to attack to open their supply lines. With Moltke's armies operating independently, ready to be brought together or dispersed as the situation changed, any number of things were possible, and indeed he had mentioned all of these possibilities and more in either staff talks or planning documents. The rapid Prussian mobilization, with three concentrated armies facing individual French corps that were still being formed into armies as the fighting began, gave him even more options. The fact that the French opened operations on August 2 by actually advancing toward Saarbrücken—roughly into the center of the Prussian position, seemed to be offering him an operational target on a platter. He would simply have to wait and see.

FRONTIER BATTLES

The first major encounter of the war, at Wissembourg (Weissenburg), set the tone for all those to follow.[88] The crown prince and his trusted chief of staff, General Albrecht von Blumenthal, put 3rd Army on the road early on the morning of August 4. They would cross the Lauter River, the French border, and begin what promised to be a long march to the west. In the van would be the II Bavarian Corps, under General von Hartmann. The sector was the operational responsibility of the French I Corps, under Marshal Patrice MacMahon. He had his four infantry divisions drawn up in an arrangement that has puzzled analysts ever since, an irregular square, with its points at Hagenau (3rd Division plus corps headquarters), Froeschwiller (1st Division), Lembach (4th Division), and Wissembourg (2nd Division). The 2nd Division and its commander, General Abel Douay, were "on point," in a sense. They were about to get hit by an entire enemy corps. MacMahon's three neighboring divisions were deployed too far apart, at least twenty miles, for mutual support.

The battle opened at 8:00 A.M., with the 4th Bavarian Division attempting to cross the river directly opposite the old walled town of Wissembourg and getting drilled by murderous French fire. It was a shocking introduction to the Chassepot. In every way—accuracy, striking power, and especially range—it outclassed the needle gun. Faced by a solid line of French (and Algerian) rifles stretching from Wissembourg to the town of Altenstadt on the right, and then back to the Geisberg Castle, a considerable number of Bavarian troops decided they'd had enough for the day, either filtering away to the rear or settling into whatever cover they could find for a long stay. The French probably could have charged out and swept them from the field altogether, but adhered to a rigid defensive doctrine. They did not maneuver, but simply shot. Eventually, the Prussians managed to wheel up some of their artillery, rifled steel guns from the firm of Krupp. They were a crucial addition to the Prussian order of battle since that horrible morning on July 3, 1866, when Austrian guns on the Chlum Heights had had their way with the Prussian infantry. Soon, Wissembourg was on fire and the defenders, too, had their share of men drifting to the rear.

The 4th Bavarian Division had failed, but it was not alone. By 10:30 A.M., the spearheads of two more of Frederick William's corps had arrived on the field: the 9th Division (of V Corps) and the 21st Division (XI Corps). The 9th Division outflanked Altenstadt and then Wissembourg to the right, while the 21st drove into the deep right flank and rear of the French position toward the Geisberg castle. The French position simply cracked apart, although there was some hard street fighting in Wissembourg and a true melee in the castle. With more Prussian troops arriving by the hour, eventually comprising the entire V and XI Corps, the 2nd Division had no choice but to retreat. There certainly was no shame in that: by now, seven thousand Frenchmen were facing fifty thousand Germans. The Prussians scratched a division off the French order of battle and resumed their advance the next day.

Meanwhile, action had already begun to unfold to the north. Here, both Steinmetz and Frederick Charles had observed the French ad-

General Karl von Steinmetz, commander of Prussian 1st Army in the war with France. His unauthorized southward advance led his army directly into the path of the neighboring 2nd and nearly unhinged Moltke's entire operational scheme.

vance toward Saarbrücken, and then—with amazement—a French retirement. Apparently the advance had been intended to satisfy Parisian public opinion and quiet doubts about Napoleon III's generalship. As the French retreated, however, the wheels nearly came off the entire Prussian operational scheme. General von Steinmetz feared that there would be a loss of contact with the French, as had happened so often in

1866—he had commanded the Prussian V Corps at Skalitz—and was determined not to let that happen. Rather than advance to the southwest, as headquarters had directed, he now ordered his two corps (VII and VIII) to advance almost due south, that is, directly into the path of the neighboring 2nd Army moving up from the east.

If there had been a true French intent to attack at this point, we might still be sorting out the traffic jam that resulted from two nineteenth-century armies and their entire supply trains suddenly hitting the same crossroads. Interestingly enough, despite the hand-wringing of analysts and historians on this singular event, Steinmetz wasn't immediately dismissed. One staff officer at Prussian headquarters in Mainz wrote that Moltke was "beginning to regret [Steinmetz's] appointment," hardly fighting words.[89] In fact, this is how operational-level command in the Prussian army operated, and how it always would operate. If the enemy was there, you attacked him and waited for neighboring divisions, corps, and armies to march to the sound of the guns. The angriest officer was probably Frederick Charles of the 2nd Army, but only because he, too, was itching to get at the French.

On August 6, the Prussian 14th Division (VII Corps of Steinmetz's army) crossed the Saar River and attacked the French in an extremely strong position near Spichern.[90] Fittingly, the divisional commander, General Kameke, had requested permission to attack from Steinmetz. It was, in many ways, a repeat of Wissembourg. There was the same shock at the horrible impact of French rifle fire, with Prussian soldiers repeatedly being shot from what they regarded as impossible ranges. There was the same murderous effectiveness of the Prussian artillery, the great equalizer in this war. Finally there were the same French passivity and the same inexorable Prussian flanking maneuvers, which simply stretched the French line until it broke.

The odds this time had been even worse for the Prussians. The 14th Division had taken on the entire French II Corps, under General Charles Frossard, one division against three. Those three, moreover, were deployed along a line of hills known as the Spichern heights, a "tremendous natural wall,"[91] between Forbach in the west and Spichern in the east. Sometimes running to the perpendicular, it was one of the strongest natural positions in this corner of France.[92] Frossard's three divisions lay abreast: his right was anchored by 3rd Division (General Laveaucoupet) on the Red Mountain (Rother Berg) north of Spichern; his center at Stiring by 1st Division (General Vergé); and his left by 2nd Division (General Bataille). The first wave of attackers, the 27th Infantry Brigade from Kameke's division, hit a wall of lead in its initial rush toward the Rother Berg, and nothing Kameke did could get it moving again. Prussian artillery came forward and began dealing out horrible punishment to the French in their trenches, but Kameke's attempt to insert his other brigade (the 28th) ran into the same blizzard of Chassepot fire.

Masses of both French and Prussian forces lay in the vicinity of Spichern. To the east, only seven miles from Frossard's right, lay the III French Corps of Marshal Bazaine, and just passing through to the northeast were the forces of both Steinmetz's 1st and Frederick Charles's 2nd Army, their units inextricably intertwined in that great traffic snarl at Saarbrücken. Predictably, it was the Prussian generals who marched to the sound of gunfire, as both generals engaged in a race to reinforce Kameke's lone division at Spichern: Steinmetz rushing his VIII Corps into action, Frederick Charles his III. Perhaps it is more accurate to say that random elements of both corps arrived on the field by late afternoon, a battalion and a battery at a time. The pressure of their numbers eventually began to tell, and the constant pounding of the Krupp guns also had its effect on French morale. By contrast, Bazaine did not decide to march to Frossard's relief until quite late in the day, and his lead units arrived just in time to crash into a wave of demoralized units falling back from Spichern. It had been a tough, firepower-intensive battle, and it had taken more than five thousand Prussian casualties, the vast majority from Kameke's division, to lever the French off the Spichern Heights. French losses were lower, some four thousand, but still significant, with casualties from artillery predominating, the pattern in this war.

That same day, Frederick William's 3rd Army fought a virtually identical battle at Wörth.[93] Reassembling the army after Wissembourg, he now faced almost due south. Heading toward Strasbourg on August 6, his units crashed into the rest of MacMahon's I Corps. The French were drawn up in a north-south line running from the village of Neehwiller in the north, through the central villages of Froeschwiller and Elsasshausen, and anchored in the village of Eberbach in the south. A heavily wooded ridge, fronted by the river Sauer, with the French everywhere on the high ground, it was once again a tough nut for the Prussians to crack.

They did crack it, however, in the by now familiar pattern. As Prussian march columns made their way south, the commander of the V Corps, General Hugo von Kirchbach, took note of the French activity on his right. Not pausing to report it to headquarters, or to request permission, he simply wheeled right near the village of Wörth and at-

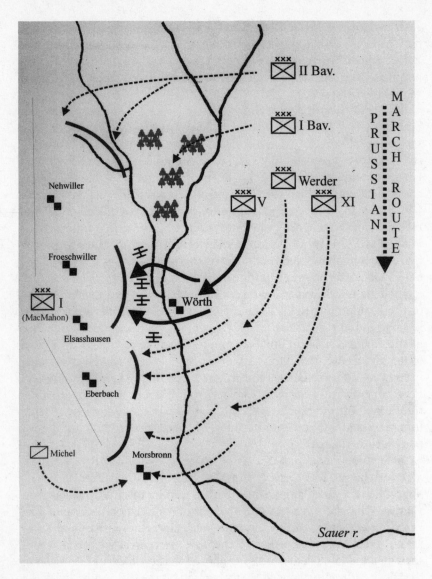

Kirchbach's Wheel: The Battle of Wörth, August 6, 1870

tacked. Frederick William and General Blumenthal alike were wary of blundering into a French trap in such difficult country and would have greatly preferred a more measured and careful approach. If so, they were in the wrong army.

Wörth was a murderous battle. Kirchbach's 10th Division was the first in, storming through Wörth and running into the standard French greeting: a hail of Chassepot fire. Casualties were enormous, and there were scenes of panic. As always, the French failed to exploit their defensive success and transform it into a counterattack. They simply kept shooting—quite well, in fact. They held their position even as the newly formed Werder Corps (comprising the two divisions from Baden and Württemberg) formed up on the left of V Corps, striking toward Elsasshausen and Eberbach, and the XI Corps came up on Werder's left. In the north, II Bavarian Army Corps arrived on the far right, thrusting toward Neehwiller. The same 4th Bavarian Division that had been so badly shot up at Wissembourg now got to take an encore and received the same treatment as in the earlier encounter. Eventually I Bavarian Corps would squeeze its way into the line between II Bavarian and V Corps. By noon, the Prussians had the defenders greatly outnumbered, an entire army of five corps facing the French I Corps. Frederick William set up a huge concentrated line of Krupp artillery, some three hundred guns, against the French center at Wörth, and the Prussians began dealing out their share of slaughter. As the immense Prussian host began lapping around both his flanks, MacMahon played his last card: a charge by the reserve cavalry, the Michel Brigade to be specific, against Morsbronn. It collapsed in an orgy of Prussian field and artillery fire—the signal for the collapse of the French position in front of Froeschwiller. It had been a savage battle, utterly without higher direction on either side. Each army suffered about eleven thousand dead and wounded, but the French collapse left some nine thousand prisoners in Prussian hands.

Was Kirchbach responsible for the high casualties in his own corps? The answer is yes. He drove his men against a firm, unshaken line of French infantry and looked on as company after company went forward bravely and vanished in a hail of enemy fire. Certainly, a better-timed and better-coordinated multicorps attack could have driven back the French with far lighter casualties, and in that sense, Kirchbach was a butcher. However, a more cautious approach would not have mauled the French I Corps in the manner it did. Moreover, Kirchbach was acting in the Prussian tradition, and he knew it. There were no repercussions for sucking 3rd Army into a battle its commanders had no intention of fighting that day, no accusations that he was somehow responsible for the lives lost. That was the way the Prussian army, more than any other army in the world, did business.

MARS-LA-TOUR

After this hectic first week, there was a lull in the fighting. All three Prussian armies had to form themselves back into march column and resume their advance into the French interior, heading west. Frederick Charles was separated from the other two armies and would have a long series of marches to get back into contact. The French Army of the Rhine, at least those parts of it that had not already been mauled in battle, were concentrated at Metz and were theoretically capable of striking a sharp blow against Prussian 1st and 2nd Armies. Command paralysis had set in, however. Napoleon III was tottering badly on his throne by now and decided to hand over the reins of supreme command. The recipient was Marshal Bazaine, a general who had proven supremely unwilling to take any action against the Prussians thus far.

The stage was set for the strangest battle of the war. It seemed to most observers that the best thing Bazaine could do was retreat from his exposed position in Metz, get back across the Moselle River, and establish himself at Paris or Chalons. In either place, he could take in reinforcements, reorganize his increasingly demoralized force, and get it back into fighting trim. Instead, he lingered for more than a week at Metz, to the amazement of Moltke and the Prussian command. Moltke now ordered all three armies to head toward Metz, a short pivot for 1st Army, forced marches for the others. As they were hurrying to the north, however, they heard bad news. On the night of August 15, Bazaine had begun his retreat toward Verdun. They were too late.

Or were they? By that evening, one Prussian formation was within striking distance of Metz. It was the spearhead of 2nd Army: Prussian III Corps under General Constantin von Alvensleben.[94] What happened should not be surprising by now. Having just crossed the Moselle River, which runs almost exactly south to north before it bends toward Metz, he could clearly see French columns retreating from Metz, moving west. Believing that Bazaine would not have waited this long to begin the retreat, a notion shared generally by the Prussian command, he thought that it had to be elements of the French rear guard. Not wanting to let it slip away, he launched an attack, without hesitation or permission from upper echelons, against the French forces opposite. This "rear guard," of course, turned out to be the main body of the Army of the Rhine, holding a line stretching from Mars-la-Tour in the west through Vionville and then to Rezonville in the east.

Alvensleben's attack was an epic moment in the history of the Prussian army, a corps taking on an army and miraculously surviving all day. In fact, it was even better than that. Alvensleben opened the at-

Lieutenant-General Konstantin von Alvensleben. At the head of III Corps, he launched a daring attack on the entire French army outside Mars-la-Tour, August 16, 1870.

tack by sending forward just a single division: the Prussian 5th under General von Stülpnagel. It drove toward Rezonville, the eastern extremity of the French position, and crashed into Frossard's II Corps, reorganized after its baptism at Spichern. Once again, Frossard's men proved they could dish out the fire, sending much of 5th Division reeling back with horrendous casualties, and pinning the rest in front of Rezonville. Alvensleben, now suspecting that there was a larger force in the neighborhood, sent in his 6th Division under General Buddenbrock, which came up on 5th Division's left. Its experience was practically identical, only here it was facing Vionville in the center of the French line, and the defenders were the French VI Corps.

Alvensleben was in trouble. Only one other major Prussian unit was over the Moselle, the X Corps. The rest of Frederick Charles's army was strung out to the south en route, too far away to help. The French III Corps, holding to the right of Vionville, was facing air. A simple approach and wheel to the east would have hit 6th Division hard and probably routed it, and there was yet another corps to its right, the IV. Geoffrey Wawro is not overstating when he calls Mars-la-Tour "a battle that the French should have won" and states that they had "the Prussians entirely at their mercy."[95]

But they didn't win. The same dynamic obtained here as in earlier battles. The French seemed satisfied to shoot whatever Prussian formation happened to appear in front of them. They made no attempt to maneuver. The Prussians gradually wheeled up the entire artillery complement of III Corps, and much of the slowly arriving X Corps as well, and established a wall of guns facing the center of the French position. The arrival of the infantry divisions of X Corps stabilized the situation, but only because the French refused to attack a force that was less than half their size. Adding a final touch of seasoning to this encounter was Bazaine's nonexistent supreme command of the French forces. In fact, he wasn't even in the midst of the battle, but on the extreme left wing at Gravelotte. He was hanging close to Metz, in other words, and preparing a retreat back to the city from the outset of the fighting. The fighting went on into the evening, and although it was a tactical draw, it had been a strategic disaster for the French. A single Prussian corps had managed to wrest away control of the road to Verdun from the entire French army.

Two moments from the battle of Mars-la-Tour would enter the lore of the Prussian-German army. The single most famous moment of the battle, and perhaps of the entire war, occurred late in the afternoon. With Alvensleben's corps mauled and barely clinging to survival, he ordered a cavalry charge by the 12th Brigade under General Friedrich Wilhelm von Bredow. The target was the gun line of the French VI Corps, which was at the time mercilessly pounding the hapless infantry of the 6th Division. Bredow launched his charge—some say reluctantly, others not—and actually managed to get forward, shrouded by the smoke of thousands of guns. One contemporary German source described Bredow's ride:

Once convinced of the necessity this general knew no hesitation, or impediment. Having at his right the three squadrons of the 16th Uhlans, under Major von Dollen, men of the Alte Mark, and to his left those of the 7th Cuirassiers, under Major von Schmettow, men of Halberstadt, he gallops across the highway up the steep path of glory. The squadrons wheel to the right, advance, and in full gallop they dash at the foe. Now their batteries are reached, and the artillerymen, amazed by this unexpected maneuver, are cut down.

He slammed into the French position, silencing the guns and hacking away at their crews, and incidentally sowing a great deal of panic in the French rear. But soon he met trouble, in a form any eighteenth-century cavalryman would have understood: "On they go to encounter a second line of infantry, but now the audacious riders get into a circle of fire, for the infantry that had been ridden through recovers again and opens fire. The much thinned squadrons are scattered by this time, the horses, after tearing along a victorious course 3000 paces long, are quite spent."[96] Indeed, it's probably not an exaggeration to say that Bredow attracted the fire of every Chassepot within range. By the time he regrouped his squadrons to return whence he had come, there wasn't much left. He returned to his start line with less than half the men who had started out, just 380 out of 800.

It was, as German officers immediately dubbed it, a "Death Ride" (*Totenritt*). As a tactical expedient, it worked, relieving the pressure on the Prussian infantry and no doubt lifting their morale. Even at the time, however, there were observers within the Prussian military establishment who pointed out that under normal circumstances of atmosphere and terrain, every single one of Bredow's troopers would have been killed long before they got to the French line—a true death ride. Even today, the argument continues, with those who argue that it proved the continued utility of cavalry on the nineteenth-century battlefield pitted against those who argue just the opposite. Frederick Charles was convinced of the former: "If instead of Bredow's one brigade, an entire division had attacked with support," he wrote, "then this attack would have been decisive."[97]

There was a second celebrated occurrence, and this one too would be a source of major postwar controversy. Late in the afternoon, the two divisions of the Prussian X Corps arrived on the field. The 20th Division formed up on Alvensleben's immediate left; the 19th Division now slid into the line to the left of the 20th. Believing that it had the French right flank, the 19th now went forward into the attack, and crashed, once again, straight into the French IV Corps (General Ladmirault). At the point of the attack was the 38th Brigade under General Wedel, who advanced with his two regiments side by side. The attack was a catastrophe, leading to the near-destruction of Wedel's Brigade—more than 2,500 casualties including seventy-two officers, in just a few minutes of combat. Recriminations over the catastrophe—who exactly ordered the brigade forward, where the divisional general was standing and what he could see from his vantage point, how General Wedel formed up the 38th for the attack, and other details besides—would feature prominently in German military literature for the next thirty years.[98] Spearheading the charge was Fritz Hoenig, who on August 16 was a lieutenant and battalion adjutant in the 19th Division. The sometimes careless manner in which he used his sources, and the arrogant and peremptory tone of the staff officers who responded to his work, kept the *Militär-Wochenblatt* lively well into the twentieth century.

ST. PRIVAT

Mars-la-Tour had been the bloodiest battle yet, with each side sustaining about fifteen thousand casualties. Although he had given as much damage as he had taken, Bazaine had nowhere to go. After pointedly inviting his officers to come up with a better idea, he retired onto the fortifications of Metz the next morning. This merely meant that there was inevitably going to be a round two, as the rest of the Prussian 1st and 2nd armies caught up with III and X Corps and arrived in front of Metz.

The battle that would be fought on August 18, just two days after Mars-la-Tour, was the most artless of Moltke's career. Although known as the battle of St. Privat, it in fact took place over much the same ground as Mars-la-Tour.[99] Indeed, the question can arise as to whether it should have been fought at all, since he had France's main field force bottled up in a fortress far too small to feed it. At its height late in the afternoon, it featured two solid and parallel lines of corps stretching north to south from St. Privat to the banks of the Moselle, five corps facing five corps. For the Prussians, moving from north to south, it was XII (Saxon), Guards, and IX Corps (of the 2nd Army), and VII and VIII (of 1st Army); facing them, again north to south, were the VI, IV, III, and II Corps, with the Guards Corps in reserve. In the morning, however, the Guards and XII Corps were not yet deployed, but were being rushed to the north as fast as they could march, to take their place in the line. Moltke's original plan called for pinning attacks by the corps on his center and right, while the Saxon XII Corps worked its way from the left around the French right. That plan broke down within the opening minutes, and the battle soon degenerated into a pure frontal assault. Although the casualties were predictably enormous, they were even higher than they had to be, because of the aggressiveness of virtually every Prussian corps commander.

For such a sprawling battle, St. Privat is remarkably easy to describe. Indeed, one hardly needs recourse to a map to study it. Frederick Charles led off with his IX Army Corps, under General Albrecht von Manstein (who by now had apparently made the acquaintance of General Moltke). His attack collapsed under murderous rifle fire. Steinmetz's 1st Army then started in, launching supporting attacks by VII and VIII Corps. They had the same result. On the Prussian left, meanwhile, the Guards Corps and the Saxon XII Corps assembled their artillery into a great line of guns and began blasting the French right, and the village of St. Privat that anchored it, to bits. In this war, causing French casualties was the job of the Prussian artillery. The French presented as stationary a target as modern war has ever seen, and their casualties, too, were horrendous. As French fire in this sector died down, Moltke's flanking maneuver around the French right seemed destined to succeed.

At this very moment, of course, there was another unauthorized Prussian advance, this time by the Guards Corps under Prince August of Württemberg. Historians work overtime trying to identify precise reasons for these seemingly inexplicable decisions. Sometimes they identify battle lust, other times incompetence, and still others the thirst for glory. In fact, these unauthorized and invariably bloody assaults were simply systemic—they were part and parcel of the Prussian command ethos. Two Guards divisions now attempted to storm St. Privat, 1st Guards on the left and 2nd on the right, grouped in thick company columns rather than the lighter skirmishing order used elsewhere along the line. They, too, ran into the buzz saw, a true hurricane of Chassepot and Mitrailleuse fire. These being the Prussian Guards, they came back for more, and then again a third time. Their casualties, Moltke would later write, were "enormous." Five battalions lost every single one of their officers, in fact, and all the others lost the majority of them. They managed to advance within needle-gun range, and drove back the foremost of the enemy positions, but got no closer than five hundred yards of St. Privat itself.[100]

It was not until 7:00 P.M. that the XII Saxon Corps, finally in position on the extreme left of the Prussian line, began its assault on Roncourt, the village anchoring the French right. With artillery raining down on the French defenders in this sector, the VI Corps, troops who had steadfastly resisted Prussian attacks all day, now simply crumbled. The commander of VI Corps, Marshal François Canrobert, ordered a retreat, but in fact most of his infantry had already anticipated him. With Canrobert pulling back out of the line, General Ladmirault's IV Corps on his left had little choice but to follow, and so it went—a "retreat" that was in fact a rout of soldiers who had stood helplessly too long under shellfire. The battle of St. Privat was over. The Army of the Rhine was streaming back into Metz. The Prussians had forced the French back from an ideal position, and lost just over 20,000 men, including 899 officers, and almost half of the Guards Corps in the process.[101] Moltke had not destroyed the Army of the Rhine, or even come close to it. French casualties were substantially lower than the Prussian. This time, however, he had bottled up France's main field force once and for all, and in effect had won the Franco-Prussian War.

Conclusions

There was one more drama yet to unfold. With the trapping of the Army of the Rhine in Metz, the French desperately tried to cobble together another one at Chalons, under MacMahon. It consisted of troops who had already suffered defeat, inferior manpower, and a thoroughly demoralized general. To this day it is not easy to explain why he set his Army of Chalons out on the march toward Reims. The reason usually adduced in the literature—a northward march around the right flank of the German armies advancing toward Paris to relieve Metz, barely passes muster on a map. Two Prussian armies, Frederick William's 3rd and the newly formed Army of the Meuse, now made a sharp wheel to the right and began to head north. The maneuver brought with it some risk. Depending on MacMahon's exact position, Moltke might have been volunteering his own flank to an attack. Instead, MacMahon swerved farther north to avoid the blow. The two Prussian armies hounded him toward the Belgian border and completely surrounded him at Sedan. Artillery, safely ensconced on the hills around Sedan, turned the French position into a "chamber pot," according to one French general. The Army of Chalons surrendered and went into captivity. Sedan was an encirclement battle, a "double envelopment," although even German official sources had to admit that "only the immobility of the enemy and the unfortunate choice of concentration at Sedan . . . allowed it to happen."[102] As important as it was politically, with Napoleon III among the prisoners, it offered nothing really new on the operational level.

Moltke's operational performance in both of his great wars was nothing short of spectacular. His "operations with separated portions of the army" (or perhaps, simply, "with separate armies") had proven itself again and again. Campaigning with separate armies, Moltke was capable of enveloping an enemy, or of moving rapidly to seize a central position. He could close on you with pincers; he could smash you suddenly with concentrated might. A simple speedometer reading would not show Moltke fighting a mobile war, but he got to everyplace he needed to be before his adversaries, both of whom followed the Napoleonic code and concentrated their forces for battle as early as possible. Benedek had done so at the start of the war at Olmütz, Napoleon III (and later Bazaine) within two weeks at Metz. The pace might not have been particularly speedy, but Moltke prosecuted the war of movement as successfully as any commander in Prussian-German history. Short and lively? He crushed Benedek's Army of the North in precisely thirteen days of campaigning; in 1870, he crushed the Army of the Rhine and shut it up helplessly in Metz in fifteen.

His operational maneuvers were nonpareil, and at Königgrätz, he crowned them with the dream of every great captain: a decisive victory in a field battle that ended the war at one stroke. "The success is complete," he proclaimed triumphantly to the king as the 1st Guards Division smashed into Benedek's flank, "Vienna lies at Your Majesty's feet." It was the climax of his career. By the Franco-Prussian War, however, systemic issues had arisen within the Prussian army that made it more difficult to win such a decisive battlefield victory. Some of these problems were beyond Moltke's control. The rise of the mass army, the huge supply demands that they generated, and the problems of controlling them with telegraph technology were endemic to all armies of the era, and the Prussians were no exception.

There were also problems that were unique to Prussia, however. The tendency of subordinate commanders (armies, divisions, and corps) to make a beeline for whatever enemy force they happened to encounter turned the battles of this war into a series of wrenching brawls that were very unlike Königgrätz. The crowning battle of the war, at St. Privat, nearly left King Wilhelm in tears as he surveyed the wreckage of his beloved Guards Corps. He wasn't even sure that he had won the battle until the French retreated. There were no triumphant proclamations this time. Moltke, although not the crying kind, could not have been much happier with the way the battle had unfolded. On the silent ride back to Pont à Mousson the day after battle, he turned to an aide and said, "One thing we learned yesterday: you cannot be strong enough at the point of decision."[103]

One problem that even the great Moltke never solved was the command and control of the Prussian army while it was in proximity to the enemy. He had his ideas, usually good ones, about how to proceed. His operational commanders were of a different type from Moltke, however, and their ideas usually cost far more blood than his would have. Indeed, Geoffrey Wawro speaks correctly of a "fault line" in Prussian military art:

> Essentially there were two types of officers in Prussia in 1870, and many in between who blended the qualities of both types. One type argued the invincibility of "moral" factors like "will," "guts," and "instinct." (Think of Steinmetz, or Bredow before his "Death Ride" muttering *koste es, was es wolle.* ["Whatever it costs."]) The other type exalted science, maneuver, and innovation, to win with a minimum of friction and casualties. That was Moltke's school.

"The continual tension between the two types," he adds, was a serious problem for Moltke during the Franco-Prussian War.[104] Blundering into battle might have been all well and good in the seventeenth and eighteenth centuries, when the firepower had not yet taken on the fierce cast of later eras. In an age of ever more terrible weaponry, "machine weapons," as the Germans would come to call every rapid-firing arm in the twentieth-century arsenal, Prussian warrior traditions could be positively dangerous, especially if you happened to be a foot soldier spearheading yet another frontal assault against a well-armed adversary.

6

From Schlieffen to World War I

An Age of Anxiety

The new order in Europe was destined to be short-lived. The sudden insertion of a powerful, unified Reich into the European state system led to a great deal of anxiety on the part of Germany's neighbors, and a general sense of instability. The new Germany was young, active, and determined to have its voice heard in international affairs. It tended to affect a peremptory tone in its foreign and military policy, especially after the accession of the new Kaiser Wilhelm II, which also did it little good. This brashness contributed in no small way to the seemingly endless series of diplomatic crises that afflicted Europe in the years before 1914: the First Moroccan Crisis of 1905, the Bosnian Crisis of 1908, and the Second Moroccan Crisis of 1911, for example. Although many of them were ostensibly about naval or colonial issues, lurking in the background was the behemoth: the German army, ready to be unleashed in a lightning campaign on the hapless neighbor of its choosing. Each of those states knew that, individually, they were no match for the German army. The only solution lay in collective security, and the eventual formation of the Triple Entente of Russia, Great Britain, and France in 1907 seemed almost inevitable.

Paradoxically, it was an age of anxiety within German military circles as well. The development of new weapons technologies—rapid-fire artillery, smokeless powder, magazine rifles, machine guns—led to a crisis in military operations. There was a tremendous increase in the firepower available to the defender, making a line of entrenched infantry for all intents and purposes attack-proof. The "infantry charge," the staple of battlefield attack for centuries, was apparently doomed. Germany did not fight a war between 1871 and 1914, but many other countries did: the Russo-Turkish War of 1877–1878, the Boer War of 1899–1902, the Russo-Japanese War of 1904–1905, and the Balkan Wars of 1912–1913. All followed the same general pattern: offensive operations started out with promise, but then bogged down into some form of stalemate. What is not generally recognized today is that this tendency toward stalemate and *Stellungskrieg* was a far more serious problem for Germany, with its long tradition of rapid and aggressive operations, than for its neighbors.

The issues went beyond firepower. As we have already seen in the era of the elder Moltke, a knotty complex of problems had also arisen in the area of command and control. As European population levels and industrial capacity continued to rise, armies grew apace. In 1914, France would field no less than five field armies in the opening battles; the Germans eight. The technology of command barely kept up, with the telephone and occasionally the radio now augmenting the telegraph. Maneuvering these unwieldy infantry-dominated masses presented serious problems to staff officers weaned on lessons from the operations of Napoleon and Moltke. "The command of an army of millions," wrote one expert, "is a problem that can scarcely be solved."[1]

The combination of rising firepower and bloated armies led to a monstrous rise in casualties. At Königgrätz, a battle involving more than 400,000 men had resulted in about 30,000 actual casualties, not counting 20,000 Austrian prisoners. The climactic battle of the Russo-Japanese War, at Mukden (February–March 1905), presented a very different picture. Of more than 500,000 men engaged, over 150,000 became casualties (again, not including 20,000 Russian prisoners). It only promised to get worse. By 1914, something like one in ten Frenchmen had passed through military training, a trained reserve of more than three million men. Russia had almost four million.

In addition, the introduction of the machine gun and rapid-fire artillery meant a steep increase in the demands on the logistics net. The fears of general staffs in the 1860s that the breech-loading rifle might lead soldiers to waste ammunition on frivolous unaimed fire seemed positively quaint by 1900. During the Russo-Japanese War, the Russian artillery expended an average of 87,000 rounds a month, seen then as an incredible figure. Less than a decade later, in the First Balkan War, the Bulgarian army's monthly rate had grown to 254,000 shells. By 1916, the French were averaging 4,500,000 rounds a month.[2] During the week-long battle for Messines Ridge (June 3–10, 1917), British guns fired 3,258,000 rounds.[3] The daily task of the supply services was to find enough supplies, material, and transport to feed and arm a force the size of a good-sized city. The huge freight capacity of the modern railroad made it possible, of course, but the complexity of the problem grew geometrically with every march away from the railhead.

All armies still relied on the horse-drawn wagon, with its slow speed and small capacity, to carry supplies to the forward troops. As a result, risky maneuvers that might endanger the moving force's supply lines, or involved moving an unacceptable distance from the railroad, became increasingly unlikely.[4]

When added together, these new problems spelled serious problems for the German way of war, with its stress on rapid offensive operations and a quick victory. How could there be triumph if there was no possibility of attacking successfully? German officers had always prided themselves on viewing war as an art, a free and creative activity, but in the years before 1914 they were having to deal with some thorny technical questions. Here is an actual passage from an article in an 1899 issue of the semiofficial *Militär-Wochenblatt*:

> Let us look at an attack over a 1,200 meter free plain which takes 35 minutes to reach the defender's position, with two opposing lines matched up man for man. As the attacking man crosses 1,200 meters of open plain, he will have to expose his entire body for 8 minutes. As a "target," the attacker will appear as a complete figure for 8 minutes and as a prone infantryman for 27 minutes. The defender, however, presents only a prone target for the entire 35 minutes; however, he serves as a "target" only for 27 minutes, since he can't really be shot during the 8 minutes that the attacker is rushing forward.... Now the vulnerable area of an unprotected prone riflemen has been reckoned at 0.189 square meters, and that of a running man 0.396 square meters.
>
> The defender fires for 8 minutes against a target of 0.396 square meters and 27 minutes against one of 0.189 square meters. The attacker, by contrast fires for 27 minutes only, and in fact at a target of just 0.189 square meters. Accordingly, the relationship of the attacker to the defender as an offered target is (8 x 0.396 square meters) + (27 x 0.189 square meters) to (27 x 0.189 square meters), or 8.27 to 5.10, rounded to 1.6 to 1.

In addition, since the defender was averaging 4.5 shots a minute during the entire 35 minutes, while the attacker was more or less placing the emphasis on getting forward over firing for 8 of those minutes, defensive fire superiority stood at something like 4 to 3. Multiplying the ratings for each side as *Scheibe* (target) and as *Schütze* (rifle), we arrived at a total of 6.4 to 3 or roughly a two to one superiority for the defender.[5]

The German art of war had never dealt in detail with these kinds of questions before. It would have been interesting to see Frederick the Great's reaction to a 1905 article, entitled "Creeping or Springing?"[6] By this time the above calculus had only gotten worse, as the murderous battles in front of Port Arthur in the Russo-Japanese War become public knowledge. At issue for the author, a captain and company commander in the 4th Silesian Infantry Regiment, was the best method for attacking infantry to get across the fire zone, whether by creeping stealthily or by rapid bounds. Although he personally answered with a ringing affirmation of rapid movement, the fact that he had to ask the question at all was significant. "Unless I'm being deceived," he wrote, "a certain preference for creeping has taken hold in large parts of our army. Indeed, this is not so only amongst theoreticians (Männer der Feder), but also in practice." Frederick the Great, let us recall, believed that the well-trained soldier simply marched at the enemy—with arms shouldered, no less—braving his fire and eventually dispatching him with the bayonet.

Contemporary wars, however, were forcing the Germans into just such analysis. In the Boer War of 1899, some of the finest regiments in the British army, units with long and storied traditions, had all experienced their black moments: lying prone under the burning South African sun being peppered by highly accurate fire from an opponent they could not even see. Moreover, the foe with the Mauser rifle and the ammunition bandolero wasn't even a trained infantryman: he was a civilian farmer.[7] Tales of Boer marksmanship were legion among armies of the day, and there were those who worried that European armies might be getting too gun-shy to carry out an assault against modern weaponry. It was a new and apparently incurable disease, they said, "acute Transvaalitis."[8]

Although the force levels, the unusual opponent, and the huge theater made the Boer War something of a sui generis event, the Russo-Japanese War seemed much closer to the kind of conditions European armies would have to face in the event of a great power conflict.[9] Again and again, at the Yalu, at Liaoyang, and at Mukden, two mass armies slammed into one another. Both sides employed huge amounts of artillery, machine guns, and hundreds of thousands of bodies, and both eventually fought from entrenchments behind barbed wire. Although the attacking Japanese were usually successful in smashing Russian defensive positions, the battles had been extremely bloody, and the Japanese never did land the Moltkean knockout blow.

The event of the war that drew the most European attention was the Japanese "siege" of the Russian fortress of Port Arthur, if *siege* is the correct term for what was, in effect, a series of very bloody assaults.[10] As armies had grown in size during the nineteenth century, it had become clear that they could use a great city as a strong, unflankable point upon which to base their defenses. Much of the fourth year of the American Civil War had revolved around bloody trench fighting in front of Petersburg. Likewise, the Franco-Prussian War consisted of six weeks of campaigning in the open and five months in front of Paris. The Russo-Turkish War of 1877–1878 came down in the end to a struggle for the fortified city of Plevna.[11] None of these were sieges in the ordinary sense, in that the fall of the city was not the primary issue. It was destroying the enemy force that was using the city as a strongpoint. Thus, siege warfare and battle in the open field had become increasingly difficult to tell apart. The Japanese assaulted Port Arthur once, then assaulted it again, and finally a third time before smashing their way through the town's outer defenses. The cost was sixty thousand casualties. The 1st Balkan War of 1912, fought on the very eve of World War I, presented a similar face, eventually coming down to a siege of the Turkish fortress city of Adrianople.

The oldest canard in military history is that the generals of all the European nations entered World War I ignorant of new technical developments, that they were "shocked" by the effect of the new firepower, especially the machine gun, and that they kept employing Napoleonic tactics in a battlefield environment where the only possible result was higher casualties. An entire generation of young European men perished as a result of the stupidity of the military mind. Virtually every general history of the war mentions the case of Ivan Bloch, a banker, of all things, who wrote *The Future of War*. In it, according to well-established myth, he desperately tried to warn the generals of what was about to happen: the machine guns, the trenches, stasis, whole nations pouring out their blood until there was no more to pour, but still, they refused to listen.

It is a compelling myth. With its cruel older villains and attractive youthful victims, it will probably never disappear entirely from modern historical discourse. There's only one thing wrong with it: it isn't true. Just for the record, Bloch's work itself is filled with howlers, including his famous dictum than nothing less than an eight-to-one superiority would do for an attacker to get across the fire-swept zone of the defender. He claimed that "the modern European feels more keenly and is much more excitable and impressionable than his forefathers," and was thus unable to bear the strain of modern war, another conclusion that proved to be wildly wrong. He also concluded that war had become so destructive of the international economy that it had now become impossible, and here too he couldn't have been further from the truth. Bloch's *Future of War* was a tendentious piece of propaganda, "something of a Bible for pacifists and socialists," not sound military analysis.[12]

As to European generals and their supposedly blinkered minds, they had been thinking about little else besides these very issues of tactics and technology in the years before 1914. In fact, battlefield conditions of the Great War were not radically new to military professionals. They had seen them before, quite recently in fact, in Manchuria and Thrace. The key role of medium and heavy artillery, the invisibility of entrenched defenders, the heavy losses to be expected crossing the fire zone between the trenches: all these were part of the mentality of trained officers in the years preceding the war. The curse of the new firepower, the "crisis of the offensive," and the recuperative power of mass armies even after great defeats had become a kind of obsession for virtually all of them.[13]

But not all of them. At the moment that the art of war seemed to be passing through an existential crisis caused by changing times and new technology, the chief of the Great General Staff of the German army was thinking of other things. Specifically, he was pondering the ancient Carthaginian general Hannibal, his inept Roman adversary Taurentius Varro, and a battle fought at an obscure Apulian town in 216 B.C. He was thinking of Cannae.

Schlieffen: Myth and Reality

Field Marshall Alfred Count von Schlieffen remains one of the most controversial figures in all of military history. In his own day, virtually everyone who knew him routinely called him a genius. Today, his image is almost completely negative. Historians have laid a weighty indictment at his door. He was, they say, the inept planner who tied the German army to an impossible timetable and an unworkable plan that ignored the role of logistics in modern warfare.[14] He was the man who let Moltke's art of war degenerate into a "mechanical schematism" with bitter results for Germany in World War I.[15] He was the man who strove in his operational planning for a "purely technical perfection, which tacitly ignored the priority Clausewitz had given to political considerations" and who frivolously promised a "miracle solution to

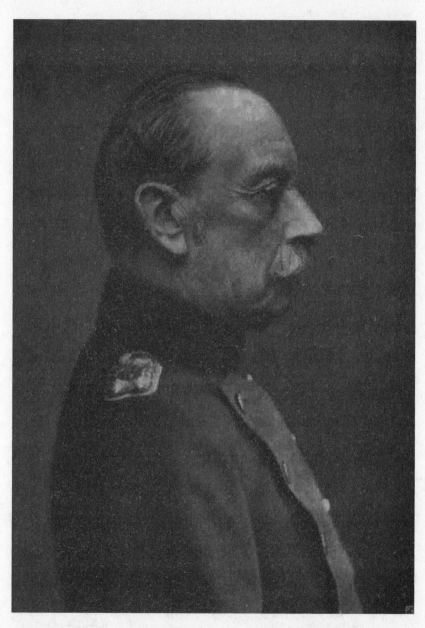

The man of Cannae: Field Marshal Count Alfred von Schlieffen. Frontispiece from Schlieffen's *Gesammelte Schriften*, volume 1 (Berlin: E. S. Mittler, 1913).

the problem of a war on two fronts."[16] They even argue that his rigid and inflexible plan for a two-front war, with its violation of Belgian neutrality, all but guaranteed that any great crisis would automatically plunge the whole world into conflict.[17] He has become, in a sense, the father of the worst catastrophe in modern history: the Great War.

It is difficult to know where to start in dissecting these arguments. Each of them is wrong, and none rests firmly on the available sources. Just to state the obvious: Schlieffen was the chief of the General Staff from 1891, when he succeeded Alfred Count von Waldersee (who served a short tenure after the departure of the great Moltke in 1888) to his retirement in 1906. The war would not even begin for another eight years, and blaming Schlieffen for it is, to put it mildly, ahistorical. His own successor, Helmuth von Moltke (the nephew of the great man, often designated "the Younger" or sometimes, more tendentiously and more than a little unfairly, "the Lesser"), would be in the post when war came in 1914, and would, in fact, command the army during the opening campaigns. Moltke's plans and generalship, therefore, are far more relevant to any analysis of 1914 than are Schlieffen's.

"Yes," Schlieffen's accusers would say, "but the plan that Schlieffen concocted for a war with Germany's neighbors was still in place, and in fact the German army marched to war with it in 1914." No one ever speaks of the "Moltke Plan" in 1914, but every student of history has heard of the famous Schlieffen Plan. It has dual meanings. The first was a strategic formula to fight a two-front war with France and Russia. Germany would concentrate enough strength in the west to overthrow France within six weeks, leaving smaller forces in the east to defend against Russia. At that point, the mass of the German army would transfer rapidly to the east using Germany's marvelous rail net and concentrate against the Russians. More specifically, on the operational level, the Schlieffen Plan called for a concentration of massive force on the German right wing against France, while leaving the left wing relatively weak. The huge right wing would swing though neutral Belgium, sweep to the west of Paris, turn and bag the entire French army between the onrushing German forces and the border, leading to the most fantastic *Kesselschlacht* of all time.

In a variation of this account, Schlieffen's defenders throw in an accusation against his successor. Moltke, they argue, inherited this perfect plan, this "recipe for victory," then threw it away by "watering it down."[18] The plan was a gamble—leaving weakness all over the board to gain strength at certain decisive points—and Moltke was no gambler. He weakened his right wing against the French, strengthened his left, and as the climactic battles approached in the west, he actually shifted two complete corps out of the theater to help Germany's beleaguered forces in East Prussia, then coming under attack by the Russians, who had shown up unexpectedly early.

This historical schema has come under attack. Historian Terence Zuber has recently argued, quite forcefully, there never was any such thing as a Schlieffen Plan, at least not as outlined above. Rather, like his predecessors, Schlieffen had drawn up several operational sketches, outlines, and memoranda. Some were more realistic than others, some dealt with hypothetical force structures and manpower levels not then available. He drafted one such document in early 1906. Published in a book by noted historian Gerhard Ritter in 1960, it is still today regarded by most historians as the Schlieffen Plan. In fact, it was little more than a *Denkschrift*, a memorandum, not unlike dozens of others prepared during Schlieffen's tenure. None of them, however, took seriously the notion of having an entire isolated German army sweep around Paris to the west—not simply a difficult operation, but an impossible one. Even a layman taking a quick glimpse at a map will see that such a maneuver would have exposed German communications and supply lines to the French interior, presumably brimming with hostiles (if the experience of the last few months of the Franco-Prussian War had been any indication). In fact, the 1906 memorandum actually included corps that did not yet exist, a strange kind of military "plan" indeed.[19]

Rather than a plan, then, Schlieffen had merely put together a deployment scheme for German forces. It was, in other words, a list of directives for an *Aufmarsch*, the only part of modern war that the commander could control carefully. As in the case of Moltke's campaigns in 1866 and 1870, the armies would operate along separate axes, seek and find the enemy's main body, and then, "using rail mobility as a force multiplier,"[20] concentrate rapidly to destroy it. Presumably, some armies would attack frontally, and others would seek to smash in one or both of the enemy's flanks. The entire force would be strongly echeloned to the right and invade Belgium—first, because that's the only spot on the map with enough open space to deploy such a huge force, and second, to work an envelopment upon the French left wing. In other words, the plan called on the German army to prosecute *Bewegungskrieg*, and to do so in the now-accepted Moltkean fashion of "cooperation between separated armies."

Whence, then, comes the accusation that Schlieffen had somehow, even after his death, been the guiding light of German operations in

1914? Oddly enough, Zuber argues, it first arose toward the end of the war, within the officer corps itself. It was clear that the war was lost and that there would be a weighty accounting after it. It was equally clear that the younger Moltke's generalship had left much to be desired in the opening campaign of the war. Even today, there is little debate on that point. Seeking an explanation for their defeat, many officers felt that it must have been Moltke's fault, that somehow he had failed to carry out the plans that Schlieffen, a much more gifted military mind, all agreed, had surely left behind. Accusations against Moltke of timidity, of "watering down," of weakening the crucial right wing all served the dual purpose of explaining the inexplicable (the lost war) and of defending the professional integrity of the officer corps. Later, those same in-house criticisms would go public and would form the basis for a long series of scholarly military histories that have fixed Schlieffen's historical image, probably for all time.

Getting at the historical Schlieffen, therefore, is an exercise in peeling away later accretions. Once we do that, we find a competent, extremely active chief of the General Staff, a man who was revered by a substantial portion of the staff officers under him and was at least respected (or feared) by the rest. He had a sarcastic streak that was either the prerogative of true genius or a hurtful character flaw, depending on one's perspective. A glance at the immense body of operational memoranda, war games, maneuvers, and tactical/strategic exercises that he drew up for his charges shows an active and agile operational mind at work. They betray no particular one-sidedness or refusal to recognize contemporary military reality. Are they brilliant? That is difficult to say—as it would be difficult for any general who never actually fought a war. One thing is certain: they are replete with rapid and bold operational maneuver, they seek the decision on the operational level, and they try to impart that preference to the large-unit commanders. Schlieffen's art of war, which never went beyond the hypothetical, is entirely in keeping with the German tradition of *Bewegungskrieg*.

We may take the Kaiser Maneuver (*Kaisermanöver*) of 1894 as a representative example of Schlieffen's methods.[21] It posed a series of operational problems involving the I and XVII Corps in East Prussia. In the first exercise, involving the I Corps, elements of a "South Army" were advancing on Königsberg, held at the time by formations belonging to a "North Army," including I Corps.[22] Noting the dispersed advance of the adversary, I Corps commander decided to launch a spoiling attack, intending to break through South Army's main position at Tharau. It

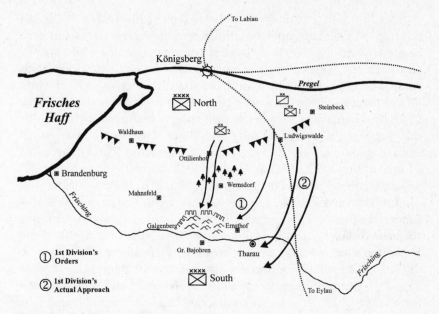

Kaisermanöver 1894: Over the Frisching

lay due south, just ten miles from Königsberg, and contained the principal bridge over the small Frisching River. As always in Schlieffen's exercises, there was a considerable amount of detail provided to the commanders:

> The latest intelligence indicated that the enemy was not expecting a blow with strong forces from the fortress, but rather intended to keep advancing on a broad front. Still, there was danger that he might be awaiting an attack behind the Frisching, in order to hold up I Corps long enough for neighboring columns to come up and launch superior forces against its flanks. It was in the interest of I Corps, then, to surprise the enemy in the area north of the Frisching in order to achieve the most rapid effect. It mustn't wait for the enemy to take possession of the wooded area north of Wernsdorf (a town about two miles north of the Frisching) and try to resist there. In order to expedite the decision, it would be useful to begin the approach in such a way that the entire corps, especially the artillery, is able to deploy in a broad front and that the attack is designed from the beginning in the form of an envelopment.[23]

It was a tricky situation. If I Corps caught South Army while it was crossing the Frisching, it might inflict a defeat on it. If it waited too long, South Army might gain the favorable terrain over the river ("the wooded area north of Wernsdorf"). Conversely, if it attacked too soon, with South Army in good position south of the river, there could be trouble.

The commander of I Corps decided on an aggressive approach. With the hostile South Army on such an extended front, he was probably facing no more than a lone division at Tharau. He brought his 2nd Division down in one column, emerging from Königsberg's line of forts near Ottilienhof, passing through Wernsdorf, and thus approaching the Tharau position from the north. This would be the column that would challenge the enemy's main body, and as such it had most of the corps' artillery. It soon got what it was looking for, a prepared South Army position on the high ground in front of the Frisching, a line of hills running from the Galgenberg in the west to the village of Ernsthof in the east, just over the river and to the west of Tharau. The terrain here was mainly flat and open, and 2nd Division's battalions had an opportunity to practice "the most difficult task that befalls infantry in war": the frontal assault against a well-established line of rifles and artillery.[24] Simultaneously, I Corps had 1st Division advancing in a separate column on the left, using the highway down toward Eylau. Accompanied by a cavalry division attached to the corps, it passed through the village of Wittenberg and was therefore moving on Tharau from the northeast.

With 2nd Division hotly engaged, yet holding its own, 1st Division now received orders to come to the rescue, "to leave the Eylau road, turn west, and launch a flank attack on the enemy position."[25] This it did in style, in a manner that anyone conversant with Prussian military operations would recognize. It turned almost due west and drove into the flank of the enemy defending the Galgenberg-Ernsthof line. With strong forces visible at Ernsthof, however, and with South Army artillery already in action south of the Frisching, the divisional commander decided to go beyond his orders. He ordered his 1st Brigade, plus most of the cavalry division, to alter its approach to the south and southwest. They crossed the river—the cavalry seizing a bridge and the infantry fording—launched a coordinated assault on the troublesome enemy artillery, and inflicted heavy casualties on the surprised defenders. Although the attack had worked its way deep into the flank and rear of the enemy position on the Frisching, the maneuver carried with it considerable risk. Indeed, the Tharau Wood separated the divisional columns during this entire sequence of events.

Nevertheless, the flanking maneuver offered the possibility of a decisive operational advantage. That was the main point of the maneuver, along with inuring the men to hard marches and twenty-four-hour days: training large-unit commanders to accept risk, to court it in fact, as an operational weapon. There was little that was "one-sided" about it. There was a great deal of hard (simulated) fighting for large portions of I Corps, especially the 1st Infantry Division carrying out the frontal maneuver. In addition, there was the warning—which would become de rigueur for the next forty years of German maneuvers—that had the battle extended into another day, I Corps might have found its position problematical. Its two divisions, indeed, were still out of contact, and if the South Army managed to recover its equilibrium, or if other enemy forces arrived in the region, there would be more hard fighting.

The rest of the maneuver would see the XVII Corps brought into action on its own in a situation parallel to the one I Corps had faced,[26] and then a highly mobile three-day encounter between the two Corps.[27] Briefly, each corps was a component of two hostile armies: an "East Army" advancing northwest toward the fortress of Elbing and a West Army advancing to the southeast, and each formed the flank of its respective force. Over the next three days, both sides had the opportunity to use just about every tool in the box: the set-piece attack, the attack from march, the mobile defense with counterattack, and the delaying attack (attempting to prevent or hinder an enemy division from rejoining its main body).

The most common accusation against German army maneuvers from this era is that the participation of the kaiser completely distorted them. William II was a vain man, and in many ways a silly one. When he attended a maneuver, the side on which he was playing invariably had to be seen as "winning." Rather than see this as invalidating the exercise, however, we should recognize that a fall maneuver of the German army was not simply a military event. It was a public display of the army at work and invariably attracted a huge audience from the local area, multigenerational family groupings from grandma and grandpa down to the youngest children. The triumphal attack of the kaiser's cavalry at the end of the maneuver was simply a punctuation mark on a splendid time had by all.[28] It had no other significance. Indeed, the professional military reportage on the 1894 Kaiser Maneuver—which otherwise went into the smallest detail of timing, terrain, and weather—did not even mention Wilhelm's presence. There is also ample evidence that many German officers found him invariably well informed and able to critique the exercise in a surprisingly competent manner, "able to speak an hour or more without looking up a place name or the name of a commander."[29]

We may gain a similar view of Schlieffen's art of war in the "tactical-strategic problems" (*taktisch-strategischen Aufgaben*) for that same year, essentially a set of test problems for General Staff students.[30] The 1894 round dealt with a situation clear across Germany, at the fortress of Metz on the Moselle River. Here, once again, two forces were operating on the flanks of much larger ones.[31] A Blue "Army Detachment" of two corps was advancing toward Metz from the northeast; Red's XVI Corps had been withdrawing before them and was now hard by the fortress city. Both had to be cognizant of their parent armies. The right wing of the (Blue) North Army was crossing the Saar River on April 1, by which time the (Red) South Army was approaching Deime. In other words, a clash of main armies was brewing well to the southeast of Metz. The actual exercise was simple. The students had to (1) come up with directives for the placement of XVI Corps on April 1; (2) prepare orders for April 2; and (3) defend their decisions.

After surveying the answers, Schlieffen began the discussion.[32] First of all, he said, even with two corps, Army Detachment Blue was no threat to Metz. Without siege artillery it couldn't harm the fortress or the XVI Corps sheltering under its guns. Second, it was clear that Blue was going to have to carry out a rapid march south to rejoin the main army before the great battle, which was sure to take place at Gross Tänchen or Mörchingen (Morhange) no later than April 3. Red's mission, therefore, was to tie up Army Detachment Blue.

Characteristically, Schlieffen recommended an attack. Troops near a friendly fortress typically turned their thoughts toward defense, he said, and neglected its offensive potential. The fortress artillery, medium and heavy, could be concentrated on Metz's eastern face and form a powerful support for the attack of XVI Corps. How to direct it? Equally characteristically, he called for using the fortress garrison troops (fourteen reserve and replacement battalions) to fix the enemy frontally, while XVI Corps came up on Blue's left (southern) flank. Hitting the southernmost of the two Blue corps would confront the other Blue corps with equally bad alternatives. It could come to the support of its hard-pressed neighbor, in which case, Army Detachment Blue certainly wouldn't be fighting at Mörchingen on April 3, "thus fulfilling the intentions of the XVI Army Corps." Equally, it could leave its neighboring corps in the lurch and try to join up with the main army, "making probable a total defeat of the southerly corps."

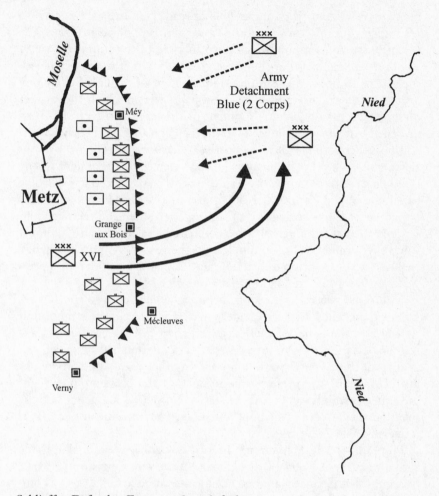

Schlieffen Defends a Fortress, 1894 *Aufgabe*

It was a solution that combined simplicity with aggression. Even when it was outnumbered two to one and had a friendly fortress at its back, the German army was trained to look for the opening and attack. That was how things had been for a good long while; it was certainly no innovation of Schlieffen's.

Another allegation against him—that he turned the battle of Cannae into a rigid, case-hardened dogma—requires careful consideration. There is no doubt that the so-called "Cannae studies," first published serially but eventually adding up to a book-length study, were the product of an obsession.[33] It is impossible to read them from start to finish without gaining the impression of a certain lack of proportion. The "Cannae studies" aim high. They are an attempt to reinterpret virtually every single battle of the three great modern captains (Frederick the Great, Napoleon, and Moltke) in the light of Hannibal's triumph over the Romans at Cannae, an improbable win in which the smaller force achieved a double envelopment of the larger. In fact, it is hard merely to sift through the 101 maps in the handsome, even ornate, 1913 edition of Schlieffen's *Complete Writings* (*Gesammelte Schriften*) without shaking one's head. The analysis beats a relentless tattoo: here is why Leuthen was not a Cannae-style victory; this is why Moltke was unable to achieve a true Cannae at Königgrätz; this is what Napoleon might have done at Ligny to achieve a Cannae. Even small and relatively obscure battles like Langensalza are compared to Cannae, although just why they should be is often unclear to the reader. As pure campaign analysis and description of battles, the "Cannae studies" have no peer. As history, they are tendentious and one-sided.

Two other pieces of evidence need to be entered into the record, however, and they are often underplayed. First of all, the studies first appeared in the issues of the *Viertelsjarhshefte für Truppenführung und Heereskunde* from 1909 to 1913, years after Schlieffen had stepped down as chief of the General Staff. They are, in other words, the product of his retirement—the perfect time to nurture an obsession, one might say. They certainly never had the status of official documents, and the role that they played in shaping actual German doctrine or operations is questionable, at best.

More important, Schlieffen's interest in Cannae was not simply the antiquarianism of an eccentric old man. At the very outset of the work, he argues that Cannae was not a question of mere form: "It was a complete victory of annihilation," he writes, "especially remarkable since, against all theory, it had been won by the smaller force." Clausewitz had warned against it ("concentric attacks against the enemy rarely benefit the weaker") and so had Napoleon ("the weaker should not seek to envelop both flanks").[34] Yet in any conceivable scenario for war, this was precisely the problem that the German army would be facing: how to achieve a rapid and complete victory over forces that outnumbered it. An obsession they might have been, but the "Cannae studies" were not completely divorced from reality.

Finally, since we have mentioned Cannae and Schlieffen's interest in things ancient, it is only fair to note that he was also the author of essays such as "Million Man Armies"[35] and "War in the Present Day."[36]

Published at almost the same time as "Cannae," they present a very different portrait of the man. Here are the words of one who has been accused of failing to read the signs of the times regarding changes in modern warfare:

The Russo-Japanese War has proven that the ordinary attack on an enemy front can still succeed despite all difficulties. The success of such an attack, however, even in the most favorable cases, is a small one. The enemy is definitely driven back, but he repeatedly takes up in another place the resistance he had temporarily abandoned. The campaign drags on. Such wars are, however, impossible in our time, in which the very existence of the nation depends upon trade and industry; a quick decision is required to set the wheels in motion once again. A strategy of attrition is impossible if it requires the support of millions and an expenditure of billions.[37]

As far back as 1901, in fact, Schlieffen had written the following prophetic words:

According to current theory, modern means of communication have made the command of million-man armies as easy and sure as an earlier corps of 15,000 to 20,000 men. While this may be true in one's own land, the telegraph will not suffice in enemy territory; it has already proven itself unreliable in maneuvers. Wet weather and difficult roads stop the cyclist; automobiles are subject to endless difficulties; the thick woods of East Prussia stop the light rays of the optical telegraph and the electrical signals of the radio telegraph alike. It is to be hoped that improvements in these areas will make the distribution of orders easier and simpler. At present, however, the armies consist of masses that are ever more difficult to control and ever less maneuverable.[38]

Indeed. Schlieffen was very much a man of his era, both cognizant of the changes that had taken place in the military sphere, and at the same time aware that some things never change. He was an important military intellectual. He was also absolutely Prussian in his insistence on the power of the offensive. "Only one idea is justified: if one is too weak to attack the whole, then one attacks a part," he once told a student. What if the enemy came on with several armies? Launch an attack on the one that offered the best target, Schlieffen said. What if one was too weak to attack an enemy army? Attack a particular column, Schlieffen answered.[39] Aggression, rapidity of maneuver, flanking maneuvers, and encirclement—these were all elements of Schlieffen's impressive classroom repertoire. Whether he would have taken a place among the great field commanders will always remain the most tantalizing unanswered question of German military history.

Decision in the West? The "Namur Campaign"

Despite the opprobrium heaped on him over the years, General Helmuth von Moltke oversaw many key reforms within the German army in the years leading up to 1914. The deployment plans that Schlieffen left behind when he retired were designed to prosecute a war against the French army of 1906. One of the underlying assumptions at the time was that the French would adopt a defensive posture, hunkering down behind their fortress line. Since that time, however, the conclusion of the Triple Entente had made it likely that the French would launch a grand offensive of their own, most probably into Lorraine. The deployments that went for 1905–1906, therefore, were no longer appropriate for 1914.[40] Of nine new divisions formed between 1906 and 1914, he assigned six to strengthen the left. Some accuse him of wasting forces on a secondary theater, but given the problems the Germans had in supplying their right wing in the course of the campaign, cramming more divisions into it might have had disastrous consequences, without increasing its fighting efficiency.[41]

No army rode off to war better equipped, and that, too, took place on Moltke's watch. Staff studies of the Russo-Japanese and Balkan Wars had shown the importance of howitzers and heavy artillery. Both the Krupp works in Germany and Skoda in Austria-Hungary had conducted what one scholar has called "aggressive research and development programs in heavy artillery."[42] By 1914, each German division had its own battalion of light field howitzers (105 mm) and each corps its own battalion of heavy field howitzers (150 mm). The German army thus went to war in 1914 with 2,280 howitzers and larger guns in its arsenal, the largest number by far of the contending powers, and each division possessed the imposing figure of seventy-two organic guns and howitzers.

Historians typically end the opening campaign in the west with the German defeat at the Marne. In fact, by the time the Germans got there they had already squandered their best chance for victory. It resulted from the interplay between each side's initial deployment, impressive German victories in the opening battles, and a certain amount of enemy blundering. One could say the same sort of thing about all the Prussian victories we have studied so far, Königgrätz and Mars-la-Tour, for example. This time, it happened at Namur.

The war in the west opened with the greatest clash of mass infantry armies in human history.[43] Nothing like it would ever be seen again. The Germans arrayed no less than seven field armies north to south (numbered 1st–7th in that direction); the French countered with five (1st–5th, south to north). Although army numbers are often random designations, these numbers say something. It was the German armies on the right wing, the 1st Army of General Alexander von Kluck, on the far right of the line, and his neighbor immediately to the left, 2nd Army under General Karl W. P. von Bülow, that were about to play the crucial role in the fighting. These two would invade neutral Belgium, head west, and then wheel left and enter France from the relatively unprotected north. Their operational target was not necessarily Paris. Paris was simply a direction, much as Gitschin had been in 1866 (and Paris in 1870, for that matter). In other words, marching on the capital was the best way to ensure that the French would place a large force, a worthy operational target, in the German path.

Likewise, the French concentrated strength on their right wing, 1st and 2nd Armies. Both of them would drive northeastward into Lorraine, crash into whatever German forces happened to be there, and show that the French army had recovered its offensive spirit since 1870. This was "Plan XVII," a scheme so primitive in its operational conception—it was, after all, a purely frontal offensive—that it makes one wonder what the first sixteen had been like.[44] When engaged simultaneously, the two operations were destined to work as a kind of revolving door upon one another, the Germans swinging down and the French swinging up.

Once things were in play, however, the door swung in Germany's favor. After a two-week mobilization, German 1st and 2nd Armies invaded Belgium. The key Belgian fortress of Liège had already fallen to a successful *coup de main* by a task force under General Erich Ludendorff. After initial attacks had failed, Ludendorff actually drove to the gates of the city in his chauffeured limousine and imperiously demanded, and received, its surrender.[45] The outlying forts, constructed on modern principles and "impregnable," were then pulverized with gigantic 405 mm and 310 mm siege mortars. With Liège reduced, the path was clear for the passage of the German right wing. The two armies entered the country on August 16 and drove forward against light resistance from the Belgian army.

A German foot soldier, twenty-two-year-old Max Albert Harmon, posing proudly for his portrait in Augsburg before departing for the front. He would survive the war and later emigrate to the United States. Courtesy Inga Smith.

Meanwhile, on August 14, the French 1st Army (General Auguste DuBail) and 2nd Army (General Noël de Castelnau) implemented Plan XVII. Over the next six days, they advanced a grand total of ten miles into Lorraine. Even for the mass army, this was slow going. On August 20, 1st Army came up to the main German position at Sarrebourg, and the 2nd Army did the same at Morhange (the very town, incidentally, that Schlieffen predicted would witness the clash of main armies in his 1894 *Aufgaben*). Unlike 1870, this time the French launched vigorous infantry attacks at both places, and both times the Germans drove them back in some confusion with machine gun and heavy artillery fire. Although we can now discount the mythology that grew up around these battles, describing them as the slaughter of two whole French armies, they were certainly bad enough.[46] The French had committed their main force to these attacks, and in both cases they collapsed with heavy loss of life.

It soon became impossible for the French to ignore the danger hurtling down on them from the north. It was now clear that the Germans had entered Belgium, and to counter them, French supreme commander General Joseph Joffre ordered two French armies (4th and 3rd) into the Ardennes in the eastern portion of the country. Prewar French calculations as to the limited size of the German army would not support any wider German sweep. Here, on August 22, they collided with two German armies, the 4th and 5th, which were serving as the "hinge" of the German wheel. Neither side had thrown out any reconnaissance patrols. The metaphorical "fog of war" lay heavy on the ground, and as at Leuthen in 1757, so did the real thing. The collision of four armies in a relatively small piece of real estate with only a few good roads had a predictable result: immense casualties. The heavier weight of German artillery was the deciding factor, as it was so often in these early battles, and the French once again received a severe mauling, tumbling back out of the Ardennes in total disarray.

If one is counting, and Joffre certainly had to be by this point, the Germans had now crossed off four French armies from the original order of battle's five. The only intact operational-level formation left to the French was the 5th Army, under General Charles Lanrezac. Like all the other French army commanders, he had opened hostilities by advancing to the north, in his case into Belgium. Often described as seeking to hold a line to the north, in fact, he intended to attack the first Germans he met. That would probably come somewhere along the Sambre River, he believed, which flowed roughly west-east and joined the Meuse River at the Belgian fortress of Namur. Consequently, Lanrezac crossed the border, heading north and establishing himself at Namur. He intended to cross the river and wheel right, driving in what he presumed to be the right flank of the entire German position in Belgium. It would certainly have made sense to wait until the British Expeditionary Force (BEF), under General Sir John French, was able to form up in strength on his left, but it was still coming up from the coast after having landed in France on August 12. Lanrezac felt that waiting much longer might rob him of his chance to attack under favorable circumstances. It was the first in a series of questionable miscommunications (and eventually willful noncommunications) between the BEF and its neighboring French army.

A look at a situation map on the morning of August 23 would lead one to believe that the German army was about to win one of the greatest victories in its history. Lanrezac held a west-east line along the high ground south of the Sambre, with his left just west of Charleroi and his right anchored at Namur.[47] Although his left was, relatively speaking, in the air, there was no real threat from this direction. Bulow's 2nd Army faced him frontally, a situation without real benefit to either side. It is on Lanrezac's right, however, that the trouble may be seen. Namur sits at the confluence of the Sambre and Meuse. The bend formed by the two rivers is far more acute than 90 degrees. Straggling far back on Lanrezac's right, therefore, was a long stretch of the Meuse from Namur through Dinant and down to Givet. Holding this crucial position was not much more than a single French unit: the 51st Reserve Division. Facing it was the entire German 3rd Army, commanded by General Max von Hausen. With his front facing west and with his main body already up to the Meuse, he was ideally placed to cross the river, get across Lanrezac's rear and, in conjunction with a frontal attack from Bulow's 2nd Army, destroy him.

Even if we no longer give credence to the existence of a Schlieffen Plan, we must pause here and pay our proper respects. The Moltke Plan had worked to perfection. It was not a detailed series of marches and countermarches. Rather, huge German forces, operating independently, had identified a target of opportunity. Now they were about to swoop down on a hapless French army and destroy it in the jaws of a pincer. By one count, 101 German battalions faced just 17 French in this critical sector, a classic example of a concentration of force at the decisive point: the *Schwerpunkt*.[48]

Getting a sizable German force across the Meuse at this point might well have been a war winner. It is easy to say that one battle might not

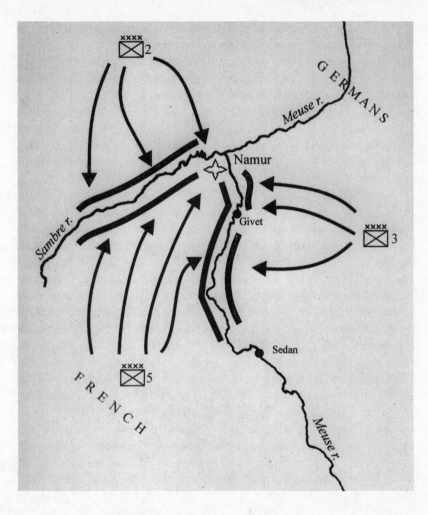

Victory in the West? Climax of the "Namur Campaign," August 23, 1914

have changed the course of the war and to argue that France would have recovered. Indeed, one can describe the history of the entire war as a series of French recoveries from disaster. French morale was a delicate and mercurial thing, however, as the rest of the opening campaign would show. Coming on top of the bad news flowing in from the other four armies, the encirclement and destruction of France's last field army, along with the huge amount of booty and hundreds of thousands of prisoners who would surely have fallen into German hands, would have had an iconic significance and would have been a difficult thing to accept or to explain to the nation. Whatever the French decided to do, such a catastrophe so early in the war would surely have forced an agonizing reappraisal of the situation on the part of the BEF, and might well have resulted in a Dunkirk-style British evacuation. Lanrezac's destruction would certainly have impelled General French to get his command as far away as possible from the Germans. In fact, subsequent events would show he needed little or no convincing on that point.[49]

The preceding scenario did not come to pass. There was a high degree of uncertainty on the part of all the army commanders around Namur. General Bülow, the commander of German 2nd Army, was also in operational control of the 1st and 3rd, the forces on either flank. He had intelligence reports from Moltke that the British lay somewhere to his right, but no definite location. On August 21, therefore, he halted his army north of the Sambre and gave 3rd Army orders to do likewise east of the Meuse. By the same token, Lanrezac could read a map, and he could see the danger of his exposed position. That same day, he too gave orders to his corps to remain concentrated on the south bank of the Sambre.

That the battle was joined at all was due to the initiative of local troop commanders on either side of the meandering rivers, in particular 2nd Army's front along the Sambre.[50] Patrols shot at patrols, were reinforced until battalions were involved, then regiments, and finally whole divisions. Pride of place goes—no surprise—to the German 2nd Guards Division, which managed to deal out serious damage to the French forces opposite, and even to get across the Sambre in a couple of places. As French forces reeled back out of contact, a gap some four miles wide opened in Lanrezac's defenses along the river. On the Meuse, things remained a bit quieter, but only because the extreme steepness of the left (French) side of the river made any large-scale crossing here quite difficult. Nevertheless, General Hausen's 3rd Army managed to put enough pressure on the French right flank to make Lanrezac nervous. With his front on the Sambre in the process of being penetrated, and his right flank vastly overextended, he ordered his army to retreat on the evening of August 23.

Even then, the crisis had not passed. Only after the armies made contact had the true nature of the situation clarified itself to the German high command. Moltke could see the opportunity that beckoned and ordered 3rd Army to get forces, any forces, across the Meuse to block the retreat of the enemy forces opposite. Hausen now passed down the order to his XIX Corps, holding the army's left (southern) flank. With most of his corps already engaged, the best that the corps commander, General of Cavalry von Laffert, could do was to assemble an ad-hoc division. It was a mixed bag: most of the 133rd Infantry Regiment, along with the 134th and 179th, the 12th and 13th Jäger Battalions, three squadrons of cavalry from the 19th Hussars, and nine batteries of artillery (portions of the 68th and 77th Field Artillery Regiments). Placed under the command of Lieutenant General Götz von Olenhusen, commander of the 40th Infantry Division, it was ordered to cross the Meuse south of Givet and drive deeply into the French right flank and rear.[51]

As the fighting was raging along the Meuse and Sambre on August 23, then, "Division Olenhusen" was marching south toward its designated crossing point: the small town of Fumay. The effort backfired completely. Simply assembling the force took all morning, the division wasn't on the road until 1:00 P.M. Two miles into its march, at Beauraing, it met up with a battalion from the VIII Corps (4th Army), part of a brigade responsible for maintaining communications between the two armies. The rest of the brigade was absent, location and destination unknown. The division was supposed to have the use of the bridge train from 40th Division, but it too was absent, and in fact it never would catch up.[52]

The division trudged south through a series of picturesque villages on the right, heavily forested bank of the Meuse. Uphill and downhill they marched, on a hot, muggy day, with the steep overhang of the left bank looking down upon the men the whole way. At each halt, both foreseen and unforeseen, the column tended to come apart, men falling out to catnap until the call of "An die Gewehre!" brought them back. By 10:00 P.M., the advance guard (134th Infantry Regiment with elements of the Jägers and hussars) stood at Willerzie, about two-thirds of the way to Fumay. Here, surprisingly, there was a brief scuffle with French forces, who weren't supposed to be over the river and who were on no one's situation maps.

The main body had gotten no farther than Bourseigne-Neuve, only about halfway to their destination. Rather than rush his forces up to Willerzie, General Olenhusen decided to suspend the fight and to rest for the night. The march had started late, and his men had been on their feet for more than nine hours. It was pitch black, and the terrain was unfamiliar. It was a reasonable decision, even if his Army commander would later criticize him for it: "Instead of prompt action to

seize the village (Willerzie) and its blocking position along the road,"
Hausen wrote, "the advance guard rested. The next morning, August
24th, they found Willerzie deserted."[53] In fact, the division needed
the rest. German records speak of wild bursts of shooting on the part
of Olenhusen's men in the town of Bourseigne-Neuve that evening,
perhaps in response to a stray French bullet, perhaps simply out of
nerves.

It wasn't until August 24, then, that Division Olenhusen reached
its destination. North of Fumay lay the village of Haybes. South of it,
the river makes a sharp loop to the east. Fumay sits within the loop
on the left bank. As elements of the 19th Hussars entered Haybes,
however, they again came under fire. They reported it, as did virtually every German soldier in Belgium suddenly taken under fire, as
"franc-tireur" activity. We now know that it was a unit of French light
infantry firing from protected positions on the left bank. At any rate,
the artillery came up and plastered the unfortunate little village. The
infantry entered Haybes next, wasting precious hours searching the
houses for civilian snipers. A later German source would declare that
"in the western portion of the village, the population kept up a lively
resistance, assisted by French customs agents," but this too seems unlikely. Although the bridge in Haybes was destroyed, a small German
force used the pontoons of the hussar regiment to fashion a temporary
bridge and establish a tiny bridgehead on the western bank. Unfortunately, they found themselves under fire the entire time, and so did all
the German troops who got too close to the river, from the steep and
rocky left bank. By the end of the day, Olenhusen had decided to leave
only his advance guard at Haybes, while pulling the main body of his
division away from the riverbank, at Hargnier.

As Lanrezac's 5th Army struggled desperately over the next few
days to extricate itself from its nearly impossible predicament, Division Olenhusen sought a crossing even farther to the south, at Revin.
Although it was just five miles south of Fumay, the intervening terrain
was so thickly forested that it required almost twenty miles of marching simply to get around it. Not until August 27 did it reach the town.
Here it rendezvoused with the long-promised bridge train and finally
got across the Meuse. Lanrezac, of course, was long gone by this time,
joining the rest of the Allied armies in the so-called Great Retreat to
the south.

The ordeal of Division Olenhusen was a microcosm of what had
happened to all the armies in the battle along the Meuse and Sambre.
Neither side knew exactly where the other was located. By the time

local forces reported enemy locations up the chain of command, and the directives had worked their way back down again, the situation had changed so dramatically that neither side could respond in a timely fashion. The German chain of command, in particular, was troublesome. Appointing Bülow a kind of ad-hoc "army group" commander (1st, 2nd, and 3rd Armies), while he still held the command of 2nd Army might have seemed like a good idea: having a man on the spot was certainly preferable to reporting everything back to Moltke at his perch in the Hotel Monopol in Coblenz. In fact, Bülow simply added another layer to the command bureaucracy, and having to function as an army commander took time and energy away from considering the needs of neighboring armies. That extra command layer had a material impact on both the tentative approach march of the 2nd and 3rd Armies toward the river line, and the preparation of orders for the Olenhusen Division. As we behold the unedifying sight of three mass armies tripping over one another in the narrow angle of the Meuse and Sambre in late August 1914, we are forced to a simple, inescapable conclusion: there were simply too many armies, too many men, and nowhere near enough command or control. What might have gone down in history as "the Namur campaign," the greatest victory in German history, would instead end on the Marne—badly.

As for that oft-analyzed battle, the Marne was like nothing so much as a metastasized version of St. Privat-Gravelotte. That encounter had matched up parallel lines of corps. The Marne would see parallel lines of armies, stretching from the Swiss border to just west of Paris.[54] As in 1870, both sides dealt out a tremendous amount of punishment, and one side eventually managed to compromise the right flank of the adversary's battle line. In 1870 it had been the crown prince of Saxony and his XII Corps that had been at the business end of things. In 1914 it was the newly formed French 6th Army under General Michel Maunoury, coming from Paris. In 1870, the flanking maneuver was enough to send General Bazaine scurrying back to Metz, a decision that some commentators have found inexplicable, given the size of the force he still had under his command. In 1914, General Moltke made an equally inexplicable decision: to retreat from a battle that he still stood a good chance of winning. The Marne was probably five times as large as St. Privat in terms of numbers engaged and certainly covered more than five times the area. Getting your troops, especially your operational-level formations (division, corps, armies) to behave under such conditions was simply beyond the command technology of the day. Lack of supply, footsore German infantrymen, the detection of "Kluck's wheel" by French aircraft, the mysteries of the "Hentsch mission," the BEF shooting the gap between German 1st and 2nd Armies—they all played a role in the German defeat on the Marne. It was the mass army and its command deficiencies, however, that were truly responsible.

Could It Have Been Different?

For the next twenty-five years, German officers and military historians alike played a kind of parlor game, asking if the campaign could have gone differently and devising their own solutions. General Wilhelm Groener led the way, penning two influential books that blamed the younger Moltke for the disaster. His argument has worked its way into our general historical consciousness and will never fully disappear. In *Das Testament der Grafen Schlieffen* (*Count Schlieffen's Testament*, 1927) and *Der Feldherr wider Willen* (*The Reluctant Warlord*, 1931),[55] Groener painted a portrait of a weak, vacillating supreme commander who consistently missed potentially decisive opportunities in the opening campaigns. More controversially, it was he who pinned the blame on Moltke for "watering down" the Schlieffen Plan, which otherwise would have been a perfect recipe for victory.

Groener's arguments generated heated responses, and their temperature increased as he became perceived as a "Republican" general—and thus seen by some as a traitor to his caste—during the Weimar era. General Ludendorff, for example, argued repeatedly that there was nothing wrong with the 1914 deployment; Schlieffen's sketch for a 1906 *Aufmarsch*, he argued, fit the times perfectly, but only because the French were inclining toward a defensive posture. It certainly would not have fit the situation in 1914, when almost half the French army (nine of twenty active corps) was preparing for a thrust into Lorraine. Ludendorff's argument became a standard one. One can see it enshrined, for example, in many dozens of articles in the *Militär-Wochenblatt* in the interwar period, including several by the journal's editor in the 1930s, General Georg Wetzell.

The emergence of a party line within the army did not stop a number of officers from trying their hand at either a better *Aufmarsch* or a more skillful handling of the armies during the fighting. To go through them all would require a book in itself, but three may stand as representative of the lot. The well-known military author Lieutenant General Ernst Kabisch, for example, remained critical of the initial deployment, since it assigned large forces to the German left that might possibly have been of use on the Marne.[56] He recognized the issues that Ludendorff had stressed, the French threat to Lorraine, and he certainly did not recommend a return to the 1906 deployment. His suggestion, however, was for the removal of the 6th Army (less the XXI Corps) from the line and its redeployment as a central army reserve behind the 3rd and 4th Armies. It covered both problems, he argued, the need to be prudent regarding the German left and the possibility of reinforcing the right. Once Moltke had sized up the true danger to the German left, and recognized that the force levels already in Lorraine were adequate for defense, he could shift the 6th Army (five corps in 1914, four in the Kabisch Plan) to the west, where it could join Kluck and Bülow on the right. It seems to be a sound plan, and there are few military analysts who would ever argue against the formation of a reserve. The main problem, not assigned sufficient weight by Kabisch, was the problem of rail transport. With the German rail net already operating at peak capacity on the right wing, getting this "Reserve Army" into the line would have been difficult. Rather than a reserve, it would instead have become a "second wave," arriving several days too late to intervene in the frontier battles no matter where Moltke decided to send it.

The Kabisch Plan was a tame one, however, compared to one devised by Lieutenant Colonel Karl Justrow.[57] Essentially, he envisioned a bold *coup de main* against the French fortress of Verdun in the opening days of the war. The fault for losing the war, he argued, lay with a General Staff that was elderly and used up in body and soul, deficient in technical knowledge and the warrior spirit alike. His plan called for boldness: the rapid concentration of four full armies (1st–4th) in the region Coblenz-Diedenhofen-Metz-Strassburg. There would be no invasion of Belgium and thus no British intervention. Instead, the Germans would launch a surprise attack against Verdun before the French were fully prepared. "Significant resistance outside of the fortified district itself was not to be expected," he wrote. The business end of the Justrow Plan included twelve early mobilized infantry brigades at full wartime strength, plus a cavalry division and strong artillery support: one field artillery regiment, two battalions of heavy field howitzers, and a mortar battalion (Justrow had been an officer on the artillery testing commission before 1914). They would sweep forward line abreast in a "heroic assault march" and sweep the disorganized and only partially deployed defenders before them. To increase the surprise, there would be a halt around noon on the first march day, and then a forced march at night. Four brigades would drive for Verdun

Alternate history? On the left, the Kabisch Plan, which argued for placing 6th Army as a general reserve (*Militär-Wochenblatt* 121, no. 14, October 11, 1936). On the right, (opposite page) the Justrow Plan for a bold coup against Verdun in the opening days of the war (*Militär-Wochenblatt* 121, no. 15, October 18, 1936).

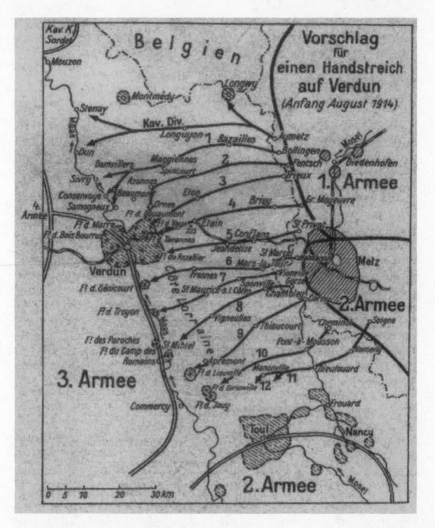

itself, the others toward the Meuse River in the north and the ridge running out of Verdun to the south, the Côte Lorraine. In two days, he argued, Verdun would be German.

It's hard to know where to start in criticizing this one. General Wetzell mocked it as the product of a "modern Alexander," who wanted to form the entire German army into a kind of "phalanx."[58] Since the French actually finished their mobilization two days before the Germans, beating them to Verdun was a fantasy. Twelve brigades was not a small or inconsiderable force—it was three full army corps, and even getting them into such a cramped position would overload the local railways. Wetzell's analysis: the twelve brigades would storm forward and get stuck in front of a position they could not take, with two dangling flanks:

> With a little imagination, one can picture the imminent catastrophe. From all sides, French reinforcements arrive: from Verdun, from Sedan, and especially from Toul. It will come to a battle on the heights of the Côte Lorraine and Woevre plain in which the stronger enemy holds all of the trumps. The commander of this "heroic undertaking" should be happy if he can rescue his "Storm Brigades" and bring them back behind the German fortifications.[59]

Such a bold venture wouldn't have worked with twelve brigades, Wetzell argued. Nor would it have worked with twelve divisions, that is to say an entire army, plus all of Germany's siege artillery. Although Justrow accused the General Staff of lacking a "modern and penetrating system" for war, he himself was in the grip of a feverish military romanticism.

Having established himself as the arbiter of alternate 1914 scenarios, Wetzell wasn't loath to try them himself. One interesting contribution was a long series of articles entitled "Der Bündniskrieg" ("Coalition War"),[60] which attributed a large share of Germany's defeat to inadequate cooperation with the Austro-Hungarian army. This was particularly true, he argued, in the war's opening campaigns. Another was his suggestion that the war might have opened with "an altered political-military objective."[61] Specifically, Wetzell analyzed an opening campaign without the invasion of Belgium. Geography split the western theater into three definite operational sectors: the Belgian west of the Meuse,[62] the central between the Meuse and the Moselle, and the southern between the Moselle and the Rhine (Lorraine). If the French stayed in their fortifications, as it seemed they would back in 1906, then getting across the Meuse, creating a *Schwerpunkt* in western Belgium, and enveloping them was the sensible course. If, however, they came forward into the offensive, as seemed increasingly likely by 1914, they would be doing the Germans a favor—Schlieffen himself had recognized that.[63] Let them come, launching simultaneous offensives into Lorraine in the south (toward Saarbrücken and Mainz) and between the Moselle and the Meuse in the north (axis Coblenz-Cologne). Between them lay the crucial breakwater, the thirty-five-mile-wide fortified front including Metz, Diedenhofen, and the so-called Nied position (*Niedstellung*). From here, 5th Army would have had its choice of operational targets. It would have overhung the French drive into Lorraine like a balcony; and it also had uppercut potential against the French thrust to the north. Either way, there was the possibility of a decisive victory. It wouldn't bag the entire French army but would have been an "annihilating partial victory," in the same way that the wins at Mars-la-Tour and St. Privat had set the table for the later feast at Sedan.[64] The Wetzell Plan wasn't naïve about British intentions. Britain would come into the war eventually. But depriving the British government of the Belgian issue might have delayed the declaration a few weeks, just long enough to inflict a punishing defeat on the French.

World War I: The War of Movement

The German failure on the Marne led to the onset of trench warfare in the west, *Stellungskrieg*, the Germans called it, the "war of position." For the next three and a half years, the Germans would sit in the line they had reached in the opening campaign, and the Allies would launch offensive after offensive to try to lever them out. The British hammered at them in Flanders, the French in the Champagne, but to no avail. Trenches, barbed wire, rapid-fire artillery, and machine guns: all conspired to rob the front of any vestige of mobility. During these years, the front in the west hardly moved an inch.[65]

It would be a mistake, however, to limit a discussion of World War I to trench warfare. On the eastern front, the war of movement began and did not stop. Here the German army was able to fight according to its preference for mobile operations, to prosecute a war that was in complete harmony with the traditions of Frederick the Great and Moltke. The difference in theaters was mainly one of size. Because of the sprawling nature of the eastern front, neither side could possibly have deployed enough formations to re-create conditions on the western front, with its wall-to-wall corps. There was, therefore, always a dangling flank to be had somewhere. The war in the east would see both sides attempting vast and daring maneuvers against the enemy's flank and rear, just as they would in a later war from 1941–1945. Although the armies were certainly in motion, however, neither side was able to solve the problem of the underdeveloped infrastructure of the region. Roads, railroads, telephone and telegraph installations: none of these was up to western European standards. Combined with the unwieldy nature of the armies themselves, these issues by and large kept either side from winning the decisive victory that so often seemed to beckon—with one stupendous exception.

TANNENBERG

The western campaign ended with a stinging defeat after a long series of victories. The German public had read dispatch after dispatch describing rapid advances, victorious encounters, and the surrender of fortresses. A week of silence followed, and then the news that the army was retreating from the Marne. By contrast, the East Prussian campaign began with a flurry of bad news—Russian invasion, Cossack raids on German villages, civilian refugees fleeing in terror. Then, suddenly, news arrived of a glorious victory, a massive *Kesselschlacht*.[66] Although the communiqué announcing it came from 8th Army headquarters at a town with the ungainly name of Frögenau, such a grand victory required a grander name. It became known almost immediately to the public as the battle of Tannenberg, site of the defeat of the Knights of the Teutonic Order in 1410. Under any name, it was unique: the only campaign in the entire war that bore any resemblance to the kind of war for which the General Staff had been preparing.

Like all the hostile powers in 1914, Russia's operational plans stressed the offensive. While the nearly unlimited masses of Russian manpower were still mobilizing, two armies would launch a simultaneous invasion of East Prussia. The 1st Army (General von Rennenkampf) would advance from the Niemen River in the east; 2nd Army (General Samsonov) from the Narew River in the south.[67] It was Moltkean warfare, a flexible, concentric advance designed to find the German main force wherever it might be, fix it frontally, and then have another army swing onto its flank. Once the armies were united and the main German force had been dispatched, they would drive on the fortress and provincial capital of Königsberg. It would be no less than the fourth time that Russian armies would be set forth on offensive operations toward Königsberg: twice in the Seven Years' War and once in 1812–1813, after driving Napoleon from Russia. There would be one more, a fifth, in 1945.

It was a sound plan, but like all excursions into the world of "operations with separated armies," it was risky. Like the Prussian armies entering Bohemia in 1866, the two Russian armies would be highly vulnerable at the start. As they advanced, they would be isolated from one another, too far apart for mutual support. In this case, the fifty-mile chain of the Masurian Lakes, thickly forested and nearly impassable, would stand between them. Coordination between the two armies was the key, but it was also bound to be a problem, given the command technology of the day.

Defending East Prussia was a single German army, the 8th (General Max von Prittwitz). It contained four corps: the elite I Corps, mainly native East Prussians under General Hermann von François; the XVII, XX, and I Reserve Corps; along with the 1st Cavalry Division; as well as fortress and replacement troops. More important than the order of battle, however, was the fact that Prittwitz had at his disposal no less than seventeen double-track rail lines, able to carry five hundred troop trains a day, enough carrying capacity for sixteen divisions. In other words, Prittwitz could theoretically shift his whole army by rail every single day of the campaign, if he wanted to. By contrast the Russians had only six lines serving the entire Warsaw district (that is, the zone of operations for Samsonov's 2nd Army).

The Russian plan fell apart immediately. Rennenkampf crossed the border first, on August 12. Cossacks, the Russian light cavalry arm, entered the German frontier village of Marggrabowa and sacked it, leading to panic on the part of the East Prussian civilian population and a great deal of heartburn within the German command. The commander of I Corps, in particular, disliked what he saw on both humanitarian and military grounds:

> The flight of the population assumed critical proportions. Thousands of these unlucky people camped on both sides of the road from Insterburg to Stallupönen with their children and everything they owned. They lay on piles of straw with their wagons, horses, and cattle. The mad rush from the land threatened to become a danger for the troop movements, as well, and the civil authorities were urgently requested to take steps against it.[68]

By August 17 all of 1st Army, three corps, had entered the province. In the south, however, Samsonov was moving much more slowly and had barely reached the border. The roads here were little more than sandy tracks through dense pine forests. They soon collapsed under the weight of men, horses, and wagons. It was not until August 19 that Samsonov crossed the border, his men already falling out of the march because of the stifling heat.

With Rennenkampf coming on and Samsonov lagging, 8th Army saw an opportunity. Prittwitz might not have been much of a general, but his staff officers were more competent. His operations officer, General Max von Hoffmann, had already drawn up a plan to smash 1st

Army at Gumbinnen. Fortified positions were carefully prepared on the Angerapp River. Once Rennenkampf, whose reconnaissance effort was feeble at best, bumped into it, a coordinated assault by three German corps (I, XVII, and I Reserve Corps) would destroy him. It was a sound plan, and it is hard to imagine it failing to work under the circumstances.

Unfortunately, it failed to take into account General François. On August 16, François began an unauthorized advance to the east, wiring his army commander that "the nearer to Russia I engage the enemy the less the risk to German territory."[69] By August 17 he was at Stallupönen on the Russian border. Here he fought a tough engagement against the lead Russian units of Rennenkampf's army. His 1st Division (General Richard von Conta) managed to hold his position against superior Russian attackers all day. The arrival later in the afternoon of the neighboring 2nd Division (General von Falk), coming up from the south, caved in the Russian left flank and captured some three thousand prisoners.[70] Stallupönen had been a tactical success and had inflicted some pain on the Russians. However, it certainly was not in harmony with the overall plan, which was to lure the Russians toward Gumbinnen and hit them there. In fact, it could well have derailed it altogether.

Today, military historians often hold up François as one of the century's classic examples of an insubordinate commander, a vainglorious idiot. Prittwitz actually wired him at Stallupönen and told him to break off the engagement and his bring his corps back to Gumbinnen. François's answer: "Tell General von Prittwitz that General von François will break off the battle when the Russians are beaten."[71] There has been a great deal of speculation as to what he thought he was doing, as well as his motivation. A typical explanation is that, as an East Prussian native, he felt that destiny had chosen him to redeem the province from the invader.[72] Others speak, more prosaically, of his thirst for action, his lust for glory, or even the desire to show off the bravery of the troops he had trained and drilled.[73]

In fact, no such explanations are necessary. As should be plain by now, the Prussian army—and now the German army—bred many such commanders through the centuries. It was such a prevalent personality type that it cannot be attributed to accidental characteristics of this or that individual. For many operational-level commanders in the German army, the art of war consisted of finding the enemy and attacking him. In fact, François had been mulling this over while commanding the *Grenzschutz* (border defense preparations) even before 8th Army became operational. Practically the first messages that came across Prittwitz's desk when he assumed command of 8th Army were from François, informing him that he intended to advance against the first Russian troops that came within reach.

Although Prittwitz did consider François insubordinate, and told him so, François got off with the same nod-and-wink routine as had other unruly commanders in previous wars.

> In January 1915 I arrived on the western front and reported to the Kaiser in Charleville. The Kaiser received me in the garden of the villa. He said some very appreciative things about Gumbinnen, Tannenberg, the Masurian Lakes, and the defense against the second Russian offensive in October and November 1914. . . . He explained to me how things stood on the western front, and then told me, with a friendly laugh, "Now with God's help, François, you'll do a good job here, too. But rein yourself in. You're too independent."[74]

François's punishment for Stallupönen? Promotion to the command of 8th Army during the fall campaign.

On August 19 Prittwitz learned that the 2nd Army had crossed the border, with its five infantry corps. Facing it was a single German formation, XX Corps. With time running out, he could not adhere to the original plan of waiting for Rennenkampf. Instead, he ordered an immediate attack on Rennenkampf at Gumbinnen on August 20. The order was a sudden one, and there was some scrambling on the German side to get the troops into position. Nevertheless, the Germans had a chance to win. They had three corps in line facing east. On the left, I Corps attacked with its usual verve, slamming into the Russian right with great force and driving it back in confusion. Moreover, the German 1st Cavalry Division got clear around the flank into the Russian rear. On the right, I Reserve Corps under General von Below also held his own against superior numbers, attacking with only one of its divisions—the other was en route. Only in the center did things go badly wrong. Here was the XVII Corps of General August von Mackensen. They had received the attack order later on August 19 and had just completed a fifteen-mile night march to get into the fight. Dazed from that experience, and with many units still intermingled, XVII Corps now crashed into a firm line of entrenched Russian infantry supported by the mass of 1st Army's artillery. Mackensen's assault troops suffered grievously, not the least from Russian sharpshooters cunningly placed in the trees, and the general had to get out on the road to stem the panic of whole units.[75]

It now seemed to Prittwitz that all was lost. He reacted in a way similar to other generals facing defeat in this early period of the war: he came apart. He announced to his astonished staff that 8th Army would have to evacuate East Prussia in order to save itself. All forces must retreat immediately behind the Vistula River. There was a general uproar among the staff, and Hoffmann later claimed that he pulled out a compass to prove to Prittwitz that the Russians were closer to the river than the Germans were, in other words that the retreat was impossible. Prittwitz pulled rank and insisted that his order be obeyed.

He then went into his private office. Here, unbeknownst to his staff, he telephoned Moltke to inform him of the decision.[76] It must have been a tough conversation; the last thing Moltke needed to hear right now was panic in the voice of one of his eight army commanders. He evidently heard just that, however, and had to tell Prittwitz to pull himself together "and rally on XX Corps,"[77] the still unengaged formation in 8th Army's order of battle.

He also decided, silently, that Prittwitz would have to be replaced. The new commander of 8th Army would be General Paul von Hindenburg, aged sixty-seven, who came out of retirement to accept the post. Although it is true that he was chosen more for his calm demeanor than for any particular military brilliance, he had certainly done his time "in battle for the greatness of Prussia,"[78] serving as a platoon leader at Königgrätz and a battalion adjutant at St. Privat. With his massive frame and deep voice, he would be the perfect reassuring figure for the shaken command structure of the 8th. It is equally true that he had not risen so high in the command structure of the German army by accident. He had held a number of staff and field assignments alike: teaching tactics at the *Kriegsakademie*, chief of staff to III Corps, service in the War Ministry, chief of staff to VIII Corps, command of IV Corps in 1905. Although he certainly relied on the advice of his chief of staff, the brilliant, somewhat unstable General Erich Ludendorff, Hindenburg was hardly the cipher that historians have portrayed.

By the time Hindenburg and Ludendorff got to East Prussia, it appears that Hoffmann had already drawn up a new plan. The simultaneous change of command and change of plan, however, means that there will always be some uncertainty as to who should get the credit for it. Rennenkampf had halted after Gumbinnen, waiting for supplies to come up. His orders to his units had been intercepted by the Germans, an easy thing to do since the Russians were transmitting *en clair*. The new plan for 8th Army, then, was to turn to the south and smash poor Samsonov—advancing blindly into enemy territory with open flanks.

Since he was known as a dawdler, there was a constant stream of messages from supreme headquarters (*Stavka* in Russian) telling him to hurry, messages that the Germans were reading.

The risks of the plan were obvious. Assigned the mission of delaying the entire Russian 1st Army was a single German cavalry division, the 1st, along with a handful of second-line *Landwehr* brigades and some local *Landsturm*, older men forming a kind of civil defense. If Rennenkampf got wind of what was happening, and if he was able to see that there was only a weak screen in front of him, he could advance not onto the flank of 8th Army, but actually into its rear as the Germans turned south. The 1st Cavalry Division had been marching and fighting since mid-August: first as part of François's *Grenzschutz*, then as part of his rogue advance to Stallupönen, and finally on the extremely active left wing at Gumbinnen, where it had driven nearly 120 miles into the Russian rear, so far it failed to get the retreat order. It was already exhausted ("little water, no supplies . . . horses exhausted, down to half fighting strength").[79] It now had the dual task of masking the transfer of its own 8th Army, as well as providing protection for its rear (*Rückendeckung*) in its new fighting position to the south. It was, in its own way, an epic: a single, exhausted division holding off an entire field army. Rennenkampf's formations advanced slowly, feeling their way forward and trying to find what out what had happened to the German army in front of them. Twice the Germans had hit Rennenkampf, once as he crossed the border and then a second time three days later, and he was in no hurry to have it happen again. Nevertheless, he didn't halt; he kept coming, slowly, to the west. By August 28, in fact, he was exchanging artillery fire with Königsberg fortress. Although we can't say that 1st Cavalry Division handled itself with any great skill, it did get in his way again and again, and it was successful in warding off Russian attempts to pierce the German veil to the south.

By August 25, all three corps that had fought at Gumbinnen were arriving in the south: I Corps by rail onto the right of XX Corps, I Reserve and XVII corps force-marching onto the left. Samsonov was unaware of all this, and on August 26 he gave orders to his units in the center to continue their advance against XX Corps. On the morning of August 27, François attacked and drove in Samsonov's left, while I Reserve and XVII corps drove in the Russian right. By evening, the Germans had encircled most of 2nd Army, 150,000 men at the start of the campaign, near the village of Tannenberg. Cut off from home, 2nd Army now dissolved into a panic-stricken mob. Herded by German machine gun fire into a shrinking perimeter, more than ninety thousand surrendered. Tales of hordes of Russian soldiers blundering into swamps or lakes in their blind panic to escape the trap and drowning are fictitious. The reality was bad enough. The final verdict on the operation should probably go to Samsonov, who shot himself.[80]

WARSAW-ŁÓDŹ

The fall of 1914 would witness one of the most unusual campaigns in the entire war. It was a highly mobile, even swirling encounter filled with near-disasters, decisive victories ripe for the plucking, and enough ups and downs satisfy a lifetime—on both sides. Although it is little remembered today, no other campaign of the war better encapsulated the German doctrine of the war of movement. Far from shaking the German military mind to its foundations, World War I in many ways reinforced very old German views on warfare.

In September 1914, Hindenburg and Ludendorff began to make preparations for another offensive, this time coming up from the south. Using rail and road, they swiftly transferred four corps from East Prussia clear around the Polish salient to Silesia in the south, one of the war's great strategic redeployments. Here they formed a new army, the 9th, consisting of XI, XVII, XX, and Guard Reserve Corps, Woyrsch's *Landwehr* Corps, the 35th Reserve Division, and the 8th Cavalry Division. The goals of this new offensive were the line of the Vistula River and Warsaw. Unbeknownst to the Germans, however, the Russians were planning an offensive at the same time. Russian supreme commander, Grand Duke Nicholas, was also deploying strong forces on the Vistula: four full armies (moving from the Russian right to left, the 2nd, 5th, 4th, and 9th), more than five hundred thousand men and 2,400 guns. Their mission: "a deep thrust into Germany with all available force," in the words of his chief of staff.[81]

The German's got their blow in first, as always, due to the more developed state of their rail net and to superior staff work, two factors that would be constant on this front. The offensive opened on September 28, took the still-assembling Russian forces by surprise, and at first made good progress. The main enemy in the first week was the horrible state of the roads due to the fall rain. Hindenburg would later say that the conditions recalled accounts he had read of Napoleon's Eylau campaign. By October 12, Mackensen's lead elements were just twelve miles from Warsaw, a single day's march. However, they were by now encountering stiff resistance. The German line faced generally northeast, with its right on the Vistula about sixty miles south of Ivangorod and its left in the air. As Russian 2nd and 5th Armies began their descent from the north, they threatened to overlap the German left flank, guarded only by a weak screen of the German 8th Cavalry Division and 35th Reserve Division. Captured Russian army orders gave the Germans a disquieting picture of Russian strength. Between the San and the Vistula Rivers, Grand Duke Nicholas disposed of some sixty divisions, against just eighteen German; in the Warsaw region alone, the balance was fourteen to five. As a result of the previous fighting in the Tannenberg campaign, and the "long and exhausting marches of more than two hundred miles over indescribable roads," many German units were down to less than half establishment, and in some cases worse than that. An increasingly anxious General Hindenburg could see trouble brewing: "What we had feared actually materialized. Fresh masses of troops poured forth from Warsaw and crossed the Vistula below it. Our far-flung battle line was firmly held in front while superior enemy forces, reaching out farther and farther west, threatened to roll up our left flank. The situation could and should not be allowed to remain thus."[82] On October 17, Hindenburg and Ludendorff ordered a limited withdrawal from the Warsaw position. It turned into a longer one when Austrian attacks ordered by Field Marshal Konrad von Hötzendorf collapsed a few days later, placing 9th Army's right flank in danger as well. The retreat concluded on the operation's original start line. Hindenburg and Ludendorff breathed a sigh of relief when the Russians did not pursue: "At first the Russians were hot on our heels, but then the distance between us began to increase."

The "Warsaw campaign" was a bold, but failed, German attempt to find the Russian left flank in Poland. Switching their *Schwerpunkt* from East Prussia to Silesia literally overnight, they had stolen a march on the Grand Duke. Then, as was typical of operations in this era, the Germans could not exploit the initial advantage. The dynamics of the mass army, whose every movement was ponderous in the extreme, took over. The German march into southern Poland was slow, and made even slower by the poor state of the roads. The Russians were able to move enough troops into Warsaw by rail to present the enemy with a solid front by the time he reached the Vistula. They even had troops to spare to begin their own flanking movement, which was hardly an exercise in rapidity in its own right. A huge and clumsy line of corps, ranged abreast, had entered Poland; an even larger line of corps, ranged abreast, had flanked it. It was about as mobile a campaign as 1914-style mass armies could conduct.

The 9th Army was back on its start line by October 24. It had escaped a greatly superior Russian force, but Hindenburg felt that the situation was still quite grim. The Russians were now poised to invade "fertile Silesia, with its highly developed coal mines and great industrial areas, both as vital to our military operations as daily bread itself!"[83] This was a strategic target, in other words, far more important to Germany than East Prussia had been.

On November 1, the emperor appointed Hindenburg commander in chief of all the German forces in the east, with Ludendorff as his chief of staff. August von Mackensen became commander of the 9th Army. Freed from operational control of the army, Hindenburg and Ludendorff could throw themselves immediately into the task of planning future operations. They faced their fair share of challenges. The men of 9th Army were exhausted by forced marches and more than a month of nonstop fighting. Nor would reinforcements be forthcoming. The new supreme commander, General Erich von Falkenhayn, was then deeply engaged in what looked to be the decisive battle raging around Ypres in the west. In this ticklish situation, Ludendorff and Hindenburg opted once again for the bold stroke. The best way to defend Silesia would be to launch another attack on the Russians.

> The consideration that formed the basis of our new plan was this: In the existing situation, if we tried to deal purely frontally with the Russian Fourth Army, a battle against overwhelming Russian superiority would take the same course as that before Warsaw. It was not thus that Silesia would be saved from a hostile invasion. The problem of saving Silesia could only be solved by an offensive. Such an offensive against the front of a far superior enemy would simply be shattered to pieces. We had to find the way to his exposed, or merely slightly protected flank.[84]

That meant the right wing of the Russian force. Hindenburg and Ludendorff would aim the German thrust at the gap between the Russian 1st Army (Rennenkampf), drawn back to the northeast along the bend of the Vistula, and the 2nd (General Scheidemann) in the region of the industrial city of Łódź. The thrust from the south had failed; why not launch a thrust from the north? It would catch the mass of the Russian forces in the Polish salient completely out of position and literally facing the wrong way.

From October 24 to 29, in another of those pieces of staff work for which the German army has become famous, the entire 9th Army was shifted back by rail from the southern to the northern face of the salient. Eighteen divisions took part and completed it in just five days. With its new base between Posen and Thorn, the army was ready for action on October 30. The new deployment left behind only weak forces in the region of Czestochowa, consisting mainly of Woyrsch's *Landwehr* Corps and other untried units. These were the only liaison between 9th Army and the left wing of the Austro-Hungarian forces, a thin screen indeed for sixty miles of front. Hindenburg allowed as much in his memoirs: "From the point of view of numbers, the Russians had only to walk into Silesia to sweep away their resistance with ease and certainty."[85] To prevent that from happening, the Germans had in the course of their retreat destroyed many of the railroads and bridges in southwestern Poland, making a Russian advance in this relatively poor area even more difficult.[86]

Once again the German offensive caught the Russians utterly by surprise. With its left wing along the Vistula River and its right north of the Warta, Mackensen's 9th Army crashed into the right flank of the Russian 2nd Army, with XXV Reserve Corps under General Scheffer taking the lead. Scheffer overran the light screen there and then drove deep into the Russian rear. The Russian Northwest Front commander, General Ruszkii, at first refused to recognize the seriousness of the German threat to his right. "I have set the beginning of the offensive of the 2nd, 5th, and 4th Armies for November 1st," he declared. By the time he realized the gravity of the situation, five full German corps were pouring through the remnants of 2nd Army's right wing, posing a direct threat to the rear of the Russian position in Poland. General Alfred Knox, British military attaché, wrote that it looked like another decisive German victory, "on a par with Cannae, Sedan, or Tannenberg."

Although 2nd Army was in trouble, Grand Duke Nicholas kept his head. He ordered Russian 1st Army to detach three divisions, the "Lovicz force," to march southwest to the aid of 2nd Army. At the same time, 5th Army (on 2nd Army's left) faced about, countermarched, and struck the flank of the encircling German forces. Just that quickly, it was Scheffer who was surrounded. Nicholas's quartermaster general, General Yuri Danilov, actually ordered the trains up to the front to haul off the prisoners that the Russians expected to bag. These were heady days for Russian headquarters. "We've won a victory, a great victory," exulted army chief of staff General Mikhail Beliaev. The number of expected prisoners kept rising. Danilov's first estimate was 50,000; soon, Beliaev was quoting a figure of 150,000.[87] In *The Unknown War* (1932), Winston Churchill opined that "a glance at the map will show that Scheffer's sixty thousand Germans were far more completely surrounded than Samsonov's army had been at Tannenberg. Moreover they were surrounded by vastly superior numbers. So far as strategy can achieve or maps record a situation, their destruction seemed certain."[88]

Alas for the Russians, it was not to be. It was Scheffer's turn to shine, as he pulled off one of the most audacious maneuvers of the war. Forming his corps into a huge, concentrated phalanx (including ten thousand Russian prisoners in the center of the square), he launched an attack in a totally unexpected direction, to the northeast, *away* from his own line. Smashing into a single, barely deployed corps here (the 6th Siberian, part of the Lovicz force), he overran it, broke into the clear, and then wheeled back left to the safety of his own lines, resuming his place in the line between the I Reserve and XX Corps. His men had fought and marched without rest for nine days, and he himself stayed awake at one point for seventy-two straight hours. Together they made it out alive from one of the great adventures of the war.

The campaign was drawing to an end. There had been fighting on a vast scale for three months, and the pace had been hard on men, horses, and equipment. The Germans had gotten the better of the fighting, for the most part, and the Russians had to abandon plans to invade Silesia. With the arrival of Falkenhayn's long-promised reinforcements, Russian resistance in front of Łódź began to collapse. The Russians evacuated the city on December 6, drawing back their line halfway to Warsaw. German troops entered Łódź just before Christmas 1914. For this victory, the emperor promoted Hindenburg to Field Marshal.

Ludendorff later called the Łódź campaign "my pride." The forces were under one strong command, he said, despite the difficulties in communications, "and the corps wheeled like companies."[89] In the end, however, the Łódź campaign saw the failure of both sides to exploit grand opportunities and was more evidence of how hard it was to control such huge forces—250,000 Germans and 600,000 Russians—within the limits of telegraph technology. The Germans had achieved operational surprise, overrun the flank of an entire Russian army, and driven deep into its rear. It had been a textbook case of the German war of movement, but it had not moved quickly enough. The Russians rushed reinforcements to the scene, and in the absence of a frontal German threat had the leisure to turn one of their armies around to counterattack the encircling force. Now it was the Russians who had a German force surrounded, but they proved as unable to close the deal as the Germans had been. Both sides had their chance at a Tannenberg, but neither had reason to be pleased with the results.

Conclusions

In 1903, at the height of Schlieffen's influence, the War History Section (*Abteilung* I) of the Great General Staff published an interesting volume entitled *Success in Battle: How Do We Strive for It? (Der Schlachter-folg)*.[90] Like the "Cannae studies," it is an ambitious attempt to look at the great campaigns of the modern era, especially the victories over Austria and France, in order to distill their lessons for the future. To that purpose, it included a companion volume of no less than sixty-five highly detailed campaign maps. Although the Germans often claimed that they saw no certainty in war and rejected all "systems" for battle-field operations, *Success in Battle* certainly does offer some grounding principles. Not surprisingly, it has little to do with better peacetime organization, or a superior logistics net, or greater industrial capacity. Here is the opening paragraph of the "Conclusion":

> The previous examples confirm convincingly the old truth that a blow against the flank of an enemy, along with a threat to his rear, corresponds to the greatest success. We must also recognize that such an intended flank attack does not always succeed. All the more credit goes to the commander who, nevertheless, tenaciously strives for the advantage of the flank attack. In modern times it was King Frederick who first set his sights on a complete victory, which a parallel battle could not provide.[91]

Hence the oblique attack. But the king went beyond that tactical device: "[Frederick] in his later battles went further than striving to gain the enemy's flank, either throwing his entire army against the rear of the opponent or, as at Torgau, falling upon him from two sides."

As with Frederick, so with Napoleon. Using the superior mobility of the revolutionary armies, facing less maneuverable forces that had dispersed their available strength all over the map, "he concentrated his own strength in a decisive direction against the flank and rear of the enemy." Marengo, Ulm, and Jena were the results. They did not arise from carefully laid plans, exact in all particulars, but the result of freedom of action, of powerful mobile forces in play, which could be brought together in "an operational flanking movement." Only when the allies fought Napoleon with his own weapons, as in Blücher's crossing of the Elbe in 1813, were they able to match strength with Napoleon on the operational level.

Finally, to Moltke. The heir to Napoleon's art of war, Scharnhorst's reorganization of the Prussian army, and Clausewitz's teachings on the necessity for a battle of annihilation, the great chief of the General Staff fought the greatest battles of the era. In each one, he sought to land heavy, operational-level blows, launching entire corps and armies against the enemy flank or rear: Königsberg, Metz, and Sedan. One could not derive a one-size-fits-all recipe for Moltke's art of war, nor draw up a detailed instruction manual for his battles. In fact he had made a career out of denying that it was possible to systematize them. "Strategy is a system of expedients," he had written. His most famous quote, "No plan survives contact with the enemy's main body," was not just the modesty of a great and successful general. It was something he firmly believed and something that the history of his wars had taught him in spades. Could any plan, no matter how clever, account for General von Steinmetz's actions in the opening phases of the Franco-Prussian War?

As they ruminated on the campaigns of World War I, contemplating what had gone wrong, officers of the German army saw no reason to discard the fundamental ideas of *Success in Battle*. Forced into a *Stellungskrieg* for which they were neither trained nor inclined, they had soldiered on professionally. In the course of the war's middle years, they had even become experts at defensive warfare, as the Allies launched offensive after offensive on the western front. They learned to ward off French strikes in the Champagne and British blows in Flanders, and they invariably inflicted more pain than they suffered themselves. Nevertheless, they had not suddenly become converts to defensive or positional warfare: "The battles of the first campaigning period in the west were lost. The *Stellungskrieg* made its appearance, a strange type of fighting to us. As we taught our troops how to dig in, however, we dug a grave for *Bewegungskrieg*, which embodies the German spirit of the attack and the tactical schooling of the officer corps."[92] Indeed. Those were the words of General Hermann von François, the hero of Stallupönen, Gumbinnen, and Tannenberg. He was typical of an officer corps, and an army, that still had an apparently unchangeable default setting: *Bewegungskrieg*.

The *Stellungskrieg* in the middle of the war interested them hardly at all. The hardening of the front into a state of near permanency, the difficulty of cracking it, the monstrous casualties on both sides—none of these had taken the Germans by surprise. That was exactly what happened in a war of position: it soon became a war of attrition, a war that Germany would almost certainly lose. It had nothing to do with firepower or machine guns per se. One staff officer condemned that common idea as "absolutely false." It was simply what happened when both sides were of equal strength, "when neither opponent had such a significant superiority in men, materiel, or leadership that he could attack in the grand style."[93] The realization had set in early for many of them—as early as November 1914 in the case of General von Falkenhayn. Although Germany had predictably succumbed to superior numbers and resources, they saw little need to spend much time contemplating the intricacies of trench warfare. Blasting through a trench line was simply a technical question, more closely related to siege and fortress warfare than to operations in the open field.[94]

Instead, they obsessed on the war's improbably early turning point: the opening campaign of 1914. It was obvious to them that there had been a very good opportunity to win a decisive victory in that campaign. The French had advanced an entire army to the north at Namur, with its right flank open, a juicy operational target indeed. Command paralysis, slow-moving infantry armies, the thick fog of war generated by mass armies in action: all these things had conspired to rob the German army of the victory that was there for the taking. As the army entered a new era, its brightest operational minds were concentrating on one thing: how once again to resurrect *Bewegungskrieg* and fight campaigns of movement on the operational level. The next time an enemy army offered its flank with a foolish and precipitate move into a position of danger, perhaps along the same Meuse River that had shielded Lanrezac's 5th Army, the German army would be ready.

Collapse and Rebirth:
From Versailles to Case White

What is the significance of 1918? Historians typically treat it as the "big break," a spectacular discontinuity with the past. In fact, Germany had been here before: in 1806, to be precise. Napoleon's destruction of the Prussian army at Jena and Auerstädt, Murat's ruthless pursuit of the fleeing remnants of the defeated force, and the complete occupation of Prussian territory had seemed to bring down the curtain on Prussia's great power status. The low point came with the Treaty of Tilsit in 1807. As Napoleon and Alexander I met to decide the fate of Europe, floating on their raft in the midst of the Niemen River, Frederick William III spent a long day riding nervously up and down the river bank, wondering if he would even have a state to rule in the morning. He got one, but the treaty terms left it greatly truncated. It was also officially disarmed, allowed to keep only an insignificant army and forced to submit to French occupation of its major fortresses.

Despite these restrictions, the Prussian state would display surprising reserves of strength. It fought French occupation both actively (defying the limits on its armed forces through use of the so-called Krümper system) and passively (participating in Napoleon's Russian campaign, for example, but dragging its feet the entire way, contributing almost nothing to the fighting, and defecting as soon as Napoleon had suffered a serious reverse). Under several far-sighted officers—Scharnhorst, Gneisenau, Boyen, Clausewitz, and others—it also carried out a thorough self-examination and reform of the army. Less then seven years after the most decisive defeat in its history, Prussia had an army in the field against Napoleon, and less than two years after that, the Prussian army would be pursuing the fleeing remnants of the French army away from the field at Waterloo. The commander of that victorious army, Marshal Blücher, was an old man, over seventy years of age, but he seemed to have found new reserves of strength and vitality. He was the Prussian army, in metaphor.

In other words, for all the ink spilled over it, the Treaty of Versailles wasn't anything particularly new. As the losing side in the greatest war of all time, Germany had paid a severe price. The disarmament clauses of the Treaty of Versailles left the German army (*Reichswehr*) with just one hundred thousand men and a ceiling of four thousand officers. The treaty also dictated its organization and armament. It was to consist of precisely seven infantry and three cavalry divisions, a huge percentage of cavalry for a post-1919 army, and it was forbidden to possess any so-called "offensive weapons": tanks, aircraft, or heavy artillery. The treaty prohibited conscription, so the force consisted solely of long-term volunteers (twelve years for the men, twenty-five years for the officers), stipulations that theoretically made it impossible for the Germans to accumulate a trained reserve. It abolished the Great General Staff, as well as the *Kriegsakademie* that had produced its members. And finally, in a move that could not help but impact military readiness, it saddled Germany with an enormous reparations bill, at the same time as its territorial clauses (occupation of the Rhineland, for example) removed a full 30 percent of the German national tax base.[1]

As it was with Tilsit, so it was with Versailles. Within a decade of signing this allegedly Carthaginian peace, the German military was on its way to a rebirth. It resisted the Allies actively, by experimenting with forbidden weapons like tanks, aircraft, and submarines. It resisted them passively, dragging its feet on weapons inspections and deadlines for the destruction of fortresses and other facilities. It created a camouflaged General Staff under the harmless-sounding rubric of the *Truppenamt* ("troops office"), it continued to train General Staff officers, under the even more harmless-sounding rubric of "commander's assistants" (*Führergehilfen*), and in the so-called "divisional schools" it created a decentralized replacement for the *Kriegsakademie*. Its small size allowed it to keep standards at the absolute highest, and it trained, drilled, and exercised more actively than any army on the planet. Erwin Rommel, a man who would show no little operational talent in the next great war, was a captain in this army, and a captain he almost certainly would have remained until retirement, if later political developments had not paved the way for a rapid rearmament.

Seeckt and the Reichswehr

During the interwar period (1919–1939), the German army dusted itself off from four years of trench warfare, not to mention defeat, and returned to its classical pattern of operational-level war making.[2] The continuities between German operations in World War II and older campaigns are far more striking than the differences. Certainly, the weapons became more technologically sophisticated. Tanks and aircraft increasingly became the strike forces; cavalry all but disappeared; the infantry soldiered on, but with far better fire support and far more sophisticated tactics. Nevertheless, the campaigns rarely departed from the pattern of independent armies maneuvering concentrically against the main enemy force (or against his capital, to force him to deploy his main field force in the path). The goal remained the destruction of the enemy army in a great *Kesselschlacht*; the means remained *Bewegungskrieg*.

This was the task of Germany's military leaders in the interwar era. The crucial figure here, as important to his era as Scharnhorst or Moltke had been to theirs, was General Hans von Seeckt.[3] Seeckt was a gentleman, a man of high refinement, and an intellectual. Like many nobles, he wore a monocle; unlike them, he refused to wear blinkers. He brought an unsentimental, objective view to his task at a time when some fellow officers were steeping themselves in nostalgia for a simpler time, when the All-Highest commanded and they obeyed. There was nothing he disliked more than *Schlagworte*, a German word that means "slogans" but which can also be translated by the twenty-first-century term *buzzwords*. These were catchy turns of phrase that were repeated until they took on the ring of truth.[4] They were a way of life, he recognized, "for all those who are unable to think for themselves." Every buzzword, he said, should leave the listener asking one question: "Is this really true?"[5] Nowhere was the problem more prevalent, or more deadly, than in the military. "Thousands of military human lives are sacrificed to military buzzwords—assuredly not from any evil intention, but simply from lack of independent thought." The term *Cannae*, for example, was permissible as a means of keeping the commander's eye fixed on the ultimate aim of all military operations: destruction of the enemy. If it became a scheme, a one-size-fits-all solution to the problems of modern warfare, it would lead only to disaster. "Cannae," he wrote, "still endures as an idea—the will to destroy—but for anyone who does not comprehend it in this way, it becomes an empty and dangerous *Schlagwort*."[6]

His dispassionate nature was never more evident than in his attitude toward the most controversial military issue of the day, the debate over mechanization. The interwar period was in many ways the age of the military enthusiast. There was J. F. C. Fuller in Britain, brimming over with enthusiasm for the tank. A modern Luther, he demanded nothing less than a "reformation of war," the abolition of the infantry, and its replacement by great fleets of tanks.[7] In Italy there was Giulio Douhet, preaching an even more extreme gospel: a vision of future wars being decided within minutes by strategic bombing, even before the armies had mobilized.[8] And back in Britain, there was B. H. Liddell Hart, whose enthusiasms—tanks, strategic bombing, the "indirect approach—changed seemingly by the month, although he preached each one with equal fervor.[9] Everywhere, great powers and small, from the United States to Hungary,[10] armies were experimenting with tanks, schemes for mechanization, and mobile formations large and small.

In Germany, the situation was different. Here, there was no real mechanization debate, at least not in the form that it took in Great Britain, with its bitterness, name-calling, and ad hominem broadsides. Although there were clashes over this or that point, especially over the future of the cavalry, the major thrust was not in dispute. Unlike commanders in Britain or France, Seeckt and his successors had a clear view of what they wanted to achieve. They wanted to fashion an army that was once again capable of fighting the war of movement on the operational level. Despite the defeat in the war, they saw no reason to jettison traditional operational doctrine as it had come down through the centuries. Tanks, aircraft, motorized infantry, and artillery were all here to stay, certainly, but the infantry wasn't going anywhere. The new weapons were valuable only insofar as they allowed the German army to return to the war-making tradition of Frederick the Great, Napoleon, and Moltke. The rise of *Maschinenwaffen* ("machine weapons"), therefore, did not mean the abolition of a distinctly German pattern of warfare. Instead, they would serve as tools of its restoration.

It is to Seeckt's credit that he kept his eye on this goal even while commanding a tiny army, in reality little more than a "militarized border police."[11] He oversaw the preparation of an entirely new set of manuals, for example, including the new field service regulations, *Führung und Gefecht der verbundenen Waffen* (Leadership and Battle with Combined Arms). It was a compendium of traditional concepts of Prussian-German war making, restated and adjusted for modern conditions. It contained, for example, what one analyst has called a "near-classic credo of German military doctrine":[12]

The attack alone dictates the law to the enemy. It is here that the superiority of leader and troops comes best into play. Especially effective is the envelopment of one or both flanks and the attack in the enemy's rear. In this way the enemy can be destroyed. All orders for the attack must bear the stamp of great decisiveness. The leader's will to victory must be shared down to the last man.[13]

They were familiar words to anyone who had studied Prussian military operations over the years—the operational heritage of Frederick the Great, Clausewitz, Moltke, and Schlieffen.

Another *Schlagwort* that Seeckt refused to accept was the notion of "the lessons of World War I." Although he had seen action on all the wartime fronts, including service on the crucial right wing in 1914, he won his wartime laurels in the east. As chief of staff to the armies under the command of General August von Mackensen, he directed the decisive breakthrough of the Russian front between Gorlice and Tarnòw in 1915, as well as the deep penetration into the Russian rear. In 1916, still assisting Mackensen, he helped to plan the lightning conquest of Romania.[14] These were the campaigns that stamped his vision of war. In the East he saw a great deal of hard fighting, but the vastness of the front and the absence of covering terrain prevented the development of the *Stellungskrieg*, or war of position, that had occurred in northern France. He did not accept the commonly held belief that there was a new "crisis of the attack,"[15] as in the pre-1914 era. The invulnerability of entrenched infantry, the futility of infantry assault, the omnipotence of the machine gun—these were buzzwords. They were not the nature of war. Rather, they were simply the outcome of the aberrational nature of the western theater: mass armies packed solidly, corps to corps and elbow to elbow, across four hundred miles of unbroken front.

If there was one common thread running through all these new documents, it was the importance of mobility. The one form of battle that the Reichswehr practiced obsessively was the meeting engagement: two forces smashing into one another unexpectedly.[16] Victory went to the commander who could recognize what was happening, react to it, and get his units out of march column into the line. The ability of the German army to perform this complicated ritual fills the World War II memoir literature from the Allied side: a seemingly uncanny ability to whip together an integrated fire team out of a handful of infantry, a single machine gun, and a light mortar. The Germans should have been good at it. They'd been practicing it for twenty years.

Meeting engagements and maneuver warfare required reforms in command and control. Seeckt believed there was no need in most cases to issue printed orders. Verbal orders were almost always preferable. Ideally, they should derive from the terrain, with the officer pointing to the actual objectives, rather than to the map. They should be "clear, positive, and simple." They must never be the product of a "war council" between the commander and his officers; there was no need for "long-winded discussions." And there was certainly no need for what he called "prolix written combat orders." There was no place in *Bewegungskrieg* for typewriters or mimeograph machines; these were accouterments of trench warfare.[17]

Seeckt was perhaps the first commander in European history to say something out loud that certainly must have been percolating in the military subconscious. It was not just technology, he recognized, but the mass army itself that had caused the *Stellungskrieg* in the first place. "The mass becomes immobile, it can no longer maneuver," he wrote, "and therefore it cannot win. It can only crush."[18] During the war, all European armies had increased in size and decreased in effectiveness. They became, in effect, huge militias: mobs of half-trained soldiers who were incapable of forcing a decision. New technology, armor and air power above all, had chewed them up, turning this "immobile, almost defenseless human mass" into "cannon fodder for a small number of elite technicians on the other side."[19] They died in huge numbers as a result and were then invariably replaced by fresh recruits even more poorly prepared to face the storm of steel. An ideal national army, Seeckt felt, only needed to be large enough to fight off a surprise enemy attack in the opening phase of a war. Once on a wartime footing, its real strength would lie not in its mass but in its mobility. It would consist of well-conditioned infantry, a large contingent of cavalry, and a full complement of motorized and mechanized units. Its superior mobility would work as a force multiplier, enabling it to wage offensive warfare even against larger enemy armies and letting it aim at a decisive battle of annihilation against the enemy. "The goal of modern strategy will be to achieve a decision with highly mobile, highly capable forces, before the masses have even begun to move," he wrote.[20]

It is often passed over with slight comment, but it is surely significant that one of his first acts as chief of the army was to designate its battalions as repositories for the traditions, memorabilia, and honors of past Prussian regiments. It was quite a popular move within the officer corps. Indeed, the shooting had barely stopped when a staff officer published an appeal in the *Militär-Wochenblatt* on behalf of "what is venerable and permanent":

We must preserve the old regiments, with their traditions dating back to Warsaw (I refer here to the famous battle of July 28th–30th, 1656, in which the Poles received such a welcome thrashing) and Fehrbellin, and extending to the most recent past. It would be a great and irreparable injustice to the people connected to these regiments of the royal era, if we rip away all connection to the past. For the common people—even if they vote Social Democrat—are conservative. Even today, every provincial newspaper carries stories of the death of an old fighter, and the assembly of his former comrades in the regimental association to pay him the last honor.[21]

This was not simply a question of tradition, but of operational doctrine. Note that the frame of reference here is not, as might be expected, the great events of the recent past, neither the Somme nor Amiens nor Passchendaele. Instead, it is the battles of Warsaw and Fehrbellin, rapid and decisive victories from the age of the Great Elector. They may have already been forgotten in the rest of Europe, and they may be virtually unknown to most people today, but they were still touchstones of Prussian-German military culture in 1919.

It is a commonplace to argue that World War I had shaken the very edifice of western thought, the belief in science and progress—for many, even the belief in God. It had apparently not, however, disturbed the German military's belief in the war of movement. Indeed, on the very eve of World War II, as European armies once again subjected their societies to the wrenching process of mobilization, the semiofficial weekly of the German army, the *Militär-Wochenblatt*, was looking to the past. In its issue of August 18, 1939, it ran a detailed analysis of the most famous German victory of World War I. This was perhaps the final version of the magazine that most German officers read before departing for the Polish border. If it is true that the high command of the army went to war in 1914 with images of Cannae on its mind, it would do so in 1939 with images of another battle, "a complete victory that achieved the only thing worth fighting for, the destruction of the enemy," one with "all the characteristics of *Bewegungskrieg*."[22] It would be dreaming of Tannenberg.

The Persistence of the Prussian Operational Pattern

EARLY REBIRTH: STORMING THE ANNABERG

Arguing that traditional operational patterns survived during the interwar era requires further discussion. After all, Seeckt's Reichswehr never fought a battle during this period. It had no Königgrätz to its credit, nor any Jena, for that matter. However, German forces did fight at least one battle between 1920 and 1939. Nearly forgotten today, it was major news at the time and is still worthy of study.

The Treaty of Versailles had called for a plebiscite in the important German industrial district of Upper Silesia. As the voting approached, tensions rose between the Germans and Poles in the province, and in fact there were Polish uprisings in August 1919 and August 1920. The plebiscite, held in March 1921, was a severe blow to the young Polish state, with the Germans winning the vote by 707,000 to 479,000. While they cried fraud and the Germans exulted, the Allies announced a decision to partition Upper Silesia—which only inflamed both population groups. On May 3, there was a third Polish uprising led by Wojciech Korfanty.[23] The uprising succeeded in seizing all the areas claimed by Poland—some two-thirds of the province and virtually all its industry. On May 9, the Poles seized Cosel and crossed to the left bank of the Oder; on May 12, further attacks in the northern sector drove the Germans out of Rosenberg. Only several small bridgeheads on the right bank of the Oder remained in German hands, the most important being at Krappitz.[24]

Opposing the Polish forces in Upper Silesia was a motley collection of German irregulars, known as the *Selbstschutz* (Self-Defense), a mix of recently demobilized veterans and men too young to have fought in the war. Coming to their aid was a large-scale influx of paramilitary formations and *Freikorps* from all over Germany. These included the *Stahlhelm*, the *Jungdeutscher Orden,* the *Organisation Escherich* (or *Orgesch*), and many others.[25] The German government could not intervene directly, which would mean war with the Allies, but it did provide transportation and supplies to groups traveling to the beleaguered province.

The German forces, although outnumbered, soon seized the initiative. This was not surprising, given the fact that many of them were highly experienced soldiers, while most of the Polish insurgents were Upper Silesian civilians. The arrival of powerful German reinforcements in the province sealed the fate of the insurrection. German counterattacks began as early as May 15, when Cosel was retaken. On May 20, the Poles launched one last great attack along the rail line leading to Kreuzburg from Zembowitz, an assault spearheaded by an armored train and two 105 mm cannon. After a preliminary bombardment, the Poles attempted to storm the German positions. The well-trained German force allowed the Poles to close to within one hundred yards, then opened fire with machine guns, "sowing panic in the ranks of the insurgents."[26] By May 22, Rosenberg was back in German hands.

Advertisements for service in the "well-disciplined units" of the *Freikorps*.
Note that joining up will be "counted as service in the active army." *Militär-
Wochenblatt* 103, nos. 96–97 (February 11 and 13, 1919).

This had been small-scale combat up till now, and the German commander, General Bernhard von Hülsen, believed that the time had come for a larger action. As one of his company commanders wrote, "it was time for a great, visible victory to take over from the wearying routine of patrols and positional battles."[27] It was, in other words, time to step up to the operational level. The major geographical feature in Upper Silesia is a chain of hills that dominate the right bank of the Oder. The most important is the Annaberg, about ten kilometers to the east of Krappitz. Standing some three hundred meters high, with a convent and large stone clock tower on the summit, it was the provincial landmark. The master of the Annaberg would be master of Upper Silesia.

By the third week of May, Hülsen had identified the Annaberg as his primary operational target. He managed to concentrate a large force by the standards of this small war: six and a half battalions. Organizing them into two columns, he quietly transferred them to the right bank of the Oder at the Krappitz bridgehead, and at 2:30 A.M. on May 21, he launched them on an offensive against the Annaberg.

The going was slow at first and Polish resistance fierce. Perhaps the Poles had got wind of the German river crossing, Hülsen believed. There also wasn't a single heavy weapon in the German arsenal. "We learned then," he wrote, "how painful it could be to mount an assault on a fortified position without a single piece of artillery."[28] The situation became particularly dire when the Poles began to launch a series of local counterattacks from their positions on the heights. The Germans, young toughs from the Bavarian-based *Freikorps Oberland*, had to beat them back with grenade and then with bayonet. Driving the Poles from Sakrau, the Germans seized a pair of guns ("made in Germany") and muscled them forward. Just after sunrise, the Bavarians made good use of their new battery, using it to support an attack on the town of Oleschka, on the western slopes of the Annaberg.

Eventually, better German training began to tell. The Imperial Army was no more, but these officers and soldiers still bore the stamp of its training regimen. Although there doesn't seem to have been an operational plan worked out in advance, the Oberlanders worked their way around the base of the hill and at 11:00 A.M. launched a well-coordinated concentric advance on the hill. The Finsterlin Battalion attacked from the northwest; the Assault Detachment Heintz from the southwest; the Oestricher Battalion with its two captured cannon from the east; the Sebringhaus Battalion and the Eicke Company from the southeast. It was over by lunch hour. "Our hearts trembled with joy," wrote one participant, "as we watched the Poles evacuate their positions and the black-

The Annaberg, with the monastery on the summit clearly visible. In the foreground is the grave of "twenty-one brave fighters of the self-defense force who fell in the days of the uprising, 1921."

white-red flag appear on the clock tower of the convent. It was the first German victory since those days of ignominy in November 1918."[29]

A victory, yes, but a small one, and one should not exaggerate it. The German force on the Annaberg hadn't even reached one thousand men. With "battalions" of volunteers that were closer in size to companies, the figure was probably somewhere around nine hundred. It had suffered a grand total of 120 casualties. The *Freikorps* involved were some of the most unsavory characters in all of German history, right-wing extremists and murderous thugs like later S.A. *Obergruppenführer* Edmund Heines[30] and Ernst von Salomon, who in the next year would take part in the plot to murder German foreign minister Walther Rathenau.[31] These were men who either could or would not demobilize psychologically after World War I. They hated civilians, frankly, and they murdered more than their fair share of them. Nevertheless, the attack on the Annaberg is significant. It had adhered to long-standing traditions of German operations, even if only subconsciously, and it showed how far down the chain of command the officers and men had internalized the concepts they had learned in training. It was all there on that hot spring day: a high degree of aggression, a concentric advance against the enemy, and, even if only in miniature, a battle of annihilation.

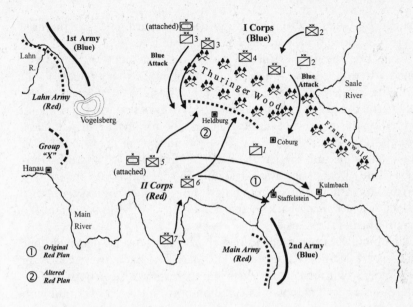

Meeting Engagement: The Fall Maneuvers of 1930

THE FALL MANEUVERS OF 1930

The Fall Maneuvers of 1930 are another example of the persistence of the Prussian operational pattern.[32] They featured a highly mobile scenario taking place in the broken terrain south of the Thuringer Wald. All ten of the army's divisions took part, along with a full complement of administrative and supply services, all the way down to the field postal service. The pinch of the Great Depression meant that some were represented only as "flag divisions" (staff and intelligence sections all the way down to battalion, with companies represented in the field by appropriately colored flags) or "cadre divisions" (divisional staff only). Nevertheless, two complete divisions were in the field, making it the largest Reichswehr maneuver since 1919.

As was the long-standing custom by now, the actual mobile units were inserted on the flanks of a larger theaterwide confrontation. In this case Blue 1st Army was retreating to the east in the face of an advance by the Red "Lahn Army" north of the Vogelsberg. Likewise, far to the southeast, Blue 2nd Army was withdrawing to the east before the advance of the Red "Main Army" (named for the river Main). In the gap between the two pairs of armies, Red's II Corps, commanded by General von Kayser (5th, 6th, and 7th Infantry Divisions, along with the 1st Cavalry Division) faced off against Blue's I Corps, commanded by General Otto von Hasse (1st, 2nd, 3rd, and 4th Infantry Divisions, 2nd and 3rd Cavalry Division).

Analyzing the initial situation, the Red commander saw an opportunity to envelop Blue 2nd Army on its open northern (right) flank. His initial orders were for 5th and 6th Divisions to advance to the east, through Staffelstein and Kulmbach; 7th Division was hurrying up to the line but would not be ready for action for another day at least. Finally, he had his 1st Cavalry Division advancing on Coburg with an eye to protecting the left flank of the advancing 5th and 6th Divisions. Blue, for its part, was advancing to the south with its entire I Corps—its principal mission to guard the right flank of the 2nd Army and allow it to swing back to the northeast and the more defensible terrain of the Frankenwald.

The mobile corps on both sides, then, had drawn up plans without being aware of the existence of the other. The maneuver opened on September 15 with the directors springing that surprise on both parties. There was a certain amount of scrambling from the very beginning in what had suddenly turned into a vast corps-level meeting engagement. Red had to forget about its envelopment plans of the Main Army, and instead swing to the north and northeast. Its new mission called for a blow against Blue I Corps as it emerged from the Thuringer Wald—a sort of Jena campaign in reverse. Blue, with a force that was two divisions stronger than Red, immediately spotted an opportunity to envelop Red's left wing south of the forest, using three infantry divisions (1st, 3rd, and 4th) and the 3rd Cavalry Division. The attack offered good prospects, made even better by the armored brigade attached to the 3rd Cavalry. The only potential problem for Blue was bad news far to the right—its 1st Army was being pushed steadily back, and the Blue commander already knew that he might have to surrender some of his divisions at any moment to reinforce it.

The morning of September 16, therefore, saw the opposing corps crash into one another, with each seeking to benefit from the difficulties of the other. Blue was having a hard time getting its main body through the Thuringer Wald; Red had a dangling left flank vulnerable to a Blue attack by infantry and armor. Red 5th Division crashed into Blue 3rd Infantry Division and fought it to a standstill, but immediately came under attack deep on its left flank and rear from the Blue 3rd Cavalry Division. The entire left wing of the Red position was now in danger from this "effectively developing concentric attack."[33] The Red commander had to do a quick survey of his front, and by and large the news was bad. His left was in trouble. To the east, 6th Division had achieved its march objectives for the day without a great deal of action developing outside of a few patrols. Red's 7th Division was just coming up now and would soon be joining the line to the right of the 6th, with 1st Cavalry Division pulling back to guard the extreme right flank. With a fully developed enemy across his entire front in strength and threatening to lap him on the left, Red II Corps commander drew back his 5th and 6th Divisions on the night of September 16–17.

The next day of the maneuver saw repeated missed opportunities by both sides. Blue I Corps commander was conscious of his superior strength by now and aimed this time for an envelopment of Red's eastern flank. Although only a single division (3rd Cavalry) had carried out the first attack, this one would attempt the grand stroke. His 4th Infantry Division would strike Red frontally near the village of Heldburg, while 1st and 2nd Infantry Divisions and 2nd Cavalry Division attacked "in an enveloping fashion," seeking the enemy's right flank, levering Red II Corps away from contact with Main Army, and perhaps threatening the left of Red's main force. Blue's 3rd Infantry Division would also join in, "continuing its concentric attack"[34] in a southeasterly direction against Red 5th Division. As was typical of Prussian-German war making, Blue's commander was a man in a hurry, working in an uncertain environment against an unknown deadline. As the situation of 1st Army far off to the right became more dire, he would almost certainly be ceding a division or two very soon.

The action on September 17 was the most interesting of the entire maneuver. Blue launched a well-coordinated double-envelopment of the Red II Corps. Red largely avoided the pain of the blow, however, through the timely withdrawal that the commander had ordered the night before. Blue's attempted envelopment, in other words, struck air. In fact, when Blue 3rd Infantry Division made its turn-in to the southeast, it offered its own right flank to a sharp counterblow from the now-revived Red 5th Division, supported by its own armored brigade. The Blue division was thrown back in some confusion. In the east, Blue's four-division *Schwerpunkt* soon came to a standstill, held up by Red's advance guard, extremely broken terrain, and some truly awful weather—hard rains that soaked both sides for the entire three days of the maneuver.

On the evening of September 17, both sides received news from the flanks. In the southeast, Blue's 2nd Army had successfully disengaged from the Red "Main Army." Pivoting with its right on Bamberg, it had drawn back to a defensible line in the Frankenwald. "The crisis on the northern flank of Blue 2nd Army was over."[35] Unfortunately, that happy news was more than balanced by events far to the west, where

Lahn Army was attacking Blue 1st Army frontally. Here a newly identi-fied "Red Group X" had assembled in Hanau and was slowly advancing against the left flank of 1st Army. The situation was not yet critical, but once again Blue I Corps commander had to be aware that upper com-mand echelons would soon be transferring one or more of his divisions.

Characteristically, while he still had his entire corps together, he ordered one last attack against Red for September 18 while Red did the same against Blue. By now the situation had stabilized enough so that both attacks would be purely frontal in nature. On the evening of September 18, however, Blue finally received orders for the immediate transfer of at least two divisions to the west to match up against Red Group X. Another stormy night allowed Blue's redeployment to go unnoticed by Red.

The three-day maneuver was over, and despite the presence of sev-eral "flag" and "cadre" divisions, the commanders, staff, and intelli-gence officers on both sides had been through a grueling workout. The officers and men had been on the move for three solid days, and the pace had been brutal. As one participant wrote, by the last day "ev-ery time an order was given without the map, Klein-Eibstadt became Gross-Eibdorf and Gross-Bardorf became Klein-Barstadt."[36] The fog of war had been present in abundance, aided in this case by rotten weather, and both teams had done a great deal of groping in the dark. Red II Corps began with what looked like an open shot on the right flank of the Blue "Main Army." It then saw that opportunity evapo-rate as a huge force (Blue I Corps) came down on it from the north, striking it a sharp blow that soon developed into a dangerous series of attempted envelopments: first against Red's left flank, then against its right. Only Blue's need to remove divisions from the combat sector and dispatch them to the west had saved Red from worse trouble. Red had difficulty dealing with Blue's tanks in direct combat, yet maneu-vered cleverly from a position of weakness to avoid the heaviest weight of Blue's intended blow—the double envelopment on September 17. Its skillful withdrawal in the face of Blue's initial attack even allowed it to deliver a solid rap in the flank of one of Blue's onrushing divisions.

The obsession with detail in these maneuvers could often go to in-credible lengths. The 1930 maneuver featured the entire supply and administrative structure of the army, as well. There was a fully func-tioning radio and telephone net; planners requisitioned the necessary railroads for the duration; chains of command were established in case of illness on the part of any of the major participants. The exercise even featured fully operational field post systems for both Blue and Red.

There were postbox numbers and arrangements for mail distribution in the field, which extended as low as individual platoons. The emphasis was on the field post system in a war of movement. On the third day of the operation, the situation required mail officers for both Blue and Red to switch the location of their principal depots, and they also had to prepare for another switch on a hypothetical fifth day. Apparently, in the German army, even the field post was expected to have a *Schwerpunkt*.[37]

Foreign observers at German maneuvers, U.S. military attachés for example, would typically send back copious, detailed reports to their home countries of what they had experienced. What is surprising is how little attention they ever paid to the operational situation. Instead, the reports bulged with tactical details, the appearance and demeanor of the men or horses, new helmet straps or belt buckles, and the occasional appearance of a new weapon or two (although this was rare in officially disarmed Germany). All these things are important, of course, and an attaché is supposed to report what he sees. Discussion of the maneuvers on the operational level, however, would have given the War Department far greater insight into just how the Germans were preparing to fight the next war.

Mechanization and the War of Movement

THE PANZER DIVISION

In the interwar period, the Germans would devise their own unique solution to the mechanization problem. Other armies had their share of false starts. Although the British had the early lead, all they managed to come up with was something called the "Armoured Division," a pure armored formation with hundreds of tanks and almost no supporting arms. Designed for speed and dash, it proved to be a disaster in the early years of the war. The French came up with a pair of new formations, a "light mechanized division" (DLM) for cavalry duties like screening and pursuit and a much slower "armored division" (DCR) for the assault; the first proved to be too light for sustained pounding, and the second too slow for maneuver. The Italians came up with one of the most spectacular doctrinal wrong turns of all time: the binary division, which consisted of two regiments instead of three. It was lighter, faster, easier to deploy, and, once again, a failure in actual combat.[38] There are those who argue that the U.S. Army's armored doctrine, employing tanks almost purely for exploitation and pursuit, rather than for fighting other tanks, rivaled the Italians for futility.[39]

The Germans came up with something quite different: the panzer division.[40] Its development was the most important military innovation in the interwar period, and it is surprising how little understood it remains. Still the most common explanation is that the Germans concentrated their tanks in large units rather than parceling them out in "penny packets" among their infantry. One of the leading German military theorists of the era, Colonel (later General) Heinz Guderian, immortalized this doctrine in the untranslatable phrase "Klotzen, nicht kleckern," usually rendered in English as "Kick 'em, don't splatter 'em," but really meaning "strike concentrated, not dispersed." Such a phrase might give the impression that a panzer division was made up of nothing but tanks. In fact, the panzer division was a combined arms formation. It included tanks, to be sure, but it also had its own organic reconnaissance, infantry, and artillery components, even its own supply columns and bridging trains. The principal innovation was that each of these supporting arms could move as rapidly as the tank. The new formation was not merely a "tank division," then, but "a self-contained combined arms team, in which tanks were backed up by other arms brought up, as far as possible, to the tanks' standards of mobility."[41]

Flexibility was its hallmark. It could assault and penetrate an enemy position, break through into the clear, and then conduct pursuit of the beaten remnants of the enemy—all by itself. It could seize key ground with its tanks, hold it with its rapidly advancing infantry and artillery, withstand the strongest enemy counterattacks, and then regroup and do it all over again. It was, in other words, the perfect weapon for the war of movement on the operational level. Panzer divisions, grouped into larger panzer corps (and eventually panzer armies), could get around or slice through virtually every infantry position they met in the opening years of World War II. Driving deep into the opponent's flank or rear, and then linking up far behind the lines, they were capable of sealing off the largest encirclements in military history.

This was not just "movement by separated armies" or "concentric advance" as in the German wars of the nineteenth century. This was actual encirclement, with hundreds of thousands of prisoners the result. It went far beyond Moltke's concept of *Kesselschlacht*, which saw armies uniting on the battlefield to launch decisive attacks from more than one compass point. In the early years of World War II, the panzer division achieved something that German staff officers had dreamed about but rarely achieved: the battle of annihilation. Even more surprisingly, they assembled this stellar record while remaining only a small portion of the German order of battle. In 1935, the German army (by now styled the

"Wehrmacht") established its first three panzer divisions. By 1939, there were still only six, along with four so-called light divisions.[42] Here was the realization of Seeckt's view of a small and highly mobile elite that would form the cutting edge of the mass army.

The panzer division arose not simply from theoretical work, however. There was a long series of maneuvers and field exercises testing mechanized war concepts. In the 1928 fall maneuvers in Silesia, simulated tank attacks twice overran the same divisional headquarters.[43] In 1931–1932, Colonel Oswald Lutz, the inspector of motor transport troops, oversaw a series of exercises involving dummy tank battalions on the maneuver grounds of Jüterbog and Grafenwöhr. From them, Lutz derived a series of lessons to be used as a basis for further training, based on the principle of independent missions for the tanks, overwhelming mass, and surprise. The armored assault, he wrote, should be "surprising, sudden, and on a broad front."[44] Most important were the exercises after the introduction of tanks in 1935. The 1936 fall maneuvers marked the first appearance of an actual armored fighting vehicle in a German field exercise. The 1937 fall maneuvers in Mecklenburg were, in a sense, a "coming-out party" for the new formations. Here the 3rd Panzer Division sliced through positional defenses on the enemy flank, turned and assaulted a bridgehead position near Lake Malchin from the rear, and then turned again and smashed the opponent's vulnerable supply and headquarters facilities. The new Luftwaffe played a key role here, as well, interdicting the Malchin position, preventing reinforcements from reaching it, and leaving it vulnerable to the bold panzer stroke.

There was one last piece of the puzzle, and that was the issue of command and control. It had been hard enough to control the mass army when it consisted almost exclusively of slow-moving infantry. With high-velocity armored units careening around the continent on far-flung and independent missions, the problem had become much more intense, and things became even worse with the insertion of aircraft into the mix. The solution was a new technological breakthrough: the radio. Although the strengths and weaknesses of the tank were the obsession of most contemporary military discourse, radio was the real breakthrough of the period. The days of the runner, the unreliable telegraph, and the Morse code were gone, replaced by direct voice messages from the commander to subordinate and vice versa.

Although all western nations shared the technology of radio, it was the Germans who put it through the most far-reaching tests, culminating in the "Radio Exercise" (*Funkübung*) of 1932. The German army was the first to realize that the radio was not simply a desirable asset. As far as the new mobile formations went, the radio was indispensable. "It is part of the unique character of motorized and mechanized units that they can only be commanded with the assistance of technical means of communication," wrote Major Friedrich Bertkau: "The masses of motor vehicles in their extraordinarily long columns or widely dispersed battle formations, the noise of the machines, the difficulty of observation from inside the tank, the speed of movement, the rapid change of the battle situation, the special difficulty in moving at night—all these demand a technical solution to command problems."[45] Only the radio could provide an instantaneous way to report the situation back to the commander and to send relevant orders to the troops. From the start, the German principle for the new panzer division was a radio in each command station and each vehicle of the unit, from the smallest motorcycle to the heaviest tank, with specialized command vehicles designed to carry radio equipment, both senders and receivers. Tank warfare on the operational level, in other words, was unthinkable without the radio.[46]

CASE WHITE

The first test for these new mobile formations came during the invasion of Poland in September 1939, and they certainly passed the test. There is still controversy over how to evaluate Case White, the code name for the operation. On the one hand, the Germans won a devastating and complete victory, with their untried panzer divisions leading the way. The word *blitzkrieg*, "lightning war," soon became part of the world's military vocabulary.[47] Yet it can't be denied that this great victory came at the expense of a far weaker, far poorer country that could not afford the kind of modern weapons the Germans had. Poland's geographical situation was nearly hopeless. Germany lay not only to the west, but also to the northwest (Pomerania) and southwest (Silesia). Directly to the south lay German-occupied Slovakia, and directly to the north the detached German province of East Prussia. It should also be added that to the east was the Soviet Union, ruled by Adolf Hitler's new treaty partner, Joseph Stalin. Nothing short of full-blown western intervention, in other words, could have saved Poland from the German assault.

The operational plan for Case White[48] featured concentric drives by two widely separated army groups, five armies, operating from Pomerania and East Prussia in the north and from Silesia and occupied Slovakia in the south. Army Group North (General Fedor von Bock) had 4th Army operating out of Pomerania and its 3rd based in East

Prussia. Army Group South (General Gerd von Rundstedt) contained three armies: 8th and 10th Armies advancing from Silesia, and 14th Army straddling the territory between Silesia and occupied Slovakia. Expressed in simplest terms, the plan called for the two army groups to smash through the Polish defensive positions along the border and catch the main body of the Polish forces in a great pincer movement (*Zangenbewegung*), with the main weight of the attack coming up from Army Group South. In fact, the unusual conformation of the border made things quite a bit more complicated than that.

Those problems were particularly evident in the northern sector. Army Group North had to deploy in completely separate areas, with its two armies divided by the Polish Corridor. As a result, the army group "had to solve two problems at the same time," one geographic and one operational.[49] First, it had to crash through enemy defenses in the corridor and establish overland communications with East Prussia. This would be the primary responsibility of 4th Army, and especially of its XIX (Motorized) Corps under General Heinz Guderian. He would begin the campaign by driving almost due east to overrun the corridor. Only then would Army Group North begin the destruction of the Polish army by launching a major attack to the south. The position of 3rd Army in East Prussia was especially problematic. It would start the war technically isolated, having to rely on a seaborne line of communications back to Germany proper, and it would stay that way until the corridor had been captured. The defense of the detached province had figured prominently in German war games during the interwar era, and the prognosis had never been optimistic.[50] Even a small Polish force, the Germans knew, could disrupt traffic and supply through the corridor.

Planning problems did not stop there. All summer long, Bock had been peppering the High Command of the Army (OKH) with plans to expand his role.[51] After overrunning the corridor, he wanted to ship his entire 4th Army from Pomerania to East Prussia, inserting it on the left of 3rd Army and sending it on a wide sweep far to the east of Warsaw. If Polish forces managed to escape the initial German blow along Poland's western border, he felt, they would attempt to regroup in the interior of the country. An encirclement might occur to the region east of Warsaw. The chief of the OKH, General Walther von Brauchitsch, took a dim view of such a major redeployment in the midst of the fighting. He warned Bock repeatedly that committing troops too far to the east of Warsaw could have serious repercussions in case of an Allied attack in the west.[52] Once again, as in all of Prussia's wars, we see the crucial role of time constraints. This war, too, had to be short and lively—a quick victory and then redeployment to the west.

There was no easy answer, however. The 4th Army had to open the corridor, and it had to launch a major and rapid attack toward the south, so as not to leave Army Group South bearing the burden of the offensive all by itself. How to weigh the two was the issue, and it hung in the air all summer. The eventual solution, however, was the only possible one from the standpoint of German military tradition:

> The General Staff of the Army emphasized that, after it reached the Vistula, the mass of the 4th Army should keep attacking in the same direction (i.e., to the southeast). Bock, however, argued that an offensive from southern East Prussia, with the *Schwerpunkt* aiming over the Narew and then east of Warsaw would be the most effective. Eventually, the OKH gave in and changed its operational directives correspondingly. The army group must have full freedom of action.[53]

Indeed, the man in the field always took precedence over the staff in German war making. Brauchitsch still envisioned the destruction of Polish forces to the west of Warsaw and felt that he had made his point; Bock now felt that he had permission for a complete redeployment of 4th Army after opening the corridor, with an eye to an envelopment and great *Kessel* somewhere to the east of the capital. As always, the German way of war left many planning issues in the air, allowing them to play out in the course of actual operations.

In the end it scarcely mattered. Army Group North crossed the border before dawn on September 1. There was some hard fighting here and there across the front, but essentially the plan worked as devised. On the left wing of 4th Army, Guderian's XIX Corps (3rd Panzer Division, 2nd and 20th Motorized Infantry Divisions) attacked out of Pomerania. It found a weak spot in the positions of the Polish Pomorze Army and soon had bridgeheads across the Brda (Brahe) River, using rubber assault boats to ferry the infantry across.[54] The other two components of 4th Army (I and III Corps) advanced on Guderian's right, objective Bydgoszcz (Bromberg). Progress was good. As early as the second day of the advance, panzer elements of XIX Corps had outrun their gasoline and ammunition supply columns.[55] He had to call a temporary halt to allow the trucks to catch up, and they, in turn, had a wild ride, having to fight their way through Polish units bypassed by the armored advance.

Nevertheless, by the end of the day, the Germans had sealed off the southern end of the corridor, trapping two Polish infantry divisions (9th and 27th) and a cavalry brigade (Pomorska). Their attempts to break out came to naught, with all three formations being smashed in the course of the fighting and fifteen thousand prisoners already in German hands by day three.[56] It is almost certainly from this sector that there arose the famous tales of Polish lancers attempting to charge German tanks. They aren't true—the German sources are extremely sketchy as to time and place—but it is likely that Polish cavalry units had contacted German armor in their attempt to escape encirclement in the corridor.[57]

Other operational details in this sector included the seizure of the free city of Danzig, accomplished by local units of the *SS-Heimwehr Danzig*, and the defeat of Polish forces defending the port of Gdynia, a mission carried out successfully by a special detachment of Border Defense Command I (*Grenzschutz Abschnittskommando* I). Although these small operations ran smoothly, there were a few missteps. An attempted landing by a marine assault company at Danzig, carried into the harbor before the outbreak of the war on a "friendship visit" by the training ship *Schleswig-Holstein*, misfired completely. The ship also formally opened hostilities by bombarding the Polish fortress of Westerplatte, but the tiny Polish garrison there managed to hold out for five days.[58] Likewise, a coup against the crucial rail bridge over the Vistula at Tczew (Dirschau) got there too late to prevent the Poles from destroying it. It was a blow to German communications between the Reich and the separated province. In a longer campaign, such failures might well have had serious consequences.

The advance of 3rd Army from East Prussia began with XXI Corps advancing to the southwest, with the Vistula River on its right, toward Grudziądz (Graudenz). It contacted Polish units almost immediately, the 16th and 4th Infantry Divisions, the right flank and rear of the same Pomorze Army being so roughly handled by 4th Army. The Poles managed heavy counterattacks the next day, but ran into a buzz saw of German artillery and air attack, and had soon fallen back into Grudziądz. From here they managed to retreat in fairly good order to the south and east.

The rest of 3rd Army had slower going against heavy Polish resistance. This was, after all, the short road to Warsaw, defended by the 8th and 20th Infantry Divisions of the Polish Modlin Army. The I Corps lay immediately to the left of XXI Corps, with an ad-hoc "Corps Wodrig" to its own left. In this sector the German spearheads

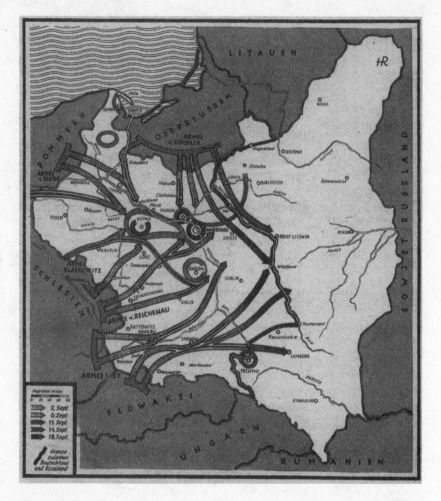

German view of the victory in Poland. *Die Wehrmacht* III, 21 (October 11, 1939), p. 7.

of Light Division Kempf ran into problems of their own—the tough Polish position at Mlawa: concrete bunkers linked by trenches, minefields, tank obstacles, and above all, well-sited antitank guns.[59] The Kempf Division was another ad-hoc unit, essentially a lighter-than-light binary unit consisting of the 7th Panzer Regiment and the S.S. Motorized Infantry Regiment. Within a few hours, the S.S. assault troops had suffered heavy casualties, and dozens of German tanks had been destroyed or damaged. No one should confuse the German tanks in this campaign with the later behemoths of 1943–1945. These were largely Panzer Mark I and Mark IIs. The former, with just 13 mm of frontal armor and a machine gun as its main armament in the turret, was already obsolete except as a trainer; the latter, with its small 20 mm gun, should probably not have been engaged in anything more dangerous than reconnaissance duty.

It was clear to the 3rd Army commander, General von Küchler, that a quick change of plan was necessary. He now shifted Division Kempf from the I Corps sector in the center to Corps Wodrig on the left. That actually entailed disengaging the division from the fight at Mlawa, motoring back into Germany at Wetzhausen, driving east through Neidenburg and Willenberg, and then reinvading Poland.[60] The infantry divisions of I Corps would assault Mlawa frontally, while Corps Wodrig (with Division Kempf in the lead) carried out an enveloping thrust around the right flank of the Polish position toward Przasnysz and then south to Ciechanów, in the rear of Mlawa. Guarding the far left of this tricky maneuver was the German 1st Cavalry Brigade. It would take three days of fighting, but in the end the combination of frontal, flank, and rear attacks had cracked the Mlawa position. Modlin Army was in headlong flight to the south, with I and Wodrig Corps in pursuit toward the Narew River.

The linkup of the two northern armies came that same day, with the right wing of XXI Corps (3rd Army) making contact with the left wing of II Corps (4th Army) on the Vistula just north of Grudziadz. With 4th Army swinging southeast, the Germans now launched a concentrated two-army drive: 4th advancing on Bydgoszcz and Thorn along the Drewenz River, a sector held by the last intact unit of Pomorze Army, the Polish 15th Infantry Division; and 3rd Army (I and Wodrig Corps) crossing the Narew and continuing its advance toward the Vistula and Bug Rivers, and from there to Warsaw.

The operations of Army Group North certainly present a unique appearance. The XXI Corps of 3rd Army was now, to all intents and purposes, attacking in concert with 4th Army. It was miles away from any contact with the rest of the 3rd Army, the mass of which lay far to the east. It was attacking almost due south, while its sister corps (I and Wodrig) were advancing to the southeast; thus the gap was widening. The army group commander, General Bock, had also removed his 10th Panzer Division from reserve and dispatched it on a quick ride across the Polish corridor, behind the rear of the combined 4th and 3rd Armies. From here, it would assist 3rd Army on the southward thrust toward Warsaw by constant threats to the Polish right flank. Joining it would soon be Guderian's entire XIX Corps. Thus far in

the campaign it had taken part in an assault, a defense against counterattacks, a pursuit of beaten remnants, an encirclement, and now a
disengagement and rapid redeployment for further action: all in the
first two days. In five days, then, the northern wing of the German
army presents a mixed picture. It had destroyed an entire Polish army
(Pomorze), mauled another one (Modlin), and was now poised for a
further advance into the interior of the country; it also lay scattered
about the countryside in a fairly high state of operational confusion.

In the south, Rundstedt was swinging a far heavier bat, the mass
of the German army. It is always easy to detect the *Schwerpunkt* of
German operations in World War II: simply count the panzer divisions. Army Group South contained four of the six then in existence,
along with three of the four light divisions. Altogether, Rundstedt had
three armies on line, from left to right the 8th, 10th, and 14th. It was
their task to destroy the mass of the Polish army by a direct thrust
to the northeast toward Warsaw. The 10th Army in the center would
form the army group spearhead, with no less than six mobile formations: two panzer divisions, two light divisions, and two motorized
infantry divisions. It was, by 1939 standards, a gigantic concentration
of force.

It should not be surprising, then, that Rundstedt broke through almost everywhere. On the left, the 8th Army reached the Prosna River
on the second day of operations, slashing through the defenses of the
Polish Łódź Army. This was largely the work of well-drilled infantry; 8th Army had no panzer elements outside the few tanks of the *SS
Leibstandtarte Adolf Hitler*, at the time just a motorized infantry regiment. On the right, 14th Army, including XXII (Motorized) Corps,
broke into Poland from the Jablunka Pass in the west to Novy Targ
(Neumarkt) in the east. It was the center of the army group that made
the most progress, however. Here 10th Army blasted through the seam
between the Łódź Army on its left and the Kraków Army on its right,
reaching the Warthe River and then crossing it in stride. This is where
the Poles got their first look at the full German mechanized package:
tank columns deploying off the road at the first sign of resistance and
bypassing the defenders on both flanks, heavy air attacks by *Stuka* dive-
bombers, their screeching siren adding a note of terror to the bombing
run; rapid advances by tank columns deep into the rear that suddenly
materialized into blocking positions when the Poles tried to retreat.

In concert with 14th Army to its right, the advance of 10th Army also
had the benefit of working concentrically against the Kraków Army,
tucked into the southwestern corner of Poland. Soon its remnants were

attempting to retreat into the interior, a task that in many places meant running a gauntlet of German armor that had already established itself in the rear, and by September 6 Kraków itself had fallen to the invaders. The collapse of the Kraków Army and the Pomorze Army far to the right in the corridor, in turn, meant disaster for the two Polish armies between them: the Łódź Army, already pressed hard by 8th Army's attacks, and, deployed deep in the section of the Polish border bulging out toward Germany, the Poznań Army under General Tadeusz Kutrzeba. Facing only German border defense commands, the latter was at the moment still largely untouched by enemy action, but it was already doomed: one hundred miles from the relative safety of Warsaw, with two complete German army groups closing in behind it.

By week two, the Germans were in full throttle all across the front of both army groups. Although the Germans themselves referred to the maneuver as a "pincers," in fact the Polish army was being pressed by two very heavy slabs of iron. The first German panzer forces reached the outskirts of Warsaw by September 8, as the armored spearheads of 10th Army slashed across the southern Polish plain toward the capital. In the course of its headlong rush, 10th Army actually overran the Polish "Prusy Army" while it was still in the process of assembling.[61] It was a truly apocalyptic moment in the history of modern military operations—troop trains arriving at the front to disgorge their occupants straight into *Luftwaffe* bombing runs, artillery bombardment, and tank attacks. Polish casualties were everywhere horrendous. The few defending formations with an open retreat path to Warsaw were desperately trying to get there, but they were gradually coming apart under unrelenting air attack. Polish command and control had broken down, and the only army still functioning as such, the only army still intact, was the isolated Poznań Army.

In fact, it was Poznań Army's belated attempt to retreat that would bring about the climax of the campaign. As it tried desperately to slither out of the jaws clamping down on it from both right and left, it smashed into the northern (left) flank guard of the advancing German 8th Army along the Bzura River west of Warsaw on September 9.[62] The 14th, 17th, and 25th Infantry Divisions, along with the Podolska and Wielkopolska Cavalry Brigades hit the overextended German 24th and 30th Infantry Divisions strung out along the river. It was half counterattack, half formless melee—the Poles were in the midst of a hurried retreat, after all. Still, the initial thrust managed to achieve surprise and made good progress at first, capturing some 1,500 German prisoners from the panic-stricken 30th Division alone. It certainly caused heartburn at German headquarters: army, army group, and OKH alike.

What it could not do, however, was have lasting repercussions. Kutrzeba and his army were trying to break out, but by this time the question was, break out to where? The attackers were acting in isolation, without any hope of support or reinforcement from forces in the rest of the country. In addition, they were facing in the German army a force that could stop on a dime, turn around, and launch large-scale operations in a way that was not yet typical of western armies. Within a day, German reinforcements were on the way to the Bzura, including the mass of 10th Army's armored units. Diverted instantaneously from the drive on Warsaw, they shifted their axis 180 degrees in effortless fashion. Faced with concentric attacks from all four points of the compass, the mass of the Polish attackers was soon hemmed into a shrinking pocket on the Bzura, along with remnants of Army Pomorze who had managed to escape the blows of Army Group North. Subjected to nonstop attack by the Luftwaffe and punished heavily by the German artillery, in a hopeless strategic situation, more than one hundred thousand men would surrender. At this point, 10th Army's armored divisions did it again, shifting their axis of advance 180 degrees for the second time in a week, and hurrying back toward Warsaw.[63] By September 19, Warsaw was the only spot on the map still in Polish hands, and the Germans, in fact, would speak of an "Eighteen Days' Campaign."[64] Surrounded and under heavy aerial bombardment, Warsaw would surrender on September 27.

CASE WHITE ANALYZED

The Germans had won this campaign in the opening days. By the end of week one, five of the seven Polish armies in the initial order of battle had been mauled (Łódź, Modlin), completely encircled (Poznań, Kraków), and in one unfortunate case (Pomorze), both. As 8th and 10th Armies (Army Group South) drove to the northeast, and 3rd and 4th Armies (Army Group North) drove southwest and south, their concentric advance caught most of the Polish army in a fantastic *Kessel*. The Poles lost 65,000 men killed in action, 144,000 wounded; German losses were just 11,000 and 30,000, respectively. The prisoner of war totals tell the tale, however: the Germans took the incredible figure of 587,000.[65]

The Polish campaign had proved once and for all that large-scale operations with mechanized forces were possible. There were the inevitable foul-ups. General Bock ended the war with two-thirds of 4th Army (the infantry corps) in northwest Poland and the rest, Guderian's

XIX (Motorized) Corps to be exact, sliding south down the Bug River far to the east of Warsaw—a strange situation map, indeed. It was a satisfying and rapid drive for the great "panzer leader," no doubt, but practically pointless. It had its roots in the prebattle controversy over what to do with 4th Army after it had seized the corridor and, we might add, in General Bock's determination to run his own campaign as he saw fit.

Nevertheless, a great deal more had gone right. In contrast to virtually every campaign since the days of Napoleon, German momentum did not flag, but increased as the first week of the campaign passed. The Germans managed to force small openings—tactical breaches—in the Polish defenses in the first few days. With tanks and aircraft, infantry and artillery all cooperating efficiently, those tactical breaches soon widened into operational ones, large enough for entire divisions to pass through in march and road column. Thus, we see Army Group South reducing the border defenses in the first few days and then lunging clear across central Poland toward Warsaw by day eight. Elements that had stalled previous campaigns, fortifications like the ones at Modlin northwest of Warsaw, for example, were now simply smothered by air attack. The *Stukas* proved especially effective throughout the campaign. Massed into a "Close Battle Division" of 160 aircraft, they destroyed the Modlin position, cracking what would have been a tough nut indeed for ground forces alone.[66]

Certainly some of this success was due to the Polish deployment. It is true that having to go it alone against the Wehrmacht presented the Polish high command under General Eduard Rydz-Śmigły with several bad options. It is equally true that he chose the worst one possible: attempting to defend every inch of the country's overlong border. Virtually all the Polish strength began the campaign hard up along the German frontier, a set of forward deployments that proved to be disastrous. With the main armies crushed in the opening days (or in the case of Poznan Army, encircled without a single shot being fired), there never was any time to deploy new armies or rush reinforcements to the front.

How did the Germans view what they had done? In its essence, this campaign would have been instantly recognizable to Moltke: two great masses maneuvering so as to take the enemy between them. More recently, German troops had campaigned in Poland throughout World War I, and this campaign looked familiar to some old hands on the General Staff.[67] "The opening situation in Silesia and Galicia," wrote one, "was highly reminiscent of the joint Central Powers offensive in the fall of 1914."[68] Then it had been German 9th Army under Hindenburg-Ludendorff attacking from Silesia on both sides of Czestochowa in the direction of Ivangorod and Warsaw. That was almost precisely the mission of German 10th Army in 1939. Likewise, the aggression, the drive to get at the enemy, the refusal to accept orders from the General Staff if they appeared to be preventing immediate and constant attacks, the proto-François machinations of General Bock: these things had been seen since the days of the Great Elector, Frederick the Great, and Blücher.

However, for all the tradition, it is important to recognize the new aspects, in particular the role of tank, aircraft, and radio. Although there have been occasional cranky voices since 1939 arguing that the new machines made little difference in the outcome, that argument flies in the face of both history and contemporary opinion at the time. Once again, it was obvious to those who had seen both campaigns:

> The essential difference between the conduct of the current eastern war and that of the World War is that the present army has both armored and motorized formations. They turn each tactical breakthrough into a rapid and comprehensive operational one. In the World War, because of our lack of tanks, this was possible only through a long continuation of the attack, sometimes stretching out for weeks, as at Gorlice and Przasnysz.[69]

In the back of the German military mind on September 1, 1939, was the nightmare of 1915–1917: the great unbreakable *Stellungskrieg*. The tanks and mechanized formations had worked well in maneuvers, true, but suspicion had lingered that real war might be different. "The demands of the soldier that *Stellungskrieg* must be avoided," wrote one officer, "had turned into a presupposition that it could be avoided," but *müssen* (must) and *können* (can) were two very different things.[70] A single week into the campaign, however, these same officers were basking in the flush of a rapid-paced, maneuver-oriented battle of annihilation: "Today, thanks to armor and rapid motorized units—as well as to a superior *Luftwaffe*—breakthroughs lead very soon to a catastrophic situation on long segments of the enemy front, as the events at Radom, Kutno, the attack on the Corridor, and the offensive out of East Prussia make clear."[71]

Perhaps Poland was not a true test of the new mechanized German army. It was a second-rate power without modern weaponry. But even countries like Poland had proved to be tough nuts to crack in World

War I: Belgium, Serbia, Romania, Bulgaria. Indeed, a huge Anglo-French force had spent years in the camp at Salonika during the war, unable to crack through a ring of Bulgarian troops dug in north of the city. Without tanks and aircraft, it is easy to imagine the 1939 campaign resembling the German invasion of Romania in 1916: an impressive win, slightly incomplete, and stretching out over four complete months.[72]

After Poland, *blitzkrieg* became a common military term. It has gained so much cachet over the years that its absence in a discussion seems jarring. Others speak of a "revolution in military affairs" or "RMA," common buzzwords in current U.S. military circles.[73] To the Germans, however, what had happened in Poland was not the creation of something new, but a renaissance. Although armor and aircraft had contributed a great deal, they had not been the essence of the enterprise. They had been useful tools. "The most important fact, indeed," one officer wrote, "is that *Bewegungskrieg*, so often pronounced dead, has risen once again in its old glory."[74] This would not be a replay of 1914, argued another:

> By the end of the first month of the world war, the *Stellungskrieg* had already begun. While we tried repeatedly to force a *Bewegungskrieg*, our opponents were content to hold us tight, in order to starve us out. In this they finally succeeded. The lesson they learned was that to prepare for *Stellungskrieg* was the best way to win a war against us, and they prepared for defense politically, economically, and militarily. . . . Our war experience was diametrically opposed. We recognized that *Bewegungskrieg* was the only path to the destruction of the enemy, and therefore we created the means—above all air power and tanks—that were necessary to a mobile conduct of the war.[75]

When they viewed the Polish campaign, far from seeing it as a tactical novelty or the result of some technological marvel, German officers saw the rebirth of an old tradition. In fact, for all the talk of German innovation and the "rise of blitzkrieg" in the interwar period, it seems that the German army had changed hardly at all.[76]

The Culmination Point

Since 1945, scholars and buffs alike have been playing a popular intellectual parlor game, similar to the one German officers played after 1918. This one might be called "Hitler's Mistakes"[1] or "Why the Germans Lost the War,"[2] and the aim is to pick out two or three bad führer decisions that lost World War II for the German army. For some, the answer is clear: it is the halt order to the panzers outside Dunkirk that snatched defeat out of the jaws of victory. The British Expeditionary Force managed to escape and lived to fight another day. For others it is the decision to switch to terror bombing of British cities at the very moment that the Luftwaffe was pressing the Royal Air Force hard in its attacks on airfields and installations. Still others question Hitler's decision to invade the Soviet Union in 1941, with an unconquered Britain still at his back. Scholars have spilled a great deal of ink over the years identifying the two-front war as the German military nightmare, and this decision simply seems inexplicable. Still others accept Operation Barbarossa's legitimacy but claim that Hitler bungled it in execution, particularly by diverting *Panzergruppe* Guderian into the Ukraine in late summer 1941, with the road to Moscow open.[3] Then there is the voluntary, even gratuitous, declaration of war on the United States in December 1941. This last decision rescued President Franklin Roosevelt from having to bring off what even that wiliest of American politicians recognized would have been a real trick: somehow transferring the anger of the American public from the Japanese who had just bombed Pearl Harbor to the regime that he saw as the real threat to the future of democracy: Hitler's Germany.

And so it goes. The bungled offensive toward Stalingrad comes in for its share of criticism and still wins recognition as the "turning point" of the war—curious, since the five decisions mentioned previously are usually said to have turned the tide as well. Hitler's refusal to follow Rommel's advice regarding deployment of the armored reserve in the west in the summer of 1944 gets a great deal of play. Rommel wanted them at the water's edge, Hitler as a reserve in the rear, a made-for-Hollywood confrontation between the evil führer and his dashing field marshal. In fact, Hollywood did make a movie of it: *The Longest Day* (1962), with Werner Hinz as Rommel, John Wayne, and a cast of thousands.

In fact, it is time to end the game altogether. Military history is the only area in all of historical scholarship where it is still necessary to devise "perfect plans," to tell the historical actors what they "should have done," how they "could have gotten it right." It is a kind of armchair generalship, interesting and even fun, but pointless. Modern warfare is such a complex phenomenon that reducing it to a specific magic moment, or in this case to a whole series of them, is impossible. Too many analysts quote Clausewitz about the uncertainty and friction of war, and then state categorically that the Germans could have won the war if only they had turned right at Dnepropetrovsk or left at Alam Halfa. The primary question for historians should never be what someone *ought* to have done, but *why* they did what they did.[4]

The Germans lost World War II for good reason. Hitler was incompetent, yes, and the buck has to stop at his desk, or perhaps on the map table around which "the greatest field general of all time" made his increasingly inexplicable decisions. Standing right there alongside him, however, was the General Staff. For all its glorious intellectual tradition, all the thought it had poured into wars both historical and theoretical over the centuries, the staff designed and launched some terrible operations in this war. Some of it was no doubt due to desperation, and it is clear that the longer the war went on, the worse the operations became: the campaign plan for Stalingrad (1942) looked like someone at the briefing had dropped the notes and hurriedly tried to reassemble them;[5] the offensive toward Kursk (1943) was a lumbering strike against the most obvious spot on the map;[6] and the Mortain counteroffensive (1944) was a nonstarter that allowed the U.S. Army to do what it did better than anyone else in World War II: smother an onrushing opponent with fire.[7] Blaming each and every one of these episodes on Hitler was a convenient way for former General Staff officers to shift the blame. He had the perfect credentials. He was dead, first of all, and therefore incapable of defending himself; and second, he was Hitler.

It is necessary to go deeper, however, than simply assigning blame. In assessing the performance of the Germans in World War II, we can say that they did some things well, very well. Maneuver on the operational level, boldness in the assault, tenacity on the defensive, the integration and cooperation of combined arms: the German army had no peer in the early years of the war, although it did decline in quality steadily as the war went on. The almost nine million casualties it suffered in the Soviet Union will do that to any army.[8] The lost war, however, was the fault of the dozens of other things that it did poorly. These included items like military intelligence (finding out what was on the other side of the hill) and counterintelligence (hiding what is on your side of the hill). The entire area of supply, from battlefield logistics to harnessing of industry to the war effort, was rarely more than an afterthought. Prussia had always needed to keep its wars "short and lively," Frederick the Great had believed, because it could not afford to sustain the effort for long. He ruled a small, infertile sandbox on the periphery of the Holy Roman Empire. Adolf Hitler ruled highly industrialized Europe, at least for a short time, and the Germans could have done much more with their conquered territories and populations than plunder the first and enslave and murder the second. Finally, the Germans once again proved, if they had not already done so to complete satisfaction in World War I, to be completely incompetent at coalition warfare.[9] The objection that Germany's only ally, Italy, was so weak as to make a true *Bündniskrieg* (coalition war) impossible is simply wrong. Germany began this war with a mighty ally indeed: the Soviet Union. Adding it all up leads to the conclusion that the defeat was due not just to Hitler's lack of ability as a field marshal, or bad generalship on the part of the officer corps. In this great conflict, the "German way of war" took on the world and was found wanting.

The War of Movement, 1940

"SHORT AND LIVELY"

In the opening years of World War II, the Wehrmacht had a run of decisive victories that was quite unlike anything in memory. It tried several new approaches—large-scale mechanized land operations, air landings, paratroop drops, even a couple of amphibious landings—and virtually all of them worked. It wasn't perfection, certainly, but it might have seemed that way to observers. It left contemporaries gasping for breath and has continued to impress later generations. No matter what the level of interest or involvement—scholar, military professional, or simply military "buff"—the Wehrmacht still demands attention.

These were campaigns that the German army had been dreaming of since 1918, of course, but their roots also go deep into the history of Prussia. There was one "short and lively" campaign after another. Case White smashed the Polish army in just eighteen days (with Warsaw holding out for another ten). Case Yellow dismantled the Anglo-French army in Flanders even more quickly. In fact, it might be argued that the 1940 campaign was to all intents and purposes over in three days. By that time the operational maneuver that won it, the huge mass of panzers passing through the Ardennes forest, had come to a successful completion, the Allies were hopelessly out of position, and the Germans were poised to slice through a carefully prepared weak spot into the open.

In between these two was a much smaller campaign in the north, the operation known as *Weserübung*.[10] The invasion of Denmark might have set a world's record for rapidity and completeness. The major fighting, including the occupation of the capital, Copenhagen, was over in four hours. It included several well-coordinated landings on the morning of April 9, 1940, including two paratroop drops, the first in military history: one against the long bridge linking the Gedser ferry terminal to Copenhagen,[11] another at Aalborg in the far north of the Jutland Peninsula to secure its important airfield. At the same time, there were five simultaneous naval landings around the coast of Jutland from west to east: at Esbjerg, Thyboron, Middelfart, Nyborg, and Gedser. Finally, there was a land drive up the peninsula by two motorized brigades and an infantry division, which covered the entire length of Denmark, well over three hundred miles, by the end of the day.[12] The "Danish campaign" lasted roughly from breakfast to lunchtime on April 9, 1940, and the German opinion that "the plan worked out in action like a precision watch"[13] seems entirely justified.

The Germans did much the same thing at the same time against much larger Norway. This time there were six simultaneous seaborne landings (from north to south, Narvik, Trondheim, Bergen, Kristiansand-Arendal, Oslo, and Egersund); a paratroop landing at Stavanger, aiming at the nearby air base at Sola; and a combined air-sea landing at Oslo. German troops in the first wave numbered somewhat less than nine thousand men, but they made up for their small numbers by appearing seemingly everywhere along the coast, all at once.[14] As in Danzig harbor, some German troops and a great deal of equipment lay in the holds of merchant vessels that had put into Norwegian ports before the start of hostilities.[15] Although there was some hard fighting here and there, Oslo fell the first afternoon and the rest of sprawling Norway in just thirty-two days. Here the Germans augmented their tiny land forces with a strong commitment of airpower, with

Luftwaffe units staging forward and operating from Norwegian bases by the end of day one. Again, the timing and precision of the landings, the cooperation between land, sea, and air, would have been impressive even for a peacetime exercise.

It happened again in the Balkans in the spring of 1941, simultaneous invasions of Greece (Operation Marita) and Yugoslavia (Operation Punishment), the former the result of serious planning over months, the latter improvised within days to respond to an anti-Axis coup d'état in Belgrade.[16] The Germans kicked the British army from one good blocking position in the mountains to the next and finally booted it off the continent altogether, its second rushed evacuation in months. The British destination this time was Crete. There the Germans hit them with a true bolt out of the blue: Operation Mercury, the first all-airborne operation in military history.[17] The British lost the fight for the island and evacuated again, this time to Egypt. Here they were destined to make the acquaintance of a German general named Erwin Rommel.

This period of the war climaxed in the opening of the campaign in the Soviet Union, Operation Barbarossa. An operational approach that had begun with individual panzer divisions had now evolved into entire panzer armies (*Panzergruppen*). No less than four of them spearheaded the invasion: one in the north, heading toward Leningrad; one in the south, toward Kiev. The central front was the *Schwerpunkt*, containing the other two. With 3rd *Panzergruppe* (General Hermann Hoth) operating the northern flank of Army Group Center, and 2nd *Panzergruppe* (General Heinz Guderian) on the southern flank, the German spearheads slashed through the Red Army formations in front of them and, again and again, turned inward, Hoth to the south, Guderian to the north. Their linkups would create the largest battles of encirclement in world history. This was the classic "concentric attack by separated armies," the obsession of German military intellectuals in the years before 1914.

All these campaigns bore the marks of long-standing Prussian tradition. They were all, in a sense, front-loaded. The Germans concentrated overwhelming force and engaged in bold and aggressive maneuvers from the outset, often quite literally in the first few minutes of the fighting. Tendencies toward decisive and rapid action that had been percolating within the Prussian-German military establishment for centuries came to full flower in the age of the tank, truck, airplane, and radio. They hit their opponents hard at the most psychologically vulnerable moment: when the war had just begun. Imagine, for a moment, the plight of a staff officer or supreme commander fighting the Wehrmacht in 1940 or 1941. A message rouses him from deep sleep at 4:00 A.M. stating that "strong German armored forces have crossed the border." A half hour later a second message arrives, telling him that his air force has been destroyed, or that there have been landings at five widely separated cities along his coast, or that paratroopers have been seen at a half dozen different sites near the capital. This exact scenario played out again and again in this era.

We should not forget one last point. The Germans prosecuted the war with a degree of ruthlessness, not just toward enemy armed forces but the civilian population as well, that hearkened back to Frederick the Great's "harrowing of Saxony" in the Seven Years' War.[18] Unfortunately, that was a historical tendency that the Wehrmacht would bring up to twentieth-century standards in the course of the war, until National Socialism's racial ideology brought the trend to a mad, simmering perfection. There can no longer be any debate on the German army's wholesale involvement in war crimes against civilians. It was not the product of defeat or desperation. It started at the very beginning with the invasion of Poland;[19] it was in full swing during the years of victory; and it continued right up until the final, bitter end. Terrorizing the civilian population wherever possible was part of the Wehrmacht's arsenal. So was terrorizing its own soldiers. This was an army that handed down no less than thirty thousand death sentences against its own soldiers in the course of the war, and executed twenty-two thousand, compared to just forty-eight in all of World War I.[20]

CASE YELLOW: THE PLAN

If one campaign defines the Wehrmacht's success in this era, it was the offensive in the west in May 1940. Although the Germans had displayed an impressive set of tools in Poland, there were too many western observers who discounted them. The Poles were too weak, too backward, they said, and the geography had been unfavorable for the defense. The arguments contained some truth, although it was certainly going too far to liken Germany's victory to a "colonial war,"[21] as more than one western analyst did. Poland's revenge, in a sense, would be to watch the Wehrmacht carve up the French army even more easily.

If Adolf Hitler had had his way, the campaign in the west would have begun within days of the victory over Poland. The original date for the offensive, November 12, 1939, would have set the Wehrmacht some interesting problems.[22] Although getting into position along the western border would have been a stretch, this was just the sort of problem that superior German staff work had solved in the past. What was more important was to have some sort of operational guideline. The first plan, drawn up in haste in October 1939 (the "OKH plan"), was about as much of a frontal assault as any in the history of the Prussian-German army. The Wehrmacht would deploy three army groups (A, B, and C), but only the first two would be part of the maneuver force. The mission of Army Group C (Ritter von Leeb), sitting on the far left of the line facing the French frontier, was simply to pin the French troops holding the Maginot Line. Army Group B (Fedor von Bock), deployed on the right wing, would form the *Schwerpunkt*. Allotted most of the armor, he would drive west, overrunning Belgium and the Netherlands. Army Group A (General Gerd von Rundstedt) was to drive to the Meuse (but not beyond it) and cover Bock's left flank. There would be no wheeling, no independent maneuver by the various army groups (or their individual armies), no concentric advance, and, frankly, as many German officers thought when they first saw it, no chance at all for decisive victory.

Thus began a period of "restless operational planning" that lasted all through the winter.[23] There was a great deal of back and forth on this issue among members of the staff, and, in fact, Hitler would postpone the operation no less than twenty-nine times. The good campaigning weather of the fall turned into the snowfalls of winter, there were "fall-ins" (orders to prepare for an attack within forty-eight hours) followed by more postponements. At one point, in January 1940, it looked like the Germans might actually be ready to go when a staff plane had engine trouble and made an emergency landing at Mechelen-sur-Meuse in Belgium. Unfortunately it was carrying crucial planning documents. Although they were certainly not the entire operational plan for the west, as they are sometimes styled, they did include instructions for the operations of Luftflotte II that clearly indicated a German advance on the right wing, as well as a general evaluation of the military situation ("Beurteilung der Lage").[24] With the cat now out of the bag—it was assumed that the Belgians would soon turn over the documents to the French, which they did—it was time for yet another postponement, and more time at the drawing board. As the spring of 1940 approached, about the only thing that everyone had agreed upon was what to call the operation, *Fall Gelb:* Case Yellow.

It is often argued that disputes over the plan betrayed the General Staff's fundamental lack of enthusiasm for a western offensive. That may be true, but it is far more likely that it resulted from a lingering mistrust of Hitler's operational judgment, as well as a disinclination for a premature move against Britain and France. For all their modernism, the General Staff also tended to look backward and think historically. The last time they'd dipped their toe into these waters they were bitten by a shark: a three-year *Stellungskrieg* that had eventually swallowed them all. Despite the success in Poland, there had to be some trepidation about moving in half-cocked. Field Marshal Walther von Brauchitsch, the OKH commander, warned Hitler, "We know the British from the last war—and how tough they are."[25]

Whatever the reason, the objectives mentioned in the first paragraph of the OKH operational plan, dated October 19, 1939, certainly did aim low: "To defeat the largest possible elements of the French and Allied armies and simultaneously to gain as much territory as possible in Holland, Belgium, and northern France as a basis for successful air and sea operations against Britain and as a broad protective zone for the Ruhr." The more specific operational objectives in paragraph two aimed lower still: "While eliminating the Dutch armed forces, to defeat as many elements of the Belgian army as possible in the vicinity of the frontier fortifications and, by rapidly concentrating powerful mechanized forces, to create a basis for the immediate prosecution of the attack with a strong right northern wing (*Nordflügel*) and the swift occupation of the Belgian coastline."[26] The German army was apparently about to mobilize its powerful new panzer and air forces and launch a great offensive in the west in order to "defeat as many elements of the Belgian army as possible." It would have been interesting to resurrect the shade of Frederick the Great and ask him what he thought of that.

Although it is easy to paint a picture of staff timidity, it also has to be said that the objections to the OKH plan arose within the officer corps almost immediately. In rewrites and revisions of the plan, we see the language toughen, with the October 29 version speaking of "engaging and destroying the largest possible elements of the French army in northern France and Belgium" and "destroying the Allied forces north of the Somme," although even now there was no talk of decisive victory. The preceding aims were to serve merely as a prelude to "creating favorable conditions for the prosecution of the war against Britain and France by land and air."

Not surprisingly, the loudest complaints came from Rundstedt's Army Group A. As always, it was the general tasked with the diversionary effort or the holding mission who found the plan wanting: Frederick Charles in 1866, Steinmetz in 1870, François in 1914, Bock in 1939. German operational commanders saw themselves not so much as officers in the same army as general contractors in the service of the king, emperor, or in this case, führer. Now it was Rundstedt's turn.

General Erich von Manstein had held several high staff and field commands in the army, including chief of the operations branch of the General Staff from 1935 to 1936 and deputy to Army Chief of Staff Ludwig Beck from 1936 to 1938. In the Polish campaign he had served as chief of staff to Rundstedt's Army Group South, and he was still attached to Rundstedt's command (now designated Army Group A) in 1940. His first reaction to the OKH plan, he would later write in his memoirs, *Lost Victories*, had been "emotional rather than intellectual":

> The strategic intentions of OKH struck me as being essentially an imitation of the famous Schlieffen Plan of 1914. I found it humiliating, to say the least, that our generation could do nothing better than repeat an old recipe, even when this was the product of a man like Schlieffen. What could possibly be achieved by turning up a war plan our opponents had already rehearsed with us once before?[27]

It was something of a repeat performance, and Manstein might have added that the previous performance had received decidedly mixed reviews. Even worse, it had none of Schlieffen's brio or determination to destroy. "Schlieffen had drafted his plan with an eye to the utter and final defeat of the entire French army": "The 1939 operation plan, on the other hand, contained no clear-cut intention of fighting the campaign to a victorious conclusion. Its object was, quite clearly, *partial* victory (defeat of the Allied forces in northern Belgium) and *territorial gains* (possession of the Channel coast as a basis for future operations)."[28]

On behalf of his commander, Manstein now drew up an alternate plan that would, by a circuitous route, wind up on Hitler's desk. It essentially reversed the roles of Bock and Rundstedt. The former would be stripped of the *Schwerpunkt*, and most of the panzer divisions that went with it, and allotted a secondary role. Bock's mission would be to invade Belgium and the Netherlands in order to attract the attention of the Allied forces in France and perhaps lure them to the north. Once they had swallowed the bait, Manstein envisioned a gigantic panzer thrust by Army Group A through the difficult terrain of the Ardennes. With its dense old-growth forest, its steep-banked rivers, and its winding roads and trails, it was hardly a place that you would think of when the phrase "tank country" came to mind.

That, of course, was exactly Manstein's point. The panzers would likely meet little if any resistance in the forest, since the French and Belgians considered it unsuitable for operations by armor. Certainly, the kind of large-scale thrust Manstein was planning wouldn't even have crossed their minds. Having passed the Ardennes, the panzers would have a single river to cross, the Meuse between Sedan and Dinant. Once over that obstacle, there would be nothing but open country all the way to the English Channel. In this manner, they would have gotten onto the rear of the Allied force that lay to the north, which could now be subjected to a concentric attack and destroyed, in the classic Prussian style.

The battle over the operations plan raged all winter. Manstein made few friends criticizing the OKH plan as unimaginative and boring, and his appointment to command a mere infantry corps in the operation has to be seen in this light as a demotion. "Staff officers," Schlieffen had once written, "should work relentlessly, accomplish much, remain in the background, and be more than they seem."[29] Moltke had once said they should be "faceless." Manstein was violating those precepts. Nevertheless, the downed plane in Mechelen made Hitler more determined than ever to come up with a more daring plan. On February 17, Hitler held a luncheon in Berlin for all the newly appointed corps commanders. He apparently knew something of the Manstein plan through his military adjutant, Colonel Rudolf Schmundt, and what he had heard intrigued him. According to Manstein,

> As we were taking our leave at the end of the meal, Hitler told me to come to his study, where he invited me to outline my views on the handling of the western offensive. I am not clear whether he had already been informed of our plan by Schmundt, and, if so, in what detail. In any case I found him surprisingly quick to grasp the points which our Army Group had been advocating for many months past, and he entirely agreed with what I had to say.[30]

It was a case of synergy. Hitler, like every ruler of Prussia-Germany before him, looked to prosecute wars rapidly, with bold offensive strokes. Although he hadn't been able to get such a plan out of his top staff officers, he knew that he had now found his man.

The synergy went deeper than the personal, however. In his exhaustive biography of Hitler, scholar Ian Kershaw has recently introduced a concept called "working toward the Führer." Hitler rarely had to issue specific decrees for the regime's most radical policies. His subordinates did it for him, and the competition at all levels of the regime was ferocious: "In the Darwinist jungle of the Third Reich, the way to power and advancement was through anticipating the 'Führer will,' and, without waiting for directives, taking initiatives to promote what were presumed to be Hitler's aims and wishes."[31] Lower administrative organs knew full well that it was the most extreme and ruthless suggestions that were to evolve into policy and that those who had put them forth were most likely to advance in the hierarchy. Arguing that rearmament should be slowed, or that construction crews should lay down fewer miles of Autobahn, or that there should be an easing of the regime's harsh anti-Semitic policies were all nonstarters. For an ambitious young bureaucrat, there was no future in arguing for a smaller air force.

The same dynamic had been at work in the Prussian and German armies for centuries. Wars came and went, regimes rose and fell, technology worked its magic ever anew, but the culture of the German army inevitably "worked towards the offensive." Only plans for the rapid and decisive operational stroke were likely to meet with widespread approval among the commanders. Anything that smacked of half-measures or timidity, even if chosen for good reason, would call forth opposition in the planning stages and often disobedience in the actual fighting. The Manstein plan, therefore, worked in two directions. It resonated not only with Hitler's restlessness and search for the radical solution to every problem, but with many other officers in the German army, not all of whom were in Army Group A.

This operational preference might help to explain why the officer corps, despite later denials, supported every one of Hitler's military initiatives for the rest of the war. Long after the initiative had slipped from his hands, Hitler continued to seek victory through the offensive: Kursk, Mortain, the Ardennes in 1944, the hopeless Lake Balaton offensive of March 1945, and many other smaller operations. Although there was a significant body of opinion within the army opposing each of these attacks, there were always hundreds of officers eager to take part in their planning and execution. This was an army that had dedicated itself for centuries to grooming such officers. It was a tradition that dated well back into history, long before the rise of Hitler in 1933. Since 1650, Brandenburg-Prussia-Germany had fought wars innumerable and had attempted to win each one with a rapid offensive blow in the opening days. We must stop treating that fact as a mere coincidence.

On February 24, 1940, army Chief of Staff General Franz Halder issued a new set of operational directives for the upcoming offensive in the west that adopted the Manstein plan in every particular.[33] Bock's now-secondary Army Group B would consist of just two armies: the 18th (General Küchler) had the mission of overrunning the Netherlands; the 6th (General Walter von Reichenau) would push into Belgium. Bock's main task was to make a great deal of noise, in a sense. It was essential that the Allies view Army Group B as the main German thrust. Thus, Bock's secondary operations actually included a hefty sampling of the new mobile units: several paratrooper and glider units, including the 7th Flieger Division and 22nd Airlanding Division; two complete panzer corps, the XVI (General Erich Hoepner) and the XXXIX (General Schmidt), as well a significant commitment of air power.

The new *Schwerpunkt* was in the south. Army Group A now included three armies: the 4th (Günther von Kluge), 12th (Wilhelm von List), and 16th (Ernst Busch), plus a newly organized Panzer Group (*Panzergruppe*) under General Ewald von Kleist. All told it contained seven of Germany's ten panzer divisions. The employment of Panzer Group von Kleist—three complete corps—brought German mechanized operations to a new stage of development and complexity. Since the Kleist group would have to pass through the Ardennes and then launch its attack on an exceedingly narrow front, the new plans had it echeloned in some depth. The first echelon would consist of Guderian's XIX Corps, now upgraded from its 1939 designation of "motorized" to "panzer"; the second the XLI Panzer Corps under General Georg-Hans Reinhardt, and the third the XIV Motorized Corps under General Gustav von Wietersheim. The I Flak Corps would advance between XIX and XLI Panzer Corps, providing protection from any Allied air that might penetrate the Luftwaffe's air umbrella.[34] It was the mightiest mechanized force—a kind of phalanx—that the world had yet seen: 134,000 men, 41,000 vehicles, 1,250 tanks, and 362 reconnaissance vehicles.

The actual operation, opening on May 10, 1940, proved to be much less troublesome than the battle over planning it. As ever in German operational planning, there was a series of shocks to the Allied commanders quite early in the war.[35] In the Netherlands, it was the use of both airborne and air-landing troops—two complete divisions—to seize airfields, bridges over the numerous watercourses, and other strategic installations.[36] In fact, the government districts of the Hague, army headquarters, and Queen Wilhelmina herself were among the targets. Not all went completely according to plan. As always, when the Germans launched special operations, some worked and some didn't. Many bridges fell to the landing forces, the Moerdijk causeway south of Rotterdam, for example. By and large, however, the jumps against the airfields were disastrous. The attempt to seize the Ockenburg, Valkenburg, and Ypenburg airfields around The Hague collapsed in the face of larger-than-expected airfield garrisons and the fact that Luftwaffe raids failed to knock out Dutch antiaircraft batteries in the area. Disaster begot disaster when the German transports arrived with the air-landing troops, expecting to land at the captured fields. At Ypenburg, for example, Dutch fire destroyed eleven of the first thirteen JU-52 transport aircraft in the air. It might be argued that the shock and panic they caused in the Dutch command, which had to face combat outside the very walls of the capital and throughout the four corners of the land from the first moment, might have made them worthwhile anyway. Whether shattering the Dutch was worth the loss of so many highly trained specialist troops is another question. The arrival of the mass of Küchler's 18th Army soon made it a moot point.

To the south, the Germans hit pay dirt with another bold coup. This was a glider assault on the modern Belgian fortress of Eben Emael, at the junction of the Meuse and the Albert Canal.[37] The glider added a new dimension to operations, its silent approach being a complement to the piercing siren of the *Stuka*. Operation Granite involved landing a force on top of the fort itself, knocking out its guns, and then forcing the surrender of the troops inside. It certainly had its share of problems. The glider carrying the commander of the operation, Lieutenant Rudolf Witzig, was one of two that released prematurely. He had his pilot glide back over the Rhine, called the nearest Luftwaffe headquarters, and got himself another tow plane. Meanwhile, the assault force landed and within ten minutes had knocked out all the guns and installations on the surface of the fort. It was an impressive debut for the hollow charge explosive, which proved highly effective against the armored cupolas of the Belgian guns.[38] The tiny force—just seventy-eight men—did have some problems with a Belgian garrison ten times its own size, although German morale rose considerably when a lone glider appeared over the fort, landed, and disgorged the fiery Lieutenant Witzig. He and his men managed to keep the garrison bottled up until German ground forces arrived the next day, elements of the 4th Panzer Division (6th Army).

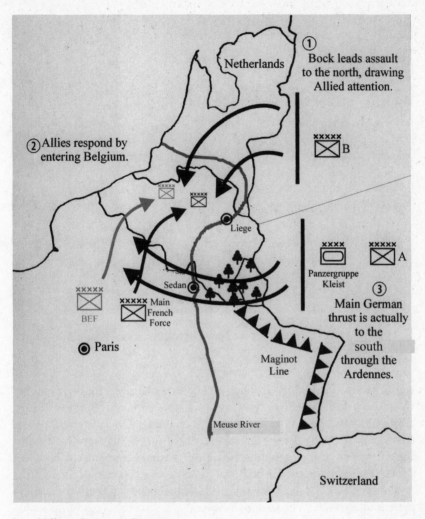

Case Yellow: *Bewegungskrieg* 1940

The rest of Army Group B played its role to the hilt. The large 6th Army (five complete corps) entered the southern Netherlands with Hoepner's XVI Panzer Corps in the van. The plan called for a quick crossing of the "Maastricht appendage" and then entry into the central Belgium plain west of the Meuse and Sambre. Unfortunately, the Dutch blew the Meuse bridges in the appendage before the Germans could seize them, and Hoepner's panzers would spend a full day immobilized in Dutch territory. On May 11 they got moving again and

German tanks in Rotterdam after the Dutch capitulation. Courtesy of
Christian Ankerstjerne.

the next day crashed into a large French mechanized force advancing
from the south. This was the Cavalry Corps of General René Prioux,
containing the 2nd and 3rd Light Mechanized Divisions. In a two-
day clash of armor near Gembloux, the French managed to handle
the Germans pretty roughly, bringing them to a standstill in many
spots. This should not surprise us, as the French tanks, especially the
medium SOMUA S-35, were in most respects superior to their German counterparts. The German captain who described the first day at
Gembloux as a "hard and bitter day" wasn't kidding.[39] Nevertheless,
the skills of the veteran and better-trained German crews eventually
began to tell against a French force that was tasting combat for the
first time. After a concentrated German attack managed to penetrate
the front of the 3rd Light Mechanized division, Prioux ordered the
Cavalry Corps to retire on May 14.

In fact, the Cavalry Corps was at Gembloux not to seek decisive
battle with the Wehrmacht's finest, but merely to cover the major Allied operational maneuver of the campaign. The Allies were following
"Plan-D," which called for the Anglo-French force to enter Belgium
and take up a strong defensive position along the Dyle River.[40] Four

Forming up! A motorcycle with sidecar joins a German reconnaissance column somewhere in the Netherlands, May 1940. Courtesy of Christian Ankerstjerne.

complete armies were involved, from west to east the 7th Army, the latest version of the British Expeditionary Force, the 1st, and the 9th. The advance would proceed in tandem with a wheel to the right, so that by the time they had finished their advance, the Allies would be facing nearly due east, from Belgian Monthermé in the south to the

Dutch border. In March, the French introduced the so-called "Breda variant" to the plan, with 7th Army on the left extending the line up to Breda in the Netherlands.[41] This "Dyle-Breda position," the Allies believed, would be an ideal place to meet the principal German thrust coming down on them out of the north. As the Belgians and Dutch armies retreated, they could plug themselves into it as well, no small consideration to the final shape of the plan.

Once again, as in 1914, French operational plans played ideally into German hands. Facing the German *Schwerpunkt*, an immense armored force aiming toward Sedan, was the French 2nd Army. Its task was simply to function as a hinge for the Allied swing into Belgium, and it was essentially performing what one modern authority has called "an economy of force operation."[42] It had low priority in manpower, in equipment, and in air support. Of its five divisions, two were over-age reservists, or "series B," one was North African, and one a colonial unit from Senegal. In 1914, the Germans had come quite close to winning a decisive victory at Namur. This time, along the same river Meuse, they would collect on that debt.

Once the two rival deployments are understood, the actual campaign in the south is a simple story. The panzers entered the Ardennes without incident—a long snake of tanks, trucks, and reconnaissance vehicles fifty miles long. The most anxious moments for the Wehrmacht were traffic delays. They brushed aside weak Belgian resistance in the forest itself, mainly light Belgian Chasseurs Ardennais, who set up roadblocks and demolitions but little else. Early in the evening of May 12—just day three of the operation—the head of the German snake emerged from the forest. It was Guderian's XIX Panzer Corps, heading toward Sedan. Rather than pause and stage a set-piece river crossing the next day, Guderian forced a crossing that evening on his own initiative. A handful of infantry in rubber assault boats, as well as a few tanks and motorcycles, managed to establish a bridgehead on the far bank. The campaign had been decided, although no one knew it yet.

The next day, the French 2nd Army took the kind of pounding that only Polish veterans could have understood. There were tanks, a huge mass of them in fact, stretching as far as the eye could see, along with heavy artillery concentrations, both 105 mm and 150 mm, and finally ceaseless dive-bombing by the *Stukas*. Units of the French 2nd Army broke in panic even before the Germans were over the river in force, and the same thing happened to French 9th Army at the two Meuse River crossings to the north, one at Monthermé (Reinhardt's XLI Panzer Corps) and one at Dinant (Hoth's XV Panzer Corps, part of

More action from the Dutch campaign, 1940. Above, a German
reconnaissance column pauses. Below, German panzers enter a Dutch town.
Courtesy of Christian Ankerstjerne.

4th Army). By the end of the day on May 13, the Germans had torn a
great gash in the French line some fifty miles wide.

It was not simply a tactical opening, but an operational one. Over
the next week, the three armies of Army Group A would pour through

Some tough fighting at the Meuse crossing point, May 1940. A German antitank gun in action. From the Wehrmacht-published *Sieg über Frankreich*, p. 64.

the gap. With the panzers in the lead, and the poor infantry forced-marching until it dropped, the Germans slid across the rear of the huge Allied army in Belgium. This had to be a satisfying moment for the German commanders, veterans all of the previous war. In 1914, the French 5th Army had offered itself up on a platter along the Meuse, and the Germans had failed to snatch it. Now they had. In 1918 they had launched a great offensive that came ever so close to final victory. Now those very place names in Flanders that had hung just tantalizingly out of reach in 1918 were falling in a rush: Arras, Amiens, Mt. Kemmel.

The Germans reached another milestone on May 20. Late in the day, the 2nd Panzer Division (XIX Panzer Corps) reached Abbeville at the mouth of the Somme River. It meant the destruction of the Allied army to the north, no less than a million and a half men. It was a *Kesselschlacht*, the greatest battle of encirclement in military history up to this point. During their drive across northern France, the panzers had been nearly unmolested. The French managed a pair of counterattacks, led by the commander of the newly formed 4th Ar-

mored Division, General Charles de Gaulle. Neither his first attack at
Montcornet (May 17), nor a second one at Crécy-sur-Serre (May 19)
managed to halt German momentum. Neither did the single British
counterstroke of the campaign, near Arras on May 21.

What they did achieve was to give the German high command,
up to and including Hitler, an attack of the shakes. Their situation
maps showed an ominous picture: long, vulnerable armored spearheads strung out on the roads, completely out of contact with their
follow-on infantry divisions. Orders actually went out to Guderian to
halt and allow time for the infantry to catch up. Once they had con-
solidated a defensive position on his flanks, he could drive on. Anyone
who has studied the centuries-long operational pattern of the German
army could not possibly be surprised at Guderian's response. He ignored his orders and continued on, undertaking a "reconnaissance in
force" that included—no surprise—his entire XIX Panzer Corps.[43] He
reached the Channel, wheeled north, and kept on attacking. The time
was coming when such independent action would no longer be tolerated in the Wehrmacht, but that time was not yet.

CASE YELLOW: THE EXULTATION

The victory in the "the battle of Flanders," as the German styled
it, seemed not only to wipe away the stain of the defeat in the World
War I, but to place a satisfying cap on centuries of Prussian-German
military operations. No one could blame German military professionals for doing a bit of gloating, and the tone of the analysis in the *Militär-Wochenblatt* over the next year was quite unlike anything that that
rather staid publication had ever known, with the possible exception of
the years immediately following 1870. The series of its weekly lead articles, entitled "Greater Germany's Freedom War 1940" (*Grossdeutschlands Freiheitskrieg 1940*), began revving into high gear in the May 24 issue. With allowances for a week of journalistic lag time, it covered events
in the west from May 10 to May 17. "The German hour had struck on
the western front!" it thundered. "The powerful strike force of Germany's million-man army, its soldiers the best-trained in the world and
equipped with the most modern weapons, entered enemy territory."[44]
On the fifth day of the great offensive, "the irresistible and fearless advancing fighting troops" won their first grand success: the capitulation
of Holland, which was thereby "saved from being destroyed."[45]

That was nothing compared to the next few weekly reports. The
German attack "had transformed *Stellungskrieg* into *Bewegungskrieg*,"
declared the next issue: "Never stopping, smashing all resistance,

the German army continued to gain ground in Belgium and northern France. Under the impression of these facts the nervousness rises in London and Paris. 'Perhaps it is necessary,' declares Reynaud in his last speech to the Chamber, 'to change our commanders and our methods.'"[46] It was too late for that, however. "The pursuit of the enemy, the English and Belgians in the north as well as the French in the south continues energetically." What the German high command was already calling "the greatest offensive operation of all times" was nearing its culmination.[47] The French 9th Army was in the process of dissolution; the commander of the 7th Army, General Giraud, was already in German captivity. The arrival of the panzers in Abbeville meant that the Allied host in Belgium would now be fighting with the sea at its back. The "ring is tightening!" it warned.[48]

By the next issue, "what our opponents had thought was impossible" had come to pass. France was cut off from England; Dover itself was now in "the German operational zone."[49] German troops stood on the streets of Calais.[50] This German drive to victory in fifteen days of unceasing attack "was without parallel in world history." The arrival of German panzers on the Channel coast had allowed the entire army to launch powerful "concentric attacks" against the enemy.[51] The following passage captures the breathless, exuberant mood:

> In this campaign, superior German troops and leadership have destroyed three French armies in three weeks and taken two army commanders prisoner; they have smashed the English expeditionary army and driven it from the continent. Only ruins of the force have accompanied its commander back to England. The Belgian army forced to capitulate. The Channel coast in German hands. Incalculable number of prisoners and captured weapons. Even London and Paris can no longer hide such a collapse. Now they call the whole battle in Artois and Flanders "a magnificently conducted retreat." On May 30th, London radio declared that the Allied lands looked on with pride at "the greatest retreat battle in world history."

"As if," the article continued, "that was the aim and objective of this struggle on the Anglo-French side, the meaning of this war that England had declared on Germany!"[52]

And so it continued into the next issue, a culmination point as far as German exultation was concerned.[53] The battle in the west was "the most successful battle of all time." It was the "greatest battle of annihilation of all time,"[54] a phrase used twice, "one of the greatest vic-

Apocalypse 1940. Allied prisoners marching into captivity near Dunkirk.
From *Sieg über Frankreich*, p. 76.

tories in world history,"[55] also used twice, and finally, "a victory in the greatest battle of all time."[56] The postbattle scene of Dunkirk appears in loving detail, a battlefield "strewn thickly with weapons and equipment both destroyed and usable, innumerable enemy dead, slaughtered cattle." It is an unparalleled scene of "devastation and destruction."[57]

The Germans would have time to savor this victory. There would be no more major land action until spring 1941 and the invasion of the Balkans, followed closely by the invasion of Russia. As more details became known about the campaign, it was clear to more and more officers that it had been a milestone in German military history, and in fact they viewed it almost exclusively through a historical lens. To one officer, it was "a new Waterloo,"[58] to another "a modern Austerlitz."[59] Just as Napoleon had exploited his opponent's flanking maneuver by launching one of his own, so had the Germans done the same. Both battles had seen the victorious side launch its attack against the pivot of the enemy maneuver, and both had forced the foe back against an obstacle and destroyed him.

It was a victory for modern weaponry, certainly, tanks and aircraft in particular, but they were only instruments of something higher:

Boldness works suggestively upon the enemy. That is the only way to explain the powerful impact of the Wehrmacht on its numerous enemies, even in places where anyone doing a rational assessment of the conditions would prophesy only a limited success at best. Our offensives in Poland and Norway, in Holland and Belgium, hit the enemy unexpectedly, like a thunderbolt, and they threw everything into terror and confusion. The flanking maneuvers were not without danger; the German command took the danger into account. The extraordinary things that happened—German land forces showing up on the Norwegian coast, breaking through the fortifications protecting Belgium and France, forcing a crossing of the Rhine—had a crippling effect on enemy morale.

German boldness found its consummation in the tank and air forces, which "robbed the Allied commanders completely of their ability to make a decision."[60]

As one Wehrmacht colonel explained, it wasn't the weapons, but the spirit of the men behind them, that had been decisive:

The English were for a long time the pioneers of the idea of mechanized formations. Not only did they write about it, they produced official regulations as well. Unfortunately, writing and deeds are two different things. They can't complain about lack of opportunity. If they really were so excited about an encounter with the German Panzer force, like they had always claimed, they had their best opportunity in Belgium. There were individual attempts, but the Royal Tank Corps soon fell apart. The tanks stayed behind, but their crews insulted us by showing us their backs in the "greatest retreat of all times."[61]

As ever in this period, the exultation was never far from the surface.[62] It was the satisfying feeling of hundreds of years of patient work and striving, finally coming to fruition.

Defeat: Barbarossa[63]

The campaign in Russia is the one that, more than any other, gets the "how could the Germans have won the war" treatment. This is particularly true of the English-speaking world. It is a result, no doubt, of the cold war. The postwar United States was now the sworn foe of world communism, and a process of identification with the Wehrmacht on the eastern front was noticeable by the 1950s. In the event of a war,

Where to now? With victory in the west assured, a German panzer
commander ponders his next campaign. Courtesy of Christian Ankerstjerne.

NATO was now facing these same Soviet hordes, tanks, and guns. It
would be outnumbered all along the line, and yet it would have to find
a way to win. Perhaps the Wehrmacht had something to teach. This
was not an unconscious development. U.S. military officials organized
captive German officers into research teams, a process that culminated
in the preparation of the Department of the Army's German Report
Series: *Russian Combat Methods in World War II* appeared in November
1950; *German Defense Tactics against Russian Breakthroughs* in October
1951; *Operations of Encircled Forces: German Experiences in Russia* in January 1953, and there were many more besides.[64] All dealt with situations
that U.S. and NATO forces might be facing in any number of near-
term scenarios.

Another facet of the same phenomenon was the great popularity in
the west of German memoirs, especially by the generals. The books
by F. W. von Mellenthin (*Panzer Battles*, 1956), Heinz Guderian (*Panzer Leader*, 1957), and Erich von Manstein (*Lost Victories*, 1958) are the
best-known examples,[65] but there were many others besides, and it is a
phenomenon that has lasted to the present day.[66] A strange view of the
war in the east arose, focusing almost exclusively on the German point
of view and asking repeatedly how the German army could have won.
One modern scholar notes the strange character of the historiography:

Barbarossa might well be the only war ever in which the losers wrote the history, rather than the victors.[67] It is only quite recently that the situation has begun to change and a more nuanced view of the war in the east has developed, especially in the numerous works of soldier-scholar David M. Glantz.[68]

In some ways, Operation Barbarossa was a new kind of war for Germany, a conflict with a "double face."[69] Hitler set the terms long before the first German soldier crossed the border: "The upcoming campaign," he told General Alfred Jodl, "is more than a mere contest of arms. It will be a struggle between two world-views."[70] This was about more than regime change, but a struggle to the death between National Socialism and "Jewish Bolshevism." Barbarossa envisioned the physical destruction of the Soviet Union, the deliberate starvation of tens of millions of Slavs—Russians, Byelorussians, Ukrainians, and others—and the helotization of the surviving remnant. What the "destruction of Jewish Bolshevism" would mean for the millions of Jews in the territories to be conquered would soon be obvious.

In one way, however, Barbarossa was completely in keeping with past German wars. The classic front-loaded campaign, its success depended on a rapid blow from the outset. It was necessary to hit the Red Army with massive force from the opening moments, to shatter it rapidly, and above all to prevent it from retreating deep into the Russian interior where only months of campaigning could root it out. According to the initial operational document ("Führer Directive #21") of December 18, 1940: "During the initial phase the bulk of the Russian Army stationed in western Russia is to be destroyed in a series of daring operations spearheaded by armored thrusts. The organized withdrawal of intact units into the vastness of interior Russia must be prevented."[71] The German nightmare was a rapid and preplanned Russian retreat behind the great river lines, especially the Dvina and the Dnepr, the same considerations that had troubled them in the Polish campaign, where the Narew, Vistula, and San were the barriers. It was likely, however, that that was precisely what the Red Army would do. Most German planners believed that it would have to be insane to meet the Wehrmacht toe-to-toe along the border.

Nevertheless, that is almost precisely what happened. Not only did the Red Army concentrate along the border, it met virtually every German advance with a counterthrust by powerful mechanized forces. Virtually all of them were disasters. Soviet forces were in most cases making their battlefield debut, and they were coming up against a veteran army with an unbroken record of victory, which simply chewed them up. Although Soviet tanks were superior to most of their Wehrmacht counterparts, and although there were plenty of them, Soviet tactics were primitive, their operations amateurish, their training wholly unrealistic. In other words, the Red Army was a fairly typical peacetime army: mountains of shiny new weapons, and little idea of how to use them.

THE CAMPAIGN

That is the backdrop for the opening months of Barbarossa, in which the Wehrmacht dealt out an ungodly amount of death and destruction on all fronts, but especially along the Warsaw-Moscow highway. In the north, Hoepner's *Panzergruppe* covered half the distance to Leningrad in the first five days. Manstein's LVI Panzer Corps drove some 50 miles on the first day alone, and 185 in the first four days.[72] In cooperation with a Finnish attack from the north, Leningrad was soon surrounded. In the south progress was somewhat slower, although the holdup here was due mainly to the conformation of the border. Rundstedt's advancing forces had to pass through a chokepoint, the narrow gateway between the Carpathian Mountains to the southwest and the impassable Pripet Marshes to the northeast. Still, by late July the panzers had broken into the open here as well, encircling Soviet forces at Uman in August, while the Romanian army drove on Odessa, the USSR's major port in the south.

Army Group Center's progress was astounding. This was the operational *Schwerpunkt*, with two of the army's four panzer groups attached, and they simply sliced through the opposition in front of them. In the first seven days of Barbarossa, *Panzergruppe* Guderian advanced 270 miles. With Hoth acting as the northern pincer and Guderian the southern, the Germans turned a series of grand encirclements. By June 26, they had formed a huge *Kessel* at Bialystok, followed by a second at Minsk, and then a third at Smolensk in July. Soviet losses in these battles were appalling. By August, there were no less than 895,000 prisoners of war in German hands. It gave a new definition to "battle of annihilation."

The only trouble was, it didn't annihilate. Although the Red Army was getting clobbered, it continued to defend tenaciously, and the Wehrmacht even found the *Kessels* to be troublesome. Sealing off a pocket of two hundred thousand men was like trying to blockade a small city, and in fact the Germans failed repeatedly. Thousands of Soviet troops managed to save themselves and rejoin their own lines or flee to the forests to join the already burgeoning partisan movement.

Reducing such pockets was even more difficult, requiring a series of pitched infantry battles that caused high casualties even to the victor.

The Red Army also never stopped counterattacking. These were often improvised, clumsy affairs, but they took their toll on the Germans. In particular, there was a series of sharp counterstrokes near Smolensk in late July, involving Soviet 20th Army (General P. A. Kurochkin), 19th Army (General I. S. Konev), and 21st Army (General F. I. Kuznetsov).[73] They were hastily planned and poorly coordinated, and in Konev's case, the men quite literally launched their attack as they dismounted from their troop trains. Although ultimately unsuccessful, however, these counterattacks seem to have been instrumental in the German decision to divert Guderian to the south to clear up the Ukraine before continuing on the road to Moscow.

Certainly, on a situation map, Army Group Center's progress had far outstripped its partners. In August, therefore, Hitler ordered a corps from Hoth's Panzer Group to the north to aid in storming Leningrad, and, more important, dispatched Panzer Group Guderian in its entirety to the south to help encircle Red Army forces in the Ukraine. With Kleist (1st Panzer Group) approaching from the west, and Guderian swooping down from the north, the Germans formed the greatest *Kessel* of all around Kiev. It trapped four full Soviet armies, the 5th, 37th, 26th, and 21st, some 665,000 prisoners in all.[74] The number of Soviet prisoners in German hands was now close to two million.

The Kiev encirclement is one of those alleged turning points in operation Barbarossa that continues to attract attention. General Staff officers would later point to it as the moment in which Hitler undid all the successes they had achieved, wasting precious time on a sideshow into the Ukraine while the road to Moscow lay open to German forces. In fact, this reasoning is specious all the way down the line. The road to Moscow was certainly not wide open. The battles in front of Smolensk had proved that, and the Germans had come to a halt on the Desna River to bring up supplies and reinforcements. Despite postwar complaints about Hitler's culpability, there was a hefty amount of support within the staff and command echelons for the turn into the Ukraine—from commander of the 4th Army, General Günther von Kluge, for example. Finally, a point rarely made: can any battle that nets 665,000 prisoners of war ever be considered a mistake? A major portion of Soviet fighting strength went into German captivity at Kiev. Certainly, from the perspective of the battle of annihilation, the only perspective most German officers had, Kiev was a masterstroke.

Besides the drive into the Ukraine, other factors began to affect the

progress of Barbarossa. Soviet equipment was far better than the prewar German estimates. Tanks, in particular the medium T-34 and the
heavy KV-1, were impervious to most German weapons. General Erhard Raus commanded 6th Panzer Division's Motorized Brigade in the
opening campaign. His memoirs describe vividly the shock of seeing
every weapon in the German antitank arsenal bounce off the armor of
the heavy KV-1 tank. On one occasion, a single KV-1 parked on a road
severed the supply line of his brigade for two full days. He describes
the action as German crews muscle a battery of four 50-mm antitank
guns into position. The tank doesn't respond to the activity around it,
and the Germans are puzzled:

> As we watched from the crest of the hill, someone suggested that
> perhaps the tank had been damaged and subsequently deserted by
> its crew, since little else could account for it simply squatting mo-
> tionless in the road, a perfect target. (The ridicule to be received
> from one's fellows, after having spent hours jockeying into position
> to finish off a dead tank, can be imagined.) Suddenly the first round
> flashed forth from one of the antitank guns, tracing a trajectory like
> a silver ray dead onto the target. In no time the armor-piercing shell
> had covered the intervening 600 meters. A glare of fire appeared,
> followed by the sound of a violent impact. A direct hit! A second
> and then a third shot followed.
>
> Officers and troops alike cheered and shouted as if spectators at a
> shooting match. "A hit! Bravo! The tank's been polished off!" The
> tank did not move until it had been pelted by at least eight direct
> hits. Then its turret rotated, it took careful aim, and methodically
> silenced our antitank battery with a few 80mm shells. Two of our
> 50mm guns were shot to pieces, and the remaining two seriously
> damaged.

Indeed, that tank sat there until drilled at point blank range by an
88-mm antiaircraft gun. German infantry crawled onto the tank and
found that only two of the seven rounds had pierced the armor.

> Suddenly the gun barrel started to move again, and our soldiers dis-
> persed in amazement. Quickly, the engineers took hand grenades
> and pushed them into the hole produced by the hit at the lower part
> of the turret. A dull explosion sounded, and the hatch lid flew open.
> In the interior of the tank lay the bodies of the brave crewmen, who
> before had apparently only fainted.[75]

"Deeply moved by such heroism," Raus concluded, "we buried the dead with all honors." A lone tank holding up the advance of an entire brigade for two full days is, admittedly, an anomaly. Yet, it would not be the last surprise for the Germans in this campaign.

Intelligence had also failed to recognize the enormity of the force that the Soviets could mobilize. The sheer size of the forces involved was beyond anything the Wehrmacht had yet faced. The Soviet regime, for example, was able to call up over *five million* reservists to the colors by the end of June. Prewar German estimates envisioned some three hundred Soviet divisions; by December the Soviets had fielded no less than six hundred. The Soviets had already lost one hundred divisions yet were everywhere still in the field, something no other contemporary army could have achieved.[76]

Finally, the Germans were often lacking in simple things like knowledge of the exact conformation of the terrain or the precise shape of the road network. Conditions in western and central Europe were common knowledge, printed on maps readily available to the public. An educated German staff officer probably didn't even need to read a map during much of Case Yellow. No one needed to look up items like the exact number of infantry marches from St. Quentin to Amiens or the depth of the Meuse River near Namur. Years of education, and centuries of campaigning on the same terrain, had burned these items into the brain of every German staff officer. It was different when the topic involved details of the terrain on the road from Maloyaroslavets to Kaluga, or the precise location of the crossing points of some remote *balka* in southern Ukraine. Maps were wholly inadequate, and German troops found themselves getting lost repeatedly in the course of Barbarossa, especially as the great early successes took them deeper into the country.

Let us call upon General Raus again, still with the 6th Panzer's motorized brigade, somewhere between Porkhov and Dno on the southern approaches to Leningrad. Orders had just come through to head north and assist 1st Panzer Division in overcoming unexpectedly tough Soviet resistance near Novoselye. "Hardly had *Kampfgruppe* Raus, then the division lead echelon, started for the trouble spot," he writes, "than the road shown on the map as leading directly through a swamp to Novoselye came to an end."

> The occupants of the wretched huts, which we came across here and there, appeared equally bewildered when we requested them to make a circle around the swampy area and lead us to a village that was

marked on our obsolete maps as being located on our line of march. These people were not familiar with the name with which the village was labeled on our maps, because the name had been changed decades earlier. Often we were left relying solely on our compasses and our instincts. With guides and engineers to the front, we took up a zigzag course, from village to village, over the best wagon roads that could be found.[77]

Even today, his account of 6th Panzer Division's passage through the swamps east of Lake Peipus is painful reading. There is even a certain comic opera nature to it all: an elite mechanized force going from village to village asking directions from a bemused peasantry.

For this combination of reasons, it wasn't until October that Army Group Center was ready to begin its drive on Moscow. Dubbed Operation Typhoon, it included three armies (9th, 4th, and 2nd, north to south), plus three panzer groups (once again north to south, 3rd, 4th, and Guderian's 2nd, now formally renamed "2nd Panzer Army"). The original plans called for a classically Prussian concentric advance against the Soviet armies in front of the Soviet capital.[78] Again, it began well. At Bryansk, the advance of 2nd Panzer Army to the northeast encircled the better part of three Soviet armies: 3rd, 13th, and 50th. At Vyazma, a near perfect Cannae-style double envelopment netted them an incredible bag of six more armies (19th, 24th, 29th, 30th, 32nd, and 43rd).[79] The combined total for both these battles was 750,000 prisoners. For the Red Army, this was like June, only worse, since it was taking place almost directly in front of the capital.

Fortunately for the Soviets, it began to rain on October 8. By the middle of the month, the roads on the way to Moscow had collapsed, with the weight of thousands of tanks, trucks, guns, and horse wagons churning them into mud. The locals knew what it meant: it was "the time without roads," a period in which no one in his right mind would try to drive by cart or truck. The Germans kept going, however, and by October 22, Hoth's Panzer Group 3 was stuck in a sea of mud outside Kalinin. On October 25, the commander of Army Group Center, Bock, complained in his diary of being "stuck fast." Then, on November 6, the freeze hit, the onset of the Russian winter. This was, in part, good news. As the muddy roads froze solid, the German drive could recommence. The bad news, of course, was that temperatures soon plunged, eventually reaching −40 F. Winter supplies were available but were piled up at depots far to the rear. The German supply service, as it always did, had prioritized items like guns and ammunition and gasoline over winter clothing, but given the state of the roads even priority items failed to arrive. The cold was horrible on the men, and just as bad on the vehicles. It's probably never a good idea to light a fire under an armored fighting vehicle jam-packed with explosive ammunition, but German crews were doing just that by November, in order to melt the oil in the pan.

Although the weather must figure prominently in any operational account of Typhoon, it wasn't the only problem. From the classical styling of its origins, Typhoon had soon collapsed into an operational mess for which virtually every commander involved must take some of the blame. In general, Army Group Center was aiming at Moscow, but it certainly failed to achieve anything like the decisive concentration of force it might have. In the south, Guderian's 2nd Panzer Army was supposed to be driving on Tula, the crucial railway town almost due south of Moscow. At the same time, however, much of its strength was tied up maintaining the Bryansk pocket. It also had orders from the OKH to drive southeast and take Kursk. Guderian was a flexible panzer leader, but even he had a difficult time going in three directions at once. On the other wing of the army group, a strong battle group of 9th Army and 3rd Panzer Group received orders to shift the axis of their advance almost due north, to make contact with the southern wing of Army Group North. Army Group Center's commander, Bock, took one look at these orders and knew that it was the end of a concentrated strike at Moscow. This was no longer concentric advance, but "excentric"—with main bodies flying away from one another.[80] It was the sort of thing one did when the enemy was defeated and one was occupying as much territory as possible.

Still, Typhoon inched forward. By December, the histories tell us, German patrols were "within sight" of the Kremlin, although the exact unit involved or the exact vantage point it had for this fortunate view has never been fully established; both 2nd Panzer Division and 258th Infantry Division claimed the honors (both part of XL Motorized Corps, 4th Panzer Group).[81] Soviet resistance had stiffened, however, and it was plain there would be no great breakthrough into the capital. The gravest threat, at least on the map, came in the south, where Panzer Group Guderian formed the southern end of the great German pincer aimed at Moscow. At the crucial railroad town of Tula, however, the Red Army succeeded in braking German momentum. Guderian's panzers overlapped Tula on both sides but never did take the city itself. In reality, he had suffered such catastrophic losses even getting to Tula that there was never much chance of taking it.[82]

It seems fairly obvious in hindsight that this would have been a good time to halt the winter attack on Moscow, carry out a short tactical withdrawal to defensible positions, and prepare to winter there. By now, Army Group North was stuck fast in front of Leningrad. The Germans had also suffered a serious check in the south, where a powerful concentration of fresh Soviet divisions had driven the German 1st Panzer Group (now styled "1st Panzer Army") back from Rostov. General von Rundstedt, Army Group South commander, had advised a withdrawal from Rostov to the line of the Mius River. Hitler had summarily dismissed him on December 1, but then ordered the retreat anyway. There was little choice.

On the central front, the drive on Moscow had sputtered out altogether, and there were ominous signs of a Soviet buildup in front of the capital. The comparisons to Napoleon and the *Grande Armée*, usually described as part of the German reaction to the upcoming Soviet counteroffensive, actually began in late November. The 4th Army chief of staff, General Günther Blumentritt, relates an unforgettable scene from this period:

> All the commanders were now asking: "When are we going to stop?" They remembered what had happened to Napoleon's army. Many of them began to re-read Caulaincourt's book grim account of 1812.[83] That book had a weighty influence at this critical time in 1941. I can still see von Kluge [4th Army commander] trudging through the mud from his sleeping quarters to his office, and there standing before the map with Caulaincourt's book in his hand. That went on day after day.[84]

Note that Kluge's reaction was not to a defeat, but to something that, to the Germans, was even more ominous. Kluge was trained to view war in a certain way, and the signs were all bad. The men were freezing and exhausted, the machinery was breaking down, and the supply services were bringing in a trickle of what the front line needed. The war of movement had come to a halt.

Nevertheless, the offensive went on. Hitler was responsible, of course, but he was not alone. General von Bock, commander of Army Group Center, was also strongly in support of continuing the attack toward Moscow. He had played the supporting role in Case White, and he had done the same in Case Yellow. The opportunity to play the lead, and to become the conqueror of Moscow, was not an opportunity he would give up lightly. Frankly, it is difficult to think of a single German commander in his place, in this or in any previous war, who would have even considered a halt. And so the Germans ground forward, fighting themselves down, quite literally in some units, to the last man, tank, and gun.

This was the precise moment that the Soviets launched their great counteroffensive in front of Moscow, on the brutally cold morning of December 5, 1941. The level of force involved showed that the Red Army had graduated to a new military league altogether: seventeen armies and two large cavalry corps (Cavalry Group Belov and 11th Cavalry Corps) grouped into four separate army fronts (Northwestern, Kalinin, Western, and Southwestern).[85] Spearheading the attack were troops of the Siberian Reserve, specially trained in winter combat and equipped with skis and heavy white parkas. These formations had just arrived after a top-secret eight thousand kilometer journey from the Far East. In overall command was the aggressive and brilliant young General G. K. Zhukov. He had shown brightly in the fighting against the Japanese in Manchuria in 1939–1940 and now had a chance to display his art of war to the Wehrmacht. It included an ability to remain cool under a German mechanized offensive, to pick out a weak spot, and then to slam into it with tremendous force. This was far from a simple frontal assault, but a combination of a sharp frontal blow with powerful thrusts on the flanks. Kalinin Front, in particular, first cleared up the German bulge pressing north of Moscow, then extended its offensive far to its own right, seeking to get around the left and into the rear of Army Group Center. For the first time since Moltke had made the "concentric advance by separated armies" his calling card, the German army was now finding out what it was like to be on the receiving end.

Surprise was total, although it shouldn't have been, and that fact demonstrates once again the inadequacy of German intelligence efforts. Many German units simply melted away, and soon Army Group Center was staring disaster in the face. Its commanders at all levels first recommended a retreat, and then began demanding one. Hitler refused, however. In one of the most famous, yet controversial, moments of the entire war, he issued a *Haltbefehl*, usually translated as "stand-fast order": each unit was to hold its position and defend it to the last, even if it had been bypassed or surrounded.[86] Frostbitten German soldiers obeyed, by and large, and went into all-around defensive positions, "hedgehogs," in whatever meager bit of shelter they had happened to find. By January 1942 Soviet momentum had worn down. The Red Army was not yet ready to go deep on the Germans; it had neither the tactics and supply services, nor systems of command and control for that. There are those who still argue that Hitler's "stand-fast order" had saved the day. The recently dismissed General Rund-stedt was not among them. "It was Hitler's decision for rigid resistance that caused the danger in the first place," he later claimed. "It would not have arisen if he had permitted a timely withdrawal."[87]

Vindicated against his generals, he now fired them en masse. Top-ping the list was Brauchitsch, the commander in chief of the OKH. He'd actually suffered a heart attack in early December, brought on by the tensions of mediating between Hitler's orders above him and the army group commanders beneath. Hitler now took his place, as-suming personal command over army operations. Both Leeb (Army Group North) and Bock (Army Group Center) joined Rundstedt in premature retirement. One of the first acts of the new commander of Army Group Center, Kluge, was to dismiss Guderian as commander of 2nd Panzer Army. It seems a fairly trivial issue today: a retreat by the 10th Motorized Division from Chern in the face of a Soviet attack on Christmas Day, 1941. Kluge accused him of directly violating both OKH and Army Group orders; Guderian answered that he had led his army as his conscience dictated; Kluge sacked him.[88] There apparently was no longer much room for independence of command in the Ger-man army.

BARBAROSSA: ANALYSIS

The Moscow counteroffensive is a good place to halt. The war wasn't over, far from it. The German army still lay deep inside the Soviet Union and in unchallenged occupation of Europe. In North Africa, General Erwin Rommel's *Afrika Korps* had only just begun to make life miserable for the British, and it would drive on to even greater triumphs in 1942. The western Allies would land in Normandy just as Soviet strength was waxing in Byelorussia, but there would be much hard fighting before the end in May 1945.

Nevertheless, December 1941 marks a definite shift in the strate-gic winds. Just two days after the Soviet counteroffensive in front of Moscow, the Japanese launched their raid on Pearl Harbor. That sur-prise blow was followed a couple of days later by another one: Hitler's declaration of war on the United States. It is instructive to pause for a moment and recall that, as of mid-June 1941, Hitler's Germany was at war with Great Britain alone, a nation that still possessed, in the form of its overseas empire, large reserves of strength. Six months later, it was still at war with Britain; it was now at war with the largest land power in the world, the Soviet Union; and it had just cavalierly, almost thoughtlessly, added the world's economic, financial, and industrial giant: the United States. Short of a wonder-weapon like the atom bomb, it is hard to conceive of a scenario that would have given Germany a decisive victory in this war.

There is another reason why December 1941 marks a great break point of German military history, however. If there has been one constant in the campaigns we have studied up to this point, from the seventeenth century to the 1940s, it is the German tradition of the independence of the commander. Today we call it *Auftragstaktik*, or speak of "flexible command" or "mission orders." By whatever name, the reality was this: no one and nothing could ever trump the independent authority of the higher German commander. He had a mission, it is true, but the methods and means were his alone. Often, even getting him to follow the mission was difficult enough. Frederick the Great didn't violate this compact, the great Moltke had tried but failed repeatedly, and Prussian-German history is filled with hard chargers like Frederick Charles in 1866, General Steinmetz in 1870, and, perhaps the classic example of them all, the incorrigible General Hermann von François, the hero of Tannenberg. Even Hitler had allowed subordinate commanders to flout orders with impunity—Guderian in Case Yellow, for example. The system had worked well enough, mainly because of the high level of aggression in most Prussian commanders. Flouting orders almost always meant one thing: making for the nearest enemy concentration and launching a vicious attack on it. It rarely meant lying down on the job.

It is easy to blame Hitler for the demise of *Auftragstaktik*. He swept away many traditions in German politics and society, and it is hard to see how he could have spared the army. His first decree as the new commander in chief was a fundamental order on reports from the higher commanders. Calling on them to report every detail, to provide plain answers to every question, and to state clearly when they had failed to carry out assigned orders, it is still an incredible thing to read. A recent German authority has noted the historic nature of the "fundamental order":

This was the very point at which the issue of reporting intersected with the renunciation of *Auftragstaktik*. For the staffs, the requirements meant a constant presentation of dates, positions, troop units, and similar details, each of which could be demanded on a daily or nightly basis. It was often difficult for an isolated unit to supply the exact strength at the moment of the required report, and the parts of a given unit that were necessarily deployed well behind the front varied locally. Since no system of reporting could ensure that "unclear positions" were not hidden somewhere, this system came more and more to resemble a game.[89]

Moreover, Hitler proved to be a supreme commander who intervened not just in operational details, such as placement of reserves, but who regularly sent directives to lower tactical units about deployment of their light mortars or their antitank guns. There were still plenty of aggressive commanders in the pipeline who soldiered on for Hitler and kept the war going for another three and a half years. In that time, however, the last three and a half years of Prussian-German military history, the independence of battlefield command became a dead letter. It wasn't simply the fact that he fired all his generals and replaced them with toadies or National Socialist fanatics. It was that he issued the "stand-fast order" in the first place.

Once again, however, we must go beyond a simple "Hitler did it" approach to the death of *Auftragstaktik*. In fact, it was also the times, and in particular, the state of technological development. In the age of the radio, the supreme commander now had virtually instantaneous access to each army group and army commander. There was nothing to stop him from going lower in the chain of command if he so desired. Beyond the radio, however, it was the introduction of air power into the mix that transformed *Auftragstaktik* from the German army's characteristic tradition into a pleasant memory. With the conduct of land warfare increasingly bound up with control of the air, and with cooperation between land and air assets now central to battlefield success, there was simply no more room for a truly independent army commander, doing as he saw fit and then reporting it later to the supreme command. Let it be recalled that it was not Hitler, but Kluge, who fired Guderian. The dash, the impetuousness, the ability to roam free, away from higher control—all these belonged to a bygone era. As warfare has become ever more technologically complex, they will never return.

The high priest of the new dispensation was not Adolf Hitler, but General Franz Halder, the army chief of staff. In a set of directives to the chiefs of staff of the army groups and armies on January 6, 1942, he stressed that it was time for a stricter system of command, one based firmly on Hitler's will. Handing down a mission whose means were the choice of the lower commander had led not only to a flouting

A long way from home. German mechanized advance into the foothills of
the Caucasus Mountains, 1942. Courtesy of Christian Ankerstjerne.

of the high command's intentions, but to "serious disadvantages for
the overall situation." It was time for clear and unambiguous orders,
he told them. "The duty of soldierly obedience leaves no room for
the sensibilities of lower headquarters. On the contrary it demands
the best and most rapid execution of orders in the sense that the one
issuing them intended."[90] Moreover, while the German army was in
the trying process of re-establishing a cohesive front in the east, he
warned that orders from the high command would necessarily be dealing with the most minute tactical details.

As for a final verdict on Operation Barbarossa, perhaps it is best
to state that, rather than the Wehrmacht "losing" it, the Soviet army
won it. In June 1941, unlike previous campaigns, the German army entered upon a campaign in which the enemy did not show his back. Although the Wehrmacht certainly did clobber the Soviets in the opening months of Operation Barbarossa, carving them up and sealing off
even larger encirclements than in the west, it now faced an enemy who
in many ways was just as aggressive. With old imperial Russian traditions of maneuver by huge, independent "army groups" (the Russian

word was "front," used in a more technical sense than in the west) now married to the twin characteristics of Stalinism—heavy industrialization and absolute ruthlessness—the Russians were able to prosecute their own, very potent version of the war of movement. They were able to do so with levels of manpower, matériel, and disdain for losses that simply dwarfed anything the Germans had at their disposal.

The move into the Soviet Union was the acid test of *Bewegungskrieg*. Despite all the impressive operational victories in the early going, the centuries-old German conception of war making ultimately failed the test. Barbarossa presented the German army with a task for which it was not suited. An army designed, trained, and equipped for short campaigns in central and western Europe, with a highly developed infrastructure and a well-manicured road network, was out of its depth fighting a winter campaign in the heart of European Russia, just as it would prove to be out of its depth in the logistics-dominated war in the desert. Conquering France was once thing; winning and controlling a vast colonial empire extending to the Urals was something else again. It would have required, at the very least, better systems of intelligence, counterintelligence, and supply, and these deal only with the operational level.[91] At the strategic level, such a war required a comprehensive program of rational, long-term economic planning by experts, not by Hitler's party cronies or his favorite of the month.[92] It also wouldn't have hurt to have a decent ally or two.

Finally, let us return to the question that opened this chapter. Was there a turning point of World War II? It is difficult to answer definitively. Such a sprawling conflict, so many complexities: in this age of chaos theory, we should beware of any simplistic attempts to provide linear analysis of it all. There is one fundamental question, however, that does have an answer. When did most German staff officers know that the war was lost? When did they know that the attempt to win the war in the Soviet Union had failed, even after all the early victories, and even after reloading the barrel for a second time in Operation Typhoon? A historical view of German operations tells us the precise date. It was December 26, 1941, a Friday. In the issue of the *Militär-Wochenblatt* appearing on that day, there is the standard weekly report of operations on all fronts, under the heading "Germany's Freedom War." Tucked away, almost unnoticeable, its significance perhaps not fully appreciated by anyone not steeped in the curriculum of the *Kriegs-akademie*, was a phrase that must have caused even the most optimistic German officer to stop short. There, in black and white, was a message of doom, a simple headline that ran, "*Stellungskrieg* in the east."[93]

Conclusion: The German Way of War

In surveying German war making from the Great Elector's victory at Warsaw in 1656 to the near-disaster suffered by Army Group Center in front of Moscow, several recurring patterns emerge. Prussia-Germany tried to keep its wars short, winning a decisive battlefield victory in the briefest possible time. Although it might be argued that every warring power desires the same thing, no other country took this trend to such extremes. No other country in European history sought victory so relentlessly through sudden or surprising operational maneuver. Prussian armies virtually always tried to get onto the flank or into the rear of their adversaries, not just with a cavalry unit or two, but with the entire force. The Great Elector and his Swedish allies marching around the Polish blocking position at Warsaw; Frederick the Great marching around the flank of Austrian foe at Leuthen or all the way around into the Russian rear at Zorndorf; Blücher crossing the Elbe at Wartenburg to challenge Napoleon; Moltke maneuvering his separated armies so they formed a great concentric mass on the battlefield at Königgrätz: these were, in living form, the Prussian way of war. They are all manifestations of *Bewegungskrieg*, the operational-level war of movement. Only in the war of movement did the possibility exist for a decisive victory of annihilation.

At the same time, keeping wars short meant that the Prussian army had to be the aggressor, not necessarily in terms of starting the war, but of carrying the action to the enemy. The Prussian army attacked. Even if it were temporarily forced onto the strategic defensive, as with 8th Army in East Prussia in 1914, it still sought an opening to deal a crushing blow against the enemy through operational maneuver. This preference extended from the staff to the field officers and all the way down to the tactical level. Prussian infantry was conditioned to attack, to give the enemy no rest. "The entire strength of our troops lies in the attack," Frederick the Great once said. "We would be fools to renounce it without good reason."[1] The Franco-Prussian War, to give one example, consisted of a series of bruising Prussian attacks, in which the aggression of Moltke's commanders and their infantry, attacking frontally, held the French in place long enough for another force or forces to work around their flank. There was little art here, but a great deal of guts and killer instinct.

It is customary to write German military history almost solely in terms of its great philosophers and theoreticians of war: Clausewitz, Moltke, and Schlieffen, for example. It is time to redress that imbalance and to suggest that the man of action played as strong a role, if not stronger, than the thinker. Virtually every great period of Prussian-German military history has a suitable candidate. At the side of the Great Elector rode the hard-charging and hard-drinking Derfflinger, a foreign import with a checkered past who became Prussia's first great military hero. For Frederick the Great it was men like the great hussar Ziethen,[2] also a hard drinker, mean tempered, unassuming in appearance, but hell in the saddle, not to mention Seydlitz, whose self-generating aggression remade the Prussian cavalry into the strike force par excellence of the era. For the reform era, typically seen as the age of Scharnhorst and Gneisenau, there was Blücher, an unusual character whose entire art of war consisted of an apparently insatiable drive to come to grips with his French enemy. Moltke's victories, typically analyzed in theoretical and doctrinal terms, would have been unthinkable without the "Red Prince," Frederick Charles, wearing the same flamboyant uniform as Ziethen. "Concentric maneuvers" with "separate portions of the army" were all well and good, Frederick Charles believed, as long as he got to attack any enemy within his reach along the way. He did just that, and he triumphed more often than not. His decision to attack an Austrian force twice as large as his own at Königgrätz, and then to hold on through a very uncomfortable morning, was the key to victory in the greatest battle of the era of railroads and rifles. Germany's twentieth-century wars are filled with the same kind of characters, warriors who drove at the enemy and attacked without asking permission from their superiors.

It is customary today, in U.S. military circles for example, to use the term *Auftragstaktik* to describe the German doctrine of command. According to the common explanation, the supreme commander (typically the chief of the General Staff) devised a mission (*Auftrag*), but left the methods and means of achieving it to the officer on the spot. They could handle their commands as they saw fit, as long as they were acting within the mission defined by the supreme commander. Analysts typically see this flexible command system as one of the secrets to German battlefield success.

In fact, defined in that way, *Auftragstaktik* is completely mythological. The Germans hardly ever used the term when discussing issues of command. Rather, they spoke of "the independence of subordinate commanders," which is a very different thing.[3] In a letter to a member of the Italian General Staff in 1874, Moltke described it this way:

> The commander, who in our days no longer leads a closed phalanx but different armies in different theaters, cannot manage without the independent action of his subordinate commanders. A victory won without—or even against—higher orders can still be part of the totality, for each victory carries with it far-reaching effects. The commander will add it into his calculations, as he does all those other facts that went into modifying the plan he originally conceived and held to steadily.[4]

Operational-level German commanders (corps and above) saw themselves, and were recognized by the General Staff, as absolutely independent in spirit and behavior; they were free agents while on campaign.

It was a view tied closely to old Prussia's social system, especially the distinct social contract between the king and the Junker nobility. They swore fealty to him and served him, typically in war but also in the civil service. In return, he allowed them near total dominance over the serfs, and later the peasants, on their domains. That arrangement extended to the general's relationship with the troops under his command, as well. Although they were not his property, they were bound to obey him, and he could launch them on any operation that he saw fit. For the king (or his deputy, the chief of the General Staff) to intervene in a detailed way in the military operations of his subordinate would have been to violate this arrangement and to call into question the sovereignty of the Prussian nobility.

In the course of a comprehensive historical survey, it is almost impossible to find an occasion when a "mission" as defined by the supreme command took precedence over the wishes of a battlefield commander. Frederick Charles did not seem overly concerned with his assigned mission as he led the 1st Army into Bohemia. He was supposed to make a beeline for Gitschin and link up with the crown prince. He did get to Gitschin eventually, but only after repeatedly going out of his path to hammer Austrian forces he met along the way. Nor was his decision to attack the Austrians as soon as he encountered them behind the Bistritz River in harmony with Moltke's own plans—the 2nd Army was still a full day's march from the battlefield, and there are those even today who argue that Frederick Charles almost upset the entire applecart with a precipitate attack on a much larger force. General Flies had a mission of his own in 1866. He was supposed to bar the gate to the Hanoverian army and force it into surrender. Instead he, too, advanced on it and launched an attack on an enemy who outnumbered him two to one. In 1914, General Hermann von François was supposed to link up with the main body of 8th Army at Gumbinnen. Instead, taking note of Russian activity at Stallupönen, he advanced to the town and launched an immediate attack on them—his I Corps taking on an entire Russian army. After smashing through the French lines at Sedan, General Guderian received a clear mission: to halt and allow the mass of Army Group A's infantry to catch up to his hard-charging panzers. It did not take the "panzer leader" long to devise a good excuse to disobey, and his entire corps continued its drive under the transparent guise of a "reconnaissance in force." These events are so common that describing them as anomalies seems ridiculous, and praising some while condemning others seems unfair. They were an integral part of the Prussian-German way of war.

Perhaps the most incredible example was the opening sequence of moves in the Franco-Prussian War. The decision of General Steinmetz to march his 1st Army due south into the path of the oncoming friendly 2nd Army (led by its own hard charger, Frederick Charles) appears, at first, to be inexplicable. He nearly derailed Moltke's entire operational scheme, which called for 2nd Army to advance in the center and the other two armies to operate as flanking forces. It caused a traffic jam of monumental proportions, and a more active and aggressive French command might have made the Prussians pay. None of these things mattered to Steinmetz. He had spotted a French force within quick marching distance, at Spichern. This was the reality of Prussian command "doctrine": attack the enemy wherever he was found. Far from being coldly rational strategists, the commanders of Prussian field armies were often like so many attack dogs, straining at any leash designed to limit their freedom of action and not infrequently snapping at each other when the prey was near.

It worked well enough until 1914, when friction between army commanders and the supreme command (Moltke the Younger) contributed materially to the failure on the Marne, however one chooses to explain that failure. In World War II, it reappeared. Once again, however one chooses to explain the German failure in Operation Barbarossa, it is difficult to say much that is positive about the Wehrmacht's command arrangements. In the end, *Auftragstaktik* or the "independence of subordinate commanders" died not merely at the hands of Adolf Hitler, but at the hands of General Franz Halder and the rest of the General Staff. The Wehrmacht killed the old command style because it no longer corresponded to modern realities. An army group is too precious a national asset to entrust to the whims of one man.

It is highly problematic, therefore, for a modern army to claim *Auftragstaktik* as a basis for its system of command. First, the Prussian system of subordinate leaders who possessed a high degree, if not absolute, operational independence grew out of a different social and historical milieu. Soldiers in the U.S. Army are citizens, with the same rights and privileges as the officer, and he will never have the right to use them independently in the manner of a Prussian field marshal. Moreover, the contemporary state of the U.S. Army, with its interplay of highly complex weapons systems and communications technology, offers little opportunity for the independence of division, corps, or army commanders. How much conceptual space for a truly independent command can there possibly be in an operation involving highly mobile ground elements, tactical air, and helicopter gunships, for example? Consider, for a moment, the coalition offensive in Operation Desert Storm (1991). Let us posit the following scenario, an alternate history, but one that will sound familiar to students of Prussian military history:

> In the initial assault, General Gary E. Luck (XVIII Airborne Corps), smarting under the relegation of his command to the status of flank guard for VII Corps's "great wheel" to the right and eager for personal glory, decides unilaterally to alter the axis of advance for his corps. Instead of north-northeast, he swings sharply to the east. The maneuver brings him into contact at numerous spots with the armor of VII Corps, and there is a great deal of confusion and tragic examples of friendly fire, before Luck smashes into the Iraqi flank.

How would General Norman Schwarzkopf have reacted to "Luck's wheel"? A wistful sigh, a chuckle, and a shake of the head? What of the reaction in the American media, with its televised images of a forty-eight-hour traffic snarl, interviews with bemused soldiers, and footage of friendly fire incidents? Or newspaper headlines that would have read, invariably, "Chaos in the Desert"? The preceding scenario is not some exaggerated fantasy. The Prussian-German supreme command had to deal with issues just like it in every single war it fought.

Another benefit of surveying German military history in the *longue durée* is that it suggests an answer to another long-controversial question. Clearly, the Germans did not invent something called *blitzkrieg* in the 1920s and early 1930s. Rather, Prussia and Germany had been trying to keep their wars short since the days of the Great Elector and Frederick the Great. They believed, rightly or wrongly, that a short war was the only kind that they could win. A long war meant a war of attrition, and poor, small Prussia would always find itself at a disadvantage against larger, better-heeled neighbors in such a contest. That tradition had carried on into the nineteenth century, and in Moltke the Elder, Prussia found the short-war commander par excellence. The attempt to achieve a repeat in 1914 of his great victories came to naught. After the failure of the opening campaign, there came the long and demoralizing *Stellungskrieg*, over three years of positional warfare that bled both sides dry, only the German side a bit more successfully than the Allied. The introduction of the tank and the aircraft, typically viewed as a revolutionary development, or indeed as part of a "revolution in military affairs," simply provided the tools that the German army needed to get back to what it had always done best: prosecute a short, violent *Bewegungskrieg*. The experience of World War I, jarring in so many areas, did not shake this venerable German view of military operations. The German analysis of these successful operations in the war's first two years—Poland, *Weserübung*, Case Yellow, the opening phase of Barbarossa—placed them squarely within that traditional context.

The end of the war saw Germany prostrate, its armies crushed, its cities pounded into rubble, its very status as a civilized nation called into question by the crimes of the Third Reich. It had to accept occupation by the victorious powers, and eventually partition into two states, each of which mirrored the political and economic system of its principal great power occupier. Germany in general, and Berlin in particular, became the poster child for the division of the world into two power blocs during the cold war. In the immediate wake of the war, it was obvious that the United States and the Soviet Union disagreed on virtually every aspect of what was once again being called the "German question." They sparred over the question of forcing Germany to pay reparations (a crucial issue to rebuilding the devastated Soviet economy); over the process of de-Nazification (whom to punish and whom to rehabilitate); even the precise content of postwar German textbooks.

In one area, however, there was unanimity. Both great powers agreed that Prussia had to be destroyed. The adjective *Carthaginian* has a long pedigree in diplomatic history, but this was the one truly Carthaginian moment of twentieth-century peacemaking. The historic state of Frederick the Great received the death penalty and disappeared from the European map. Not only did the former Allies believe that Prussia was too large, relative to the other German states, to coexist without dominating them,[5] they also viewed Prussia as a danger to the peace of Europe. On February 25, 1947, the members of the Allied Control Commission (Generals Lucius Clay, Sir Brian Robertson, Joseph Pierre Koenig, and Vassily Sokolovsky), issued "Decree 46":

> The Prussian state, which from early days had been the bearer of militarism and reaction in Germany, has *de facto* ceased to exist.
>
> Guided by the interest of preservation of peace and security of peoples and with the desire to assume further reconstruction of the political life of Germany on a democratic basis, the Control Council enacts as follows:
>
> Article I. The Prussian state with its central government and all its agencies is abolished.[6]

Apparently, in the age of nuclear weapons, the world could no longer tolerate a state in the heart of Europe dedicated to the prosecution of "short and lively" wars.

Notes

Preface

1. *König-Feldherr* or, to use the French with which Frederick himself was more comfortable, *roi-connétable*. German historians of Frederick's reign have been using the latter term more and more frequently. For a discussion of the advantages accruing to Frederick by virtue of combining the political leadership and military command in one person, see Reed Browning, "New Views on the Silesian Wars," *Journal of Military History* 69, no. 2 (April 2005), pp. 532–533.

2. Carl von Clausewitz, *On War*, edited and translated by Michael Howard and Peter Paret (Princeton, N.J.: Princeton University Press, 1984), book 2, chapter 2, p. 136.

3. For a survey of the recent literature on German federalism, see Abigail Green, "The Federal Alternative? A New View of Modern German History," *Historical Journal* 46, no. 1 (March 2003), pp. 187–202, with its attempt to restore a balance between the traditional Prusso-centric "Borussian narrative" and one willing to recognize the importance and legitimacy of other historical alternatives.

4. See Michael Stürmer, *The German Empire: A Short History* (New York: Modern Library, 2000), pp. 12–13.

5. See the article by Dennis E. Showalter, "German Grand Strategy: A Contradiction in Terms?" *Militärgeschichtliche Mitteilungen* 48, no. 2 (1990), pp. 65–102.

6. See the seminal essay by Fernand Braudel, "Histoire et sciences socials: la longue durée," *Annales: Economies, sociétés, civilisations* 13, no. 4 (October–December 1958), pp. 725–754.

7. A point made by Stig Förster, "Operationsgeschichte heute: Eine Einführung," *Militärgeschichtliche Zeitschrif* 62 (2002), pp. 309–313, who warns of leaving operational history in the hands of "pied Pipers and so-called experts of doubtful provenance" (p. 310). For arguments on behalf of the continued relevance of operational history, see also Bernd Wegner, "Wozu Operationsgeschichte?" and Dennis E. Showalter, "Militärgeschichte als Operationsgeschichte," both in *Was ist Militärgeschichte?* ed. Benjamin Ziemann and Thomas Kühne (Paderborn: Ferdinand Schöningh, 2000).

1. The Great Elector and the Origins of Prussian War Making

1. The encounter in the Teutoburgerwald between Hermann and Varus traditionally makes the list of history's most decisive battles, although we still are not

sure where, when, or exactly why it was fought. See the classic account by Sir Edward Creasy, *The Fifteen Decisive Battles of the World from Marathon to Waterloo* (New York: A. L. Burt, 1890), pp. 134–161, as well as J. F. C. Fuller, *The Decisive Battles of the Western World, and Their Influence upon History*, vol. 1, *From the Earliest Times to the Battle of Lepanto* (London: Eyre & Spottiswoode, 1954). For the debate over exactly where the battle took place, as well as analysis of the punitive expedition under Germanicus, see Hans Delbrück, *History of the Art of War*, vol. 2, *The Barbarian Invasions* (Lincoln: University of Nebraska Press, 1990), pp. 69–148. For a view that disagrees with Delbrück on the location of both Varus's camp and the site of the actual battle, see Major General Wolf, "Die Schlacht im Teutoburger Walde," *Beihefte zum Militär-Wochenblatt 1902* (Berlin: E. S. Mittler, 1902), pp. 267–284, with an extremely useful map.

2. Our sources on Adrianople are still quite sketchy and are likely to remain that way. The pertinent volume of the *West Point Atlas*, for example, contains what might be called "generic battle map number 1," a standard portrayal of Visigothic cavalry on the flanks driving off their Roman counterparts, turning in, and striking the flanks of the infantry. Elmer C. May, Gerald P. Stadler, and John F. Votaw, *Ancient and Medieval Warfare. West Point Military History Series* (Wayne, N.J.: Avery, 1984), p. 87.

3. For a more sophisticated view of a specific Germanic barbarian tribe, see Thomas S. Burns, *A History of the Ostrogoths* (Bloomington: Indiana University Press, 1984), who describes the interplay and interpenetration of Roman and German civilization along the frontier, and who also argues for the magnetic pull of the latter: "The primary stimulus for this gradual migration was the Roman frontier, which increasingly offered service in the army and work for pay around the camps" (p. 21). See also the sophisticated analysis of the *Völkerwanderung* in Herwig Wolfram, *History of the Goths* (Berkeley: University of California Press, 1988), pp. 5–9. For a recent synthesis displaying the state of the question, see Steven Ozment, *A Mighty Fortress: A New History of the German People* (New York: HarperCollins, 2004), pp. 17–33.

4. To his credit, Charlemagnes's own biographer, Einhard, goes into great detail on the Saxon Wars, "waged for thirty-three long years and with immense hatred on both sides." See the combined biographies of Einhard and Notker the Stammerer, *Two Lives of Charlemagne* (New York: Penguin, 1969), pp. 61–64.

5. Frederick Wilhelm has attracted a great deal of attention from German-language scholars, much less in English. The venerable biography by Martin Philippson, *Der Grosse Kurfürst Friedrich Wilhelm von Brandenburg*, 3 vols. (Berlin: Verlag Siegfried Cronbach, 1897–1903), is still a towering work, combining judgments that have stood the test of time with wonderful writing. See also Hans Kania, *Der Grosse Kurfürst* (Leipzig: Teubner, 1930), a shorter work based heavily on Philippson, with a large dash of operational detail included. The modern successors to Philippson, both well grounded in the primary and secondary literature, are Ernst Opgenoorth, *Friedrich Wilhelm: der Grosse Kurfürst von Brandenburg*, 2 vols. (Frankfurt: Musterschmidt Göttingen, 1971–1978), and Ludwig Hüttl, *Friedrich Wilhelm von Brandenburg* (München: Süddeutscher Verlag, 1981). Gerhard Oestreich,

Friedrich Wilhelm, der Grosse Kurfürst (Frankfurt: Musterschmidt Göttingen, 1971) is a useful handbook. A popular work worth consulting is Barbara Beuys, *Der Grosse Kurfürst: Der Mann, der Preussen schuf* (Reinbek bei Hamburg: Rowohlt, 1979). The pickings in English are still quite slim. A good short introduction to the historical problems of the Elector's reign is to be found in Margaret Shennan, *The Rise of Brandenburg-Prussia* (London: Routledge, 1995). Ferdinand Schevill, *The Great Elector* (Chicago: University of Chicago Press, 1947) is outdated and filled with extremely opaque writing. See also the chapter entitled "The Great Elector" in H. W. Koch, *A History of Prussia* (New York: Dorset Press, 1978), pp. 43–64.

6. The same root shows up in the place-name "Mercia," one of the kingdoms of the Anglo-Saxon heptarchy in early medieval Britain, and "Ostmark," the original Carolingian name for the province that would eventually become Austria. The Nazis would resurrect the latter name after the *Anschluss* of 1938.

7. The other electors of the original seven were the archbishops of Mainz, Trier, and Cologne; the king of Bohemia; the count palatine (*Pfalzgraf*) of the Rhine; and the duke of Saxony.

8. The official name of the Teutonic Knights (*Deutschritter Orden*) was The Servants of St. Mary of the German House. Their devotion to the Blessed Virgin is evident in place-names, such as Marienwerder and Marienburg. For the details of their conquest of the province, see Delbrück, *History of the Art of War*, vol. 3, *Medieval Warfare*, pp. 377–383, and Koch, *History of Prussia*, pp. 1–22.

9. For Tannenberg, perhaps the first attempt to get behind the mythmaking and written in his typically prickly style, see Delbrück, *History of the Art of War*, vol. 3, pp. 523–527.

10. For a pre–World War I account of the order's battle with its "hate-filled enemies," striving for "a destruction of Germandom," see Lieutenant General Noetzel, "Die Schlacht bei Tannenberg am 15. Juli 1410: Kampf des Deutschen Ordens gegen Polen," *Militär-Wochenblatt* 95, no. 86 (July 14, 1910), pp. 2034–2041; and for a Russian construction (plus the German reaction), see "Gedanken zur 500-Jahrfeier des Allslavischen Sieges am 15. Juli 1410 über die Deutschen bei Tannenberg," *Militär-Wochenblatt* 95, no. 102 (August 18, 1910), pp. 2378–2382.

11. Representative samplings of the Borussian school include Heinrich von Treitschke, *Deutsche Geschichte im neunzehnten Jahrhundert*, 5 vols. (Leipzig: S. Hirzel, 1879–1895); Johann Gustav Droysen, *Friedrich I: König von Preussen* (Berlin: De Gruyter, 2001); and Heinrich von Sybel, *Die Begrundung des Deutschen Reiches durch Wilhelm I*, 7 vols. (München: R. Oldenbourg, 1889–1894). For the origins of Treitschke's thought, see Andreas Dorpalen, "Treitschke," *Journal of Contemporary History* 7, nos. 3–4 (July–October 1972), pp. 21–35. For a critique of the Borussian school in the light of new approaches, see Abigail Green, "The Federal Alternative? A New View of Modern German History," *Historical Journal* 46, no. 1 (March 2003), pp. 187–202.

12. The military revolution, its exact definition, and the controversies that swirl around it have dominated early modern military historiography for the last thirty years. The term "military revolution" first appeared in the literature in Michael Roberts, *The Military Revolution, 1560–1660: An Inaugural Lecture Delivered before*

the Queen's University of Belfast (Belfast: M. Boyd, 1956). Geoffrey Parker's article "The Military Revolution, 1550–1660: A Myth?" *Journal of Modern History* 48, no. 2 (June 1976), pp. 195–214, was both a critique of Roberts and a broadening of the argument away from Sweden (Roberts's main interest) toward a European-wide interpretation. In particular, Parker saw the rise of a new type of fortress, the so-called *trace italienne*, its expense, and the huge number of soldiers required to man it as being crucial to explaining why armies grew so rapidly in the period. He expanded the argument into a book, *The Military Revolution: Military Innovation and Rise of the West, 1500–1800* (Cambridge: Cambridge University Press, 1988). See also John A. Lynn, one of the leading contributors to this debate, who has subjected Roberts's and Parker's findings to a rigorous test case in the French army: "The *Trace Italienne* and the Growth of Armies: The French Case," *Journal of Military History* 55, no. 3 (July 1991), pp. 297–330, and "Recalculating French Army Growth during the Grand Siecle, 1610–1715," *French Historical Studies* 18, no. 4 (Autumn 1994), pp. 881–906. One could not find a better guide to the controversies and generally fascinating nature of the debate than to consult Clifford J. Rogers, *The Military Revolution Debate: Readings on the Military Transformation of Early Modern Europe* (Bouder, Colo.: Westview Press, 1995). It contains reprints of the seminal articles by Roberts, Parker, and Lynn mentioned above, and much more.

13. For the origins of Brandenburg's claim to Pomerania, see Opgenoorth, *Friedrich Wilhelm*, vol. 1, pp. 28–29, 75; Philippson, *Grosse Kurfürst*, vol. 1, pp. 9, 84–85; and Hüttl, *Friedrich Wilhelm*, p. 44.

14. For period engravings of Oder-Spree canal, see Ingrid Mittenzwei and Erika Herzfeld, *Brandenburg-Preussen, 1648 bis 1789: Das Zeitalter des Absolutismus in Text und Bild* (Köln: Pahl-Rugenstein, 1987), pp. 75–77.

15. One name associated with the *Primat der Aussenpolitik* is the father of modern scholarly historiography, Leopold von Ranke. See especially his masterwork, *Memoirs of the House of Brandenburg and History of Prussia during the Seventeenth and Eighteenth Centuries* (London: J. Murray, 1849). After years of attack by historians on the left, especially social and political critics of the so-called "Bielefeld School" like Hans-Ulrich Wehler, the idea made a qualified comeback in the 1980s and 1990s in the writings of Michael Stürmer, Andreas Hillgruber, and others, part of the conservative turn (*Wende*) in Germany during those years. See, for example, Stürmer's essay "A Nation State against History and Geography: The German Dilemma," in *Escape into War? The Foreign Policy of Imperial Germany*, ed. Gregor Schöllgen (New York: Berg, 1990).

16. See Eckart Kehr, *Battleship Building and Party Politics in Germany, 1894–1901: A Cross-Section of the Political, Social, and Ideological Preconditions of German Imperialism* (Chicago: University of Chicago Press, 1973), as well as *Der Primat der Innenpolitik: Gesammelte Aufsätze zur preussish-deutschen Sozialgeschichte im 19. und 20 Jahrhundert* (Berlin: W. de Gruyter, 1965).

17. Shennan, *Rise of Brandenburg-Prussia*, p. 14.

18. For a thoughtful account of Louis XIV's wars, see David Kaiser, *Politics and War: European Conflict from Phillip II to Hitler* (Cambridge, Mass.: Harvard University Press, 1990).

19. Delbrück, *History of the Art of War*, vol. 4, *The Dawn of Modern Warfare*, p. 247.

20. Gordon A. Craig, *The Politics of the Prussian Army 1640–1945* (Oxford: Oxford University Press, 1955), pp. 3–4.

21. Outside the Great Northern War involving Peter the Great and Charles XII, the other Northern Wars—a tangled nest of conflicts involving Sweden, Poland, Russia, and Brandenburg—have not received the attention that is their due, at least in English. A refreshing exception is the work of the Polonist Robert I. Frost. His *The Northern Wars: War, State, and Society in Northeastern Europe, 1558–1721* (Essex: Longman, 2000) is unlikely to be superseded for some time. For an analysis of the Swedish-Brandenburger war on Poland, see his *After the Deluge: Poland-Lithuania and the Second Northern War, 1655–1660* (Cambridge: Cambridge University Press, 1993). There is confusion of terminology within the field. Many refer to the 1655–1660 conflict as the "First Northern War"; Frost refers to it as the second, with the first having taken place after the collapse of the truce between Poland and Muscovy (1562–1570). See *Northern Wars*, pp. 12–13.

22. Philippson, *Grosse Kurfürst*, vol. 1, p. 231.

23. For Labiau, see Koch, *History of Prussia*, p. 54; Hüttl, *Friedrich Wilhelm*, p. 217.

24. The Battle of Warsaw deserves far more attention than it has received in English. Those seeking to reconstruct it from the Brandenburger side must rely on older works. The best account is still Gerhard von Pelet-Narbonne, *Der Grosse Kurfürst* (Berlin: B. Behr, 1905). Pelet-Narbonne was a lieutenant general in the German army at the time, and the work is part of the series *Erzieher des preussischen Heeres*, 12 vols. (Berlin: B. Behr, 1905–1907), which he edited. One should supplement it with the pertinent chapters in the masterful work by Curt Jany, *Geschichte der königlich preussischen Armee*, 4 vols. (Berlin: Karl Siegismund, 1928–1933), especially vol. 1, pp. 123–130; Philippson, *Grosse Kurfürst*, vol. 1, pp. 233–236; Kania, *Grosse Kurfürst*, pp. 64–65; and Opgenoorth, *Friedrich Wilhelm*, vol.1, pp. 336–341. From the Polish side, see Frost, *Northern Wars*, pp. 173–176, with its extremely useful maps. The present account follows Pelet-Narbonne's most carefully.

25. The seventy-thousand figure comes from Philippson, the two hundred thousand figure is mentioned in Opgenoorth, *Friedrich Wilhelm*, vol. 1, p. 337, n268, though it remains uncited. See Jany, *Geschichte der königlich preussischen Armee*, vol. 1, p. 123, for the forty thousand figure.

26. For the postbattle Swedish claims, see Opgenoorth, *Friedrich Wilhelm*, vol. 1, pp. 342–343. The Elector felt it necessary to write a rejoinder, published in Amsterdam.

27. Pelet-Narbonne, *Grosse Kurfürst*, p. 74.

28. For the struggle over the Colline, see Jany, *Geschichte der königlich preussischen Armee*, vol. 1, pp. 126–128; see also the map on p. 127, reprinted forty-three years later in Opgenoorth, *Friedrich Wilhelm*, vol. 1, p. 339.

29. Pelet-Narbonne, *Grosse Kurfürst*, p. 75.

30. For the charge of the Połubinski Hussars, as well as a passionate and entirely justified plea for a more objective reading of Polish military history in general, see Frost, *Northern Wars*, pp. 16–18, 174.

31. Philippson, *Grosse Kurfürst*, vol. 1, p. 236, maintains that the Polish fort was garrisoned by mercenary German infantry. Frost, *Northern Wars*, doesn't accept a third day of battle at all, arguing that the Poles had already retreated and that "the Allies rolled forward across the open plain" (p. 174).

32. Philippson, *Grosse Kurfürst*, vol. 1, p. 23; Pelet-Narbonne, *Grosse Kurfürst*, p. 74, calls it "the first great victory."

33. For Frederick Wilhelm's carefully detailed operational order for the Ahlsen landing, see Pelet-Narbonne, *Grosse Kurfürst*, pp. 78–81, who reproduces it in toto. For the disappointment in front of Stettin in 1660, see Lieutenant General Roessel, "Vor zweihundertfünfzig Jahren," part 12, "Die Belagerung von Stettin durch Kaiserliche Truppen unter Feldzeugmeister de Souches und Brandenburgische unter dem Grafen Dohna—Beendigung des Feldzuges in Pommern," *Militär-Wochenblatt* 95, nos. 17–19 (February 3, 1910, February 5, 1910, and February 8, 1910), pp. 382–387, 402–407, and 427–430.

34. Craig, *Politics of the Prussian Army*, p. 2; Shennan, *Rise of Brandenburg-Prussia*, p. 28. For Frederick William's distrust of military coalitions, see Delbrück, *History of the Art of War*, vol. 4, p. 245.

35. Fehrbellin may be better known than Warsaw, but it is still necessary to consult older German works to reconstruct the encounter. The primary source is still that of the Elector's great grandson, King Frederick II (the Great) of Prussia. See his "Fehrbellin," in *Ausgewählte Werke Friedrichs des Grossen*, vol. 1: *Historische und militärische Schriften, Briefe*, ed. Gustav Berthold Volz (Berlin: Reimar Hobbing, 1900), pp. 9–13, as well as his "Charakterbild," pp. 13–17, which compares the personality of the Elector with that of Louis XIV. See also the useful operational history in W. von Unger, "Feldmarschall Derfflinger," *Beihefte zum Militär-Wochenhblatt 1896* (Berlin: E. S. Mittler, 1896), pp. 295–439, especially the section "Rathenow und Fehrbellin," pp. 355–373, as well as Philippson, *Grosse Kurfürst*, vol. 2, pp. 332–361; Pelet-Narbonne, *Grosse Kurfürst*, pp. 86–90; Jany, *Geschichte der königlich preussischen Armee*, vol. 1, p. 229–244; and Kania, *Grosse Kurfürst*, pp. 149–160.

36. This tendency even appears in otherwise ceremonial anniversary articles. See, for example, the article by General Friedrichfranz Feeser, "Friedrich Wilhelm, der Grosse Kurfürst: zur Erinnerung an der zweihundertfünfzigjährigen Todestag, 9. May 1688," *Militär-Wochenblatt* 122, no. 46 (May 13, 1938), pp. 2945–2948.

37. Philippson, *Grosse Kurfürst*, vol. 2, p. 390.

38. For the debate over whether to attack at Marlenheim, see Pelet-Narbonne, *Grosse Kurfürst*, pp. 83–84, as well as Unger, "Feldmarschall Derfflinger," pp. 346–355.

39. Frost, *Northern Wars*, p. 213, is the only source in English to mention the "deeply unfavourable circumstances" in which the Swedes undertook the campaign, as well as their extreme reluctance.

40. Frederick the Great, "Fehrbellin," p. 9.

41. Pelet-Narbonne, *Grosse Kurfürst*, p. 86.

42. Koch, *History of Prussia*, p. 62. Kania, *Grosse Kurfürst*, p. 151, tells us that Derfflinger was "seventy years old, as vigorous as a boy" ("siebzigjährig, rüstig wie ein Jüngling").

43. See Frederick the Great, "Fehrbellin," p. 10; for minor variations, see Jany, *Geschichte der königlich preussischen Armee*, vol. 1, p. 239, and Pelet-Narbonne, *Grosse Kurfürst*, p. 87.

44. Frederick the Great, "Fehrbellin," p. 10, and Kania, *Grosse Kurfürst*, pp. 151–152, describe a ruse; Jany, *Geschichte der königlich preussischen Armee*, vol. 1, p. 240, and Pelet-Narbonne, *Grosse Kurfürst*, p. 88, an assault.

45. For the Hennigs mission, one of the major pieces of patriotic Prussian lore of this campaign, see Jany, *Geschichte der königlich preussischen Armee*, vol. 1, pp. 240–241. Philippson, *Grosse Kurfürst*, vol. 3, p. 501, calls him "Henni(n)ges"; Schevill, *Great Elector*, pp. 318–319, calls him "Henning."

46. Kania, *Grosse Kurfürst*, pp. 156–157, has a solidly reasoned discussion of Swedish numbers. See also Frederick the Great, "Fehrbellin," p. 11.

47. Kania, *Grosse Kurfürst*, p. 157, and Jany, *Geschichte der königlich preussischen Armee*, vol. 1, p. 242, both name Derfflinger as the commander who first identified the hills as the key piece of battlefield terrain. Pelet-Narbonne, *Grosse Kurfürst*, p. 89, and Frederick the Great, "Fehrbellin," p. 12, credit it to the Elector.

48. Opgenoorth makes this point of comparison between Marlenheim and Fehrbellin explicitly (*Friedrich Wilhelm*, vol. 2, p. 169).

49. For the "schematic" accusation, a term of high insult in later German military literature, see Pelet-Narbonne, *Grosse Kurfürst*, p. 89.

50. The tale of Emanuel Froben, Master of the Elector's Horse and a servant who laid down his life for his lord, is a key part of the Fehrbellin narrative—recurring in virtually every analysis of the battle. The classic account is Frederick the Great, "Fehrbellin," p. 12, but see also Philippson, *Grosse Kurfürst*, vol. 2, p. 359; Jany, *Geschichte der königlich preussischen Armee*, vol. 1, p. 242; and Kania, *Grosse Kurfürst*, p. 159, the last of whom eyes it most critically. Froben was indeed killed at the side of his master, and Frederick William later did exchange a horse with one of his cavalrymen. Kania argues that postbattle narratives have conflated the two tales.

51. See Frost, *Northern Wars*, pp. 213–214.

52. See Opgenoorth, *Friedrich Wilhelm*, vol. 2, p. 170.

53. The phrase "vom Rhein bis an den Rhin" is Pelet-Narbonne's, *Grosse Kurfürst*, p. 90.

54. Jany, *Geschichte der königlich preussischen Armee*, vol. 1, pp. 244–261, has the most comprehensive analysis of this difficult campaign. See also Opgenoorth, *Friedrich Wilhelm*, pp. 180–187.

55. For the winter campaign of 1678–1679, see Jany, *Geschichte der königlich preussischen Armee*, vol. 1, pp. 261–271; Pelet-Narbonne, *Grosse Kurfürst*, 94–99; Kania, *Grosse Kurfürst*, pp. 176–178; Lieutenant Colonel Ponath, "Einwirkung von Gewässern und Sümpfen auf winterliche Kriegführung," 2 parts, *Militär-Wochenblatt* 113, nos. 26–27 (January 11, 1929; January 18, 1929), pp. 1035–1040, 1081–1085, especially part 2, pp. 1081–1082; and Major Heinz Guderian, "Bewegliche Truppenkörper: Ein kriegsgeschichtliche Studie," part 1, "Die Schlittenfahrt des Grossen Kurfürsten im Winterfuldzug 1678–79," in *Militär-Wochenblatt* 112, no. 18 (November 11, 1927), pp. 649–652.

56. For numbers in the winter campaign, see Jany, *Geschichte der königlich preussischen Armee*, vol. 1, pp. 261–266.

57. Guderian, "Die Schlittenfahrt," p. 650.

58. Jany, *Geschichte der königlich preussischen Armee*, vol. 1, p. 269.

59. Phillipson, *Grosse Kurfürst*, vol. 2, p. 412.

60. Phillipson, *Grosse Kurfürst*, vol. 2, p. 411.

61. Pelet-Narbonne, *Grosse Kurfürst*, p. 96.

62. For a representative sampling, see two articles by F. L. Carsten, "The Great Elector and the Foundation of the Hohenzollern Despotism," *English Historical Review* 65, no. 255 (April 1950), pp. 175–202, and "The Resistance of Cleves and Mark to the Despotic Policy of the Great Elector," *English Historical Review* 66, no. 259 (April 1951), pp. 219–241.

63. For the Kölln story, see Ernst Fischer, "Georg Derfflinger: Bruchstücke seines Lebensbildes," *Beihefte zum Militär-Wochenblatt 1894* (Berlin: E. S. Mittler, 1894), pp. 397–451.

64. See the fascinating personality profile of Derfflinger in Rudolf Thiel, *Preussische Soldaten* (Berlin: Paul Neff, 1940), pp. 15–37.

65. Guderian, "Die Schlittenfahrt," p. 651. See also by Guderian, "Schnelle Truppen einst und jetzt," in *Militärwissenschaftliche Rundschau* 4, no. 2 (1939), pp. 229, 243, esp. pp. 230–231.

2. The Origins of Frederician Warfare

1. Russell F. Weigley, *The Age of Battles: The Quest for Decisive Warfare from Breitenfeld to Waterloo* (Bloomington: Indiana University Press, 1991), p. 168.

2. Christopher Duffy, *The Military Experience in the Age of Reason* (London: Routledge and Kegan Paul, 1987), p. 190.

3. Hans Delbrück, "Über die Verschiedenheit der Strategie Friedrichs und Napoleons," in *Historische und politische Aufsätze* (Berlin: Georg Stilke, 1907), pp. 241–242.

4. A typical example is to be found in Weigley, *Age of Battles*, p. 168, who argues that one can actually grow "nostalgic" contrasting "the comparatively civilized warfare of the eighteenth century with the barbarities of our own time," but who also allows that the Seven Years' War, aiming at the humbling of Prussia and its removal from the ranks of the great powers "was therefore by no means a paradigm of limited conflict."

5. The literature on Frederick the Great is immense. To begin with the primary source, Frederick was a polymath of the Enlightenment who wrote widely about politics, about war, and about himself. Indeed, his collected papers, published in Berlin from 1846–1856 as *Oeuvres de Frédéric le Grand*, run to thirty volumes. The German edition, *Die Werke Friedrichs des Grossen* (1913) assembles them in ten. A good short introduction is Gustav Berthold Volz, ed., *Ausgewählte Werke Friedrichs des Grossen*, vol. 1., *Historische und militärische Schriften, Briefe* (Berlin: Reimar Hobbing, 1900). Frederick's military writings are available in English translation in *Frederick the Great on the Art of War*, ed. Jay Luvaas (New York: Free Press, 1966).

It combines Frederick's *Instruction militaire du roi de Prusse pour ses généraux* (1753) with his later writings, although the transitions from one document to the next are not always as noticeable as they ought to be.

There are enough biographies to keep any interested reader happy for a long time. The standard in German is still the comprehensive work by Reinhold Koser, *Geschichte Friedrichs des Grossen* (Berlin: J. G. Cotta, 1912–1913). See also Lieutenant Colonel W. von Bremen, *Friedrich der Grosse* (Berlin: B. Behr, 1905), vol. 3 of the series *Erzieher des preussischen Heeres*, 12 vols. (Berlin: B. Behr, 1905–1907). In English, the classic is Thomas Carlyle, *History of Friedrich the Second, Called Frederick the Great* (Albany: J. B. Lyon, 1900). Many will thrill to the breathless Victorian prose; others will blanch; a good way to tell which way you turn is the one-volume abridgment of the work edited by John Clive, *History of Frederick the Great* (Chicago: University of Chicago Press, 1969). Cyril Ransome, ed., *The Battles of Frederick the Great* (New York: Scribner's, 1892) abstracts the military portions of Carlyle's massive narrative. Another older work that still contains much useful information is W. F. Reddaway, *Frederick the Great and the Rise of Prussia* (New York: Putnam, 1904).

There are many useful and readable modern biographies, as well. Foremost among the scholarly works are Gerhard Ritter, *Frederick the Great: A Historical Profile* (Berkeley: University of California Press, 1968); Walther Hubatsch, *Frederick the Great of Prussia: Absolutism and Administration* (London: Thames and Hudson, 1973); and Theodor Schieder, *Frederick the Great* (London: Longman, 2000). For compilations of primary source materials by and about the king, see also Peter Paret, ed., *Frederick the Great: A Profile* (New York: Hill and Wang, 1973) and Louis L. Snyder, *Frederick the Great* (Englewood Cliffs, N.J.: Prentice Hall, 1971). Among more popular works, the best are Robert B. Asprey, *Frederick the Great: The Magnificent Enigma* (New York: Ticknor & Fields, 1986), with a foreword by Dennis E. Showalter; and David Fraser, *Frederick the Great: King of Prussia* (New York: Fromm, 2001).

Regarding Frederick's military operations, the best place to start is the dominant body of work by Christopher Duffy, who has spent a career as a one-man Frederick the Great industry. Beyond *The Military Experience in the Age of Reason*, he is the author of *The Army of Frederick the Great* (London: David & Charles, 1974); *Frederick the Great: A Military Life* (London: Routledge and Kegan Paul, 1985), as well as *The Fortress in the Age of Vauban and Frederick the Great, 1660–1789* (London: Routledge and Kegan Paul, 1985), the second volume of his *Siege Warfare* series. One of the deans of military history in the United States, Dennis E. Showalter, has recently weighed in with *The Wars of Frederick the Great* (London: Longman, 1996), which skillfully places operational details in their eighteenth-century historical context and wraps them in a delightful package of his always formidable writing.

And from Germany, see the crucial body of work by Johannes Kunisch on Frederick's abilities as military commander, including *Friedrich der Grosse: Der König und seine Zeit* (München: Beck, 2004), a comprehensive biography, and the seminal article "Friederich der Grosse als Feldherr," in Oswald Hauser, ed., *Friedrich der Grosse in seiner Zeit*, vol. 8, *Neue Forschungen zur brandenburg-preussischen Geschichte*

(Köln: Böhlau Verlag, 1987). The latter essay appears also in the essential compilation of Kunisch's essays, *Fürst—Gesellschaft—Krieg: Studien zur bellizistischen Disposition des absoluten Fürstenstaates* (Köln: Böhlau Verlag, 1992), pp. 83–106.

6. Showalter, *Wars of Frederick the Great*, p. 67.

7. For the best short discussion of the reign of Frederick I (III), see H. W. Koch, *A History of Prussia* (New York: Dorset Press, 1978), pp. 65–77.

8. The standard work on Frederick William I is still Carl Hinrichs, *Friedrich Wilhelm I., König in Preussen: eine Biographie: Jugend und Aufstieg* (Darmstadt: Wissenschaftliche Buchgesellschaft, 1968). The work is an expansion of the author's original 1943 volume. See also Reinhold Dorwart, *The Administrative Reforms of Frederick William I of Prussia* (Westport: Greenwood Press, 1971). Frederick William I has also had his share of bad press. For representative examples, see Robert R. Ergang, *The Potsdam Führer: Frederick William I, Father of Prussian Militarism* (New York: Columbia University Press, 1941) and Fernand Fizaine, *Frédéric-Guillaume 1er: père du militarisme allemand* (Paris: La Nef de Paris, 1958), an interesting accusation about a king who never went to war or fought a battle. See also Koch, *History of Prussia*, pp. 78–101.

9. Duffy, *Army of Frederick the Great*, p. 88. See also Showalter, *Wars of Frederick the Great*, for a discussion of the importance of drill.

10. Duffy, *Army of Frederick the Great*, p. 89.

11. On the first two Silesian Wars, there is one essential English-language work, and it is doubtful that it will be superseded anytime soon: Reed Browning, *The War of the Austrian Succession* (New York: St. Martin's Press, 1993). Browning is an expert in the political and diplomatic background to the conflict, writes very thoughtfully of the linkages between politics, society, and war, yet departs sufficiently from the "new military history" to stress the importance of strategic, operational, and even tactical detail.

12. As the first battle of Frederick's career, the Battle of Mollwitz has caught the attention of historians seeking the roots of his art of war. The accounts are often impressionistic rather than detailed, however. Begin with the German General Staff Study: *Die Kriege Friedrichs des Grossen*, part 1, *Der Erste Schlesische Krieg 1740–1742*, vol. 1, *Die Besetzung Schlesiens und die Schlacht bei Mollwitz* (Berlin: E. S. Mittler, 1890), the best source of operational details and excellent maps. The source and critical notes to the account of the battle are indispensable. Nevertheless, criticisms against the series were not uncommon when it appeared, since it was written over many years by different officers, without a unified redaction. See the criticisms of an earlier edition in "Friedrich der Grosse als Feldherr," *Militär-Wochenblatt* 67, no. 12 (February 11, 1882), pp. 235–251. Frederick's own account of the battle, "Mollwitz," included in Volz, *Ausgewählte Werke Friedrichs des Grossen*, pp. 79–86, requires caution in its use. The king, writing many years after the fact, misnames rivers, lays unfair blame on various subordinates, and makes mistakes in outlining the admittedly complex order of battle. Other detailed accounts of the battle appear in Asprey, *Frederick the Great*, pp. 195–203, although his literary technique of switching to the present tense for battle scenes is pointless and annoying; Browning, *Austrian Succession*, pp. 51–54; Duffy, *Army of Frederick the Great*, pp.

160–161, and *Military Life*, pp. 28–34; Fraser, *Frederick the Great*, pp. 77–106; Curt Jany, *Geschichte der königlich preussischen Armee bis zum Jahre 1807*, 4 vols. (Berlin: Karl Siegismund, 1928–1933), vol. 2, *Die Armee Friedrichs des Grossen 1740 bis 1763*, pp. 32–39; Ransome, *Battles of Frederick the Great*, pp. 10–24 (which gives Carlyle's account, see n. 5 above), and, most recently, Showalter, *Wars of Frederick the Great*, pp. 45–50. Both Bremen, *Friedrich der Grosse*, pp. 9–10, and Weigley, *Age of Battles*, pp. 170–173, offer shorter, impressionistic accounts.

13. See the German General Staff account, *Schlacht bei Mollwitz*, pp. 375–387, "Parallelmarsch der Preussischen und Oesterreichischen Armee von 6ten bis 9ten April."

14. Duffy, *Military Life*, p. 30; German General Staff, *Schlacht bei Mollwitz*, p. 391. The source notes of the latter also contain a detailed discussion of the Austrian numbers, which may have ranged as high as 10,600 infantry and 8,600 cavalry. See note 127, pp. 448–449.

15. In "Mollwitz," p. 83, Frederick lays the blame for the problem almost exclusively on the shoulders of his right wing cavalry commander, Count Adolf Friedrich von der Schulenberg.

16. German General Staff, *Schlacht bei Mollwitz*, pp. 394–395.

17. Frederick, "Mollwitz," p. 83.

18. German General Staff, *Schlacht bei Mollwitz*, p. 397. Identical phrasing appears in Jany, *Geschichte der königlich preussischen Armee*, p. 34.

19. German General Staff, *Schlacht bei Mollwitz*, p. 399.

20. For the controversy about the status of Schulenberg's wing at the moment of the Austrian charge, see Frederick, "Mollwitz," p. 83, and Jany, *Geschichte der königlich preussischen Armee*, p. 35, which follows Frederick's account closely; and German General Staff, *Schlacht bei Mollwitz*, p. 400.

21. For the controversy about the formation of Römer's charging cavalry, see Frederick, "Mollwitz," p. 83, and German General Staff, *Schlacht bei Mollwitz*, p. 454.

22. Duffy, *Military Biography*, p. 32, attributes at least part of the poor showing of the Prussian cavalry to the grenadiers, "who got in their way."

23. German General Staff, *Schlacht bei Mollwitz*, p. 400.

24. Frederick, "Mollwitz," p. 84.

25. Showalter, *Wars of Frederick the Great*, p. 47.

26. Frederick, "Mollwitz," p. 84.

27. German General Staff, *Schlacht bei Mollwitz*, p. 406.

28. Frederick, "Mollwitz," p. 84.

29. Jany, *Geschichte der königlich preussischen Armee*, p. 37.

30. Frederick, "Mollwitz," p. 85.

31. German General Staff, *Schlacht bei Mollwitz*, p. 406.

32. Jany, *Geschichte der königlich preussischen Armee*, p. 36.

33. German General Staff, *Schlacht bei Mollwitz*, pp. 407–408.

34. Both the German General Staff, *Schlacht bei Mollwitz*, p. 410, and Jany, *Geschichte der königlich preussischen Armee*, p. 38, declare it so; Duffy, *Military Life*, p. 33, brings the tactical curtain down on the battle after Frederick's departure.

35. Jany, *Geschichte der königlich preussischen Armee*, p. 38.

36. Browning, *Austrian Succession*, p. 53.

37. German General Staff, *Schlacht bei Mollwitz*, p. 412.

38. Showalter, *Wars of Frederick the Great*, pp. 7–8, speaks of the "underdeveloped nervous system" of the eighteenth-century army.

39. German General Staff, *Schlacht bei Mollwitz*, p. 419.

40. Bremen, *Friedrich der Grosse*, p. 9.

41. Showalter, *Wars of Frederick the Great*, p. 48.

42. Frederick, "Mollwitz," pp. 85–86. The Prussian General Staff, *Schlacht bei Mollwitz*, pp. 415–417 disagreed, however, and so do most modern commentators. See Duffy, *Military Life*, pp. 30–31, and Showalter, *Wars of Frederick the Great*, pp. 49–50.

43. Prussian General Staff, *Schlacht bei Mollwitz*, p. 417.

44. Bremen, *Friedrich der Grosse*, pp. 9–10.

45. For Chotusitz, see Showalter, *Wars of Frederick the Great*, pp. 58–61; Duffy, *Military Life*, pp. 41–45; and Fraser, *Frederick the Great*, pp. 116–120.

46. Bremen, *Friedrich der Grosse*, pp. 14–17.

47. See Brent Nosworthy, *The Anatomy of Victory: Battle Tactics, 1689–1763* (New York: Hippocrene Books, 1990), pp. 281–283.

48. Hugo von Freytag-Loringhoven, *Feldherrngrösse: Von Denken und Handeln hervorragender Heerführer* (Berlin: E. S. Mittler, 1922), p. 56.

49. See the profile of Ziethen in Rudolf Thiel, *Preussische Soldaten* (Berlin: Paul Neff, 1940), pp. 89–91.

50. For the birth and development of the Prussian Hussars, see "Der Zusammenhang der Husaren der heutigen Armee mit denen der Armee Friedrichs des Grossen," *Militär-Wochenblatt* 76, no. 67 (August 1, 1891), pp. 1705–1720; the quote is from p. 1707.

51. For detailed analysis of the *Grenzer*, see Gunther E. Rothenberg, *The Austrian Military Border in Croatia, 1522–1747* (Urbana: University of Illinois Press, 1960).

52. The best and most detailed analysis of the "oblique order" is to be found in Nosworthy, *Anatomy of Victory*, pp. 192–197.

53. Quoted in Freytag-Loringhoven, *Feldherrngrösse*, p. 57.

54. See, for example, the pertinent volume of the *West Point Atlas*, where the term *oblique order* is used specifically for both battles. Elmer C. May, Gerald P. Stadler, and John F. Votaw, *Ancient and Medieval Warfare* (Wayne, N.J.: Avery, 1984), p. 16, map 6 (chapter 1) and p. 35, map 3 (chapter 2).

55. Duffy, *Military Experience in the Age of Reason*, pp. 52–53.

56. See the unsigned article "Zum Friedrichstage," *Militär-Wochenblatt* 79, no. 7 (January 24, 1894), pp. 175–178.

57. The sources on Hohenfriedeberg are sufficient to describe the battle itself, although the operational maneuvers preceding it require care in their reconstruction. Begin, as always, with the German General Staff Study, *Die Kriege Friedrichs des Grossen*, part 2, *Der Zweite Schlesische Krieg 1744–1745*, vol. 2, *Hohenfriedeberg* (Berlin: E. S. Mittler, 1895), which is particularly good on just those operational-level details that receive less attention in most works. The focus is so different from the Mollwitz volume's emphasis on the tactical details of the battle itself

(see note 12, above) that they may well be the work of different authors. Again, see the criticisms of the series in the *Militär-Wochenblatt* article "Friedrich der Grosse als Feldherr." See also Jany, *Geschichte der königlich preussischen Armee*, vol. 2, pp. 128–139, which follows the General Staff account closely, but also apparently works from other sources of information. Frederick's own account of the battle, "Hohenfriedberg" [sic], is to be found in Volz, *Ausgewählte Werke Friedrichs des Grossen*, pp. 89–97, and once again, is a simplified and at times inaccurate portrayal of the battle. Other worthy accounts of the battle appear in Asprey, *Frederick the Great*, pp. 317–324, once again switching to the present tense, and Browning, *Austrian Succession*, pp. 213–218. The latter is typically thoughtful, although the use of modern Czech and Polish place names can be jarring (Hradec Karlove for Königgrätz, for example, and Zabkowice Slaskie for Frankenstein). It leads to immense difficulties in trying to follow the action and penalizes most heavily those readers who already know something of the campaign. As anyone who has worked in the field will attest, the problem is endemic to the historiography of East Central Europe, and there is no ideal solution. Duffy's two works (*Army of Frederick the Great*, pp. 160–161, and *Military Life*, pp. 163–165) are both excellent. See also Fraser, *Frederick the Great*, pp. 178–184, Ransome, *Battles of Frederick the Great*, pp. 34–49, which gives Carlyle's account (see n. 5 above), and, once again, the fine account in Showalter, *Wars of Frederick the Great*, pp. 78–84. Weigley, *Age of Battles*, pp. 175–176, offers, again, an impressionistic account.

58. The best accounts of the Bohemian campaign of 1744 are to be found in Jany, *Geschichte der königlich preussischen Armee*, vol. 2, pp. 105–115, who recognizes "the brilliant success of Traun's art of maneuver" (p. 113), Duffy, *Military Life*, pp. 51–56, and Showalter, *Wars of Frederick the Great*, pp. 74–77. Duffy and Showalter both reference French pressure as a reason for Frederick's march southward from Prague; Jany sees it as part of the original plan, if the Austrians did not come out in defense of Prague.

59. Both quotes are found in Duffy, *Military Life*, p. 57.

60. Frederick, "Hohenfriedberg," p. 91.

61. The "man from Schöneberg" is from Frederick, "Hohenfriedberg," p. 90; the General Principles of War, article XII, gives the "Italian from Schmiedeberg" reference. See Luvaas, ed., *Frederick the Great on the Art of War*, p. 122. See also the German General Staff, *Hohenfriedeberg*, p. 216, which misidentifies the first reference as a man from "Schömberg."

62. For the preliminary engagement (*Vorgefecht*) at Landeshut, see German General Staff, *Hohenfriedeberg*, pp. 194–203.

63. Frederick, *Hohenfriedberg*, pp. 91–92.

64. The best source for these operational movements is German General Staff, *Hohenfriedeberg*, "Die Heeresbewegung vom 22. Mai bis zur Vorabend der Schlacht von Hohenfriedeberg," pp. 203–222.

65. Frederick, *Hohenfriedberg*, p. 92.

66. German General Staff, *Hohenfriedeberg*, p. 208.

67. Duffy, Military Life, gives Frederick's impression of the scene. See also Asprey, p. 320, and Jany, *Geschichte der königlich preussischen Armee*, vol. 2, p. 126.

68. Jany, *Geschichte der königlich preussischen Armee*, vol. 2, p. 126.

69. German General Staff, *Hohenfriedeberg*, p. 218.

70. German General Staff, *Hohenfriedeberg*, pp. 210–211.

71. See German General Staff, *Hohenfriedeberg*, p. 226, and 66. Jany, *Geschichte der königlich preussischen Armee*, vol. 2, p. 127.

72. See Duffy, *Military Life*, p. 61; Showalter, *Wars of Frederick the Great*, p. 79; Jany, *Geschichte der königlich preussischen Armee*, vol. 2, pp. 129–130; and German General Staff, *Hohenfriedeberg*, pp. 224–225.

73. German General Staff, *Hohenfriedeberg*, p. 229, uses the phrase "ein allgemeines Handgemenge."

74. Duffy, *Military Life*, p. 62, calls it an "improvised line of battle."

75. German General Staff, *Hohenfriedeberg*, p. 230.

76. For the battle against the Austrians, see Jany, *Geschichte der königlich preussischen Armee*, vol. 2, pp. 134–138; German General Staff, *Hohenfriedeberg*, pp. 232–239 ; and Duffy, *Military Life*, pp. 62–64.

77. German General Staff, *Hohenfriedeberg*, p. 238.

78. See the opening of Showalter's *Wars of Frederick the Great*, pp. 1–2, which contrasts military history's "Whigs" and "Calvinists," with the former seeing war as "a contest between progress and obscurantism, with progress . . . inevitably emerging triumphant."

79. See, for example, the highly debatable assertions in Weigley, *Age of Battles*, p. 175, and Fraser, *Frederick the Great*, pp. 178–179.

3. Frederick in the Seven Years' War

1. For a detailed account of the debate, generally supporting Delbrück, see Arden Bucholz, *Hans Delbrück and the German Military Establishment* (Iowa City: Iowa University Press, 1985), especially pp. 2–18 and 36–37. See also the numerous works of Delbrück himself, of which the following are a representative sampling: Hans Delbrück, *History of the Art of War*, vol. 4, *The Dawn of Modern Warfare* (Lincoln: University of Nebraska Press, 1990), especially pp. 369–383; *Die Strategie des Perikles erläutert durch die Strategie Friedrichs des Grossen* (Berlin: Georg Reimer, 1890), especially pp. 30–48, and most important, his essay, "Über die Verschiedenheit der Strategie Friedrichs und Napoleons," in *Historische und politische Aufsätze* (Berlin: Georg Stilke, 1907), pp. 223–301. For a fair-minded overview, see Antulio J. Echevarria II, *After Clausewitz: German Military Thinkers before the Great War* (Lawrence: University Press of Kansas, 2000), pp. 183–188, and for a sympathetic analysis of one of Delbrück's principal critics, see Echevarria's "General Staff Historian Hugo Freiherr von Freytag-Loringhoven and the Dialectics of German Military Thought," *Journal of Military History* 60, no. 3 (July 1996), pp. 471–494.

2. Theodor von Bernhardi, *Friedrich der Grosse als Feldherr*, 2 vols. (Berlin: Ernst Miller, 1881). See the detailed synopsis and review, arguably read by ten times as many German officers, "Friedrich der Grosse als Feldherr," *Militär-Wochenblatt* 67, no. 12 (February 11, 1882), pp. 235–252.

3. Delbrück, *History of the Art of War*, vol. 4, p. 369.

4. Delbrück, *History of the Art of War*, vol. 1, *Warfare in Antiquity*, p. 425.

5. Delbrück, *History of the Art of War*, vol. 3, *Medieval Warfare*, pp. 608–612.

6. Hans Delbrück, "Friedrich der Grosse als Feldherr: eine methodologische Parodie," in *Die Strategie des Perikles*, pp. 30–48.

7. Delbrück's own characterization of the parody, *History of the Art of War*, vol. 4, p. 379.

8. "Friedrich der Grosse als Feldherr: eine methodologische Parodie," p. 42.

9. Delbrück, *History of the Art of War*, vol. 1, p. 35. See also Bucholz, *Hans Delbrück*, pp. 32–34.

10. Bucholz, *Hans Delbrück*, p. 38.

11. It is interesting to note that the currently dominant scholars on Frederick take a harder view of Delbrück. Dennis E. Showalter, *The Wars of Frederick the Great* (London: Longman, 1996), argues that "Frederick was neither an 'attritionist' nor an 'annihilationist,'" since "both approaches tend to make war an abstraction, an end in itself," (p. 106) and criticizes both positions as suffering "from the same form of hindsight" (p. 146). Christopher Duffy, *Frederick the Great: A Military Life* (London: Routledge and Kegan Paul, 1985), p. 284, labels Delbrück "one of those people who draw their vital force from confrontation and controversy."

12. For examples, see "Friedrich der Grosse als Feldherr" (the *Militär-Wochenblatt* review of Bernhardi's book, note 2, above), p. 238; Hugo Freiherr von Freytag-Loringhoven, *Feldherrngrösse: Von Denken und Handeln hervorragender Heerführer* (Berlin: E. S. Mittler, 1922), p. 5; and especially A. von Taysen, *Zur Beurtheilung des siebenjähriges Krieges* (Berlin: E. S. Mittler, 1882), which takes issue with several of Bernhardi's points regarding Frederick's preference for the battle of annihilation. See also the review of Taysen's book by von Ollech in *Militär-Wochenblatt* 67, no. 67 (August 19, 1882), pp. 1310–1323, and *Militär-Wochenblatt* 67, no. 68 (August 23, 1882), pp. 1343–1352.

13. Duffy, *Frederick the Great: A Military Life*, p. 285.

14. Delbrück, *History of the Art of War*, vol. 4, p. 379. Delbrück's student Richard Schmitt also took up the cudgel for his dissertation adviser in *Prinz Heinrich als Feldherr im Siebenjährigen Kriege*, 2 vols. (Greifswald: Julius Abel, 1885–1899). See the extremely negative review of the second volume in *Militär-Wochenblatt* 84, no. 55 (June 21, 1899), pp. 1439–1444. For a more modern look at the prince, an important figure due for an updated biography, see Chester V. Easum, *Prince Henry of Prussia: Brother of Frederick the Great* (Westport, Conn.: Greenwood Press, 1971), a reprint of the 1942 work.

15. "Friedrich der Grosse als Feldherr" (the *Militär-Wochenblatt* review of Bernhardi's book, note 2, above), p. 237.

16. Echevarria, *After Clausewitz*, p. 185.

17. For the German view of "inner" and "outer" lines, see General Ludwig, "Die Operation auf der inneren und der äusseren Linie im Lichte underer Zeit," *Militär-Wochenblatt* 126, no. 1 (July 4, 1941), pp. 7–10.

18. For Prussian military operations in the Seven Years' War, begin with Frederick's own accounts, found (in German translation) in *Ausgewählte Werke Fried-*

richs des Grossen, vol. 1., *Historische und militärische Schriften, Briefe*, ed. Gustav Berthold Volz (Berlin: Reimar Hobbing, 1900), especially "Die Siebenjährige Krieg," pp. 99–161. Frederick must be used with caution, however. He wrote these memoirs long after the event, and they are often wrong on the details of the military encounters. Three secondary works are absolutely essential today, two by the dean of Frederick scholars, Christopher Duffy: *The Army of Frederick the Great* (London: David & Charles, 1974), and *Frederick the Great: A Military Life;* the other is Dennis Showalter's marvelous *Wars of Frederick the Great.* Also indispensable is Curt Jany, *Geschichte der königlich preussischen Armee*, vol. 2, *Die Armee Friedrichs des Grossen 1740 bis 1763* (Berlin: Karl Siegismund, 1928–1933). Other useful works include the numerous biographies of Frederick the Great, especially Reinhold Koser, *Geschichte Friedrichs des Grossen* (Berlin: J. G. Cotta, 1912–1913), and W. von Bremen, *Friedrich der Grosse* (Berlin: B. Behr, 1905). Bremen was a lieutenant colonel in the German army at the time, and the work is volume 3 of the series *Erzieher des preussischen Heeres*, 12 vols. (Berlin: B. Behr, 1905–1907). Scholarly works include Gerhard Ritter, *Frederick the Great: A Historical Profile* (Berkeley: University of California Press, 1968); Walther Hubatsch, *Frederick the Great of Prussia: Absolutism and Administration* (London: Thames and Hudson, 1973); and Theodor Schieder, *Frederick the Great* (London: Longman, 2000). The two biographies that deal most carefully with Frederick's operations are Robert B. Asprey, *Frederick the Great: The Magnificent Enigma* (New York: Ticknor & Fields, 1986) and David Fraser, *Frederick the Great: King of Prussia* (New York: Fromm, 2001). Joseph Miranda, "The Gentlemen's World War: The Seven Years' War in Europe, 1756–1763," *Strategy and Tactics* 163 (September 1993), pp. 5–28, has a great deal of hard information on weaponry, tactics, and doctrine, as well as an interesting simulation game on the conflict.

19. See the series of maps in Waldemar Erfurth, "Das Zusammenwirken getrennter Heeresteile," part 1, *Militärwissenschaftliche Rundschau* 4, no. 1 (1939), pp. 16–18, which also links the 1757 and 1866 campaigns to Frederick's campaign of maneuver in the War of the Bavarian Succession (1778), all of which look remarkably similar on the map.

20. Frederick the Great, "Schlacht bei Prag," in Volz, *Ausgewählte Werke*, pp. 110–113; the quote is from p. 112.

21. See Jeremy Black, *European Warfare, 1660–1815* (New Haven, Conn.: Yale University Press, 1994), p. 75.

22. Frederick the Great, "Kolin," in Volz, *Ausgewählte Werke*, pp. 118–121. The quote is from p. 121.

23. Delbrück, *History of the Art of War*, vol. 4, p. 344.

24. See Robert A. Kann, *A History of the Habsburg Empire 1526–1918* (Berkeley: University of California Press, 1974), pp. 174–175.

25. The phrase is from David Lloyd George, at the Versailles conference in 1919. See Robert M. Citino, *Evolution of Blitzkrieg Tactics: Germany Defends Itself against Poland, 1918–1933* (Westport, Conn.: Greenwood Press, 1987), p. 7.

26. For details and analysis of the Rossbach campaign, one should start with the official history by the German General Staff, *Die Kriege Friedrichs des Grossen*, part 3, *Die siebenjährige Krieg*, vol. 5, *Hastenbeck und Rossbach* (Berlin: E. S. Mittler, 1903),

and the useful summary in Curt Jany, *Geschichte der königlich preussischen Armee bis zum Jahre 1807*, vol. 2, *Die Armee Friedrichs des Grossen 1740 bis 1763* (Berlin: Karl Siegismund, 1928), pp. 426–445. Freytag-Loringhoven, *Feldherrngrösse*, pp. 65–67, provides another view from the German General Staff. See also Frederick the Great's accounts in Volz, ed., *Ausgewählte Werke*, "Wider die Reichsarmee und die Franzosen" (pp. 126–131) and "Rossbach" (pp. 131–136), although as always one must use them with caution. Pride of place in the secondary literature goes to Showalter, *Wars of Frederick the Great*, pp. 177–192, Duffy, *Army of Frederick the Great*, 174–176, and Duffy, *Frederick the Great: A Military Life*, pp. 134–143. Asprey, *Frederick the Great*, pp. 464–473 and Fraser, *Frederick the Great* both contain useful narratives and maps.

27. Russell F. Weigley, *The Age of Battles: The Quest for Decisive Warfare from Breitenfeld to Waterloo* (Bloomington: Indiana University Press, 1991), p. 183.

28. For the significance of Seydlitz for later German war making, see *Friedrich Wilhelm von Seydlitz: Königlich Preussischer General der Kavallerie: Der Deutschen Reiterei gewidmet von einem Deutschen Reiteroffizier* (Kassel: Theodor Kay, 1882), an enthusiastic portrayal, though certainly not the work of a scholar. See Kähler's review in *Militär-Wochenblatt* 67, no. 25 (March 29, 1882), pp. 495–506. See also Kunhardt von Schmidt, "Seydlitz," *Militär-Wochenblatt* 90, no. 31 (March 14, 1905), pp. 726–731.

29. Delbrück, "Über die Verschiedenheit der Strategie Friedrichs und Napoleons," p. 235.

30. Weigley, *Age of Battles*, p. 183.

31. See Jany, *Geschichte der königlich preussischen Armee*, p. 435, for one such argument.

32. German General Staff, *Hastenbeck und Rossbach*, p. 203.

33. For a detailed look at this little-remembered episode, see "Die Streifzug des F. M. L. Grafen Hadik nach Berlin," in German General Staff, *Hastenbeck und Rossbach*, pp. 173–182, complete with a map of the battle in the Köpenicker Vorstadt.

34. For numbers, see German General Staff, *Hastenbeck und Rossbach*, pp. 207–208.

35. German General Staff, *Hastenbeck und Rossbach*, p. 200.

36. Ibid.

37. Frederick the Great, "Rossbach," p. 131.

38. German General Staff, *Hastenbeck und Rossbach*, pp. 205–206.

39. According to Duffy, *Frederick the Great: A Military Life*, p. 140, by November 4 the allies had been "seven days now without shelter or regular rations."

40. Frederick the Great, "Rossbach," p. 132.

41. German General Staff, *Hastenbeck und Rossbach*, p. 209. See also Jany, *Geschichte der königlich preussischen Armee*, p. 437.

42. Duffy, *Frederick the Great: A Military Life*, p. 142. See also German General Staff, *Hastenbeck und Rossbach*, p. 212.

43. Showalter, *Wars of Frederick the Great*, pp. 187–188.

44. German General Staff, *Hastenbeck und Rossbach*, pp. 214–215.

45. German General Staff, *Hastenbeck und Rossbach*, pp. 215–216.

46. Showalter, *Wars of Frederick the Great*, pp. 186.

47. German General Staff, *Hastenbeck und Rossbach*, p. 222.

48. "Friedrich der Grosse als Feldherr: eine methodologische Parodie," p. 47.

49. See, for example, Jany, *Geschichte der königlich preussischen Armee*, p. 429. In *Wars of Frederick the Great*, Showalter offers particular insight into the motivation of the allied armies at Rossbach, with the French having to deal with the increasingly antimilitary tone of their own society's intellectuals (pp. 167–175) and the Imperial army having to keep on the move or risk disintegrating (pp. 181–185).

50. Frederick the Great, "Rossbach," p. 136.

51. Delbrück, "Über die Verschiedenheit der Strategie Friedrichs und Napoleons," p. 235.

52. Showalter, *Wars of Frederick the Great*, pp. 194–195, contains the best account of Frederick's morale boosting activities at this time, with a particularly effective evocation of the famous speech: "Like all great performances, Frederick's blended sincerity and artifice in a way impossible for anyone to separate" (p. 195). For the complete text of the speech, see Miranda, "The Gentlemen's World War: The Seven Years' War in Europe, 1756–1763," p. 19.

53. Frederick the Great, "Marsch nach Schlesien," in Volz, ed., *Ausgewählte Werke*, p. 138.

54. For details and analysis of Leuthen, see the official history by the German General Staff, *Die Kriege Friedrichs des Grossen*, part 3, *Die siebenjährige Krieg*, vol. 6, *Leuthen* (Berlin: E. S. Mittler, 1904), and, once again, a distillation of the discussion in Jany, *Geschichte der königlich preussischen Armee*, pp. 445–459. Freytag-Loringhoven, *Feldherrngrösse*, pp. 67–72, provides a good detailed account from a general staff perspective. Frederick the Great's account in Volz, ed., *Ausgewählte Werke*, "Leuthen," pp. 139–143, is still the classic primary source, much more detailed on troop movements and tactics than other of the king's writings—it is likely that Leuthen impressed itself more firmly upon his mind. Once again, Showalter *Wars of Frederick the Great*, pp. 192–206, Duffy, *Army of Frederick the Great*, 176–179, and Duffy, *Frederick the Great: A Military Life*, pp. 148–154 set the standard in the secondary literature. Among the popular histories, see Asprey, *Frederick the Great*, pp. 475–481, and Fraser, *Frederick the Great*, pp. 368–375. For a representative Austrian account, see Gilbert Anger, ed., *Illustrirte Geschichte der k.k. Armee*, vol. 2 (Vienna: Gilbert Anger, 1887), pp. 1038–1039.

55. German General Staff, *Leuthen*, pp. 9, 17.

56. Jany, *Geschichte der königlich preussischen Armee*, p. 450.

57. German General Staff, *Leuthen*, p. 18; Freytag-Loringhoven, *Feldherrngrösse*, p. 71.

58. German General Staff, *Leuthen*, p. 25. See also Bremen, *Friedrich der Grosse*, p. 70. Freytag-Loringhoven, *Feldherrngrösse*, p. 71, Asprey, *Frederick the Great*, p. 478, and Showalter, *Wars of Frederick the Great*, p. 198, offer variations.

59. German General Staff, *Leuthen*, p. 25.

60. German General Staff, *Leuthen*, p. 30.

61. German General Staff, *Leuthen*, p. 41.

62. Duffy, *Frederick the Great: A Military Life*, attributes the loss of Breslau to "mental confusion" on the part of Charles (p. 179).

63. See, for example, Duffy, *Frederick the Great: A Military Life*, p. 311: "The Oblique Order worked to near-perfection at Leuthen, and Frederick held throughout his life to the ideal of attacking with a single wing."

64. German General Staff, *Leuthen*, pp. 63–64.

65. Lieutenant Colonel Rudolf von Friederich, "Die Schlacht bei Zorndorf am 25. August 1758," *Beiheft, Militär-Wochenblatt*, vol. 7 (1908), pp. 293–322. The quote is found on p. 293.

66. Friederich, "Schlacht bei Zorndorf," p. 294; Bremen, *Friedrich der Grosse*, p. 74; *Geschichte der königlich preussischen Armee*, pp. 483–484.

67. Showalter, *Wars of Frederick the Great*, p. 211.

68. For the Zorndorf campaign, see first of all the official history by the German General Staff, *Die Kriege Friedrichs des Grossen*, part 3, *Die siebenjährige Krieg*, vol. 8, *Zorndorf und Hochkirch* (Berlin: E. S. Mittler, 1910), and, once again, the pertinent pages in Jany, *Geschichte der königlich preussischen Armee*, pp. 470–495. See also the synopsis and review of this volume of the General Staff history, "Das Generalstabswerk über den siebenjährigen Krieg," *Militär-Wochenblatt* 95, no. 87 (July 16, 1910), pp. 2057–2062. Other German sources worth consulting are Lieutenant Colonel von Friederich's article "Schlacht bei Zorndorf" and M. von Poseck, "Zorndorf," *Militär-Wochenblatt* 126, no. 9 (August 29, 1941), pp. 235–238. Friederich's piece was originally the "Frederick Day" lecture to the Military Society (*Militärische Gesellschaft*) of Berlin in 1908, with Kaiser Wilhelm II in attendance. Friederich was the Chief of Military History Section of the General Staff (*Abteilung II*), which oversaw the preparation of the volumes in the *Kriege Friedrichs des Grossen* series, as well as serving as an instructor at the *Kriegsakademie*. As always, Showalter, *Wars of Frederick the Great*, pp. 212–221, Duffy, *Army of Frederick the Great*, pp. 181–184, and Duffy, *Frederick the Great: A Military Life*, pp. 163–172 dominate the secondary literature. Asprey, *Frederick the Great*, pp. 493–499, and Fraser, *Frederick the Great*, pp. 387–396 both succeed in capturing the savage nature of the fighting.

69. Friederich, "Schlacht bei Zorndorf," p. 299.

70. For Frederick's maneuver scheme, see German General Staff, *Zorndorf und Hochkirch*, pp. 122–123; Friederich, "Schlacht bei Zorndorf," pp. 299–301, and Poseck, "Zorndorf," pp. 235–236.

71. For Delbrück's assessment of the wagon park episode, see *History of the Art of War*, vol. 4, pp. 352–353.

72. Friederich, "Schlacht bei Zorndorf," pp. 301–302, is useful here.

73. The attack was not an example of the oblique order. The advance guard and left wing were to form a concentrated mass, and there was to be no wheel. See German General Staff, *Zorndorf und Hochkirch*, pp. 132n, 468. Showalter, *Wars of Frederick the Great* (p. 221) and Duffy, *Frederick the Great: A Military Life*, p. 165, disagree with this assessment.

74. Friederich, "Schlacht bei Zorndorf," p. 306.

75. See the judgment by Poseck, "Zorndorf," p. 236, who describes Kanitz's advance as "contrary to the king's orders." Also, the German General Staff, *Zorndorf und Hochkirch*, p. 135, describe Kanitz as "departing from the king's order on his own responsibility." See Prince Moritz's concurring opinion on pp. 468–469n29.

76. German General Staff, *Zorndorf und Hochkirch*, p. 137.

77. Poseck, "Zorndorf," p. 237, has Seydlitz emerging out of a "cloud of smoke."

78. Friederich, "Schlacht bei Zorndorf," pp. 311–312.

79. See German General Staff, *Zorndorf und Hochkirch*, Anlage 4, "Abstufung des blutigen Verlustes der preussischen Bataillone" for the breakdown of Prussian losses. See also Friederich, "Schlacht be Zorndorf," p. 317.

80. Poseck, "Zorndorf," p. 238.

81. German General Staff, *Zorndorf und Hochkirch*, p. 165.

82. Friederich, "Schlacht bei Zorndorf," p. 321, notes the king's judgment with approval.

83. Quote taken from Showalter, *Wars of Frederick the Great*, p. 216. Duffy, *Frederick the Great: A Military Life*, p. 167, notes that the story was first related only in 1797, in the biography by Blankenberg (*Karakter- und Lebensgeschichte des Herrn von Seydlitz*). The anonymous cavalryman-author of *Friedrich Wilhelm von Seydlitz: Königlich Preussischer General der Kavallerie* explicitly rejects the story's historicity. Since we are dealing here with a popular history cum adventure story, his judgment, on this point at least, should stand as definitive. For discussion of another Seydlitz legend, the famous "spring over the bridge" in the king's presence during the Berlin maneuvers of 1743 (or perhaps at Frankfurt on the Oder), see "Seydlitz' Brückensprung," *Militär-Wochenblatt* 67, no. 96 (November 25, 1882), pp. 1912–1914.

84. Delbrück, *History of the Art of War*, vol. 4, pp. 373–374.

85. Delbrück, *History of the Art of War*, vol. 4, p. 376.

86. Delbrück, *History of the Art of War*, vol. 4, p. 353.

87. Bremen, *Friedrich der Grosse*, pp. 99–100.

88. The quote shows up frequently in German military literature. See, for example, the review of Colonel Blume, *Strategie* (Berlin: E. S. Mittler, 1882), in *Militär-Wochenblatt* 67, no. 103 (December 16, 1882), pp. 2042–2052, especially p. 2046.

89. "Neuzeitliche Lehren aus der Kriegführung Friedrichs des Grossen," *Militär-Wochenblatt* 115, no. 29 (February 4, 1931), pp. 1113–1118. The quote is from p. 1114.

90. "Neuzeitliche Lehren aus der Kriegführung Friedrichs des Grossen," p. 1113.

4. "Disgrace and Redemption"

1. The phrase appears in the title of the work by German General Staff officer and noted military writer Colmar Baron von der Goltz, *Jena to Eylau: The Disgrace and the Redemption of the Old-Prussian Army* (New York, E. P. Dutton, 1913).

2. Walter Görlitz, *History of the German General Staff, 1657–1945* (New York: Opraeger, 1953), p. 27.

3. Jules Michelet, *History of the French Revolution*, edited and with an introduction by Gordon Wright (Chicago: University of Chicago Press, 1967), p. 9.

4. For representative samples of the argument, with varying degrees of nuance, see David G. Chandler, *The Art of Warfare on Land* (New York: Penguin, 1974), p. 149; Michael Howard, *War in European History* (Oxford: Oxford University Press, 1976), pp. 79–80; and Cyril Falls, *The Art of War from the Age of Napoleon to the Present Day* (Oxford: Oxford University Press, 1961), pp. 22–31. For a good, detailed account of the impact of the Revolution on the French army, see Theodore Ropp, *War in the Modern World* (Baltimore, Md.: Johns Hopkins University Press, 2000), pp. 102–117. For a crucial contribution in the revision, incorporating detailed research in the French primary sources with findings from sociology and social psychology, see John A. Lynn, *The Bayonets of the Republic: Motivation and Tactics in the Army of Revolutionary France, 1791–94* (Urbana: University of Illinois Press, 1984), especially pp. xi–xii.

5. "Poetry, never reality" ("C'est la poésie, jamais la réalité") is the description of bayonet attacks found in the seminal work of French military intellectual Charles-Ardant du Picq, *Battle Studies: Ancient and Modern Battle* (New York: Macmilllan, 1921). See also Stefan T. Possony and Etienne Mantoux, "Du Picq and Foch: The French School," in *Makers of Modern Strategy: Military Thought from Machiavelli to Hitler*, ed. Edward Mead Earle (New York: Atheneum, 1966), pp. 206–233.

6. The classic account of Valmy is found in Gaetano Salvemini, *The French Revolution, 1788–1792* (New York: Norton, 1962), pp. 322–324.

7. For revolutionary and Napoleonic infantry tactics, see David G. Chandler, *The Campaigns of Napoleon* (New York: Macmillan, 1966), pp. 332–367; Albert A. Nofi, ed., *Napoleon at War: Selected Writings of F. Loraine Petre* (New York: Hippocrene, 1984), pp. 43–51; Steven S. Ross, *From Flintlock to Rifle: Infantry Tactics, 1740–1866* (London: Frank Cass, 1996); and Gunther E. Rothenberg, *The Art of Warfare in the Age of Napoleon* (Bloomington: Indiana University Press, 1978), pp. 149–156.

8. See, for example, Brian Bond, *The Pursuit of Victory: From Napoleon to Saddam Hussein* (Oxford: Oxford University Press, 1996), p. 30, which discusses the "articulation of the formerly unitary and unwieldy mass armies into divisions and corps."

9. Martin van Creveld, *Command in War* (Cambridge, Mass.: Harvard University Press, 1985), p. 55.

10. German General Staff, *Studien zur Kriegsgeschichte und Taktik*, vol. 3, *Der Schlachterfolg: mit welchen Mitteln wurde er erstrebt?* (Berlin: E. S. Mittler, 1903), with accompanying atlas. The quote is from p. 6.

11. For Napoleon, see first of all, Chandler, *Campaigns of Napoleon*, a towering work in every way, marrying vivid writing with scholarly knowledge like few books out there, supplemented with Rory Muir's more recent work, *Tactics and the Experience of Battle in the Age of Napoleon* (New Haven, Conn.: Yale University Press, 1998), which focuses on the British army in the Peninsular Campaign. Other useful works include two by Gunther E. Rothenberg, *The Art of Warfare in the Age of Napoleon* and *Napoleon's Great Adversaries: The Archduke Charles and the Austrian Army, 1792–1814* (Bloomington: Indiana University Press, 1982); J. F. C. Fuller, *The Conduct of War, 1789–1961* (New York: Da Capo, 1992), especially

Chapter 3, "Napoleonic Warfare," pp. 42–58; and Larry H. Addington, *The Patterns of War Since the Eighteenth Century* (Bloomington: Indiana University Press, 1994), pp. 1–42, all of which offer good introductions. Robert Holtman, *The Napoleonic Revolution* (New York: J. B. Lippincott, 1967) is still the best synthesis of the dramatic impact of Napoleon on European history. For a specific focus on the operational level, see two works by Robert M. Epstein, "Patterns of Change and Continuity in Nineteenth-Century Warfare," *Journal of Military History* 56, no. 3 (July 1992), pp. 375–388, and *Napoleon's Last Victory and the Emergence of Modern War* (Lawrence: University Press of Kansas, 1994), an operational analysis of the Wagram campaign of 1809.

12. German General Staff, *Der Schlachterfolg*, p. 21.

13. For the best analysis of the problem of supply in the Napoleonic campaign, see Martin van Creveld, *Supplying War: Logistics from Wallenstein to Patton* (Cambridge: Cambridge University Press, 1977), pp. 40–74.

14. Epstein, "Patterns of Change and Continuity in Nineteenth-Century Warfare," attributes Napoleon's success to "flexible tactics and superior command and control" (p. 378).

15. F. Loraine Petre, *Napoleon's Conquest of Prussia, 1806* (London: John Lane, 1914), p. 8. See also the introduction by Field Marshal Earl Roberts, pp. ix–xvii ("Such was the punishment Prussia met with for her selfishness and her unpreparedness," p. xvi).

16. The title of chapter 39 in Chandler, *Campaigns of Napoleon*, pp. 443–451.

17. "As Napoleon sarcastically remarked, the address of these congratulations had been changed by the result of the battle." Petre, *Napoleon's Conquest of Prussia*, pp. 14–15.

18. A huge popular literature grew up around the figure of Queen Luise and her relationship to Napoleon. See, for example, the historical novel by well-known nineteenth-century German author Luise Mühlbach, *Napoleon and the Queen of Prussia* (New York: D. Appleton, 1888), with its tear-jerking account of the meeting between the Emperor and the Queen at Tilsit (pp. 126–132). It is apparently based on the account in Jean-Baptiste Marbot, *The Memoirs of Baron de Marbot, Late Lieutenant-General in the French Army*, vol. 1 (London: Longmans, Green, 1892), pp. 232–233. For a no less patriotic account, see Lieutenant Colonel von Bremen, "Königin Luise von Preussen: Zum Gedächtnis ihres Todestages, 19, Juli 1810," *Militär-Wochenblatt* 95, no. 88 (July 19, 1910), pp. 2079–2089.

19. Chandler, *Campaigns of Napoleon*, p. 454.

20. Quoted in Petre, *Napoleon's Conquest of Prussia*, p. 21.

21. Rothenberg, *Art of Warfare in the Age of Napoleon*, p. 188.

22. Ibid., p. 189.

23. Much of the work done on Jena is now quite old, although it is by no means obsolete. See the account by the German General Staff, *Der Schlachterfolg*, pp. 28–38, as well as two early twentieth-century works by English authors, Colonel F. N. Maude, *1806: The Jena Campaign* (London: Swan Sonnenschein, 1909), recently reprinted as *The Jena Campaign, 1806* (London: Greenhill, 1998) and Petre's aforementioned *Napoleon's Conquest of Prussia*, reprinted by Hippocrene Books, New

York, in 1972. Petre may occasionally puzzle American readers, as for example his description of the village of Lobstadt on the Jena battlefield as "a village occupying much the same position in reference to Jena that Betchworth occupies in respect to Dorking" (p. 121). The analytical treatment in Görlitz, *History of the German General Staff*, pp. 26–28, is still worthy. More modern accounts include Chandler, *Campaigns of Napoleon*, pp. 479–488, 502–506; and Robert B. Asprey, *The Reign of Napoleon Bonaparte* (New York: Basic Books, 2001), pp. 20–34.

24. See Maude, *Jena Campaign*, p. 70.

25. Carl von Clausewitz, *On War*, edited and translated by Michael Howard and Peter Paret (Princeton, N.J.: Princeton University Press, 1984), p. 493. See also Petre, *Napoleon's Conquest of Prussia*, pp. 116–117.

26. German General Staff, *Der Schlachterfolg*, pp. 28–29.

27. Chandler, *Campaigns of Napoleon*, p. 465; German General Staff, *Der Schlachterfolg*, p. 29.

28. German General Staff, *Der Schlachterfolg*, p. 28.

29. German General Staff, *Der Schlachterfolg*, p. 29; Chandler, *Campaigns of Napoleon*, p. 464.

30. German General Staff, *Der Schlachterfolg*, p. 29.

31. Ibid., p. 31.

32. For Saalfeld, see Petre, *Napoleon's Conquest of Prussia*, pp. 93–102, plus the map facing p. 102 ("Plan for Action at Saalfeld").

33. German General Staff, *Der Schlachterfolg*, pp. 34–35.

34. Chandler, *Campaigns of Napoleon*, p. 471.

35. Maude, *Jena Campaign*, p. 132; Petre, *Napoleon's Conquest of Prussia*, pp. 106, 112.

36. For Napoleon's wheel, see German General Staff, *Der Schlachterfolg*, p. 34.

37. Chandler, *Campaigns of Napoleon*, pp. 482–484.

38. The ordeal of Grewart's grenadiers has been an irresistible moment for historians of Jena. See Maude, *Jena Campaign*, pp. 156–157; Petre, *Napoleon's Conquest of Prussia*, pp. 136–137; and Chandler, *Campaigns of Napoleon*, pp. 484–485.

39. For Auerstädt, see Maude, *Jena Campaign*, pp. 164–175; Petre, *Napoleon's Conquest of Prussia*, pp. 149–164; and Chandler, *Campaigns of Napoleon*, pp. 489–502.

40. The best discussion of Bernadotte's conduct is still Maude, *Jena Campaign*, pp. 175–177.

41. See *Kolberg* (1945, directed by Veit Harlan), with Heinrich George as Nettelbeck, Horst Caspar as Gneisenau, and a cast of thousands of Wehrmacht extras. It cost eight million Reichsmarks, making it one of the most expensive films ever produced by the Third Reich.

42. For Blücher's retreat to Lübeck, see Petre, *Napoleon's Conquest of Prussia*, pp. 254–287, complete with the surrender note, "I capitulate, since I have neither bread nor ammunition—Blücher" (p. 286).

43. For the Pultusk campaign, see Raymond E. Bell, Jr., "Eylau—Winter War," *Strategy and Tactics* 138 (October 1990), pp. 20–43, especially the excellent map on p. 24.

44. Goltz, *Jena to Eylau*, pp. 117–118.

45. For the Eylau campaign, see Chandler, *Campaigns of Napoleon*, pp. 535–555; F. Loraine Petre, *Napoleon's Campaign in Poland, 1806–7* (London: The Bodley Head, 1901), recently reprinted by Hippocrene Books (New York, 1975), especially pp. 161–212; Bell, "Eylau—Winter War"; Albert A. Nofi, "Eylau," a sidebar to Nofi's "Napoleon's Art of War," *Strategy and Tactics* 75 (July–August 1979), pp. 4–19; and for a typically German operational focus, Captain Meltzer, "Betrachtungen zum Feldzug und zum Schlacht von Pr. Eylau," *Militär-Wochenblatt* 121, no. 31 (February 12, 1937), pp. 1773–1776. For a critique of Baron Marbot's memoirs, a source still used as an authority on Eylau, despite the presence of some obvious fables, see Oscar von Lettow-Vorbeck, "Mémoires du general Baron de Marbot," *Militär-Wochenblatt* 84, no. 49 (June 3, 1899), pp. 1297–1301. The battle of Eylau with its swirling snow, frozen lakes, and massive cavalry charges has had a magnetic attraction to war gamers, and in fact there have been at least four commercially available war games (or "conflict simulations" to many of those who play them): "Napoleon's Art of War: Eylau and Dresden," appearing in *Strategy and Tactics* 75 (Simulations Publications, Inc., 1979), designed by Omar DeWitt, Bob Jervis, and Redmond A. Simonsen; "Winter War: Napoleon at Eylau," appearing in *Strategy and Tactics* 138 (Simulations Publications, Inc., 1990), designed by Ken Broadhurst; "Eylau: Napoleon's Winter Battle, 1807" (Game Designer's Workshop, 1980), designed by Rik Fontana; and, most recently, "Preussisch Eylau, February 1807" (Avalanche Press, 1998). It may well be the best-known Napoleonic battle of all with this knowledgeable military history subculture.

46. Field Marshal Count Alfred von Schlieffen, "Cannae," in *Gesammelte Schriften*, vol. 1 (Berlin: E. S. Mittler, 1913), p. 44. The translation *Cannae: Authorized Translation* (Ft. Leavenworth, Kans.: Command and General Staff School Press, 1931), is quite clumsy. See also Meltzer, "Betrachtungen zum Feldzug und zum Schlacht von Pr. Eylau," p. 1773.

47. See the map in Meltzer, "Betrachtungen zum Feldzug und zum Schlacht von Pr. Eylau," p. 1774, as well as the map in Bell, "Eylau—Winter War," p. 37.

48. Meltzer, "Betrachtungen zum Feldzug und zum Schlacht von Pr. Eylau," p. 1774.

49. Meltzer, "Betrachtungen zum Feldzug und zum Schlacht von Pr. Eylau," p. 1775.

50. As always, Petre, *Napoleon's Campaign in Poland, 1806–7*, gives a description that may puzzle American readers, writing that the terrain "bears a strong resemblance to some of the open valley of Norfolk and Suffolk" (p. 161).

51. Meltzer, "Betrachtungen zum Feldzug und zum Schlacht von Pr. Eylau," p. 1775.

52. Chandler, *Campaigns of Napoleon*, pp. 538–539.

53. The classic description of Murat's grand charge is Petre, *Napoleon's Campaign in Poland, 1806–7*, pp. 184–187. See also Chandler, *Campaigns of Napoleon*, pp. 543–544.

54. Goltz, *Jena to Eylau*, pp. 272–273.

55. See "Zur Phänomen von Deutsch-Eylau," *Militär-Wochenblatt* 95, no. 42 (April 5, 1910), p. 1027, wherein author "P. v. J." describes a similar phenomenon

that he experienced in a March 1909 exercise on the maneuver ground at Posen. The author means "Preussisch-", not "Deutsch-" Eylau.

56. Meltzer, "Betrachtungen zum Feldzug und zum Schlacht von Pr. Eylau," p. 1773.

57. Goltz, *Jena to Eylau*, pp. 288–289.

58. Goltz, *Jena to Eylau*, pp. 273–275.

59. Eduard Höpfner, *Der Krieg von 1806 und 1807* (Berlin: Simon Schropp, 1855), second edition, vol. 3, p. 236. Quoted in Goltz, *Jena to Eylau*, p. 287.

60. Chandler, *Campaigns of Napoleon*, p. 548.

61. Quoted in Goltz, *Jena to Eylau*, pp. 305, 306.

62. See J. Hildebrand, *Die Schlacht bei Pr. Eylau* (Quedlinburg: H. C. Huch, 1906). Quoted in Goltz, *Jena to Eylau*, p. vii.

63. Goltz, *Jena to Weimar*, pp. vi, 325, 326.

64. Meltzer, "Betrachtungen zum Feldzug und zum Schlacht von Pr. Eylau," p. 1776.

65. "La Prusse n'est pas un État qui possède une armée; c'est une armée qui a conquis une nation." Quoted in Jacques Benoist-Mechin, *Histoire de L'Armée Allemande*, vol. 1 (Paris: Albin Michel, 1938), p. 13.

66. See George Rudé, *Revolutionary Europe, 1783–1815* (New York: Harper, 1964), p. 145.

67. Gordon A. Craig, *The Politics of the Prussian Army, 1640–1945* (Oxford: Oxford University Press, 1955), p. 1.

68. There is a large literature on the Prussian reform era, although little new has appeared in some time. Begin with Walter M. Simon, *The Failure of the Prussian Reform Movement, 1807–1819* (Ithaca, N.Y.: Cornell University Press, 1955), a pessimistic work produced with the shadow of the Nazi experience still looming; Craig, *Politics of the Prussian Army*, pp. 37–53; Görlitz, *History of the German General Staff*, pp. 15–49; and Rothenberg, *The Art of Warfare in the Age of Napoleon*, pp. 190–194. Peter Paret, *Yorck and the Era of Prussian Reform* (Princeton, N.J.: Princeton University Press, 1966) and Charles E. White, *The Enlightened Soldier: Scharnhorst and the Militärische Gesellschaft in Berlin, 1801–1805* (Westport, Conn.: Praeger, 1989) highlight two of the most crucial figures. For a tightly focused analysis of one crucial area, see Dennis E. Showalter, "Manifestation of Reform: The Rearmament of the Prussian Infantry, 1806–13," *Journal of Modern History* 44, no. 3 (September 1972), pp. 364–380, and for a more synthetic analysis of the reform package and its implications by the same author, "The Retaming of Bellona: Prussia and the Institutionalization of the Napoleonic Legacy, 1815–1876," *Military Affairs* 44, no. 2 (April 1980), pp. 57–63. The agenda is clear: a comprehensive military biography, in English, of Gneisenau.

69. See Daniel Moran's review of White, *Enlightened Soldier*, in *Journal of Military History* 56, no. 1 (January 1992), pp. 131–132.

70. Rothenberg, *The Art of Warfare in the Age of Napoleon*, p. 191, as well as Keith Simpson, *History of the German Army* (Greenwich, Conn.: Bison Books, 1985), p. 43. The latter is a pictorial history with a refreshingly erudite and analytical text.

71. It certainly does not appear to have derived from "krumm," the German for "crooked" or "devious," still the most common explanation in the literature. For the roots of the term, probably deriving from the extra length of cloth on a garment before it was taken in, see Dierk Walter, *Preussische Heeresreformen 1807–1870: Militärische Innovation und der Mythos der "Roonschen Reform"* (Paderborn: Ferdinand Schöningh, 2003), pp. 253–254n111. Walter's book is an extremely important contribution to the history of the nineteenth-century Prussian army, an energetic and utterly successful attack on the traditional view that the "Roon reforms" of the 1860s magically transformed the Prussian army from incompetence to brilliance overnight.

72. Walter, *Preussische Heeresreformen*, p. 256.

73. Rothenberg, *The Art of Warfare in the Age of Napoleon*, pp. 193–194.

74. See Detlef Bald, "The Impact of Tradition of the Education of the Military in Germany," *Military Affairs* 45, no. 3 (October 1981), pp. 109–112.

75. See the article by Baron von Manteuffel, "Zur Jahrhundertfeier der Kriegsakademie," *Militär-Wochenblatt* 95, no. 36 (March 19, 1910), pp. 813–820. Manteuffel was director of the *Kriegsakademie* at the time. See also the work published in conjunction with the centennial of the academy: Captain von Scharfenort, *Die Königliche Preussische Kriegsakademie 1810–1910* (Berlin: E. S. Mittler, 1910). Finally, the former chief of the General Staff, Count Alfred von Schlieffen, was the keynote speaker at the centennial festivities. See the text of his speech in "Rede des Generaloberst Graf Schlieffen auf die Kriegsakademie am 15. October 1910," *Militär-Wochenblatt* 95, no. 138 (November 5, 1910), pp. 3207–3209.

76. Craig, *Politics of the Prussian Army*, p. 45.

77. The Leipzig campaign, unlike Jena or Eylau, continues to excite the interest of historians. For Prussian involvement, see Baron Carl von Müffling, *Memoirs of Baron von Müffling: A Prussian Officer in the Napoleonic Wars* (London: Greenhill, 1997), primary source testimony from the senior quartermaster of Blücher's Army of Silesia. See also the three-part series "Der Herbstfeldzug 1813," parts 1–3, *Militär-Wochenblatt* 90, nos. 5–7 (January 12, 1905, January 14, 1905, January 17, 1905), pp. 100–105, 124–128, and 141–146. It is a synopsis and review of the first two volumes of Lieutenant Colonel Rudolf von Friederich, *Geschichte des Herbstfeldzuges 1813*, 3 vols. (Berlin: E. S. Mittler, 1903–1906); as always, these *Wochenblatt* articles were of enormous importance as a way of mediating large and detailed scholarly works to German army officers. For a review of the three-volume work, see "Zur Jahrhundertfeier der Befreiungskriege," *Militär-Wochenblatt* 95, no. 128 (October 13, 1910), pp. 2963–2967. For other German professional literature, see Karl Linnebach, "Die Völkerschlacht bei Leipzig," *Militär-Wochenblatt* 123, no. 17 (October 21, 1938), pp. 1065–1069, and Major General Klingbeil, "Die operative Bedeutung der befestigten Elb-Linie für die Heerführung Napoleons im Herbstfeldzug 1813 unter neuzeitlicher Betrachtung," *Militär-Wochenblatt* 123, no. 24 (December 9, 1938), pp. 1561–1567.

There is also an immense body of recent literature. See, for example, the collections of eyewitness accounts in Antony Brett-James, *Europe against Napoleon: The Leipzig Campaign 1813 from Eyewitness Accounts* (London: Macmillan, 1970); Digby

Smith, *1813: Leipzig: Napoleon and the Battle of Nations* (London: Greenhill, 2000). For an analysis tied specifically to modern-day concerns, see Brigadier J. P. Riley, *Napoleon and the World War of 1813: Lessons in Coalition Warfighting* (London: Frank Cass, 2000). Pride of place at the present time, however, goes to Michael V. Leggiere, *Napoleon and Berlin: The Franco-Prussian War in North Germany* (Norman: University of Oklahoma Press, 2002), an exhaustive work by a formidable scholar who is as well versed in the political and social literature as he is the military sources, able to discuss the works of Thomas Nipperdey, for example, as well as those of F. Loraine Petre.

78. Chandler, *Campaigns of Napoleon*, p. 887.

79. For the best account of this difficult period of the campaign, see Lieutenant General Waldemar Erfurth, "Die Zusammenwirken getrennter Heeresteile," part 1, *Militärwissenschaftliche Rundschau* 4, no. 1 (1939), pp. 28–41.

80. Clausewitz, *On War*, p. 323.

81. For Dresden, see Chandler, *Campaigns of Napoleon*, pp. 903–912.

82. "Der Herbstfeldzug 1813," pp. 101–102; Chandler, *Campaigns of Napoleon*, pp. 911–912.

83. Erfurth, "Zusammenwirken getrennter Heeresteile," pp. 30, 33.

84. For Yorck's crossing of the Elbe, see Major General Klingbeil, "Yorcks Elb-Übergang bei Wartenburg an 3. October 1813," *Militär-Wochenblatt* 123, no. 14 (September 30, 1938), pp. 857–861.

85. Chandler, *Campaigns of Napoleon*, p. 918.

86. Quoted in Erfurth, "Zusammenwirken getrennter Heeresteile," p. 41.

87. Indeed, Leggiere, *Napoleon and Berlin*, pp. 294–297, goes so far as to argue that "the Prussian army . . . still preferred to fulfill a national desire for vengeance rather than comply with the international requisites for a durable peace" and that "the Prussian military establishment" was "committed to destroying the French Empire to satisfy its lust for revenge" (p. 295). If so, then Blücher was truly the embodiment of the Prussian ideal.

88. Erfurth, "Zusammenwirken getrennter Heeresteile," p. 40.

89. See, most recently, Brian R. Sullivan, "Intelligence and Counter-Terrorism: A Clausewitzian-Historical Analysis," *Journal of Intelligence History* 3, no. 1 (2003), pp. 1–18, and Jon Tetsuro Sumida, "The Relationship of History and Theory in *On War:* The Clausewitzian Ideal and Its Implications," *Journal of Military History* 65, no. 2 (April 2001), pp. 333–354, one of the most intriguing articles ever to appear on the philosopher. Sumida argues that there was an instrumental purpose behind Clausewitz's synthesis of history and theory—he intended it as a means of helping an officer who had never served in a war "to grapple with the moral dilemmas that accompanied critical operational decision making and thus improve the person's ability to learn from actual experience." It is an intriguing argument that helps break us out of the "Is Clausewitz still relevant?" box. The last great flurry of Clausewitz books came in the early 1990s, due no doubt to the sudden and surprising end of the cold war. See, for example, Martin van Creveld, *The Transformation of War* (New York: Free Press, 1991); Azar Gat, *The Origins of Military Thought: From the Enlightenment to Clausewitz* (Oxford: Oxford University Press, 1992);

Peter Paret, *Understanding War: Essays on Clausewitz and the History of Military Power* (Princeton, N.J.: Princeton University Press, 1992); and Christopher Bassford, *Clausewitz in English: The Reception of Clausewitz in Britain and America, 1815–1945* (Oxford: Oxford University Press, 1994).

90. Antulio J. Echevarria II, "General Staff Historian Hugo Freiherr von Freytag-Loringhoven and the Dialectics of German Military Thought," *Journal of Military History* 60, no. 3 (July 1996), pp. 471–494.

91. Daniel J. Hughes, "Schlichting, Schlieffen, and the Prussian Theory of War in 1914," *Journal of Military History* 59, no. 2 (April, 1995), pp. 257–277.

92. Andrew Roberts, *Napoleon and Wellington: The Battle of Waterloo and the Great Commanders Who Fought It* (New York: Simon and Schuster, 2001), p. 84. His book embodies the problem of English-language Waterloo scholarship in its title. For a scholarly corrective, see the two-volume work by Peter Hofschröer that restores the Prussian contribution to its rightful place: *1815: The Waterloo Campaign*, vol. 1, *Wellington, His German Allies, and the Battles of Ligny and Quatre Bras* (London: Greenhill, 1998), and vol. 2, *The German Victory* (London: Greenhill, 1999). For a late nineteenth-century German view, see Colonel Keim, "Waterloo-Legenden," parts 1–3, *Militär-Wochenblatt* 84, nos. 77–79 (August 30, 1899, September 2, 1899, and September 6, 1899), pp. 1917–1922, 1953–1958, and 1978–1982), especially part 3, including the legend that "Wellington was the real victor at Waterloo and that Prussian help was only an epilog to an already won battle."

93. See Hans Delbrück, "Prinz Friedrich Karl," in *Historische und Politische Aufsätze* (Berlin: Georg Stilke, 1907), pp. 302–316.

94. The phrase comes from Russel H. S. Stolfi, *A Bias for Action: The German 7th Panzer Division in France and Russia, 1940–1941. Marine Corps University Series Perspectives on Warfighting* 1 (Quantico, Va.: Marine Corps Association, 1991). For the latest word on the Desert Fox, see the comparative biography by Dennis E. Showalter, *Patton and Rommel: Men of War in the Twentieth Century* (New York: Berkley Caliber, 2005). Showalter portrays Rommel as the quintessential "muddy boots commander," impatient with staff and bureaucracy and overly intellectualized methods of warfare.

95. See Bruce Condell and David T. Zabecki, eds., *On the German Art of War: Truppenführung* (Boulder, Colo.: Lynne Rienner, 2001), p. 19, and Robert M. Citino, *The Path to Blitzkrieg: Doctrine and Training in the German Army, 1920–1939* (Boulder, Colo.: Lynne Rienner, 1999), p. 224. See also Colonel Friedrich von Cochenhausen, "Untätigkeit belastet schwerer als ein Fehlgreifen in der Wahl der Mittel: Gedanken über Lilienstein—Maxen," *Militär-Wochenblatt* 112, no. 6 (August 11, 1927), pp. 196–203.

96. Erfurth, "Zusammenwirken getrennter Heeresteile," p. 40.

5. Moltke's Art of War

1. Golo Mann, *The History of Germany Since 1789* (New York: Praeger, 1968), pp. 156–198.

2. Among German nationalists, the *kleindeutsch* faction preferred a smaller Germany centered on Prussia, with multinational Austria excluded. They faced a *grossdeutsch* ("greater German") party, who wished a larger Reich centered around the Habsburg Empire. The two groupings first arose during the revolutions of 1848 and the subsequent Frankfurt Parliament. See Charles Breunig and Matthew Levinger, *The Revolutionary Era* (New York: Norton, 2002), pp. 280–285; Wolfram Siemann, *The German Revolution of 1848–49* (New York: St. Martin's Press, 1998), pp. 190–193; and Steven Ozment, *A Mighty Fortress: A New History of the German People* (New York: HarperCollins, 2004), pp. 170–174.

3. See, for example, the blizzard of articles in the late 1980s in *Military Review*, the journal of the U.S. Army Command and General Staff College at Ft. Leavenworth, Kansas—the U.S. equivalent, in other words, of the *Militär-Wochenblatt* or the *Militärwissenschaftliche Rundschau:* Roger A. Beaumont, "On the Wehrmacht Mystique," *Military Review* 66, no. 7 (July 1986), pp. 44–56; Antulio Echevarria II, *"Auftragstaktik:* In Its Proper Perspective," *Military Review* 66, no. 10 (October 1986); Daniel J. Hughes, "Abuses of German Military History," *Military Review* 66, no. 12 (December 1986), pp. 66–76; and Martin van Creveld, "On Learning from the Wehrmacht and Other Things," *Military Review* 68, no. 1 (January 1988), pp. 62–71. The Hughes article, especially, is essential on the difficulty of the U.S. military learning from other national armies when there is so little knowledge of foreign languages within the officer corps.

4. The standard English translation is Carl von Clausewitz, *On War*, edited and translated by Michael Howard and Peter Paret (Princeton, N.J.: Princeton University Press, 1984), with introductory essays by Paret, Howard, and Bernard Brodie.

5. The title of the first chapter in Federico Chabod's magisterial *Italian Foreign Policy: The Statecraft of the Founders* (Princeton, N.J.: Princeton University Press, 1984), pp. 5–66.

6. "Preface by Marie von Clausewitz to the Posthumous Edition of Her Husband's Works," Clausewitz, *On War*, p. 65.

7. Clausewitz, *On War*, book 6, chapters 15–17, pp. 417–432.

8. Clausewitz, *On War*, book 7, chapter 19, pp. 557–561.

9. Michael Howard, "The Influence of Clausewitz," Clausewitz, *On War*, p. 27.

10. Hans Rothfels, "Clausewitz," in *Makers of Modern Strategy: Military Thought from Machiavelli to Hitler*, ed. Edward Mead Earle (New York: Atheneum, 1966), pp. 93–113. The quote is from p. 93 ("le plus Allemand des Allemands . . . A tout instant chez lui on a la sensation d'être dans le brouillard métaphysique").

11. Clausewitz, *On War*, book 6, chapter 14, p. 416; and book 6, chapter 28, pp. 492–494. For Clausewitz as a military historian (and an eyewitness), see also his *The Campaign of 1812 in Russia* (London: Greenhill Books, 1992).

12. For Clausewitz's "military Romanticism," see John Lynn, *Battle: A History of Combat and Culture* (Boulder, Colo.: Westview Press, 2003), pp. 192–216.

13. The best introduction to Jomini's work is still John Shy, "Jomini," in *Makers of Modern Strategy from Machiavelli to the Nuclear Age*, ed. Peter Paret (Princeton, N.J.: Princeton University Press, 1986), pp. 143–185.

14. The *Précis* has been translated into English as *The Art of War* (Westport, Conn.: Greenwood Press, reprint of 1862 edition). The maxims are taken from p. 63.

15. See Jomini, *Art of War*, pp. 112–115, in which he has to execute some fancy intellectual footwork to prove that his point remains valid even in a case where it clearly does not—the Leipzig campaign of 1813. For commentary, see also the article by General of Artillery Ludwig, "Die Operation auf der inneren und der äußeren Linie im Lichte unserer Zeit," *Militär-Wochenblatt* 126, no. 1 (July 4, 1941), pp. 7–10.

16. The German phrase is "eine wunderliche Dreifaltigkeit," Clausewitz, *On War*, book 1, chapter 1, p. 89.

17. Clausewitz, *On War*, book 1, chapter 1, p. 75.

18. Clausewitz, *On War*, book 1, chapter 4, p. 113.

19. Clausewitz, *On War*, book 1, chapter 7, p. 119.

20. Clausewitz, *On War*, book 2, chapter 2, p. 140.

21. Clausewitz, *On War*, book 1, chapter 1, p. 85.

22. Clausewitz, *On War*, book 2, chapter 2, p. 136.

23. See, to give just one example, Dennis E. Showalter, "The Retaming of Bellona: Prussia and the Institutionalization of the Napoleonic Legacy, 1815–1876," *Military Affairs* 44, no. 2 (April 1980), pp. 57–63: "*On War* became for soldiers what the Bible is for Christians: a book to be quoted rather than understood, sources of support for the reader's preconceptions" (p. 60).

24. See, for example, the discussion of Clausewitz in the article "Taktische und strategische Grundsätze der Gegenwart," *Beiheft zum Militär-Wochenblatt* (1896), pp. 193–229, especially pp. 193–196. The piece is anonymous, but evidently the work of General Sigismund von Schlichting, who would a short time later publish a three-volume work with the same title (Berlin: E. S. Mittler, 1898–1899).

25. Clausewitz, *On War*, book 4, chapter 3, p. 228.

26. Clausewitz, *On War*, book 4, chapter 5, p. 236.

27. Clausewitz, *On War*, book 8, chapter 1, p. 577.

28. The one failing of the otherwise excellent book by Jehuda L. Wallach, *The Dogma of the Battle of Annihilation: The Theories of Clausewitz and Schlieffen and Their Impact on the German Conduct of Two World Wars* (Westport, Conn.: Greenwood, 1986) is that the theory of the annihilating battle springs to life, fully blown, out of the writings of Clausewitz, rather than out of Prussian military praxis.

29. "Eine Ehrenschuld der Armee," *Militär-Wochenblat* 90, no. 26 (March 2, 1905), pp. 615–616.

30. See Dennis E. Showalter's article, "Mass Multiplied by Impulsion: The Influence of Railroads on Prussian Planning for the Seven Weeks' War," *Military Affairs* 38, no. 2 (April 1974), pp. 62–67, as well as his seminal book, *Railroads and Rifles: Soldiers, Technology, and the Unification of Germany* (Hamden, Conn.: Archon Books, 1976).

31. Martin van Creveld, *Command in War* (Cambridge, Mass.: Harvard University Press, 1985), pp. 105–106.

32. Creveld, *Command in War*, p. 107.

33. See John A. English and Bruce I. Gudmundsson, *On Infantry* (Westport, Conn.: Praeger, 1994), pp. 1–14.

34. The professional journals of the German military are the source of many hundreds of articles on Moltke. In 1891, for example, the year of Moltke's death, see emperor William II's "Trauer um den verewigten General-Feldmarschall Grafen von Moltke," *Militär-Wochenblatt* 76, no. 37 (April 26, 1891), n.p.—an unusual, single-sheet "special edition"; as well as Major General von Estorff, "General-Feldmarschall Graf von Moltke," *Militär-Wochenblatt* 76, no. 38 (April 29, 1891), pp. 967–970; Lieutenant Colonel Leszczynski, "Gesammelte Schriften und Denk-würdigkeiten des General-Feldmarschalls Grafen Helmuth von Moltke," a review of the volumes of Moltke's papers published by his family, in *Militär-Wochenblatt* 76, nos. 71, 73, 98 (August 15, 1891, August 22, 1891, November 7, 1891), pp. 1808–1811, 1867–1872, 2533–2536; "Das Verdienst der Armee um Moltke," *Militär-Wochenblatt* 76, no. 108 (December 12, 1891), p. 2795, which compares Moltke's writings with those of Goethe in favor of the former, which "have no equal in German literature." The articles never stopped until the demise of the *Wochenblatt* at the end of World War II. See, for example, General of Artillery Ludwig, "Moltke als Erzieher" and the unsigned article, "Generalfeldmarschall Graf von Schlieffen über den großen Feldherrn der preußisch-deutschen Armee," both in *Militär-Wochenblatt* 125, no. 17 (October 25, 1940), pp. 802–804 and 805–807. Moltke's complete writings are found in the fourteen-volume collection edited by the Great General Staff, *Militärische Werke* (Berlin: E. S. Mittler & Son, 1892–1912). For those without access, Daniel J. Hughes, ed., *Moltke on the Art of War: Selected Writings* (Novato, Calif.: Presidio, 1993) is absolutely indispensable, combining a judicious selection of Moltke's works, smooth translation, and penetrating commentary.

35. Hughes, *Moltke on the Art of War*, p. 176.

36. For Moltke's views on maneuvers, war games, and exercises, see Arden Bucholz, *Moltke, Schlieffen, and Prussian War Planning* (Providence, R.I.: Berg, 1991), pp. 31–43.

37. Quoted in General von Voigts-Rhetz, "Erklärung," *Militär-Wochenblatt* 84, no. 37 (April 26, 1899), p. 1013.

38. For a diagram of the needle gun, along with a solid analysis of its advantages and disadvantages, see Paul Dangel, "Blood and Iron," *Command* 21, March–April 1993, p. 16.

39. A point made by Hans Delbrück, "Prinz Friedrich Karl," in *Historische und Politische Aufsätze* (Berlin: Georg Stilke, 1907), pp. 309–310: "Moltke was no philosopher, but a hero. The fine books that he wrote as a captain would have been forgotten today, if he had not fought his battles."

40. Hughes, *Moltke on the Art of War*, p. 91.

41. Here the best available source—with a discussion rich in operational insight—is the four-part article by Lieutenant General Waldemar Erfurth, "Das Zusammenwirken getrennter Heeresteile," 4 parts, *Militärwissenschaftliche Rundschau* 4, nos. 1–4, 1939.

42. The German is "eine Kalamität," taken from the "Instruktion für die höheren Truppenführer," June 24, 1869. It is one of Moltke's most famous quotes,

appearing in German General Staff, *Studien zur Kriegsgeschichte und Taktik*, vol. 3, *Der Schlachterfolg: mit welchen Mitteln wurde er erstrebt?* (Berlin: E. S. Mittler, 1903), p. 311; Lieutenant General Waldemar Erfurth, "Die Zusammenwirken getrennter Heeresteile," part 2, *Militärwissenschaftliche Rundschau* 4, no. 2 (1939), pp. 156–178 (p. 170); and Lieutenant General von Caemmerer, "Zwei Bemerkungen zu Moltke's Stragtegie im Jahre 1866," *Militär-Wochenblatt* 90, no. 156 (December 21, 1905), pp. 3603–3608, to list just a few examples. See also Hughes, *Moltke on the Art of War*, p. 175, where "calamity" is rendered (in a perfectly acceptable manner) as "catastrophe."

43. Hughes, *Moltke on the Art of War*, p. 175; Martin van Creveld, *Technology and War* (New York: Free Press, 1991), p. 169; Creveld, *Command in War*, p. 105; Erfurth, "Die Zusammenwirken getrennter Heeresteile," p. 170.

44. Hughes, *Moltke on the Art of War*, p. 11n32.

45. Still a worthy addition to the literature on the *Kesselschlacht* doctrine and the role it would play in twentieth-century German war making is Larry H. Addington, *The Blitzkrieg Era and the German General Staff, 1865–1941* (New Brunswick, N.J.: Rutgers University Press, 1971).

46. The German phrase is "Getrennt marschieren, vereint schlagen." Ludwig, "Moltke als Erzieher," p. 803.

47. See, for example, General Ernst Kabisch, "Systemlose Strategie," *Militär-Wochenblatt* 125, no. 26 (December 27, 1940), p. 1235.

48. For the derivation of the term *Auftragstaktik*, see Antulio J. Echevarria II, *After Clausewitz: German Military Thinkers before the Great War* (Lawrence: University Press of Kansas, 2000), pp. 32–42, and pp. 94–103. Arising in a post-Moltkean debate over infantry tactics, *Auftragstaktik* stood for a flexible system of organization, with units and doctrines being formed for specific missions in battle; it was opposed to *Normaltaktik*, the use of standardized formations and procedures in battle. Echevarria warns that "the term *Auftragstaktik* has been greatly abused in military publications in recent years" (p. 38), and argues successfully that the Germans managed a synthesis of contending concepts in the years before 1914: with a stress on proper planning at the small unit level and more openness and flexibility for the higher commanders. On the debate, see Daniel J. Hughes, "Schlichting, Schlieffen, and the Prussian Theory of War in 1914," *Journal of Military History* 59, no. 2 (April 1995), pp. 257–277; and, for Schlieffen, Bucholz, *Moltke, Schlieffen, and Prussian War Planning*, especially pp. 109–157, 213.

49. Hughes, *Moltke on the Art of War*, pp. 184–185.

50. For the context of the famous question uttered by General Albrecht von Manstein, commander of the 6th Infantry Division at Königgrätz, see the detailed analysis by Lieutenant Colonel Obkircher, "Moltke, der 'unbekannte' General von Königgrätz: Zur Errinerung an den 75. Gedenktag der Schlacht bei Königgrätz am 3. Juli 1866," *Militär-Wochenblatt* 125, no. 52 (June 27, 1941), pp. 1994–1997.

51. Until recently, the standard work on the war of 1866 was Gordon Craig, *The Battle of Königgrätz: Prussia's Victory over Austria, 1866* (Philadelphia: Lippincott, 1964). It has now been superseded by two works: Geoffrey Wawro, *The Austro-Prussian War: Austria's War with Prussia and Italy in 1866* (Cambridge: Cambridge

University Press, 1996), a work of meticulous research, extremely good writing, and judgments so bold (especially on the Austrian commander Ludwig Benedek) that they may occasionally make the reader wince; and Dennis E. Showalter, *The Wars of German Unification* (London: Arnold, 2004), an equally felicitous marriage of world-class scholarship and excellent writing. Wawro does the scholarly world a special favor by including detailed and insightful analysis on the campaign in northern Italy that culminated in the Austrian victory at Custoza. See also Arden Bucholz, *Moltke and the German Wars, 1864–1871* (New York: Palgrave, 2001), pp. 103–138. There is also an immense Prussian-German literature on the war. For the professional military view, the best place to start is with Helmuth von Moltke, *Strategy, Its Theory and Application: The Wars for German Unification, 1866–1871* (Westport, Conn.: Greenwood, 1971), a reprint of his selected correspondence; Hughes, *Moltke on the Art of War*, pp. 59–63, 134–137; and Field Marshal Count Alfred von Schlieffen, "Cannae," in *Gesammelte Schriften*, vol. 1 (Berlin: E. S. Mittler, 1913), pp. 72–164. See also the translation *Cannae: Authorized Translation* (Ft. Leavenworth, Kans.: Command and General Staff School Press, 1931), pp. 60–179. See also Major General Oscar von Lettow-Vorbeck, *Geschichte des Krieges von 1866 in Deutschland*, 3 vols. (Berlin: E. S. Mittler, 1896–1902, accompanied by very useful maps. For a general account by one of Germany's most brilliant and renowned literary figures, see Theodor Fontane, *Der deutsche Krieg von 1866*, 2 vols. (Berlin: R. v. Decker, 1870–1871).

52. For the western campaign of 1866, see Wawro, *Austro-Prussian War*, pp. 75–81; Lettow-Vorbeck, *Geschichte des Krieges von 1866*, vol. 1, *Gastein-Langensalza*; and Fontane, *Der deutsche Krieg von 1866*, vol. 2, *Der Feldzug in West- und Mitteldeutschland*.

53. Lettow-Vorbeck, *Gastein-Langensalza*, p. 258.

54. Fontane, *Der Feldzug in West- und Mitteldeutschland*, p. 8.

55. Reproduced in Lettow-Vorbeck, *Gastein-Langensalza*, p. 268.

56. Wawro, *Austro-Prussian War*, p. 80.

57. Lettow-Vorbeck, *Gastein-Langensalz*a, p. 302.

58. Ibid., p. 308.

59. Lettow-Vorbeck also included the Hanoverian cavalry pursuit in his tactical handbook *Kriegsgeschichtliche Beispiele* (Berlin: R. v. Decker, 1899), pp. 99–101.

60. Lettow-Vorbeck, *Gastein-Langensalza*, p. 315; Fontane, *Der Feldzug in West- und Mitteldeutschland*, pp. 26–29, underplays the effects of the cavalry pursuit.

61. The Königgrätz campaign has generated an enormous body of literature over the years. Wawro, *Austro-Prussian War* and Showalter, *Wars of German Unification* are the required volumes. One should also consult Theodor Fontane, *Der deutsche Krieg von 1866*, vol. 1, *Der Feldzug in Böhmen und Mähren* (isssued in two "half-volumes," *Bis Königgrätz* and *Königgrätz. Bis vor Wien*), and the mountain of professional German military literature. Begin with Lettow-Vorbeck, *Geschichte des Krieges von 1866*, vol. 2, *Der Feldzug in Böhmen*, supplemented by the pertinent sections in German General Staff, *Der Schlachterfolg*, pp. 162–188; Hugo Freiherr von Freytag-Loringhoven, *Feldherrngrösse: Von Denken und Handeln hervorragender Heerführer* (Berlin: E. S. Mittler, 1922), pp. 158–170, and Erfurth, "Das Zusammen-

wirken getrennter Heeresteile," pp. 163–170. See also Major Keim, "Der Feldzug 1866 in Böhmen," *Militär-Wochenblatt* 84, nos. 10–11 (February 1, 1899, February 4, 1899), pp. 273–279, pp. 299–305; and Caemmerer, "Zwei Bemerkungen zu Moltke's Stragtegie im Jahre 1866."

62. See the comparative series of maps in Erfurth, "Das Zusammenwirken getrennter Heeresteile," part 1: "Der bayrische Erbfolgekrieg" (p. 16); "Versammlung am 18.6.1866" (p. 17); and "Die Eröffnung des siebenjährigen Krieges 1757" (p. 18).

63. German General Staff, *Der Schlachterfolg*, p. 164.

64. Wawro, *Austro-Prussian War*, pp. 126–127, is particularly effective in describing the ruinous impact of Benedek's flank march on the battle readiness of his army.

65. For 2nd Army's battles as it tried to cross the Riesengebirge, see Paul Dangel, "Blood and Iron," pp. 20–24, especially the superb maps.

66. For the origins of Austrian shock tactics, see Geoffrey Wawro, "'An Army of Pigs': The Technical, Social, and Political Bases of Austrian Shock Tactics, 1859–1866," *Journal of Military History* 59, no. 3 (July 1995), pp. 407–433.

67. Showalter, *Wars of German Unification*, p. 197.

68. For casualty figures at Nachod, Trautenau, Burkersdorf, and Skalitz, see Lettow-Vorbeck, *Der Feldzug in Böhmen*, pp. 217, 244, 312, and 294, respectively.

69. Lettow-Vorbeck, *Der Feldzug in Böhmen*, p. 2.

70. Wawro, *Austro-Prussian War*, p. 208, calls Benedek's line at Chlum "the worst of all possible deployments."

71. Craig, *Battle of Königgrätz*, pp. 84–85.

72. Wawro, *Austro-Prussian War*, p. 212; Craig, *Battle of Königgrätz*, p. 85.

73. Quoted in Craig, *Battle of Königgrätz*, p. 85.

74. Creveld, *Command in War*, pp. 137–138; Craig, *Battle of Königgrätz*, p. 111.

75. Craig, *Battle of Königgrätz*, p. 85. It is highly unlikely that even the chief of the General Staff would have said such a thing to his king.

76. Wawro, *Austro-Prussian War*, pp. 204–207, contains the first comprehensive account of this "council of war." It is shocking—and central to the author's indictment of Benedek—that the *Feldzeugmeister* spent several hours on administrative trivia, yet said not one word to his subordinates about actual operational plans for the next day's battle.

77. For events in the Swiepwald, or Svib Forest, see Wawro, *Austro-Prussian War*, pp. 221–227, which credits it with success in threatening the Prussian left, and argues that it might have yielded victory to the Austrians if Benedek had been willing to support it with his reserve. According to Showalter, *Railroads and Rifles*, pp. 130–134, the fighting in Swiepwald sucked up forty-nine Austrian battalions, and destroyed twenty-eight of them (p. 133).

78. "Plauschen Sie nicht so dumm, das it ja gar nicht möglich!" Keim, "Der Feldzug 1866 in Böhmen," p. 304.

79. Quoted in Edgar Feuchtwanger, *Bismarck* (London: Routledge, 2002), p. 148.

80. German General Staff, *Studien zur Kriegsgeschichte und Taktik*, vol. 6, *Heeresverpflegung* (Berlin: E. S. Mittler, 1913), p. 105.

81. There is dispute over just what General von Manstein meant by his ques-

tion. Showalter, *Wars of German Unification*, p. 188, argues that it was an "expression of sarcasm, not ignorance." That has not always been the idea within the German military community. In his speech at the unveiling of the Moltke monument in Berlin on October 26, 1905, for example, Field Marshal Alfred von Schlieffen implied that Manstein did not, in fact, know the name Moltke. See Field Marshal Count Alfred von Schlieffen, "Rede bei Enthüllung des Moltke-Denkmals auf dem Königsplatz in Berlin am 26. Oktober 1905," *Gesammelte Schriften*, vol. 2 (Berlin: E. S. Mittler, 1913), pp. 442–445. In best official history style, Obkircher, "Moltke, der 'unbekannte' General von Königgrätz," preserves everyone's honor by arguing that it was neither ignorance nor sarcasm. Manstein was simply being loyal to the chain of command. He already had an explicit order to join in the attack across the Bistritz from his army commander, Frederick Charles, and it would have been an act of indiscipline simply to disregard it.

82. Creveld, *Command in War*, pp. 137–138. For Frederick Charles's operational conception of an early concentration, see his letter to King Wilhelm of June 11, 1866, reproduced in Lettow-Vorbeck, *Gastein-Langensalza*, pp. 110–111, in which he assures the monarch that he can effect a preinvasion linkup with 2nd Army in "10–14 days."

83. Delbrück, *Friedrich Karl*, p. 308.

84. Geoffrey Wawro continues to carve out an empire for himself as the historian of record for the wars of Bismarck and Moltke. See his most recent book, *The Franco-Prussian War* (Cambridge: Cambridge University Press, 2003), which has now largely superseded the work by Michael Howard, *The Franco-Prussian War* (New York: Macmillan, 1962). Dennis Showalter's *Wars of German Unification* places the individual wars deeply and firmly into their contexts, and, continuing a tradition he began with *Wars of Frederick the Great* (London: Longman, 1996), is nonpareil on the motivation of soldiers and commanders under fire. See also Bucholz, *Moltke and the German Wars*, pp. 139–184. The primary source is Helmuth von Moltke, *The Franco-German War of 1870–71* (New York: Howard Fertig, 1988); here speaks the voice of the calm technician, practically devoid of emotion or anecdote. See also Moltke, *Strategy, Its Theory and Application;* Hughes, *Moltke on the Art of War*, pp. 38–44, 115–121, 137–154; and Spenser Wilkinson, ed., *Moltke's Military Correspondence, 1870–71* (Aldershot: Gregg Revivals, 1991). Once again, there is a beautifully written account for the general reader (in German) by noted novelist and observer of Prussian life, Theodor Fontane, *Der Krieg gegen Frankreich, 1870–1871*, 4 vols. (Zürich: Manesse, 1985). For the view of German military professionals, see German General Staff, *Studien zur Kriegsgeschichte und Taktik*, vol. 2, *Das Abbrechen von Gefechten* (Berlin: E. S. Mittler, 1903), a series of divisional-level studies from the war, with an unsurpassed companion volume of maps; German General Staff, *Der Schlachterfolg*, pp. 189–305; and German General Staff, *Heeresverpflegung*, pp. 134–224. The chief of staff to Crown Prince Frederick William has published his memoirs, quite revealing as to the commander–staff officer relationship, Count Albrecht von Blumenthal, *Journals of Field-Marshal Count von Blumenthal for 1866 and 1870–71* (London: Edward Arnold, 1903). Two British memoirs offer interesting details on the personalities, soldiers, and terrain. See

Archibald Forbes, *My Experiences of the War between France and Germany*, 2 vols. (Leipzig: Berhnard Tauchnitz, 1871), and Alexander Innes Shand, *On the Trail of the War* (New York: Harper, 1871). The latter was a correspondent for the London *Times*. Finally, see two collections of translated German works, *St. Privat: German Sources* (Ft. Leavenworth, Kans.: Staff College Press, 1914), and Major General Sir F. Maurice, ed., *The Franco-German War, by Generals and Other Officers Who Took Part in the Campaign* (London: Allen & Unwin, 1899).

85. Freytag-Loringhoven, *Feldherrngrösse*, p. 171.

86. Kabisch, "Systemlose Strategie," p. 1235.

87. The version in Moltke, *Franco-German War*, p. 8, contains the infelicitous translation "from the fertile southern states into the narrower tract on the north." For the original, see Kabisch, "Systemlose Strategie," p. 1235.

88. For the engagement at Wissembourg (Weissenburg), see Wawro, *Franco-Prussian War*, pp. 95–107; German General Staff, Der Schlachterfolg, pp. 199–200; German General Staff, *Das Abbrechen von Gefechten*, pp. 1–30, with its detailed account of the fight of the French Douay Division; and A. von Pfister, "Weissenberg," (sic) in Maurice, *Franco-German War*, pp. 73–80.

89. Wawro, *Franco-Prussian War*, p. 110.

90. For Spichern, see Wawro, *Franco-Prussian War*, pp. 107–120; German General Staff, *Der Schlachterfolg*, pp. 205–209; German General Staff, *Das Abbrechen von Gefechten*, pp. 31–69, a close reading of the experience of Frossard's Corps, and Hans von Kretschman, "From Spicheren to Vionville," in Maurice, *Franco-German War*, pp. 106–130.

91. Shand, *On the Trail of the War*, p. 22.

92. Ibid., p. 23.

93. For Wörth (Froeschwiller), see Wawro, *Franco-Prussian War*, pp. 121–137; German General Staff, *Der Schlachterfolg*, pp. 201–204; A. von Pfister, "The Battle of Wörth," (sic) in Maurice, *Franco-German War*, pp. 81–105, and Major Keim, "Die Schlacht von Wörth," 3 parts, *Militär-Wochenblatt* 76, nos. 87–89 (October 3, 1891, October 7, 1891, October 10, 1891), pp. 2239–2251, 2265–2275, 2293–2304.

94. For Mars-la-Tour, see Wawro, *Franco-Prussian War*, pp. 138–163; David Ascoli, *A Day of Battle: Mars-la-Tour, 16 August 1870* (London: Harrap, 1987); Hans von Kretschman, "The Battle of Vionville—Mars-la-Tour," in Maurice, *Franco-German War*, pp. 131–153, and for the view of a later generation of German military professionals, Lieutenant Colonel Obkircher, "General Constantin von Alvbensleben: Zu Seinem 50. Todestag, 28 März," *Militär-Wochenblatt* 126, no. 39 (March 7, 1942), pp. 1111–1115.

95. Wawro, *Franco-Prussian War*, pp. 152, 155.

96. Kretschman, "The Battle of Vionville—Mars-la-Tour," p. 146.

97. See the discussion in Eric Dorn Brose, *The Kaiser's Army: The Politics of Military Technology in Germany during the Machine Age, 1870–1918* (Oxford: Oxford University Press, 2001), p. 10, as well as Obkircher, "General Constantin von Alvbensleben," p. 1113, with the latter arguing that it was the "dispersal" of the charge that turned it into a death ride.

98. One does not know where to start with the Hoenig controversy—it went on and on, and in the end generated its own library of polemical articles filled with exclamation points. It deserves a monograph from a modern scholar. Its origins date to 1881, with the publication of Hoenig's book *Zwei Brigaden* (Two Brigades), a comparison of the successful attack of the 28th Infantry Brigade at Bor during the battle of Königgrätz and the catastrophic defeat of the 38th Brigade at Mars-la-Tour. Focusing on the latter, he heaped blame on the commander of the 19th Division, General von Schwartzkoppen, railing against his "complete incompetence." The book is a remarkable reconstruction of the 38th Brigade's destruction, in an almost minute-by-minute fashion, and was popular both inside and outside Germany. By 1894, it had gone through four editions and had expanded its title into *Untersuchungen über die Taktik der Zukunft,* translated into English as *Inquiries concerning the Tactics of the Future* (London: Longmans, Green, 1899). Although the German General Staff was an institution remarkable for its intense self-criticism, it was also a closed guild that tolerated no comment from anyone on the outside. Hoenig may not have been the historian that Hans Delbrück was, but in many ways the controversy hit the officers of the General Staff closer to home. This was not an argument over typology of the long-dead Frederick the Great, but one that dealt with a war they themselves had run. The articles in the *Militär-Wochenblatt* never stopped coming attacking Hoenig's views; he responded in kind (often in the pages of the same journal); and both sides' views underwent subtle modulations over time, as is typical of such *Federkriegen.* Simply to gain a handle on the controversy, start with these articles from both sides: Major Meissner, "Fritz Hoenigs 'Taktik der Zukunft' und die Brigade Wedell bei Mars la Tour," 3 parts, *Militär-Wochenblatt* 76, nos. 61–63 (July 15, 1891, July 18, 1891, July 22, 1891), pp. 1559–1573, 1589–1597, 1617–1623; Fritz Hoenig's response to Meissner, "Die Brigade Wedell bei Mars la Tour," 7 parts, *Militär-Wochenblatt* 76, nos. 71–73, 75–78 (August 15, 1891, August 19, 1891, August 22, 1891, August 26, 1891, August 29, 1891, September 2, 1891, September 5, 1891), pp. 1814–1826, 1853–1858, 1887–1891, 1939–1948, 1955–1959, 1988–1994, 2001–2006. Eight years later, things were still going strong, with the General Staff by now wheeling out heavier artillery. See General von Scherff, "Fritz Hoenigs 'Wahrheit,'" 2 parts, *Militär-Wochenblatt* 84, nos. 34, 36 (April 19, 1899, April 22, 1899), pp. 911–916, 971–986, and General Friedrich von Bernhardi, "Zur Beurtheilung der militärwissenschaftlichen Arbeiten F. Hoenigs," 2 parts, *Militär-Wochenblatt* 84, nos. 41–42 (May 10, 1899, May 13, 1899), pp. 1087–1103, 1119–1134.

99. For St. Privat, Wawro, *Franco-Prussian War,* pp. 164–185, "Der Kampf um St. Privat," *Militär-Wochenblatt* 84, no. 1 (January 4, 1899), pp. 18–26, and Colmar von der Goltz, "St. Privat-La Montagne, and Metz," in Maurice, *Franco-German War,* pp. 154–201.

100. See Moltke, *Franco-German War,* p. 61; and Captain Arnold Helmuth, "The Prussian Guard on the 18th of August, 1870," in *St. Privat: German Sources,* pp. 1–43.

101. Goltz, "St. Privat-La Montagne, and Metz," p. 181.

102. German General Staff, *Der Schlachterfolg*, pp. 243–244.

103. Lieutenant General Marx, "Operative Zersplitterung in der Kriegsge-schichte," *Militär-Wochenblatt* 125, no. 3 (July 19, 1940), p. 86.

104. Wawro, *Franco-Prussian War*, p. 168.

6. From Schlieffen to World War I

1. Field Marshal Count Alfred von Schlieffen, "Über die Millionenheere," *Gesammelte Schriften*, vol. 1 (Berlin: E. S. Mittler, 1913), p. 24.

2. David T. Zabecki, *Steel Wind: Colonel Georg Bruchmüller and the Birth of Modern Artillery* (Westport, Conn.: Praeger, 1994), p. 8.

3. Colonel Terence Cave, "Foreword," in *The War Diary of the Master of Belhaven (Ralph Hamilton), 1914–1918* (Barnsley: Wharncliffe, 1990), p. i.

4. The only book to deal solely with the issue of wartime logistics is Martin van Creveld, *Supplying War: Logistics from Wallenstein to Patton* (Cambridge: Cambridge University Press, 1977). It has not pleased everyone. See, for example, the negative critique by John Lynn, "The History of Logistics and *Supplying War*," in *Feeding Mars: Logistics in Western Warfare from the Middle Ages to the Present*, ed. John Lynn (Boulder, Colo.: Westview Press, 1993), pp. 9–27, which faults Creveld on conceptual and statistical grounds. The critique focuses on Creveld's analysis of the early modern period, however, not World War I.

5. "Kampf und Gefecht," *Militär-Wochenblatt* 84, no. 27 (March 25, 1899), pp. 694–698.

6. Captain Langemak, "Kriechen oder Springen? Ein Beitrag zu unserer Gefechts-ausbildung," *Militär-Wochenblatt* 84, no. 28 (March 7, 1905), pp. 653–660.

7. For operations in South Africa, see Robert M. Citino, *Quest for Decisive Victory: From Stalemate to Blitzkrieg in Europe, 1899–1940* (Lawrence: University Press of Kansas, 2002), pp. 31–63.

8. See Joseph C. Arnold, "French Tactical Doctrine, 1870–1914," *Military Affairs* XLII, 2 (April 1978), pp. 63–64, as well as Michael Howard, "Men against Fire: The Doctrine of the Offensive in 1914," in *Makers of Modern Strategy from Machiavelli to the Nuclear Age*, ed. Peter Paret (Princeton, N.J.: Princeton University Press, 1986), p. 516.

9. For the Russo-Japanese War, begin with Bruce Menning, *Bayonets before Bullets: The Imperial Russian Army, 1861–1914* (Bloomington: Indiana University Press, 1992), a solid history of the war (pp. 152–199) in the context of an analysis of doctrine, training, and organization in the Russian army throughout the period; Richard W. Harrison, *The Russian Way of War: Operational Art, 1904–1940* (Lawrence: University Press of Kansas, 2001), pp. 7–23; and Citino, *Quest for Decisive Victory*, pp. 65–99. For an analysis comparing and contrasting the German and British official histories of the war, see Gary P. Cox, "Of Aphorisms, Lessons, and Paradigms: Comparing the British and German Official Histories of the Russo-Japanese War," *Journal of Military History* 56, no. 3 (July 1992), pp. 389–401. Cox sees the thirteen-volume German work as laying stress on the importance of the

operational art, characterized by a "relentless emphasis" on the importance of "boldness in offensive operations" (p. 397), as opposed to the British view that highlighted the importance of new technologies during the war.

10. The account by David H. James, *Daily Telegraph* correspondent, has never been bettered: *The Siege of Port Arthur: Records of an Eye-Witness* (London: T. Fisher Unwin, 1905). For contemporary German views, see "Port Arthur," *Militär-Wochenblatt* 90, no. 20 (February 16, 1905), pp. 477–482, and Captain Hüther, "Nochmals Port Arthur," *Militär-Wochenblatt* 90, no. 30 (March 11, 1905), pp. 702–708.

11. For a discussion of the siege of Plevna, see Menning, *Bayonets before Bullets*, pp. 60–64; William McElwee, *The Art of War: Waterloo to Mons* (Bloomington: Indiana University Press, 1974), pp. 199–205, as well as Paddy Griffith, *Forward into Battle: Fighting Tactics from Waterloo to the Near Future* (Novato, Calif.: Presidio, 1990), pp. 69–76. More recently, see the article (and simulation game) by Joseph Miranda, "The Battle of Plevna," *Strategy and Tactics* 218 (September–October 2003), pp. 23–26.

12. For a balanced view of Bloch, without cant or cliché, see Antulio Echevarria II, *After Clausewitz: German Military Thinkers before the Great War* (Lawrence: University Press of Kansas, 2000), pp. 85–93. The quote is from p. 87. See also Tim Travers, "Technology, Tactics, and Morale: Jean de Bloch, the Boer War, and British Military Theory, 1900–1914," *Journal of Modern History* 51, no. 2 (June 1979), pp. 264–286.

13. See, for example, the body of work by Stig Förster, especially "Dreams and Nightmares: German Military Leadership and the Images of Future Warfare, 1871–1914," in *Anticipating Total War: The German and American Experiences, 1871–1914*, ed. Manfred F. Boemeke, Roger Chickering, and Stig Förster (Cambridge: Cambridge University Press, 1999), pp. 343–376, an attack on the very notion of the "short war illusion" supposedly shared by all of Europe's generals.

14. This is the argument of Gerhard Ritter, who more than anyone else is responsible for shaping contemporary views on the plan. See *Der Schlieffenplan: Kritik eines Mythos* (Munich: R. Oldenbourg, 1956), especially pp. 13–81, which included Schlieffen's *Denkschrift* of early 1906, the first time it had appeared in published form. Ritter's verdict ("the Schlieffen Plan was never a sound recipe for victory," but "a bold, even over-bold gamble, whose success depended on many lucky breaks," p. 68) has been the basis for virtually every historical analysis of the German war plan in 1914.

15. Jehuda L. Wallach, *The Dogma of the Battle of Annihilation: The Theories of Clausewitz and Schlieffen and Their Impact on the German Conduct of Two World Wars* (Westport, Conn.: Greenwood, 1986), p. 60.

16. Hans-Ulrich Wehler, *The German Empire, 1871–1918* (Dover, N.H.: Berg, 1985), p. 151. With the publication of Fritz Fischer, *Griff nach der Weltmacht: die Kriegszielpolitik des kaiserlichen Deutschland, 1914–18* (Düsseldorf: Droste Verlag, 1961), the belief that Germany had been largely, if not solely, responsible for the outbreak of World War I became an article of faith among leftist historians in Germany. It found particular resonance in the work of the so-called "critical

school," several of whom, like Wehler, taught at the University of Bielefeld (hence, "Bielefeld school").

17. Ritter, *Der Schlieffenplan*, p. 90.

18. This conclusion, still widely accepted, first appeared in two books by the former quartermaster general of the army, General Wilhelm Groener: *Das Testament des Grafen Schlieffen: Operative Studien über den Weltkrieg* (Berlin: E. S. Mittler, 1927) and *Der Feldherr wider Willen: Operative Studien über den Weltkrieg* (Berlin: E. S. Mittler, 1931).

19. Terence Zuber, *Inventing the Schlieffen Plan: German War Planning, 1871–1914* (Oxford: Oxford University Press, 2002) is the most important book on World War I in decades. Presented first in his seminal article, "The Schlieffen Plan Reconsidered," *War in History* 6, no. 3 (July 1999), pp. 262–305, Zuber's argument is essentially that the "Schlieffen Plan" is a postwar construction, that Schlieffen never had firm plans to march an army corps around the west of Paris to encircle the entire French army, and that consequently, there was nothing for Moltke to "water down." Noting that there is no reference at all to the plan in print until 1920, and that the first operational history of the war, the Swiss historian Hermann Stegemann's *Geschichte des Krieges* (Stuttgart: Deutsche Verlags-Anstalt, 1918) doesn't mention it at all, he posits that German officers, anxious to preserve their reputations, attempted to heap the blame onto Moltke by claiming that he had failed to carry out the plan bequeathed to him by his genius-predecessor, Schlieffen. The idea took hold in the 1920s, particularly in the works of General Groener (cited earlier, note 18). Not only is Zuber's argumentation convincing, but his thesis explains several heretofore puzzling aspects of the opening campaign, such as why Kluck's 1st Army surrendered two corps to the investment of Antwerp (a "blunder" taught in every staff school since 1914) on his way to the Marne, or why, if Kluck was supposed to be the business end of the Schlieffen Plan, he was actually placed under the operational control of Bülow, commander of the neighboring 2nd Army but also responsible for both neighboring armies (1st and 3rd). There has never been a satisfactory explanation for either one of these problems. Since there never was a plan for a vast encirclement of the French from the right wing, however, Kluck's importance is cut down to size. It wasn't his job to win the war; he was merely the flank guard on the right.

Like all "grand statements," Zuber overreaches at times. His repeated attempts to exculpate Schlieffen and the German army from charges of aggression, militarism, and war guilt are a good example. He may be right and he may be wrong, but certainly it will take more than the shape of Schlieffen's actual operational scheme to establish the point, and his arguments in their current state are underdeveloped and tendentious. He argues that the Schlieffen Plan has been used as proof of Germany's malignant and warlike intentions in the years before 1914 ("The Schlieffen plan is one of the principal pieces of evidence for German war guilt. . . . The great arrows of the Schlieffen plan slashing across the map of France are interpreted as graphic representations of German aggression." p. 302). In fact, by 1920, the year that Zuber himself claims that the Schlieffen Plan was "invented," the Allies had already imposed the Treaty of Versailles on Germany, requiring it to admit guilt for starting the war.

20. Zuber, *Inventing the Schlieffen Plan*, pp. 302–303.

21. Major Keim, "Ueberblick über den Verlauf der Kaisermanöver," 5 parts, *Militär-Wochenblatt* 79, nos. 91, 93, 101–103 (October 27, 1894, November 3, 1894, December 1, 1894, December 5, 1894, December 8, 1894), pp. 2403–2410, 2448–2454, 2669–2676, 2696–2700, 2721–2733.

22. Keim, "Ueberblick über den Verlauf der Kaisermanöver," part 1, "Manöver des I. Armeekorps gegen einen markirten Feind am 6. September."

23. Keim, "Manöver des I. Armeekorps," pp. 2405–2406.

24. Ibid., p. 2410.

25. Ibid., p. 2409.

26. Keim, "Ueberblick über den Verlauf der Kaisermanöver," part 2, "Manöver des XVII. Armeekorps gegen einen markirten Feind am 8. September."

27. Keim, "Ueberblick über den Verlauf der Kaisermanöver," parts 3–5, "Manöver des I. und XVII. Armeekorps gegeneinander."

28. A point made well in Arden Bucholz, *Moltke, Schlieffen, and Prussian War Planning* (New York: Berg, 1991), p. 144: As far as Schlieffen was concerned, "It was a once-a-year public display and Wilhelm could do what he liked."

29. Major General von Kurnatowski, "Die grossen Feldmanöver unter Wilhelm II," *Militär-Wochenblatt* 103, no. 137 (May 22, 1919), pp. 1541–2544.

30. For the entire set of staff problems from 1891 to 1905, see Field Marshal Count Alfred von Schlieffen, *Dienstschriften des Chefs des Generalstabes der Armee General-feldmarschalls Graf von Schlieffen*, vol. 1, *Die Taktisch-Strategischen Aufgaben aus den Jahren 1891–1905* (Berlin: E. S. Mittler, 1937), with six detailed maps and sketches for the various problems. For more on Schlieffen's teaching exercises, see the imposing second volume, *Die Grossen Generalstabsreisen—Ost—aus den Jahren 1891–1905*, which presents the staff rides in the east for 1894, 1897, 1899, 1901, and 1903, replete with a comprehensive selection of maps and sketches. For a review of the first volume, see Major F. von Unger, "Grundsätzliches in Graf Schlieffens Generalstabsaufgaben," *Militär-Wochenblatt* 122, no. 15 (October 8, 1937), pp. 910–913.

31. Schlieffen, *Taktisch-Strategischen Aufgaben*, "1894," pp. 23–26.

32. Ibid., p.24.

33. Field Marshal Count Alfred von Schlieffen, "Cannae," in *Gesammelte Schriften*, vol. 1 (Berlin: E. S. Mittler, 1913), pp. 25–266.

34. Schlieffen, *Cannae*, p. 29.

35. Schlieffen, "Über die Millionenheere."

36. Field Marshal Count Alfred von Schlieffen, "Der Krieg in der Gegenwart," *Gesammelte Schriften*, vol. 1 (Berlin: E. S. Mittler, 1913), pp. 11–22.

37. Schlieffen, "Der Krieg in der Gegenwart," p. 17.

38. Schlieffen, *Die Taktisch-Strategischen Aufgaben*, "1901," p. 84. Quoted in Colonel Fuppe, "Neuzeitliches Nachrichtenverbindungswesen als Führungsmittel im Kriege," *Militärwissenschaftliche Rundschau* 3, no. 6 (1938), p. 750.

39. See Unger, "Grundsätzliches in Graf Schlieffens Generalstabsaufgaben," pp. 911–912.

40. The was the view of General Erich Ludendorff and a dominant group of German staff officers in the 1930s. See General Georg Wetzell, "Schlieffens Ver-

mächtnis," *Militär-Wochenblatt* 122, no. 39 (March 25, 1938), pp. 2483–2489, especially pp. 2484–2485. For a representative example of the case against Moltke, see, J. F. C. Fuller, *A Military History of the Western World*, vol. 3, *From the American Civil War to the End of World War II* (New York: Da Capo, 1957), pp. 196–198.

41. For the difficulties that Schlieffen's loaded right wing would have posed to the German rail net, see the articles by Colonel von Mantey, "Die Eisenbahnlage im Westen bei Kriegsbeginn 1914," *Militär-Wochenblatt* 122, no. 48 (May 27, 1938), pp. 3081–3089; "Nachschub und Operationsplan," 2 parts, *Militär-Wochenblatt* 124, nos. 1–2 (July 1, 1939, July 7, 1939), pp. 1–6, 76–81; and "Einfluss der Verkehrsmittel, insbesondere der Eisenbahn auf den Verlauf der Marneschlacht," *Militär-Wochenblatt* 124, no. 37 (March 15, 1940), pp. 1731–1732. Mantey criticizes Groener, among others, for underestimating the impact of both sides' railroads on the course of the operation in the west.

42. Zabecki, *Steel Wind*, pp. 11, 166; Boyd L. Dastrup, *The Field Artillery: History and Sourcebook* (Westport, Conn.: Greenwood, 1994), pp. 44–45.

43. The literature on World War I is copious and keeps growing. The most useful recent work is Niall Ferguson, *The Pity of War* (London: Penguin, 1999), a powerful argument against British participation in the war. Hew Strachan, *The First World War*, vol. 1, *To Arms* (Oxford: Oxford University Press, 2001) is a scholarly account of the war in all its military, diplomatic, and political complexity. It is also 1,227 pages long—and this is just the first volume of a projected three. For a shorter introduction to his oeuvre, see Hew Strachan, ed., *World War I: A History* (Oxford: Oxford University Press, 1998), a collection of articles by leading scholars and authors. Besides Strachan's introduction (pp. 1–8), the most notable contributions are Dennis E. Showalter, "Manoeuvre Warfare: The Eastern and Western Fronts, 1914–1915," pp. 39–53; B. J. C. McKercher, "Economic Warfare," pp. 119–133; and Tim Travers, "The Allied Victories, 1918," pp. 278–290. John Keegan, *The First World War* (London: Hutchinson, 1998), contains a solid and quite readable operational history marred only by its Anglocentric approach. James L. Stokesbury, *A Short History of World War I* (New York: William Morrow, 1981) is still the best-written work on the topic, part of a series of works by Stokesbury, including short histories of World War II and Korea.

For tactics in the war, see the prickly revisionist works by Paddy Griffith: *Forward into Battle: Fighting Tactics from Waterloo to the Near Future* (Novato, Calif.: Presidio, 1990) and *Battle Tactics of the Western Front: The British Army's Art of Attack* (New Haven, Conn.: Yale University Press, 1994); Shelford Bidwell and Dominick Graham, *Fire-Power: British Army Weapons and Theories of War, 1904–1945* (London: Allen and Unwin, 1982); and the large body of work by Tim Travers, including *The Killing Ground: The British Army, the Western Front, and the Emergence of Modern Warfare, 1900–1918* (London: Allen and Unwin, 1987); "The Evolution of British Strategy and Tactics on the Western Front in 1918: GHQ, Manpower, and Technology," *Journal of Military History* 54, no. 2 (April 1990), pp. 173–200; "Could the Tanks of 1918 Have Been War-Winners for the British Expeditionary Force?" *Journal of Contemporary History* 27, no. 3 (July 1992), pp. 389–406; and *How the War Was Won: Command and Technology in the British Army on the Western Front,*

1917–1918 (New York: Routledge, 1992). Even General Douglas Haig's reputation, the victim of the Liddell Hart-Fuller school in the interwar era, is in process of revision, especially on the question of his openness to the tank and other new technology. See Brian Bond and Nigel Cave, eds., *Haig: A Reappraisal 70 Years On* (London: Leo Cooper, 1999).

44. For professional German opinion of the French *Aufmarsch* and operational plans, see Wolfgang Foerster, *Aus der Gedankenwerkblatt des Deutschen Generalstabes* (Berlin: E. S. Mittler, 1931), pp. 105–141. Foerster was the section chief of the *Reichsarchiv* responsible for the volumes of the German official history of the war in the west to 1916. Still useful is the short piece by R. L. Dinardo, "French Military Planning, 1871–1914," *Strategy and Tactics* 118 (March–April 1988), pp. 10–13. It includes diagrams of Plans XI, XIV, XV, XV (modified), XVI (1905), XVI (modified), and XVII.

45. For a German view of Ludendorff's coup at Liège, see Lieutenant General Schwarte, "General Ludendorffs Lebenswerk," 2 parts, *Militär-Wochenblatt* 104, nos. 23–24 (August 21, 1919; August 23, 1919), pp. 433–446, 467–472, especially part 1, pp. 437–438. Still the most readable account of German operations in 1914 is Correlli Barnett, *The Swordbearers: Supreme Command in the First World War* (Bloomington: Indiana University Press, 1963), pp. 1–98.

46. For the traditional view of the battle, replete with the French "advancing as if at Waterloo," moving to the attack "in long lines in perfect order," only to be slaughtered en masse by German machine guns, see Stokesbury, *Short History*, 40–41. For a more sober account of the opening battles in Lorraine, see Griffith, *Forward into Battle*, pp. 90–94.

47. For Namur, the German official history still dominates the historiography. Reichsarchiv, *Der Weltkrieg 1914–1918*, vol. 1, *Die Grenzschlachten im Westen* (Berlin: E. S. Mittler, 1925), pp. 346–430, 479–504. The maps are essential.

48. Zuber, *Inventing the Schlieffen Plan*, p. 43.

49. For the German view—thoroughly negative—of French generalship, see General von Zwehl, "Die Operationen des Feldmarschalls French gegen die 1. Armee und das VII. Reservekorps im Sommer 1914," *Militär-Wochenblatt* 104, nos. 35–38 (September 18, 1919, September 20, 1919, September 23, 1919, and September 25, 1919), pp. 673–678, 689–698, 717–722, 737–742.

50. Keegan, *First World War*, pp. 94–97, is particularly useful here.

51. For the adventures of the Olenhusen Division, see Captain Niemann, "Der vereitelte Maas-Übergang bei Haybes-Fumay," *Militär-Wochenblatt* 123, no. 3 (July 15, 1938), pp. 134–138.

52. Niemann, "Der vereitelte Maas-Übergang," p. 135.

53. Ibid.

54. For the Marne, see two older works: Robert B. Asprey, *The First Battle of the Marne* (Philadelphia: Lippincott, 1962) and Georges Blond, *The Marne* (London: Macdonald, 1965). For contemporary and postwar German views, see Walther Kolbe, *Die Marneschlacht* (Bielefeld: Velhagen und Klasing, 1917); General Alexander von Kluck, *Der Marsch auf Paris und die Marneschlacht 1914* (Berlin: E. S. Mittler, 1920), especially pp. 140–147; Colonel Bauer, *Der grosse Krieg in Feld und Hei-*

mat: Errinerungen und Betrachtungen (Tübingen: Osiander'sche Buchhandlung, 1921), a snarling work by a former staff officer; Lieutenant General Ernst Kabisch, *Die Marneschlacht 1914* (Berlin: Otto Schlegel, 1933). See also the seemingly infinite mass of articles in the professional literature, of which the following are representative examples: Lieutenant General von Görtz, "Mouvement tourné?" *Militär-Wochenblatt* 104, no. 36 (September 20, 1919), pp. 697–700; General von Kuhl, "Die Marneschlacht," *Militär-Wochenblatt* 104, no. 39 (September 27, 1919), pp. 753–758; General von Kuhl, "Die beiden Marneschlachten," *Militär-Wochenblatt* 113, no. 27 (January 18, 1929), pp. 1069–1072; and General Georg Wetzell, "Die Führung im Marne-Feldzug 1914: Betrachtungen zu dem Buche von Oberstleutnant a. D. Müller-Loebnitz," 4 parts, *Militär-Wochenblatt* 124, nos. 32–35 (February 2, 1940, February 9, 1940, February 16, 1940, February 23, 1940), pp. 1524–1528, 1564–1570, 1604–1611, 1643–1649. Finally, see Karl Lange, *Marneschlacht und deutsche Öffentlichkeit 1914–1939: eine verdrängte Niederlage und ihre Folgen* (Düsseldorf: Bertelsmann, 1974) for the issues of how public knowledge about the battle and historical memory were intertwined after 1914.

55. See the review by Lieutenant Colonel Theobald von Schäfer, "Der Feldherr wider Willen," *Militär-Wochenblatt* 114, no. 2 (May 11, 1930), pp. 1641–1643.

56. See the discussion of the Kabisch plan in General Georg Wetzell, "Studie über Operationspläne und Kriegswirklichkeit," 3 parts, *Militar-Wochenblatt* 121, nos. 13–15 (October 4, 1936, October 11, 1936, October 18, 1936), pp. 629–636, 696–701, and 753–762. See especially part 1, "Grundsätzliches," pp. 635–636, and part 2, "Ein besserer Aufmarsch 1914?" pp. 696–700.

57. For the original version of the plan, including the employment of field armies of 12–15 corps apiece, see Karl Justrow, *Feldherr und Kriegstechnik: Studien über den Operationsplan des Grafen Schlieffen und Lehren für unseren Wehraufbau und unsere Landesverteidigung* (Oldenburg: Gerhard Stalling, 1933), pp. 259–289. See the discussion by Wetzell of a later version in "Studie über Operationspläne und Kriegswirklichkeit," part 3, "Ein Operationsplan, der es uns ermöglicht hätte, den Krieg zu gewinnen?" pp. 753–762.

58. Wetzell, "Studie über Operationspläne und Kriegswirklichkeit," p. 756.

59. Ibid., p. 761.

60. General Georg von Wetzell, "Der Bündniskrieg: Eine militärpolitisch operative Studie des Weltkrieges," 5 parts, *Militär-Wochenblatt* 122, nos. 14–18 (October 1, 1937, October 8, 1937, October 15, 1937, October 22, 1937, October 29, 1937), pp. 833–841, 897–903, 961–967, 1025–1030, and 1089–1094. By the same author, see "'Der Bündniskrieg' und die Kritik," 2 parts, *Militär-Wochenblatt* 122, nos. 28–29 (January 7, 1938, January 14, 1938), pp. 1745–1754, 1812–1818; "Nochmals: 'Der Bündniskrieg' und die Kritik," *Militär-Wochenblatt* 122, no. 35 (February 25, 1938), pp. 2209–2215; and "Bismarck-Moltke und der Bündniskrieg," *Militär-Wochenblatt* 122, no. 45 (May 6, 1938), pp. 2873–2881.

61. General Georg Wetzell, "Der Kriegsbeginn 1914 unter einer anderen politisch-militärischen Zielsetzung," *Militär-Wochenblatt* 121, no. 32 (February 19, 1938), pp. 1845–1853.

62. Wetzell, "Studie über Operationspläne und Kriegswirklichkeit," p. 631.

63. Schlieffen had described any such French attack as a "personal favor" (*Liebesdienst*). Wetzell, "Studie über Operationspläne und Kriegswirklichkeit," p. 634.

64. Wetzell, "Der Kriegsbeginn 1914 unter einer anderen politisch-militärischen Zielsetzung," pp. 1850–1851.

65. For a powerful evocation of life in the trenches from the British perspective, see Denis Winter, *Death's Men: Soldiers of the Great War* (New York: Penguin, 1978).

66. See General Hermann von François, *Marneschlacht und Tannenberg: Betrachtungen zur deutscher Kriegsführung der ersten sechs Kriegswochen* (Berlin: Scherl, 1920), pp. 115–117.

67. The best book by far on the Tannenberg campaign is Dennis E. Showalter, *Tannenberg: Clash of Empires* (Washington, D.C.: Brassey's, 2004). It is carefully researched, a delight to read, and perceptive in its insight (the true strength of all Showalter's operational histories) into what makes men fight. For Moltke's decision to send what proved to be unnecessary reinforcements to the East, see pp. 193–196. Norman Stone, *The Eastern Front, 1914–1917* (London: Hodder and Stoughton, 1975), is still indispensable for any inquiry into the war between the Central Powers and Russia, and so is Holger H. Herwig, *The First World War: Germany and Austria-Hungary, 1914–1918* (London: Arnold, 1997). Still quite useful is Sir Edmund Ironside, *Tannenberg: The First Thirty Days in East Prussia* (Edinburgh: William Blackwood, 1933). A detailed account of operations, with essential maps, is to be found in an article by Lieutenant Colonel Ponath, "Die Schlacht bei Tannenberg 1914 in kriegsgeschichtlicher, taktischer, und erzieherischer Auswertung," *Militär-Wochenblatt* 124, no. 8 (August 18, 1939), pp. 476–482.

68. François, *Marneschlacht und Tannenberg*, p. 159.

69. Quoted in Alan Clark, *Suicide of the Empires: The Battles on the Eastern Front, 1914–18* (New York: American Heritage Press, 1971), p. 29. For a focus on the operations of François and his I Corps, see Randy R. Talbot, "General Hermann von François and Corps-Level Operations during the Tannenberg Campaign, August 1914," Masters Thesis, Eastern Michigan University, 1999.

70. Showalter, *Tannenberg: Clash of Empires*, contains the best account in English of Stallupönen. See also François, *Marneschlacht und Tannenberg*, pp. 169–179, and Talbot, "General Hermann von François and Corps-Level Operations during the Tannenberg Campaign," pp. 57–64.

71. François, *Marneschlacht und Tannenberg*, p. 171.

72. Winston Churchill, *The Unknown War: The Eastern Front* (New York: Charles Scribner's Sons, 1932), p. 177. This is the point made in the German official history, as well.

73. Groener, *Testament des Grafen Schlieffen*, p. 127.

74. François, *Marneschlacht und Tannenberg*, p. 177.

75. Talbot, "General Hermann von François and Corps-Level Operations during the Tannenberg Campaign," pp. 67–68.

76. Who said what, to whom, and in which tone of voice has been a matter of controversy since the day it happened. The sources even contradict one another on the exact day of Prittwitz's phone call to Moltke. See Showalter, *Tannenberg: Clash of Empires*, pp. 193–194, as well as his article, "Even Generals Wet Their

Pants: The First Three Weeks in East Prussia, August 1914," *War & Society* 2, no. 2 (1984), pp. 61–86, which assesses the "psychological effects of the telephone," as well as its impact on operations.

77. Talbot, "General Hermann von François and Corps-Level Operations during the Tannenberg Campaign," p. 80.

78. The title of chapter 2 of Field Marshall Paul von Hindenburg, *Out of my Life*, vol. 1 (New York: Harper, 1921), pp. 20–64.

79. Captain Meier-Welcker, "Die Rückendeckung der 8. Armee während der Schlacht bei Tennenberg," *Militär-Wochenblatt* 121, no. 4 (July 25, 1926), pp. 165–170.

80. See Keegan, *First World War*, p. 150.

81. Quoted in W. Bruce Lincoln, *Passage through Armageddon: The Russians in War and Revolution, 1914–1918* (New York: Simon and Schuster, 1986), p. 84.

82. Hindenburg, *Out of My Life*, vol. 1, p. 148. For the Warsaw campaign, see also Stone, *Eastern Front*, pp. 92–100; Churchill, *Unknown War*, pp. 239–250; Curt Matthes, *Die 9. Armee im Weichselfeldzug 1914* (Berlin: Junker & Dünnhaupt, 1937); Herwig, *Germany and Austria-Hungary*, pp. 106–108; and Keegan, *First World War*, pp. 176–179.

83. Hindenburg, *Out of My Life*, vol. 1, p. 151.

84. Ibid., p. 153.

85. Ibid., p. 154. For the Lodz campaign, see also Stone, *Eastern Front*, pp. 100–107; Churchill, *Unknown War*, pp. 251–271; Herwig, *Germany and Austria-Hungary*, pp. 108–111; and Keegan, *First World War*, pp. 180–181.

86. From peacetime maneuvers, the Germans had calculated that in a resource-poor area like Poland, any advance more than seventy-five miles from the railhead was extremely hazardous. See Lieutenant Colonel Theobald von Schäfer, "Die Enstehung des Entschlusses zur Offensive auf Lods: Zum Gedenken an General Ludendorff," *Militärwissenschaftliche Rundschau* 3, no. 1 (1938), p. 20.

87. Lincoln, *Passage through Armageddon*, pp. 86–87.

88. Churchill, *Unknown War*, p. 262. An interesting comparison of Rennen-kampf's command failures in both East Prussia and Poland, based on studies done by the Red Army, is found in Colonel Achsenbrandt's article, "Rennenkampf als Führer der 1. Armee im Herbst 1914," *Militär-Wochenblatt* 124, no. 5 (July 28, 1939), pp. 272–275.

89. Schäfer, "Enstehung des Entschlusses zur Offensive auf Lods," p. 25.

90. German General Staff, *Studien zur Kriegsgeschichte und Taktik*, vol. 3, *Der Schlachterfolg: mit welchen Mitteln wurde er erstrebt?* (Berlin: E. S. Mittler, 1903).

91. German General Staff, *Der Schlachterfolg*, p. 306.

92. François, *Marneschlacht und Tannenberg*, p. 123.

93. Bauer, *Der grosse Krieg in Feld und Heimat*, p. 59.

94. The Germans had become extremely interested in tactics of storming fortress positions well before 1914. See the flurry of articles, for example, that appeared in Germany during the Russo-Japanese War, focusing on the similarities of the fighting to siege warfare. They include the anonymous "Port Arthur" and Hüther, "Nochmals Port Arthur" (see note 10, earlier), as well as Baron von der Goltz, "Welchen Weg hat die kriegsmässige Ausbildung der Infanterie einzuschla-

gen?" *Militär-Wochenblatt* 90, no. 1 (January 3, 1905), pp. 18–21; "Die Festung in den Kriegen Napoleons und der Neuzeit," *Militär-Wochenblatt* 90, no. 23 (February 23, 1905), pp. 543–550; and Lieutenant Colonel Ludwig, "Ueber Festungskriegfragen," *Militär-Wochenblatt* 90, no. 26 (March 2, 1905), pp. 619–627.

7. Collapse and Rebirth

1. There has been a veritable library of books devoted to the pluses and minuses of the Versailles Treaty, most of it highly condemnatory. Setting the tone early on, of course, was J. M. Keynes, *The Economic Consequences of the Peace* (New York: Harcourt, Brace and Howe, 1920). Following in his path, historians laid a weighty indictment at the door of the treaty, blaming it for everything from the Great Depression to the fall of the Weimar Republic to the rise of Hitler. It is only recently that a revisionist view has arisen. It began with Andreas Hillgruber, *Grossmachtpolitik und Militarismus im 20. Jahrhundert: Drei Beiträge zum Kontinuitätsproblem* (Düsseldorf: Droste, 1974), who pointed out that the treaty had left Germany intact and in a position to once again become a great power. With Austria-Hungary gone, he argued, German industry had a golden opportunity to penetrate eastern and southeastern European markets. Hillgruber's thesis has become the consensus among German historians. See, for example, the treatment of Versailles in two recent general texts on the Weimar Republic: Edgar Feuchtwanger, *From Weimar to Hitler: Germany, 1918–33* (New York: St. Martin's Press, 1993), pp. 45–54, and Detlev J. K. Peukert, *The Weimar Republic: The Crisis of Classical Modernity* (New York: Hill and Wang, 1992), pp. 42–46.

2. For an overview of the interwar era, with a special eye to its role as an incubator of a "revolution in military affairs," two works are indispensable: Williamson Murray and Allan R. Millett, eds., *Military Innovation in the Interwar Period* (Cambridge: Cambridge University Press, 1996), and Harold R. Winton and David R. Mets, eds., *The Challenge of Change: Military Institutions and New Realities, 1918–1941* (Lincoln: University of Nebraska Press, 2000). The list of works dealing with the era is large and getting larger. See, among others, the works by Robert M. Citino, *The Path to Blitzkrieg: Doctrine and Training in the German Army, 1920–1939* (Boulder, Colo.: Lynne Rienner, 1999), *Quest for Decisive Victory: From Stalemate to Blitzkrieg in Europe, 1899–1940* (Lawrence: University Press of Kansas, 2002), *Blitzkrieg to Desert Storm: The Evolution of Operational Warfare* (Lawrence: University Press of Kansas, 2004), and "'Die Gedanken sind frei': The Intellectual Culture of the Interwar German Army," *Army Doctrine and Training Bulletin* 4, no. 3 (Fall 2001); James S. Corum, *The Roots of Blitzkrieg: Hans von Seeckt and German Military Reform* (Lawrence: University Press of Kansas, 1992); Eugenia C. Kiesling, *Arming against Hitler: France and the Limits of Military Planning* (Lawrence: University Press of Kansas, 1996); David E. Johnson, *Fast Tanks and Heavy Bombers: Innovation in the U.S. Army, 1917–1945* (Ithaca, N.Y.: Cornell University Press, 1998); William O. Odom, *After the Trenches: The Transformation of U.S. Army Doctrine, 1918–1939* (College Station: Texas A&M University Press, 1999); and the seminal work by

Harold R. Winton, *To Change an Army: General Sir John Burnett-Stuart and British Armored Doctrine, 1927–1938* (Lawrence: University Press of Kansas, 1988).

3. The dominant book in the historiography on Seeckt is James S. Corum, *Roots of Blitzkrieg*. See also Citino, *Evolution of Blitzkrieg Tactics*, pp. 41–94, and *Path to Blitzkrieg*, especially pp. 7–69.

4. Hans von Seeckt, "Schlagworte," in *Gedanken eines Soldaten* (Leipzig: K. F. Koehler, 1935), pp. 7–18. There is a translated volume of an earlier edition. See "Catchwords," *Thoughts of a Soldier* (London: Ernest Benn, 1930), pp. 3–17. For pro and con reviews of Seeckt's book in the professional literature, see General Metzsch, "Gedanken eines Soldaten," *Militär-Wochenblatt* 113, no. 14 (October 11, 1928), pp. 525–527, and the anonymous "Das Gesicht des wirklichen Krieges," *Militär-Wochenblatt* 113, no. 21 (December 4, 1928), pp. 817–823, respectively.

5. Seeckt, "Schlagworte," p. 9.

6. Ibid., p. 15.

7. See J. F. C. Fuller, *The Reformation of War* (London: Hutchinson, 1923), especially pp. 152–169. See the discussion of Fuller's military thought in Robert M. Citino, *Armored Forces: History and Sourcebook* (Westport, Conn.: Greenwood, 1994), pp. 33–39, as well as the biographical sketch on pp. 233–235.

8. See Giulio Douhet, *The Command of the Air* (New York: Coward-McCann, 1942). See also Phillip S. Meilinger, "The Historiography of Airpower: Theory and Doctrine," *Journal of Military History* 64, no. 2. (April 2000), pp. 467–501.

9. The classic statement of the indirect approach is B. H. Liddell Hart, *The Decisive Wars of History* (London: G. Bell, 1929), later reprinted as *Strategy*, second revised edition (New York: Holt, 1967). See the discussion of Liddell Hart's military thought in Robert M. Citino, *Armored Forces: History and Sourcebook* (Westport, Conn.: Greenwood, 1994), pp. 39–43, as well as the biographical sketch on pp. 250–251.

10. For Hungarian maneuvers, see "Die grossen ungarischen Herbstmanöver," *Militär-Wochenblatt* 122, no. 24 (December 10, 1937), pp. 1503–1506, discussing field maneuvers of a "motorized brigade." For a report on the U.S. Army maneuvers of August 1940 in the Adirondacks, with a spotlight on operations of the 7th Mechanized Cavalry Brigade, see Colonel Rudolf Ritter von Xylander, "Die grossen Übungen der 1. amerikanischen Armee," *Militär-Wochenblatt* 124, no. 32 (February 2, 1940), pp. 1528–1531.

11. See Lieutenant General von der Leyen, "Friedrich Wilhelm I.—Scharnhorst—Seeckt: Vom Werk dreier Schöpfer des preussisch-deutschen Heeres," 2 parts, *Militär-Wochenblatt* 126, nos. 24–25 (December 12, 1941; December 19, 1941), pp. 661–664, 691–697. The quote is from p. 695.

12. Heinz-Ludger Borgert, "Grundzüge der Landkriegführung von Schlieffen bis Guderian," *Handbuch zur deutschen Militärgeschichte 1648–1939*, vol. 9: *Grundzüge der militärischen Kriegführung* (München: Bernard & Graefe, 1979), p. 543.

13. *Führung und Gefecht der verbundenen Waffen* (Berlin: Offene Worte, 1921), paragraph 10. For a comprehensive discussion of the manual, see Adolf Reinicke, *Das Reichsheer 1921–1934: Ziele, Methoden der Ausbildung und Erziehung sowie der Dienstgestaltung* (Osnabrück: Biblio Verlag, 1986), pp. 92–100.

14. The Romanian campaign attracted a great deal of attention at the time among

the interwar era German military professionals but has almost faded from the view of modern scholars. For the primary source, see General Erich von Falken-hayn, *Der Feldzug der 9, Armee gegen die Rumänen und Russen, 1916/17* (Berlin: E. S. Mittler, 1921). For an analysis of the campaign, including both Falkenhatyn's crossing of the Carpathians and Mackensen's drive across the Danube, see Jacob Lee Hamric, "Germany's Decisive Victory: Falkenhayn's Campaign in Romania, 1916," Masters Thesis, Eastern Michigan University, 2004.

15. See, for example, Lieutenant Colonel Lothar Rendulic, "Kann der Krise des Angriffes überwunden werden?" ("Can the Crisis of the Attack Be Overcome"), *Militär-Wochenblatt* 114, no. 36 (March 25, 1930), pp. 1401–1405, as well as the anon-ymous article in response, "Die Krise des Angriffs kann überwunden werden," *Militär-Wochenblatt* 114, no. 40 (April 25, 1930), pp. 1569–1570, which answers the question affirmatively: yes it can, with tanks.

16. For the meeting engagement, see *Führung und Gefecht der verbundenen Waffen*, 246, 255, 262; Borgert, "Grundzüge der Landkriegführung von Schlieffen bis Guderian," pp. 544–545; and Friedrich von Rabenau, *Seeckt: Aus seinem Leben, 1918–1936* (Leipzig: von Hase und Koehler Verlag, 1940), p. 511.

17. For more discussion on all these points, see Citino, *Path to Blitzkrieg*, p. 55.

18. Hans von Seeckt, "Moderne Heere," *Gedanken eines Soldaten*, p. 54. See also the comments in "Moderne Heere: Betrachtungen über die 'Gedanken eines Sol-daten' des Generalobersten von Seeckt," *Militär-Wochenblatt* 113, no. 31 (February 11, 1929), pp. 1193–1198.

19. Seeckt, "Moderne Heere," p. 56.

20. Hans von Seeckt, "Grundsätze moderner Landesverteidigung," *Gedanken eines Soldaten*, p. 77.

21. See Major General von Scriba, "Die Traditionen müssen der künftigen Preussischen Armee erhalten bleiben," *Militär-Wochenblatt* 103, no. 104 (March 1, 1919), pp. 1891–1894.

22. See Lieutenant Colonel Ponath, "Die Schlacht bei Tannenberg 1914 in kriegsge-schichtlicher, taktischer und erjieherischer Auswertung," *Militär-Wochenblatt* 124, no. 8 (August 18, 1939), pp. 476–482.

23. For a solid account of the 1921 Polish uprising, see Harald von Riekhoff, *German-Polish Relations, 1918–1933* (Baltimore, Md.: Johns Hopkins University Press, 1971), pp. 41–47.

24. The best scholarly analysis of the entire Upper Silesian problem is T. Hunt Tooley, *National Identity and Weimar Germany: Upper Silesia and the Eastern Bor-der, 1918–1922* (Lincoln: University of Nebraska Press, 1997). For the third Pol-ish uprising and the subsequent fighting, see Jacques Benoist-Mechin, *Histoire de L'Armée Allemande*, vol. 2 (Paris: Albin Michel, 1938), pp. 163–210.

25. For the role of the various *Freikorps* in Upper Silesia, see Robert G. L. Waite, *Vanguard of Nazism: The Free Corps Movement in Postwar Germany 1918–1923* (New York: Norton, 1952), pp. 227–232.

26. Benoist-Mechin, *Histoire de L'Armée Allemande*, p. 184.

27. See Manfred von Killinger, a Freikorps company commander in the fighting, *Kampf um Oberschlesien* (Leipzig: K. F. Koehler, 1934), p. 53.

28. Benoist-Mechin, *Histoire de L'Armée Allemande*, p. 195.

29. Ibid., p. 196.

30. Waite, *Vanguard of Nazism*, p. 230.

31. See *The Answers of Ernst von Salomon to the 131 Questions of the Allied Military Government "Fragebogen"* (London: Putnam, 1954), pp. 86–91. See, especially, Salomon's analysis of Freikorps motivation in Upper Silesia.

32. For the fall 1930 maneuvers, see Robert M. Citino, "The Weimar Roots of German Military Planning in the 1930s," B. J. C. McKercher and Roch Legault, eds., *Military Planning and the Origins of the Second World War in Europe* (Westport, Conn.: Praeger, 2001), pp. 59–87, especially pp. 63–69. For the primary sources, see "Die Grosse Rahmenübung 1930," *Militär-Wochenblatt* 115, no. 14 (October 11, 1930), pp. 513–520; General M. von Poseck, "Die Kavallerie im Manöver 1930," *Militär-Wochenblatt* 115, no. 21 (December 4, 1930), pp. 793–797; "Rückblick eines Infanterie-Nachrichtenoffiziers auf die grosse Rahmenübung 1930," *Militär-Wochenblatt* 115, no. 21 (December 4, 1930), pp. 797–801; and "Die Grosse Rahmenübung von der Truppe aus gesehen," *Militär-Wochenblatt* 115, no. 22 (December 11, 1930), pp. 844–846.

33. "Die Grosse Rahmenübung 1930," p. 516.

34. Ibid., p. 517.

35. Ibid., p. 518.

36. "Die Grosse Rahmenübung von der Truppe aus gesehen," p. 846.

37. For more of the intricate detail of the 1930 maneuvers, which amounted to nothing less than a full mobilization exercise, see Citino, *Path to Blitzkrieg*, pp. 190–195.

38. For Italian armor in the era, see the essential work, John J. T. Sweet, *Iron Arm: The Mechanization of Mussolini's Army, 1920–1940* (Westport, Conn.: Greenwood Press, 1980), as well as Enzio Rivus, "Die Tankwaffe Italiens," *Militär-Wochenblatt* 121, no. 4 (July 25, 1936), pp. 179–182. For the binary division, see Lieutenant Colonel Braun, "Motorisierte Gedankensplitter aus aller Welt," part 6, "Die neue italienische Inf.-Versuchsdivision 'Binaria,'" *Militär-Wochenblatt* 123, no. 21 (November 18, 1938), pp. 1345–1347. For a modern verdict, see Brian R. Sullivan, "Fascist Italy's Military Involvement in the Spanish Civil War," *Journal of Military History* 59, no. 4 (October 1995), p. 709: the divisions were "too weak against opponents better armed than the Ethiopians and—lacking a third infantry regiment, too inflexible in maneuver."

39. Fighting enemy tanks was the mission of a hybrid vehicle known as the "tank destroyer." See the still-standard work by Charles M. Baily, *Faint Praise: American Tanks and Tank Destroyers during World War II* (Hamden, Conn.: Archon, 1983). For a more recent demolition of the concept, see Roman Johann Jarymowycz, *Tank Tactics: From Normandy to Lorraine* (Boulder, Colo.: Lynne Rienner, 2001), p. 149: "There were forty-five tank destroyer battalions available to Bradley—a force equivalent to fifteen armored divisions except for the drawback of their being incapable of offensive operations." For a newer, more positive analysis of U.S. armored doctrine, see Dennis E. Showalter, "America's Armored Might," *World War II* (April 2005), pp. 50–56.

40. For the rise of the panzer division, see W. Heinemann, "The Development of German Armoured Forces 1918–1940," in *Armoured Warfare*, ed. J. P. Harris and F. H. Toase (London: B. T. Batsford Ltd., 1990). The works of Richard L. DiNardo are essential. See, for example, *Germany's Panzer Arm* (Westport, Conn.: Greenwood Press, 1997).

41. Richard M. Ogorkiewicz, *Armoured Warfare: A History of Armoured Forces and Their Vehicles* (New York: Arco, 1971), p. 73.

42. Citino, *Armored Forces*, p. 57.

43. "Das Gesicht des wirklichen Krieges," p. 821. See also Lieutenant General Ernst Kabisch, "Die grossen Manöver in Schlesien, 24./25. September 1928," *Militär-Wochenblatt* 113, no. 17 (November 4, 1928), pp. 651–656.

44. See the discussion in Citino, *Quest for Decisive Victory*, pp. 202–203.

45. Major Friedrich Bertkau, "Die nachrichtentechnische Führung mechanisierter Verbände," *Militär-Wochenblatt* 120, no. 15 (October 18), 1935, p. 612, as well as Colonel Fuppe, "Neuzeitliches Nachrichtenverbindungswesen als Führungsmittel im Kriege," *Militärwissenschaftliche Rundschau* 3, no. 6 (1938), pp. 750–758.

46. Heinz Guderian, "Die Panzertruppen und ihr Zusammenwirken mit den anderen Waffen," *Militärwissenschaftliche Rundschau* 1, no. 5 (1936), pp. 607–626, especially p. 621.

47. The word *blitzkrieg* had already been floating around for some time in the late 1930s. Sometimes credited to western, specifically American, correspondents writing about the dramatic German victories in the war's early years, it can actually be found here and there in pre-1939 professional literature of the prewar period. It signified any rapid and complete victory, and the Germans never did use it in any precise sense—yet another supposedly crucial German term used far more in the west than in Germany itself. For the earliest printed use of the term that I have found, see Lieutenant Colonel Braun, "Der strategische Überfall," *Militär-Wochenblatt* 123, no. 18 (October 28, 1938), pp. 1134–1136, although the sense is that the word has already been in use: "Nach dem Zeitungsnachrichten hatten die diesjährigen französischen Manöver den Zweck, die Bedeutung des strategischen Überfalls—auch 'Blitzkrieg' genannt—zu prüfen" (p. 1134). For later uses, see Lieutenant Colonel Köhn, "Die Infanterie im 'Blitzkrieg,'" *Militär-Wochenblatt* 125, no. 5 (August 2, 1940), pp. 165–166, where "Blitzkrieg" is used only in quotation marks and is described as a "catch-phrase" (*Schlagwort*), as well as Colonel Rudolf Theiss, "Der Panzer in der Weltgeschichte," *Militär-Wochenblatt* 125, no. 15 (October 11, 1940), pp. 705–708, which likewise uses the term in quotes. By 1941, German usage had dropped the quotes, although the word was still not used in any precise technical sense. See Lieutenant Colonel Gaul, "Der Blitzkrieg in Frankreich," *Militär-Wochenblatt* 125, no. 35 (February 28, 1941), pp. 1513–1517.

48. For Case White, begin with the belated "official history" commissioned by the Militärgeschichtliches Forschungsamt, *Das Deutsche Reich und Der Zweite Weltkrieg*, vol. 2, *Die Errichtung der hegemonie auf dem Europäischen Kontinent* (Stuttgart: Deutsche Verlags-Anstalt, 1979), especially "Hitler's Erster 'Blitzkrieg' und seine Auswirkungen auf Nordosteuropa," pp. 79–156. Labeling this "official history" is misleading—it is meticulously researched, scholarly, and extremely criti-

cal throughout. Robert M. Kennedy, *The German Campaign in Poland, 1939*, Department of the Army Pamphlet no. 20, p. 255 (Washington, D.C.: Department of the Army, 1956) continues to be useful, and so does Matthew Cooper, *The German Army, 1933–1945* (Chelsea, Mich.: Scarborough House, 1978), pp. 169–176. See a pair of articles written for the popular audience: Pat McTaggart, "Poland '39," *Command* 17 (July–August 1992), p. 57, and David T. Zabecki, "Invasion of Poland: Campaign That Launched a War," *World War II* 14, no. 3 (September 1999), pp. 26ff. See also the pertinent sections in the memoir literature: Heinz Guderian, *Panzer Leader*, pp. 46–63; Erich von Manstein, *Lost Victories* (Novato, Calif.: Presidio, 1982), pp. 22–63; and F. W. von Mellenthin, *Panzer Battles: A Study of the Employment of Armor in the Second World War* (New York: Ballantine, 1956), pp. 3–9. A good revisionist work, drawn from Polish sources, is Steven Zaloga and Victor Madej, *The Polish Campaign* (New York: Hippocrene, 1991). For a blow-by-blow account while it was happening, see "Deutschlands Abwehrkrieg von 1939," part 1, "Die Ereignisse im Osten vom 1. bis 9. September," *Militär-Wochenblatt* 124, no. 12 (September 15, 1939), pp. 729–733; part 2, "Die Ereignisse im Osten vom 9. September bis 16. September," *Militär-Wochenblatt* 124, no. 13 (September 22, 1939), pp. 769–774; and part 3, "Die Ereignisse in Polen vom 17. bis 24. September," *Militär-Wochenblatt* 124, no. 14 (October 1, 1939), pp. 809–813.

49. *Die Errichtung der hegemonie auf dem Europäischen Kontinent*, p. 95.

50. Among the veritable mountain of documents on this point, see, for example, "Ostseeverteidigung Pillau," *German Naval Archives*, University of Michigan Microfilming Project #2, reel 31, serial PG 34089, frames 539–559. See also the documentation in "Führerkriegsspiel Dezember 1927: Part III, Allgemeine Lage," reel 33, serial PG 34005, frames 728–729.

51. For the dispute over the German operational plan, see *Die Errichtung der hegemonie auf dem Europäischen Kontinent*, pp. 92–99, and Kennedy, *German Campaign in Poland*, pp. 58–63 and 73–77.

52. Kennedy, *German Campaign in Poland*, p. 62.

53. *Die Errichtung der hegemonie auf dem Europäischen Kontinent*, p. 96.

54. McTaggart, "Poland '39," p. 57.

55. Kennedy, *German Campaign in Poland*, p. 81.

56. Ibid., p. 83.

57. Zalog and Madej, *The Polish Campaign*, puts to rest the old tale of "cavalry charging tanks" once and for all on pp. 110–112. They describe a successful charge by the 18th Lancer Regiment and its commander, Colonel Kazimierz Mastelarz, against a weak German infantry position that later came to grief when several German armored cars happened on the scene, and they also note that Polish cavalry was well acquainted with the capabilities of tanks, since each cavalry brigade had an armored troop attached to it.

58. American correspondent William L. Shirer visited Westerplatte just days after the battle and was shocked at the accuracy of the *Stuka* dive-bombers, which managed several direct hits with five-hundred-pound bombs. *Berlin Diary* (New York: Knopf, 1941), pp. 215–216.

59. For the engagement at Mlawa, replete with extremely detailed maps, see

Major Wim Brandt, "Eine motorisierte Aufklärungsabteilung im Polenfeldzug," part 1, "Mlawa-Przasnysz,-Ciechanow," *Militär-Wochenblatt* 124, no. 25 (December 15, 1939), pp. 1252–1256. Brandt was the commander of the motorized reconnaissance detachment in question.

60. Brandt, "Eine motorisierte Aufklärungsabteilung im Polenfeldzug," p. 1253.

61. *Die Errichtung der hegemonie auf dem Europäischen Kontinent*, p. 117.

62. For the battle of the Bzura, see Zaloga and Madej, *The Polish Campaign*, 131–138. For German primary sources, see Johann Adolf Graf Kielmansegg, *Panzer zwischen Warschau und Atlantik* (Berlin: Verlag "Die Wehrmacht": 1941), especially pp. 60–71 ("Die Schlacht an der Bzura"), as well as Christian Kinder, *Männer der Nordmark an der Bzura* (Berlin: E. S. Mittler, 1940), the former by the chief of staff to one of the 10th Army's panzer divisions and later divisional commander in the postwar *Bundeswehr*, the latter by a captain and company commander of the infantry divisions hit hard in the fight.

63. See James Lucas, *Battle Group! German Kampfgruppen Action of World War Two* (London: Arms and Armour, 1993), pp. 10–24, which focuses on the operations of 4th Panzer Division in Warsaw and on the Bzura.

64. See, for example, Rolf Bathe, *Der Feldzug der 18 Tage: die Chronik des polnischen Dramas* (Oldenburg: Gerhard Stalling, 1939). Zaloga and Madej, *The Polish Campaign*, p. 158, address the "myth of the 'eighteen-day war,'" pointing out that Army Group South "lost more men killed in the final half of the war than in the first two weeks."

65. Zaloga and Madej, *The Polish Campaign*, p. 156. *Die Errichtung der hegemonie auf dem Europäischen Kontinent*, p. 133, gives a figure of one million Polish prisoners: seven hundred thousand to Germany and three hundred thousand to the Soviet Union.

66. For the role of the Luftwaffe in the Polish campaign, see James S. Corum, *The Luftwaffe: Creating the Operational Air War, 1918–1940* (Lawrence: University Press of Kansas, 1997), pp. 272–275. For a detailed operational account of the fighting around Modlin, see Major Wim Brandt, "Bilder aus der Belagerung von Modlin," *Militär-Wochenblatt* 124, no. 30 (January 19, 1940), pp. 1451–1454.

67. See, for example, General Georg Wetzell, "Einst und Jetzt," *Militär-Wochenblatt* 124, no. 14 (October 1, 1939), pp. 813–817.

68. Ibid., p. 815.

69. Ibid.

70. "Das Gesicht des wirklichen Krieges," p. 817.

71. Wetzell, "Einst und Jetzt," p. 815.

72. For German views of the Romanian campaign, see "Truppen-Kriegsgeschichte, Beispiel 9: Turnu Severin 1916," 2 parts, *Militär-Wochenblatt* 123, no. 17–18 (October 21, 1938; October 28, 1938), pp. 1078–1081, 1146–1150, and Lieutenant Colonel Ponath, "Feuerüberfalle gegen lohnende Augenblicksziele: Kämpfe der Abteilung Picht (verst. I./I.R. 148) vom 20.11. bis 6.12. 1916 bei Turnu-Severin und am Alt in der Schlacht in Rumänien," *Militär-Wochenblatt* 112, no. 35 (March 18, 1928), pp. 1344–1346, and by the same author, "Aus grosser Zeit vor zwanzig Jahren: Der Einbruch in die rumänische Ebene," *Militär-Wochenblatt* 121, no. 21 (December 4, 1936), pp. 1101–1103.

73. For an argument that places the alleged German "revolution in military affairs" in its rightful—narrowly circumscribed—place, see the typically hard-nosed article by Williamson Murray, "May 1940: Contingency and Fragility of the German RMA," in *The Dynamics of Military Revolution, 1300–2050*, ed. MacGregor Knox and Williamson Murray (Cambridge: Cambridge University Press, 2001), pp. 154–174, in which he scores the "naïve technological determinists whose views have shaped the debates at the turn of the twenty-first century" (p. 156).

74. Lieutenant General Marx, "Der Sprung vom Wissen zum Können," *Militär-Wochenblatt* 124, no. 15 (October 6, 1939), p. 853.

75. Colonel Theiss, "Kriegserfahrung," *Militär-Wochenblatt* 125, no. 6 (August 9, 1940), pp. 205–207.

76. A point made by Dennis E. Showalter, "Military Innovation and the Whig Perspective of History," in *The Challenge of Change: Military Institutions and New Realities, 1918–1941*, ed. Harold R. Winton and David R. Mets (Lincoln: University of Nebraska Press, 2000), p. 229.

8. The Culmination Point

1. See Ronald Lewin, *Hitler's Mistakes: New Insights into What Made Hitler Tick* (New York: Morrow, 1984), which ranges more widely than the war into areas of politics and economy.

2. See Kenneth Macksey, *Why the Germans Lose at War: The Myth of German Military Superiority* (London: Greenhill, 1996).

3. For the definitive statement on how Germany could have won the war in the east, see Russel H. S. Stolfi, *Hitler's Panzers East: World War II Reinterpreted* (Norman: University of Oklahoma Press, 1992).

4. For the same point regarding French military preparations for World War II—another subject over which historians tend to lecture the historical actors—see Eugenia C. Kiesling, *Arming against Hitler: France and the Limits of Military Planning* (Lawrence: University Press of Kansas, 1996), pp. xii–xiii.

5. For a detailed critique of Case Blue, the drive on Stalingrad, see Robert M. Citino, *Blitzkrieg to Desert Storm: The Evolution of Operational Warfare* (Lawrence: University Press of Kansas, 2004), pp. 85–93.

6. Kursk has been the subject of intense scholarly scrutiny of late, a welcome change from all those years when western historians virtually ignored it. See the definitive study by David M. Glantz and Jonathan M. House, *The Battle of Kursk* (Lawrence: University Press of Kansas, 1999), who call Kursk "a turning point in the war strategically, operationally, and tactically" (p. 280), as well as David M. Glantz and Harold S. Orenstein, eds., *The Battle for Kursk 1943: The Soviet General Staff Study* (London: Frank Cass, 1999). Finally, see the indispensable collection of scholarly articles edited by Roland G. Foerster, *Gezeitenwechsel im Zweiten Weltkrieg? Die Schlachten von Char'kov und Kursk im Frühjahr und Sommer 1943 in operativer Anlage, Verlauf und politischer Bedeutung* (Berlin: E. S. Mittler, 1996), vol. 14 of the *Militärgeschichtliches Forschungsamt* series *Vorträge zur Militärgeschichte*.

The papers, delivered at a 1993 symposium in Ingolstadt, range far and wide over the battle, its origins, and its effects, but special mention goes to the contributions by Glantz, "Prelude to Kursk: Soviet Strategic Operations, February–March 1943" (pp. 29–56); Karl-Heinz Frieser's comparative analysis of the battles of Kharkov and Kursk, "Schlagen aus der Nachhand—Schlagen aus der Vorhand: Die Schlachten von Char'kov und Kursk 1943," pp. 101–135; Johann Adolf Graf von Kielmansegg, "Bemerkungen eines Zeitzeugen zu den Schlachten von Char'kov und Kursk aus der Sicht des damaligen Generalstabsoffiziers Ia in der Operationsabteilung des Generalstabs des Heeres," pp. 137–148, from an officer in the Operations Section of the German General Staff, and Gerhard L. Weinberg, "Zur Frage eines Sonderfriedens im Osten" (pp. 173–183).

7. See Mark J. Reardon, *Victory at Mortain: Stopping Hitler's Panzer Counteroffensive* (Lawrence: University Press of Kansas, 2002) and Alwyn Featherston, *Saving the Breakout: The 30th Division's Heroic Stand at Mortain, August 7–12, 1944* (Novato, Calif.: Presidio, 1993).

8. See, for example, David M. Glantz, and Jonathan M. House, *When Titans Clashed: How the Red Army Stopped Hitler* (Lawrence: University Press of Kansas, 1995), p. 284.

9. For an analysis of just how incompetent the Germans were at coalition warfare, see Richard L. DiNardo, *Germany and the Axis Powers: From Coalition to Collapse* (Lawrence: University Press of Kansas, 2005).

10. For *Weserübung*, see Adam R. A. Claasen, *Hitler's Northern War: The Luftwaffe's Ill-Fated Campaign, 1940–1945* (Lawrence: University Press of Kansas, 2001), a definitive portrait of German combined operations in the north, ranging far beyond Luftwaffe activity to include land and naval combat, not to mention the interplay of all three arms. Another important work by a contemporary scholar is James S. Corum, "The German Campaign in Norway as a Joint Operation," *Journal of Strategic Studies* 21, no. 4 (December 1998), pp. 50–77, which not only looks carefully at the successes of German interservice cooperation in the campaign, but also Allied failures in the same area. For a new edition of a venerable primary source, see Erich Raeder's memoir, *Grand Admiral* (New York: Da Capo Press, 2001), especially pp. 300–318. Finally, see Chris Smith, "Strike North: Germany Invades Scandinavia, 1940," *Command* 39 (September 1996), pp. 18–27, for sound analysis and the trademark of this now defunct military history/war-game magazine, excellent maps.

11. For a fine operational summary of the Danish campaign, see Major Macher, "Die Besetzung Dänemarks," *Militär-Wochenblatt* 125, no. 45 (May 9, 1941), pp. 1791–1793, written on the occasion of the campaign's first anniversary.

12. See Claasen, *Hitler's Northern War*, pp. 62–65.

13. Macher, "Die Besetzung Dänemarks," p. 1793.

14. Still useful for the initial German landings and the Norwegian response to them, see two articles in the *History of the Second World War* series: J. L. Moulton, "Hitler Strikes North," no. 3, pp. 68–74, and Leif Bohn, "The Norwegian View," pp. 77–78.

15. For the German naval order of battle, see Tom Dworschak, "Operation

Weser Exercise: The German Navy in Norway, 1940," *Command* 39 (September 1996), pp. 28–33.

16. For the campaigns in Yugoslavia and Greece, see Alex Buchner, *Der deutsche Griechenland-Feldzug: Operationen der 12. Armee 1941* (Heidelberg: Kurt Vowinckel, 1957), part of the still very useful *Die Wehrmacht im Kampf* series, vol. 14. See also *The German Campaigns in the Balkans* (spring 1941), part of the *German Report Series* (Washington, D.C.: Department of the Army, 1953). For the *German Report Series* and its impact on the postwar U.S. Army, see Kevin Soutor, "To Stem the Red Tide: The German Report Series and Its Effect on American Defense Doctrine, 1948–1954," *Journal of Military History* 57, no. 4 (October 1993), pp. 653–688.

17. For Operation Mercury, see Robert M. Citino, *Blitzkrieg to Desert Storm: The Evolution of Operational Warfare* (Lawrence: University Press of Kansas, 2004), pp. 42–49.

18. The phrase is Dennis E. Showalter's, *The Wars of Frederick the Great* (London: Longman, 1996), p. 145n11. See also the discussion on pp. 144–145, where he speaks of "systematic policies of hostage-taking and *dragonnades.*"

19. For details on the Wehrmacht's crimes in Poland, see Alexander B. Rossino, *Hitler Strikes Poland: Blitzkrieg, Ideology, and Atrocity* (Lawrence: University Press of Kansas, 2003). For France, see Julien Fargettas, "Les Massacres de Mai–Juin 1940," in Christine Levisse-Touzé, *La Campagne de 1940: Actes du colloque, 16 au 18 Novembre 2000* (Paris: Tallandier, 2001), pp. 448–464.

20. Manfred Messerschmidt, "Das Bild der Wehrmacht in Deutschland seit 1945," *Revue d'Allemagne* 30, no. 2 (April–June 1998), pp. 117–125.

21. Colonel Rudolf Theiss, "Der Panzer in der Weltgeschichte," *Militär-Wochenblatt* 125, no. 15 (October 11, 1940), p. 706.

22. See the seminal article by Hans-Adolf Jacobsen, "Hitlers Gedanken zur Kriegführung im Westen," *Wehrwissenschaftliche Rundschau* 5, no. 10 (October 1955), pp. 433–446. All subsequent work on the topic has been a commentary on this article, including the author's own *Fall Gelb: der Kampf um den deutschen Operationsplan zur Westoffensive 1940* (Wiesbaden: F. Steiner, 1957).

23. Jacobsen, "Hitlers Gedanken zur Kriegführung im Western," p. 433.

24. For a discussion of the Mechelen incident, including detailed analysis of the actual documents taken by the Belgians, see Jean Vanwelkenhuyzen, "Die Krise vom Januar 1940," *Wehrwissenschaftliche Rundschau* 5, no. 2 (February 1955), pp. 66–90.

25. The crucial primary source in English is B. H. Liddell Hart, *The German Generals Talk* (New York: Quill, 1979). See p. 109 for the Brauchitsch quote. At first accepted uncritically by historians, then later scored by them, the book can still be used with profit by those who are careful to understand its origin. The result of interviews that he conducted with German staff officers just after the war (published originally as *The Other Side of the Hill* in 1948), it arose out of several diverse elements: factual and apparently objective judgments in many cases, a huge amount of special pleading by the German officers (heaping all blame for every mistake onto Hitler's shoulders), and a relationship between the author and his subjects laden with subtext—they eager to find a friend in the western camp, he eager to establish himself as the "father of blitzkrieg."

26. For discussion of the planning documents, see the primary source by General Erich von Manstein, *Lost Victories* (Novato, Calif.: Presidio, 1982), pp. 97–98. See also Jacobsen, "Hitlers Gedanken zur Kriegführung im Western," p. 438.

27. Manstein, *Lost Victories*, p. 98.

28. Ibid., p. 99.

29. Quoted in Florian K. Rothbrust, *Guderian's XIXth Panzer Corps and the Battle of France: Breakthrough in the Ardennes, May 1940* (Westport, Conn.: Praeger, 1990), p. 94.

30. Manstein, *Lost Victories*, pp. 120–121; see also Jacobsen, "Hitlers Gedanken zur Kriegführung im Western," pp. 442–443.

31. See Kershaw's biography, *Hitler*, 2 vols. (New York: Norton, 1998–2000), especially vol. 1, *1889–1936: Hubris*, pp. 527–589. The quote is from p. 530. For reviews of the book, discussing the concept of "working towards the Führer," see Jeffrey Hart, "The Hitler Problem," *National Review* 53, no. 1 (January 2001), pp. 47–49, and Omer Bartov, "A Man without Qualities," *New Republic* 224, no. 11 (March 12, 2001), pp. 34–40.

32. For the German offensive in the west, see *Das Deutsche Reich und der Zweite Weltkrieg*, vol. 2, *Die Errichtung der Hegemonie auf dem Europäischen Kontinent* (Stuttgart: Deutsche Verlags-Anstalt, 1979), especially the portions written by Hans Umbreit, "Der Kampf um die Vormachtstellung in Westeuropa," pp. 233–327. The standard works in English are Jeffrey A. Gunsburg, *Divided and Conquered: The French High Command and the Defeat in the West, 1940* (Westport, Conn.: Greenwood, Press, 1979), and Robert A. Doughty, *The Breaking Point: Sedan and the Fall of France, 1940* (Hamden, Conn.: Archon, 1990). For the role of Guderian's panzers in the campaign, see Florian K. Rothbrust, *Guderian's XIXth Panzer Corps and the Battle of France*.

33. *Die Errichtung der Hegemonie auf dem Europäischen Kontinent*, p. 254.

34. Rothbrust, *Guderian's XIXth Panzer Corps and the Battle of France*, p. 29.

35. For these "Sonderunternehmen," see *Die Errichtung der Hegemonie auf dem Europäischen Kontinent*, pp. 259–260.

36. For the campaign in the Netherlands, including detailed orders of battle for the Dutch army, see David Meyler, "Missed Opportunities: The Ground War in Holland," *Command*, no. 42 (March 1997), pp. 58–69.

37. For Eben Emael, James E. Mrazek, *The Fall of Eben Emael* (Novato, Calif.: Presidio, 1970), has long held pride of place: a popular work, yet well grounded in the sources, including interviews with General Kurt Student and Colonel Rudolf Witzig. See also Stephen B. Patrick, "Paratroop: A History of Airborne Operations," *Strategy and Tactics*, no. 77 (December 1979), pp. 4–13.

38. See Mrazek, *Fall of Eben Emael*, p. 56, for a diagram of the *Hohlladung*.

39. Jeffrey A. Gunsburg, "The Battle of the Belgian Plain, 12–14 May 1940: The First Great Tank Battle," *Journal of Military History* 56, no. 2 (April 1992), pp. 207–244. See especially pp. 222–223. See also Colonel Gérard Saint-Martin, "Le Corps de Cavalerie en Belgique du 10 au 14 Mai 1940," in Levisse-Touzé, *La Campagne de 1940*, pp. 168–176, including the extremely useful map on p. 176.

40. For the Dyle Plan, see Gunsburg, *Divided and Conquered*, pp. 119–146 and

265–292, which argues that the plan was potentially a "strategy for victory," but that it also "carried the risk of degenerating into an encounter battle in which the enemy, operating under unified command from nearby bases with air superiority, would have the advantage" (p. 270), a sound judgment. See also Doughty, *Breaking Point*, pp. 12–14. For a useful recent sampling of French scholarly and military opinion, see Levisse-Touzé, *La Campagne de 1940*. Especially thought provoking are the contributions by General Bruno Chaix, "Les plans opérationnels de 1940: Aller ou non en Belgique?" pp. 52–62, which argues that the Dyle Plan was flawed in conception and execution, but that it was the least of the Allied problems, and that "erreurs stratégiques ne sont probablement que d'un poids limité comparées aux erreurs tactiques commises et aux surprises tactiques subies par les Alliés sur le canal Albert et sur la Meuse" (p. 61); Jean Vanwelkenhuyzen, "Le Rôle de l'Armée Belge," pp. 63–83; General Jean Delmas, "La manoeuvre générale: surprise allemande, défense française," pp. 117–125; and Olivier Forcade, on the thorny problem of Allied intelligence during the campaign, "Le Renseignement face à l'Allemagne au printemps 1940 et au début de la campagne de France," pp. 126–155, including maps from French military intelligence.

41. For the Breda variant, see Doughty, *Breaking Point*, pp. 14–17; Gunsburg, *Divided and Conquered*, pp. 138–139, 270–271, which argues that it "siphoned off almost all of the mobile reserves" (p. 138) and "strained the limits of French doctrine" (p. 270); and Chaix, "Les plans opérationnels de 1940," who agrees that "l'envoi de la 7ᵉ armée en Hollande prive aussi le front de Meuse de reserves à bonne portée" (p. 61).

42. Doughty, *Breaking Point*, p. 102.

43. For the "reconnaissance in force," see the primary source, Heinz Guderian, *Panzer Leader* (New York: Ballantine, 1957), pp. 87–88.

44. "Grossdeutschlands Freiheitskrieg 1940," part 41, "Die deutsche Maioffensive auf der Westfront in den Tagen vom 10. bis 17. Mai 1940," *Militär-Wochenblatt* 124, no. 47 (May 24, 1940), p. 2122.

45. Ibid., p. 2125.

46. "Grossdeutschlands Freiheitskrieg 1940," part 42, "Die deutsche Maioffensive in den tagen vom 17. bis 23. Mai 1940," *Militär-Wochenblatt* 124, no. 48 (May 31, 1940), p. 2164.

47. Ibid., p. 2166.

48. Ibid., p. 2169.

49. "Grossdeutschlands Freiheitskrieg 1940," part 43, "Die Kapitulation der belgischen Armee und die Vernichtung der englischen und französischen Armeen in Flandern und im Artois in den tagen vom 24. Mai bis 1. Juni 1940," *Militär-Wochenblatt* 124, no. 49 (June 7, 1940), p. 2201.

50. Ibid., p. 2202.

51. Ibid., p. 2203, 2205.

52. Ibid., p. 2207.

53. "Grossdeutschlands Freiheitskrieg 1940," part 44, "Der Abschluss der Vernichtungsschlacht in Flandern und im Artois sowie der Beginn der neuen deutschen Offensive über die Somme und den Oise-Aisne Kanal in der Woche vom 2. bis 8.6.1940," *Militär-Wochenblatt* 124, no. 50 (June 7, 1940), p. 2245.

54. Ibid., pp. 2245, 2246.

55. Ibid., pp. 2246, 2247.

56. Ibid., p. 2247.

57. Ibid., p. 2246.

58. Werner Freiherr von Rheinbaben, "Einem neuen 'Waterloo' entgegen," *Militär-Wochenblatt* 125, no. 39 (March 28, 1941), pp. 1630–1631.

59. Lieutenant Colonel Dr. Guse, "Ein modernes Austerlitz," *Militär-Wochenblatt* 125, no. 20 (November 15, 1940), pp. 947–949.

60. Rittmeister F. Kronberger, "Es gibt Fälle, wo das höchste Wagen die höchste Weisheit ist," *Militär-Wochenblatt* 125, no. 7 (August 16, 1940), pp. 249–251.

61. Theiss, "Der Panzer in der Weltgeschichte, p. 707.

62. For more of this "literature of exultation," see the numerous works intended for the popular audience and produced by the Wehrmacht itself in the immediate wake of its victorious campaigns. For example, *Sieg über Frankreich: Berichte und Bilder* (Berlin: Wilhelm Andermann, 1940), issued by the *Oberkommando der Wehrmacht* (OKW), featured a collection of short "you are there" vignettes of the fighting, such as "Eine Kompanie Infanterie" (pp. 33–36), "Kampftage einer Flak-batterie" (pp. 47–49), "Die Schlacht im Raume von Sedan" (pp. 67–70), and "Wie Gent durch Handstreich fiel" (pp. 78–80), plus a large selection of photographs. See also Willy Beer, Fritz Dettmann, Karl Erck, Georg Engelbert Graf, General Ernst Kabisch, Peter Stronn, Kapitän Widemann, and Hans Zielinski, *Unser Kampf in Frankreich* (Munich: F. Bruckmann, 1941), the companion to two earlier works, *Unser Kampf in Polen: Die Vorgeschichte—Strategische Einführung—Politische und kriegerische Dokumente* (Munich: F. Bruckmann, 1940); and Dr. H. H. Ambrosius, Kriegsberichter Fritz Dettmann, Darl Erck, Georg Engelbert Graf, and Rear Admiral Lützow, *Unser Kampf in Norwegen* (Munich: F. Bruckmann, 1940). Other worthy examples include Hugo Amstark, *Panzerjäger in Frankreich* (Vienna: Deutscher Verlag für Jugend und Volk, 1941); Gerhard Starcke, *"Die roten Teufel sind die Hölle": Kriegstagebuchblätter vom Westfeldzug 1940* (Berlin: Buchergilde Gutenberg, 1941); Heinrich Müller, *Division Sintzenich: Erlebnisberichte aus dem Feldzuge in Frankreich 1940* (Frankfurt am Main: Hans Schäefer, 1943), and Walter Best, *Mit der Leibstandarte im Westen* (München: Zentralverlag der NSDAP, 1944). All of this literature displays similar characteristics: a personalist, heroic tone, a very light dose of operational detail (sometimes omitting the name of particular divisions or corps, for example), and a swaggering sense of German military superiority. There is no other body of war literature quite like it, save perhaps French memoirs from the Napoleonic period. The contribution by Best is particularly interesting, an encomium to "eine der jüngsten Waffen der deutschen Wehrmacht," the propaganda company, where writers "neben ihren Kameraden der Presse, des Films, und des Funks gleichfalls als Soldaten zum unmittelbaren Einsatz im Kampf kamen" (p. 7).

63. With regards to the historiography of Operation Barbarossa, we are now living in the "Glantz era." As once-closed Soviet archives began to open in the 1990s, historians were able to draw a much more detailed portrait of the Red Army than was heretofore possible. The point man in this development was David M.

Glantz, the leading western authority on the Soviet military. For the buildup to Barbarossa, see David M. Glantz, *Stumbling Colossus: The Red Army on the Eve of World War II* (Lawrence: University Press of Kansas, 1998); for the Russo-German war itself, see David M. Glantz and Jonathan House, *When Titans Clash: How the Red Army Stopped Hitler* (Lawrence: University Press of Kansas, 1995), a welcome change from traditional analysis that saw Barbarossa strictly in terms of how the Wehrmacht lost it; and more recently, he and House have penned the definitive history of the war's greatest tank battle, *The Battle of Kursk*. Other scholars whose investigation of the Russian sources has born fruit include Richard W. Harrison, *The Russian Way of War: Operational Art, 1904–1940* (Lawrence: University Press of Kansas, 2001), and Carl van Dyke, *The Soviet Invasion of Finland* (London: Frank Cass, 1997). Another recent and influential work placing Soviet operational art at the center of twentieth-century military history is Shimon Naveh, *In Pursuit of Military Excellence: The Evolution of Operational Theory* (London: Frank Cass, 1997), a difficult work steeped in the murky depths of systems logic. Still worthy among the older works is Alan Clark, *Barbarossa: The Russian-German Conflict, 1941–1945* (New York: Quill, 1985). Although previous works had tended to lay all the blame for the disaster that befell the Wehrmacht in 1941 on Hitler, a view encouraged by the surviving German generals and best expressed in Liddell Hart's *The German Generals Talk*, Clark argued persuasively that the German field commanders and General Staff shared a great deal of the responsibility. The culmination point of that thesis is Geoffrey P. Megargee, *Inside Hitler's High Command* (Lawrence: University Press of Kansas, 2000), a passionate and convincing demolition of the notion of an infallible German General Staff.

64. *Russian Combat Methods in World War II* (Washington, D.C.: Department of the Army, 1950); *German Defense Tactics against Russian Breakthroughs* (Washington, D.C.: Department of the Army, 1951); *Operations of Encircled Forces: German Experiences in Russia* (Washington, D.C.: Department of the Army, 1952). See also *Military Improvisations during the Russian Campaign* (Washington, D.C.: Department of the Army, 1951).

65. The original editions in English are Heinz Guderian, *Panzer Leader* (London: M. Joseph, 1952); Erich von Manstein, *Lost Victories* (Chicago: H. Regnery, 1958); F. W. von Mellenthin, *Panzer Battles: A Study of the Employment of Armor in the Second World War* (New York: Ballantine, 1956).

66. See, for example, Erhard Raus, *Panzer Operations: The Eastern Front Memoir of Erhard Raus, 1941–1945* (New York: Da Capo, 2003), compiled and translated by Stephen H. Newton. Although Raus was one of wartime Germany's most proficient panzer commanders, he had been almost unknown until recently. He began Operation Barbarossa leading the 6th Panzer Division's Motorized Brigade, got the division in September, rose to corps and then army command, and took part in virtually every major operation in the East from the heady drive on Leningrad to the hopeless defense of Pomerania. He wound up the war in American captivity where, along with several fellow officers, he helped to write the pamphlets in the Department of the Army's *German Reports* series. More recently, Peter G. Tsouras edited a volume dedicated solely to Raus's writings, *Panzers on the Eastern Front: General*

Erhard Raus and His Panzer Divisions in Russia, 1941–1945 (London: Greenhill, 2002). Interest in Raus has never been higher than it is today, proving that even sixty years later we are still "discovering" new things about the greatest of wars.

67. See Geoffrey P. Megargee, *War of Annihilation: Combat and Genocide on the Eastern Front, 1941* (Lanham, Md.: Rowman & Littlefield, 2005), p. vi.

68. A milestone was the 1983 appearance of the Barbarossa volume of the German official history. See *Das Deutsche Reich und der Zweite Weltkrieg*, vol. 4, *Der Angriff auf die Sowjetunion* (Stuttgart: Deutsche Verlags-Anstalt, 1983), especially the sections authored by Jürgen Förster, "Das Unternhemen 'Barbarossa' als Eroberungs- und Vernichtungskrieg" (pp. 413–447); Ernst Klink, "Die Operationsführung: Heer und Kriegsmarine" (pp. 451–652); and Horst Boog, "Die Operationsführung: Die Luftwaffe" (pp. 652–712).

69. *Der Angriff auf die Sowjetunion*, p. 413.

70. Ibid., p. 414.

71. *The German Campaign in Russia: Planning and Operations, 1940–1942* (Washington, D.C.: Department of the Army, 1955), p. 22, another in the *German Reports* series, contains the complete text of Führer Directive number 21.

72. For the drive of LVI Panzer Corps, see Manstein, *Lost Victories*, pp. 175–188.

73. For these still little-known battles in front of Smolensk and their impact, see Glantz and House, *When Titans Clashed*, pp. 58–61.

74. Glantz and House, *When Titans Clashed*, pp. 75–78. For a vivid account of Kiev, see also Alexander Werth, *Russia at War* (New York: Carroll and Graf, 1992), pp. 202–212.

75. Raus, *Panzer Operations*, pp. 26–33.

76. Glantz and House, *When Titans Clashed*, p. 68.

77. Raus, *Panzer Operations*, p. 46.

78. The OKH diary itself referred to Typhoon as "utterly classical" ("geradezu klassisch"). See *Der Angriff auf die Sowjetunion*, p. 577.

79. The characterization is that of General Günther Blumentritt, chief of staff of German 4th Army. Liddell Hart, *German Generals Talk*, p. 184.

80. See the lucid discussion of Typhoon's operational shortcomings in *Der Angriff auf die Sowjetunion*, pp. 575–579.

81. General Blumentritt mentions both units. Liddell Hart, *German Generals Talk*, pp. 186, 187.

82. Something Guderian himself admits. *Panzer Leader*, pp. 194–195.

83. The reference is to the memoirs of Napoleon's personal aide during the Russian campaign: Armand Augustin Louis de Caulaincourt, *With Napoleon in Russia: The Memoirs of General de Caulaincourt, duke of Vicenza* (New York: Grosset & Dunlap, 1935).

84. Liddell Hart, *German Generals Talk*, p. 185.

85. For expert narration and analysis of the Moscow counteroffensive—no mean feat, considering its sprawling nature—see Glantz and House, *When Titans Clashed*, pp. 87–97.

86. For the *Haltbefehl* and its later military-political consequences, see *Der Angriff auf die Sowjetunion*, pp. 605–619.

87. Liddell Hart, *German Generals Talk*, p. 189.

88. Guderian, *Panzer Leader*, pp. 209–210, and *Der Angriff auf die Sowjetunion*, pp. 617–618, are in substantial agreement on the details.

89. *Der Angriff auf die Sowjetunion*, p. 619.

90. Ibid., p. 618.

91. There has been a flood of work of late on intelligence and counterintelligence in the war. See, for example, Jim deBrosse and Colin Burke, *The Secret in Building 26: The Untold Story of America's Ultra War against the U-Boat Enigma Codes* (New York: Random House, 2004); Wladyslaw Kozaczuk and Jerzy Straszak, *Enigma: How the Poles Broke the Nazi Code* (New York: Hippocrene, 2004); Thaddeus Holt, *The Deceivers: Allied Military Deception in the Second World War* (New York: Simon and Schuster, 2004); and Michael Dobbs, *Saboteurs: The Nazi Raid on America* (New York: Knopf, 2004), the last throwing a harsh light on the amateurish nature of German efforts in the area of espionage.

92. A comparison between economic planning in the United States and Germany's primitive effort is instructive. On the former, see Paul A. C. Koistinen, *Arsenal of World War II: The Political Economy of American Warfare, 1940–1945* (Lawrence: University Press of Kansas, 2004).

93. "Grossdeutschlands Freiheitskrieg," part 124, "Der Stellungskrieg im Osten," *Militär-Wochenblatt* 126, no. 26 (December 26, 1941), p. 715.

9. Conclusion

1. Rittmeister F. Kronberger, "Es gibt Fälle, wo das höchste Wagen die höchste Weisheit ist," *Militär-Wochenblatt* 125, no. 7 (August 16, 1940), pp. 249–251.

2. Rudolf Thiel, *Preussische Soldaten* (Berlin: Paul Neff, 1940), pp. 89–91.

3. See, for example, Major Bigge, "Ueber Selbstthätigkeit der Unterführer im Kriege," *Beihefte zum Militär-Wochenblatt 1894* (Berlin: E. S. Mittler, 1894), pp. 17–55, from the text of a lecture given to the Military Society in Berlin on November 29, 1893. See also General von Blume, "Selbstthätigkeit der Führer im Kriege," *Beihefte zum Militär-Wochenblatt 1896* (Berlin: E. S. Mittler, 1896), pp. 479–534.

4. Bigge, "Ueber Selbstthätigkeit der Unterführer im Kriege," pp. 17–18.

5. See Jean Edward Smith, ed., *The Papers of Lucius D. Clay*, vol. 1, *Germany 1945–1949* (Bloomington: Indiana University Press, 1974), p. 103.

6. See the article by T. C. W. Blanning, "The Death and Transfiguration of Prussia," *Historical Journal* 29, no. 2 (June 1986), pp. 433–459, for a discussion of the revival of interest in Prussia within the Federal Republic in the early 1980s, manifested in a huge outpouring of new Prusso-centric books that became known as the *Preussenwelle* (Prussian wave). It was a phenomenon not without its critics. See, for example, the ever-contrary Hans-Ulrich Wehler, *Preussen ist wieder chic . . . Politik und Polemic in zwanzig Essays* (Frankurt am Main: Suhrkamp, 1983).

Bibliography: Works Cited

"Das Generalstabswerk über den siebenjährigen Krieg." *Militär-Wochenblatt* 95, no. 87, July 16, 1910.

"Das Gesicht des wirklichen Krieges." *Militär-Wochenblatt* 113, no. 21, December 4, 1928.

"Das Verdienst der Armee um Moltke." *Militär-Wochenblatt* 76, no. 108, December 12, 1891.

"Der Herbstfeldzug 1813." Parts 1–3. *Militär-Wochenblatt* 90, nos. 5–7, January 12, 1905, January 14, 1905, January 17, 1905.

"Der Kampf um St. Privat." *Militär-Wochenblatt* 84, no. 1, January 4, 1899.

"Der Zusammenhang der Husaren der heutigen Armee mit denen der Armee Friedrichs des Grossen." *Militär-Wochenblatt* 76, no. 67, August 1, 1891.

"Deutschlands Abwehrkrieg von 1939." Part 1. "Die Ereignisse im Osten vom 1. bis 9. September." *Militär-Wochenblatt* 124, no. 12, September 15, 1939.

"Deutschlands Abwehrkrieg von 1939." Part 2. "Die Ereignisse im Osten vom 9. September bis 16. September." *Militär-Wochenblatt* 124, no. 13, September 22, 1939.

"Deutschlands Abwehrkrieg von 1939." Part 3. "Die Ereignisse in Polen vom 17. bis 24. September." *Militär-Wochenblatt* 124, no. 14, October 1, 1939.

"Die Festung in den Kriegen Napoleons und der Neuzeit." *Militär-Wochenblatt* 90, no. 23, February 23, 1905.

"Die Grosse Rahmenübung 1930." *Militär-Wochenblatt* 115, no. 14, October 11, 1930.

"Die Grosse Rahmenübung von der Truppe aus gesehen." *Militär-Wochenblatt* 115, no. 22, December 11, 1930.

"Die grossen ungarischen Herbstmanöver." *Militär-Wochenblatt* 122, no. 24, December 10, 1937.

"Die Krise des Angriffs kann überwunden werden." *Militär-Wochenblatt* 114, no. 40, April 25, 1930.

"Die Schlacht im Raume von Sedan." *Oberkommando der Wehrmacht. Sieg über Frankreich: Berichte und Bilder.* Berlin: Wilhelm Andermann, 1940.

"Eine Ehrenschuld der Armee." *Militär-Wochenblatt* 90, no. 26, March 2, 1905.

"Eine Kompanie Infanterie." *Oberkommando der Wehrmacht. Sieg über Frankreich: Berichte und Bilder.* Berlin: Wilhelm Andermann, 1940.

"Friedrich der Grosse als Feldherr." *Militär-Wochenblatt* 67, no. 12, February 11, 1882.

"Gedanken zur 500-Jahrfeier des Allslavischen Sieges am 15. Juli 1410 über die Deitschen bei Tannenberg." *Militär-Wochenblatt* 95, no. 102, August 18, 1910.

"Generalfeldmarschall Graf von Schlieffen über den großen Feldherrn der preußisch-deutschen Armee." *Militär-Wochenblatt* 125, no. 17, October 25, 1940.

"Grossdeutschlands Freiheitskrieg 1940." Part 41. "Die deutsche Maioffensive auf der Westfront in den Tagen vom 10. bis 17. Mai 1940." *Militär-Wochenblatt* 124, no. 47, May 24, 1940.

————. Part 42. "Die deutsche Maioffensive in den tagen vom 17. bis 23. Mai 1940." *Militär-Wochenblatt* 124, no. 48, May 31, 1940.

————. Part 43. "Die Kapitulation der belgischen Armee und die Vernichtung der englischen und französischen Armeen in Flandern und im Artois in den tagen vom 24. Mai bis 1. Juni 1940." *Militär-Wochenblatt* 124, no. 49, June 7, 1940.

————. Part 44. "Der Abschluss der Vernichtungsschlacht in Flandern und im Artois sowie der Beginn der neuen deutschen Offensive über die Somme und den Oise-Aisne Kanal in der Woche vom 2. bis 8.6.1940." *Militär-Wochenblatt* 124, no. 50, June 14, 1940.

"Grossdeutschlands Freiheitskrieg." Part 124. "Der Stellungskrieg im Osten." *Militär-Wochenblatt* 126, no. 26, December 26, 1941.

"Kampf und Gefecht." *Militär-Wochenblatt* 84, no. 27, March 25, 1899.

"Kampftage einer Flakbatterie." *Oberkommando der Wehrmacht. Sieg über Frankreich: Berichte und Bilder.* Berlin: Wilhelm Andermann, 1940.

"Moderne Heere: Betrachtungen über die 'Gedanken eines Soldaten' des Generalobersten von Seeckt." *Militär-Wochenblatt* 113, no. 31, February 11, 1929.

"Neuzeitliche Lehren aus der Kriegführung Friedrichs des Grossen." *Militär-Wochenblatt* 115, no. 29, February 4, 1931.

"Port Arthur." *Militär-Wochenblatt* 90, no. 20, February 16, 1905.

"Prinz Heinrich als Feldherr im Siebenjährigen Kriege." *Militär-Wochenblatt* 84, no. 55, June 21, 1899.

"Rückblick eines Infanterie-Nachrichtenoffiziers auf die grosse Rahmenübung 1930." *Militär-Wochenblatt* 115, no. 21, December 4, 1930.

"Seydlitz' Brückensprung." *Militär-Wochenblatt* 67, no. 96, November 25, 1882.

"Strategie: eine Studie von Blume, Oberst und Kommandeur des Magdeburgischen Füsilier-Regiments Nr. 36." *Militär-Wochenblatt* 67, no. 103, December 16, 1882.

"Taktische und strategische Grundsätze der Gegenwart." *Beihefte zum Militär-Wochenblatt 1896.* Berlin: E. S. Mittler, 1896.

"Truppen-Kriegsgeschichte, Beispiel 9: Turnu Severin 1916." 2 parts. *Militär-Wochenblatt* 123, no. 17–18, October 21, 1938; October 28, 1938.

"Wie Gent durch Handstreich fiel." *Oberkommando der Wehrmacht. Sieg über Frankreich: Berichte und Bilder.* Berlin: Wilhelm Andermann, 1940.

"Zum Friedrichstage." *Militär-Wochenblatt* 79, no. 7, January 24, 1894.

"Zur Jahrhundertfeier der Befreiungskriege." *Militär-Wochenblatt* 95, no. 128, October 13, 1910.

"Zur Phänomen von Deutsch-Eylau." *Militär-Wochenblatt* 95, no. 42, April 5, 1910.

Achsenbrandt, Colonel. "Rennenkampf als Führer der 1. Armee im Herbst 1914." *Militär-Wochenblatt* 124, no. 5, July 28, 1939.

Addington, Larry H. *The Blitzkrieg Era and the German General Staff, 1865–1941.* New Brunswick, N.J.: Rutgers University Press, 1971.

———. *The Patterns of War Since the Eighteenth Century.* Bloomington: Indiana University Press, 1994.

Ambrosius, Dr. H. H., Kriegsberichter Fritz Dettmann, Darl Erck, Georg Engelbert Graf, and Rear Admiral Lützow. *Unser Kampf in Norwegen.* Munich: F. Bruckmann, 1940.

Amstark, Hugo. *Panzerjäger in Frankreich.* Vienna: Deutscher Verlag für Jugend und Volk, 1941.

Anger, Gilbert, ed. *Illustrirte Geschichte der k.k. Armee.* Vol. 2. Vienna: Gilbert Anger, 1887.

Arnold, Joseph C. "French Tactical Doctrine, 1870–1914." *Military Affairs* 42, no. 2, April 1978.

Ascoli, David. *A Day of Battle: Mars-la-Tour, 16 August 1870.* London: Harrap, 1987.

Asprey, Robert B. *The First Battle of the Marne.* Philadelphia: Lippincott, 1962.

———. *Frederick the Great: The Magnificent Enigma.* New York: Ticknor & Fields, 1986.

———. *The Reign of Napoleon Bonaparte.* New York: Basic Books, 2001.

Baily, Charles M. *Faint Praise: American Tanks and Tank Destroyers during World War II.* Hamden, Conn.: Archon, 1983.

Bald, Detlef. "The Impact of Tradition of the Education of the Military in Germany." *Military Affairs* 45, no. 3, October 1981.

Barnett, Correlli. *The Swordbearers: Supreme Command in the First World War.* Bloomington: Indiana University Press, 1963.

Bartov, Omer. "A Man without Qualities." *New Republic* 224, no. 11, March 12, 2001.

Bassford, Christopher. *Clausewitz in English: The Reception of Clausewitz in Britain and America, 1815–1945.* Oxford: Oxford University Press, 1994.

Bathe, Rolf. *Der Feldzug der 18 Tage: die Chronik des polnischen Dramas.* Oldenburg: Gerhard Stalling, 1939.

Bauer, Colonel. *Der grosse Krieg in Feld und Heimat: Errinerungen und Betrachtungen.* Tübingen: Osiander'sche Buchhandlung, 1921.

Beaumont, Roger A. "On the Wehrmacht Mystique." *Military Review* 66, no. 7, July 1986.

Beer, Willy, Fritz Dettmann, Karl Erck, Georg Engelbert Graf, General Ernst Kabisch, Peter Stronn, Kapitän Widemann, and Hans Zielinski. *Unser Kampf in Frankreich.* Munich: F. Bruckmann, 1941.

Bell, Raymond E., Jr. "Eylau—Winter War." *Strategy and Tactics* 138, October 1990.

Benoist-Mechin, Jacques. *Histoire de L'Armée Allemande.* 2 vols. Paris: Albin Michel, 1938.

Bernhardi, General Friedrich von. "Zur Beurtheilung der militärwissenschaftlichen Arbeiten F. Hoenigs." 2 parts. *Militär-Wochenblatt* 84, nos. 41–42, May 10, 1899; May 13, 1899.

Bernhardi, Theodor von. *Friedrich der Grosse als Feldherr.* 2 volumes. Berlin: Ernst Miller, 1881.

Bertkau, Major Friedrich. "Die nachrichtentechnische Führung mechanisierter Verbände." *Militär-Wochenblatt* 120, no. 15, October 18, 1935.

Best, Walter. *Mit der Leibstandarte im Westen.* München: Zentralverlag der NSDAP, 1944.

Beuys, Barbara. *Der Grosse Kurfürst: Der Mann, der Preussen schuf.* Reinbek bei Hamburg: Rowohlt, 1979.

Bidwell, Shelford, and Dominick Graham. *Fire-Power: British Army Weapons and Theories of War, 1904–1945.* London: Allen and Unwin, 1982.

Bigge, Major. "Ueber Selbstthätigkeit der Unterführer im Kriege." *Beihefte zum Militär-Wochenblatt 1894.* Berlin: E. S. Mittler, 1894.

Black, Jeremy. *European Warfare, 1660–1815.* New Haven, Conn.: Yale University Press, 1994.

Blanning, T. C. W. "The Death and Transfiguration of Prussia." *Historical Journal* 29, no. 2, June 1986.

Blond, Georges. *The Marne.* London: Macdonald, 1965.

Blume, Colonel. *Strategie: eine Studie.* Berlin: E. S. Mittler, 1882.

Blume, General von. "Selbstthätigkeit der Führer im Kriege." *Beihefte zum Militär-Wochenblatt 1896.* Berlin: E. S. Mittler, 1896.

Blumenthal, Count Albrecht von. *Journals of Field-Marshal Count von Blumenthal for 1866 and 1870–71.* London: Edward Arnold, 1903.

Boemeke, Manfred F., Roger Chickering, and Stig Förster, eds. *Anticipating Total War: The German and American Experiences, 1870–1914.* Cambridge: Cambridge University Press, 1999.

Bohn, Leif. "The Norwegian View." *History of the Second World War* no. 3, 1978.

Bond, Brian. *The Pursuit of Victory: From Napoleon to Saddam Hussein.* Oxford: Oxford University Press, 1996.

—— and Nigel Cave, eds. *Haig: A Reappraisal 70 Years On.* London: Leo Cooper, 1999.

Borgert, Heinz-Ludger. "Grundzüge der Landkriegführung von Schlieffen bis Guderian." *Handbuch zur deutschen Militärgeschichte 1648–1939.* Vol. 9. *Grundzüge der militärischen Kriegführung.* München: Bernard & Graefe, 1979.

Brandt, Major Wim. "Bilder aus der Belagerung von Modlin." *Militär-Wochenblatt* 124, no. 30, January 19, 1940.

——. "Eine motorisierte Aufklärungsabteilung im Polenfeldzug." Part 1. "Mlawa-Przasnysz,-Ciechanow." *Militär-Wochenblatt* 124, no. 25, December 15, 1939.

Braudel, Fernand. "Histoire et sciences socials: la longue durée." *Annales: Economies, sociétés, civilisations* 13, no. 4, October–December 1958.

Braun, Lieutenant Colonel. "Der strategische Überfall." *Militär-Wochenblatt* 123, no. 18, October 28, 1938.

——. "Motorisierte Gedankensplitter aus aller Welt." Part 6. "Die neue italienische Inf.-Versuchsdivision 'Binaria.'" *Militär-Wochenblatt* 123, no. 21, November 18, 1938.

Bremen, Lieutenant Colonel W. von. *Friedrich der Grosse.* Berlin: B. Behr, 1905.

———. "Königin Luise von Preussen: Zum Gedächtnis ihres Todestages, 19, Juli 1810." *Militär-Wochenblatt* 95, no. 88, July 19, 1910.

Brett-James, Antony. *Europe against Napoleon: The Leipzig Campaign 1813 from Eyewitness Accounts.* London: Macmillan, 1970.

Breunig, Charles, and Matthre Levinger. *The Revolutionary Era.* New York: Norton, 2002.

Brose, Eric Dorn. *The Kaiser's Army: The Politics of Military Technology in Germany during the Machine Age, 1870–1918.* Oxford: Oxford University Press, 2001.

Browning, Reed. *The War of the Austrian Succession.* New York: St. Martin's Press, 1993.

———. "New Views on the Silesian Wars." *Journal of Military History* 69, no. 2, April 2005.

Buchner, Alex. *Der deutsche Griechenland-Feldzug: Operationen der 12. Armee 1941.* Heidelberg: Kurt Vowinckel, 1957.

Bucholz, Arden. *Hans Delbrück and the German Military Establishment.* Iowa City: Iowa University Press, 1985.

———. *Moltke and the German Wars, 1864–1871.* New York: Palgrave, 2001.

———. *Moltke, Schlieffen, and Prussian War Making.* Providence, RI: Berg, 1991.

Burns, Thomas S. *A History of the Ostrogoths.* Bloomington: Indiana University Press, 1984.

Caemmerer, Lieutenant General von. "Zwei Bemerkungen zu Moltke's Stragtegie im Jahre 1866." *Militär-Wochenblatt* 90, no. 156, December 21, 1905.

Carlyle, Thomas. *History of Friedrich the Second, Called Frederick the Great.* Albany: J. B. Lyon, 1900.

Carsten, F. L. "The Great Elector and the Foundation of the Hohenzollern Despotism." *English Historical Review* 65, no. 255, April 1950.

———. "The Resistance of Cleves and Mark to the Despotic Policy of the Great Elector." *English Historical Review* 66, no. 259, April 1951.

Caulaincourt, Armand Augustin Louis de. *With Napoleon in Russia: The Memoirs of General de Caulaincourt, Duke of Vicenza.* New York: Grosset & Dunlap, 1935.

Chabod, Federico. *Italian Foreign Policy: The Statecraft of the Founders.* Princeton, N.J.: Princeton University Press, 1984.

Chaix, General Bruno. "Les plans opérationnels de 1940: Aller ou non en Belgique?" In *La Campagne de 1940: Actes du Colloque, 16 au 18 Novembre 2000,* edited by Christine Levisse-Touzé. Paris: Tallandier, 2001.

Chandler, David G. *The Art of Warfare on Land.* New York: Penguin, 1974.

———. *The Campaigns of Napoleon.* New York: Macmillan, 1966.

Churchill, Winston. *The Unknown War: The Eastern Front.* New York: Charles Scribner's Sons, 1932.

Citino, Robert M. *Armored Forces: History and Sourcebook.* Westport, Conn.: Greenwood, 1994.

———. *Blitzkrieg to Desert Storm: The Evolution of Operational Warfare.* Lawrence: University Press of Kansas, 2004.

———. *Evolution of Blitzkrieg Tactics: Germany Defends Itself against Poland, 1918–1933.* Westport, Conn.: Greenwood Press, 1987.

————. "'Die Gedanken sind frei': The Intellectual Culture of the Interwar German Army." *Army Doctrine and Training Bulletin* 4, no. 3, Fall 2001.

————. *The Path to Blitzkrieg: Doctrine and Training in the German Army, 1920–1939.* Boulder, Colo.: Lynne Rienner, 1999.

————. *Quest for Decisive Victory: From Stalemate to Blitzkrieg in Europe, 1899–1940.* Lawrence: University Press of Kansas, 2002.

————. "The Weimar Roots of German Military Planning in the 1930s." B. J. C. McKercher and Roch Legault, eds. *Military Planning and the Origins of the Second World War in Europe.* Westport, Conn.: Praeger, 2001.

Claasen, Adam R. A. *Hitler's Northern War: The Luftwaffe's Ill-Fated Campaign, 1940–1945.* Lawrence: University Press of Kansas, 2001.

Clark, Alan. *Barbarossa: The Russian-German Conflict, 1941–1945.* New York: Quill, 1985.

————. *Suicide of the Empires: The Battles on the Eastern Front, 1914–18.* New York: American Heritage Press, 1971.

Clausewitz, Carl von. *The Campaign of 1812 in Russia.* London: Greenhill Books, 1992.

————. *On War.* Edited and translated by Michael Howard and Peter Paret. Princeton, N.J.: Princeton University Press, 1984.

Clive, John, ed. *History of Frederick the Great.* Chicago: University of Chicago Press, 1969.

Cochenhausen, Colonel Friedrich von. "Untätigkeit belastet schwerer als ein Fehlgreifen in der Wahl der Mittel: Gedanken über Lilienstein—Maxen." *Militär-Wochenblatt* 112, no. 6, August 11, 1927.

Condell, Bruce, and David T. Zabecki, eds. *On the German Art of War: Truppenführung.* Boulder, Colo.: Lynne Rienner, 2001.

Cooper, Matthew. *The German Army, 1933–1945.* Chelsea, Mich.: Scarborough House, 1978.

Corum, James S. "The German Campaign in Norway as a Joint Operation." *Journal of Strategic Studies* 21, no. 4, December 1998.

————. *The Luftwaffe: Creating the Operational Air War, 1918–1940.* Lawrence: University Press of Kansas, 1997.

————. *The Roots of Blitzkrieg: Hans von Seeckt and German Military Reform.* Lawrence: University Press of Kansas, 1992.

Cox, Gary P. "Of Aphorisms, Lessons, and Paradigms: Comparing the British and German Official Histories of the Russo-Japanese War." *Journal of Military History* 56, no. 3, July 1992.

Craig, Gordon A. *The Battle of Königgrätz: Prussia's Victory over Austria, 1866.* Philadelphia: Lippincott, 1964.

————. *The Politics of the Prussian Army, 1640–1945.* Oxford: Oxford University Press, 1955.

Creasy, Sir Edward. *The Fifteen Decisive Battles of the World from Marathon to Waterloo.* New York: A. L. Burt, 1890.

Creveld, Martin van. "On Learning from the Wehrmacht and Other Things." *Military Review* 68, no. 1, January 1988.

————. *Command in War.* Cambridge, Mass.: Harvard University Press, 1985.

————. *Supplying War: Logistics from Wallenstein to Patton.* Cambridge: Cambridge University Press, 1977.

————. *Technology and War.* New York: Free Press, 1991.

————. *The Transformation of War.* New York: Free Press, 1991.

Dangel, Paul. "Blood and Iron." *Command* 21, March–April 1993.

Dastrup, Boyd L. *The Field Artillery: History and Sourcebook.* Westport, Conn.: Greenwood, 1994.

deBrosse, Jim, and Colin Burke. *The Secret in Building 26: The Untold Story of America's Ultra War against the U-Boat Enigma Codes.* New York: Random House, 2004.

Delbrück, Hans. "Friedrich der Grosse als Feldherr: eine methodologische Parodie." *Die Strategie des Perikles erläutert durch die Strategie Friedrichs des Grossen.* Berlin: Georg Reimer, 1890.

————. "Prinz Friedrich Karl." *Historische und Politische Aufsätze.* Berlin: Georg Stilke, 1907.

————. "Über die Verschiedenheit der Strategie Friedrichs und Napoleons." *Historische und politische Aufsätze.* Berlin: Georg Stilke, 1907.

————. *Die Strategie des Perikles erläutert durch die Strategie Friedrichs des Grossen.* Berlin: Georg Reimer, 1890.

————. *Historische und politische Aufsätze.* Berlin: Georg Stilke, 1907.

————. *History of the Art of War.* 4 volumes. Lincoln: University of Nebraska Press, 1990.

Delmas, General Jean. "La manoeuvre générale: surprise allemande, défense française." In *La Campagne de 1940: Actes du Colloque, 16 au 18 Novembre 2000,* edited by Christine Levisse-Touzé. Paris: Tallandier, 2001.

Dinardo, Richard L. "French Military Planning, 1871–1914." *Strategy and Tactics* 118, March–April 1988.

————. *Germany and the Axis Powers: From Coalition to Collapse.* Lawrence: University Press of Kansas, 2005.

————. *Germany's Panzer Arm.* Westport, Conn.: Greenwood Press, 1997.

Dobbs, Michael. *Saboteurs: The Nazi Raid on America.* New York: Knopf, 2004.

Dorpalen, Andreas. "Treitschke." *Journal of Contemporary History* 7, nos. 3–4, July–October 1972.

Dorwart, Reinhold. *The Administrative Reforms of Frederick William I of Prussia.* Westport, Conn.: Greenwood Press, 1971.

Doughty, Robert A. *The Breaking Point: Sedan and the Fall of France, 1940.* Hamden, Conn.: Archon, 1990.

Douhet, Giulio. *The Command of the Air.* New York: Coward-McCann, 1942.

Droysen, Johann Gustav. *Friedrich I: König von Preussen.* Berlin: De Gruyter, 2001.

Duffy, Christopher. *The Army of Frederick the Great.* London: David & Charles, 1974.

————. *The Fortress in the Age of Vauban and Frederick the Great, 1660–1789.* London: Routledge and Kegan Paul, 1985.

————. *Frederick the Great: A Military Life*. London: Routledge and Kegan Paul, 1985.

————. *The Military Experience in the Age of Reason*. London: Routledge and Kegan Paul, 1987.

Dworschak, Tom. "Operation Weser Exercise: The German Navy in Norway, 1940." *Command* 39, September 1996.

Earle, Edward Mead, ed. *Makers of Modern Strategy: Military Thought from Machiavelli to Hitler*. New York: Atheneum, 1966.

Easum, Chester V. *Prince Henry of Prussia: Brother of Frederick the Great*. Westport, Conn.: Greenwood Press, 1971.

Echevarria II, Antulio. *After Clausewitz: German Military Thinkers before the Great War*. Lawrence: University Press of Kansas, 2000.

————. "*Auftragstaktik*: In Its Proper Perspective." *Military Review* 66, no. 10, October 1986.

————. "General Staff Historian Hugo Freiherr von Freytag-Loringhoven and the Dialectics of German Military Thought." *Journal of Military History* 60, no. 3, July 1996.

Einhard and Notker the Stammerer. *Two Lives of Charlemagne*. New York: Penguin, 1969.

English, John A., and Bruce I. Gudmundsson. *On Infantry*. Westport, Conn.: Praeger, 1994.

Epstein, Robert M. *Napoleon's Last Victory and the Emergence of Modern War*. Lawrence: University Press of Kansas, 1994.

————. "Patterns of Change and Continuity in Nineteenth-Century Warfare." *Journal of Military History* 56, no. 3, July 1992.

Erfurth, Lieutenant General Waldemar. "Das Zusammenwirken getrennter Heeresteile." 4 parts. *Militärwissenschaftliche Rundschau* 4, nos. 1–4, 1939.

Ergang, Robert R. *The Potsdam Führer: Frederick William I, Father of Prussian Militarism*. New York: Columbia University Press, 1941.

Estorff, Major General von. "General-Feldmarschall Graf von Moltke." *Militär-Wochenblatt* 76, no. 38, April 29, 1891.

Falkenhayn, General Erich von. *Der Feldzug der 9, Armee gegen die Rumänen und Russen, 1916/17*. Berlin: E. S. Mittler, 1921.

Falls, Cyril. *The Art of War from the Age of Napoleon to the Present Day*. Oxford: Oxford University Press, 1961.

Fargettas, Julien. "Les Massacres de Mai–Juin 1940." In *La Campagne de 1940: Actes du Colloque, 16 au 18 Novembre 2000*, edited by Christine Levisse-Touzé. Paris: Tallandier, 2001.

Featherston, Alwyn. *Saving the Breakout: The 30th Division's Heroic Stand at Mortain, August 7–12, 1944*. Novato, Calif.: Presidio, 1993.

Feeser, General Friedrichfranz. "Friedrich Wilhelm, der Grosse Kurfürst: zur Erinnerung an der zweihundertfünfzigjährigen Todestag, 9. May 1688." *Militär-Wochenblatt* 122, no. 46, May 13, 1938.

Ferguson, Niall. *The Pity of War*. London: Penguin, 1999.

Feuchtwanger, Edgar. *Bismarck*. London: Routledge, 2002.

————. *From Weimar to Hitler: Germany, 1918–33.* New York: St. Martin's Press, 1993.

Fischer, Ernst. "Georg Derfflinger: Bruchstücke seines Lebensbildes." *Beihefte zum Militär-Wochenblatt 1894.* Berlin: E. S. Mittler, 1894.

Fischer, Fritz. *Griff nach der Weltmacht: die Kriegszielpolitik des kaiserlichen Deutschland, 1914–18.* Düsseldorf: Droste Verlag, 1961.

Fizaine, Fernand. *Frédéric-Guillaume 1er: père du militarisme allemand.* Paris: La Nef de Paris, 1958.

Foerster, Roland G., ed. *Gezeitenwechsel im Zweiten Weltkrieg? Die Schlachten von Char'kov und Kursk im Frühjahr und Sommer 1943 in operativer Anlage, Verlauf und politischer Bedeutung.* Berlin: E. S. Mittler, 1996.

Foerster, Wolfgang. *Aus der Gedankenwerkblatt des Deutschen Generalstabes.* Berlin: E. S. Mittler, 1931.

Fontane, Theodor. *Der deutsche Krieg von 1866.* Vol. 1. *Der Feldzug in Böhmen und Mähren.* Berlin: R. v. Decker, 1870.

————. *Der deutsche Krieg von 1866.* Vol. 2. *Der Feldzug in West- und Mitteldeutschland.* Berlin: R. v. Decker, 1871.

————. *Der Krieg gegen Frankreich, 1870–1871.* Vol. 1. *Der Krieg gegen das Kaiserreich bis Gravelotte, 18. August 1870.* Zürich: Manesse, 1985.

————. *Der Krieg gegen Frankreich, 1870–1871.* Vol. 2. *Der Krieg gegen das Kaiserreich von Gravelotte bis zur Kapitulation von Metz, 19. August 1870 bis 27. Oktober 1870.* Zürich: Manesse, 1985.

Forbes, Archibald. *My Experiences of the War between France and Germany.* 2 volumes. Leipzig: Berhnard Tauchnitz, 1871.

Forcade, Olivier. "Le Renseignement face à l'Allemagne au printemps 1940 et au début de la campagne de France." In *La Campagne de 1940: Actes du Colloque, 16 au 18 Novembre 2000,* edited by Christine Levisse-Touzé. Paris: Tallandier, 2001.

Förster, Stig. "Operationsgeschichte heute: Eine Einführung." *Militärgeschichtliche Zeitschrift* 62 (2002).

————. "Dreams and Nightmares: German Military Leadership and the Images of Future Warfare, 1871–1914." Manfred F. Boemeke, Roger Chickering, and Stig Förster, eds. *Anticipating Total War: The German and American Experiences, 1871–1914.* Cambridge: Cambridge University Press, 1999.

François, General Hermann von. *Marneschlacht und Tannenberg: Betrachtungen zur deutscher Kriegsführung der ersten sechs Kriegswochen.* Berlin: Scherl, 1920.

Fraser, David. *Frederick the Great: King of Prussia.* New York: Fromm, 2001.

Freytag-Loringhoven, Hugo von. *Feldherrngrösse: Von Denken und Handeln hervorragender Heerführer.* Berlin: E. S. Mittler, 1922.

Friederich, Lieutenant Colonel Rudolf von. "Die Schlacht bei Zorndorf am 25. August 1758." *Beihefte zum Militär-Wochenblatt 1908.* Berlin: E. S. Mittler, 1908.

————. *Geschichte des Herbstfeldzuges 1813.* 3 volumes. Berlin: E. S. Mittler, 1903–1906.

Friedrich Wilhelm von Seydlitz: Königlich Preussischer General der Kavallerie: Die Deutschen Reiterei gewidmet von einem Deutschen Reiteroffizier. Kassel: Theodor Kay, 1882.

Frieser, Karl-Heinz. "Schlagen aus der Nachhand—Schlagen aus der Vorhand: Die Schlachten von Char'kov und Kursk 1943." In *Gezeitenwechsel im Zweiten Weltkrieg? Die Schlachten von Char'kov und Kursk im Frühjahr und Sommer 1943 in operativer Anlage, Verlauf und politischer Bedeutung*, edited by Roland G. Foerster. Berlin: E. S. Mittler, 1996.

Frost, Robert I. *After the Deluge: Poland-Lithuania and the Second Northern War, 1655–1660*. Cambridge: Cambridge University Press, 1993.

———. *The Northern Wars: War, State, and Society in Northeastern Europe, 1558–1721*. Essex: Longman, 2000.

Führung und Gefecht der verbundenen Waffen. Berlin: Offene Worte, 1921.

Fuller, J. F. C. *The Conduct of War, 1789–1961*. New York: Da Capo, 1992.

———. *The Decisive Battles of the Western World, and Their Influence upon History*. Vol. 1. *From the Earliest Times to the Battle of Lepanto*. London: Eyre & Spottiswoode, 1954.

———. *A Military History of the Western World*. Vol. 3. *From the American Civil War to the End of World War II*. New York: Da Capo, 1957.

———. *The Reformation of War*. London: Hutchinson, 1923.

Fuppe, Colonel. "Neuzeitliches Nachrichtenverbindungswesen als Führungsmittel im Kriege." *Militärwissenschaftliche Rundschau* 3, no. 6, 1938.

Gat, Azar. *The Origins of Military Thought: From the Enlightenment to Clausewitz*. Oxford: Oxford University Press, 1992.

Gaul, Lieutenant Colonel. "Der Blitzkrieg in Frankreich." *Militär-Wochenblatt* 125, no. 35, February 28, 1941.

The German Campaign in Russia: Planning and Operations, 1940–1942. Washington, D.C.: Department of the Army, 1955.

The German Campaigns in the Balkans (Spring 1941). Washington, D.C.: Department of the Army, 1953.

German Defense Tactics against Russian Breakthroughs. Washington, D.C.: Department of the Army, 1951.

German General Staff. *Die Kriege Friedrichs des Grossen*. 19 volumes. Berlin: E. S. Mittler, 1890–1914.

———. *Die Kriege Friedrichs des Grossen*. Part 1. *Der Erste Schlesische Krieg 1740–1742*. Berlin: E. S. Mittler, 1890–1893.

———. *Die Kriege Friedrichs des Grossen*. Part 1. *Der Erste Schlesische Krieg 1740–1742*. Vol. 1. *Die Besetzung Schlesiens und die Schlacht bei Mollwitz*. Berlin: E. S. Mittler, 1890.

———. *Die Kriege Friedrichs des Grossen*. Part 2. *Der Zweite Schlesische Krieg 1744–1745*. Berlin: E. S. Mittler, 1895.

———. *Die Kriege Friedrichs des Grossen*. Part 2. *Der Zweite Schlesische Krieg 1744–1745*. Vol. 2. *Hohenfriedeberg*. Berlin: E. S. Mittler, 1895.

———. *Die Kriege Friedrichs des Grossen*. Part 3. *Der siebenjährige Krieg, 1756–1763*. 13 volumes. Berlin: E. S. Mittler, 1901–1914.

———. *Die Kriege Friedrichs des Grossen*. Part 3. *Der siebenjährige Krieg, 1756–1763*. Vol. 5. *Hastenbeck und Rossbach*. Berlin: E. S. Mittler, 1903.

————. *Die Kriege Friedrichs des Grossen.* Part 3. *Der siebenjährige Krieg, 1756–1763.* Vol. 6. *Leuthen.* Berlin: E. S. Mittler, 1904.

————. *Die Kriege Friedrichs des Grossen.* Part 3. *Der siebenjährige Krieg, 1756–1763.* Vol. 8. *Zorndorf und Hochkirch.* Berlin: E. S. Mittler, 1910.

————. *Studien zur Kriegsgeschichte und Taktik.* Vol. 2. *Das Abbrechen von Gefechten.* Berlin: E. S. Mittler, 1903.

————. *Studien zur Kriegsgeschichte und Taktik.* Vol. 3. *Der Schlachterfolg: mit welchen Mitteln wurde er erstrebt?* Berlin: E. S. Mittler, 1903.

————. *Studien zur Kriegsgeschichte und Taktik.* Vol. 6. *Heeresverpflegung.* Berlin: E. S. Mittler, 1913.

Glantz, David M. "Prelude to Kursk: Soviet Strategic Operations, February–March 1943." *Gezeitenwechsel im Zweiten Weltkrieg? Die Schlachten von Char'kov und Kursk im Frühjahr und Sommer 1943 in operativer Anlage, Verlauf und politischer Bedeutung,* edited by Roland G. Foerster. Berlin: E. S. Mittler, 1996.

————. *Stumbling Colossus: The Red Army on the Eve of World War II.* Lawrence: University Press of Kansas, 1998.

————, and Jonathan M. House. *The Battle of Kursk.* Lawrence: University Press of Kansas, 1999.

————, and Jonathan M. House. *When Titans Clashed: How the Red Army Stopped Hitler.* Lawrence: University Press of Kansas, 1995.

————, and Harold S. Orenstein, eds. *The Battle for Kursk 1943: The Soviet General Staff Study.* London: Frank Cass, 1999.

Goltz, Colmar Baron von der. *Jena to Eylau: The Disgrace and the Redemption of the Old-Prussian Army.* New York: E. P. Dutton, 1913.

————. "St. Privat-La Montagne, and Metz." In *The Franco-German War, by Generals and Other Officers Who Took Part in the Campaign,* edited by Major General Sir F. Maurice. London: Allen & Unwin, 1899.

————. "Welchen Weg hat die kriegsmässige Ausbildung der Infanterie einzuschlagen?" *Militär-Wochenblatt* 90, no. 1, January 3, 1905.

Görlitz, Walter. *History of the German General Staff, 1657–1945.* New York: Opraeger, 1953.

Görtz, Lieutenant General von. "Mouvement Tourné?" *Militär-Wochenblatt* 104, no. 36, September 20, 1919.

Green, Abigail. "The Federal Alternative? A New View of Modern German History." *Historical Journal* 46, no. 1, March 2003.

Griffith, Paddy. *Battle Tactics of the Western Front: The British Army's Art of Attack.* New Haven, Conn.: Yale University Press, 1994.

————. *Forward into Battle: Fighting Tactics from Waterloo to the Near Future.* Novato, Calif.: Presidio, 1990.

Groener, General Wilhelm. *Das Testament des Grafen Schlieffen: Operative Studien über den Weltkrieg.* Berlin: E. S. Mittler, 1927.

————. *Der Feldherr wider Willen: Operative Studien über den Weltkrieg.* Berlin: E. S. Mittler, 1931.

Guderian, Heinz. "Bewegliche Truppenkörper: Ein kriegsgeschichtliche Studie."

Part 1. "Die Schlittenfahrt des Grossen Kurfürsten im Winterfuldzug 1678–79." *Militär-Wochenblatt* 112, no. 18, November 11, 1927.

———. "Die Panzertruppen und ihr Zusammenwirken mit den anderen Waffen." *Militärwissenschaftliche Rundschau* 1, no. 5, 1936.

———. *Panzer Leader.* London: M. Joseph, 1952.

———. *Panzer Leader.* New York: Ballantine, 1957.

———. "Schnelle Truppen einst und jetzt." *Militärwissenschaftliche Rundschau* 4, no. 2, 1939.

Gunsburg, Jeffrey A. "The Battle of the Belgian Plain, 12–14 May 1940: The First Great Tank Battle." *Journal of Military History* 56, no. 2, April 1992.

———. *Divided and Conquered: The French High Command and the Defeat in the West, 1940.* Westport, Conn.: Greenwood Press, 1979.

Guse, Lieutenant Colonel Dr. "Ein modernes Austerlitz." *Militär-Wochenblatt* 125, no. 20, November 15, 1940.

Hamilton, Ralph. *The War Diary of the Master of Belhaven (Ralph Hamilton), 1914–1918.* Barnsley: Wharncliffe, 1990.

Hamric, Jacob Lee. "Germany's Decisive Victory: Falkenhayn's Campaign in Romania, 1916." Masters Thesis, Eastern Michigan University, 2004.

Harris, J. P., and F. H. Toase, eds. *Armoured Warfare.* London: B. T. Batsford Ltd., 1990.

Harrison, Richard W. *The Russian Way of War: Operational Art, 1904–1940.* Lawrence: University Press of Kansas, 2001.

Hart, Jeffrey. "The Hitler Problem." *National Review* 53, no. 1, January 2001.

Hauser, Oswald, ed. *Friedrich der Grosse in seiner Zeit.* Vol. 8. *Neue Forschungen zur Brandenburg-preussischen Geschichte.* Koln: Bohlau Verlag, 1987.

Heinemann, W. "The Development of German Armoured Forces 1918–1940." J. P. Harris and F. H. Toase, eds. *Armoured Warfare.* London: B. T. Batsford Ltd., 1990.

Helmuth, Captain Arnold. "The Prussian Guard on the 18th of August, 1870." *St. Privat: German Sources.* Ft. Leavenworth, Kans.: Staff College Press, 1914.

Herwig, Holger H. *The First World War: Germany and Austria-Hungary, 1914–1918.* London: Arnold, 1997.

Hildebrand, J. *Die Schlacht bei Pr. Eylau.* Quedlinburg: H. C. Huch, 1906.

Hillgruber, Andreas. *Grossmachtpolitik und Militarismus im 20. Jahrhundert: Drei Beiträge zum Kontinuitätsproblem.* Düsseldorf: Droste, 1974.

Hindenburg, Field Marshall Paul von. *Out of My Life.* Vol. 1. New York: Harper, 1921.

Hinrichs, Carl. *Friedrich Wilhelm I., König in Preussen: eine Biographie: Jugend und Aufstieg.* Darmstadt: Wissenschaftliche Buchgesellschaft, 1968.

Hoenig, Fritz. "Die Brigade Wedell bei Mars la Tour." 7 parts. *Militär-Wochenblatt* 76, nos. 71–73, 75–78, August 15, 1891; August 19, 1891; August 22, 1891; August 26, 1891; August 29, 1891; September 2, 1891; September 5, 1891.

———. *Inquiries concerning the Tactics of the Future.* London: Longmans, Green, 1899.

Hofschröer, Peter. *1815: The Waterloo Campaign.* Vol. 1. *Wellington, His German Allies, and the Battles of Ligny and Quatre Bras.* London: Greenhill, 1998.

———. *1815: The Waterloo Campaign.* Vol. 2. *The German Victory.* London: Greenhill, 1999.

Holt, Thaddeus. *The Deceivers: Allied Military Deception in the Second World War.* New York: Simon and Schuster, 2004.

Holtman, Robert. *The Napoleonic Revolution.* New York: J. B. Lippincott, 1967.

Höpfner, Eduard. *Der Krieg von 1806 und 1807.* Berlin: Simon Schropp, 1855.

Howard, Michael. *The Franco-Prussian War.* New York: Macmillan, 1962.

———. "The Influence of Clausewitz." Carl von Clausewitz. *On War.* Edited and translated by Michael Howard and Peter Paret. Princeton, N.J.: Princeton University Press, 1984.

———. "Men against Fire: The Doctrine of the Offensive in 1914." In *Makers of Modern Strategy from Machiavelli to the Nuclear Age,* edited by Peter Paret. Princeton, N.J.: Princeton University Press, 1986.

———. *War in European History.* Oxford: Oxford University Press, 1976.

Hubatsch, Walther. *Frederick the Great of Prussia: Absolutism and Administration.* London: Thames and Hudson, 1973.

Hughes, Daniel J. "Abuses of German Military History." *Military Review* 66, no. 12, December 1986.

———. "Schlichting, Schlieffen, and the Prussian Theory of War in 1914." *Journal of Military History* 59, no. 2, April 1995.

———. ed. *Moltke on the Art of War: Selected Writings.* Novato, Calif.: Presidio, 1993.

Hüther, Captain. "Nochmals Port Arthur." *Militär-Wochenblatt* 90, no. 30, March 11, 1905.

Hüttl, Ludwig. *Friedrich Wilhelm von Brandenburg.* München: Süddeutscher Verlag, 1981.

Ironside, Sir Edmund. *Tannenberg: The First Thirty Days in East Prussia.* Edinburgh: William Blackwood, 1933.

Jacobsen, Hans-Adolf. *Fall Gelb: der Kampf um den deutschen Operationsplan zur Westoffensive 1940.* Wiesbaden: F. Steiner, 1957.

———. "Hitlers Gedanken zur Kriegführung im Westen." *Wehrwissenschaftliche Rundschau* 5, no. 10, October 1955.

James, David H. *The Siege of Port Arthur: Records of an Eye-Witness.* London: T. Fisher Unwin, 1905.

Jany, Curt. *Geschichte der königlich preussischen Armee.* 4 volumes. Berlin: Karl Siegismund, 1928–1933.

Jarymowycz, Roman Johann. *Tank Tactics: From Normandy to Lorraine.* Boulder, Colo.: Lynne Rienner, 2001.

Johnson, David E. *Fast Tanks and Heavy Bombers: Innovation in the U.S. Army, 1917–1945.* Ithaca, N.Y.: Cornell University Press, 1998.

Jomini, Baron Antoine Henri de. *The Art of War.* Westport, Conn.: Greenwood Press, reprint of 1862 edition.

Justrow, Karl. *Feldherr und Kriegstechnik: Studien über den Operationsplan des Grafen Schlieffen und Lehren für unseren Wehraufbau und unsere Landesverteidigung.* Oldenburg: Gerhard Stalling, 1933.

Kabisch, Lieutenant General Ernst. "Die grossen Manöver in Schlesien, 24./25. September 1928." *Militär-Wochenblatt* 113, no. 17, November 4, 1928.

————. *Die Marneschlacht 1914*. Berlin: Otto Schlegel, 1933.

————. "Systemlose Strategie." *Militär-Wochenblatt* 125, no. 26, December 27, 1940.

Kähler. "Friedrich Wilhelm von Seydlitz: Königlich Preussischer General der Kavallerie: Der Deutschen Reiterei gewidmet von einem Deutschen Reiteroffizier." *Militär-Wochenblatt* 67, no. 25, March 29, 1882.

Kaiser, David. *Politics and War: European Conflict from Phillip II to Hitler*. Cambridge, Mass.: Harvard University Press, 1990.

Kania, Hans. *Der Grosse Kurfürst*. Leipzig: Teubner, 1930.

Kann, Robert A. *A History of the Habsburg Empire 1526–1918*. Berkeley: University of California Press, 1974.

Keegan, John. *The First World War*. London: Hutchinson, 1998.

Kehr, Eckart. *Battleship Building and Party Politics in Germany, 1894–1901: A Cross-Section of the Political, Social, and Ideological Preconditions of German Imperialism*. Chicago: University of Chicago Press, 1973.

————. *Der Primat der Innenpolitik: Gesammelte Aufsätze zur preussish-deutschen Sozialgeschichte im 19. und 20 Jahrhundert*. Berlin: W. de Gruyter, 1965.

Keim, Colonel. "Der Feldzug 1866 in Böhmen." *Militär-Wochenblatt* 84, nos. 10–11, February 1, 1899; February 4, 1899.

————. "Die Schlacht von Wörth." 3 parts. *Militär-Wochenblatt* 76, nos. 87–89, October 3, 1891; October 7, 1891; October 10, 1891.

————. "Ueberblick über den Verlauf der Kaisermanöver." 5 parts. *Militär-Wochenblatt* 79, nos. 91, 93, 101–103, October 27, 1894; November 3, 1894; December 1, 1894; December 5, 1894; December 8, 1894.

————. "Waterloo-Legenden." Parts 1–3. *Militär-Wochenblatt* 84, nos. 77–79, August 30, 1899; September 2, 1899; and September 6, 1899.

Kennedy, Robert M. *The German Campaign in Poland, 1939*. Pamphlet no. 20. Washington, D.C.: Department of the Army, 1956.

Kershaw, Ian. *Hitler*. Vol. 1. *1889–1936: Hubris*. New York: Norton, 1998.

Keynes, J. M. *The Economic Consequences of the Peace*. New York: Harcourt, Brace and Howe, 1920.

Kielmansegg, Johann Adolf Graf von. "Bemerkungen eines Zeitzeugen zu den Schlachten von Char'kov und Kursk aus der Sicht des damaligen Generalstabsoffiziers Ia in der Operationsabteilung des Generalstabs des Heeres." In *Gezeitenwechsel im Zweiten Weltkrieg? Die Schlachten von Char'kov und Kursk im Frühjahr und Sommer 1943 in operativer Anlage, Verlauf und politischer Bedeutung*, edited by Roland G. Foerster. Berlin: E. S. Mittler, 1996.

————. *Panzer zwischen Warschau und Atlantik*. Berlin: Verlag, 1941.

Kiesling, Eugenia C. *Arming against Hitler: France and the Limits of Military Planning*. Lawrence: University Press of Kansas, 1996.

Killinger, Manfred von. *Kampf um Oberschlesien*. Leipzig: K. F. Koehler, 1934.

Kinder, Christian. *Männer der Nordmark an der Bzura*. Berlin: E. S. Mittler, 1940.

Klingbeil, Major General. "Die operative Bedeutung der befestigten Elb-Linie für die Heerführung Napoleons im Herbstfeldzug 1813 unter neuzeitlicher Betrachtung." *Militär-Wochenblatt* 123, no. 24, December 9, 1938.

———. "Yorcks Elb-Übergang bei Wartenburg an 3. October 1813." *Militär-Wochenblatt* 123, no. 14, September 30, 1938.

Kluck, General Alexander von. *Der Marsch auf Paris und die Marneschlacht 1914*. Berlin: E. S. Mittler, 1920.

Knox, MacGregor, and Williamson Murray, eds. *The Dynamics of Military Revolution, 1300–2050*. Cambridge: Cambridge University Press, 2001.

Koch, H. W. *A History of Prussia*. New York: Dorset Press, 1978.

Köhn, Lieutenant Colonel. "Die Infanterie im 'Blitzkrieg.'" *Militär-Wochenblatt* 125, no. 5, August 2, 1940.

Koistinen, Paul A. C. *Arsenal of World War II: The Political Economy of American Warfare, 1940–1945*. Lawrence: University Press of Kansas, 2004.

Kolbe, Walther. *Die Marneschlacht*. Bielefeld: Velhagen und Klasing, 1917.

Kolberg (film). Directed by Veit Harlan, 1945.

Koser, Reinhold. *Geschichte Friedrichs des Grossen*. Berlin: J. G. Cotta, 1912–1913.

Kozaczuk, Wladyslaw, and Jerzy Straszak. *Enigma: How the Poles Broke the Nazi Code*. New York: Hippocrene, 2004.

Kretschman, Hans von. "The Battle of Vionville—Mars-la-Tour." In *The Franco-German War, by Generals and Other Officers Who Took Part in the Campaign*, edited by Major General Sir F. Maurice. London: Allen & Unwin, 1899.

———. "From Spicheren to Vionville." In *The Franco-German War, by Generals and Other Officers Who Took Part in the Campaign*, edited by Major General Sir F. Maurice. London: Allen & Unwin, 1899.

Kronberger, Rittmeister F. "Es gibt Fälle, wo das höchste Wagen die höchste Weisheit ist." *Militär-Wochenblatt* 125, no. 7, August 16, 1940.

Kuhl, General von. "Die beiden Marneschlachten." *Militär-Wochenblatt* 113, no. 27, January 18, 1929.

———. "Die Marneschlacht." *Militär-Wochenblatt* 104, no. 39, September 27, 1919.

Kunisch, Johannes. *Friedrich der Grosse: Der Konig und seine Zeit*. München: Beck, 2004.

———. "Friedrich der Grosse als Feldherr." Oswald Hauser, ed., *Friedrich der Grosse in seiner Zeit*, vol. 8, *Neue Forschungen zur brandenburg-preussischen Geschichte*. Köln: Böhlau Verlag, 1987.

———. *Fürst—Gesellschaft—Krieg: Studien zur bellizistischen Disposition des absoluten Fürstenstaates*. Köln: Böhlau Verlag, 1992.

Kurnatowski, Major General von. "Die grossen Feldmanöver unter Wilhelm II." *Militär-Wochenblatt* 103, no. 137, May 22, 1919.

Lange, Karl. *Marneschlacht und deutsche Öffentlichkeit 1914–1939: eine verdrängte Niederlage und ihre Folgen*. Düsseldorf: Bertelsmann, 1974.

Langemak, Captain. "Kriechen oder Springen? Ein Beitrag zu unserer Gefechtsausbildung." *Militär-Wochenblatt* 84, no. 28, March 7, 1905.

Leggiere, Michael V. *Napoleon and Berlin: The Franco-Prussian War in North Germany*. Norman: University of Oklahoma Press, 2002.

Leszczynski, Lieutenant Colonel. "Gesammelte Schriften und Denkwürdigkeiten des General-Feldmarschalls Grafen Helmuth von Moltke." *Militär-Wochenblatt* 76, nos. 71, 73, 98, August 15, 1891; August 22, 1891; November 7, 1891.

Lettow-Vorbeck, Major General Oscar von. *Geschichte des Krieges von 1866 in Deutschland.* Vol. 1. *Gastein-Langensalza.* Berlin: E. S. Mittler, 1896.

———. *Geschichte des Krieges von 1866 in Deutschland.* Vol. 2. *Der Feldzug in Böhmen.* Berlin: E. S. Mittler, 1899.

———. *Geschichte des Krieges von 1866 in Deutschland.* Vol. 3. *Der Main-Feldzug.* Berlin: E. S. Mittler, 1902.

———. *Kriegsgeschichtliche Beispiele.* Berlin: R. v. Decker, 1899.

———. "Mémoires du General Baron de Marbot." *Militär-Wochenblatt* 84, no. 49, June 3, 1899.

Levisse-Touzé, Christine. *La Campagne de 1940: Actes du Colloque, 16 au 18 Novembre 2000.* Paris: Tallandier, 2001.

Lewin, Ronald. *Hitler's Mistakes: New Insights into What Made Hitler Tick.* New York: Morrow, 1984.

Leyen, Lieutenant General von der. "Friedrich Wilhelm I.—Scharnhorst—Seeckt: Vom Werk dreier Schöpfer des preussisch-deutschen Heeres." 2 parts. *Militär-Wochenblatt* 126, nos. 24–25, December 12, 1941; December 19, 1941.

Liddell Hart, B. H. *The Decisive Wars of History.* London: G. Bell, 1929.

———. *The German Generals Talk.* New York: Quill, 1979.

———. *Strategy.* New York: Holt, 1967.

Lincoln, W. Bruce. *Passage through Armageddon: The Russians in War and Revolution, 1914–1918.* New York: Simon and Schuster, 1986.

Linnebach, Karl. "Die Völkerschlacht bei Leipzig." *Militär-Wochenblatt* 123, no. 17, October 21, 1938.

Lucas, James. *Battle Group! German Kampfgruppen Action of World War Two.* London: Arms and Armour, 1993.

Ludwig, General of Artillery. "Moltke als Erzieher." *Militär-Wochenblatt* 125, no. 17, October 25, 1940.

———. "Die Operation auf der inneren und der äußeren Linie im Lichte unserer Zeit." *Militär-Wochenblatt* 126, no. 1, July 4, 1941.

Ludwig, Lieutenant Colonel. "Ueber Festungskriegfragen." *Militär-Wochenblatt* 90, no. 26, March 2, 1905.

Luvaas, Jay, ed. *Frederick the Great on the Art of War.* New York: Free Press, 1966.

Lynn, John A. *Battle: A History of Combat and Culture.* Boulder, Colo.: Westview Press, 2003.

———. *The Bayonets of the Republic: Motivation and Tactics in the Army of Revolutionary France, 1791–94.* Urbana: University of Illinois Press, 1984.

———. "The History of Logistics and Supplying War." In *Feeding Mars: Logistics in Western Warfare from the Middle Ages to the Present,* edited by John Lynn. Boulder, Colo.: Westview Press, 1993.

———. "Recalculating French Army Growth during the Grand Siecle, 1610–1715." *French Historical Studies,* 18, no. 4, Autumn 1994.

———. "The *Trace Italienne* and the Growth of Armies: The French Case," *Journal of Military History*, 55, no. 3, July 1991.

———, ed. *Feeding Mars: Logistics in Western Warfare from the Middle Ages to the Present.* Boulder, Colo.: Westview Press, 1993.

Macher, Major. "Die Besetzung Dänemarks." *Militär-Wochenblatt* 125, no. 45, May 9, 1941.

Macksey, Kenneth. *Why the Germans Lose at War: The Myth of German Military Superiority.* London: Greenhill, 1996.

Mann, Golo. *The History of Germany Since 1789.* New York: Praeger, 1968.

Manstein, Field Marshall Erich von. *Lost Victories.* Chicago: H. Regnery, 1958.

———. *Lost Victories.* Novato, Calif.: Presidio, 1982.

Manteuffel, Freiherr von. "Zur Jahrhundertfeier der Kriegsakademie." *Militär-Wochenblatt* 95, no. 36, March 19, 1910.

Mantey, Colonel von. "Die Eisenbahnlage im Westen bei Kriegsbeginn 1914." *Militär-Wochenblatt*, 122, no. 48, May 27, 1938.

———. "Einfluss der Verkehrsmittel, insbesondere der Eisenbahn auf den Verlauf der Marneschlacht." *Militär-Wochenblatt* 124, no. 37, March 15, 1940.

———. "Nachschub und Operationsplan." 2 parts. *Militär-Wochenblatt* 124, nos. 1–2, July 1, 1939; July 7, 1939.

Marbot, Jean-Baptiste. *The Memoirs of Baron de Marbot, Late Lieutenant-General in the French Army.* London: Longmans, Green, 1892.

Marx, Lieutenant General. "Der Sprung vom Wissen zum Können." *Militär-Wochenblatt* 124, no. 15, October 6, 1939.

———. "Operative Zersplitterung in der Kriegsgeschichte." *Militär-Wochenblatt* 125, no. 3, July 19, 1940.

Matthes, Curt. *Die 9. Armee im Weichselfeldzug 1914.* Berlin: Junker & Dünnhaupt, 1937.

Maude, Colonel F. N. *1806: The Jena Campaign.* London: Swan Sonnenschein, 1909.

———. *The Jena Campaign, 1806.* London: Greenhill, 1998.

Maurice, Major General Sir F., ed. *The Franco-German War, by Generals and Other Officers Who Took Part in the Campaign.* London: Allen & Unwin, 1899.

May, Elmer C., Gerald P. Stadler, and John F. Votaw. *Ancient and Medieval Warfare.* West Point Military History Series. Wayne, N.J.: Avery, 1984.

McElwee, William. *The Art of War: Waterloo to Mons.* Bloomington: Indiana University Press, 1974.

McKercher, B. J. C. "Economic Warfare." In *World War I: A History*, edited by Hew Strachan. Oxford: Oxford University Press, 1998.

———, and Roch Legault, eds. *Military Planning and the Origins of the Second World War in Europe.* Westport, Conn.: Praeger, 2001.

McTaggart, Pat. "Poland '39." *Command* 17, July–August 1992.

Megargee, Geoffrey P. *Inside Hitler's High Command.* Lawrence: University Press of Kansas, 2000.

———. *War of Annihilation: Combat and Genocide on the Eastern Front, 1941.* Lanham, Md.: Rowman & Littlefield, 2005.

Meier-Welcker, Captain. "Die Rückendeckung der 8. Armee während der Schlacht bei Tennenberg." *Militär-Wochenblatt* 121, no. 4, July 25, 1926.

Meilinger, Phillip S. "The Historiography of Airpower: Theory and Doctrine." *Journal of Military History* 64, no. 2, April 2000.

Meissner, Major. "Fritz Hoenigs 'Taktik der Zukunft' und die Brigade Wedell bei Mars la Tour." 3 parts. *Militär-Wochenblatt* 76, nos. 61–63, July 15, 1891; July 18, 1891; July 22, 1891.

Mellenthin, F. W. von. *Panzer Battles: A Study of the Employment of Armor in the Second World War*. New York: Ballantine, 1956.

Meltzer, Captain. "Betrachtungen zum Feldzug und zum Schlacht von Pr. Eylau." *Militär-Wochenblatt* 121, no. 31, February 12, 1937.

Menning, Bruce. *Bayonets before Bullets: The Imperial Russian Army, 1861–1914*. Bloomington: Indiana University Press, 1992.

Messerschmidt, Manfred. "Das Bild der Wehrmacht in Deutschland seit 1945." *Revue d'Allemagne* 30, no. 2, April–June 1998.

Metzsch, General. "Gedanken eines Soldaten." *Militär-Wochenblatt* 113, no. 14, October 11, 1928.

Meyler, David. "Missed Opportunities: The Ground War in Holland." *Command*, no. 42, March 1997.

Michelet, Jules. *History of the French Revolution*. Edited and with an introduction by Gordon Wright. Chicago: University of Chicago Press, 1967.

Militärgeschichtliches Forschungsamt. *Das Deutsche Reich und Der Zweite Weltkrieg*. Vol. 2. *Die Errichtung der hegemonie auf dem Europäischen Kontinent*. Stuttgart: Deutsche Verlags-Anstalt, 1979.

———. *Das Deutsche Reich und Der Zweite Weltkrieg*. Vol. 4. *Der Angriff auf die Sowjetunion*. Stuttgart: Deutsche Verlags-Anstalt, 1983.

Military Improvisations during the Russian Campaign. Washington, D.C.: Department of the Army, 1951.

Miranda, Joseph. "The Battle of Plevna." *Strategy and Tactics* 218, September–October 2003.

———. "The Gentlemen's World War: The Seven Years' War in Europe, 1756–1763." *Strategy and Tactics* 163, September 1993.

Mittenzwei, Ingrid, and Erika Herzfeld. *Brandenburg-Preussen, 1648 bis 1789: Das Zeitalter des Absolutismus in Text und Bild*. Köln: Pahl-Rugenstein, 1987.

Moltke, Field Marshal Helmuth Graf von. *The Franco-German War of 1870–71*. New York: Howard Fertig, 1988.

———. *Militärische Werke*. 14 volumes. Berlin: E. S. Mittler, 1892–1912.

———. *Strategy, Its Theory and Application: The Wars for German Unification, 1866–1871*. Westport, Conn.: Greenwood, 1971.

Moulton, J. L. "Hitler Strikes North." *History of the Second World War*. No. 3, 1978.

Mrazek, James E. *The Fall of Eben Emael*. Novato, Calif.: Presidio, 1970.

Müffling, Baron Carl von. *Memoirs of Baron von Müffling: A Prussian Officer in the Napoleonic Wars*. London: Greenhill, 1997.

Mühlbach, Luise. *Napoleon and the Queen of Prussia*. New York: D. Appleton, 1888.

Muir, Rory. *Tactics and the Experience of Battle in the Age of Napoleon*. New Haven, Conn.: Yale University Press, 1998.

Müller, Heinrich. *Division Sintzenich: Erlebnisberichte aus dem Feldzuge in Frankreich 1940*. Frankfurt am Main: Hans Schäefer, 1943.

Murray, Williamson. "May 1940: Contingency and Fragility of the German RMA." In MacGregor Knox and Williamson Murray, eds. *The Dynamics of Military Revolution, 1300–2050*. Cambridge: Cambridge University Press, 2001.

———, and Allan R. Millett, eds. *Military Innovation in the Interwar Period*. Cambridge: Cambridge University Press, 1996.

Naveh, Shimon. *In Pursuit of Military Excellence: The Evolution of Operational Theory*. London: Frank Cass, 1997.

Niemann, Captain. "Der vereitelte Maas-Übergang bei Haybes-Fumay." *Militär-Wochenblatt* 123, no. 3, July 15, 1938.

Noetzel, Lieutenant General. "Die Schlacht bei Tannenberg am 15. Juli 1410: Kampf des Deutschen Ordens gegen Polen." *Militär-Wochenblatt* 95, no. 86, July 14, 1910.

Nofi, Albert A. "Eylau." *Strategy and Tactics* 75, July–August 1979.

———. "Napoleon's Art of War." *Strategy and Tactics* 75, July–August 1979.

———, ed. *Napoleon at War: Selected Writings of F. Loraine Petre*. New York: Hippocrene, 1984.

Nosworthy, Brent. *The Anatomy of Victory: Battle Tactics, 1689–1763*. New York: Hippocrene Books, 1990.

Oberkommando der Wehrmacht. *Sieg über Frankreich: Berichte und Bilder*. Berlin: Wilhelm Andermann, 1940.

Obkircher, Lieutenant Colonel. "General Constantin von Alvbensleben: Zu Seinem 50. Todestag, 28 März." *Militär-Wochenblatt* 126, no. 39, March 7, 1942.

———. "Moltke, der 'unbekannte' General von Königgrätz: Zur Errinerung an den 75. Gedenktag der Schlacht bei Königgrätz am 3. Juli 1866." *Militär-Wochenblatt* 125, no. 52, June 27, 1941.

Odom, William O. *After the Trenches: The Transformation of U.S. Army Doctrine, 1918–1939*. College Station: Texas A&M University Press, 1999.

Oestreich, Gerhard. *Friedrich Wilhelm, der Grosse Kurfürst*. Frankfurt: Musterschmidt Göttingen, 1971.

Ogorkiewicz, Richard M. *Armoured Warfare: A History of Armoured Forces and Their Vehicles*. New York: Arco, 1971.

Ollech, von. "Zur Beurtheiling des siebenjähriges Krieges." *Militär-Wochenblatt* 67, nos. 67–68, August 19, 1882; August 23, 1882.

Operations of Encircled Forces: German Experiences in Russia. Washington, D.C.: Department of the Army, 1952.

Opgenoorth, Ernst. *Friedrich Wilhelm: der Grosse Kurfürst von Brandenburg*. 2 volumes. Frankfurt: Musterschmidt Göttingen, 1971–1978.

Ozment, Steven. *A Mighty Fortress: A New History of the German People*. New York: HarperCollins, 2004.

Paret, Peter, ed. *Frederick the Great: A Profile.* New York: Hill and Wang, 1973.

———, ed. *Makers of Modern Strategy from Machiavelli to the Nuclear Age.* Princeton, N.J.: Princeton University Press, 1986.

———. *Understanding War: Essays on Clausewitz and the History of Military Power.* Princeton, N.J.: Princeton University Press, 1992.

———. *Yorck and the Era of Prussian Reform.* Princeton, N.J.: Princeton University Press, 1966.

Parker, Geoffrey. "The Military Revolution, 1550–1660: A Myth?" *Journal of Modern History* 48, no. 2, June 1976.

———. *The Military Revolution: Military Innovation and Rise of the West, 1500–1800.* Cambridge: Cambridge University Press, 1988.

Patrick, Stephen B. "Paratroop: A History of Airborne Operations." *Strategy and Tactics*, no. 77, December 1979.

Pelet-Narbonne, Gerhard von. *Der Grosse Kurfürst.* Berlin: B. Behr, 1905.

———, ed. *Erzieher des preussischen Heeres.*12 volumes. Berlin: B. Behr, 1905–1907.

Petre, F. Loraine. *Napoleon's Campaign in Poland, 1806–7.* London: The Bodley Head, 1901.

———. *Napoleon's Campaign in Poland, 1806–7.* New York: Hippocrene, 1975.

———. *Napoleon's Conquest of Prussia, 1806.* London: John Lane, 1914.

———. *Napoleon's Conquest of Prussia, 1806.* New York: Hippocrene, 1972.

Peukert, Detlev J. K. *The Weimar Republic: The Crisis of Classical Modernity.* New York: Hill and Wang, 1992.

Pfister, A. von. "The Battle of Wörth." In *The Franco-German War, by Generals and Other Officers Who Took Part in the Campaign,* edited by Major General Sir F. Maurice. London: Allen & Unwin, 1899.

———. "Weissenberg." In *The Franco-German War, by Generals and Other Officers Who Took Part in the Campaign,* edited by Major General Sir F. Maurice. London: Allen & Unwin, 1899.

Philippson, Martin. *Der Grosse Kurfürst Friedrich Wilhelm von Brandenburg.* 3 volumes. Berlin: Verlag Siegfried Cronbach, 1897–1903.

Picq, Charles-Ardant du. *Battle Studies: Ancient and Modern Battle.* New York: Macmilllan, 1921.

Ponath, Lieutenant Colonel. "Aus grosser Zeit vor zwanzig Jahren: Der Einbruch in die rumänische Ebene." *Militär-Wochenblatt* 121, no. 21, December 4, 1936.

———. "Einwirkung von Gewässern und Sümpfen auf winterliche Kriegführung." 2 parts. *Militär-Wochenblatt* 113, nos. 26–27, January 11, 1929; January 18, 1929.

———. "Feuerüberfalle gegen lohnende Augenblicksziele: Kämpfe der Abteilung Picht (verst. I./I.R. 148) vom 20.11. bis 6.12. 1916 bei Turnu-Severin und am Alt in der Schlacht in Rumänien." *Militär-Wochenblatt* 112, no. 35, March 18, 1928.

———. "Die Schlacht bei Tannenberg 1914 in kriegsgeschichtlicher, taktischer, und erzieherischer Auswertung." *Militär-Wochenblatt* 124, no. 8, August 18, 1939.

Poseck, General M. von. "Die Kavallerie im Manöver 1930." *Militär-Wochenblatt* 115, no. 21, December 4, 1930.

———. "Zorndorf." *Militär-Wochenblatt* 126, no. 9, August 29, 1941.

Possony, Stefan T., and Etienne Mantoux. "Du Picq and Foch: The French School." Edward Mead Earle, ed. *Makers of Modern Strategy: Military Thought from Machiavelli to Hitler.* New York: Atheneum, 1966.

Rabenau, Friedrich von. *Seeckt: Aus seinem Leben, 1918–1936.* Leipzig: von Hase und Koehler Verlag, 1940.

Raeder, Erich. *Grand Admiral.* New York: Da Capo Press, 2001.

Ranke, Leopold von. *Memoirs of the House of Brandenburg and History of Prussia during the Seventeenth and Eighteenth Centuries.* London: J. Murray, 1849.

Ransome, Cyril, ed. *The Battles of Frederick the Great.* New York: Scribner's, 1892.

Raus, Erhard. *Panzer Operations: The Eastern Front Memoir of Erhard Raus, 1941–1945.* New York: Da Capo, 2003.

Reardon, Mark J. *Victory at Mortain: Stopping Hitler's Panzer Counteroffensive.* Lawrence: University Press of Kansas, 2002.

Reddaway, W. F. *Frederick the Great and the Rise of Prussia.* New York: Putnam, 1904.

Reichsarchiv. *Der Weltkrieg 1914–1918.* Vol. 1. *Die Grenzschlachten im Westen.* Berlin: E. S. Mittler, 1925.

Reinicke, Adolf. *Das Reichsheer 1921–1934: Ziele, Methoden der Ausbildung und Erziehung sowie der Dienstgestaltung.* Osnabrück: Biblio Verlag, 1986.

Rendulic, Lieutenant Colonel Lothar. "Kann der Krise des Angriffes überwunden werden?" *Militär-Wochenblatt* 114, no. 36, March 25, 1930.

Rheinbaben, Werner Freiherr von. "Einem neuen 'Waterloo' entgegen." *Militär-Wochenblatt* 125, no. 39, March 28, 1941.

Riekhoff, Harald von. *German-Polish Relations, 1918–1933.* Baltimore, Md.: Johns Hopkins University Press, 1971.

Riley, J. P. *Napoleon and the World War of 1813: Lessons in Coalition Warfighting.* London: Frank Cass, 2000.

Ritter, Gerhard. *Frederick the Great: A Historical Profile.* Berkeley: University of California Press, 1968.

———. *Der Schlieffenplan: Kritik eines Mythos.* Munich: R. Oldenbourg, 1956.

Rivus, Enzio. "Die Tankwaffe Italiens." *Militär-Wochenblatt* 121, no. 4, July 25, 1936.

Roberts, Andrew. *Napoleon and Wellington: The Battle of Waterloo and the Great Commanders Who Fought It.* New York: Simon and Schuster, 2001.

Roberts, Michael. *The Military Revolution, 1560–1660: An Inaugural Lecture Delivered before the Queen's University of Belfast.* Belfast: M. Boyd, 1956.

Roessel, Lieutenant General. "Vor zweihundertfünfzig Jahren." Part 12. "Die Belagerung von Stettin durch Kaiserliche Truppen unter Feldzeugmeister de Souches und Brandenburgische unter dem Grafen Dohna—Beendigung des Feldzuges in Pommern." *Militär-Wochenblatt* 95, nos. 17–19, February 3, 1910; February 5, 1910; and February 8, 1910.

Rogers, Clifford J., ed. *The Military Revolution Debate: Readings on the Miltary Transformation of Early Modern Europe.* Boulder, Colo.: Westview Press, 1995.

Ropp, Theodore. *War in the Modern World.* Baltimore, Md.: Johns Hopkins University Press, 2000.

Ross, Steven S. *From Flintlock to Rifle: Infantry Tactics, 1740–1866*. London: Frank Cass, 1996.

Rossino, Alexander B. *Hitler Strikes Poland: Blitzkrieg, Ideology, and Atrocity*. Lawrence: University Press of Kansas, 2003.

Rothbrust, Florian K. *Guderian's XIXth Panzer Corps and the Battle of France: Breakthrough in the Ardennes, May 1940*. Westport, Conn.: Praeger, 1990.

Rothenberg, Gunther E. *The Art of Warfare in the Age of Napoleon*. Bloomington: Indiana University Press, 1978.

———. *The Austrian Military Border in Croatia, 1522–1747*. Urbana: University of Illinois Press, 1960.

———. *Napoleon's Great Adversaries: The Archduke Charles and the Austrian Army, 1792–1814*. Bloomington: Indiana University Press, 1982.

Rothfels, Hans. "Clausewitz." In *Makers of Modern Strategy: Military Thought from Machiavelli to Hitler*, edited by Edward Mead Earle. New York: Atheneum, 1966.

Rudé, George. *Revolutionary Europe, 1783–1815*. New York: Harper, 1964.

Russian Combat Methods in World War II. Washington, D.C.: Department of the Army, 1950.

Saint-Martin, Colonel Gérard. "Le Corps de Cavalerie en Belgique du 10 au 14 Mai 1940." In *La Campagne de 1940: Actes du Colloque, 16 au 18 Novembre 2000*, edited by Christine Levisse-Touzé. Paris: Tallandier, 2001.

Salomon, Ernst von. *The Answers of Ernst von Salomon to the 131 Questions of the Allied Military Government "Fragebogen."* London: Putnam, 1954.

Salvemini, Gaetano. *The French Revolution, 1788–1792*. New York: Norton, 1962.

Schäfer, Lieutenant Colonel Theobald von. "Die Enstehung des Entschlusses zur Offensive auf Lods: Zum Gedenken an General Ludendorff." *Militärwissenschaftliche Rundschau* 3, no. 1, 1938.

———. "Der Feldherr wider Willen." *Militär-Wochenblatt* 114, no. 2, May 11, 1930.

Scharfenort, Captain von. *Die Königliche Preussische Kriegsakademie 1810–1910*. Berlin: E. S. Mittler, 1910.

Scherff, General von. "Fritz Hoenigs 'Wahrheit.'" 2 parts. *Militär-Wochenblatt* 84, nos. 34, 36, April 19, 1899; April 22, 1899.

Schevill, Ferdinand. *The Great Elector*. Chicago: University of Chicago Press, 1947.

Schieder, Theodor. *Frederick the Great*. London: Longman, 2000.

Schlichting, General Sigismund von. *Taktische und strategische Grundsätze der Gegenwart*. 3 volumes. Berlin: E. S. Mittler, 1898–1899.

Schlieffen, Field Marshal Count Alfred von. "Cannae." *Gesammelte Schriften*. Vol. 1. Berlin: E. S. Mittler, 1913.

———. *Cannae: Authorized Translation*. Ft. Leavenworth, Kans.: Command and General Staff School Press, 1931.

———. *Dienstschriften des Chefs des Generalstabes der Armee Generalfeldmarschalls Graf von Schlieffen*. Vol. 1. *Die Taktisch-Strategischen Aufgaben aus den Jahren 1891–1905*. Berlin: E. S. Mittler, 1937.

———. *Dienstschriften des Chefs des Generalstabes der Armee Generalfeldmarschalls Graf von Schlieffen*. Vol. 2. *Die Grossen Generalstabsreisen—Ost—aus den Jahren 1891–1905*. Berlin: E. S. Mittler, 1938.

———. *Gesammelte Schriften*. 2 volumes. Berlin: E. S. Mittler, 1913.

———. "Der Krieg in der Gegenwart." *Gesammelte Schriften*. Vol. 1. Berlin: E. S. Mittler, 1913.

———. "Rede bei Enthüllung des Moltke-Denkmals auf dem Königsplatz in Berlin am 26. Oktober 1905." *Gesammelte Schriften*. Vol. 2. Berlin: E. S. Mittler, 1913.

———. "Rede des Generaloberst Graf Schlieffen auf die Kriegsakademie am 15. October 1910." *Militär-Wochenblatt* 95, no. 138, November 5, 1910.

———. "Über die Millionenheere." *Gesammelte Schriften*. Vol. 1. Berlin: E. S. Mittler, 1913.

Schmidt, Kunhardt von. "Seydlitz." *Militär-Wochenblatt* 90, no. 31, March 14, 1905.

Schmitt, Richard. *Prinz Heinrich als Feldherr im Siebenjährigen Kriege*. 2 volumes. Greifswald: Julius Abel, 1885–1899.

Schöllgen, Gregor, ed. *Escape into War? The Foreign Policy of Imperial Germany*. New York: Berg, 1990.

Schwarte, Lieutenant General. "General Ludendorffs Lebenswerk." 2 parts. *Militär-Wochenblatt* 104, nos. 23–24, August 21, 1919; August 23, 1919.

Scriba, Major General von. "Die Traditionen müssen der künftigen Preussischen Armee erhalten bleiben." *Militär-Wochenblatt*, no. 104, March 1, 1919.

Seeckt, Hans von. *Gedanken eines Soldaten*. Leipzig: K. F. Koehler, 1935.

———. *Thoughts of a Soldier*. London: Ernest Benn, 1930.

Shand, Alexander Innes. *On the Trail of the War*. New York: Harper, 1871.

Shennan, Margaret. *The Rise of Brandenburg-Prussia*. London: Routledge, 1995.

Shirer, William L. *Berlin Diary*. New York: Knopf, 1941.

Showalter, Dennis E. "America's Armored Might." *World War II*. April 2005.

———. "Even Generals Wet Their Pants: The First Three Weeks in East Prussia, August 1914." *War & Society* 2, no. 2, 1984.

———. "German Grand Strategy: A Contradiction in Terms?" *Militärgeschichtliche Mitteilungen* 48, no. 2, 1990.

———. "Manifestation of Reform: The Rearmament of the Prussian Infantry, 1806–13." *Journal of Modern History* 44, no. 3, September 1972.

———. "Manoeuvre Warfare: The Eastern and Western Fronts, 1914–1915." In *World War I: A History*, edited by Hew Strachan. Oxford: Oxford University Press, 1998.

———. "Mass Multiplied by Impulsion: The Influence of Railroads on Prussian Planning for the Seven Weeks' War." *Military Affairs* 38, no. 2, April 1974.

———. "Militärgeschichte als Operationsgeschichte." In *Was ist Militärgeschichte?* edited by Benjamin Ziemann and Thomas Kühne. Paderborn: Ferdinand Schöningh, 2000.

———. "Military Innovation and the Whig Perspective of History." In *The*

Challenge of Change: Military Institutions and New Realities, 1918–1941, edited by Harold R. Winton and David R. Mets. Lincoln: University of Nebraska Press, 2000.

———. *Patton and Rommel: Men of War in the Twentieth Century.* New York: Berkley Caliber, 2005.

———. *Railroads and Rifles: Soldiers, Technology, and the Unification of Germany.* Hamden, Conn.: Archon Books, 1976.

———. "The Retaming of Bellona: Prussia and the Institutionalization of the Napoleonic Legacy, 1815–1876." *Military Affairs* 44, no. 2, April 1980.

———. *Tannenberg: Clash of Empires.* Washington, D.C.: Brassey's, 2004.

———. *The Wars of Frederick the Great.* London: Longman, 1996.

———. *The Wars of German Unification.* London: Arnold, 2004.

Shy, John. "Jomini." In *Makers of Modern Strategy from Machiavelli to the Nuclear Age,* edited by Peter Paret. Princeton, N.J.: Princeton University Press, 1986.

Siemann, Wolfram. *The German Revolution of 1848–49.* New York: St. Martin's Press, 1998.

Simon, Walter M. *The Failure of the Prussian Reform Movement, 1807–1819.* Ithaca, N.Y.: Cornell University Press, 1955.

Simpson, Keith. *History of the German Army.* Greenwich, Conn.: Bison Books, 1985.

Smith, Chris. "Strike North: Germany Invades Scandinavia, 1940." *Command* 39, September 1996.

Smith, Digby. *1813: Leipzig: Napoleon and the Battle of Nations.* London: Greenhill, 2000.

Smith, Jean Edward, ed. *The Papers of Lucius D. Clay.* Vol. 1, *Germany 1945–1949.* Bloomington: Indiana University Press, 1974.

Snyder, Louis L., ed. *Frederick the Great.* Englewood Cliffs, N.J.: Prentice Hall, 1971.

Soutor, Kevin. "To Stem the Red Tide: The German Report Series and Its Effect on American Defense Doctrine, 1948–1954." *Journal of Military History* 57, no. 4, October 1993.

St. Privat: German Sources. Ft. Leavenworth, Kans.: Staff College Press, 1914.

Starcke, Gerhard. *"Die roten Teufel sind die Hölle": Kriegstagebuchblätter vom Westfeldzug 1940.* Berlin: Buchergilde Gutenberg, 1941.

Stegemann, Hermann. *Geschichte des Krieges.* Stuttgart: Deutsche Verlags-Anstalt, 1918.

Stokesbury, James L. *A Short History of World War I.* New York: William Morrow, 1981.

Stolfi, Russel. H. S. *A Bias for Action: The German 7 Panzer Division in France and Russia, 1940–1941. Marine Corps University Series Perspectives on Warfighting.* No. 1. Quantico, Va.: Marine Corps Association, 1991.

———. *Hitler's Panzers East: World War II Reinterpreted.* Norman: University of Oklahoma Press, 1992.

Stone, Norman. *The Eastern Front, 1914–1917.* London: Hodder and Stoughton, 1975.

Strachan, Hew. *The First World War*. Vol. 1. *To Arms*. Oxford: Oxford University Press, 2001.

———, ed. *World War I: A History*. Oxford: Oxford University Press, 1998.

Stürmer, Michael. *The German Empire: A Short History*. New York: Modern Library, 2000.

———. "A Nation State against History and Geography: The German Dilemma." In *Escape into War? The Foreign Policy of Imperial Germany*, edited by Gregor Schöllgen. New York: Berg, 1990.

Sullivan, Brian R. "Fascist Italy's Military Involvement in the Spanish Civil War." *Journal of Military History* 59, no. 4, October 1995.

———. "Intelligence and Counter-Terrorism: A Clausewitzian-Historical Analysis." *Journal of Intelligence History* 3, no. 1, 2003.

Sumida, Jon Tetsuro. "The Relationship of History and Theory in *On War*: The Clausewitzian Ideal and Is Implications." *Journal of Military History* 65, no. 2, April 2001.

Sweet, John J. T. *Iron Arm: The Mechanization of Mussolini's Army, 1920–1940*. Westport, Conn.: Greenwood Press, 1980.

Sybel, Heinrich von. *Die Begrundung des Deutschen Reiches durch Wilhelm I*. 7 volumes. München: R. Oldenbourg, 1889–1894.

Talbot, Randy R. "General Hermann von François and Corps-Level Operations during the Tannenberg Campaign, August 1914." Masters Thesis, Eastern Michigan University, 1999.

Taysen, A. von. *Zur Beurtheilung des siebenjähriges Krieges*. Berlin: Mittler, 1882.

Theiss, Colonel Rudolf. "Kriegserfahrung." *Militär-Wochenblatt* 125, no. 6, August 9, 1940.

———. "Der Panzer in der Weltgeschichte." *Militär-Wochenblatt* 125, no. 15. October 11, 1940.

Thiel, Rudolf. *Preussische Soldaten*. Berlin: Paul Neff, 1940.

Tooley, T. Hunt. *National Identity and Weimar Germany: Upper Silesia and the Eastern Border, 1918–1922*. Lincoln: University of Nebraska Press, 1997.

Travers, Tim. "The Allied Victories, 1918." In *World War I: A History*, edited by Hew Strachan. Oxford: Oxford University Press, 1998.

———. "Could the Tanks of 1918 Have Been War-Winners for the British Expeditionary Force?" *Journal of Contemporary History* 27, no. 3, July 1992.

———. "The Evolution of British Strategy and Tactics on the Western Front in 1918: GHQ, Manpower, and Technology." *Journal of Military History* 54, no. 2, April 1990.

———. *How the War Was Won: Command and Technology in the British Army on the Western Front, 1917–1918*. New York: Routledge, 1992.

———. *The Killing Ground: The British Army, the Western Front, and the Emergence of Modern Warfare, 1900–1918*. London: Allen and Unwin, 1987.

———. "Technology, Tactics, and Morale: Jean de Bloch, the Boer War, and British Military Theory, 1900–1914." *Journal of Modern History* 51, no. 2, June 1979.

Treitschke, Heinrich von. *Deutsche Geschichte im neunzehnten Jahrhundert.* 5 volumes. Leipzig: S. Hirzel, 1879–1895.

Tsouras, Peter G., ed. *Panzers on the Eastern Front: General Erhard Raus and His Panzer Divisions in Russia, 1941–1945.* London: Greenhill, 2002.

Unger, Major F. von. "Grundsätzliches in Graf Schlieffens Generalstabsaufgaben." *Militär-Wochenblatt* 122, no. 15, October 8, 1937.

Unger, W. von. "Feldmarschall Derfflinger." *Beihefte zum Militär-Wochenhblatt 1896.* Berlin: E. S. Mittler, 1896.

Unser Kampf in Polen: Die Vorgeschichte—Strategische Einführung—Politische und kriegerische Dokumente. Munich: F. Bruckmann, 1940.

van Dyke, Carl. *The Soviet Invasion of Finland.* London: Frank Cass, 1997.

Vanwelkenhuyzen, Jean. "Die Krise vom Januar 1940." *Wehrwissenschaftliche Rundschau* 5, no. 2, February 1955.

———. "Le Rôle de l'Armée Belge." In *La Campagne de 1940: Actes du Colloque, 16 au 18 Novembre 2000,* edited by Christine Levisse-Touzé. Paris: Tallandier, 2001.

Voigts-Rhetz, General von. "Erklärung." *Militär-Wochenblatt* 84, no. 37, April 26, 1899.

Volz, Gustav Berthold, ed. *Ausgewählte Werke Friedrichs des Grossen.* Vol. 1. *Historische und militärische Schriften, Briefe.* Berlin: Reimar Hobbing, 1900.

Waite, Robert G. L. *Vanguard of Nazism: The Free Corps Movement in Postwar Germany 1918–1923.* New York: Norton, 1952.

Wallach, Jehuda L. *The Dogma of the Battle of Annihilation: The Theories of Clausewitz and Schlieffen and Their Impact on the German Conduct of Two World Wars.* Westport, Conn.: Greenwood, 1986.

Walter, Dierk. *Preussische Heeresreformen 1807–1870: Militärische Innovation und der Mythos der "Roonschen Reform."* Paderborn: Ferdinand Schöningh, 2003.

Wawro, Geoffrey. "'An Army of Pigs': The Technical, Social, and Political Bases of Austrian Shock Tactics, 1859–1866." *Journal of Military History* 59, no. 3, July 1995.

———. *The Austro-Prussian War: Austria's War with Prussia and Italy in 1866.* Cambridge: Cambridge University Press, 1996.

———. *The Franco-Prussian War.* Cambridge: Cambridge University Press, 2003.

Wegner, Bernd. "Wozu Operationsgeschichte?" In *Was ist Militärgeschichte?* edited by Benjamin Ziemann and Thomas Kühne. Paderborn: Ferdinand Schöningh, 2000.

Wehler, Hans-Ulrich. *The German Empire, 1871–1918.* Dover, N.H.: Berg, 1985.

———. *Preussen ist wieder chic . . . Politik und Polemic in zwanzig Essays.* Frankurt am Main: Suhrkamp, 1983.

Weigley, Russell F. *The Age of Battles: The Quest for Decisive Warfare from Breitenfeld to Waterloo.* Bloomington: Indiana University Press, 1991.

Weinberg, Gerhard L. "Zur Frage eines Sonderfriedens im Osten." In *Gezeitenwechsel im Zweiten Weltkrieg? Die Schlachten von Char'kov und Kursk im Frühjahr und Sommer 1943 in operativer Anlage, Verlauf und politischer Bedeutung,* edited by Roland G. Foerster. Berlin: E. S. Mittler, 1996.

Werth, Alexander. *Russia at War*. New York: Carroll and Graf, 1992.

Wetzell, General Georg. "Bismarck-Moltke und der Bündniskrieg." *Militär-Wochenblatt* 122, no. 45, May 6, 1938.

———. "Der Bündniskrieg: Eine militärpolitisch operative Studie des Weltkrieges." 5 parts. *Militär-Wochenblatt* 122, nos. 14–18, October 1, 1937; October 8, 1937; October 15, 1937; October 22, 1937; October 29, 1937.

———. "'Der Bündniskrieg' und die Kritik." 2 parts. *Militär-Wochenblatt* 122, nos. 28–29, January 7, 1938; January 14, 1938.

———. "Einst und Jetzt." *Militär-Wochenblatt* 124, no. 14, October 1, 1939.

———. "Die Führung im Marne-Feldzug 1914: Betrachtungen zu dem Buche von Oberstleutnant a. D. Müller-Loebnitz." 4 parts. *Militär-Wochenblatt* 124, nos. 32–35, February 2, 1940; February 9, 1940; February 16, 1940; February 23, 1940.

———. "Der Kriegsbeginn 1914 unter einer anderen politisch-militärischen Zielsetzung." *Militär-Wochenblatt* 121, no. 32, February 19, 1938.

———. "Nochmals: 'Der Bündniskrieg' und die Kritik." *Militär-Wochenblatt* 122, no. 35, February 25, 1938.

———. "Schlieffens Vermächtnis." *Militär-Wochenblatt* 122, no. 39, March 25, 1938.

———. "Studie über Operationspläne und Kriegswirklichkeit." 3 parts. *Militär-Wochenblatt* 121, nos. 13–15, October 4, 1936; October 11, 1936; October 18, 1936.

White, Charles E. *The Enlightened Soldier: Scharnhorst and the Militärische Gesellschaft in Berlin, 1801–1805*. Westport, Conn.: Praeger, 1989.

Wilkinson, Spenser, ed. *Moltke's Military Correspondence, 1870–71*. Aldershot: Gregg Revivals, 1991.

William II. "Trauer um den verewigten General-Feldmarschall Grafen von Moltke." *Militär-Wochenblatt* 76, no. 37, April 26, 1891.

Winter, Denis. *Death's Men: Soldiers of the Great War*. New York: Penguin, 1978.

Winton, Harold R. *To Change an Army: General Sir John Burnett-Stuart and British Armored Doctrine, 1927–1938*. Lawrence: University Press of Kansas, 1988.

———, and David R. Mets, eds. *The Challenge of Change: Military Institutions and New Realities, 1918–1941*. Lincoln: University of Nebraska Press, 2000.

Wolf, Major General. "Die Schlacht im Teutoburger Walde." *Beihefte zum Militär-Wochenblatt 1902*. Berlin: E. S. Mittler, 1902.

Wolfram, Herwig. *History of the Goths*. Berkeley: University of California Press, 1988.

Xylander, Colonel Rudolf Ritter von. "Die grossen Übungen der 1. amerikanischen Armee." *Militär-Wochenblatt* 124, no. 32, February 2, 1940.

Zabecki, David T. "Invasion of Poland: Campaign That Launched a War." *World War II* 14, no. 3, September 1999.

———. *Steel Wind: Colonel Georg Bruchmüller and the Birth of Modern Artillery*. Westport, Conn.: Praeger, 1994.

Zaloga, Steven, and Victor Madej. *The Polish Campaign*. New York: Hippocrene, 1991.

Ziemann, Benjamin, and Thomas Kühne, eds. *Was ist Militärgeschichte?* Paderborn: Ferdinand Schöningh, 2000.

Zuber, Terence. *Inventing the Schlieffen Plan: German War Planning, 1871–1914.* Oxford: Oxford University Press, 2002.

———. "The Schlieffen Plan Reconsidered." *War in History* 6, no. 3, July 1999.

Zwehl, General von. "Die Operationen des Feldmarschalls French gegen die 1. Armee und das VII. Reservekorps im Sommer 1914." 4 parts. *Militär-Wochenblatt* 104, nos. 35–38, September 18, 1919; September 20, 1919; September 23, 1919; and September 25, 1919.

Index